Singapore Mandarin Grammar I

As the first volume of a two-volume set that presents a comprehensive syntactical picture of Singapore Mandarin, this title discusses the distinguishing characteristics of the Chinese language and describes the grammar of Singapore Mandarin.

The book first provides an overview of the grammar of Singapore Mandarin and compares it with Chinese Mandarin (Putonghua). As a variety of Mandarin Chinese, Singapore Mandarin is also characterised by syntactic rules taking precedence over morphological rules. Therefore, it is argued that word order and functional words are specifically important in the study of Singapore Mandarin. Then the author explicates the properties and functions of the following nine grammatical components: the five most basic phrase types, word classes, sentences, subjects and predicates, predicates and objects, predicates and complements, attributes and adverbials, complex predicate phrases, and prepositions and prepositional phrases.

With rich and authentic language examples, the book will serve as a must-read for learners and teachers of Mandarin Chinese and linguistics scholars interested in global Chinese and especially Singapore Mandarin.

Lu Jianming is a professor and doctoral supervisor in the Chinese Department at Peking University, China. He has been teaching and researching on modern Chinese studies for more than 60 years and has served as President of the World Chinese Teaching Association and President of the International Chinese Linguistic Society.

China Perspectives

The *China Perspectives* series focuses on translating and publishing works by leading Chinese scholars, writing about both global topics and China-related themes. It covers Humanities & Social Sciences, Education, Media and Psychology, as well as many interdisciplinary themes.

This is the first time any of these books have been published in English for international readers. The series aims to put forward a Chinese perspective, give insights into cutting-edge academic thinking in China, and inspire researchers globally.

To submit proposals, please contact the Taylor & Francis Publisher for the China Publishing Programme, Lian Sun (Lian.Sun@informa.com)

Titles in linguistics currently include:

Modern Chinese Grammar II
Grammatical Constituents
WANG Li

Modern Chinese Grammar III
Substitution and Numeration
WANG Li

Modern Chinese Grammar IV
Special Forms and Europeanized Grammar
WANG Li

Singapore Mandarin Grammar I
Lu Jianming

Cognitive Neural Mechanism of Semantic Rhetoric
Qiaoyun Liao, Lijun Meng

For more information, please visit https://www.routledge.com/China-Perspectives/book-series/CPH

Singapore Mandarin Grammar I

Lu Jianming

LONDON AND NEW YORK

This book is published with financial support from the Chinese Fund for the Humanities and Social Sciences.

First published in English 2023
by Routledge
4 Park Square, Milton Park, Abingdon, Oxon OX14 4RN

and by Routledge
605 Third Avenue, New York, NY 10158

Routledge is an imprint of the Taylor & Francis Group, an informa business

© 2023 Lu Jianming

Translated by Peng Guozhen, Wang Luming, Jiang Huili, Yang Xiaodong

The right of Lu Jianming to be identified as author of this work has been asserted in accordance with sections 77 and 78 of the Copyright, Designs and Patents Act 1988.

All rights reserved. No part of this book may be reprinted or reproduced or utilised in any form or by any electronic, mechanical, or other means, now known or hereafter invented, including photocopying and recording, or in any information storage or retrieval system, without permission in writing from the publishers.

Trademark notice: Product or corporate names may be trademarks or registered trademarks, and are used only for identification and explanation without intent to infringe.

English version by permission of The Commercial Press.

British Library Cataloguing-in-Publication Data
A catalogue record for this book is available from the British Library

Library of Congress Cataloging-in-Publication Data
Names: Lu, Jianming, author.
Title: Singapore Mandarin grammar/Lu Jianming.
Other titles: Xinjiapo Hua yu yu fa. English
Description: Abingdon, Oxon; New York: Routledge, 2023. | Series: China perspectives | Includes bibliographical references and index. |
Identifiers: LCCN 2022016441 (print) | LCCN 2022016442 (ebook) |
Subjects: LCSH: Mandarin dialects—Singapore—Grammar. | Mandarin dialects—Singapore—Syntax.
Classification: LCC PL1893. L813 2022 (print) | LCC PL1893 (ebook) | DDC 495.15—dc23/eng/20220418
LC record available at https://lccn.loc.gov/2022016441
LC ebook record available at https://lccn.loc.gov/2022016442

ISBN: 978-1-032-34813-1 (hbk)
ISBN: 978-1-032-34953-4 (pbk)
ISBN: 978-1-003-32395-2 (ebk)

DOI: 10.4324/b23129

Typeset in Times New Roman
by Apex CoVantage, LLC

Contents

List of Translators		vi
Foreword		vii
1	Introduction	1
2	Five Basic Types of Phrase	15
3	Word Classes	31
4	Sentences	76
5	Subjects and Predicates	94
6	Predicates and Objects	151
7	Predicates and Complements	227
8	Attributes and Adverbials	283
9	Complex Predicate Phrases	353
10	Prepositions and Prepositional Phrases	401
	Appendix 1 English-Chinese Term List	484
	Appendix 2 Translation of Examples and Glossary	491
	Appendix 3 The Sources of Examples	493
	Bibliography	498
	Index	501

Translators

Peng Guozhen is a professor of linguistics at Zhejiang University of Technology. Her research interest is language typology and Chinese syntax.

Wang Luming is an associate professor at Zhejiang University of Technology. Her research interest is neurolinguistics.

Jiang Huili is a lecturer at Zhejiang University of Technology. Her research interest is second language acquisition and teaching.

Yang Xiaodong is a lecturer at Zhejiang University of Technology. His research interest is Chinese syntax and corpus linguistics.

Foreword

Professor Lu Jianming's new book, *Singapore Mandarin Grammar I*, is to be published, and I have been invited to write the foreword for it as I am connected to this work in some ways. Many of my views on language relate to the content of this book. Reading this manuscript in advance not only brings me enjoyment but takes me back to the 1990s. This foreword, therefore, will elaborate upon the intellectual merits of the volume, as well as some pleasant recollections.

I. Recollections of the Past

The late former Prime Minister Lee Kuan Yew was a staunch supporter of the Chinese language during his lifetime, and in 1979 he initiated the Speak Mandarin Campaign.[1] To make it easier for Singaporeans to learn Mandarin and to use it, the authorities also launched the programme "Dial for Mandarin", helping Singaporeans interested in learning Mandarin to do so through telephone calls. At that time, we were using modern Chinese Mandarin as the standard language. As one of the consultants for the course, I was sceptical about the standardness of the expression 贵也贵不到哪里去 *guì yě guì bùdào nǎlǐ qù* 'It won't be too expensive'. Such a sentence is well-formed in dialects, but was it grammatical in Chinese Mandarin? I had no idea because I had never been to China, and there was no explanation about it in any of the grammar texts I could find, including Lü Shuxiang and Zhu Dexi's 《语法修辞讲话》 *Yǔfǎ xiūcí jiǎnghuà* '*Speech on Grammar and Rhetoric*' and Chao Yuen Ren's *A Grammar of Spoken Chinese*. Later, I was relieved to discover such a usage in Lao She's work and thus decided to keep the expression in the textbook for "Dial for Mandarin".

In 1985, the First International Conference on Chinese Language Teaching and Research was held at Xiangshan, Beijing, and I attended the conference with Lu Shaochang, Chen Chongyu, Xie Zewen and Xie Shiya. That was my first visit to Beijing. During the several days I stayed there, I became aware that there were differences between Chinese Mandarin and Singapore Mandarin. But what exactly were the differences? In response to my question, Professor Lu Jianming said, "It is necessary to understand, identify and describe the features of Singapore Mandarin, which will lay the groundwork for its standardization." Only by doing so, these differences may be properly addressed and handled in the teaching of Singapore Mandarin. These are the things I have kept in mind all this time.

Following China's reform and opening up, a large number of Chinese intellectuals arrived in Singapore, bringing a variety of viewpoints about the language used in *Zaobao*. At that time, I was a member of the newspaper's advisory board, so I got the chance to see the expressions that they were critical of. Most of those expressions, with the exception of some clearly incorrect or ill-formed ones, were also used by the majority of Singaporeans. Therefore I advised the then-Prime Minister Lee Kuan Yew that *Zaobao* should engage a language expert to review the journalists' vocabulary. At the same time, I was wondering whether it was necessary for Singapore Mandarin to be entirely normalised according to the standards of Chinese Mandarin.

In 1994, Nanyang Technological University established the Chinese Language and Culture Centre, with myself as the director and Professor Li Yunwei as the deputy director. For linguistic research, we then launched three research programs: (1) a study of Chinese languages in Southeast Asia; (2) a comparative study of Singapore Mandarin and the modern standard Mandarin; (3) a study of language usage of Chinese people in Singapore.

Professor Lu Jianming was our Centre's first visiting faculty. I have always believed that mainland China's first-class intellectuals should receive their due respect. Thus the payment for Professor Lu Jianming at the Centre was the same as that for professors from Europe and the United States. My peers at a Hong Kong tertiary colleges then criticized me, saying, "You have violated the market", for at that time it was the prevailing practice in Hong Kong to give unfair salaries to mainland Chinese specialists and scholars.

Professor Lu Jianming came to the Centre to work on the comparative study of Singapore Mandarin and the modern standard Mandarin, and wrote an article entitled "Characteristics of Singapore Mandarin Grammar". At that time, I was unable to participate in the research due to my heavy administrative responsibilities, but I attended every seminar of the research group and was quite familiar with the research process. Professor Lu's research had a two-fold influence on me. First, it changed my view from regarding Chinese Mandarin as the absolute standard for every aspect of Singapore Mandarin to advocating a normative standard close to Chinese Mandarin for Singapore Mandarin. Second, it led to my advocating the compilation of the 《全球华语词典》 *quánqiú huáyǔ cídiǎn* 'Global Chinese Dictionary' and 《全球华语大词典》 *quánqiú huáyǔ dà cídiǎn* 'Great Global Chinese Dictionary', as well as researching Global Chinese Grammar to address issues that arose in global Chinese language communication.

While Professor Lu Jianming was in Singapore we struck up a friendship through our research sessions and daily interactions and communications. From 1994 to the present, over the course of more than two decades, he has become a sincere and real friend for me, a friend I can rely on in Beijing.

Upon returning to China in 1995, he deliberately took with him a number of works by local writers, planning to write a grammar book on the Chinese language in Singapore. Thus *Singapore Mandarin Grammar I* is a description of the grammar features of Singapore Mandarin during the 1980s and 1990s, based on the corpus of written language.

II. Features and Contributions of *Singapore Mandarin Grammar I*

Firstly, the author reviewed the local research on Singapore Mandarin grammar conducted in the 1980s and 1990s and made the following comments: (1) Singaporean scholars paid little attention to the boundaries between the common language and dialects, and tended to regard everything that was different from Chinese Mandarin as characteristics of Singapore Mandarin grammar. In fact, many of the grammatical phenomena discussed were merely dialectal components, not features of Singapore Mandarin as a common language. (2) There were some overgeneralisations about Singapore Mandarin. For instance, in the discussion about the word order of double object constructions, it is stated that due to the influence of Min and Cantonese, the object referring to things (i.e. direct object) precedes the object referring to the person (i.e. indirect object) in Singapore Mandarin (e.g. 他给三本书我 *tā gěi sān běn shū wǒ* 'He gave me three books'). Such a generalisation gives a false impression that this is the only possible word order for double object constructions. The fact is that apart from the order mentioned, the reverse order, in which the indirect object precedes the direct object, is also allowed in Singapore Mandarin (e.g. 给他五块钱 *gěi tā wǔ kuài qián* 'Give him five dollars' or 告诉他一个好消息 *gàosù tā yī gè hǎo xiāoxī* 'Tell him the good news'). In addition, this order is even more prevalent in written texts, while the use of the first order is rather limited. These comments are all quite pertinent. Moreover, the Singapore Mandarin grammatical studies at that time mixed up written and spoken languages and would usually use examples to demonstrate the differences between Singapore Mandarin and Chinese Mandarin. However, none of the researchers spoke Chinese Mandarin nor were familiar with its syntax, and what they were referring to were only grammar books published at that time or before.

Unlike those researchers, Professor Lu lives in a contemporary Chinese Mandarin-speaking environment and has conducted extensive research on the grammar of this language. Having him study Singapore Mandarin grammar, we can avoid the trap of failing to 'make out the true face'.[2] As a result, there are so many findings in the book that we, as Singapore Mandarin speakers, have not been able to discover. Currently, the differences highlighted in the book still exist in Singapore Mandarin.

Secondly, the book mainly examines the written language of Singapore Mandarin, while also taking the spoken language into account. Professor Lu gives the following reasons: (1) Written language is substantially more standardised since it has been modified and refined. (2) The common language of an ethnic group usually contains both spoken and written forms, though with a different historical formation process. Generally speaking, the written language will become the common language before the spoken form does. (3) In the case of Singapore Mandarin, the spoken form has not yet matured into the common language for

Singaporeans. If the spoken language should be the focus of linguistic investigation, one will inevitably include some non-Singapore-Mandarin usages as characteristics of it. Therefore, Professor Lu Jianming chose to investigate the written language of more than 110 works by Singaporean authors and scholars, including novels, dramas, essay collections, travelogues, academic essay collections and Singapore Mandarin textbooks for primary and secondary schools (see Appendix 3, The Origins of Examples). He also examined several Chinese newspapers circulated in Singapore, focusing on *Zaobao* as a representative example, and collected data from some Chinese programmes broadcast on Singapore TV's Channel 8. He made strenuous efforts to make the corpus universal and representative in order to "describe and explain characteristics that are compatible with Chinese Mandarin, and to specify characteristics that are inconsistent with Chinese Mandarin".

I once held the view that the influence of foreign languages on spoken Singapore Mandarin was far greater than that on written forms, since spoken Singapore Mandarin had not developed into a common and mature language as the written language had. This is in line with Professor Lu's view that "spoken Singapore Mandarin is immature". On the other hand, from the perspective of language contact, spoken Singapore Mandarin has more grammatical variations than the written form. Some variations have become conventional and are also found in other Chinese-speaking regions, such as Malaysia. These phenomena need to be studied in the future. If these instances occur in other Chinese-speaking regions as well, can they be labelled as "grammatical features of Singapore Mandarin"?

Thirdly, this book is the first monograph that systematically discusses the grammar of Singapore Mandarin. Readers will learn the grammatical features of Singapore Mandarin, understand the reasons for these features and the detailed differences between Singapore Mandarin and Chinese Mandarin. Meanwhile, they are also learning a whole grammatical system, some aspects of which are listed here.

1. 一般上 *yībānshàng* 'in general' is an adverb particularly and frequently used in Singapore Mandarin.
2. In Chinese Mandarin, only *de* 得 'DE' can be used in predicate-state complement constructions, but not 到 *dào* 'DAO'. There is no 使到 *shǐdào* 'make' in Chinese Mandarin either.
3. 来 *lái* 'come' is a very unique auxiliary in Singapore Mandarin, which usually follows the predicate-complement structure V 好 *hǎo* 'well'. V 好来 *hǎolái* 'well' is semantically equivalent to V 好 *hǎo* 'well' but with an emphasis of hoping to achieve the desired good results.
4. Unstressed 是 *shì* 'be' is used in adjective predicate sentences, such as 我认为这是不公平 *wǒ rènwéi zhè shì bù gōngpíng* 'I don't think it is fair'. This kind of Europeanised sentence is not found in Chinese Mandarin.
5. Due to the influence of English, the BEI construction is extensively utilised in Singapore Mandarin, not exclusively found in translated works.

The foregoing features make this text particularly well suited as a reference book for those working in the local press and media, as a textbook for Chinese language teacher education in tertiary institutions, and for Chinese language or comparative linguistics courses in Chinese departments. Professor Lu Jianming said modestly that the publication of the monograph was simply a way to leave his mark. As an ex-practitioner in Chinese language teachers' education who has spent my entire career promoting and working on the development and application of Chinese language in Singapore, I replied that this mark was never small.

Finally, I would like to reaffirm Professor Lu Jianming's view on the regulation of Singapore Mandarin. "Of the two, universality and systematicity, universality is primary, and systematicity is ultimately subordinate to universality." It was with this view in mind that I came up with the notion of 大华语 *dà huáyǔ* 'Great Chinese'. I also put forward the principle of "strict teaching and lenient evaluation" in the teaching of Mandarin. "Strict teaching" means that the selection of teaching materials should tilt towards Chinese Mandarin, while "lenient evaluation" means that language usage in Singapore should be taken fully into account in evaluation.

Chew Ching Hai

Notes

1 Translator's note: For detailed discussion about different terms used for Chinese language in Singapore and other Chinese speaking regions, see section 1.2.
2 The author cited a famous Chinese poem by Li Bai here, which goes 不识庐山真面目，只缘身在此山中 'Of Mountain Lu we cannot make out the true face, for we are lost in the heart of the very place' (translated by Xu Yuanchong). It implies that one may not find the real characteristics of a grammar if one is immersed in it.

1 Introduction

Lu Jianming

1.1 What Is Grammar?

What is grammar? In simple terms, grammar refers to the rules of our words. The way we speak or write is determined by certain rules and principles, as can be shown by the following examples:

(1) 老爸　　　最　　　喜欢　　　吃　　　榴莲。
　　lǎobà　　*zuì*　　*xǐhuān*　　*chī*　　*liúlián*
　　Dad　　　most　　like　　　eat　　durian
　　'Dad's favourite fruit is durian.'

(2) 榴莲　　　老爸　　　最　　　喜欢　　　吃。
　　liúlián　　*lǎobà*　　*zuì*　　*xǐhuān*　　*chī*
　　durian　　dad　　　most　　like　　　eat
　　'Durian is the favourite fruit for dad.'

(3) *老爸　　　喜欢　　　最　　　吃　　　榴莲。[1]
　　lǎobà　　*xǐhuān*　　*zuì*　　*chī*　　*liúlián*
　　Dad　　　like　　　most　　eat　　durian

(4) *老爸　　　榴莲　　　吃　　　最　　　喜欢。
　　lǎobà　　*liúlián*　　*chī*　　*zuì*　　*xǐhuān*
　　Dad　　　durian　　eat　　most　　like

(5) *吃　　　喜欢　　　最　　　榴莲　　　老爸。
　　chī　　*xǐhuān*　　*zuì*　　*liúlián*　　*lǎobà*
　　eat　　like　　　most　　durian　　dad

DOI: 10.4324/b23129-1

All the sentences from (1) to (5) contain the same language components: 老爸 *lǎobà* 'dad', 最 *zuì* 'most', 喜欢 *xǐhuān* 'like', 吃 *chī* 'eat' and 榴莲 *liúlián* 'durian'. However, Singapore Mandarin native speakers would intuitively acknowledge that sentences (1) and (2) are acceptable while sentences (3) to (5) are not. This is because sentences (1) and (2) conform to Singapore Mandarin speaking rules. The sentences in (3) to (5) violate these rules. Although both sentences in (1) and (2) are well structured, the meaning of sentence (1) differs very subtly from that of sentence (2) (sentence (1) emphasises the fact that the dad's favourite food is durian, whereas sentence (2) focuses on durian as being dad's favourite food), as they are constructed according to different rules. It is evident from these examples that the five components – 老爸 *lǎobà* 'dad', 最 *zuì* 'most', 喜欢 *xǐhuān* 'like', 吃 *chī* 'eat' and 榴莲 *liúlián* 'durian' – are not juxtaposed together randomly. They have to follow certain rules when forming a meaningful sentence, and different construction rules will lead to different interpretations. Perceptibly, the formation of our speech is determined by rules. We are usually not aware of the existence of these rules because we take them for granted. These rules are called the grammar of a language.

When we say "grammar refers to the rules we follow when speaking", it is a convenient yet loose definition because the principles of speech are not only concerned with the grammar but also with phonology, semantics and pragmatics. To put it in more scientific terms, grammar refers to the way in which we can and cannot combine words to form phrases and sentences in a language. Our speech consists of sentences made up of words that can be further divided into morphemes. So, we can redefine grammar as the rules of how to combine words into phrases and sentences. Although this definition is correct about the domains of grammar, it is, however, descriptively inadequate, because there are rules which are beyond the description of this generalisation. For example, in the case of pictophonetic characters which are composed of a pictophonetic element and a phonetic element, the part that signifies the sound of the character is neither a word nor a morpheme. Thus, the formation rule of pictophonetic characters is not covered by this definition of grammar. So far, it is more accurate to say that grammar is the set of rules by which larger units of meaning and sound are formed out of smaller ones. It is known to all that language is a semiotic system of sound and meaning, while the units are of different sizes. As a result, smaller units form larger units, according to what we call grammar, in a language.

Grammar is generally subdivided into two areas of study – syntax and morphology. Syntax is concerned with the ways in which words can be combined to form sentences. Morphology is the study of how words are formed out of morphemes. For Mandarin Chinese, the common language of the Han people, including Singapore Mandarin, syntactic rules are of greater importance than morphological rules. Thus, studying Singapore Mandarin grammar basically means the study of the syntax from a practical perspective. So, this book will mainly focus on the description and interpretation of the syntactic rules of Singapore Mandarin.

We cannot talk about grammar without mentioning its relations with logic, which is quite intricate and complex. In particular, the boundaries between the two need special attention.

Although ungrammatical sentences certainly make no sense, it does not mean that grammatical sentences will always be intelligible. For example, in Singapore Mandarin, there is such a construction "X bǎ Y VP", as illustrated here:

(6) 哥哥　　　把　　汽车　　修好　　了。
　　 gēge　　 bǎ　 qìchē　 xiūhǎo　 le
　　 older.brother　BA　car　　fix　　LE
　　 'The older brother had the car fixed.'

(7) 他　　把　　车　　卖　　了。
　　 tā　 bǎ　 chē　 mài　 le
　　 3SG　BA　car　 sell　 LE
　　 'He sold off the car.'

(8) 弟弟　　　　把　　杯子　　打破　　了。
　　 dìdi　　　 bǎ　 bēizi　 dǎpò　　le
　　 younger.brother　BA　cup　　break　LE
　　 'The younger brother broke the cup.'

(9) 风　　把　　门　　吹开　　了。
　　 fēng　 bǎ　 mén　 chuīkāi　 le
　　 wind　 BA　door　blow.open　LE
　　 'The wind blew the door open.'

The following sentence also conforms to this sentence configuration.

(10) *蚂蚁　　把　　灯　　吹灭　　了。
　　 mǎyǐ　 bǎ　 dēng　 chuīmiè　 le
　　 ant　　BA　fire　　blow.out　 LE
　　 Lit: 'The ant blew out the fire.'

However, this sentence is semantically bizarre since an ant cannot be interpreted as the agent of the blowing action (unless in a fairy story). Therefore, a grammatically well-structured sentence might not be semantically logical and meaningful. The sentences in (11) are another example:

(11) 鬼子兵　　　一下子　　倒　　了　　一大片，　死了　　的、
　　　guǐzibīng　　yíxiàzi　　dǎo　le　　yídàpiàn　sǐle　　de
　　　devil.soldiers　at.once　fall　LE　a.swarm　dead　DE

半死不活　　　的　　都　　躺　　在　　血泊里　　　乱喊乱叫。
bànsǐbùhuó　　de　　dōu　tǎng　zài　xuèpōlǐ　　luànhǎnluànjiào
dying　　　　DE　　all　lie　in　pool.of.blood　scream.and.cry

'A large swarm of devil soldiers fell down at once. The dead ones and the dying ones are all screaming and crying.'

These sentences are grammatically correct, but semantically illogical, since the dead devil soldiers cannot possibly scream and cry as the dying ones do.

On the contrary, other sentences which seem to have no logic on the surface are accepted and understood by every native speaker. Therefore, those should be regarded as completely well-structured sentences in Singapore Mandarin. For example, it is acceptable to say 你吃大碗 nǐ chī dàwǎn, 我吃小碗 wǒ chī xiǎowǎn 'you eat the big bowl of food, and I eat the smaller one'. The literal meaning of this sentence seems to go against our common world knowledge (especially in comparison with 你吃米饭 nǐ chī mǐfàn, 我吃面条 wǒ chī miàntiáo 'you eat the rice and I eat the noodle'). However, Singapore Mandarin native speakers would not interpret this sentence literally as 'you eat that big bowl and I eat the small one'. Another example is the phrase 恢复疲劳 huīfùpíláo 'to refresh', which also appears to be illogical in its literal sense 'to restore the fatigue' (in comparison with 恢复体力 huīfù tǐlì 'restore energy'). But again, this phrase is conventional and grammatical, which should not be discarded mechanically as being ungrammatical.

Hence, grammar closely relates to logic but it is not completely equal. Logic is the rule of thinking and reasoning. Since the ability to think and reason are shared by all human beings, logical rules remain the same across the different languages. Nevertheless, grammar is the rule of language which is the carrier of thinking. Different people use different languages, which involve different grammatical rules that do not correspond to logical rules. Thus, we need to avoid replacing grammatical analysis with logical analysis in grammar teaching or grammar research.

Lastly, one point needs to be mentioned and that is the word "grammar" is used in two senses. The first sense refers to the grammatical rule itself, which is used in sentences such as "This sentence violates the grammar" or "Singapore Mandarin grammar differs from Chinese Mandarin Grammar". The second sense of grammar indicates the description and illustration of the rules of a certain language. This sense is used in sentences like "He bought a grammar book today" and "There will be a grammar test tomorrow morning". The grammar rules of a language are of objective existence, and one language has only one grammar. However, the description of the grammar of a language might not be the same because of different views and perspectives from different researchers. We have to make it clear that any type of grammar book can only serve as a tool which helps us to observe and understand language phenomena that offers us a way to analyse and study the grammar. But, we should not let the grammar books lead us by the nose and mistake them as being 100 percent accurate during the learning process. It is essential that we constantly test the grammar rules against authentic language facts to provide continuous modification and complementation for the existing rules in grammar books.

1.2 What Is the Grammar of Singapore Mandarin?

The grammar of Singapore Mandarin refers to the rules of forming phrases and sentences in the language. Singapore Mandarin is the common language of all Singaporean Chinese people, which is also an essential part of the Standard Chinese that is adopted in modern Chinese societies around the world. The standard variety of Chinese is known as 普通话 *Pǔtōnghuà* 'the common language' in mainland China (which is referred to as Chinese Mandarin hereafter); 国语 *Guóyǔ* 'the national language' in Taiwan and Hong Kong of China; and 华语 *Huáyǔ* 'the language of the Chinese people' in Singapore, Malaysia and many other places. Singapore Mandarin and Chinese Mandarin can be traced to the same origin. They share similarities in that both are based on the northern Chinese varieties, with Beijing pronunciation being the standard. However, the two varieties are distinct from each other in phonetic, lexical and syntactic aspects. In phonetics, one significant difference is that rhotacisation of syllable finals and neutral tone are hardly present in Singapore Mandarin but very common in Chinese Mandarin. On the lexical level, words such as 组屋 *zǔwū* 'public housing', 使到 *shǐdào* 'make', 太过 *tàiguò* 'too much' and 摆放 *bǎifàng* 'arrange' are commonly used in Singapore Mandarin but rare in Chinese Mandarin. The words 服务员 *fúwùyuán* 'waiter', 乘客 *chéngkè* 'passenger', 宇航员 *yǔhángyuán* 'astronaut', 救护车 *jiùhùchē* 'ambulance', 摩托车 *mótuōchē* 'motorcycle', 洗澡 *xǐzǎo* 'take a shower' and 劫持 *jiéchí* 'hijack' in Chinese Mandarin are replaced with 侍应生 *shìyīngshēng*, 搭客 *dākè*, 太空人 *tàikōngrén*, 救伤车 *jiùshāngchē*, 电单车 *diàndānchē*, 冲凉 *chōngliáng* and 骑劫 *qíjié* respectively in Singapore Mandarin. There are also apparent differences on the grammatical level. For example, the VP-Neg question formed by two-syllable verbs (or adjectives) has to be in the form of "AB *bū* AB" in Chinese Mandarin (e.g. 参观不参观 *cānguān bū cānguān* 'whether to visit', 干净不干净 *gānjìng bū gānjìng* 'whether to be clean'), however the form of "A *bū* AB" (e.g. 参不参观 *cān bū cānguān*, 干不干净 *gān bū gānjìng*) is not only grammatical but also more frequently used in Singapore Mandarin. The other example is that Singapore Mandarin allows *yǒu* insertion ahead of the matrix verb, such as 我也有想过 *wǒ yě yǒu xiǎngguò* 'I have also thought about it' or 你妈妈有在家吗 *nǐ māmā yǒu zàijiā ma* 'Is your Mum at home?'; whereas in Chinese Mandarin, the preceding two sentences have to be 我也想过 *wǒ yě yǒu xiǎngguò* and 你妈妈在家吗 *nǐ māmā yǒu zàijiā ma*. In general,

Singapore Mandarin has its own characteristics and grammatical features. In this book, the similarities between Singapore Mandarin and Chinese Mandarin are well described and explicated. Meanwhile the differences are highlighted. The reasons that Singapore Mandarin grammar distinguishes itself from Chinese Mandarin grammar are discussed in Chapter 5, Volume II.

This book mainly concentrates on the grammar of written data of Singapore Mandarin, and also takes oral data into consideration at the same time. There are two reasons why written Singapore Mandarin is regarded as the main research target: (1) Written language is substantially more standardised since it has been modified and refined. (2) The common language of an ethnic group usually contains both spoken and written forms, though with a different historical formation process. Generally speaking, the written language will become the common language before the spoken form does; in the case of Chinese language, the time that written Chinese had become the lingua franca of the Han nationality can be dated back to the end of the Tang Dynasty (the 9th century AD). During the following Song (12th century) and Yuan (13th century) Dynasties, written Chinese became better developed. This type of written Chinese is based on the northern varieties of Chinese and spread widely throughout China. Comparatively, the oral form of the lingua franca of the Han nationality emerged between the Yuan and Ming Dynasties (14th century AD), which was called *Guanhua* (官话, Mandarin). It became well developed only in the Qing Dynasty (17th to 18th centuries).

As a city and island nation, Singapore boasts ethnic diversity. The Singaporean government has decided to adopt a bilingual language policy in response to the country's social and economic features. This was absolutely a wise and correct decision. The initiation of such a type of bilingual policy results in the fact that most Chinese Singaporean, especially the younger generations, can speak both Chinese and English. This is conducive to the unity of the various ethnic groups in Singapore, which significantly benefits their economic development. It is also helpful to the work and study of every Singaporean as well. However, this has adverse effects on the study of Singapore Mandarin grammar, and the main negative impact is the mechanical application of English grammar when studying Singapore Mandarin grammar. It should be pointed out that these two grammars are remarkably different from each other. More specifically, Singapore Mandarin is a kind of non-morphological language that "lacks of morphological transformation" (Lü 1979) compared to English, which has distinct morphological markers and transformations. Take the follow sentences as an example.

(1) 他　　　　正在　　　　　　吃饭。
　　 tā　　　　zhèngzài　　　　chīfàn
　　 3SG.　　 in.process　　　 have.lunch
　　 'He is having his lunch.'

(2) 大家　　　都　　　尊重　　　他。
　　 dàjiā　　 dōu　　 zūnzhòng　 tā
　　 everybody　all　　respect　　 3SG
　　 'Everybody respects him.'

(3) 他　　爸爸　　从　　　中国　　　回来　　了。
　　 tā　　bàba　　cóng　　zhōngguó　 huílái　　le
　　 3SG　father　 from　　China　　　return　　LE
　　 'His father has come back from China.'

The third person pronoun 他 *tā* in (1) to (3) has different grammatical statuses and functions. But, in each example, the word 他 *tā* remains identical in form. When these sentences are translated into English, different lexical forms of the third person pronoun should be selected, as shown in (4) to (6).

(4) He is having his lunch.

(5) Everybody respects him.

(6) His father has come back from China.

See more examples as follows.

(7) 我们　　　调查　　　　事故　　　的　　　原因。
　　 wǒmen　　diàochá　　shìgù　　 De　　 yuányīn
　　 1Pl　　　investigate　accident　DE　　 cause
　　 'We will investigate the cause of the accident.'

(8) 调查　　　　事故　　　的　　 原因　　　是　　必要的。
　　 diàochá　　shìgù　　　de　　 yuányīn　　shì　 bìyàode
　　 investigate　accident　DE　　cause　　　be　　necessary
　　 'It is necessary to investigate the cause of the accident.'

(9) 我们　　正在　　　　对　　　事故　　　进行　　　调查。
　　 wǒmen　zhèngzài　　duì　　 shìgù　　 jinxing　　diàochá
　　 1Pl　　 in.process　 about　accident　proceed　 investigation
　　 'We are investigating the accident.'

The word 调查 *diàochá* 'investigation' functions differently here in each sentence in the same lexical form. It is a different story in English. For the English equivalent sentences we have to use 'investigate' in (10), 'investigating' in (11) and 'investigation' in (12).

(10) We will investigate the cause of the accident.
(11) Investigating the cause of the accident is necessary.
(12) We are making an investigation the accident.

The aforementioned features have to be noted when studying the Singapore Mandarin grammar. It is not proper to apply English grammar directly to Singapore Mandarin grammar.

Two more points should be considered since Singapore Mandarin lacks morphological changes.

First, we should put emphasis on word order. Word order is a significant mechanism in Singapore Mandarin due to the lack of morphological change. The conversion of the word order may change the structure and meaning of the original sentence. For example, 买榴莲了 *mǎiliúlián le* '<Someone> bought durian' and 榴莲买了 *liúliánmǎi le* 'As for durian, it is bought' have different meanings because of the alteration of the structural relationship of the grammatical elements. The former is an example of verb-object construction, whereas the latter is an example of a subject-predicate construction. Therefore, it is important to be fully aware of the word order when studying Singapore Mandarin grammar.

Second, we should attach importance to the application of functional words. Functional words here refer to words such as 的 *de* 'DE', 了 *le* 'LE', 呢 *ne* 'SFP', 吗 *ma* 'SFP', 而 *ér* 'and', 又 *yòu* 'and/again', 也 *yě* 'also', 把 *bǎ* 'BA', 被 *bèi* 'BEI' and so on. The major function of these types of words in a sentence is to express the grammatical relationship between words and phrases and to provide certain grammatical meanings to particular words and phrases. For example, 借书 *jiè shū* 'to borrow books' expresses a kind of grammatical relationship. The insertion of 的 *de* between the two characters, that is, 借的书 *jiè de shū* 'books that are borrowed', expresses another kind of grammatical relationship with a dissimilar meaning. The other example is as follows:

(13) 只有　　好　　政府　　　　和　　好　　公民，
　　　zhīyǒu　*hǎo*　*zhèngfǔ*　　*hé*　*hǎo*　*gōngmín*
　　　only　　good　government　and　good　citizens

　　　才　　能　　让　　我们　　赖以　　自强不息，　　而　　面对
　　　cái　*néng*　*rang*　*wǒmén*　*làiyǐ*　*zìqiángbūxī*　　*ér*　*miànduì*
　　　just　can　let　1PL　rely　self-improvement　and　face

千变万化　　　　的　　　国际局势。（早报 1995 年 8 月 21 日 7 版）
qiānbiànwànhuà　de　guójìjúshì
ever-changing　DE　international.situation
'Only a good government and good citizens can let us rely on self-improvement and face the ever-changing international situation.' (*Zaobao*, 7th edition, Aug. 21, 1995)

If the two functional words 只有 *zhǐyǒu* 'only' and 才 *cái* 'just' are deleted in example (13), then the relationship between the subject and the predicate will not remain the same. The deletion of these words erases the meaning expressed in the original sentence, which shows that "a good government and good citizens" is a prerequisite of "relying on self-improvement and facing the ever-changing international situation".

Functional words take significant roles in every language. They are extremely important in Singapore Mandarin grammar due to the lack of morphological changes in this language. Those who would like to improve their language proficiency and those who would like to learn Singapore Mandarin as a foreign language have to pay great attention to the use of functional words.

As for the research of Singapore Mandarin grammar, some representative researches include Chen (1993), The Grammar Section of Singapore Standard Chinese Committee (1985) and Goh (1986), among others. Their researches is worth referring to. However, some shortcomings still remain. First, their research focuses more on the oral instead of the written form of Singapore Mandarin. The oral language spoken in Singapore appears not to be as mature as a common language to all Singaporean Chinese. The result produced by focusing on oral language is to treat non-Singapore-Mandarin phenomena as characteristics of Singapore Mandarin. Second, the distinction between the common language and dialects are not fully noticed. It seems that any features that are different from Chinese Mandarin are considered to be the features of Singapore Mandarin grammar. In fact, many linguistic phenomena they mentioned are dialectical phenomena, not features of the common language. Third, some of their research findings are over-generalisations from isolated incidents. For example, in their research, the double object construction is said to be in an order where the thing-denoting object (i.e. direct object) is ahead of the person-denoting object (i.e. indirect object) in Singapore Mandarin due to the influence of Cantonese and Min dialects, as in 他给三本书我 *tā gěi sānběnshū wǒ* 'He gave three books to me'. This gives an incorrect impression that there is only one possible word order for double object construction in Singapore Mandarin. The actual situation is that in Singapore Mandarin the indirect object can either follow the direct object or precede it, as in 给他五块钱 *gěi tā wǔkuàiqián* 'give him five dollars' and 告诉他一个好消息 *gàosù tā yígè hǎoxiāoxī* 'tell him a piece of good news'. Furthermore, the latter form is more common in written Singapore Mandarin than the former, while the use of the former form is strictly constrained.

Considering the fact that the written form of Singapore Mandarin is more representative as the Singaporean common language compared to the oral form, we will concentrate on written Singapore Mandarin as our target language in this book. We have investigated more than 110 Chinese books published in Singapore during the 1980s and 90s. These were all written by Singaporean writers and scholars, and range in style from novels, dramas, proses, travel notes, academic papers and Singapore Mandarin textbooks for elementary and middle schools (see Appendix 3, The Sources of Examples, for details). We have also surveyed Chinese newspapers published in Singapore as well, with a focus on the *Zaobao*. Some Chinese broadcast programs, such as MediaCorp Channel 8, are also within our scope. Thus, the texts we selected in this book are representative and universal. To be more specific, according to the data we observed, the grammar described in this book is the grammar of Singapore Mandarin in the 1980s and 90s.

All the example sentences are marked with their sources. For the sake of universality, the example sentences after each grammatical description of a language phenomenon are not limited to just one particular resource, but adopted from different resources.

1.3 Grammatical Units

In order to describe or explain grammatical rules in one language, we need to choose certain forms of the sentence constituent as the unit for linguistic analysis. These are usually referred to as grammatical units. We must be very clear about these grammatical units when we learn and study a language grammar.

Singapore Mandarin sentences are often thought of as composed of characters. However, we do not use 'character' but 'word' or 'morpheme' as grammatical units when we talk about grammar. For example, instead of saying the sentence 今年葡萄丰收 *jīnnián pútáo fēngshōu* 'The grapes have been harvested this year' is formed by six characters, we should say that it is formed by three words – 今年 *jīnnián* 'this year', 葡萄 *pútáo* 'grape', 丰收 *fēngshōu* 'to be harvested' – or by five morphemes, 今 *jīn*, 年 *nián*, 葡萄 *pútáo*, 丰 *fēng*, 收 *shōu*. Before we learn and study the Singapore Mandarin grammar, we need to understand clearly the concept of character, morpheme and word. However, to understand the latter two we should first start from the notion of character.

Most of the characters we use are meaningful. Only some of them are not. According to whether the character is meaningful or not, we can divide them into two types:

A Meaningful characters such as 人 *rén* 'person', 好 *hǎo* 'good', 红 *hóng* 'red', 吃 *chī* 'eat', 走 *zǒu* 'walk', 吝 *lìn* 'stingy', 机 *jī* 'machine', 了 *le* 'LE', 的 *de* 'DE', 呢 *ne* 'SFP'.

B Meaningless characters such as 垃 *lā*, 橄 *gǎn*, 蜻 *qīng*, 葡 *pú*, 徘 *pái*, 蚯 *qiū*, 圾 *jī*, 榄 *lǎn*, 蜓 *tíng*, 萄 *táo*, 徊 *huái*.

All the characters in Group A are meaningful and these types of characters account for the majority of Chinese language. All the characters in Group B however are meaningless. For example, 垃 *lā* and 圾 *jī* do not have meanings as separate words unless they are combined together to express the meaning 'rubbish'. In grammar, characters in Group A can be regarded as morphemes, whereas the separate characters in Group B are not morphemes, and only the combinations of two characters are morphemes, such as 垃圾 *lājī* 'rubbish', 橄榄 *gǎnlǎn* 'olive', 蜻蜓 *qīng tíng* 'dragonfly', 葡萄 *pútáo* 'grape'. Although each character in Group A is a morpheme, we cannot draw a conclusion that one character is one morpheme because the relation between the character and the morpheme is quite complicated.

First, one character can represent several morphemes. There are two subtypes:

A One character represents different morphemes that have the same pronunciation but different meanings. For example, 信 *xìn* represents at least four morphemes, as follows:

   a The first morpheme means 'to believe', for example 信不信由你 *xìnbúxìnyóunǐ* 'whether you believe or not is up to you' and 别信他的话 *bié xìn tā de huà* 'don't believe his words'.
   b The second morpheme means 'letter', for example 写了一封信 *xiě le yìfēngxìn* 'wrote a letter' and 第一封介绍信 *dìyī fēng jièshàoxìn* 'the first letter of introduction'.
   c The third morpheme means 'credit', for example 言而有信 *yánéryǒuxìn* 'keep a promise' and 别失信于民 *bié shīxìnyúmín* 'don't disappoint people by breaking your promise'.
   d The fourth morpheme means 'as one pleases', for example 信步走来 *xìnbùzǒulái* 'come over at will' and 信口开河 *xìnkǒukāihé* 'speak carelessly'.

B One character represents different morphemes that have different pronunciations and meanings. For example, the character 乐 represents at least two different morphemes with two pronunciations: One means 'music' with the pronunciation *yuè*, the other means 'happy' with the pronunciation *lè*, as illustrated by the following examples in group *a* and group *b* respectively.

   a 音乐 *yīnyuè* 'music'   奏乐 *zòuyuè* 'play music'   乐器 *yuèqì* 'instrument'
   b 快乐 *kuàilè* 'happy'   欢乐 *huānlè* 'happy'   他乐了 *tālè le* 'he flipped out'

Second, the same morpheme can be represented by different characters. A typical example is numeral characters. One number can be represented by different characters. For example, the number 1 can be expressed by two characters, 一 *yī* and 壹 *yī*, the number 2 can be expressed by 二 *èr* and 贰 *èr*, the number 7 can be expressed by 七 *qī* and 柒 *qī* and so on.

Third, one character contains two morphemes. For example, 仨 *sā* is a one-syllable character but contains two morphemes, that is 三 *sān* 'three' and 个 *gè* 'CL'. It is also the same for 俩 *liǎ*, which contains two morphemes, 两 *liǎng* 'two' and 个 *gè* 'CL'.

Lastly, some characters are morphemes in one word but not in the other. For example, 沙 *shā* in the word 泥沙 *níshā* 'mud and sand' or the word 沙土 *shātǔ* 'sandy soil' is a morpheme. 发 *fā* in the word 发展 *fāzhǎn* 'develop' or the word 发达 *fādá* 'developed' is also a morpheme. But 沙 *shā* and *fā* in the word 沙发 *shāfā* 'sofa' are not morphemes independently. They are syllables because they are transliterated from English and express the meaning 'sofa' only when they are used as a whole.

Therefore, the notion of the character is not equal to that of the morpheme. Characters are the written unit used for recording languages, while morphemes are the smallest meaningful unit in grammar. We cannot talk about grammar on the basis of characters.

As far as Singapore Mandarin is concerned, there are four grammatical units. They are morpheme, word, phrase and sentence. Morpheme is the smallest grammatical unit and sentence is the largest. In Singapore Mandarin, the relations between the four units are: Morphemes form words, words form phrases and words/phrases with intonation form sentences. We will introduce morphemes and words in the following section.

1.4 Morphemes and Words

Morphemes and words are closely related because a word is composed of one or several morphemes.

A morpheme is the smallest meaningful grammatical unit in regards to the relationship between sound and meaning. For instance, the sentence 妹妹不吃白菜 *mèimei bū chībáicài* 'My sister doesn't eat cabbage' is composed of six morphemes, including 妹 *mèi* 'sister', 妹 *mèi* 'sister', 不 *bū* 'NEG', 吃 *chī* 'eat', 白 *bái* 'white', 菜 *cài* 'vegetable'. Every morpheme has its sound and meaning, which cannot be divided into smaller units. For example, as for the sound of *mèi*, it can be divided into smaller units – a rising tone, an initial consonant /m/ and a dual vowel /ei/ which can then be further divided into /e/ and /i/. However, from the sound-meaning perspective, it cannot be further divided. Thus, 妹 *mèi* 'sister' is considered as a morpheme in Singapore Mandarin. Most of the morphemes in Singapore Mandarin are monosyllable. Only a few of them are two-syllable or multi-syllable morphemes such as 葡萄 *pútáo* 'grape', 咖啡 *kāfēi* 'coffee', 巴刹 *bāshā* 'bazaar', 甘榜 *gānbǎng* 'kampong', 巧克力 *qiǎokèlì* 'chocolate', 比基尼 *bǐjīní* 'bikini' and 迪斯科 *dísīkē* 'disco'. These morphemes are mostly transliterated from foreign languages. The function of morphemes is to form words. In other words, morphemes are the building blocks of words.

A word is a grammatical unit that is larger than a morpheme. It is the smallest meaningful unit which can stand alone. In Singapore Mandarin, a word formed by a single morpheme is called a mono-morphemic word. For example, 不 *bū* 'NEG', 吃 *chī* 'eat', 人 *rén* 'person', 水 *shuǐ* 'water', 酒 *jiǔ* 'alcohol', 大 *dà* 'big', 红 *hóng* 'red', 亮 *liàng* 'bright', 拿 *ná* 'take', 坐 *zuò* 'sit', 买 *mǎi* 'buy', 他 *tā* 'he', 我 *wǒ* 'I'.

A word made of two or more morphemes is called a compound word; for example, 妹妹 *mèimei* 'sister', 白菜 *báicài* 'cabbage', 衣服 *yīfú* 'cloth', 组屋 *zǔwū* 'public house', 学校 *xuéxiào* 'school', 电脑 *diànnǎo* 'computer', 漂亮 *piàoliàng* 'beautiful', 伟大 *wěidà* 'great', 参观 *cānguān* 'visit', 研究 *yánjiū* 'research', 刚才 *gāngcái* 'just now', 但是 *dànshì* 'however', 因为 *yīnwéi* 'because', 工程师 *gōnchéngshī* 'engineer', 房地产 *fángdìchǎn* 'real estate', 建屋局 *jiànwūjú* 'Housing Development Board', 地球仪 *dìqiúyí* 'tellurian', 太空梭 *tàikōngsuō* 'space shuttle', 江湖医生 *jiānghúyīshēng* 'quack doctor', 帝国主义 *dìguózhǔyì* 'imperialism'.

Given that the single morpheme 妹 *mèi* 'sister' can also express the meaning of 'sister', one may ask why 妹妹 *mèimei* 'sister' but not 妹 *mèi* 'sister' is identified as a word? This is because 妹 *mèi* cannot stand on its own. For example, we never say *妹不吃白菜 *mèi bū chī báicài* 'My sister doesn't eat cabbage', *我有一个妹 *wǒ yǒuyí gè mèi* 'I have a sister', *妹很漂亮 *mèihěn piàoliàng* 'My sister is very beautiful' or *我很喜欢妹 *wǒ hěn xǐhuān mèi* 'I like my sister very much'. These examples show that 妹 *mèi* 'sister' is only a morpheme and the reduplicated form 妹妹 *mèimei* 'sister' is a word in Singapore Mandarin. However, 白 *bái* 'white' and 菜 *cài* 'vegetable' can both be used independently and are separate words. For instance, 白 *bái* is a word in the sentence 这张纸很白 *zhè zhāng zhǐ hěn bái* 'This paper is very white', and 菜 *cài* is a word in the sentence 妈妈买了许多菜 *māmamǎi le xǔduō cài* 'Mum bought a lot of vegetables'. However, why is 白菜 *báicài* 'cabbage' considered as one word but not two words? This is because 白 *bái* and 菜 *cài* are closely related in this case. The meaning 'cabbage' is not equal to the combined meaning of 白 *bái* 'white' and 菜 *cài* 'vegetable'. In other words, 白菜 *báicài* 'cabbage' cannot be considered as 白的菜 *bái de cài* 'white vegetable' because they denote different things. Thus, 白 *bái* 'white' and 菜 *cài* 'vegetable' are morphemes in the word 白菜 *báicài* 'cabbage'.

By contrast, although 不 *bū* 'not' and 吃 *chī* 'eat' are also adjacent in 不吃 *bū chī* 'not eat', they are considered as two words. This is because they not only have a meaning as a whole but can also be used on their own separately. For example, 不吃 *bū chī* 'not eat', 不说 *bū shuō* 'not say', 不看 *bú kàn* 'not watch', 不写 *bū*xiě 'not write', 不去 *búqù* 'not go', 不想 *bū xiǎng* 'not think' and 吃白菜 *chī báicài* 'eat cabbage', 吃樱桃 *chī yīngtáo* 'eat cherry', 吃面包 *chī miànbāo* 'eat bread', 吃冰淇淋 *chī bīngqílín* 'eat ice cream', 吃中国菜 *chī zhōngguócài* 'eat Chinese food'. In addition, we can insert other words between 不 *bū* 'not' and 吃 *chī* 'eat', such as 不吃 *būchī* 'not eat' → 不怎么吃 *būzěnmechī* 'not eat very much'/不常吃 *būchángchī* 'not often eat'/不天天吃 *būtiāntiān chī* 'not eat everyday'/不少吃 *būshǎo chī* 'not moderately eat'/不好好吃 *būhǎohao chī* 'not eat well' and so on. Therefore, 不吃 *būchī* cannot be regarded as one word but two words, because 不吃 *būchī* 'not eat' can be further analysed into two smaller units, each of which can stand on its own.

In brief, the word is the smallest grammatical unit that can be used on its own. Words form the sentences as building blocks.

In the next chapter we will further discuss word classes and sentences.

1.5 Explanations of the Examples

First of all, some examples in the book have sources but some do not. For the examples that include sources, there is one special case, in which the book being cited was missed in our Appendix 3, The Sources of Examples, and now there is no available access to its publisher and year of publication due to negligence of the work. For these cases, △ is added in front of the book name being cited to indicate that these examples have a source but the source is missing from Appendix 3. For example, there are two such cases in Section 3.4: 传统文化△趣谈 *chuántǒng wénhuà* 'traditional culture' (△*Qùtán*, 70) and 中学的大门(△含羞草 8) *zhōngxué de dàmén* 'the middle school gate' (△*Hánxiūcǎo*, 8). In addition, one example in Section 4.19 in Volume II was cited from *Shin Min Daily News*, which I just happened to read one day. This paper was not subscribed to by our research centre, and thus was not included in our corpus. However, the feasibility of those examples without sources has been confirmed by Huang Zuming and Cai Meili as being acceptable in Singapore Mandarin. They were born in Singapore and were studying at Peking University during that time. Both of them are now working in Singapore's education sector.

Second, characters are used differently in Singapore and mainland China in some phrases. Examples are as follows:

Singapore	Mainland China	Pinyin	Meaning
噜嗦	噜苏/啰嗦/啰唆	*luōsuō*	to chatter
毛毛絮雨	毛毛细雨	*máomáoxìyǔ*	drizzling
好象	好像	*hǎoxiàng*	to look like
腊烛	蜡烛	*làzhú*	candle
多脑河	多瑙河	*duōnǎohé*	the Danube
伊莉莎白	伊丽莎白	*yīlìshābái*	Elizabeth
座落	坐落	*zuòluò*	to be located in

All the words used in the book are standard characters in Mainland China, which will not influence the description of Singapore Mandarin grammar.

Third, the adverbial marker 地 *de* 'DE' in written language is written as 的 *de* 'DE' in Singapore Mandarin. All the examples in this book will be cited according to the original text, and 的 *de* 'DE' will remain unchanged.

Note

1 The asterisk in this book indicates that the expression is not grammatical.

2 Five Basic Types of Phrase

Lu Jianming

2.1 What Are Phrases?

A phrase is a grammatical unit that is larger than words and it is formed by combining words together according to grammatical rules. The function of a phrase is to form larger phrases or to be realised as sentences. For example, 骑马 *qímǎ* 'ride a horse' is a phrase which consists of two words: 骑 *qí* 'riding' and 马 *mǎ* 'horse'. 骑马 *qímǎ* *'ride a horse'* as a constituent may be embedded in a larger phrase, as in example (1).

(1) 朵丽丝   教   我   骑马…（大胡子 11）
    duǒlìsī *jiāo*   *wǒ*   *qímǎ*
    Dorothy   teach   1SG   ride.horse
    'Dorothy teaches me how to ride a horse.' (*Dàhúzi* 11)

The phrase 骑马 *qímǎ* 'ride a horse' can be a sentence in a given context, as shown in example (2). Here 骑马 *qímǎ* 'ride a horse' is a sentence, realised by the phrase 骑马 *qímǎ* 'ride a horse' with an intonation for questioning.

(2) 马丁   侧头   问   我： "要   骑马   吗？"
    mǎdīng *cètóu*   *wèn*   *wǒ*   *yào*   *qímǎ*   *ma*
    Martin   lean.head ask   1SG   want   ride.horse SFP
    'Martin turned his head around and asked me, "Want to ride a horse?"'

    "骑马？"   我   反问：   "上   哪儿   骑？"（大胡子 8）
    qímǎ   *wǒ*   *fǎnwèn* *shàng* *nǎr*   *qí*
    ride.horse 1SG   back.ask go   where   ride
    '"Ride a horse?" I asked him, "where?"' (*Dàhúzi* 8)

Different types of phrases are formed by linking up words with different grammatical rules. There are five basic types of phrase in Singapore Mandarin:

A Modifier-head phrases 偏正词组

小鱼 *xiǎo yú* 'small fish' 空瓶子 *kōng píngzi* 'empty bottle'
很深 *hěn shēn* 'very deep' 刚出世 *gāng chūshì* 'just born'

B Predicate-object phrases 述宾词组

读书 *dú shū* 'read books' 看电视 *kàn diànshì* 'watch TV'
听唱片 *tīng chàngpiān* 'listen to records'

C Predicate-complement phrases 述补词组

拉	长	借	来	挤	出
lā	*cháng*	*jiè*	*lái*	*jǐ*	*chū*
pull	long	borrow	come	squeeze	out
'to extend'		'to borrow'		'squeeze out'	

看	得	完
kàn	*de*	*wán*
read	DE	finish

'be able to finish reading'

D Subject-predicate phrases 主谓词组

时间	过	得	快,	孩子	要	念书,
shíjiān	*guò*	*de*	*kuài*	*háizi*	*yào*	*niànshū*
time	go	DE	fast	children	should	read.book

'time goes fast'   'children should go to school'

船	开	了（万花筒 62–63）
chuán	*kāi*	*le*
ship	leave	LE

'The ship is leaving.' (*Wànhuātǒng* 62–63)

E Coordinative phrases 联合词组

父亲、	母亲,	亲戚	和	朋友们
fùqīn	*mǔqīn*	*qīnqī*	*hé*	*péngyǒumen*
father	mother,	relatives	and	friends

'father, mother, relatives and friends'

（他们	的	恋爱	始终	建立	在）	健康、	理智
tāmen	de	liànài	shǐzhōng	jiànlì	zài	jiànkāng	lǐzhì
3PL	DE	love	always	built	on	healthy	rational

（的	基础	上）,
de	jīchǔ	shàng
DE	base	on

'(Their love is always built on a) healthy and rational (base).'

生男	生女	（都	一样）（无弦月 4–5）
shēngnán	shēngnǚ	dōu	yíyàng
have.boy	have.girl	all	same

'having a boy or a girl (are the same)' (*Wúxiányuè* 4–5)

This chapter focuses on the aforementioned five types of phrases. What needs to be clarified to the readers first is the significant difference between Singapore Mandarin and English in terms of grammatical units due to the lack of morphological transformations in Singapore Mandarin. In English, morphemes, words, phrases and sentences are in a "forming relationship", that is, morphemes form words, words form phrases and phrases form sentences. However, in Singapore Mandarin, such a "forming relationship" is only effective to morphemes and words (i.e. morphemes form words), as well as to words and phrases (i.e. words form phrases). The relationship between words, phrases and sentences is a "realising relationship", which means that sentences in Singapore Mandarin are not combinations of phrases but are realised by words or phrases integrating a given intonation. Such differences between Singapore Mandarin and English are illustrated as follows, where → indicates the "forming relationship" and ↓ indicates the "realising relationship".

English: morphemes ⟶ words ⟶ phrases ⟶ sentences

Singapore Mandarin: morphemes ⟶ words ⟶ phrases
                                          ↘ ↙
                                      sentences

As Zhu (1985) points out, "Chinese sentence structure is understood as long as the structure and function of Chinese phrases are made clear". Thus, this book starts from the basic types of phrases in Singapore Mandarin.

2.2 Modifier-Head Phrases

The word 鱼 *yú* 'fish' denotes the category of fish, including all kinds of fish in the world. If 小 *xiǎo* 'small' is added ahead of it, that is, 小鱼 *xiǎo yú* 'small fish', the scope is reduced to small-sized fish. Thus, it can be seen that the modifier

小 *xiǎo* 'small' serves to modify and restrict the head noun, that is, 鱼 *yú* 'fish'. The phrase 小鱼 *xiǎo yú* 'small fish' is a typical example of the modifier-head phrases.

Generally, the modifier-head phrase consists of two components: The main part is the head of the phrase, such as 鱼 *yú* 'fish' in 小鱼; the modification and restriction part is the modifier, such as 小 *xiǎo* 'small' in 小鱼 *xiǎo yú* 'small fish', which modifies or semantically restricts the head. The relationship between the modifier and the head is modification. More examples of modifier-head phrases are grouped here, based on the semantic relation between the modifier and the head.

A 新   车   干净   衣服   欢乐   的   气氛
   xīn   *chē*   *gānjìng* *yīfú*   *huānlè*   *de* *qìfēn*
   new   car   clean   clothes   happy   DE   atmosphere
   'new car'   'clean clothes'   'happy atmosphere'

B 木头   桌子   塑料   雨伞   棉布   的   衣服
   mùtóu   *zhuōzi* *sùliào*   *yǔsǎn*   *miánbù*   *de* *yīfú*
   wood   table   plastic   umbrella cotton   DE   clothes
   'wooden table'   'plastic umbrella'   'cotton clothes'

C 红红   的   太阳   雪白   的   衬衣
   hónghóng *de* *tàiyáng*   *xuěbái*   *de* *chènyī*
   red   DE   sun   white   DE   shirt
   'red sun'   'white shirt'

   阴森森   的   感觉
   yīnsēnsēn *de* *gǎnjué*
   gloomy   DE   feeling
   'gloomy feeling'

D 我们   学校   他   弟弟   公司   的   利益
   wǒmén   *xuéxiào* *tā* *dìdi*   *gōngsī*   *de* *lìyì*
   1Pl   school   3SG   brother   company   DE   profit
   'our school'   'his brother'   'the company's profit'

E 三   辆   车   五   粒   鸡蛋   许多   礼物
   sān   *liàng* *chē*   *wǔ*   *lì* *jīdàn*   *xǔduō*   *lǐwù*
   three   Cl.   car   five   Cl.   egg   many   gift
   'three cars'   'five eggs'   'many gifts'

F	细细	研究	认真	地	学习	慢慢	写
	xìxì	*yánjiū*	*rènzhēn*	*de*	*xuéxí*	*mànmàn*	*xiě*
	carefully	research	carefully	DE	study	slowly	write
	'to research carefully'		'to study carefully'			'to write slowly'	

G	马上	走	刚	来	已经	看	了
	mǎshàng	*zǒu*	*gāng*	*lái*	*yǐjīng*	*kàn*	*le*
	right.away	go	just	come	already	see	LE
	'to go right away'		'just came'		'already seen'		

H	很	高	非常	地	重要	十分	安静
	hěn	*gāo*	*fēicháng*	*de*	*zhòngyào*	*shífēn*	*ānjìng*
	very	high	very	DE	important	extremely	quiet
	'very high'		'very important'			'extremely quiet'	

In Class A, the head denotes an object, and the modifier conveys the characteristic of the head (e.g. 新 *xīn* 'new' in 新车 *xīn chē* 'new car' expresses the characteristic of the newness of 车 *chē* 'car'). In Class B, the modifier expresses the texture of the object (i.e. the head). For example, 木头 *mùtóu* 'wooden' in 木头桌子 *mùtóu zhuōzi* 'a wooden table' indicates that the table is made of wood. In Class C, the modifier describes or explains properties or stative traits of the object (i.e. the sun). For example, 红红的 *hónghóng de* 'red' in 红红的太阳 *hónghóng de tàiyáng* 'a red sun' describes the red colour of the sun. In Class D, the modifier specifies the possessor of the head, such that 学校 *xuéxiào* 'school' is possessed by 我们 *wǒmen* '1PL' in 我们学校 *wǒmén xuéxiào* 'our school'. In Class E, the modifier indicates the quantity of the object. For example, 三辆 *sān liàng* 'three' expresses that the quantity of 车 *chē* 'car' is three. In Class F, the head denotes an activity, whereas the modifier specifies the manner of the activity (e.g. 细细 *xìxì* 'carefully') indicates that 研究 *yánjiū* 'research' is conducted in a careful manner. In Class G, the modifier states the time of the action or activity, such as 马上 *mǎshàng* 'right away' indicates that the action 走 *zǒu* 'go' is about to take place in a very short time. In Class H, the adjective head denotes a kind of quality or property, whereas the modifier expresses the degree of the quality. For example, 很 *hěn* 'very' in 很高 *hěn gāo* 'very high' indicates that it is very high.

Clearly, the eight classes of modifier-head phrases can be categorised into two classes according to the property of the head. The head in Class A to Class E denotes objects, so the whole phrase denotes objects as well. By comparison, the head in Class F to Class H doesn't denote objects but activities or properties. Hence, the whole phrase doesn't represent objects. Later it will be shown that the functions of the two types of modifier-head phrases also differentiate from each other in constructing sentences. For the sake of distinction, the modifiers in the first type are called attributes (定语 *dìngyǔ*), with the phrases being called attribute-head phrases

(定-中偏正词组 *dìng - zhōng piānzhèng cízǔ*); whereas the modifiers in the second type are called adverbials (状语 *zhuàngyǔ*), with the phrases being called adverbial-head phrases (状-中偏正词组 *zhuàng - zhōng piānzhèng cízǔ*).

Some of the examples discussed contain the auxiliary word 的 *de* 'DE' or 地 *de* 'DE', such as 欢乐的气氛 *huānlè de qìfēn* 'happy atmosphere', 棉布的衣服 *miánbù de yīfú* 'cotton clothes', 红红的太阳 *hónghóng de tàiyáng* 'red sun', 公司的利益 *gōngsī de lìyì* 'the profit of the company', 认真地学习 *rènzhēn de xuéxí* 'to study carefully' and 非常地重要 *fēicháng de zhòngyào* 'very important'. Generally, 的 *de* 'DE' is used in attribute-head phrases (定-中偏正词组 *dìng - zhōng piānzhèng cízǔ*) while 地 *de* 'DE' is used in adverbial-head phrases (状-中偏正词组 *zhuàng - zhōng piānzhèng cízǔ*). Other examples do not contain 的 *de* or 地 *de*. However, in these cases it is also possible to insert 的 *de* 'DE' or 地 *de* 'DE' between the modifier and the head, as indicated here.

新	车		新	的	车
xīn	*chē*		*xīn*	*de*	*chē*
new	car		new	DE	car
'new car'			'new car'		

木头	桌子		木头	的	桌子
mùtóu	*zhuōzi*		*mùtóu*	*de*	*zhuōzi*
wood	table		wood	DE	table
'wooden table'			'wooden table'		

我们	学校		我们	的	学校
wǒmén	*xuéxiào*		*wǒmén*	*de*	*xuéxiào*
1Pl	school		1Pl	DE	school
'our school'			'our school'		

细细	研究		细细	地	研究
xìxì	*yánjiū*		*xìxì*	*de*	*yánjiū*
carefully	research		carefully	DE	research
'to research carefully'			'to research carefully'		

十分	安静		十分	地	安静
shífēn	*ānjìng*		*shífēn*	*de*	*ānjìng*
extremely	quiet		extremely	DE	quiet
'extremely quiet'			'extremely quiet'		

Whether 的 *de* 'DE' or 地 *de* 'DE' is inserted or not does not affect the semantic meaning or the property of the phrase. For example, 新车 *xīn chē* 'new car' and

细细研究 *xìxì yánjiū* 'to research carefully' are modifier-head phrases without 的/地 *de* '*DE*'. Comparatively, 新的车 *xīn de chē* 'new car' (新的 *xīn de* 'new' is the modifier and 车 *chē* 'car' the head) and 细细地研究 *xìxì de yánjiū* 'to research carefully' (细细地 *xìxì de* 'carefully' is the modifier and 研究 *yánjiū* 'research' the head) are also modifier-head phrases with 的/地 *de* '*DE*'.

2.3 Predicate-Object Phrases

As discussed in the previous section, 小鱼 *xiǎo yú* 'small fish' is a modifier-head phrase. If 小 *xiǎo* 'small' is replaced by the verb 钓 *diào* 'to fish' or 吃 *chī* 'to eat', 钓鱼 *diàoyú* 'to catch fish' and 吃鱼 *chīyú* 'to eat fish' distinguish themselves from 小鱼 *xiǎo yú* 'small fish' not only in semantic meaning but also in the structural relations between the two words. The phrases such as 钓鱼 *diàoyú* 'to catch fish' or 吃鱼 *chīyú* 'to eat fish' are called predicate-object phrases.

Generally, a predicate-object phrase also consists of two parts: The first part is the matrix verb, indicating the activity; the following part is the object that is affected by the activity. For example, 钓 *diào* 'to fish' in 钓鱼 *diàoyú* 'to catch fish' is an activity of fishing, whereas 鱼 *yú* 'fish' is the object of what is being fished. The first part of the predicate-object phrase is usually called the predicate (述语 *shùyǔ*), and the following part is called the object (宾语 *bīnyǔ*). The predicate dominates the object. Some more examples follow.

洗	衣服	读	书	盖	楼房
xǐ	*yīfú*	*dú*	*shū*	*gài*	*lóufáng*
wash	clothes	read	book	build	building
'to wash clothes'		'to read books'		'to build high buildings'	

写	信	想	办法	考虑	问题
xiě	*xìn*	*xiǎng*	*bànfǎ*	*kǎolǜ*	*wèntí*
write	letter	think	way	consider	problem
'to write letters'		'to find a way'		'to consider a problem'	

坐	德士	去	牛车水	吃	大碗
zuò	*déshì*	*qù*	*niúchēshuǐ*	*chī*	*dàwǎn*
take	taxi	go	China.Town	eat	big.bowl
'to take a taxi'		'to go to China Town'		'to eat with a big bowl'	

写	毛笔	爱	干净	喜欢	唱歌
xiě	*máobǐ*	*ài*	*gānjìng*	*xǐhuān*	*chànggē*
write	brush.pen	like	clean	like	sing
'to write with a brush'		'to love to be clean'		'to like singing'	

做	实验	接受	训练
zuò	shíyàn	jiēshòu	xùnliàn
do	experiment	receive	training
'to do experiments'		'to receive training'	

Auxiliary words such as 了 *le 'LE'*, 着 *zhe 'ZHE'* or 过 *guò 'GUO'* are usually inserted in predicate-object phrases, as in the following:

洗	衣服	洗	了	衣服
xǐ	yīfú	xǐ	le	yīfú
wash	clothes	wash	LE	clothes
'to wash clothes'		'have washed clothes'		

盖	楼房	盖	着	楼房
gài	lóufáng	gài	zhe	lóufáng
build	building	build	ZHE	building
'to build high buildings'		'is building high buildings'		

想	办法	想	过	办法
xiǎng	bànfǎ	xiǎng	guò	bànfǎ
think	way	think	GUO	way
'to think about a way'		'have thought about a way'		

The nature of the predicate-objective phrase doesn't change even though 了 *le 'LE'*, 着 *zhe 'ZHE'* or 过 *guò 'GUO'* is inserted. 洗衣服 *xǐ yīfú* 'to wash clothes' and 洗了衣服 *xǐ le yīfú* 'have washed clothes' are both predicate-objective phrases, in the latter of which 洗了 *xǐ le* 'have washed' is the predicate and 衣服 *yīfú* 'clothes' is the object.

It seems that 的 *de 'DE'* can be inserted in predicate-object phrases as well, as shown here.

洗	衣服	洗	的	衣服
xǐ	yīfú	xǐ	de	yīfú
wash	clothes	wash	DE	clothes
'to wash clothes'		'clothes that have been washed'		

盖	楼房	盖	的	楼房
gài	lóufáng	gài	de	lóufáng
build	building	build	DE	building
'to build high buildings'		'buildings that have been built'		

想	办法		想	的	办法
xiǎng	*bànfǎ*		*xiǎng*	*de*	*bànfǎ*
think	way		think	DE	way
'to find a way'			'the way that is found'		

Nevertheless, the property of the phrase changes from a predicate-object phrase (e.g. 洗衣服 *xǐ yīfú* 'to wash clothes') into a modifier-head phrase (such as 洗的衣服 *xǐ de yīfú* 'clothes that have been washed') after 的 *de* '*DE*' insertion. Meanwhile, the interpretation of the phrase changes as well.

2.4 Predicate-Complement Phrases

洗衣服 *xǐyīfu* 'wash the clothes' is one example of the aforementioned predicate-object construction. If 衣服 *yīfú* 'clothes' is replaced by 干净 *gānjìng* 'clean', the property of the construction changes. In 洗干净 *xǐgānjìng* 'wash clean' the predicate 洗 *xǐ* 'wash' represents an action, 干净 *gānjìng* 'clean' denotes a result of the action. The same action may have different results as illustrated here.

洗	干净		洗	白	（了）
xǐ	*gānjìng*		*xǐ*	*bái*	*le*
wash	clean		wash	white	(LE)
'wash (until it is) clean'			'wash (until it is) white'		

洗	丢	（了）	洗	破	（了）
xǐ	*diū*	*le*	*xǐ*	*pò*	*le*
wash	lost	(LE)	wash	break	(LE)
'wash (until it is) lost'			'wash (until it is) broken'		

Note that the same result can also be realised by different methods which are indicated by the verbs, as shown here.

洗	干净		刷	干净
xǐ	*gānjìng*		*shuā*	*gānjìng*
wash	clean		brush	clean
'wash (until it is) clean'			'brush (until it is) clean'	

扫	干净		擦	干净
sǎo	*gānjìng*		*cā*	*gānjìng*
sweep	clean		scrub	clean
'sweep (until it is) clean'			'scrub (until it is) clean'	

Constructions like 洗干净 xǐ gānjìng 'wash clean' are called predicate-complement phrases. The predicate-complement phrase consists of two constituents: The main constituent, which is usually called the predicate, and the complement, which completes the meaning of the predicate.

说	清楚	写	明白	看	完
shuō	qīngchǔ	xiě	míngbái	kàn	wán
speak	clear	write	explicit	read	finish
'explain clearly'		'write clearly'		'read (until it is) finished'	

抓	紧	跑	出去	拿	进来
zhuā	jǐn	pǎo	chūqù	ná	jìnlái
grasp	firm	run	go.out	take	come.in
'firmly grasp'		'run outside'		'take inside'	

走	开	关	上
zǒu	kāi	guān	shàng
go	away	close	up
'go away'		'close fully'	

In these cases, a complement marker 得 de 'DE' can be inserted between the predicate and the complement.

洗	干净	→	洗	得	干净
xǐ	gānjìng		xǐ	de	gānjìng
wash	clean		wash	DE	clean
'wash (until it is) clean'			'be able to wash it clean'		

说	清楚	→	说	得	清楚
shuō	qīngchǔ		shuō	de	qīngchǔ
speak	clear		speak	DE	clear
'speak clearly'			'be able to speak it clearly'		

看	完	→	看	得	完
kàn	wán		kàn	de	wán
read	finish		read	DE	finish
'read (until it is) finished'			'be able to finish reading'		

跑	出去	→	跑	得	出去
pǎo	chūqù		pǎo	de	chūqù
run	out		run	DE	go.out
'run outside'			'be able to run outside'		

关	上	→	关	得	上
guān	*shàng*		*guān*	*de*	*shàng*
close	off		close	DE	off
'close fully'			'be able to close'		

The insertion does not change the property of the phrase. For example, 洗干净 *xǐgānjìng* 'wash clean' is a predicate-complement phrase, and 洗得干净 *xǐdegānjìng* 'be able to wash it clean' is also a predicate-complement phrase, with 洗得 *xǐde* 'wash DE' being the predicate and 干净 *gānjìng* 'clean' being the complement. However, the meaning of the phrase will undergo a slight change after 得 *de* 'DE' insertion (see Section 7.4).

2.5 Subject-Predicate Phrases

The subject-predicate phrase consists of a subject and a predicate. The subject, which states what or who the sentence is about, comes first; the predicate, which predicates what or how the subject is, comes after. For example, 爸爸回来了 *bàba huíláile* 'dad came back' is a subject-predicate phrase. 爸爸 *bàba* 'dad' is the subject, indicating what the sentence states; 回来了 *huíláile* 'came back' is the predicate explaining what the subject did. 这是芒果 *zhè shì mángguǒ* 'This is a mango' is another example of subject-predicate phrase, in which 这 *zhè* 'this' is the subject and 是芒果 *shì mángguǒ* 'is a mango' is the predicate. More examples follow.

阿宋	去	妈妈	不	看
āsòng	*qù*	*māmā*	*bú*	*kàn*
Asong	go	mum	not	look
'Asong will go.'		'Mum won't look.'		

我们	走	这	本	书	看	过
wǒmen	*zǒu*	*zhè*	*běn*	*shū*	*kàn*	*guò*
1Pl	go	this	CL	book	read	GUO
'Let's go.'		'(I) have read the book.'				

江鱼仔	不	吃	杯子	打破	了
jiāngyúzǎi	*bù*	*chī*	*bēizi*	*dǎpò*	*le*
Ikan.Bilis	NEG	eat	cup	broken	LE
'(Someone) does not eat Ikan Bilis.'			'The cup is broken.'		

观点	很	明确	新加坡	很	美
guāndiǎn	*hěn*	*míngquè*	*xīnjiāpō*	*hěn*	*měi*
viewpoint	very	explicit	Singapore	very	beautiful
'The viewpoint is explicit.'			'Singapore is very beautiful.'		

这里	干净		爸爸	是	司机
zhèlǐ	gānjìng		bàba	shì	sījī
here	clean		father	be	driver
'It is clean here.'			'My father is a driver.'		

我	是	公务员		今天	星期一
wǒ	shì	gōngwùyuán		jīntiān	xīngqīyī
1SG	be	civil.servant		today	Monday
'I am a civil servant'				'It is Monday today.'	

是不是 *shìbushì* 'be not be' can be inserted between the subject and the predicate to transform the phrase into the interrogative form. The insertion will not change the property of the phrase. It remains a subject-predicate phrase. Consider the following examples.

阿宋	去		→	阿宋	是不是	去?	
āsòng	qù			āsòng	shìbúshì	qù	
Asong	go			Asong	be.not.be	go	
'Asong will go.'				'Will Asong go?'			

这	本	书	看	过	→	这	本	书	是不是	看	过?
zhè	běn	shū	kàn	guò		zhè	běn	shū	shìbushì	kàn	guò
this	CL	book	read	ASP		this	CL	book	be.not.be	read	ASP
'I have read the book.'						'Have you read the book?'					

观点	很	明确	→	观点	是不是	很	明确
guāndiǎn	hěn	míngquè		guāndiǎn	shìbushì	hěn	míngquè
viewpoint	very	explicit		viewpoint	be.not.be	very	explicit
'The viewpoint is explicit.'				'Is the viewpoint explicit?'			

爸爸	是	司机	→	爸爸	是不是	司机
bàba	shì	sījī		bàba	shìbushì	sījī
Dad	be	driver		Dad	be.not.be	driver
'My dad is a driver.'				'Is your dad a driver?'		

2.6 Coordinative Phrases

A phrase formed by coordinating together several words of equal grammatical statuses is called a coordinative phrase. The difference between the coordinative phrase and the aforementioned four types of phrases is that the former is not necessarily made of two parts, as illustrated here.

Five Basic Types of Phrase

爸爸	妈妈		分析	研究		活泼	可爱
bàbà	māmā		fēnxī	yánjiū		huópō	kěài
Dad	Mum		analyse	research		lively	cute
'Dad and Mum'			'analyse and research'			'lively and cute'	

听、	说、	读、	写		春	夏	秋	冬
tīng	shuō	dú	xiě		chūn	xià	qiū	dōng
listen	speak	read	write		spring	summer	autumn	winter
'listen, speak, read and write'					'spring, summer, autumn and winter'			

北京、	上海、	天津		酸、	甜、	苦、	辣
běijīng	shànghǎi	tiānjīn		suān	tián	kǔ	là
Beijing	Shanghai	Tianjin		sour	sweet	bitter	spicy
'Beijing, Shanghai and Tianjin'				'sour, sweet, bitter and spicy'			

哥哥、	姐姐、	弟弟、	妹妹
gēgē	jiějiě	dìdì	mèimèi
elder.brother	elder.sister	younger.brother	younger.sister
'elder brother, elder sister, younger brother and younger sister'			

Some coordinate phrases don't have a pause between words, such as 爸爸妈妈 *bàbà māmā* 'dad mum', 分析研究 *fēnxī yánjiū* 'analyse and research', while others do have a pause, which is usually indicated by an slight-pause mark ' 、 ' in written Singapore Mandarin. Sometimes words can also be coordinated by a conjunction word, as shown in the following examples.

爸爸	和	妈妈		北京、	上海	和	天津
bàbà	hé	māmā		běijīng	shànghǎi	hé	tiānjīn
dad	and	mum		Beijing	Shanghai	and	Tianjin
'dad and mum'				'Beijing, Shanghai and Tianjin'			

分析	并	研究		活泼	而	可爱
fēnxī	bìng	yánjiū		huópō	ér	kěài
analyse	and	research		lively	and	cute
'analyse and research'				'lively and cute'		

The preceding coordinate phrases express a meaning of addition. There is also another kind of coordinative phrase which expresses an alternative meaning. This is illustrated by the following examples:

银行	或	保险公司		法学院	或者	文学院
yínháng	huò	bǎoxiǎngōngsī		fǎxuéyuàn	huòzhě	wénxuéyuàn
bank	or	insurance.company		faculty.of.law	or	faculty.of.arts

'bank or insurance company'   'faculty of law or faculty of arts'

珍珠坊	还是	文理坊		去	香港	还是	去	台湾
zhēnzhūfāng	háishì	wénlǐ fāng		qù	xiānggǎng	háishì	qù	táiwān
Pearl.Square	or	Wenlifang		go	HongKong	or	go	Taiwan

'Pearl Square or Wenlifang'   'go to Hong Kong or Taiwan'

吃	不	吃		有	没	有
chī	bù	chī		yǒu	méi	yǒu
eat	NEG	eat		have	NEG	have

'eat or not eat'   'have or not have'

是	男	是	女，	是	扁	是	圆？	（金狮奖（四）111）
shì	nán	shì	nǚ	shì	biǎn	shì	yuán	
be	male	be	female	be	flat	be	round	

'Male or female, flat or round?' (*Jīnshī jiǎng* (*sì*) 111)

2.7 Complex Phrases

So far, we have briefly introduced five types of the most important and basic phrases of Singapore Mandarin. In previous discussions, simple phrases, the constituents of which are merely one word, were selected for better comprehension. However, the constituents of phrases can be not only words but also phrases, which are even more frequent in actual language usage. Here is one example.

提高	马来	社会	的	教育	及	生活	水平
tígāo	mǎlái	shèhuì	de	jiàoyù	jí	shēnghuó	shuǐpíng
improve	Malay	society	DE	education	and	living	standard

'improve the educational and living standard of the Malay society' (*Zaobao*, 7th edition, Aug. 21, 1995)

The preceding example is a predicate-object phrase made up with a predicate 提高 *tígāo* 'improve' and an object 马来社会的教育及生活水平 *mǎlái shèhuì de jiàoyù jí shēnghuó shuǐpíng* 'the educational and living standard of the Malay society'. The predicate is a word, while the object itself is an attribute-head endocentric phrase with an attribute 马来社会 (的) *mǎlái shèhuì de* '(of) the Malay society' – which again is an attribute-head endocentric phrase – and a head 教育及生活水平 *jiàoyù jí shēnghuó shuǐpíng* 'education and living standard'. The head itself is an attribute-head endocentric phrase, with an attribute 教育及生活 *jiàoyù jí shēnghuó* 'education and living' modifying the headword 水平 *shuǐpíng* 'standard'. The attribute 教育及生活 *jiàoyù jí shēnghuó* can be further analysed as a coordinative phrase. Thus, the whole phrase could be analysed in the diagram as follows.

```
提高    马来 社会 (的) 教育 及 生活    水平
tígāo   mǎlái shèhuì (de) jiàoyù jí shēnghuó shuǐpíng
  1             2                              (predicate-object phrase)
          3              4                     (attribute-head endocentric phrase)
        5   6         7        8               (5-6, 7-8, attribute-head endocentric phrases)
                    9   10                     (coordinative phrase)
```

A phrase whose constituents are also phrases is called a complex phrase. The aforementioned phrase is one example. It has eight words: 提高 *tígāo* 'improve', 马来 *mǎlái* 'Malay', 社会 *shèhuì* 'society', 的 *de* 'DE', 教育 *jiàoyù* 'eucation', 及 *jí* 'and', 生活 *shēnghuó* 'living', 水平 *shuǐpíng* 'standard'. On the surface, these words are lined up one by one just as we stand in a queue; nevertheless, they are not at the same layer in terms of the internal structure of the phrase. The adjacent words are not simply joined together in a linear order. As a matter of fact, words of a complex phrase are linked up layer by layer according to certain syntactic rules, which suggests that the internal structure of the complex phrase is hierarchical. It's important to keep this in mind when we analyse a complex phrase or even a complicated sentence. We should analyse them layer by layer based on their internal structure and figure out the immediate constituents of each layer until we reach the last layer of single words. To dismantle a grammatical construction in this way is called Immediate Constituent Analysis (IC analysis, 成分分析法) or Hierarchical Analysis (层次分析法). Take another complex phrase for example.

孟紫   也   相当   注重   人物   （的）   心理   刻画
mèngzǐ   yě   xiāngdāng zhùzhòng   rénwù   de   xīnlǐ   kèhuà
Mengzi   also quite   pay.attention.to character   DE   psychological depict

'Mengzi also attaches great importance to the psychological depiction of characters.' (*Zhixing* 118)

The phrase could be analysed as follows.

孟紫	也	相当	注重	人物	（的）	心理	刻画
mèngzǐ	yě	xiàngdāng	zhùzhòng	rénwù	(de)	xīnlǐ	kèhuà

```
 1              2                              (subject-predicate phrase)
       3                4                      (adverbial-head endocentric phrase)
             5                6                (adverbial-head endocentric phrase)
                    7         8                (predicate-object phrase)
                         9       10            (attribute-head endocentric phrase)
                                 11   12       (attribute-head endocentric phrase)
```

3 Word Classes

Lu Jianming

3.1 Why Is It Necessary to Have Word Classes?

Word classes refer to the grammatical classification of words. Why is it necessary to classify words into different grammatical categories? As is known, each language contains numerous words, which are just like construction materials such as bricks, tiles, wood, cement and nails for building houses. Each and every sentence we utter is "built" up with words. Just as construction materials function differently in building houses, different words play different roles in constructing discourses. For example:

A 看 *kàn* 'read'   洗 *xǐ* 'wash'
  吃 *chī* 'eat'   借 *jiè* 'borrow'
  了解 *liǎojiě* 'understand'

B 报纸 *bàozhǐ* 'newspaper'   衣服 *yīfu* 'clothes'
  木瓜 *mùguā* 'papaya'   小说 *xiǎoshuō* 'novel'
  情况 *qíngkuàng* 'situation'

C 正在 *zhèngzài* 'in the process of'   刚 *gāng* 'just'
  常常 *chángcháng* 'often'   马上 *mǎshàng* 'immediately'
  十分 *shífēn* 'very'

These three groups of words play different roles in constructing sentences. If we take pair combinations of the three groups, we'll see that a word in Group A and a word in Group B can be combined together with either one preceding the other. The only difference lies in the property of thus formed phrases: When words in Group A precede those in Group B (i.e. A+B), predicate-object constructions are formed, such as 看报纸 *kàn bàozhǐ* 'to read a newspaper', 洗衣服 *xǐ yīfu* 'to wash clothes', 吃木瓜 *chī mùguā* 'to eat papaya', 借小说 *jiè xiǎoshuō* 'to borrow a novel', 了解情况 *liǎojiě qíngkuàng* 'to understand the situation'. When words in Group B precede those in Group A (i.e. B+A), subject-predicate constructions are formed, such as 报纸看（了） *bàozhǐ kàn (le)* 'newspaper has been read', 衣服洗（了）*yīfu xǐ (le)* 'clothes have been washed', 木瓜吃（了）*mùguā chī (le)* 'papaya has been eaten', 小说借（了）*xiǎoshuō jiè (le)* 'the novel has been borrowed', 情况了解（了）*qíngkuàng liǎojiě (le)* 'the situation has been understood'. However, words in Group A and words in Group C can be combined together in only one possible order, with Group C preceding Group A (i.e., C+A is grammatical, A+C is ungrammatical) to form adverbial-predicate constructions, such as 正在看 *zhèngzài kàn* 'in the process of reading', 刚洗 *gāng xǐ* 'just washed', 常常吃 *chángcháng chī* 'often eat', 马上借 *mǎshàng jiè* 'to borrow immediately', 十分了解 *shífēn liǎojiě* 'to understand very much'. In contrast with the previous combinations, words in Group B and words in Group C cannot be combined in either order. There are no phrases in the form of "B+C" construction in Singapore Mandarin, the following examples being ungrammatical: *报纸正在 *bàozhǐ zhèngzài*, * 衣服刚 *yīfu gāng*, * 木瓜常常 *mùguā chángcháng*, * 小说马上 *xiǎoshuō mǎshàng*, * 情况十分 *qíngkuàng shífēn*. Neither are there expressions in the form of "C+B" construction, the following examples being ungrammatical as well: * 正在报纸 *zhèngzài bàozhǐ*, * 刚衣服 *gāng yīfu*, * 常常木瓜 *chángcháng mùguā*, * 马上小说 *mǎshàng xiǎoshuō*, *十分情况 *shífēn qíngkuàng*. It is evident from such simple comparisons that words in a language indeed belong to different groups. Classifying words into different categories helps to describe the real usage of language truthfully and is conducive to grammar research and grammar teaching. Thus, it is necessary to set up the concept of "word class" based on the function of words in forming sentences in grammar research and grammar teaching.

This will make the analysis, description and explanation of grammatical rules much easier. For example, if the preceding three groups of words are defined as three categories, namely "words in group A are verbs; words in group B are nouns; and words in group C are adverbs", then phrases such as 看报纸 *kàn bàozhǐ* 'to read a newspaper', 洗衣服 *xǐ yīfu* 'to wash clothes', 吃木瓜 *chī mùguā* 'to eat papaya', 借小说 *jiè xiǎoshuō* 'to borrow a novel' and 了解情况 *liǎojiě qíngkuàng* 'to understand the situation' can be described and explained as the following: These are predicate-object phrases indicating a dominating grammatical relation. The predicate positions can be filled with verbs and the object positions can be filled with nouns. Similarly, phrases such as 正在看 *zhèngzài kàn* 'in the process of reading', 刚洗 *gāng xǐ* 'just washed', 常常吃 *chángcháng chī* 'often eat', 马上借 *mǎshàng jiè* 'to borrow immediately' and 十分了解 *shífēn liǎojiě* 'to understand very much' can be described as adverbial-head phrases with the adverbs modifying the head verbs. Obviously, with the concept of "word class" (i.e. words are classified into different groups), the description and explanation of grammatical rules will be simple and straightforward; otherwise, it will be wordy and obscure.

Classifying words into different categories will also help people to understand the grammatical features of each group of words, so that they can use each word correctly. The following sentences are ungrammatical due to negligence of the grammatical features of different word classes:

(1)* 我　　只　　觉得　　她　　很　　面熟，
　　　wǒ　　zhǐ　　juéde　　tā　　hěn　　miànshú
　　　1SG　only　feel　　3SG　very　familiar
　　　Intended meaning: 'I just find her familiar,

　　　可　　怎么　　也　　**记忆**　　不　　起　　她　　的　　名字　　了
　　　kě　　zěnme　　yě　　**jìyì**　　bù　　qǐ　　tā　　de　　míngzì　　le
　　　but　how　　too　**memory**　NEG　up　3SG　DE　name　LE
　　　but I can't remember her name no matter how (hard I try).'

(2)* 我　　恐怕　　天　　下雨，
　　　wǒ　　**kǒngpà**　　tiān　　xiàyǔ
　　　1SG　**perhaps**　sky　　rain
　　　Intended meaning: 'I am afraid that it was going to rain,

　　　所以　　早早地　　把　　晾　　在　　外面　　的　　衣服
　　　suǒyǐ　　zǎozǎode　　bǎ　　liàng　　zài　　wàimiàn　　de　　yīfu
　　　so　　early　　BA　hang.up　at　outside　DE　clothes

　　　都　　收　　了　　进来。
　　　dōu　　shōu　　le　　jìnlái
　　　all　collect　LE　enter.come
　　　So I brought inside all the clothes hanging outside in advance'.

(3)* 老人家　　很　　**感触**　　地　　说：　　"真　　是
　　　lǎorénjiā　　hěn　　**gǎnchù**　　de　　shuō　　zhēn　　shì
　　　Old man　very　**sentiment**　DE　say　real　be
　　　Intended meaning: 'The old man said sentimentally:

　　　青　　出于　　蓝　　　胜于　　蓝，
　　　qīng　　chūyú　　lán　　shèngyú　　lán
　　　indigo.blue　come.out.of　indigo.plant　better.than　indigo.plant
　　　"Indigo blue comes from the indigo plant but bluer than where it comes from,

　　　后生可畏　　　　　　　　　　　　　　　　　呀！"
　　　hòushēngkěwèi　　　　　　　　　　　　　　ya
　　　young people are really to be regarded with respect　SFP
　　　young people are really to be regarded with respect!"'

(4)* 大家　　一　　　　走进　　展览　　大厅，
　　　dàjiā　　yì　　　　zǒujìn　zhǎnlǎn　dàtīng
　　　Everyone　as.soon.as　walk.enter　exhibition　hall
　　　Intended meaning: 'As soon as everyone enters the exhibition hall,

就　　兴致　　地　　观赏　　　着　　每　　一　　幅　　画。
jiù　　xìngzhì　de　　guānshǎng　zhe　měi　yī　fú　　huà
then　interest　DE　enjoy　　　ZHE　each　one　CL　painting
they start enjoying each painting.'

In example (1), the word 记忆 *jìyì* 'memory' belongs to Group B (nouns), and it is not allowed to take a complement or object. Therefore, 记忆 *jìyì* 'memory' should be changed to 记 *jì* 'remember' to correct the sentence (记 *jì* 'remember' belongs to Group A (verbs)). In example (2), the word 恐怕 *kǒngpà* 'perhaps' belongs to Group C (adverbs), which cannot take an object. It should be replaced by 怕 *pà* 'be afraid', which belongs to Group A (verbs), to make the sentence correct. In example (3), the word 感触 *gǎnchù* 'sentiment' belongs to Group B (nouns), and it cannot be modified by 很 *hěn* 'very'. To make the sentence grammatically correct, another word – 感慨 *gǎnkǎi* 'sentimental' – should be selected, since 感慨 *gǎnkǎi* 'sentimental' is an adjective which can be modified by 很 *hěn* 'very'. In example (4), 兴致 *xìngzhì* 'interest' also belongs to Group B (nouns) and thus cannot function as an adverbial. So we had better change it to another phrase – 兴致勃勃 *xìngzhìbóbó* 'interestedly' – which can function as an adverbial.

The preceding analysis shows that classifying words into different classes is not only possible but also necessary in grammar research and grammar teaching.

3.2 An Overview of Word Classes in Singapore Mandarin

Words in Singapore Mandarin can be classified into the following 15 groups according to their functions in sentences:

Nouns, such as:

书 *shū* 'book'　　　　　　水 *shuǐ* 'water'　　　　　　桌子 *zhuōzi* 'desk'
面包 *miànbāo* 'bread'　　学生 *xuéshēng* 'student'　　国家 *guójiā* 'country'
情况 *qíngkuàng* 'situation'　作风 *zuòfēng* 'work-style'　今天 *jīntiān* 'today'
伦敦 *lúndūn* 'London'　　新加坡 *xīnjiāpō* 'Singapore'　后面 *hòumiàn* 'back'
左边 *zuǒbiān* 'left'

Verbs, such as:

走 *zǒu* 'walk'　　　　　　吃 *chī* 'eat'　　　　　　　看 *kàn* 'look'
参观 *cānguān* 'visit'　　　调查 *diàochá* 'investigate'　希望 *xīwàng* 'hope'
相信 *xiāngxìn* 'believe'　　能够 *nénggòu* 'able'　　　可以 *kěyǐ* 'can'

来 *lái* 'come'　　　去 *qù* 'go'　　　游行 *yóuxíng* 'parade'
鞠躬 *jūgōng* 'bow'　　是 *shì* 'be'　　有 *yǒu* 'have'

Adjectives, such as:

好 *hǎo* 'good'　　坏 *huài* 'bad'　　高 *gāo* 'tall'　　大 *dà* 'big'
深 *shēn* 'deep'　　宽 *kuān* 'wide'　　甜 *tián* 'sweet'　　胖 *pàng* 'fat'
矮 *ǎi* 'short'　　干净 *gānjìng* 'clean'　　重要 *zhòngyào* 'important'
美丽 *měilì* 'beautiful'　　大方 *dàfāng* 'generous'　　严重 *yánzhòng* 'serious'
深刻 *shēnkè* 'profound'

Stative words, such as:

通红 *tōnghóng* 'completely red'　　雪白 *xuěbái* 'snow white'
蜡黄 *làhuáng* 'wax yellow'　　红通通 *hóngtōngtōng* 'brightly red'
绿油油 *lǜyóuyóu* 'green'　　亮晶晶 *liàngjīngjīng* 'glittering'
干干净净 *gāngānjìngjìng* 'perfectly clean'　　认认真真 *rènrènzhēnzhēn* 'seriously'
大大方方 *dàdàfāngfāng* 'generously'　　肮里肮脏 *āngliāngzāng* 'dirty'
马里马虎 *mǎlǐmǎhu* 'careless'　　小里小气 *xiǎolǐxiǎoqì* 'stingy'

Distinguishing words, such as:

男 *nán* 'man'　　女 *nǚ* 'woman'　　金 *jīn* 'gold'
银 *yín* 'silver'　　雌 *cí* 'female'　　雄 *xióng* 'male'
急性 *jíxìng* 'acute'　　慢性 *mànxìng* 'chronic'　　良性 *liángxìng* 'benign'
恶性 *èxìng* 'malignant'　　大型 *dàxíng* 'large-scale'　　微型 *wēixíng* 'miniature'
野生 *yěshēng* 'wild'　　人造 *rénzào* 'man-made'　　彩色 *cǎisè* 'colourful'
唯一 *wéiyī* 'only'　　公共 *gōnggòng* 'public'

Numerals, such as:

一 *yī* 'one'　　二 *èr* 'two'
四 *sì* 'four'　　七 *qī* 'seven'
十二 *shíèr* 'twelve'　　二十三 *èrshísān* 'twenty-three'
一百零八 *yìbǎilíngbā* 'one hundred and eight'
百 *bǎi* 'hundred'　　千 *qiān* 'thousand'
万 *wàn* 'ten thousand hundred'　　亿 *yì* 'million'
两 *liǎng* 'two'　　半 *bàn* 'half'
第一 *dìyī* 'first'　　第三 *dìsān* 'third'
第一千五百六十三 *dìyìqiānwǔbǎiliùshísān* 'one thousand five hundred and sixty-third'
三分之一 *sānfēnzhīyī* 'one third'
三点一四一六 *sāndiǎnyīsìyīliù* 'three point one four one six'

Classifiers, such as:

个 *gè*	粒 *lì*	只 *zhī*	间 *jiān*
匹 *pǐ*	条 *tiáo*	张 *zhāng*	
群 *qún* 'flock'		双 *shuāng* 'pair'	
公斤 *gōngjīn* 'kilogram'		公里 *gōnglǐ* 'kilometre'	
趟 *tàng* 'time'		遍 *biàn* 'time'	回 *huí* 'time'
阵子 *zhènzi* 'while'		下 *xià* 'bit'	
年 *nián* 'year'		天 *tiān* 'day'	

The use of 回 *huí* 'time', 下 *xià* 'bit' and 天 *tiān* 'day' as classifiers for events are shown in the following verb phrases:

去	过	两	回		等	一	下
qù	*guo*	*liǎng*	*huí*		*děng*	*yí*	*xià*
go	GUO	two	time		wait	one	bit
'have been there two times'					'wait for a second'		

看	了	三	天
kàn	*le*	*sān*	*tiān*
read	LE	three	day
'read for three days'			

Pronouns, such as:

你 *nǐ* '2SG'　　　我 *wǒ* '1SG'
他 *tā* '3SG'[1]　　她 *tā* '3SG'
它 *tā* '3SGn'　　你们 *nǐmen* '2Pl'
我们 *wǒmen* '1Pl'　　他们 *tāmen* '3Pl'
她们 *tāmen* '3Pl'　　它们 *tāmen* '3Pl'
这 *zhè* 'this'　　那 *nà* 'that'
这里 *zhèlǐ* 'here'　　那里 *nàlǐ* 'there'
这样 *zhèyàng* 'this way'　　那样 *nàyàng* 'that way'
这么 *zhème* 'like this'　　那么 *nàme* 'like that'
谁 *shuí* 'who'　　什么 *shénme* 'what'
哪 *nǎ* 'which'　　哪里 *nǎlǐ* 'where'
多少 *duōshǎo* 'how many'　　几 *jǐ* 'several'

Adverbs, such as:

不 *bù* 'NEG/not'　　很 *hěn* 'very'
没 *méi* 'NEG/not'　　都 *dōu* 'all'

也 yě 'also'
刚 gāng 'just'
忽然 hūrán 'suddenly'
简直 jiǎnzhí 'simply'
只 zhǐ 'only'

亲自 qīnzì 'in person'
马上 mǎshàng 'immediately'
常常 chángcháng 'often'
已经 yǐjīng 'already'
就 jiù 'only/immediately/thereupon (then)'

For example, the use of 只 zhǐ 'only' is shown in the following phrase:

只	学	了	一	年
zhǐ	xué	le	yì	nián
only	study	LE	one	year

'only studied for one year'

Prepositions, such as:

把 bǎ 'BA'   被 bèi 'BEI'   比 bǐ 'than'   往 wǎng 'toward'
从 cóng 'from'   朝 cháo facing   向 xiàng 'facing' 由 yóu 'from'
关于 guānyú 'as to' 自从 zìcóng 'since'   在 zài 'at'   以 yǐ 'with'
对于 duìyú 'concerning/with regard to'

The use of 比 bǐ 'than' and 在 zài 'at' are examplified here.

我	比	他	高。
wǒ	bǐ	tā	gāo
1SG	than	3SG	tall

'I'm taller than him.'

我	在	抽屉	里	发现	一	只	蟑螂。
wǒ	zài	chōutì	lǐ	fāxiàn	yì	zhī	zhāngláng
1SG	at	drawer	inside	find	one	CL	cockroach

'I found a cockroach in the drawer.'

Conjunctions, such as:

和 hé 'and'   或 huò 'or'   并 bìng 'and'
不但 búdàn 'not only' 而且 érqiě 'but also'   因为 yīnwèi 'because'
所以 suǒyǐ 'so'   虽然 suīrán 'although'   但是 dànshì 'but'
或者 huòzhě 'or'   即使 jíshǐ 'even if'   如果 rúguǒ 'if'

For example, the conjunction 和 hé 'and' can be used in the coordinative phrase 爸爸和妈妈 bàba hé māma 'Dad and Mum'.

Auxiliaries, such as:

了 *le* 'LE' 　　着 *zhe* 'ZHE' 　　过 *guo* 'GUO'
的 *de* 'DE' 　　得 *de* 'DE' 　　地 *de* 'DE'
所 *suǒ* 'DE' 　　似的 *shìde* 'like'

了 *le* 'LE', 着 *zhe* 'ZHE' and 过 *guo* 'GUO' are attached to verbs indicating aspectual information, as shown in the following verb phrases respectively (see Section 3.13):

写	了	一	封	信	说	着	话
xiě	*le*	*yì*	*fēng*	*xìn*	*shuō*	*zhe*	*huà*
write	LE	one	CL	letter	talk	ZHE	word
'wrote a letter'					'be talking'		

吃	过	榴莲
chī	*guo*	*liúlián*
eat	GUO	durian
'have eaten durian'		

The three auxiliary words 的 *de* 'DE', 得 *de* 'DE', 地 *de* 'DE' with the same pronunciation *de* indicate structural meanings. 的 *de* 'DE' is attached to certain words or phrases to denote a genitive or nominalised phrase. 得 *de* 'DE' is inserted between a predicate and its non-nominal complement. 地 *de* 'DE' is suffixed to an adverbial phrase (see Section 3.13). Examples are shown in the following constructions respectively.

我	的、	红	的、	吃	的
wǒ	*de*	*hóng*	*de*	*chī*	*de*
1SG	DE	red	DE	eat	DE
'my/mine'		'red/the red'		'the (food) for eating'	

他	爽快	地	答应	了。	唱	得	好
tā	*shuǎngkuài*	*de*	*dāying*	*le*	*chàng*	*de*	*hǎo*
3Sg	readily	DE	agree	LE	sing	DE	well
'He agreed readily.'					'sing well'		

似的 *shìde* 'like' and 所 *suǒ* 'SUO' are also structural auxiliaries. 似的 *shìde* 'like' is attached to various types of phrases or sentences to form an adjectival or adverbial phrase, for example 木头似的 *mùtóu shìde* 'like a log'. 所 *suǒ* 'SUO' precedes a transitive verb phrase to transform it to a nominalised phrase, as shown here.

他	所	写	的	文章
tā	suǒ	xiě	de	wénzhāng
3SG	SUO	write	DE	article

'articles written by him'

Sentence-final particles, such as:

啊 a   吗 ma   吧 ba   了 le   呢 ne   啦 la

The use of 啊 a 'SFP' and 了 le 'SFP' are illustrated in the following examples:

真	漂亮	啊！
zhēn	piàoliang	a
really	beautiful	SFP

'How beautiful!'

爷爷	回	唐山	了。
yéye	huí	tángshān	le
grandpa	return	Tangshan	SFP

'Grandpa has returned to Tangshan.'

Interjections, such as:

啊 à 'Ah'   哎 āi 'oh'   唉 ài 'Ah'
喂 wèi 'hi'   呸 pēi 'Yuck'   哼 hèng 'humph'

For example, 啊 à 'Ah' can be used in the following sentence:

啊！	我	的	祖国！
à	wǒ	de	zǔguó
Ah	1SG	DE	motherland

'Ah! My motherland.'

Onomatopoeias, such as:

啪 pā 'cracking'   咝 sī 'hissing'   叮 dīng 'ting'
哗啦啦 huālālā 'clattering'   乒呤乓啷 pīnglīngpānglāng 'rattling'

Of the 15 groups of words, nouns, verbs, adjectives, stative words, distinguishing words, numerals, classifiers and pronouns are often called content words, whereas adverbs, prepositions, conjunctions, auxiliary words and sentence-final particles are called function words. Interjections and onomatopoeias are regarded as two special word classes.

Content words and function words have distinctive grammatical features and play different roles in languages. Content words have concrete meanings that are easy to observe or perceive, while function words express abstract grammatical meanings. If we compare the noun 作风 *zuòfēng* 'work-style' and the auxiliary 得 *de* 'DE', we will find that although the meaning of 作风 *zuòfēng* 'work-style' is abstract, we can still fathom what it refers to, but the meaning of 得 *de* 'DE' is difficult to explain or fathom. We may only say that it's often suffixed to a verb or an adjective to enable them to take a complement indicating a kind of state achieved (such as 写得清清楚楚 *xiě de qīngqīngchǔchǔ* 'to write clearly and neatly', 亮得耀眼 *liàng de yàoyǎn* 'dazzling bright'). As for their grammatical functions, content words can serve as the core constituent of the five types of phrases mentioned in Chapter 2 – subject, predicate, head – while function words cannot take these roles. Function words are much fewer in number than content words but are more frequently used. Their importance to language is the same as arteries and veins are to our body. If some content words like 狗 *gǒu* 'dog', 桌子 *zhuōzi* 'desk', 面包 *miànbāo* 'bread', 看 *kàn* 'look', 喝 *hē* 'drink', 好 *hǎo* 'good' are removed from Singapore Mandarin, the language will certainly be affected but still works pretty well. However, if several function words like 的 *de* 'DE', 了 *le* 'LE/SFP', 不 *bù* 'NEG', 也 *yě* 'also', 吗 *ma* 'SFP' are removed, it is simply impossible to speak the language. Thus, the importance of function words is self-evident.

3.3 The Criteria for Word Classification

In the previous section, words in Singapore Mandarin are classified into 15 groups based on their grammatical function (i.e. the role of the words in sentence formation) and their grammatical meaning, the two of which are closely related. Words classified according to grammatical function also inevitably share some similarities in their grammatical meaning. For example, nouns, verbs, adjectives, stative words and distinguishing words are all defined according to their grammatical function. Words in each of these groups share similar grammatical meaning as well – nouns refer to things; verbs represent events and actions; adjectives describe properties; stative words denote the stative property of things; and distinguishing words represent discriminative features of things and so on. Theoretically speaking, it is also possible to classify words according to their grammatical meanings. In fact, numerals, onomatopoeia and pronouns are thus classified. However, the meaning of words is extremely complicated, so if we only consider the grammatical meaning and neglect the grammatical function, it is not easy to give a perfect classification in line with the needs of grammar research and grammar teaching. Particularly, words with the same meaning may not necessarily belong to the same word class. For example, 忽然 *hūrán* and 突然 *tūrán* are close in meaning (both meaning 'suddenly') and seem to be in the same class, but in fact they are not.

In terms of the grammatical function, they can both function as an adverbial as illustrated in the following examples:

(1) 他　　忽然　　　病倒　　　了。
　　 tā　　hūrán　　 bìngdǎo　　le
　　 3SG　suddenly　sick.fall　　LE
　　 'He suddenly fell sick.'

(2) 他　　突然　　　病倒　　　了。
　　 tā　　tūrán　　 bìngdǎo　　le
　　 3SG　suddenly　sick.fall　　LE
　　 'He suddenly fell sick.'

Yet, 忽然 *hūrán* cannot play any role other than adverbial, whereas 突然 *tūrán* can take on many other grammatical functions: First, 突然 *tūrán* can be modified by adverbs like 不 *bù* 'NEG', 很 *hěn* 'very' and so on. For example, 并不突然 *bìng bù tūrán* 'not surprising at all', 很突然 *hěn tūrán* 'very unexpectedly', 太突然 *tài tūrán* 'too abruptly' (*Tài yáng* 58). Second, it can function as the predicate, for example:

这　　　件　　事情　　　突然,　　太　　突然　　　了。
zhè　　 jiàn　 shìqíng　　tūrán,　 tài　　tūrán　　 le
This　　CL　　thing　　 surprising　too　surprising　LE
'This thing came as a surprise. It's too surprising.'

Third, it can function as the object, for example:

我　　并不　　　　感到　　突然。
wǒ　　bìng bù　　 gǎndào　tūrán
1SG　 not.at.all　feel　　surprised
'I am not at all surprised.'

Fourth, it can function as the verb complement, for example:

一切　　　　　来　　　　　　得　　　　　突然。
yíqiè　　　　 lái　　　　　 de　　　　　 tūrán
everything　　come　　　　 DE　　　　　 abrupt
'Everything comes abruptly.' (*Xún miào* 15)

These grammatical functions of 突然 *tūrán* are not shared by 忽然 *hūrán*. Hence, these two verbs are not interchangeable in the preceding examples. Thus, based on their distinctive grammatical functions, 忽然 *hūrán* is an adverb while 突然 *tūrán* is an adjective. Similar examples follow:

刚刚 *gānggāng* 'just' (adverb) – 刚才 *gāngcái* 'just now' (noun)
害怕 *hàipà* 'be afraid' (verb) – 恐怕 *kǒngpà* 'perhaps' (adverb)
经常 *jīngcháng* 'frequent' (adjective) – 常常 *chángcháng* 'often' (adverb)
阻碍 *zǔài* 'obstruct' (verb) – 障碍 *zhàngài* 'obstruction' (noun)
勇敢 *yǒnggǎn* 'courageous' (adjective) – 勇气 *yǒngqì* 'courage' (noun)
干脆 *gāncuì* 'straight' (adjective) – 索性 *suǒxìng* 'straightforward' (adverb)
偶尔 *ǒuěr* 'occasionally' (adverb) – 偶然 *ǒurán* 'occasional' (adjective)
战争 *zhànzhēng* 'war' (noun) – 打仗 *dǎzhàng* 'fight' (verb) – 战斗 *zhàndòu* 'battle' (noun)
红 *hóng* 'red' (adjective) – 红色 *hóngsè* 'the red' (noun) – 通红 *tōnghóng* 'red all through' (stative word)

In fact, this phenomenon (i.e. words with the same or similar meaning belonging to different word classes) exists in all languages. The following are examples in English:

construct (verb)   construction (noun)
kind (adjective)   kindness (noun)
quick (adjective)   quickly (adverb)

In summary, both the meaning and the grammatical function of words should be examined in word classification.

In western languages, words are normally classified into groups based on word morphology. In English, for example, nouns are marked differently based on numbers (normally the suffix -s is used for plural nouns); adjectives are marked differently based on grade (the comparative is marked with suffix -*er*, or 'more' before the adjective; the superlative is marked with suffix -*est* or 'most' before the adjective); and verbs are marked differently based on person, tense and so on (for example, verbs marked with the suffix ending with -*s* are used for third person, singular, present tense). Thus nouns, verbs and adjectives can be confirmed according to word morphology in English. Yet, although morphology is explicit and easy to operate, it cannot be applied to Singapore Mandarin, which is a language lacking morphological changes. One point needs to be mentioned here that the criteria of word classification based on word morphology is ultimately decided by the grammatical function of words, since morphology is merely the manifestation of grammatical function. For example, some words in English have no morphological inflections to indicate numbers, such as 'sheep', 'deer'. They represent both singular and plural forms. However, researchers on English grammar still classify them as nouns, since they are similar with nouns having plural inflections in terms of their grammatical functions. In addition, words like 'female', 'round' and 'vertical' do not have comparative forms, but researchers still regard them as adjectives because they share the same grammatical functions with adjectives that do have morphological changes.

A very important point to note is that an accurate classification of a word needs an overall analysis of its grammatical functions in different contexts. In other words, all possible grammatical functions of this word in different constructions should be examined before deciding which class it belongs to. Classifying a word based on only one of its grammatical functions is misleading and thus must be avoided. For example, the word 认真 *rènzhēn* 'serious' can function as an adverbial (e.g. 认真学习 *rènzhēn xuéxí* 'study attentively'), but it should not be thoughtlessly classified as adverbs like 都 *dōu* 'all', 也 *yě* 'also', 常常 *chángcháng* 'often', 已经 *yǐjīng* 'already'. These words are defined as adverbs because they can solely function as adverbials. The word 认真 *rènzhēn* 'serious', however, has multiple functions: It can serve as both predicate (态度认真 *tàidù rènzhēn* 'serious attitude') and verb complement (e.g. 做得认真 *zuò de rènzhēn* 'do the job in earnest'). Moreover, it can be modified by adverbs like 不 *bù* 'NEG' and 很 *hěn* 'very' (e.g. 不认真 *bú rènzhēn* 'not serious', 很认真 *hěn rènzhēn* 'very serious'). Thus it is more appropriate to classify 认真 *rènzhēn* 'serious' into the group of adjectives.

In the following sections we will give brief introductions to each word class.

3.4 Nouns

3.4.1 What Are Nouns?

Nouns denote things. Here 'thing' is a very broad concept. It can refer to something specific, such as 书 *shū* 'book', 桌子 *zhuōzi* 'table', 学生 *xuéshēng* 'student', 钢笔 *gāngbǐ* 'pen', 猪 *zhū* 'pig', 狗 *gǒu* 'dog', 汽车 *qìchē* 'car', 房子 *fángzi* 'house', 苹果 *píngguǒ* 'apple' and so on; or something abstract, such as 友谊 *yǒuyì* 'friendship', 感情 *gǎnqíng* 'emotion', 作风 *zuòfēng* 'style', 勇气 *yǒngqì* 'courage', 压力 *yālì* 'pressure', 弹性 *tánxìng* 'flexibility', 政治 *zhèngzhì* 'politics', 文化 *wénhuà* 'culture', 道理 *dàolǐ* 'truth', 机会 *jīhuì* 'opportunity' and so on. Words that express time, location and direction are also nouns, for example:

Words indicating time:

现在 *xiànzài* 'now'　　　　　　去年 *qùnián* 'last year'
明天 *míngtiān* 'tomorrow'　　　刚才 *gāngcái* 'just now'
元旦 *yuándàn* 'New Year's Day'　国庆节 *guóqìngjié* 'National Day'

Words indicating location:

新加坡 *xīnjiāpō* 'Singapore'　　中国 *zhōngguó* 'China'
北京 *běijīng* 'Beijing'　　　　　纽约 *niǔyuē* 'New York'
牛车水 *niúchēshuǐ* 'Chinatown'　裕廊 *yùláng* 'Jurong'

Words indicating direction:

东 *dōng* 'East'	南 *nán* 'south'	西 *xī* 'west'	北 *běi* 'north'
里 *lǐ* 'inside'	外 *wài* 'outside'	前 *qián* 'front'	后 *hòu* 'back'
后面 *hòumiàn* 'back'	左边 *zuǒbiān* 'left'		

3.4.2 Grammatical Functions of Nouns

The grammatical functions of nouns are mainly as follows:

1 Often used as subjects and objects. The follow sentences are examples of nouns being subjects:

(1) 三姐　　　　分娩　　　　了。（无弦月 3）
　　 sānjiě　　 *fēnmiǎn*　　 *le*
　　 sister　　　 deliver　　　 LE
　　 'The third sister gave birth to a child.' (*Wúxiányuè* 3)

(2) 妻子　　　当然　　　不会　　　同意。（女儿 108）
　　 qīzǐ　　　 *dāngrán*　　 *búhuì*　　 *tóngyì*
　　 wife　　　 of.course　　 NEG　　　 agree
　　 'Of course the wife would not agree.' (*Nǚér* 108)

(3) 木棉花　　　　掉了。（寻庙 34）
　　 mùmiánhuā　　 *diàole*
　　 kapok　　　　 drop
　　 'The kapok dropped.' (*Xúnmiào* 34)

(4) 艺术　　　是　　　什么？（科学 55）
　　 yìshù　　 *shì*　　 *shénme*
　　 art　　　 be　　　 what
　　 'What is art?' (*Kēxué* 55)

The following are examples of nouns as objects:

(5) 决　　　不　　　求　　　人。（青青 80）
　　 jué　　 *bù*　　 *qiú*　　 *rén*
　　 never　 NEG　　 beg　　　 people
　　 'Never ask for help.' (*Qīngqīng* 80)

(6) 她   立即   竖起   耳朵。（梦 159）
    tā   lìjí   shùqǐ   ěrduǒ
    3SG   immediately raise   ear
    'She immediately picked up her ears.' (*Mèng* 159)

(7) 他   留在   学府   里   温习   功课。（大胡子 70）
    tā   liúzài   xuéfǔ   lǐ   wēnxí   gōngkè
    3SG   stay   college   inside review   homework
    'He stayed at college to review his homework.' (*Dàhúzi* 70)

2 Generally speaking, things differ in quantity, so nouns can generally be modified by numeral-classifier phrases (see Section 3.8 for "numerals and classifiers"), as shown in the following examples:

(8) 一   名   士兵（金狮奖 11）
    yì   míng   shìbīng
    one   CL   soldier
    'a soldier' (*Jīnshīijiǎng* 11)

(9) （还有）   一   粒   苹果（微型 39）
    háiyǒu   yī   lì   píngguǒ
    still   an   CL   apple
    '(There is still) an apple.' (*Wēixíng* 39)

(10) （渐渐地   变成   了）   一   粒   气球（跳舞 129）
     jiànjiànde biànchéng le   yì   lì   qìqiú
     gradually   become   LE   one   CL   balloon
     '(Gradually become) a balloon.' (*Tiàowǔ* 129)

(11) （又   是）   一   个   病房（心情 21）
     yòu   shì   yí   gè   bìngfáng
     again   be   one   CL   ward
     'one more ward' (*Xīnqíng* 21)

(12) （哭   了）   一   个   晚上（心情 20）
     （kū   le）   yí   gè   wǎnshàng
     cry   LE   one   CL   night
     '(cried) for one night' (*Xīnqíng* 20)

3 One typical grammatical characteristic of nouns is that they can be modified by attributives. For example:

小	动物 (壁虎 4)	传统	文化 (△趣谈)
xiǎo	dòngwù	chuántǒng	wénhuà
small	animal	tradition	culture

'small animals' (*Bìhǔ* 4)   'traditional culture' (*Qùtán* 70)

玉	手镯 (跳舞 63)	深远	意义 (薪传 101)
yù	shǒuzhuó	shēnyuǎn	yìyì
jade	bracelet	far-reaching	significance

'jade bracelet' (*Tiàowǔ* 63)   'far-reaching significance' (*Xīnchuán* 101)

中学	的	大门 (△含羞草 8)	东方	色彩 (冰灯 76)
zhōngxué	de	dàmén	dōngfāng	sècǎi
middle.school	DE	gate	orient	colour

'the middle school gate' (*Hánxiūcǎo* 8)   'oriental style' (*Bīngdēng* 76)

清迈	的	周围 (华文教材 2B)	星期六	晚上 (追云 87)
qīngmài	de	zhōuwéi	xīngqīliù	wǎnshàng
Chiang.Mai	DE	outskirts	Saturday	night

'the outskirts of Chiang Mai' (*Huáwénjiàocái* 2B)   'Saturday night' (*Zhuīyún* 87)

4   A noun can also directly modify another noun (without 的 *de* 'DE'). For instance, in the preceding examples the attributive modifiers 传统 *chuántǒng* 'tradition', 玉 *yù* 'jade', 东方 *dōngfāng* 'Orient' and 星期六 *xīngqīliù* 'Saturday' are all nouns, and they directly modify the nouns 文化 *wénhuà* 'culture', 手镯 *shǒuzhuó* 'bracelet', 色彩 *sècǎi* 'colour' and 晚上 *wǎnshàng* 'night' respectively. More examples follow:

儒家	思想 (文艺 19)	话剧	演员 (话剧 39)
rújiā	sīxiǎng	huàjù	yǎnyuán
Confucian	thought	drama	actor

'Confucianism' (*Wényì* 19)   'drama actor' (*Huàjù* 39)

华文	作品 (新华文学 250)	美学	效果 (至性 43)
huáwén	zuòpǐn	měixué	xiàoguǒ
Chinese	work	aesthetic	effect

'Chinese works' (*Xīnhuáwénxué* 250)   'aesthetic effect' (*Zhìxìng* 43)

新闻	事业 (中国作家 181)	政治	领袖 (伦理中三 82)
xīnwén	shìyè	zhèngzhì	lǐngxiù

news	business	politics	leader

'journalism' (*Zhōngguózuòjiā* 181) 'political leaders' (*Lúnlǐzhōngsān* 382)

3.4.3 Negative Grammatical Functions of Nouns

1. Nouns cannot be modified by the negative adverb 不 *bù* 'NEG'. For example, we cannot say 不狗 *bùgǒu* 'not dog', 不猫 *bùmāo* 'not cat', 不桌子 *bùzhuōzi* 'not table', 不文化 *bùwénhuà* 'not culture', 不学生 *bùxuéshēng* 'not student' and so on.
2. Nouns cannot be modified by the degree adverb 很 *hěn* 'very'. For instance, it is ungrammatical to say 很人 *hěnrén* 'very people', 很狗 *hěngǒu* 'very dog', 很芒果 *hěnmángguǒ* 'very mango', 很学校 *hěnxuéxiào* 'very school', 很态度 *hěntàidù* 'very attitude' and so on.
3. Nouns cannot appear in a predicate-complement phrase. Neither can they be used as a predicate nor as a complement.
4. Nouns never take objects.
5. Nouns are rarely used as predicates (for occasional conditions under which nouns can be used as predicates, see Section 5.10).

These properties of nouns distinguish themselves from verbs, adjectives and stative words.

In addition, most nouns generally cannot be used as adverbials except for a few nouns indicating time and location, and they cannot be reduplicated either. There are very few exceptions. For instance, 人 *rén* 'people' can be reduplicated as 人人 *rénrén*, which means 'every person', as illustrated by the following examples:

(13) 儒家　　　理论　　　流传　　　到　　今日，　成为　　　一　　套
　　 rújiā　　　*lǐlùn*　　　*liúchuán*　*dào*　*jīnrì*,　*chéngwéi*　*yī*　*tào*
　　 Confucianism　theory　spread　to　today　become　one　CL

人人　　适用　　　的　　人生　　　哲理。（伦理·中三 31）
rénrén　*shìyòng*　*de*　*rénshēng*　*zhélǐ*
everyone　suitable　DE　life　wisdom

'Confucian theory has spread to this day and has become a life philosophy applicable to everyone.' (*Lúnlǐzhōngsān* 31)

(14) 如果　　人人　　都　　讲　　　礼貌，　家庭　　　就　　能　　　和睦，
　　 rúguǒ　*rénrén*　*dōu*　*jiǎng*　*lǐmào*,　*jiātíng*　*jiù*　*néng*　*hémù*
　　 if　everyone　all　have　manner　family　then　can　in.harmony

社会	就	能	和谐	安宁。（南风 24）
shèhuì	jiù	néng	héxié	ānníng
society	then	can	harmonious	peaceful

'If everyone is polite, the family can be in harmony and the society can be harmonious and peaceful.' (*Nánfēng* 24)

3.5 Verbs and Adjectives

Verbs and adjectives have a lot in common in grammatical functions, so we will discuss them together in the same section. They are also different. That's why they are divided into two categories.

3.5.1 What Are Verbs? What Are Adjectives?

1 Verbs indicate action, and action is also a very broad concept. The following are all verbs:

A 走 *zǒu* 'go'　　　吃 *chī* 'eat'　　　洗 *xǐ* 'wash'
　敲 *qiāo* 'knock'　挖 *wā* 'dig'　　　说 *shuō* 'say'
B 学习 *xuéxí* 'learn'　　研究 *yánjiū* 'study'
　参观 *cānguān* 'visit'　批判 *pīpàn* 'criticise'
C 喜欢 *xǐhuan* 'like'　　害怕 *hàipà* 'afraid'
　同意 *tóngyì* 'agree'　考虑 *kǎolǜ* 'consider'
D 看见 *kànjiàn* 'see'　　听见 *tīngjiàn* 'hear'
　感到 *gǎndào* 'feel'　　觉得 *juéde* 'think'
E 来 *lái* 'come'　　　去 *qù* 'go'　　　　进 *jìn* 'in'
　出 *chū* 'out'　　　进来 *jìnlái* 'come in'　出去 *chūqù* 'go out'
F 存在 *cúnzài* 'exist'　　出现 *chūxiàn* 'appear'
　消失 *xiāoshī* 'disappear'　变成 *biànchéng* 'become'
G 是 *shì* 'be'　　　　　有 *yǒu* 'have'
H 能够 *nénggòu* 'can'　　可以 *kěyǐ* 'may'
　应该 *yīnggāi* 'should'　会 *huì* 'will'
I 加以 *jiāyǐ* 'do'　　　　进行 *jìnxíng* 'conduct'

Group A represents concrete action; Group B represents abstract behaviour; Group C indicates psychological activity; Group D indicates sensory activity; Group E indicates direction of movement; Group F expresses existence or change of state; Group G expresses affirmation or possession; Group H means willingness and volition; and Group I represents abstract action and behaviour.

2 Adjectives denote property or attribute of things, such as 红 *hóng* 'red', 小 *xiǎo* 'small' 冷 *lěng* 'cold', 强 *qiáng* 'strong', 高 *gāo* 'high', 轻 *qīng* 'mild', 急 *jí* 'urgent', 干净 *gānjìng* 'clean', 秀丽 *xiùlì* 'beautiful', 清楚 *qīngchǔ* 'clear', 正确 *zhèngquè* 'correct' and so on.

3.5.2 Commonality of Verbs and Adjectives in Grammatical Functions

1. In terms of grammatical functions, verbs and adjectives can both be used as predicates. The following are examples of verbs being used as predicates.

(1) 她   吃 (短篇 23)
  tā   *chī*
  3SG eat
  'She will eat.' (*Duǎnpiān* 23)

(2) 我   同意 (笑眼 137)
  wǒ   *tóngyì*
  1SG agree
  'I agree.' (*Xiàoyǎn* 137)

(3) 你   选 (跳舞 27)
  nǐ   *xuǎn*
  2SG choose
  'Please choose.' (*Tiàowǔ* 27)

(4) 宝晴   问 (金狮奖(四) 25)
  bǎoqíng *wèn*
  baoqing ask
  'Baoqing asked.' (*Jīnshījiǎng(sì)* 25)

(5) 林伯 走 了 (华韵 33)
  línbó *zǒu* *le*
  limbo leave LE
  'Limbo left.' (*Huáyùn* 33)

Here are some examples of adjectives being used as predicates:

(6) 天气   冷 (扶轮 52)
  tiānqì *lěng*
  weather cold
  'The weather is cold.' (*Fúlún* 52)

(7) 能力   强 (风筝 77)
  nénglì *qiáng*
  ability strong
  'The ability is strong.' (*Fēngzhēng* 77)

(8) 灯光　　　　暗淡 (△南凤 13)
　　 dēngguāng　àndàn
　　 light　　　　dim
　　 'The light is dim.' (△ Nánfēng 13)

(9) 情绪　　　　低落 (一心 100)
　　 qíngxù　　　dīluò
　　 mood　　　　low
　　 'The mood is low.' (Yìxīn 100)

(10) 国土　　　　小 (华文教材 4B1)
　　 guótǔ　　　 xiǎo
　　 territory　　small
　　 'The territory is small.' (Huáwénjiàocái 4B, 1)

Verbs and adjectives can generally take complements and form predicate complement phrases. The following are examples of verbs taking complements:

(11) 看　　　　　清楚 (梦 96)
　　 kàn　　　　 qīngchǔ
　　 see　　　　 clearly
　　 'see clearly' (Mèng 96)

(12) 挖　　　　　出来 (△含羞草 45)
　　 wā　　　　　chūlái
　　 dig　　　　 out
　　 'dig out' (△ Hánxiūcǎo 45)

(13) 握　　　得　　　紧紧的 (女儿 123)
　　 wò　　　de　　　jǐnjǐnde
　　 hold　　DE　　　tight
　　 'hold tightly' (Nǚér 123)

(14) 说　　　得　　　眉飞色舞 (回忆 54)
　　 shuō　　de　　　méifēisèwǔ
　　 say　　　DE　　　excited
　　 'said excitedly' (Huíyì 54)

(15) 用　　　　　不　　　　　完（八方 100）
　　 yòng　　　　bù　　　　 wán
　　 use　　　　 NEG　　　　finish
　　 'can't use it up' (*Bāfāng* 100)

Here are examples of adjectives taking complements:

(16) 急　　　　　坏　　　　　了（撞墙 4）
　　 jí　　　　　huài　　　　le
　　 anxious　　 bad　　　　 LE
　　 'very anxious' (*Zhuàngqiáng* 4)

(17) 舒服　　　　得　　　　　多（风雨 59）
　　 shūfu　　　 de　　　　　duō
　　 comfortable　DE　　　　 much
　　 'much more comfortable' (*Fēngyǔ* 59)

(18) 荒谬　　　　得　　　　　令人懊恼（寻庙 16）
　　 huāngmiù　　de　　　　　lìngrénàonǎo
　　 ridiculous　 DE　　　　　upset
　　 'so ridiculous that it is upsetting' (*Xúnmiào* 16)

(19) 静　　　　　下来（燃烧 3）
　　 jìng　　　　 xiàlái
　　 quiet　　　　come.down
　　 'becomes quiet' (*Ránshāo* 3)

2 Both verbs and adjectives can be modified by adverbials as follows:

Verbs with adverbial:

不　　　　　　　吃 (患病 123)　　　没　　　　　　睡（大胡子 50）
bù　　　　　　　chī　　　　　　　 méi　　　　　　shuì
NEG　　　　　　 eat　　　　　　　NEG　　　　　 sleep
'not eat' (*Huànbìng* 123)　　　　'didn't sleep' (*Dàhúzi* 50)

(大家)　　　都　　　　知道 (平心 72)　　　(大家)　　　慢慢　　　　商量（短篇 61）
dàjiā　　　　dōu　　　　zhīdào　　　　　　 (dàjiā)　　　mànmàn　　 shāngliáng
everybody　 all　　　　 know　　　　　　　 everybody　 slowly　　　 discuss
'(Everybody) knows' (*Píngxīn* 72)　　　　　'(we will) discuss slowly' (*Duǎnpiān* 61)

Adjectives with adverbial:

不	合理 (怀旧 65)	太过	便宜（南北 58)
bù	hélǐ	tài guò	piányi
NEG	reasonable	too.much	cheap

'unreasonable' (*Huáijiù* 65)   'too cheap' (*Piányi* 58)

十分	严肃 (渐行 39)	非常	困难（冰灯 85)
shífēn	yánsù	fēicháng	kùnnán
very	serious	very	difficult

'very serious' (*Jiànxīn* 39)   'very difficult' (*Bīngdēng* 85)

3   Verbs and adjectives can be both preceded by the negative adverb 不 *bù* 'NEG', as shown in the following examples:

不 *bù* 'NEG' + verb:
不吃 *bùchī* 'not eat'   不喝 *bùhē* 'not drink'
不走 *bù zǒu* 'not go'   不看 *bù kàn* 'not look'
不说 *bù shuō* 'not say'   不学习 *bù xuéxí* 'not learn'
不研究 *bù yánjiū* 'not study' 不同意 *bù tóngyì* 'not agree'
不休息 *bù xiūxi* 'not rest'   不知道 *bù zhīdào* 'not know'
不出现 *bù chūxiàn* 'not appear' 不认为 *bù rènwéi* 'think not'
不愿意 *bù yuànyì* 'will not'   不能够 *bù nénggòu* 'can not'

不 + adjectives:
不好 *bù hǎo* 'not good'   不大 *bú dà* 'not big'
不红 *bù hóng* 'not red'   不细 *bù xì* 'not thin'
不灵 *bù líng* 'not work'   不漂亮 *bù piàoliang* 'not pretty'
不干净 *bù gānjìng* 'not clean' 不清楚 *bù qīngchǔ* 'not know'
不严重 *bù yánzhòng* 'not serious' 不认真 *bù rènzhēn* 'not serious'
不聪明 *bù cōngmíng* 'not smart' 不舒服 *bù shūfu* 'not well'
不便宜 *bù piányi* 'not cheap'   不正确 *bù zhèngquè* 'not correct'

These grammatical functions are sufficient to distinguish verbs and adjectives from nouns.

3.5.3 Differences Between Verbs and Adjectives in Grammar Functions

Though verbs and adjectives have many similar grammatical functions, they are two classes of words after all and thus they also differ in many aspects. Here are two evident differences:

1 Most verbs can have objects as shown by the following examples, while adjectives cannot.

吃香蕉 *chī xiāngjiāo* 'eat a banana'   喝啤酒 *hē píjiǔ* 'drink beer'
走大路 *zǒu dàlù* 'walk on the road'   看电视 *kàn diànshì* 'watch TV'
学习文化 *xuéxí wénhuà* 'learn culture'   认为好 *rènwéi hǎo* 'think (it is) good'
研究新加坡经济 *yánjiū xīnjiāpō jīngjì* 'research on Singapore's economy'
同意多给一点 *tóngyì duō gěi yìdiǎn* 'agree to give a little bit more'
休息三个人 *xiūxī sāngèrén* 'let three people rest'
知道这件事 *zhīdào zhèjiànshì* 'know this thing'
同意他的意见 *tóngyì tāde yìjiàn* 'agree with his opinion'
出现新情况 *chūxiàn xīnqíngkuàng* 'a new situation appeared'
能够洗干净 *nénggòu xǐ gānjìng* 'can wash clean'

2 Adjectives can all be modified by the degree adverbs, such as 很 *hěn* 'very', which is shown as follows:

很好 *hěn hǎo* 'very good'   很大 *hěn dà* 'very big'
很红 *hěn hóng* 'very red'   很细 *hěn xì* 'very thin'
很灵 *hěn líng* 'very effective'   很漂亮 *hěn piàoliàng* 'very beautiful'
很干净 *hěn gānjìng* 'very clean'   很清楚 *hěn qīngchǔ* 'very clear'
很严重 *hěn yánzhòng* 'very serious'   很认真 *hěn rènzhēn* 'very careful'
很聪明 *hěn cōngmíng* 'very brilliant'   很舒服 *hěn shūfu* 'very comfortable'
很便宜 *hěn piányi* 'very cheap'   很正确 *hěn zhèngquè* 'very right'
很伟大 *hěn wěidà* 'very great'   很实在 *hěn shízài* 'very honest'

Verbs, on the contrary, generally cannot accept modification of degree adverbs, as evidenced by the following ungrammatical expressions:

*很吃 *hěn chī* 'very eat'   *很喝 *hěn hē* 'very drink'
*很走 *hěn zǒu* 'very walk'   *很看 *hěn kàn* 'very look'
*很学习 *hěn xuéxí* 'very study'   *很研究 *hěn yánjiū* 'very research'

There are a small number of verbs that cannot take an object, for instance 游泳 *yóuyǒng* 'swim', 咳嗽 *késòu* 'cough', 游行 *yóuxíng* 'parade', 示威 *shìwēi* 'demonstrate', 办公 *bàngōng* 'work', 出发 *chūfā* 'depart', 崩溃 *bēngkuì* 'breakdown', 鞠躬 *jūgōng* 'bow'. However, they cannot be preceded by degree adverbs like 很 *hěn* 'very'. Thus, they are still distinguished from adjectives. Usually verbs that can have objects are called transitive verbs and those that cannot are called intransitive verbs.

There are a few verbs indicating mental activities that can also be modified by 很 *hěn* 'very', including 想 *xiǎng* 'miss', 爱 *ài* 'love', 怕 *pà* 'afraid', 喜欢 *xǐhuān* 'like', 愿意 *yuànyì* 'be willing to', 害怕 *hàipà* 'afraid', 赞成 *zànchéng* 'approve' and 同意 *tóngyì* 'agree', as can be seen in the following:

很想 *hěn xiǎng* 'miss very much'   很爱 *hěn ài* 'love very much'
很怕 *hěn pà* 'afraid a lot'   很喜欢 *hěn xǐhuān* 'like very much'
很愿意 *hěn yuànyì* 'be quite willing to'   很害怕 *hěn hàipà* 'afraid a lot'
很赞成 *hěn zànchéng* 'quite approve'   很同意 *hěn tóngyì* 'quite agree'

However, these verbs can take objects, and the degree adverb 很 *hěn* 'very' can still precede the verb object phrase, as illustrated by the following phrases.

想她 *xiǎng tā* 'miss her'
爱祖国 *ài zǔguó* 'love the motherland'
喜欢男孩子 *xǐhuān nánháizi* 'like boys'
怕猫 *pà māo* 'be afraid of cats'
愿意参加 *yuànyì cānjiā* 'be willing to attend'
害怕考试 *hàipà kǎoshì* 'be afraid of exams'
赞成他的意见 *zànchéng tā de yìjiàn* 'approve of his opinion'
同意这种观点 *tóngyì zhèzhǒng guāndiǎn* 'agree with this opinion'
很想她 *hěn xiǎngtā* 'miss her so much'
很爱祖国 *hěn ài zǔguó* 'love the motherland very much'
很喜欢男孩子 *hěn xǐhuān nánháizi* 'like boys very much'
很怕猫 *hěn pà māo* 'be very afraid of cats'
很愿意参加 *hěn yuànyì cānjiā* 'be very willing to attend '
很害怕考试 *hěn hàipà kǎoshì* 'be very afraid of exams'
很赞成他的意见 *hěn zànchéng tā de yìjiàn* 'quite approve of his opinion'
很同意这种观点 *hěn tóngyì zhèzhǒng guāndiǎn* 'quite agree with this opinion'

3.5.4 Different Reduplication Forms of Verbs and Adjectives

There are quite a few number of verbs and adjectives that can be reduplicated, a property that is not shared by nouns. However, verbs and adjectives reduplicate in different ways, as indicated next.

Monosyllable verbs reduplicate in the form of A·A, with the second syllable taking the neutral tone. For example:

想想 *xiǎngxiang* 'think about' (*Zàijiàn* 74)
等等（我） *děngdengwǒ* 'wait for me' (*Wànhuātǒng* 53)
听听 *tīngting* 'listen to' (*Xiàoyǎn* 12）
试试 *shìshi* 'have a try' (*Fēngyǔ* 78)

Disyllabic verbs reduplicate in the form of A·BA·B, with the second and forth syllables taking the neutral tone. For example:

教训教训 *jiàoxun jiàoxun* 'teach a leasson' (*Wǔtǔ·xìjù* 148)
研究研究 *yánjiu yánjiu* 'do research' (*Wǔtǔ·xiǎoshuōshàng* 20)

考虑考虑 kǎolü kǎolü 'think about' (Shènglì 44)
欢聚欢聚 huānju huānju 'get together happily' (Lúnlǐ·zhōngsān 79)
照顾照顾 zhàogu zhàogu 'take care of' (Wǔtǔ·xiǎoshuōshàng 134)

Monosyllable adjectives reduplicate in the form of AA, in which the second syllable does not take the neutral tone. For example:

轻轻 qīngqīng 'light' (Zàijiàn 70)　　远远 yuǎnyuān 'far' (Bìhǔ 28）
好好 hǎohāo 'good' (Fēngyǔ 68)　　甜甜 tiántiān 'sweet' (Wànhuātǒng 28)
小小 xiǎoxiāo 'small' (Zhuīyún 25)　　高高 gāogāo 'high' (Wúxiányuè 83)

In Chinese Mandarin, the second syllable of the reduplication forms of monosyllable adjectives always takes form of rhotacisation in pronunciation and reads the level tone, as shown in the following examples. This form of reduplication does not exist in Singapore Mandarin, for there is no rhotacisation of syllable finals in this language.

轻轻儿 qīngqīnger 'light'　远远儿 yuǎnyuāner 'far'　小小儿 xiǎoxiāoer 'small'
甜甜儿 tiántiāner 'sweet'　好好儿 hǎohāoer 'good'　慢慢儿 mànmāner 'slow'

Disyllabic adjectives reduplicate in the form of AABB, in which the second and forth syllables do not have to change into the neutral tone. For example:

清清楚楚 qīngqīng chǔchǔ 'very clear' (Yǒuyuán 66)
结结实实 jiējiē shíshí 'very solid' (Wànhuātǒng 35)
端端正正 duānduān zhèngzhèng 'very upright' (Shènglì 92)
正正式式 zhèngzhèng shìshì 'very official' (Wǔtǔ·xìjù 83)

In a word, compared to nouns, verbs and adjectives share some similarities. However, ultimately they belong to two different word categories, and thus also differ from each other in grammatical functions.

3.6 Stative Words

Look at the following words.

碧绿 bìlǜ 'dark green'　　　　　　马里马虎 mǎlǐmǎhu 'careless'
雪白 xuěbái 'snow-white'　　　　　肮里肮脏 āanglǐāngzāng 'dirty' (报 1995
　　　　　　　　　　　　　　　　年 3 月 15 日 (Bào, Mar. 15, 1995,
　　　　　　　　　　　　　　　　supplementary edition, Issue no. 11))
红通通 hóngtōngtōng 'bright red'　糊里糊涂 húlǐhútú 'muddle-headed'
冰冷（吾土·小说上 16）bīnglěng 'ice-cold' (Wǔtǔ·xiǎoshuōshàng 16)
通红（金狮奖 7）tōnghóng 'glowing' (Jīnshījiǎng 7)

冷冰冰（万花筒 31）lěngbīngbīng 'ice cold' (*Wànhuātǒng* 31)
绿油油（晚上 158）lǜyóuyóu 'shiny green' (*Wǎnshang* 158)
黑漆漆（跳舞 3）hēiqīqī 'pitch dark' (*Tiàowǔ* 3)

These words are generally considered adjectives, but they are very different from adjectives. In terms of grammatical function, there are two obvious differences:

1 Adjectives can be modified by 不 *bù* 'NEG' and 很 *hěn* 'very', but these words can neither be modified by 不 *bù* 'NEG' nor by 很 *hěn* 'very'.
2 Adjectives can take complements, while none of the stative words can take complements.

In terms of grammatical meaning, they are also different from adjectives. Adjectives describe properties of things. But stative words indicate the state of things. Let's compare:

(1) 那　　孩子　的　　脸　　黄，　这　　孩子　的　　脸　　红。
    nà　*háizi*　*de*　*liǎn*　**huáng**,　*zhè*　*háizi*　*de*　*liǎn*　**hóng**
    that　child　DE　face　**yellow**　this　child　DE　face　**red**
    'That child's face is yellow, while this child's face is red.'

(2) 这　　孩子　的　　脸　　通红。
    zhè　*háizi*　*de*　*liǎn*　**tōnghóng**
    this　child　DE　face　**glowing**
    'The child's face is very red.'

Example (1) expresses an opinion, in which 红 *hóng* 'red' states the fact that the child's face has the property of being red. Example (2) is descriptive. The stative word 通红 *tōnghóng* 'glowing' describes the state of the child's face.

In view of the above differences, we put these words in a separate category – stative words. In terms of grammatical function, the reduplicated forms of adjectives mentioned earlier are also stative words. Stative words will be discussed further in later chapters.

3.7 Distinguishing Words

Distinguishing words are as follows:

公 *gōng* 'male'　　　　母 *mǔ* 'female'　　　　雌 *cí* 'female'
雄 *xióng* 'male'　　　　男 *nán* 'male'　　　　女 *nǚ* 'female'
荤 *hūn* 'meaty'　　　　素 *sù* 'vegetarian'　　　单 *dān* 'single'

夹 jiā 'double'　　　金 jīn 'gold'　　　银 yín 'silver'
阴 yīn 'Yin'　　　阳 yáng 'Yang'　　　公 gōng 'fair'
私 sī 'selfish'　　　正 zhèng 'deputy'　　　副 fù 'vice'
大型 dàxíng 'large'　　　微型 wēixíng 'small'　　　急性 jíxìng 'acute'
慢性 mànxìng 'chronic'　　　唯一 wéiyī 'unique'　　　公共 gōnggòng 'public'
彩色 cǎisè 'colourful'　　　黑白 hēibái 'monochrome'　　　野生 yěshēng 'wild'
人造 rénzào 'artificial'　　　良性 liángxìng 'benign'　　　恶性 èxìng 'malignant'
日常 rìcháng 'habitual'　　　高等 gāoděng 'higher'　　　首要 shǒuyào 'primary'
次要 cìyào 'secondary'　　　温 (～水)wēn(~shuǐ) 'warm(water)'
本 (～国)běn(~guó) 'native'　　　粉 (～色)fěn(~sè) 'pink(colour)'

These words are special in that they have only two grammatical functions. One is to modify nouns, functioning as attributives. Examples are 男同学 nántóngxué 'male classmate', 女同学 nǚtóngxué 'female classmate', 正班长 zhèngbānzhǎng 'monitor', 副班长 fùbānzhǎng 'deputy monitor', 急性肝炎 jíxìnggānyán 'acute hepatitis', 慢性肝炎 mànxìnggānyán 'chronic hepatitis', 恶性肿瘤 èxìngzhǒngliú 'malignant tumour'. The other is to form nominal phrases with the auxiliary 的 de 'DE', such as 公的 gōngde 'male', 母的 mǔde 'female', 单的 dānde 'single', 夹的 jiāde 'double', 良性的 liángxìngde 'benign', 恶性的 èxìngde 'malignant'. In terms of grammatical function, they are different from nouns, verbs, adjectives and stative words. Thus it is necessary to classify them as a separate category. Semantically speaking, these words can distinguish things, thus we call them distinguishing words.

3.8 Numerals and Classifiers

Numerals represent numbers or sequence of numbers. Examples of numbers are 一 yī 'one', 三 sān 'three', 八 bā 'eight', 十 shí 'ten', 五十六 wǔshíliù 'fifty-six' and so on, and examples of orders are 第一 dìyī 'first', 第三 dìsān 'third', 第八 dìbā 'eighth', 第十 dìshí 'tenth', 第五十六 dìwǔshíliù 'fifty-sixth' and so on. Classifiers are units of measurement of objects, actions or time. Classifiers such as 个 gè 'CL', 粒 lì 'CL', 条 tiáo 'CL', 间 jiān 'CL' are used to describe objects. 次 cì 'CL', 回（看一～） huí (kànyī~) 'CL (look a ~)', 下（打一～） xià (dǎyī~) 'CL (hit a ~)' can describe actions. And 年 nián 'year', 天 tiān 'day', 秒 miǎo 'second' describe time.

　　Numerals are often combined with classifiers, while classifiers can be combined only with numerals or demonstrative pronouns, such as 这 zhè 'this' and 那 nà 'that'. Thus, numerals and classifiers are often used together. The following are examples:

三个 sāngè 'three CL'　　　五粒 wǔlì 'five CL'　　　八位 bāwèi 'eight CL'
两间 liǎngjiān 'two CL'　　　一下 yíxià 'one bit'　　　三次 sāncì 'three times'

两回 liǎnghuí 'twice'	四趟 sìtàng 'four times'	三年 sānnián 'three years'
七天 qītiān 'seven days'	五秒 wǔmiǎo 'five seconds'	十分钟 shífēnzhōng 'ten minutes'
这个 zhège 'this one'	那个 nàge 'that one'	这位 zhèwèi 'this one'
那位 nàwèi 'that one'	这次 zhècì 'this time'	那次 nàcì 'that time'
这回 zhèhuí 'this time'	那回 nàhuí 'that time'	这年 zhènián 'this year'
那年 nànián 'that year'	这天 zhètiān 'this day'	那天 nàtiān 'that day'

Numerals generally do not directly modify nouns. When modifying nouns, numerals must be followed by classifiers. This is a major difference between Singapore Mandarin and English, as shown in the following contrasting examples:

'five students'	五个学生 wǔgèxuéshēng	(*五学生)(*wǔxuéshēng)
'a company'	一间公司 yījiāngōngsī	(*一公司)(*yīgōngsī)
'four eggs'	四粒鸡蛋 sìlìjīdàn	(*四鸡蛋)(*sìjīdàn)
'three books'	三本书 sānběnshū	(*三书)(*sānshū)

The combination of numerals and classifiers is called numeral-classifier phrase or numeral-classifier compound. They are used to measure the quantity of objects, the number of times an action takes place or the duration of time. Numeral-classifier phrases are modifier-head phrases. For instance, in the phrase 三个 sāngè 'three CL', 三 sān 'three' is the attribute and 个 gè 'CL' is the head.

3.9 Pronouns

Pronouns are a class of words used to refer to someone or something. According to their functions, pronouns are generally divided into three types.

A Personal pronouns:

你 nǐ 'you'	我 wǒ 'I'	他 tā 'he'
你们 nǐmen 'you'	我们 wǒmen 'we'	他们 tāmen 'they'

B Demonstrative pronouns:

这 zhè 'this'	这样 zhèyàng 'this way'	这么样 zhèmeyàng 'this way'
那 nà 'that'	那样 nàyàng 'that way'	那么样 nàmeyàng 'that way'

C Interrogative pronouns:

谁 shuí 'who'	什么 shénme 'what'	怎样 zěnyàng 'how'
怎么样 zěnmeyàng 'how'	哪儿 nǎer 'where'	

3.10 Adverbs

Adverbs are functional words, which can only serve as adverbials. Examples are as follows.

(1) 往   医院   的   第一   趟   巴士   **终于**   来   了。（青青 50）
    wǎng   yīyuàn   de   dìyī   tàng   bāshì **zhōngyú** lái   le
    to   hospital DE   first   CL   bus   **finally** come LE
    'The first bus to the hospital finally arrived.' (*Qīngqīng* 50)

(2) 我   **只**   写   了   几   页。（心情 127）
    wǒ   **zhī**   xiě   le   jǐ   yè
    1SG **only** write   LE   few   page
    'I've only written a few pages.' (*Xīnqíng* 127)

(3) 这   一切   **都**   是   上帝   所   赋予   给   他们   的。（科学 43）
    zhè   yíqiè   **dōu** shì   shàngdì   suǒ   fùyǔ   gěi   tāmen de
    this all   **all** be   god   SUO   give   to   3PL   DE
    'All this was given to them by God.' (*Kēxué* 43)

(4) **又**   **不**   是   要   举行   什么   庆典，
    yòu   **bú**   shì   yào   jǔxíng   shénme   qìngdiǎn
    again   **NEG** be   will   hold   what   celebration
    注个册   **就**   行   了。（追云 21）
    zhù-gè-cè   **jiù**   xíng   le
    register   **just** fine   LE
    'It's not a celebration. Just have a registration.' (*Zhuīyún* 21)

(5) 我   **已经**   闯   过   了   数不清的   关。（△含羞草 6）
    wǒ   **yǐjīng**   chuǎng   guò   le   shǔ-bù-qīng-de   guān
    1SG **already** pass   GUO   LE   countless   barrier
    'I've already broken through countless barriers.' (△*Hánxiūcǎo* 6)

In examples (1) through (5), 终于 *zhōngyú* 'finally', 只 *zhī* 'only', 都 *dōu* 'all', 又 *yòu* 'again', 不 *bù* 'NEG', 就 *jiù* 'just', 已经 *yǐjīng* 'already' are all adverbs. They can only be used as adverbials. Please note that not all adverbials are adverbs. See the following example.

(6) 我…… **努力**   朝   一   个   箭步   距离   之外   的
    wǒ   **nǔlì**   cháo   yí   gè   jiànbù   jùlí   zhīwài   de
    1SG   **trying.hard**   towards   one   CL   lunge   distance   outside   DE

行人	天桥	缓行而去。（撞墙 16）
xíngrén	tiānqiáo	huǎn-xíng-ér-qù
pedestrian	footbridge	walk.slowly

'I struggled towards the footbridge a short distance away.' (*Zhuàngqiáng* 16)

In the preceding example, 努力 *nǔlì* 'trying hard' is used as an adverbial, but it is not an adverb. It can be modified by 不 *bù* 'NEG' and 很 *hěn* 'very', such as 不努力 *bùnǔlì* 'not trying hard' and 很努力 *hěnnǔlì* 'trying very hard'; can be used as a predicate, as in 他努力，你不努力 *tānǔlì, nǐbùnǔlì* 'He is trying hard, but you are not'; can take a complement, as in 努力极了 *nǔlìjíle* 'trying very hard'. Therefore, 努力 *nǔlì* 'trying hard' is an adjective.

3.11 Prepositions

Prepositions are words like 把 *bǎ* 'BA', 被 *bèi* 'BEI', 由 *yóu* 'by', 使 *shǐ* 'AM', 从 *cóng* 'from', 向 *xiàng* 'towards', 往 *wǎng* 'to', 对于 *duìyú* 'for', 关于 *guānyú* 'about', 按 *àn* 'according to', 为 *wèi* 'for' and 比 *bǐ* 'than'. Prepositions are also functional words, mainly used to introduce the object related to the actions (including the location and time). See the following examples.

(1)
杨成	已经	**把**	雪云	忘记	了。（梦 65）
yángchéng	yǐjīng	**bǎ**	xuěyún	wàngjì	le
3SG	already	**BA**	XueYun	forget	LE

'Yang Cheng has already forgotten Xue Yun.' (*Mèng* 65)

(2)
我......	脑海	中，	却	一直	看到	"自己"	**被**
wǒ	nǎohǎi	zhōng	què	yìzhí	kàndào	zìjǐ	**bèi**
1SG	mind	inside	but	always	see	oneself	**BEI**

自己	杀害！（华韵 73）
zìjǐ	shāhài
oneself	kill

'But in my mind, I always see that "I" was killed by myself.' (*Huáyùn* 73)

(3)
从	北边	回来	了。（回忆 54）
cóng	běibiān	huílái	le
from	north	come.back	LE

'... came back from the north.' (*Huíyì* 54)

In example (1), 把 *bǎ* 'BA' introduces the object of the verb 忘记 *wàngjì* 'forget', which is 雪云 *xuěyún* 'Xue Yun'. In example (2), 被 *bèi* 'BEI' introduces the actor of the verb 杀害 *shāhài* 'kill', which is 自己 *zìjǐ* 'oneself'. In example (3), 从 *cóng* 'from' introduces the starting point of the action of 回来 *huílái* 'come back'. Thus, a preposition can never be a stranded syntactic component, that is, it cannot be the subject, predicate or object by itself. It must collocate with nouns, pronouns or other words to compose a prepositional phrase, as shown in 把雪云 *bǎxuěyún* 'BA Xue Yun', 被自己 *bèizìjǐ* 'by oneself', 从北边 *cóngběibiān* 'from the north'. The basic function of a prepositional phrase is to be an adverbial of a sentence, as illustrated by the preceding three examples, in which 把雪云 *bǎxuěyún* 'BA Xue Yun', 被自己 *bèizìjǐ* 'by oneself', 从北边 *cóngběibiān* 'from the north' are all adverbials.

For further discussion of prepositions and prepositional phrases, see Chapter 10.

3.12 Conjunctions

Conjunctions are functional words which are used to connect other words, phrases or clauses. Let's look at the following sentences.

(1) 地铁   投入   使用   后，   相信   巴士   **和**   德士   的
    dìtiě *tóurù*   *shǐyòng* *hòu*   *xiāngxìn* *bāshì* **hé** *déshì* *de*
    subway put.into   use   after   believe   bus   **and** taxi   DE

   生意   将   不会   受到   影响。（华文教材 1B6）
   shēngyì *jiāng* *búhuì*   *shòudào* *yǐngxiǎng*
   business   will   NEG   get   influence

   'Once the subway goes into operation, (I) don't think the bus and taxi business will be affected.' (*Huáwénjiàocái* 1B, 6)

(2) 对于   鼻子   扁   了、   嘴巴   歪   了   **或是**   秃了头   的
    duìyú *bízi* *biǎn* *le*   *zuǐba* *wāi*   *le* **huòshì**   *tū-le-tóu* *de*
    for   nose   flat   LE   mouth   crooked   LE   **or**   bald   DE

   人，   我们   都   觉得   那   是   丑的。（科学 125）
   rén   *wǒmēn*   *dōu*   *juéde*   *nà* *shì*   *chǒude*
   people 1PL   all   think   that be   ugly

   'We all assume that people with a flat nose, crooked mouth or bald head are ugly.' (*Kēxué* 125)

(3) **虽然**   岁月   在   每   个   人   的   脸   上   留下
    suīrán *suìyuè* *zài*   *měi*   *gè*   *rén*   *de* *liǎn*   *shàng*   *liúxià*
    although time   at   each   CL   person   DE   face   on   leave

   了   明显的   痕迹， **但**   "老"   字   似乎   变成   了
   le *míngxiǎnde* *hénjì* **dàn** *lǎo* *zì*   *sìhū*   *biànchéng* *le*
   LE   obvious   mark   **but** old   word   seem   become   LE

一	种	讳，	没有	人	愿意	去	触犯	它。（冰灯 12）
yī	zhǒng	huì	méiyǒu	rén	yuànyì	qù	chùfàn	tā
a	CL	taboo	not.have	people	willing	go	offend	3SG

'Although time has left obvious marks on everyone's face, the word "old" seems to have become a kind of taboo, and no one wants to use it.' (*Bīngdēng* 12)

In example (1), 和 *hé* 'and' connects two words 巴士 *bāshì* 'bus' and 德士 *déshì* 'taxi'. In example (2), 或是 *huòshì* 'or' connects three phrases 鼻子扁了 *bízi biǎnle* 'flat nose', 嘴巴歪了 *zuǐba wāile* 'crooked mouth' and 秃了头 *tūletóu* 'bald head'. In example (3), 虽然 *suīrán* 'although' and 但 *dàn* 'but' connects the two clauses. All of them are conjunctions. There will be further discussion about conjunctions in Chapter 3, Volume II.

3.13 Auxiliary Words

There are two types of auxiliary words, dynamic auxiliary words, such as 了 *le* 'LE', 着 *zhe* 'ZHE', 过 *guo* 'GUO', and structural auxiliary words, such as 的 *de* 'DE', 地 *de* 'DE', 得 *de* 'DE', 到 *dào* 'DAO', 所 *suǒ* 'SUO', 似的 *shìde* 'like'.

The words 了 *le* 'LE', 着 *zhe* 'ZHE', 过 *guo* 'GUO' are mainly suffixed to verbs and take the neutral tone in sentences. 了 *le* 'LE' indicates that an action has been completed, as exemplified in the following sentence.

(1)
黎明	的	天空	露出	了	鱼肚白。（金狮奖 102）
límíng	de	tiānkōng	lùchū	le	yúdùbái
dawn	DE	sky	appear	LE	a.grayish.colour

'At dawn the sky turned into a greyish colour.' (*Jīnshījiǎng* 102)

着 *zhe* 'ZHE' indicates the duration of actions, as in the following sentence.

(2)
老黄	正在	整理	着	农具。（短篇 85）
lǎohuáng	zhèngzài	zhěnglǐ	zhe	nóngjù
Laohuang	in.process	sort.out	ZHE	farm.tools

'Laohuang is sorting out his farm tools.' (*Duǎnpiān* 85)

过 *guò* 'GUO' indicates the past experience of actions or events. See the following example.

(3)
我	曾经	参观	过	无数	次。（晚上 159）
wǒ	céngjīng	cānguān	guo	wúshù	cì
1SG	previously	visit	GUO	countless	times

'I have visited it countless times.' (*Wǎnshàng* 159)

As for structural auxiliary words, 的 *de* 'DE', 地 *de* 'DE', 得 *de* 'DE', 所 *suǒ* 'SUO' will be discussed here. The rest will be introduced in later chapters. 的 *de* 'DE', 地 *de* 'DE', 得 *de* 'DE' all take the neutral tone *de*, however they have different functions.

的 *de* 'DE' has two main functions. First, 的 *de* 'DE' can be attached after specific words or phrases to show that they are attributes. See the following examples.

光华	乒乓	队	的	功臣（薪传 56）
guānghuá	pīngpāng	duì	**de**	gōngchén
Guanghua	table.tennis	team	**DE**	hero

'the hero of the Guanghua table tennis team' (*Xīnchuán* 56)

最后	的	牛车水（牛车水 14）
zuìhòu	**de**	niúchēshuǐ
real	**DE**	Chinatown

'the last Chinatown' (*Niúchēshuǐ* 14)

真正	的	人才（八方 73）
zhēnzhèng	**de**	réncái
last	**DE**	talent

'the real talents' (*Bāfāng* 73)

Second, 的 *de* 'DE' is attached to certain words or phrases to form a nominal structure which is often called *de* 'DE' construction. This kind of construction is equivalent to a noun in that it also refers to things. For example, 穿 *chuān* 'wear' and 吃 *chī* 'eat' are verbs that represent actions. If we add 的 *de* 'DE' after them, the resulting phrases 穿的 *chuānde* 'something to wear' and 吃的 *chīde* 'something to eat' are nominal structures representing clothes and food, as shown in the sentence 穿的，吃的，哪样缺你 *chuānde, chīde, nǎyàngquēnǐ* 'what kind of clothes and food do you lack' (*Jīnshíjiǎng* IV, 9). In the sentence 日本的不要，买德国的（再见 75） *rìběndebúyào, mǎidéguóde* 'buy German products instead of Japanese ones' (*Zàijiàn* 75), 日本的 *rìběnde* and 德国的 *déguóde* products are both DE constructions, meaning products made in Japan and products made in Germany respectively. Here is one more example.

(4) 净化不了 的 是 你 重重的 心事， 层层的
    jìng-huà-bù-liǎo **de** shì nǐ chóngchóngde xīnshì céngcéngdē
    cannot.be.purified **DE** be 2SG heavy thoughts layers

记忆。（牛车水 24）
jìyì
memory

'What cannot be purified are your heavy thoughts and layers of memory.' (*Niúchēshuǐ* 24)

In this example, 净化不了的 *jìnghuà bùliǎode* 'what cannot be purified' is a 的 *de* 'DE' construction which consists of a predicate-complement construction 净化不了 *jìnghuà bùliǎo* 'cannot be purified' and the auxiliary word 的 *de* 'DE'.

地 *de* 'DE' is attached to some words or phrases to show that those words or phrases are adverbials, as shown in the following examples.

日以继夜	地	工作 （华文教材 2A12）
rìyǐjìyè	*de*	*gōngzuò*
round the clock	DE	work

'work round the clock' (*Huáwénjiàocái* 2A, 12)

严格	地	要求	自己（伦理・中三 68）
yángé	*de*	*yāoqiú*	*zìjǐ*
strict	DE	require	oneself

'be strict with oneself' (*Lúnlǐzhōngsān* 68)

文艺	工作者	正	认真	地	树立起	他	的	形象。（至性 94）
wényì	*gōngzuòzhě*	*zhèng*	*rènzhēn*	*de*	*shùlìqǐ*	*tā*	*de*	*xíngxiàng*
Art	worker	is	carefully	DE	build	2SG	DE	image

'The artist is carefully building up his image.' (*Zhìxìng* 94)

Some people use 的 *de* 'DE' instead of 地 *de* 'DE' after adverbials, however this is not standard Chinese Mandarin and thus should be corrected.

得 *de* 'DE' is attached to a verb or an adjective to show that the word after 得 *de* 'DE' is the complement.

生活	得	愉快（金狮奖 177）	忙	得	昏头转向（南风 51）
shēnghuó	*de*	*yúkuài*	*máng*	*de*	*yūntóuzhuànxiàng*
life	DE	happy	busy	DE	dizzy

'have a happy life' (*Jīnshījiǎng* 177)   'have a hectic schedule' (*Nánfēng* 51)

Some people also use 的 *de* 'DE' instead of 得 *de* 'DE' in the middle of a verb-complement structure. This is also nonstandard and should be corrected.

In classical Chinese 所 *suǒ* 'SUO' is a functional word. It always precedes transitive verbs to form a nominal phrase which describes what one sees or hears or says and so on, such as 所见 *suǒjiàn* 'things one sees', 所闻 *suǒwén* 'things one hears', 所述 *suǒshù* 'things one says'. In modern Singapore Mandarin, 所 *suǒ* 'SUO' often collocates with 的 *de* 'DE' and forms a '(noun) + 所 + verb + 的' structure, in which it is also possible for the noun before 所 *suǒ* 'SUO' to be absent. This structure is nominal, mainly used as an attribute, as exemplified in the following examples.

(5) 他   那   支   诗   笔   所   写出   的   诗，   又
    tā   nà   zhī   shī   bǐ   **suǒ** xiěchū   de   shī   yòu
    3SG   that CL   poetry pen **SUO** write.out DE   poem   and

   犹如   筷子   所   夹   的   "五千年的芬芳"。（△新华 167）
   yóurú   kuàizī   **suǒ**   jiā   de   wǔ-qiān-nián-de-fēn-fāng
   like   chopsticks **SUO**   clip   DE   fragrance.of.five.thousand.years

   'The poems written by his poetry pen are just like the "fragrance of five
   thousand years" caught by chopsticks.' (△*Xīnhuá* 167)

Sometimes this structure is also used as a subject or an object, as it is in the
following two examples.

(6) 上面   所   谈   的   都   说明   了   条例   在
    shàngmiàn   **suǒ**   tán   de   dōu   shuōmíng   le   tiáolì   zài
    above   **SUO**   discuss DE   all   illustrate LE   regulation   at

   法治   社会   里   有   存在   的   必要。（风筝 217）
   fǎzhì   shèhuì   lǐ   yǒu   cúnzài   de   bìyào
   legal   society   inside have   exist   DE   necessity

   'What has been discussed so far all illustrate the necessity of the existence
   of regulations in a legal society.' (*Fēngzhēn* 217)

(7) 人   最终   是   艺术   所   要   关注   的。（科学 110）
    rén   zuìzhōng   shì   yìshù   **suǒ**   yào   guānzhù   de
    man   ultimate   be   art   **SUO**   want   concern   DE

   'Man is the ultimate concern of art.' (*Kēxué* 110)

However, unlike the *de* 'DE' construction, the structure of 所 *suǒ* . . . 的 *de*
'SUO . . . DE' cannot be used as a predicate.

3.14 Sentence Final Particles

Sentence final particles (e.g. 啊 *ā*, 了 *le*, 啦 *lā*, 吧 *bā*, 吗 *mā*, 呢 *nē*, 而已 *éryǐ*) often appear at the end of a sentence, indicating sentence mood, including the indicative mood, the imperative mood, the interrogative mood, the exclamative mood, and so on. Details about sentence final particles are given in Section 4.13 in Volume II.

3.15 Interjections

Interjections (e.g. 嗳 *āi* 'ah', 哦 *ò* 'oh', 嗨 *hāi* 'hi', 喂 *wèi* 'hi', 啊 *ā* 'ah', 哟 *yō* 'yo', 哼 *hēng* 'humph', 咳 *ké* 'eh', 咦 *yí* 'huh', 哇 *wā* 'wow', 哗 *huá* 'wow', 唉 *āi* 'um', 嘿 *hēi* 'hey', 哎哟 *āiyō* 'whoops', 哎呀 *āiya* 'oh') are used to respond, to call for attention or to express exclamation. The grammatical characteristic of interjections is that they do not form a constituent with other words. There will be a pause before and after an interjection. The following sentences are taken from the article "*Nightmare in the Bookstore*" in *Golden Lion Award Winners Collection I (1981–1982)*.

(1) | 哦， | 真 | 抱歉， | 我 | 还 | 以为 | 你 | 是 | 一 | 年级 |
| --- | --- | --- | --- | --- | --- | --- | --- | --- | --- |
| *ò* | *zhēn* | *bàoqiàn* | *wǒ* | *hái* | *yǐwéi* | *nǐ* | *shì* | *yī* | *niánjí* |
| oh | really | sorry | 1SG | also | think | 2SG | be | first | grade |

的	新生	呢。(68)
de	*xīnshēng*	*ne*
DE	freshman	SFP

'Oh, I'm so sorry, I thought you were a freshman in the first grade.' (68)

(2) | "子宇 | 走 | 了？" | 政生 | 关心地 | 问。 |
| --- | --- | --- | --- | --- | --- |
| *zǐyǔ* | *zǒu* | *le* | *zhèngshēng* | *guānxīnde* | *wèn* |
| Ziyu | go | LE | Zhengsheng | concernedly | ask |

"哎，	走	了。" (77)
ài	*zǒu*	*le*
yes	go	LE

' "Is Ziyu gone?" Zhengsheng asked with concern.
"Yes, he's gone." ' (77)

(3) | "你 | 也 | 这么 | 清楚？" | 朱穆郎 | 冷笑 | 道。 |
| --- | --- | --- | --- | --- | --- | --- |
| *nǐ* | *yě* | *zhème* | *qīngchǔ* | *zhūmùláng* | *lěngxiào* | *dào* |
| 2SG | also | so | clear | Zhu Mulang | sneer | say |

' "You also know it so well?" Zhu Mulang sneered and said.' (72)

"嗳，	除了	这个，	还	会	有	什么	其他	理由？" (72)
ài	*chúle*	*zhège*	*hái*	*huì*	*yǒu*	*shénme*	*qítā*	*lǐyóu*
ah	besides	this	still	will	have	what	other	reason

' "Ah, what else can be the reason?" ' (72)

(4) A: "喂, 又 闹 思乡病 了。"
　　　　wèi yòu nào xiāngsībìng le
　　　　hey again have homesick LE
　　　'Hey, you are homesick again.'

　　B: "没有, 想 些 东西。"
　　　　méiyǒu xiǎng xiē dōngxi
　　　　No think some thing
　　　'No, just thinking of something.'

　　A: "想 爱人。"
　　　　xiǎng àirén
　　　　think wife
　　　'Missing your wife.'

　　B: "..."
　　　　"..."
　　　　"..."
　　　　"..."

　　A: "唉, 猜得 没 错 吧。"（138）
　　　　ài cāide méi cuò ba
　　　　ah guess NEG wrong SFP
　　　'Ah, maybe I guessed it right.' (138)

(5) 喂, 你 到 哪里 去?（71）
　　wèi nǐ dào nǎli qù
　　hey 2SG get to where go
　　'Hey, where are you going?' (71)

(6) "咦, 怎 不 见 方愫?" 政生 看了看 腕表。（81）
　　yí zěn bú jiàn fāngsù zhèngshēng kàn-le-kàn wǎnbiǎo
　　huh how NEG see Fang Su Zhengsheng look wristwatch
　　'"Huh, where is Fang Su?" Zhengsheng looked at his wristwatch and said.' (81)

嗨 *hāi* 'hi' and 哇 *wā* 'wow' (also written as 哗 *huá* 'wow') are two interjections peculiar to Singapore Mandarin. There is no such interjection in Chinese

Mandarin. 嗨 *hāi* 'hi' is often used to extend greetings or call attention. This is borrowed from English (嗨 *hāi* 'hi' is the transliteration of the English word 'hi'). For example:

(7)   "嗨,   密斯   游"
     hāi   *mìsī*   *yóu*
     hi   Miss   You
     'Hi, Miss You.'

     "嗨,   柏斯   教授,   早"（金狮奖 127）
     hāi   *bósī*   *jiàoshòu*   *zǎo*
     hi   Perth   professor   good.morning
     'Hi, Professor Perth. Good morning.' (*Jīnshījiǎng* 127)

(8)   杰: 嗨!
     jié   ***hāi***
     Jay   **hi**
     'Jay: Hi!'

     妮: 嗨!
     nī   ***hāi***
     Ni   **hi**
     'Ni: Hi!'

     杰: 一   个   人?
     jié   *yí*   *gè*   *rén*
     Jay   one   CL   person
     'Jay: Alone?'

     妮: 两   个   人。（吾土·戏剧 79）
     nī   *liǎng*   *gè*   *rén*
     Ni   two   CL   person
     'Ni: Two people.' (*Wútǔxìjù* 79)

(9)   嗨,   想   不   想   去   游泳?（青青 67）
     hāi   *xiǎng*   *bù*   *xiǎng*   *qù*   *yóuyǒng*
     hi   want   NEG   want   go   swim
     'Hi, do you want to go swimming?' (*Qīngqīng* 67)

Word Classes 69

(10) 嗨！ 阿X 正在 隔壁 替 那 家 新 开张
hāi ā X zhèngzài gébì tì nà jiā xīn kāizhāng
hi X now next door for that CL newly opened

的 美容院 剪彩 呢。（微型 219）
de měiróngyuàn jiǎncǎi ne
DE beauty salon cut ribbon SFP

'Hi! X is cutting the ribbon for the newly opened beauty salon next door.' (*Wēixíng* 219)

哇 *wā* (哗 *huá*) 'wow' comes from Cantonese and expresses admiration or unexpected emotions.

(11) 哇， 九十二 分， 我 的 宝贝，
wā jiǔshí'èr fēn wǒ de bǎobèi
wow ninety two points 1SG DE baby

你 真 行。（胜利82）
nǐ zhēn xíng
2SG really good

'Wow, ninety-two points! Well done, my baby.' (*Shènglì* 82)

(12) 哗！ 好 美 的 丝带 花球！（今后 86）
huá hǎo měi de sīdài huāqiú
wow so beautiful DE ribbon flower ball

'Wow! What a beautiful ribbon flower ball!' (*Jīnhòu* 86)

(13) 哇！ 这么 苛刻！（醒醒 46）
wā zhème kēkè
wow so harsh

'Wow! That's harsh!' (*Xǐngxǐng* 46)

(14) 哗， 想 不到 几 个 月 不 见，
huà xiǎng búdào jǐ gè yuè bú jiàn
wow believe NEG several CL month NEG see

你 倒 发福 了！（恶梦 83）
nǐ dào fāfú le
2SG actually gain.weight LE

'Wow, haven't seen you for a few months. You've actually gained some weight.' (*Èmèng* 83)

In examples (11) and (12) the purpose of 哇 wā 'wow' and 哗 huá 'wow' is to express admiration, while their purpose is to express surprise in examples (13) and (14).

3.16 Onomatopoeias

Onomatopoeias are words that mimic sounds, such as 砰 pēng 'bang', 噔 dēng 'thud', 乒 pīng 'bang', 轰 hōng 'boom', 卜 bo 'pita-pat', 嘟 dū, 咔嚓 kāchā 'click', 哗啦 huāla 'crash', 唧唧喳喳 jījīzhāzhā 'twiter'. Onomatopoeias are often used as modifiers and can be used repeatedly. See the following examples.

(1) 老人　　　听到　　　　**砰**　　　一　　声，　　　有　　　人
　　 lǎorén　　Tīngdào　　　**pēng**　　yī　　sheng　　 yǒu　　rén
　　 old man　hear　　　　　**bang**　　one　CL　　　 have　someone

　　 打破　　　厨房　　　　的　　　窗。（万花筒 26）
　　 dǎpò　　　chúfáng　　 de　　 chuāng
　　 break　　kitchen　　　DE　　window

'The old man heard a "bang". Someone had broken the kitchen window.' (Wànhuātǒng 26)

(2) 她　　喜欢　　　看　　他　　走起　　　路　　来　　**"噔，噔，噔"**
　　 tā　　Xǐhuān　kàn　　tā　　zǒuqǐ　　lù　　lái　　**dēngdēngdēng**
　　 3SG　like　　 see　　3SG　walk　　　road　come　**thud thud thud**

　　 的　　步子。（太阳 10）
　　 de　　Bùzi
　　 DE　　step

'She likes to see him walk with a "thud, thud, thud".' (Tàiyáng 10)

(3) **"咔嚓"**　　一　　声，　　　摄影记者　　　　　高　　　叫　　　"OK"，
　　 kāchā　　yī　　shēng　　shèyǐngjìzhě　　　gāo　　 jiào　　OK
　　 click　　one　sound　　 photojournalist　loudly　shout　OK

　　 众人　　　　一齐　　　　发出　　 **"轰"**　　的　　一　　声。（扶轮 66）
　　 zhòngrén　　yìqí　　　　fāchū　　**hōng**　　de　　yī　　shēng
　　 everybody　together　　make　　**boom**　　DE　　one　sound

'"Click", the photojournalist shouted "OK" loudly, then everybody together let out a roar.' (Fúlún 66)

(4) "哗啦！ 哗啦！" 的 河 水 汹涌 而来。（晚上 180）
    huālā *huālā* *de* *hé* *shuǐ* *xiōngyǒng* *érlái*
    splash **splash** DE river water surge come
    '"Crash! Crash!" the river surged.' (*Wǎnshàng* 180)

Onomatopoeias can form sentences by themselves and can also be used repeatedly, as in the following two examples.

(5) "轰——"。 一 声 巨 响 后，
    hōng *yī* *shēng* *jù* *xiǎng* *hòu*
    boom one sound huge noise later

    山头 后方 被 燃 得 一 片 通红。（金狮奖 7）
    shāntóu *hòufāng* *bèi* *rán* *de* *yí* *piàn* *tōnghóng*
    mountain back BEI burn DE one CL Glowing.red
    '"Boom!" After a huge noise, the back of the mountain was burnt glowing red.' (*Jīnshījiǎng* 7)

(6) 两 个 人 心跳 的 声音，
    liǎng *gè* *rén* *xīntiào* *de* *shēngyīn*
    two CL people heartbeat DE sound

    突然 放大 了 几十 倍。
    tūrán *fàngdà* *le* *jǐshí* *bèi*
    suddenly amplify LE dozens.of times

    卜、 卜、 卜、 卜、 卜、 卜、 卜、 卜。（跳舞 19）
    bo *Bo* *bo* *bo* *bo* *bo* *bo* *bo*
    pit-a- Pat pit-a- pat pit-a- pat pit-a- pat
    'The two people's heartbeats suddenly became amplified, pit-a-pat, pit-a-pat, pit-a-pat, pit-a-pat.' (*Tiàowǔ* 19)

3.17 Multi-category Words

Word classes are divided according to their grammatical functions, each class with its own characteristics. We should say that the distinction between different classes are rather clear. Nonetheless, for some specific words, they might display two or more types of grammatical characteristics at the same time. These are the so-called multi-category words, or words of overlapping categories.

Multi-category words can be understood in both a narrow sense and a broad sense. In a narrow sense, they refer to words that have the same meaning but belong to different word classes. For example, 活跃 *huóyuè* 'active' is originally an adjective, which has all the grammatical properties of an adjective. Particularly it can be modified by 很 *hěn* 'very', as in 很活跃 *hěn huóyuè* 'very active'. On the other hand, it can also take objects, as in 活跃我们的思维（华文121）*huóyuè wǒmén de sīwéi* 'activate our minds' (*Huáwén* 121), where 活跃 *huóyuè* 'activate' has the characteristics of a verb. It is worth noting that it can no longer be modified by 很 *hěn* 'very' when carrying an object. For instance, we do not say 很活跃我们的思维 *hěn huóyuè wǒmén de sīwéi* '*very activate our minds'. Therefore, 活跃 *huóyuè* 'active/activate' has the grammatical features of both adjectives and verbs, a multi-category word in the narrow sense, but its meaning remains unchanged. Similar examples are 方便 *fāngbiàn*, 巩固 *gǒnggù* and 高速 *gāosù*.

方便 *fāngbiàn* is both an adjective (meaning 'convenient') and a verb (meaning 'to make convenience for somebody'), as shown in examples (1a) and (1b).

(1a) 这里　　　　交通　　　　很　　　　**方便**
　　　zhèlǐ　　　 jiāotōng　　　hěn　　　***fāngbiàn***
　　　here　　　 transport　　 very　　　**convenient**
　　　'The transport here is very convenient.'

(1b) **方便**　　　　　　顾客
　　　fāngbiàn　　 gùkè
　　　convenient　　customer
　　　'to make it convenient for customers'

巩固 *gǒnggù* is both an adjective (meaning 'solid') and a verb (meaning 'to consolidate something'), as shown in examples (2a) and (2b).

(2a) 我们　　　的　　　友谊　　　很　　　**巩固**
　　　Wǒmen　　de　　　yǒuyì　　 hěn　　　***gǒnggù***
　　　1PL　　　 DE　　　friendship very　　 **solid**
　　　'Our friendship is very solid.'

(2b) **巩固**　　　　　我们　　　的　　　国防
　　　gǒnggù　　wǒmen　　 de　　　guófáng
　　　consolidate　1PL　　　 DE　　　national.defense
　　　'Consolidate our national defence.'

高速 *gāosù* is both a distinguishing word (meaning 'high speed') and an adverb (meaning 'highly'), as in examples (3a) and (3b).

(3a) 高速　　　　　　公路
　　 gāosù　　　　　*gōnglù*
　　 high.speed　　　road
　　 'express highway'

(3b) 高速　　　　发展　　　　电子　　　　工业
　　 gāosù　　 *fāzhǎn*　　 *diànzǐ*　　 *gōngyè*
　　 highly　　　develop　　　electronic　industry
　　 'to highly develop the electronics industry'

In a broad sense, multi-category words refer to words that have different but related meanings and will fall into different types of word classes. For example, 锁 *suǒ* 'lock' is both a verb and a noun. When used as a verb, it refers to some kind of action, as in 大门锁了 *dàménsuǒle* 'The door is locked'. When used as a noun, it refers to a lock, as in the phrase 买了一把锁 *mǎileyìbǎsuǒ* 'bought a lock'. The two have different, but related, meanings. Thus 锁 *suǒ* 'lock' is an example of a multi-category word in the broad sense. Similar examples are as follows.

导演 *dǎoyǎn* is both a verb (meaning 'to direct') and a noun (meaning 'director'), as in examples (4a) and (4b).

(4a) 他　　　导演　　　了　　　一　　　部　　　影片。
　　 tā　　 *dǎoyǎn*　　 *le*　　 *yí*　　 *bù*　　 *diànyǐng*
　　 2SG　　 direct　　　LE　　　one　　　CL　　　movie
　　 'He directed a movie.'

(4b) 他　　　是　　　一　　　位　　　导演
　　 tā　　 *Shì*　　 *yí*　　 *wèi*　　 *dǎoyǎn*
　　 2SG　　 Be　　　one　　　CL　　　director
　　 'He is a director.'

代表 *dàibiǎo* is both a verb (meaning 'to represent') and a noun (meaning 'representative'), as in example (5a) and (5b).

(5a) 他　　　代表　　　大家　　　讲话
　　 tā　　 *dàibiǎo*　　 *dàjiā*　　 *jiǎnghuà*
　　 2SG　　 represent　　 everybody　speak
　　 'He represented everybody to give a speech.'

(5b) 他　　　是　　　南大　　　　　　的　　　**代表**
　　　tā　　　Shì　　　nándà　　　　　 de　　　**dàibiǎo**
　　　2SG　　Be　　　Nanjing University　DE　　**representative**
　　　'He is the representative of Nanjing University.'

报告 *bàogào* is both a verb (meaning 'to make a report') and a noun (meaning 'a report'), as in examples (6a) and (6b).

(6a) **报告**　　大家　　　一　　　个　　　好　　　消息
　　　bàogào　dàjiā　　 yí　　　gè　　　hǎo　　xiāoxī
　　　report　everybody　one　　CL　　　good　news
　　　'to report a piece of good news to everybody'

(6b) 校长　　　　作　　　了　　　一　　　个　　　**报告**
　　　xiàozhǎng　zuò　　 le　　　yí　　　gè　　　**bàogào**
　　　headmaster　make　LE　　 one　　CL　　　**report**
　　　'The headmaster made a report.'

Please note that homophones are not multi-category words. For example, 会 *huì* can be used as a noun meaning 'meeting', as in 开了一个会 *kāileyígèhuì* 'had a meeting', and can also serve as a verb meaning 'can', as in 她会弹钢琴 *tāhuìdàngāngqín* 'She can play the piano'. However, these two words are not related in meaning. They are homophones and should be regarded as two different words. Similar examples are as follows.

花 *huā* is both a noun (meaning 'flower') and a verb (meaning 'spend'), as in examples (7a) and (7b).

(7a) 送　　　她　　　一　　　束　　　**花**
　　　sòng　　tā　　　yī　　　shù　　**huā**
　　　give　　2SG　　one　　 CL　　**flower**
　　　'Give her a bunch of flowers.'

(7b) 今天　　　**花**　　　了　　　一百　　　块
　　　jīntiān　　**huā**　　le　　　yībǎi　　 kuài
　　　today　　**spend**　LE　　 a hundred　yuan
　　　'Spent a hundred *yuan* today.'

制服 *zhìfú* is a noun (meaning 'uniform') and a verb (meaning 'subdue'), as in examples (8a) and (8b).

(8a) 他   穿   了   一   身   学校   的   制服
     tā   chuān   le   yī   shēn   xuéxiào   de   **zhìfú**
     2SG   wear   LE   one   CL   school   DE   **uniform**
     'He is wearing a school uniform.'

(8b) 大家   制服   了   那个   歹徒
     dàjiā **zhìfú**   le   nàgè   dǎitú
     1PL   **subdue**   LE   that   gangster
     'People subdued the gangster.'

只 zhī is a classifier and an adverb (meaning 'only'), as in examples (9a) and (9b).

(9a) 捉   了   一   只   蟋蟀
     zhuō   Le   yī   **zhī**   xīshuài
     catch LE   one   **CL**   cricket
     'caught a cricket'

(9b) 我   只   吃   了   一   粒   鸡蛋
     wǒ   **Zhǐ**   chī   le   yī   lì   jīdàn
     1SG   **only**   eat   le   one   CL   egg
     'I only ate an egg.'

Finally, it should be pointed out that for any word classification methods multi-category words should be restricted to a very small proportion of the word family. The reason is as follows: If we divide A and B into two categories, where a considerable number of words from Group A share the characteristics of Group B and can also fall into Group B, then the criteria on which we divide A and B are not soundly based.

Note

1   Translator's note: 他 tā is used for third person, masculine, 她 tā for third person, feminine, and 它 tā for third person, non-human.

4 Sentences

Lu Jianming

4.1 An Overview of Sentences in Singapore Mandarin

When we talk about grammar, we stop at the sentence level, because a sentence is the largest grammatical unit. Units beyond a sentence, for example, a sentence group, a paragraph and a text, fall within the domain of literature or discourse linguistics.

A sentence is the basic unit of expression. Only a sentence can express a relatively complete meaning. Therefore, when people use language to think or to express their thoughts, sentences are always employed as the basic units. We always speak sentence by sentence and it is also true of our writing: a paragraph is composed of sentences and in turn a text is composed of paragraphs.

As the basic unit of expression, a sentence differs from the other grammatical units in two ways: First, each sentence has a certain intonation; second, there is always a relatively long pause before and after a sentence. The function of intonation is to express different moods. In written Singapore Mandarin, full stops "。", or question marks "?", or exclamation marks "!" are used at the ends of sentences to indicate mood and to signal a pause. Here are three sentences extracted from 撞墙 *Zhuàngqiáng* 'Knocking on the Wall', a collection of novels by Hu Yuebao.

(1) 我　　决定　　自己　　闯　　天下。(43)
　　wǒ　　Juédìng　zìjǐ　　chuǎng　tiānxià
　　1SG　 decide　 myself　break　　world
　　'I decided to carve a niche in the world for myself.' (43)

(2) 怎么样　　　的　　价格　　才　　叫　　合理? (21)
　　zěnmeyàng　　de　　jiàgé　　cái　　jiào　　hélǐ
　　what.kind.of　　DE　　price　　only　　call　　reasonable
　　'What kind of price is reasonable?' (21)

(3) 抬起　　头　　来! (47)
　　táiqǐ　　Tóu　　lái
　　raise　　Head　　up
　　'Raise your head!' (47)

DOI: 10.4324/b23129-4

These three sentences have different intonations and moods, so they end with different punctuation marks. The full stop "。" in example (1) shows a declarative mood; the question mark "?" in example (2) indicates an interrogative mood; and the exclamation mark "!" in example (3) indicates an imperative mood, which is used to make a command here.

Sentences in Singapore Mandarin, unlike English, are not formed by using phrases, but rather by using words or phrases with a certain intonation. In other words, a phrase or a word plus an intonation is a sentence as long as it can stand on its own (that is, can be spoken alone). The phrase or the word that is realised as a sentence is usually referred as a 'sentence-making unit'. Therefore, in comparison with English, we should not assume that in Singapore Mandarin a sentence must have a subject and a predicate. Conversely, a linguistic component with a subject and a predicate is not necessarily a sentence. Here is an example:

(4) a 天！ 真 是 人心叵测！
     tiān   zhēn   shì   rěnxīnpǒcè
     god   really be   one's.heart.is.unpredictable
     'Oh, my god! Man's heart is really unpredictable!'

   b 原本 还 以为 她 是 个
     yuánběn   hái   yǐwéi   tā   shì   gè
     originally still believe 3SG be   CL

   c "雪中送炭" 的 大 好 人 哪！（狮子 56）
     xuězhōngsòngtàn   de   dà   hǎo   rén   na
     offer.timely.help   DE   big   good   person   SFP
     'I thought she was a good person who could offer timely help!' (*Shīzi,* 56)

There are three sentences in example (4): a. 天！ *tiān* 'Oh, my god'; b. 真是人心叵测！ *zhēn shì rěnxīnpǒcè* 'Man's heart is really unpredictable!'; c. 原本还以为她是个 "雪中送炭" 的大好人哪！ *yuánběn hái yǐwéi tā shì gè xuězhōngsòngtàn de dà hǎo rén na* 'I thought she was a good person who could offer timely help!' However, none of them are sentences that have a subject and a predicate. Notably, although the constituent 她是个 "雪中送炭" 的大好人 has a subject and a predicate, it is not a sentence, because there is no long pause before and after it and it is not a complete intonation unit. It is embedded in sentence (c), in which it actually functions as a phrase. To clarify, let's dismantle the grammatical construction of sentence (c).

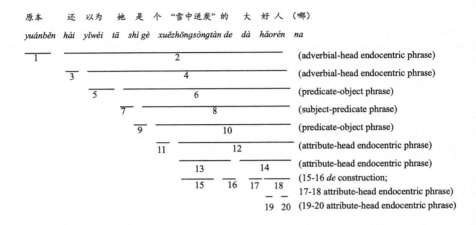

Sentences can be classified from different perspectives, which will be introduced and explained in the following sections.

4.2 Subject-Predicate Sentences and Non-Subject-Predicate Sentences

Speaking from a structural perspective, many sentences contain a subject and a predicate, which means that those sentences are realised by subject-predicate phrases. For example:

(1) 你   不要   太   激动。（追云 36）
    nǐ   búyào   tài   jīdòng
    2SG   NEG   so   excited

'Don't get so excited.' (*Zhuīyún* 36)

(2) 我   轻轻地   点   了   点   头。   （大胡子 31）
    wǒ   qīngqīngde   diǎn   le   diǎn   tóu
    1SG   gently   nod   LE   nod   head
    'I nodded gently.'(*Dàhúzi*, 31)

(3) 温朵朵   是   荷兰村   的   常客。 （跳舞 23）
    Wēnduǒduǒ   shì   héláncūn   de   chángkè
    Wen Duoduo   be   Helan.village   DE   regular.visitor
    'Wen Duoduo is a regular visitor to Helan village.' (*Tiàowǔ* 23)

A typical sentence contains a subject and a predicate. These are usually referred to as subject-predicate sentences. In contrast, non-subject-predicate sentences are composed of non-subject-predicate phrases or simple words. For example:

(4) 有人　趋　前　来　问："要　换　钱　吗？"（石头 113）
yǒurén　qū　qián　lái　wèn yào　huàn　qián　ma
someone come forward come ask　want change money SFP
'Someone came forward and asked, "want to change some money?"' (*Shítou* 113)

(5) 欢迎　　　光临　　　　"茶渊"！（华韵 39）
huānyíng　guānglín　cháyuān
welcome　　come　　　chayuan
'Welcome to "Chayuan"!' (*Huáyùn* 39)

(6) 可怜　　的　　孩子！（金狮奖（四） 90）
kělián　de　háizi
poor　DE　kid
'Poor kids.' (*Jīnshījiǎng(sì)* 90)

In general, there is a predominance of subject-predicate sentences in written genres and non-subject-predicate sentences in spoken genres; within written genres, subject-predicate sentences predominate over non-subject-predicate sentences in scientific and political texts, while in dialogues of literary works, the situation is quite the opposite.

4.3 The Classification of Subject-Predicate Sentences

The subject-predicate sentence can be subdivided into five types according to the different properties of its predicate. They are verbal predicate sentences, adjectival predicate sentences, stative word predicate sentences, nominal predicate sentences and subject-predicate predicate sentences.

1   Verbal predicate sentences are those sentences with verbal phrases as the predicate. Examples are as follows:

(1) 您老　　　夸奖　　　了。（扶轮 62）
nínlǎo　kuājiǎng　le
2SG　　praise　　　LE
'Thank you for your compliment, sir.' (*Fúlún* 62)

(2) 你们　　看　　不　　　见。（心情 18）
    nǐnmen　Kàn　bù　　jiàn
    2PL　　look　NEG　see
    'You can't see it.' (*Xīnqíng* 18)

(3) 我　　很　　爱　　养　　蝌蚪。（△南风 54）
    wǒ　　hěn　ài　　yǎng　kēdǒu
    1SG　very　love　raise　tadpole
    'I love raising tadpoles very much.' (*Nánfēng* 54)

(4) 你们　　吵　　不　　吵架？（壁虎 94）
    nǐmen　chǎo　bù　　chǎojià
    2PL　　quarrel　NEG　quarrel
    'Do you quarrel with each other?' (*Bìhǔ* 94)

(5) 这　　句　　话　　不　　一定　　是　　真理。（八方 52）
    zhè　jù　　huà　bù　　yīdìng　shì　zhēnlǐ
    this　CL　sentence　NEG　certain　be　truth
    'This statement is not necessarily true.' (*Bāfāng* 52)

2　Adjectival predicate sentences are those sentences with adjectives as the predicate. Examples are as follows:

(6) 我　　茫然。（△南风 67）
    wǒ　　mángrán
    1SG　at.a.loss
    'I'm at a loss.' (*Nánfēng* 67)

(7) 功课　　　相当　　　繁重。（华文教材 1 A 3）
    gōngkè　　xiāngdāng　fánzhòng
    schoolwork　quite　　onerous
    'The schoolwork is quite heavy.' (*Huáwénjiàocái* 1A3)

(8) 那　　太　　好　　了！（追云 14）
    nà　　tài　　hǎo　　le
    that　too　　good　LE
    'That's great.' (*Zhuīyún* 14)

(9) 她   愚昧   而   可怜。（短篇 32）
    tā   yúmèi   ér   kělián
    3SG   ignorant LIG   pathetic
    'She is ignorant and pitiful.' (*Duǎnpiān* 32)

(10) 文人   也   实在   并不   清高。（笑眼 65）
     wénrén   yě   shízài   bìng bù   qīnggāo
     scholars also   in.fact   not.at.all   proud.and.lofty
     'In fact, scholars are not so proud and lofty.' (*Xiàoyǎn* 65)

3 Stative word predicate sentences are those sentences with stative words as the predicate. Examples are as follows:

(11) 周围   朦朦胧胧的（寻庙 31）
     zhōuwéi   méngménglónglóngde
     surrounding hazy
     'It's hazy all around.' (*Xúnmiào* 31)

(12) 她   脸色   青青的（金狮奖（四）46）
     tā   liǎnsè   qīngqīngde
     3SG   complexion   green
     'Her face is green.' (*Jīnshīijiǎng(sì)* 46)

(13) 她们   讲话   总是   疯疯癫癫（梦 33）
     tāmen   jiǎnghuà   zǒngshì   fēngfēngdiāndiān
     3PL   speak   always   maniac
     'They always talk like lunatics.' (*Mèng* 33)

(14) 屋子   黑漆漆的（跳舞 3）
     wūzi   hēiqīqīde
     room   dark
     'The room is dark.' (*Tiàowǔ* 3)

(15) 天空   灰蒙蒙的（青青 79）
     tiānkōng   huīméngméngde
     sky   grey
     'The sky is grey.' (*Qīngqīng* 79)

4 Nominal predicate sentences are those sentences with nominal phrases (including classifiers) as the predicate. Examples are as follows:

(16) 杜运燮， 福建 古田 人。（△中国作家 143）
     dùyùnxiè fújiàn gǔtián rén
     Du Yunxie Fujian Gutian person
     'Du Yunxie is from Gutian, Fujian province.' (*Zhōngguózuòjiā* 143)

(17) 天边 一 片 鱼肚白（短篇 95）
     tiānbiān yī piàn yúdùbái
     rim.of.the.sky one CL grey
     'It is grey on the horizon.' (*Duǎnpiān* 95)

(18) 你 臭 人！（△含羞草 46）
     nǐ chòu rén
     2SG stink person
     'You are a terrible person.' (*Hánxiūcǎo* 46)

(19) 多少 钱 一 块 香皂。（风雨 13）
     duōshǎo qián yī kuài xiāngzào
     how.much money one CL soap
     'How much is a bar of soap?' (*Fēngyǔ* 13)

5 Subject-predicate predicate sentences are those sentences with subject-predicate phrases as the predicate. Examples are as follows:

(20) 我 的 技术 你 尽管 放心 好 了。（撞墙 80）
     wǒ de jìshù nǐ jǐnguǎn fàngxīn hǎo le
     1SG DE skill 2SG feel.free at.ease good LE
     'You can count on my skills.' (*Zhuàngqiáng* 80)

(21) 钱 我 是 没有。（华文教材 3A 57）
     qián wǒ shì méiyǒu
     money 1SG SHI not.have
     'I don't have the money.' (*Huáwénjiàocái* 3A57)

(22) 热带 的 人 性格 便 比
     rèdài de rén xìnggé biàn bǐ
     tropic DE person character just than

温带		的	人		直率		单纯。（寻庙 16）
wēndài		de	rén		zhíshuài		dānchún
temperate.zone		DE	person		straightforward		simple

'People in the tropics are more straightforward and simpler than those in temperate zones.' (*Xúnmiào* 16)

(23)
这	一	带	的	人家	多数	迟睡。（风雨 22）
zhè	yī	dài	de	rénjiā	duōshù	chíshuì
this	one	CL	DE	household	majority	sit.up

'Most people in this region stay up late.' (*Fēngyǔ* 22)

(24)
苹果、	橙、	梨，	一	种	一	包。（胜利 26）
píngguǒ	chéng	lí	yī	zhǒng	yī	bāo
apple	orange	pear	one	CL	one	pack

'Apples, oranges, and pears, pack them one kind in each bag respectively.' (*Shènglì* 26)

4.4 The Classification of Non-Subject-Predicate Sentences

In general, non-subject-predicate sentences are heavily dependent on the context. According to the degree of dependence on context, they can be further classified into independent non-subject-predicate sentences, as in (1) through (3), and dependent non-subject-predicate sentences, as in (4) and (5).

(1)
"救	火	啊！	失火	啦！"（△南风 59）
jiù	huǒ	a	shīhuǒ	la
rescue	fire	SFP	on.fire	SFP

'It's on fire! Put out the fire!' (*Nánfēng* 59)

(2)
好	一	个	晴朗	的	天气！（撞墙 77）
hǎo	yī	gè	qínglǎng	de	tiānqì
good	one	CL	sunny	DE	weather

'What a lovely, sunny day!' (*Zhuàngqiáng* 77)

(3)
一	个	毛毛细雨	的	夜晚！（短篇 45）
yī	gè	máomáoxìyǔ	de	yèwǎn
one	CL	drizzling	DE	night

'A drizzling night!' (*Duǎnpiān* 45)

(4) "你   上   学期   有   修   柏斯   的   课   吗？"
    nǐ   shàng xuéqī yǒu   xiū   bǎisī   de   kè   ma
    2SG   last   term   YOU   choose Perth   DE   class SFP
    'Did you choose Shuperth's class last term?'

"有。"（金狮奖 162－163）
yǒu
YOU
'Yes, I did.' (Jīnshījiǎng 162–163)

(5) 平： 你   吃   什么   药？
    Píng nǐ   chī   shénme   yào
    Ping 2SG   take what   medicine
    'Ping: What medicine are you taking?'

玲：   避孕   药。（金狮奖（四）129）
Líng   bìyùn   yào
Ling   contraceptive   medicine
'Ling: Contraceptives.' (Jīnshījiǎng(sì) 130)

As shown in examples (1) through (3), an independent non-subject-predicate sentence can express a complete meaning without depending on certain context. In fact, nothing is omitted, and therefore there is no need to recover a particular subject or predicate. In example (1), both 救火啊 *jiùhuǒa* 'put out the fire' and 失火啦 *shīhuǒla* 'it's on fire' are non-subject-predicate sentences composed of predicate-object phrases. We can easily understand what the sentence means without any contextual information. It is also impossible to add subjects for these sentences. In example (3), 一个毛毛细雨的夜晚 *yígè máomáo xìyǔ de yèwǎn* 'a drizzling night' is a non-subject-predicate sentence realised by a nominal attribute-head endocentric phrase. Again, the meaning is clear even without a context, and actually we cannot find a particular predicate for it.

By contrast, dependent non-subject-predicate sentences rely heavily on context for interpreting their meanings. They cannot express a complete meaning without context. Otherwise, the readers or listeners will be confused. As shown in example (4), the meaning of 有 *yǒu* 'yes, I do' is clear via its preceding context. An isolated 有 *yǒu* 'yes, I do' will lead to a confusion. Likewise, in example (5), Ling's answer of 避孕药 *bìyùnyào* 'contraceptives' would be unintelligible if there was no preceding question. Sentences of this type are elliptical sentences, as they lack a subject, a predicate or other constituents, which could only be inferred from the preceding context. Therefore, independent non-subject-predicate sentences are also referred to as 'null subject sentences' and dependent non-subject-predicate sentences as 'incomplete subject-predicate sentences', meaning that they are subject-predicate sentences with certain constituents omitted.

4.5 Declarative Sentences, Imperative Sentences, Interrogative Sentences, Exclamative Sentences and Vocative Sentences

According to the meanings and moods expressed, sentences can be classified into five types: declarative sentences, imperative sentences, interrogative sentences, exclamative sentences and vocative sentences, which we will examine in greater detail.

1. Declarative Sentences

Declarative sentences are used to report or state a fact, and end with a full stop in written genres. Here are two examples:

(1) 强奸　　是　一　项　极其　　严重　　的　罪行。（平心 85）
    qiángjiān shì yī xiàng jíqí yánzhòng de zuìxíng
    rape   be one CL   extremely serious DE crime
    'Rape is an extremely serious crime.' (*Píngxīn* 85)

(2) 我　居住　的　这　个　住宅区　　里，
    wǒ jūzhù de zhè gè zhùzháiqū lǐ
    1SG live   DE this CL neighborhood inside

    也　洋溢　　着　节日　的　气氛。（回忆 87）
    yě yángyì   zhe jiérì de qìfēn
    also be.full.of ZHE festival DE atmosphere
    'In my neighbourhood, there is also a festive atmosphere.' (*Huíyì* 87)

Declarative sentences can be long or short, as shown in (3) and (4). Example (3) is a long sentence of 39 words, while example (4) only contains one word:

(3) 以　华语　　　　的　特性　　　为　基础，
    yǐ huáyǔ   de tèxìng   wéi jīchǔ
    BA Singapore.Mandarin DE characteristic as basis

    根据　　　学习者　　的　程度　　和　需要，
    gēnjù   xuéxízhě   de chéngdù   hé xūyào
    according.to learner   DE level   and need

以	提高	学习者	的	学习	能力
yǐ	tígāo	xuéxízhě	de	xuéxí	nénglì
BA	improve	learner	DE	learning	ability

为	目标，	而	设计	的	语文	练习，
wei	mùbiāo	ér	shèjì	de	yǔwén	liànxí
as	goal	LIG	design	DE	Chinese	exercise

就	能	将	语法	教学	和	语文	教学
jiù	néng	jiāng	yúfǎ	jiàoxué	hé	yǔwén	jiàoxué
then	can	BA	grammar	teaching	and	Chinese	teaching

结合	起来。（华文 159）
jiéhé	qǐlái
combine	up

'Designing Chinese language exercises based on the characteristics of Singpore Mandarin, according to the levels and needs of learners and aiming at improving learners' learning abilities, can combine grammar teaching and Chinese teaching.' (*Huáwén* 195)

(4) （"老师， 还 记得 我 吗？"） "记得。"（牛车水 124）
    lǎoshī hái jìde wǒ ma jìde
    Teacher still remember 1SG SFP remember
    'Sir, do you still remember me?' 'Yes, I do.' (*Niúchēshuǐ* 124)

2. Imperative Sentences

Imperative sentences are used to express certain types of wishes, including requests, commands, consultations, persuasion, warnings and so on. They are usually short and always end with a full stop or an exclamation mark in written genres, as shown in (5) and (6):

(5) 快 开 门！（女儿 70）
    kuài kāi mén
    quickly open door
    'Open the door quickly!' (*Nǚér* 70)

(6) 不 准 在 房 里 吃 东西。（石头 103）
    bù zhǔn zài fáng lǐ chī dōngxī
    NEG allow in room inside eat food
    'No eating in the room.' (*Shítou* 103)

3. Interrogative Sentences

Interrogative sentences are used to ask questions. They are generally short, and usually end with a question mark in written genres, as exemplified in (7) through (9):

(7) 你   的   父母，   是   种田   的   吗？（跳舞 14）
    nǐ   de   fùmǔ   shì   zhòngtián   de   ma
    2SG   DE   parents be   farm   DE   SFP
    Are your parents farmers? (*Tiàowǔ* 14)

(8) 那些   小   鸭子   大概   全都   长成   大   鸭子
    nàxiē   xiǎo   yāzi   dàgài   quándōu   zhǎngchéng   dà   yāzi
    those   small   duck   probably   all   grow   big   duck

    了   吧？（怀旧 30）
    le   ba
    LE   SFP
    'Probably all those little ducks have grown up, right?' (*Huáijiù* 30)

(9) 做   儿女   的，   应该   怎样   孝顺   父母   呢？（伦理·中三 91）
    zuò   érnǚ   de   yīnggāi   zěnyàng   xiàoshùn   fùmǔ   ne
    being   children DE   should   how   be.filial.to   parents SFP
    'How should children be filial to their parents?' (*Lúnlǐzhōngsān* 91)

4. Exclamative Sentences

Exclamative sentences are used to express strong emotions, like joy, admiration, anger, surprise, grief, regret and so on. They are also short, in general, and end with an exclamation mark.

(10) 哗！   真   美   啊！（△南风 25）
     huà   zhēn   měi   a
     wow   really   beautiful   SFP
     'Wow! It's really beautiful.' (*Nánfēng* 25)

(11) 这个   徐勤丽   和   坐   在   课室   里   那个
     zhège   xúqínlì   hé   zuò   zài   kèshì   lǐ   nàge
     This   Xu Qinli   and   sit   at   classroom   inside   that

     呆呆的、   静静的   徐勤丽，   简直   判若两人！（跳舞 75）
     dāidāide   jìngjìngde   xúqínlì   jiǎnzhí   pànruòliǎngrén
     dull   quiet   Xu Qinli   simply   be.no.longer.one's.old.self
     'This Xu Qinli is totally different from that one in the classroom, who used to be dull and quiet.' (*Tiàowǔ* 75)

(12) 陈老太太，　　　你　　　安息　　　　　　吧！
　　　chénlǎotàitài　　nǐ　　ānxī　　　　　　ba
　　　Old Mrs. Chen　　2SG　rest.in.peace　SFP
　　　'Mrs. Chen, rest in peace.'

5. Vocative Sentences

Vocative sentences are used to greet or respond to others. A vocative sentence usually consists of a noun referring to a person or an exclamative word. For example:

(13) （小薇　　在　　门口　　　轻轻　　　咳　　了　　一　　声。）
　　　xiǎowēi　zài　　ménkǒu　qīngqīng　ké　　le　　yī　　shēng
　　　Xiaowei　at　　door　　lightly　　cough　LE　one　sound

　　　"妈。"（"小薇，　回来　　了？……"）（短篇 69）
　　　mā　　　xiǎowēi　huílái　　le
　　　mum　　Xiaowei　return　　LE
　　　'(Xiaowei coughed softly at the door.) "Mum." (Is Xiaowei back?...)' (*Duǎnpiān* 69)

(14) "喂！　　（穿上　　　　拖鞋　　吧？）"（追云 51）
　　　wèi　　　chuānshàng　tuōxié　　ba
　　　hi　　　wear　　　　slippers　SFP
　　　'Hi, (please put on your slippers.)' (*Zhuīyún* 51)

(15) （姚老师　　　双目如炬，　　　扫　　　向　　　　他，　　喊：）
　　　yáolǎoshī　　shuāngmùrújù　sǎo　　xiàng　　　tā　　　hǎn
　　　Mr. Yao　　　eyes.burning　glance　towards　3SG　　shout

　　　"麦齐荣！（站　　起来！）"（狮子 36）
　　　màiqíróng　　zhàn　qǐlái
　　　Mai Qirong　stand　up
　　　'(Mr. Yao, eyes burning, glanced at him and shouted.) "Mai Qirong! (stand up!)"' (*Shīzi* 36)

It should be noted that 喂 *wèi* 'hey' is used between two persons with close relationship. It is impolite to greet someone unfamiliar. In written genre, the vocative sentences end with a full stop or an exclamative mark. Commas are also very common, as shown in (17) and (18):

(17) "喂， （怎么 是 你？）"（金狮奖 78）
    wèi   zěnme shi   ni
    hello how   be   2SG
    'Hello, how come it's you?' (*Jīnshījiǎng* 78)

(18) "国伟，（为什么 洗澡 洗 得 那么 久 啊？）"
                                                    （狮子 25）
    guówěi wèishénme xǐzǎo xǐ   de   nàme jiǔ   a
    Guowei why   bath   wash DE   that long SFP
    'Guowei, (why did you take so long to bathe?)' (*Shīzi* 25)

Examples of vocative sentences for response are given in (19) and (20).

(19) ("我 刚 在 马路 上 碰到 你 妈。") "哦！"(金狮奖 248)
    wǒ   gāng zài mǎlù shàng pèngdào nǐ   mā   ò
    1SG just at   road on   meet   2SG   mom   oh
    '(I have met with your mom on the road just now.) "Oh, ok."' (*Jīnshījiǎng* 248)

(20) ("……您 可以 帮 我 补 一 补 吗？")
    nín   kěyǐ bāng wǒ   bǔ   yī   bǔ   ma
    2SG   can   help 1SG mend one repair SFP

    "行！"（涵珊 一 口 应承。）（跳舞 3）
    xíng hánshān yī   kǒu   yìngchéng
    Yes   Hanshan one mouth agree
    '("Could you help me mend it?") "Yes!" (Hanshan replied at once.)' (*Tiàowǔ* 3)

(21) ("……回去 吧。") "是。（老师， 我 走 了。
    huíqù   ba   shì   lǎoshī wǒ   zǒu le
    return   SFP   yes   teacher 1SG go   LE

    再见！）"（追云 45）
    zàijiàn
    bye
    '"You can go home now" "Yes, sir. I'm leaving. Goodbye."' (*Zhuīyún* 45)

Vocatives sentences as response are usually marked by words such as 唉 *ai* 'alas', 嗯 *en* 'uhhuh', 啊 *a* 'ah', 哦 *o* 'oh' or 行 *xíng* 'ok', 好 *hǎo* 'good', 是 *shì* 'yes', 对 *duì* 'right'. They end with a full stop or an exclamation mark in written form.

4.6 Simple Sentences and Composite Sentences

In order to make it easy for the reader to understand, the examples previously shown through our discussions of different types of sentences all consist of only one phrase (simple or complex) or one word plus intonation. These types of sentences, composed of one sentence-making unit (i.e., a phrase or a word), are generally called simple sentences.

The opposite of simple sentences are composite sentences, which connect two or more sentence-making units according to logical connections, plus a sentence intonation to express more complex meanings. The sentence-making units used in the composite sentence are called clauses. These always have a pause between clauses, which is usually expressed by a comma or semicolon. For example:

(1) 这 是 个 可爱 的 小岛， 这 是 个 幸福 的
zhè shì gè kěài de xiǎodǎo zhè Shì gè xìnfú de
this be CL lovely DE small.island this be CL happy DE

小岛！（独上 36）
xiǎodǎo
small.island
'This is a lovely island; this is a happy island.' (*Dúshàng* 36)

(2) 格物、 致知 是 学问 的 基础； 诚意、
géwù zhìzhī shì xuéwèn de jīchǔ chéngyì
learn.things acknowledge be study DE foundation sincerity

正心 是 道德 的 基础。（伦理·中三 64）
zhèngxīn shì dàodé de jīchǔ
righteousness be morality DE foundation
'The foundation of learning is the study of things to acquire knowledge; the foundation of morality is sincerity and righteousness.' (*Lúnlǐ·zhōngsān* 64)

Sometimes a single word can constitute a clause. As shown in (3) and (4), 奇怪 *qíguài* 'strange' and 有 *yǒu* 'have' are also clauses.

(3) **奇怪，** 你 对 她 又 没 意思， 袒护 她
qíguài nǐ duì tā yòu méi yìsi tǎnhù tā
strange 2SG towards 3SG again not.have interest protect 3SG

干嘛？（金狮奖 96）
gànmá
what

'It's strange, you don't have any interest in her, so why are you defending her?' (*Jīnshījiǎng* 96)

(4) 有， 就 给 一点； 你 没有， 也 没关系。
yǒu jiù gěi yìdiǎn nǐ méiyǒu yě méiguānxì
have then give little 2SG not.have also Ok

'If you have (something), then give me a little; if you don't, that's fine.'

Some connective words are often used, especially in written genres, to make the logical connection between clauses more obvious. For example, 不但 *búdàn* 'not only' in (5) and 只要 *zhǐyào* 'as long as' in (6) are both connective words.

(5) 美学 不但 与 艺术 发生 联系，
měixué **búdàn** yǔ yìshù fāshēng liánxì
aesthetics **not.only** with art generate relation

与 其他 学科 也 有 着 极大 的 关系。（科学 115）
yǔ qítā xuékē yě yǒu zhe jídà de guānxi
With other discipline also have ZHE strong DE relation

'Aesthetics is not only linked to art but also has a strong relation with other disciplines.' (*Kēxué* 115)

(6) 只要 你们 团结一致 支持 我 和 我 的
zhǐyào nǐmen tuánjiéyízhì zhīchí wǒ hé wǒ de
as.long.as 2PL united support 1SG and 1SG DE

政府， 我 将会 继续 服务 下去。（报 1995
年 8 月 21 日 8 版）
zhèngfǔ wǒ jiānghuì jìxù fúwù xiàqù
government 1SG will continue serve on

As long as you are united in support of me and my government, I will continue to serve.' (*Bào*, Aug. 21, 1995, Issue no. 8)

Composite sentences will be discussed in more detail in Chapter 3, Volume II.

* * * *

Over the course of Chapter 1 to Chapter 4, we have introduced morphemes, words, phrases, sentences and word classes, which are the most basic grammatical concepts required for readers to have a comprehensive understanding of Singapore Mandarin. However, there are a few points which need to be further emphasised:

1. Since the principle of sentence formation in Singapore Mandarin is basically the same as the principle of phrase formation, it is important to understand and master those formation rules. In Chapter 2, we introduced the five most basic types of phrases in Singapore Mandarin, whose formation rules can also apply to sentences, leading to the five most basic types of sentences. In order to master these sentence formats, one must be able to clearly identify them and then do lots of practice.

2. As regards phrases, we establish such terms as subjects, predicates, objects, complements, attributes, adverbials, heads and so on; when we illustrate word classes, we have nouns, verbs, adjectives, stative words and so on. It is important to note that phrases are defined in terms of grammatical relations, whereas word classes are defined in terms of the grammatical nature of the word itself. Let us make an analogy to distinguish these two notions. For a person, whether a person is Singaporean, Chinese, Japanese or British is a matter of his nationality; while at home he is a husband to his wife, a father to his son, and at school a teacher to his students, which is all about his relationships with others. The nationality of a person is relatively fixed; whether he is a husband, a father or a teacher can only be identified when he has relations with different people. Similarly, the class to which a word belongs, whether it is a noun or a verb or an adjective, is fixed. However, whether it is the subject or the predicate or the object of a sentence can only be identified when it has a relation with other words. A verb, for example, remains a verb whether it is used as a predicate, a subject or an object in a sentence.

3. While talking about phrases, we do not consider whether they are independent (a sentence) or not (not a sentence). For example:

(7) 他 不 会 写 的 字 很多。
    tā bú huì xiě de zì hěnduō
    3SG NEG can write DE word many
    'There are many words he can't write.'

(8) 我 知道 他 不 会 写。
    wǒ zhīdào tā bú huì xiě
    1SG know 3SG NEG can write
    'I know that he can't write.'

(9) 他　　　不　　　会　　　写。
　　tā　　*bú*　　*huì*　　*xiě*
　　3SG　　NEG　　can　　write
　　'He can't write.'

In examples (7) through (9), 他不会写 *tābúhuìxiě* 'he cannot write' is a subject-predicate phrase. When it is embedded in a sentence, as in (7) and (8), it is just a phrase; when it is used alone, as in (9), it is a sentence, in which case we could say that it is a sentence realised by a subject-predicate phrase and a sentence intonation.

A phrase can be a sentence, so can a word. For example:

(10) "谁？"
　　 shéi
　　 who
　　 'Who?'

　　 "我。"
　　 wǒ
　　 1SG
　　 'Me.'

　　 "进来。"
　　 jìnlái
　　 come.in
　　 'Come in.'

(11) "蛇！"　　王小姐　　　　突然　　　　惊呼　　　　起来。
　　 shé　　*wángxiǎojiě*　　*tūrán*　　　*jīnghū*　　　*qǐlái*
　　 snake　　3SG　　　　suddenly　　exclaim　　up
　　 '"Snake!" Miss Wang suddenly exclaimed.'

谁 *shéi* 'who', 我 *wǒ* '1SG', 进来 *jìnlái* 'come in' and 蛇 *shé* 'snake' are all sentences, for they meet all the requirements of being a sentence. Such sentences are commonly referred to as one-word sentences.

5 Subjects and Predicates

Lu Jianming

5.1 Two Structural Relations in Phrases

From this section onwards, we will describe and illustrate various phrases in further detail. Since all phrases in Singapore Mandarin can be independent sentences, the principles of sentence construction are basically identical with those of phrase construction. This means while we are describing various phrases, we are actually also explaining the various constructions of sentences.

Before describing and explaining various phrases, it is necessary to mention the co-existence of two structural relations in phrases. Any phrases composed of two content words, without exception, have two structural relations: The grammatical relation and the semantic relation, as examplified in (1) through (3).

(1) 哥哥 / 正在 游泳
    gēge   ***zhèngzài***   ***yóuyǒng***
    brother   in.process   **swim**
    'My brother is swimming.'

(2) 苹果 / 已经 吃 了
    píngguǒ   ***yǐjīng***   ***chī***   ***le***
    apple   already   **eat**   LE
    'The apple has already been eaten.'

(3) 那 衣服 / 很 漂亮
    nà ***yīfu***   *hěn*   ***piàoliàng***
    that **garment**   very   **nice**
    'That garment is very nice.'

The two parts in sentences (1) through (3) all share the same grammatical relation of subjects and predicates; in terms of semantic relation, however, they are different. In sentence (1), 哥哥 *gēge* 'brother' is the agent and 游泳 *yóuyǒng* 'swim' is the action. In sentence (2), 苹果 *píngguǒ* 'apple' is the patient and 吃 *chī* 'eat' is the action, and in sentence (3), 衣服 *yīfu* 'clothes' is the theme and 漂亮 *piàoliàng* 'pretty' describes its property. The so-called grammatical relation refers to the relation between the immediate components of a phrase, such as the relation between the subject and the predicate, the predicate and the object, the attributive and the head and so on. The semantic relation refers to the relation between the content words in a phrase, such as the relation between the agent and the action, the patient and the action, the theme and its property and so on. These two structural relations always co-exist in phrases composed of content words.

Sentences (1) through (3) also illustrate that the same grammatical relation can represent different semantic relations. Let's look at more examples:

(4) 洗 / 衣服
    xǐ   *yīfu*
    wash   clothes
    'wash the clothes'

(5) 衣服 / 洗 了
    yīfu   *xǐ*   *le*
    clothes wash   LE
    'The clothes are washed.'

(6) 洗 的 / 衣服
    xǐ *de*   *yīfu*
    wash DE   clothes
    'the clothes that are washed'

The preceding examples are different types of phrases. Example (4) is a predicate-object phrase, example (5) a subject-predicate phrase and example (6) an attribute-head endocentric phrase. They have different grammatical relations, but share the same semantic relation, that is, the relation between the action 洗 *xǐ* 'wash' and the patient 衣服 *yīfu* 'clothes'.

Examples (4) through (6), once again, not only show that grammatical relation and semantic relation always exist simultanenously in phrases composed of content words but also reveal that the same semantic relation can be represented by different grammatical relations according to the needs of expression. Thus, the following summary can be made:

1 Grammatical and semantic relations always co-exist in phrases composed of content words.
2 The same grammatical relation can represent different semantic relations.
3 The same semantic relation can be represented by different grammatical relations.

In grammatical research and teaching, it is extremely important to be clear about the ideas just summarised. For example, while talking about the subject and the predicate, we must be careful not to confuse the subject with the agent of an action. In Singapore Mandarin, although the agent of an action often appears in the subject position, what appears in this position is not always the agent. This will be described and explained further in this chapter.

5.2 Subjects and Predicates in Singapore Mandarin

A subject in Singapore Mandarin can be understood as the topic of a sentence and a predicate can be understood as a statement about the topic.

5.2.1 Subjects

Since the subject of a sentence is a topic and a topic's scope can be very broad, subjects in Singapore Mandarin are not limited to ordinary nouns. When compared to English, the following two phenomena are particularly noteworthy.

A   Words denoting time, place and direction can function as subjects, as they can also be topics.

(1) 去年　　　发生　　　了　　　一　　　件　　　小　　　事。（寻庙 78）
    qùnián　　*fāshēng*　*le*　　　*yī*　　　*jiàn*　　*xiǎo*　　*shì*
    last.year　happen　LE　　　one　　　CL　　　slight　　incident
    'Last year some slight incident happened.' (*Xúnmiào* 78)

(2) 新加坡　　　很　　　热。
    xīnjiāpō　　*hěn*　　*rè*
    Singapore　very　　hot
    'It is very hot in Singapore.'

(3) 前面　　　就　　　是　　　大海。（短篇 40）
    qiánmiàn　*jiù*　　*shì*　　*dàhǎi*
    front　　just　　be　　　sea
    'The sea is over there.' (*Duǎnpiān* 40)

Generally speaking, in English, words denoting time, place and direction cannot function as subjects. If the preceding three sentences were to be translated into English, 去年 *qùnián* 'last year', 新加坡 *xīnjiāpō* 'Singapore' and 前面 *qiánmiàn* 'front' would not possibly be subjects.

B Verbs and adjectives can also function as subjects, because a behaviour, an action or properties of things can be topics, too.

(4) 去   是   可以   的。
    qù   **shì**   **kěyǐ** **de**
    go   be   ok   DE
    'It's ok to go.'

(5) 成长   是   一   种   解放。（青青 21）
    chéngzhǎng **shì** **yī** **zhǒng** **jiěfàng**
    grow.up   be   one CL   liberation
    'Growing up is a kind of liberation.' (*Qīngqīng* 21)

(6) 勤   或   能   补   拙。（渐行 50）
    qín   **huò** **néng** **bǔ**   **zhuō**
    diligent may   can   complement dullness
    'Diligence may complement dullness.' (*Jiànxíng* 50)

(7) 骄傲   不   好。
    jiāoào **bù** **hǎo**
    proud NEG   good
    'Being proud is bad.'

Neither verbs nor adjectives can be used as subjects in English, whereas they can in Singapore Mandarin. One may be influenced by English grammar to think that a verb or adjective is converted into a noun when they are being the subject in Singapore Mandarin. However, this is not the case. In sentence (4), 去 *qù* 'go', as a subject, does not lose its grammatical properties as a verb. Please consider the following sentences.

不   去   是   可以   的   (去 *qù* 'go' is modified by 不 *bù* 'not')
bù **qù** **shì** **kěyǐ** **de**
NEG **go** be   ok   DE
'It's ok not to go.'

去   英国   是   可以   的   (去 *qù* 'go' is followed by an object)
qù **yīngguó** **shì** **kěyǐ** **de**
go **Britain** be   ok   DE
'It's ok to go to Britain.'

去   得   晚   一点   是   可以   的   (去 qù 'go' is followed
qù   de   wǎn   yìdiǎn   shì   kěyǐ   de   by a complement)
go   DE   late   a.little   be   ok   DE
'It's ok to go a little bit later.'

早   去   是   可以   的   (去 qù 'go' is modified by an adverbial)
zǎo   qù   shì   kěyǐ   de
earlier   go   be   ok   DE
'It's ok to go earlier.'

他   去   是   可以   的   (去 qù 'go' serves as a predicate)
tā   qù   shì   kěyǐ   de
3SG   go   be   ok   DE
'It is ok for him to go.'

Obviously, 去 qù 'go' is still a verb even after being the subject. Therefore, in Singapore Mandarin, nouns, verbs and adjectives can all serve as subjects.

5.2.2 Predicates

In Singapore Mandarin, since the predicate can be understood as a declarative statement or comment on the subject, the scope of which can be very broad. Therefore, unlike English, predicates in Singapore Mandarin are not limited to verbs. For instance:

A   Adjectives and stative words can serve directly as predicates without a copula verb. Adjectives serving as predicates are examplified in (8) through (10) and stative words serving as predicates are shown in (11) through (13).

(8) 高   山   **青**，   涧   水   **蓝**。（△南风 91）
    gāo   *shān*   ***qīng***   *jiàn*   *shuǐ*   ***lán***
    tall   mountain   green   gully   water   blue
    'The mountain is green and the stream is blue.' (*Nánfēng* 91)

(9) 天气   **冷**。（扶轮 52）
    tiānqì   ***lěng***
    weather   cold
    'It's cold.' (*Fúlún* 52)

(10) 心地　　善良（华文 157）
    xīndì　　***shànliáng***
    heart　　**kind**
    'The heart is kind.' (*Huáwén* 157)

(11) 她　　脸色　　**青青**　　**的**。（金狮奖（四）76）
    tā　*liǎnsè*　***qīngqīng***　***de***
    3SG　face　**green**　**DE**
    'She looked green.' (*Jīnshījiǎng* IV 76)

(12) 天空　　**灰蒙蒙**　　**的**。（青青 79）
    tiānkōng　***huīméngméng***　***de***
    sky　**grey**　**DE**
    'The sky is overcast.' (*Qīngqīng* 79)

B   Subject-predicate phrases can serve as predicates.

(13) 我　的　技术　**你**　**尽管**　**放心**　好了。（撞墙 80）
    wǒ　*de*　*jìshù*　***nǐ***　***jǐnguǎn***　***fàngxīn***　*hǎole*
    1SG　DE　skill　**2SG**　**feel.free.to**　**at.ease**　it.is.ok
    'You can count on my skills.' (*Zhuàngqiáng* 80)

(14) 冻　咖啡　一　**杯**　**八**　**角钱**。（梦 101）
    dòng　*kāfēi*　*yī*　***bēi***　***bā***　***jiǎoqián***
    iced　coffee　one　**CL**　**eight**　**CL**
    'It costs eighty cents to buy a cup of iced coffee.' (*Mèng* 101)

The preceding points represent the most basic knolwledge about subjects and predicates in Singapore Mandarin.

5.2.3 The Relations Between the Subjects and the Predicates

It should be pointed out that, since the subject in Singapore Mandarin can be understood as the topic of a sentence and the predicate can be understood as the comment or statement of the topic, the semantic relation between the subject and the predicate is not necessarily the relation between an agent and an action, even in subject-predicate sentences with verbal phrases. Nevertheless the predicates do not differ in form to mark different semantic relations. Let's consider the following sentences.

(15) a 我　　给　　他　　了。 (The subject is the agent)
　　　　wǒ　　gěi　　tā　　le
　　　　1SG　give　3SG　LE
　　　　'I have given (the book) to him.'

　　b 书　　给　　他　　了。 (The subject is the patient)
　　　　shū　　gěi　　tā　　le
　　　　book　give　3SG　LE
　　　　'The book has been given to him.'

(16) a 你　　切　　肉。 (The subject is the agent)
　　　　nǐ　　qiē　　ròu
　　　　2SG　cut　　meat
　　　　'You cut the meat.'

　　b 这　　把　　刀　　切　　肉。 (The subject is the tool)
　　　　zhè　　bǎ　　dāo　　qiē　　ròu
　　　　this　BA　knife　cut　　meat
　　　　'This knife is used to cut meat.'

The semantic relations between the subject and the predicate verb 给 *gěi* 'give' in (15a) and (15b) are different, though their predicates are identical in form. Likewise, the semantic relation between the subject and the predicate verb 切 *qiē* 'cut' in (16a) differs from that in (16b), but their predicates share the same form.

One more point that needs to be noted is that since a subject in Singapore Mandarin is understood as the topic, and a predicate as the statement about the topic of a sentence, the relation between the subject and the predicate is comparatively loose compared to English, as is evident in the following three aspects:

A Subjects can often be omitted. Because of this, there are a large number of dependent subject-predicate sentences, or incomplete subject-predicate sentences in Singapore Mandarin (see Section 4.4).
B There may be a pause between the subject and the predicate, and sometimes a particle may be inserted between the two, as in (17) through (20).
C Subjects and predicates can be transposed, as in (21) through (24).

(17) 我们　　两　　个，　　一定　　会　　参加！（梦 112）
　　　wǒmén　liǎng　gè　　yídìng　huì　　cānjiā
　　　1PL　　two　　CL　　certainly　will　participate
　　　'We two will certainly participate.' (*Mèng* 112)

(18) 你   的   父母,   是   种田   的   吗?（跳舞 14）
     nǐ   de   fùmǔ   shì   zhòngtián   de   ma
     2SG   DE   parents be   till.the.land DE SFP
     'Are your parents farmers?' (*Tiàowǔ* 14)

(19) 弟弟   呢,   和   他   正好   相反。（狮子 72）
     dìdi   ne   hé   tā   zhènghǎo   xiāngfǎn
     brother SEP   with 3SG   just   opposite
     'My brother's (condition) is the opposite.' (*Shīzǐ* 72)

(20) 我   啊,   吃   了。（华韵 43）
     wǒ   a   chī   le
     1SG   TOP   eat   LE
     'I have eaten.' (*Huáyùn* 43)

(21) 说话   呀,   你!（跳舞 72）
     shuōhuà ya   nǐ
     say   SFP 2SG
     'Say something!' (*Tiàowǔ* 72)

(22) 怎么   啦,   你?（想飞 124）
     zěnme   la   nǐ
     what.happen SFP   2SG
     'What happened to you?' (*Xiǎngfēi* 124)

(23) 不   要   乱说   啦,   你。（想飞 124）
     bù   yào   luànshuō   la   nǐ
     NEG   want   talk.nonsense SFP   2SG
     'Don't talk nonsense.' (*Xiǎngfēi* 124)

(24) 干   什么   呀,   你?（吾土·戏剧 189）
     gàn   shénme ya   nǐ
     do   what   SFP 2SG
     'What do you want to do?' (*Wútǔ·xìjù* 189)

In sentence (21), although the subject 你 *nǐ* '2SG' is moved to the end, the meaning of the sentence does not change. Other sentences can also be understood in this way. However, it should be noted that the subject placed after the predicate must be pronounced in a light tone.

5.3 Nominal Subjects

For the convenience of grammar research and teaching, content words such as nouns, distinguishing words, numerals and classifiers are generally called nominal words; while verbs, adjectives and stative words are called predicative words.

Within the pronouns, the personal pronouns, the demonstrative pronouns like 这 *zhè* 'this', 那 *nà* 'that', 这里 *zhèlǐ* 'here' 那里 *nǎlǐ* 'there', and the interrogative pronouns like 谁 *shuí* 'who', 什么 *shénme* 'what', 哪里 *nǎlǐ* 'where', 多少 *duōshǎo* 'how many/how much', 几 *jǐ* 'how many' belong to nominal words. The demonstrative pronouns like 这样 *zhèyàng* 'this way', 那样 *nàyàng* 'that way', 这么 *zhème* 'like this' 那么 *nàme* 'like that' 这么样 *zhèmeyàng* 'like this way', 那么样 *nàmeyàng* 'like that way' and interrogative pronouns like 怎样 *zěnyàng* 'how' 怎么样 *zěnmeyàng* 'how about' are predicate words.

There are two major differences between the nominal word and the predicative word: (1) Nominal words cannot serve as the predicate, while predicate words can. (2) Nominal words are generally not modified by adverbs, while predicates are. Accordingly, phrases can be divided into nominal phrases and predicative phrases. The former includes attribute-head endocentric phrases, coordinative noun phrases and 的 *de* 'DE' phrases; the latter consists of adverbial-head endocentric phrases, predicate-object phrases, predicate-complement phrases, subject-predicate phrases and coordinative phrases made up of verbs, adjectives or stative words. This section begins with the nominal subjects first.

5.3.1 Nouns as Subjects[1]

Most nouns can serve as subjects, as exemplified in (1) through (3).

(1) 温朵朵　　站　　在　　床边。（跳舞 22）
    wēnduǒduǒ　*zhàn*　*zài*　*chuángbiān*
    Wen Duoduo　stand　at　bedside
    'Wen Duoduo stood at the bedside.' (*Tiàowǔ* 22)

(2) 姐姐　　不　　同意。（太阳 68）
    jiějiě　*bù*　*tóngyì*
    sister　NEG　agree
    'The elder sister disagreed.' (*Tàiyáng* 68)

(3) 鸟　　会　　飞。（独上 75）
    niǎo　*huì*　*fēi*
    bird　can　fly
    'The bird can fly.' (*Dúshàng* 75)

However, a single noun is much less likely than a nominal phrase to be the subject, whether in written or spoken language. In other words, a nominal phrase being subject is more common in practical or daily communication. There are two types of nominal phrase:

A   The attribute-head phrase as the subject.

(4) 许多   新加坡   人   都   看过   李连杰   主演
    xǔduō   *xīnjiāpō* *rén*   *dōu* *kànguò* *lǐliánjié* *zhǔyǎn*
    many   Singapore person all   see   Jet Li   star

    的   "少林寺"   影片。（平心 118）
    de *shàolínsì*   *yǐngpiān*
    DE   Shaolin Temple movie

    'Many Singaporeans have watched the movie Shaolin Temple starring Jet Li.' (*Píngxīn* 118)

(5) 池塘   里   的   水   是   活水。（晚上 77）
    chítáng *lǐ*   *de*   *shuǐ*   *shì* *huóshuǐ*
    pond   inside DE   water   be   flowing. water

    'The water in the pond is flowing water.' (*Wǎnshàng* 77)

(6) 美妙   的   声音   能   把   人   吸引   住。(万花筒 32)
    měimiào   *de*   *shēngyīn*   *néng*   *bǎ*   *rén*   *xīyǐn*   *zhù*
    beautiful   DE   sound   can   BA   person   attract   hold

    'The wonderful sound can pull people in.' (*Wànhuātǒng* 32)

B   The coordinative noun phrase as the subject.

(7) 被褥、   枕头、   床单   黏黏腻腻   地   堆
    bèirù   *zhěntóu*   *chuángdān*   *niánniánnìnì*   *de*   *duī*
    bedding   pillow   bedsheet   sticky. and. greasy   DE   pile

    在   一起。（万花筒 24）
    zài   *yīqǐ*
    at   together

    'The bedding, pillow and bedsheet were piled up and stuck together.' (*Wànhuātǒng* 24)

(8) 振威　　　和　　　忠浩，　　靠　　　　墙　　　而　　　坐。（狮子 83）
　　 zhènwēi　 hé　　zhōnghào　kào　　 qiáng　　ér　　zuò
　　 Zhenwei　and　 Zhonghao　lean.against　wall　 LIG　 sit
　　 'Zhenwei and Zhonghao sit against the wall.' (*Shīzǐ* 83)

(9) 邓文茵　　　　和　　　几　　　位　　　女孩子　　　负责
　　 dèngwényīn　 hé　　jǐ　　 wèi　　nǚháizi　　　fùzé
　　 Deng Wenyin　and　several　CL　　girl　　　　be.responsible.for

　　 剥　　　 虾。（跳舞 82）
　　 bō　　　xiā
　　 shell　 shrimp
　　 'Deng Wenyin and several girls were shelling shrimps.' (*Tiàowǔ* 82)

5.3.2 DE Construction as Subjects

的 *de* 'DE' construction is nominal and often serves as a subject, as illustrated in (10) through (12).

(10)　男　　　的　　　死　　　了。（笑眼 145）
　　　nán　　de　　　sǐ　　　le
　　　man　 DE　　　die　　 LE
　　　'The man died.' (*Xiàoyǎn* 145)

(11)　他　　　跳　　　的　　　是　　　霹雳舞。（跳舞 12）
　　　tā　　　tiào　　de　　　shì　　 pīlìwǔ
　　　3SG　　jump　 DE　　　be　　　breakdancing
　　　'What he dances is breakdancing.' (*Tiàowǔ* 12)

(12)　雄　　　的，　　尾巴　　较　　　　　　长。（壁虎 62）
　　　xióng　 de　　　wěibā　 jiào　　　　　cháng
　　　male　　DE　　　tail　　comparatively　long
　　　'The male one has a longer tail.' (*Bìhǔ* 62)

有的 *yǒude* 'some' is also one of the nominal phrases which includes 的 *de* 'DE'. When 有的 *yǒude* 'some' is used in a subject-predicate sentence, it indicates partial stating. Thus, 有的 *yǒude* 'some' is usually used more than once in a sentence, as in (13) and (14).

(13)　稻田　　　　的　　颜色，　　深浅不一。　　　　有的　　　土黄色，
　　　dàotián　　　de　　yánsè　　　shēnqiǎnbùyī　　　yǒude　　　tǔhuángsè
　　　rice.field　　DE　 color　　　various　　　　　some　　　　khaki-yellow

有的	浅褐色，	有的	暗灰色。（八方 21）
yǒude	*qiǎnhèsè*	*yǒude*	*ànhuīsè*
some	light.brown	**some**	dark.gray

'The rice field is of varying shades of color: some are khaki-yellow, some are light brown, and some are dark gray.' (*Bāfāng* 21)

(14)
没有	浴室，	冲凉	成	了	大	问题，	有的
méiyǒu	*yùshì*	*chōngliáng*	*chéng*	*le*	*dà*	*wèntí*	*yǒude*
not.have	bathroom	shower	be	LE	big	problem	**some**

到	朋友	家	去	冲，	有的	去	澡场。（怀旧 14）
dào	*péngyǒu*	*jiā*	*qù*	*chōng*	*yǒude*	*qù*	*zǎochǎng*
go.to	friend	home	go	wash	**some**	go	public.bathhouse

'Without a bathroom, having a shower becomes a big problem. Some people go to a friend's home for a shower, some to the public bathhouse.' (*Huáijiù* 14)

5.3.3 Words Indicating Time, Place and Position as Subjects

Words indicating time and place can be subjects, as in (15) and (16) respectively.

(15)
九月一日	是	教师节。（平心 90）
jiǔyuèyírì	*shì*	*jiàoshījié*
September 1st	be	Teacher's Day

'September 1st is Teacher's Day.' (*Píngxīn* 90)

(16)
纽约	是	个	艺术	之	都。（怀旧 71）
niǔyuē	*shì*	*gè*	*yìshù*	*zhī*	*dū*
New York	be	CL	art	LIG	metropolis

'New York is a capital of the arts.' (*Huáijiù* 71)

More examples of those types of words being the subject are given in (17) through (19).

(17)
今晚	我	喝	了	点	酒。（梦 6）
jīnwǎn	*wǒ*	*hē*	*le*	*diǎn*	*jiǔ*
tonight	1SG	drink	LE	a.bit	alcohol

'Tonight I had a few drinks.' (*Mèng* 6)

(18) 远处   又   传   来   子弹   的   呻吟。（无弦月 11）
    yuǎnchù   yòu   chuán   lái   zǐdàn   de   shēnyín
    in.the.distance again spread come   bullet   DE   sound
    'There was again the sound of the bullets in the distance.' (*Wúxiányuè* 11)

(19) 窗   外   下   着   大   雨。
    chuāng   wài   xià   zhe   dà   yǔ
    window   outside pour   ZHE   heavy   rain
    'It is raining heavily outside.'

There are two reasons why the preceding words can be analysed as subjects:

A   They can be regarded as the topic of the sentence. Taking sentence (17) as an instance, 今晚 *jīnwǎn* 'tonight' is the topic and 我喝了点酒 *wǒhēlediǎnjiǔ* 'I had a drink' is a declarative statement of 今晚 *jīnwǎn* 'tonight'. Other sentences can be understood in the same way.

B   是不是 *shìbushì* 'be not be' can be inserted after the topics to transform those sentences into interrogative sentences, a way in which a subject-predicate relation differs from other grammatical relations.

(17)' 今晚   **是不是**   我   喝   了   点   酒？
     jīnwǎn   **shi-bu-shi**   wǒ   hē   le   diǎn   jiǔ
     tonight   be-NEG-be   1SG   drink   LE   a. bit alcoholic.drink
     'Did I have a few drinks tonight?'

(18)' 远处   **是不是**   又   传   来   子弹
     yuǎnchù   **shi-bu-shi**   yòu   chuán   lái   zǐdàn
     in. the. distance be-NEG-be again spread come   bullet

     的   呻吟？
     de   shēnyín
     DE   sound
     'Was there again the sound of the bullets in the distance?'

(19)' 窗   外   **是不是**   下   着   大   雨？
     chuāng   wài   **shi-bu-shi**   xià   zhe   dà   yǔ
     window   outside be-NEG-be   pour   ZHE   heavy   rain
     'Is it heavily raining out of the window?'

5.3.4 Nominal Pronouns as Subjects

Nominal pronouns, including personal pronouns, often serve as subjects as well.

(20) 她　　　还是　　　那么　　　美。（梦 47）
　　　tā　　　háishì　　　nàme　　　měi
　　　3SG　　still　　　　so　　　　beautiful
　　'She is still so beautiful.' (*Mèng* 47)

(21) 你　　　不要　　　介意。（变调 47）
　　　nǐ　　　búyào　　　jièyì
　　　2SG　　NEG　　　　mind
　　'Don't mind it.' (*Biàndiào* 47)

It is worth noting that the attribute-head phrases formed by pronouns and attributives are usually subjects as well. This is a characteristic of the grammar of Singapore Mandarin.

(22) 肚子　　饿　　得　　呱呱叫　　的　　她　　只　　那么
　　　dùzǐ　　è　　de　　guāguājiào　de　　tā　　zhǐ　　nàme
　　　tummy　hungry DE　rumbling　　DE　　3SG　only　so

　　　几　　口　　就　　吃　　完　　了。（恶梦 121）
　　　jǐ　　kǒu　jiù　　chī　wán　le
　　　several CL　just　eat　finish LE
　　'She was so hungry that she ate it in just a few bites.' (*Èmèng* 121)

(23) 目前　　　育　　　有　　　一　　　个　　　三岁　　　女儿
　　　mùqián　　yù　　　yǒu　　yī　　　gè　　　sānsuì　　nǚér
　　　present　　born　　have　　one　　CL　　three.age　daughter

　　　的　　他　　说："……"（报 1995 年 3 月 10 日 6 版）
　　　de　　tā　　shuō
　　　DE　　3SG　say
　　'He, who currently has a three-year-old daughter, said . . .' (*Bào*, Mar. 10, 1995, Issue no. 6)

The expression of personal pronouns taking attributives is influenced by English grammar. It is rarely seen in Chinese Mandarin.

5.3.5 Numerals as Subjects

A Numerals can be subjects in equations. Both examples in (24) are subject-predicate phrases, in which 八 *bā* 'eight' is the subject.

(24) a 八   加   二   （是   十）
        bā   *jiā*   *èr*   *shì*   *shí*
        eight plus   two   be   ten
        'Eight plus two (is ten).'

    b 八   乘以   二   （是   十六）
        bā   *chéngyǐ* *èr*   *shì*   *shíliù*
        eight multiply   two   be   sixteen
        'Eight multiplied by two (is sixteen).'

B Numerals can be subjects of sentences expressing the relationship between different digit words.

(25) 六   万   就   是   六十   千。（撞墙 26）
     liù   *wàn*   *jiù*   *shì*   *liùshí*   *qiān*
     six ten.thousand just   be   sixty   thousand
     'Six ten thousands are sixty thousand.' (*Zhuàngqiáng* 26)

C Numerals can be subjects when they are the omitted forms of numeral-classifier phrases.

(26) 四十   是   人生   的   开始。（八方 82）
     sìshí   *shì*   *rénshēng*   *de*   *kāishǐ*
     forty be   life   DE   start
     'Life begins at forty.' (*Bāfāng* 82)

(27) 二十   不   多   啊！
     èrshí   *bù*   *duō*   *a*
     twenty NEG   many   SFP
     'Twenty yuan is not too much!'

In sentence (26), 四十 *sìshí* 'forty' actually refers to 四十岁 *sìshí suì* 'forty years old'. In sentence (27), 二十 *èrshí* 'twenty' refers to 二十元 *èrshí yuán* 'twenty yuan'. Notably, the numeral cannot be monosyllabic in this case, for example, 七元不多啊 *qīyuán bù duō a* 'seven yuan is not a lot' cannot be omitted, as 七不多啊 *qī bù duō ā* 'seven is not too much'.

5.3.6 Numeral-Classifier Phrases as Subjects

Although classifiers are nominal, they cannot function as subjects unless they are combined with numerals to form phrases.

(28) 万 里 犹如 咫尺。（华文教材 3B 21）
    wàn **lǐ** yóurú zhǐchǐ
    ten.thousand **kilometer** like short.distance
    'Ten thousand kilometers is a short distance.' (*Huáwénjiàocái* 3B 21)

(29) 五 毛 行 吗？
    wǔ **máo** xíng ma
    five **ten.cent** ok SFP
    'Is fifty cents ok?' (*Duǎnpiān* 37)

5.3.7 Distinguishing Words as Subjects

Although distinguishing words are nominal, they seldom act as subjects in written genres. In spoken Singapore Mandarin, however, there are a few cases of distinguishing words being subjects.

(30) （肝炎，） 急性 好 治， 慢性 难 治。
    gānyán **jíxìng** hǎo zhì **mànxìng** nán zhì
    hepatitis **acute** easy cure **chronic** hard cure
    '(With regard to hepatitis,) acute hepatitis is easy to cure, but chronic hepatitis is hard.'

(31) 男 女 同工同酬 了。（华文教材 2A 156）
    nán **nǚ** tónggōngtóngchóu le
    male **female** same.work.same.salary LE
    'Man and woman have the same salary for the same work.'
    (*Huáwénjiàocái* 2A 156)

In sentence (30), the distinguishing words are subjects of the two clauses. In sentence (31), the coordinative phrase consisting of distinguishing words is the subject of the sentence. There are two points worth mentioning for distinguishing words to appear in the subject position: First, they are always used in pairs; second, they no longer describe a state of things but refer to things. In sentence (30), they refer to 急性肝炎 *jíxìng gānyán* 'acute hepatitis' and 慢性肝炎 *mànxìng gānyán* 'chronic hepatitis' respectively. In sentence (31), they refer to 男人和女人 *nánrén hé nǔrén* 'man and woman'.

5.4 Predicative Subjects

5.4.1 Verb and Adjective Phrases as Subjects

As mentioned in Section 5.2, both verbs and adjectives can serve as subjects, with verb phrases being the subjects examplied in (1) through (4) and adjective phrases being the subjects shown in (5) through (7).

(1) 修养　　品德，　是　　每　　个　　人　　应该
　　xiūyǎng *pǐndé* *Shì* *měi* *gè* *rén* *yīnggāi*
　　cultivate morality Be every CL person should

　　做　　　的　　　事。（伦理·中三 44）
　　zuò *de* *shì*
　　do DE Thing

'Cultivating one's morality is something that everyone should do.' (*Lúnlǐ* III 44)

(2) 学　　走　　象棋，　始　　于　　两　　年　　前。
　　xué *zǒu* *xiàngqí* *shǐ* *yú* *liǎng* *nián* *qián*
　　learn play chess begin at two CL ago

'I began to learn to play chess two years ago.'

(3) 搬家　　　已经　　快　　三　　年　　了。（壁虎 23）
　　bānjiā *yǐjīng* *kuài* *sān* *Nián* *le*
　　move.house already nearly three CL LE

'It is nearly three years since I moved house.' (*Bìhǔ* 23)

(4) 写字　　可以　　修身。（渐行 50）
　　xiězì *kéyǐ* *xiūshēn*
　　write can self-cultification

'Writing can cultivate one's moral character.' (*Jiànxíng* 50)

(5) 兴奋，　　那　　是　　一　　种　　难以言喻　　的　　开怀。（渐行 15）
　　xīngfèn *nà* *shì* *yī* *zhǒng* *nányǐyányù* *de* *kāihuái*
　　excite that be one CL unspeakable DE relief

'Excitement is a kind of relief that is beyond expression.' (*Jiànxíng* 15)

(6) 生气　　是　　浪费　　时间　　和　　精力。（报 1995 年 8 月 21 日 6 版）
　　shēnqì　**shì**　**làngfèi**　**shíjiān**　**hé**　**jīnglì**
　　angry　be　waste　time　and　energy

'Being angry is a waste of time and energy.' (*Bào*, Aug. 21, 1995, Issue no. 6)

(7) 恐惧、　惊慌、　失望　　　　与　　不安，　使　　许仙
　　kǒngjù　**jīnghuāng**　**shīwàng**　**yǔ**　**bùān**　**shǐ**　**xǔxiān**
　　fear　　panic　　disappoint　and　anxious　make　Xu Xian

　　在　　台上　　团团转。（华文教材 2A 208）
　　zài　**táishàng**　**tuántuánzhuàn**
　　at　stage　buzz.about

'Fear, panic, disappointment and anxiety made Xu Xian buzz about on the stage.' (*Huáwénjiàocái* 2A 208)

5.4.2 *Stative Words as Subjects*

Before talking about stative words as subjects there are some things which we should explain further. There are actually two types of stative words: One without 的 *de* 'DE' (as introduced in Section 3.6) and one with 的 *de* 'DE'. The latter can be further divided into three subtypes:

1 Stative words + 的 *de* 'DE':

　　碧绿的 *bìlǜde* 'green'　　　　　雪白的 *xuěbáide* 'white as snow'
　　红通通的 *hóngtōngtōngde* 'red'　　绿油油的 *lǜyōuyōude* 'green'
　　糊里糊涂的 *húlihútúde* 'confused'　马里马虎的 *mǎlīmǎhūde* 'careless'

2 Reduplicated forms of adjectives[2] + 的 *de* 'DE':

　　好好的 *hǎohǎode* 'good'　　　　慢慢的 *mànmànde* 'slow'
　　干干净净的 *gāngānjìngjìngde* 'clean'　　清清楚楚的 *qīngqīngchǔchǔde* 'clear'

3 Reduplicated forms of disyllabic stative words + 的 *de* 'DE':

　　碧绿碧绿的 *bìlǜbìlǜde* 'green'　　雪白雪白的 *xuěbáixuěbáide* 'white as snow'

In Singapore Mandarin, we find no examples of stative words as subjects, be it with or without 的 *de* 'DE', at least in written genres. However, in Chinese Mandarin, a modifier-head phrase composed of "那 *nà* 'that'/这 *zhè* 'this' + stative words with 的 *de* 'DE'" may act as the subject in spoken genres, as in sentences (8) and (9).

(8) 那　　　胖乎乎　　　的　　　是　　　阿毛。
　　nà　　*pànghūhū*　*de*　　*shì*　　*āmáo*
　　that　　chubby　　　DE　　be　　　Amao
　'That chubby one is Amao.'

(9) 这　　　黑不溜秋　　　的　　　是　　　什么？
　　zhè　　*hēibùliūqiū*　*de*　　*shì*　　*shénme*
　　this　　black　　　　DE　　be　　　what
　'What is this black thing?'

5.4.3 Subject-Predicate Phrases as Subjects

A subject-predicate phrase can be a subject.

(10) 你　　母亲　　　骂　　　　你　　也　　是　　为了　你　　好。（狮子 66）
　　　nǐ　*mǔqīn*　　*mà*　　　*nǐ*　*yě*　*shì*　*wèile*　*nǐ*　*hǎo*
　　　2SG　mother　　criticise　2SG　also　be　　for　　　2SG　good
　'Your mother criticise you for your own good.' (*Shīzi* 66)

(11) 他　　待　　　人　　　和蔼可亲（华文教材 1A 166）
　　　tā　*dài*　　*rén*　　*héǎikěqīng*
　　　3SG　treat　　people　kind
　'He treats people kindly.' (*Huáwénjiàocái* 1A 166)

We need to mention two more points about predicative subjects here:

1　Predicative phrases are far less likely than nominal phrases to be subjects.
2　When serving as subjects, predicative phrases often imply the speaker's judgement about one event.

5.5 Verbal Predicates

After introducing subjects in Singapore Mandarin, we move on to predicates. We will talk about verb phrases as predicates first.

It is generally assumed that verbs can always function as predicates, but this is not true. Among all the common languages of modern Chinese ethic groups, including Singapore Mandarin, the use of verbs alone as predicates is very limited. A number of verbs cannot be predicates unless they are combined with other words. Here are some examples.

安慰 *ānwèi* 'comfort': 他安慰我 *tā ānwèi wǒ* 'he comforts me'
我去安慰 *wǒ qu ānwèi* 'I go to comfort (someone)'
(*我安慰 *wǒ ānwèi* 'I comfort')

告诉 *gàosù* 'tell': 我告诉他 *wǒ gàosù ta* 'I tell him'
我告诉了 *wǒ gàosù le* 'I told'
(*我告诉 *wǒ gàosù* 'I tell')

企图 *qǐtú* 'try': 他企图逃跑 *tā qǐtú táopǎo* 'he tried to escape'
(*他企图 *tā qǐtú* 'he tried')

Although some verbs can serve as predicates in sentences without being combined with other words, the use of such sentences is limited. More specifically speaking, a single verb predicate is only allowed under the following three conditions:

A Indicating willingness:

我去 *wǒ qù* 'I will go'
我说 *wǒ shuō* 'I will say'
他吃 *tā chī* 'he will eat'

B Indicating contrast:

我买 *wǒ mǎi* 'I buy (instead of not buying)'
牛肉吃 *niúròu chī* 'I eat beef (instead of mutton)'

C Indicating an imperative:

您坐 *nín zuò* 'have a seat please'
大家请 *dàjiā qǐng* 'everybody please'

Thus it is rare for a single verb to be the predicate. On the other hand, verb phrases are frequently used as predicates. Take the single verb 写 *xiě* 'write' for example; it can be used freely as a predicate if combined with other words, as shown here. These subject-predicate phrases can form complete sentences without restrictions.

我没有写 wǒ méiyǒu xiě 我写了 wǒ xiě le 'I have written'
'I didn't write'

我正写呢 wǒ zhèng xiě ne 我写过 wǒ xiě guò 'I wrote'
'I am writing'

我不写 wǒ bù xiě 我写好了 wǒ xiěhǎo le 'I finished writing'
'I do not write'

我刚写 wǒ gāng xiě 我写得很慢 wǒ xiě de hěnmàn
'I was just writing' 'I write slowly'

我常写 wǒ cháng xiě 我写了一封信 wǒ xiě le yìfēngxìn
'I write a lot' 'I wrote a letter'

我能写 wǒ néng xiě 我写不好 wǒ xiě bùhǎo
'I can write' 'I can't write well'

When a verb phrase serves as a predicate, the subject is not necessarily the agent of the action. In fact, the semantic relation between the subject and the predicate may vary. Let us consider the following examples.

agent: 警察　　　来　　　了。（石头 65）
jǐngchá　lái　le
police　come　LE
'The police came.' (*Shítóu* 65)

patient: a　会考　　成绩　　公布　　了。（撞墙 3）
huìkǎo　chéngjì　gōngbù　le
exam　grade　announce　LE
'The exam results were announced.' (*Zhuàngqiáng* 3)

b　奖杯　　失去　　了。（渐行 41）
jiǎngbēi　shīqù　le
trophy　lost　LE
'The trophy was lost.' (*Jiànxíng* 41)

instrument: 这　　把　　刀　　切　　肉。
zhè　bǎ　dāo　qiē　ròu
this　CL　knife　cut　meat
'This knife is used to cut meat.'

theme: 他　　分　　了　　三　　公斤　　苹果。
tā　fēn　le　sān　gōngjīn　píngguǒ

```
          3SG    get      LE     three   kilogram  apple
```
'He was given three kilograms of apples.'

place: a 外面   正在   下雨。
           wàimiàn   zhèngzài   xiàyǔ
           outside   in.process   rain

'It's raining outside.'

b 车   上   已   几乎   坐   满   了   搭客。（短篇 16）
   chē shàng   yǐ   jīhū   zuò   mǎn   le   dākè
   bus above   already nearly sit   full LE   passengers

'The bus was almost full of passengers.' (*Duǎnpiān* 16)

time: 下午   小组   讨论。
       xiàwǔ   xiǎozǔ   tǎolùn
       afternoon   group   discussion

'There is a group discussion in the afternoon.'

晚上   欣赏   南曲   表演。（壁虎 47）
wǎnshàng   xīnshǎng   nánqǔ   biǎoyǎn
evening   enjoy   Southern   performance
                          style opera

'(We) will enjoy the performance of Southern style opera in the evening.' (*Bìhǔ* 47)

The preceding examples show that the subject and the predicate can have different semantic relations.

5.6 是 shì 'Be'... as a Predicate

From the perspective of grammatical function, 是 *shì* 'be' is a verb and the '是 *shì*...' phrase predicate is a verb predicate. But 是 *shì* 'be' has some peculiarites, which should be discussed separately.

5.6.1 Notes on 是 shì 'Be'

是 *shì* 'be' is a verb, but it is different from ordinary verbs.[3] First, it can only be negated by 不 *bù* 'NEG' (e.g. 不是 *bushì* 'not be'), but not 没 *méi* 'NEG' (there is no such expression like *没有是 in Singapore Mandarin). Second, it cannot precede the following three dynamic auxiliaries: 了 *le* 'LE', 着 *zhe* 'ZHE', 过 *guò* 'GUO'. Third, it cannot take complements.

5.6.2 Usages of 是 shì 'Be'

7 shì has the following four usages:

1 是 shì alone can be an independent sentence, indicating a positive response to a request or confirmation, meaning 'ok' or 'yes'.

(1) "你   就   特别   多嘴,   没   问   你,
    nǐ   jiù   tèbié   duōzuǐ   méi   wèn   nǐ
    2SG   just particularly speak.too.much NEG   ask   2SG

    你   给   我   安静!"
    nǐ   gěi   wǒ   ānjìng
    2SG   GEI   1SG   quiet
    'You speak too much. We are not asking you now. Please be quiet!'

    "是,   生。 ……."（追云 45）
    shì   shēng
    ok   Sheng
    'Ok, Sheng.' (Zhuīyún 45)

(2) "我   一   飞   开,   你   就   可以   动手   了。"
    wǒ   yī   fēi   kāi   nǐ   jiù   kěyǐ   dòngshǒu le
    1SG   once   fly   away   2SG   just   can   start   LE
    'As soon as I leave, you can start.'

    "是,   是,   我   就   来   试试   看   吧!"（追云 116）
    shì   shì   wǒ   jiù   lái   shìshì   kàn   ba
    ok   ok   1SG   then   come   try   see   SFP
    'Ok, Ok, let me try it.' (Zhuīyún 116)

(3) "她   没   和   你们   一起   住?"
    tā   méi   hé   nǐmén   yìqǐ   zhù
    3SG   NEG   with   2PL   together   live
    'Doesn't she live with you?'

    "是。 她   自己   租   了   一   个   房子（金狮奖 79）
    shì   tā   zìjǐ   zū   le   yī   gè   fángzi

| yes | 3SG | self | rent | LE | one | CL | house |

'Yes, she rented a house for herself.' (*Jīnshījiǎng* 79)

(4) "请 问 这儿 是 罗永健 的 家 吗？"
| qǐng | wèn | zhèer | shì | luóyǒngjiàn | de | jiā | ma |
| please | ask | here | be | Luo Yongjian | DE | house | SFP |

Excuse me. Is this Luo Yongjian's house?

"是。"（狮子 147）

shì

yes

'Yes.' (*Shīzǐ* 147)

是 *shì* 'be' in sentences (1) and (2) shows a positive response to others' requests, while it indicates confirmation in sentences (3) and (4). An affirmative 是 *shì* 'be' is always followed by 啊 *ā* 'ah' and 的 *de* 'DE'.

(5) "免费？"

miǎnfèi

free

'For free?'

"是 啊！……"（金狮奖 112）
| shì | a |
| yes | SFP |

'Yes!' (*Jīnshījiǎng* 112)

(6) "她 就 是 张妈 吧！" 王邦富 问。
| tā | jiù | shì | zhāngmā | ba | wángbāngfù | wèn |
| 3SG | then | be | Aunt Zhang | SFP | Wang Bangfu | ask |

'Is she Aunt Zhang?' Wang Bangfu asked.

"是 的，……"（短篇 82）
| shì | de |
| yes | DE |

'Yes, …' (*Duǎnpiān* 82)

2 是 *shì* 'be' functions as a predicate on its own. This usage is not common, which is occasionally seen in oral conversations and often with a contrastive meaning.

(7) "你们　　都　　是　　南大　　学生？"
　　　nǐmén　dōu　shì　nándà　xuéshēng
　　　2PL　　all　　be　　NTU　　student
　　　'Are you all NTU students?'

　　　"他们　是，　我　　不　　是。"
　　　tāmen　shì　wǒ　bù　shì
　　　3PL　　be　　1SG　NEG　be
　　　'They are, but I'm not.'

3　　"是 *shì* 'be' + predicative words" functions as a predicate. In this case there are two different ways in which we can use sentence stress to express meanings.

　　A　是 *shì* 'be' can be used to express a contrastive meaning. When this happens, the stress is natually placed on the predicative words following 是 *shì* 'be', as in (8) and (9). Take sentence (9) for example. Although there is no context showing an overt contrast, there is an implied contrastive meaning: Your mother is doing it for you, not for other purposes.

(8)　今天　　的　　辩题　　　　是　谈　　生产力　　　　和　　经济
　　　jīntiān　de　biàntí　　　　shì　tán　shēngchǎnlì　hé　jīngjì
　　　today　　DE　debate.topic　be　talk　productivity　and　economic

　　　发展　　　　　问题，　（不　　是　谈　　什么　　　社会　　问题、
　　　fāzhǎn　　　　wèntí　　bù　　shì　tán　shénme　shèhuì　wèntí
　　　development　issue　　NEG　be　talk　what　　　social　　issue

　　　教育　　　　问题。）　（华文教材 2B 122）
　　　jiàoyù　　　wèntí
　　　educational　issue

　　　'The topic of today's debate is about productivity and economic development, (but not social and educational issues . . .)' (*Huáwénjiàocái* 2B 122)

(9)　你　　妈妈　　　是　　为　　你　　好　　啊！（撞墙 25）
　　　nǐ　　māma　　shì　　wèi　nǐ　　hǎo　a
　　　2SG　mother　be　　for　　2SG　good　SFP
　　　'Your mother is doing it for you!' (*Zhuàngqiáng* 25)

　　B　When 是 *shì* 'be' is used for emphasis, the stentence stress is on 是 *shì* 'be' itself, as in (10) and (11). In this usage, 是 *shì* 'be' is often preceded by the adverb 的确 *díquè* 'indeed', as in (12).

(10) "（是，） 你 是 比 我 大 五 岁，
  shì   *nǐ* *shì* *bǐ* *wǒ* *dà* *wǔ* *suì*
  yes   2SG be than 1SG older five years

  （但 我 并 不 介意……）"（再见 40）
  dàn *wǒ* *bìng* *bù* *jièyì*
  but 1SG however NEG mind

  '(Yes), you are five years older than me, (but I don't mind . . .)' (*Zàijiàn* 40)

(11) 这么 复杂 的 问题，是 不 容易 一下子
  zhème *fùzá* *de* *wèntí* *shì* *bù* *róngyì* *yīxiàzi*
  such complicated DE issue be NEG easy right.off

  弄 清楚。（报 1995 年 6 月 17 日 8 版）
  nòng *qīngchǔ*
  make clear

  'It is not easy to make such a complicated issue clear right off.' (*Bào*, June 17, 1995, Issue no. 8)

(12) 我 的确 是 结过婚 了。（撞墙 39）
  wǒ *díquè* *shì* *jié-guò-hūn* *le*
  1SG indeed be married LE

  'I did once marry.' (*Zhuàngqián*, 39)

4 "是 *shì* 'be' + a nominal phrase" functions as a predicate. This is the most common usage of 是 *shì* 'be', as illustrated in (13) through (15).

(13) 这位 是 杨铭。（金狮奖 69）
  zhèwèi *shì* *yángmíng*
  this be Yang Ming

  'This is Yang Ming.' (*Jīnshījiǎng* 69)

(14) 这 是 你 孩子 的 成绩。（再见 62）
  zhè *shì* *nǐ* *háizi* *de* *chéngjì*
  this be 2SG kid DE grade

  'This is your kid's grade.' (*Zàijiàn* 62)

(15) 九月 一 日 是 教师节。（平心 90）
  jiǔyuè *yī* *rì* *shì* *jiàoshījié*
  September first day be Teacher's Day

  'September 1st is Teacher's Day.' (*Píngxīn* 90)

Moreover, "是 *shì*...的 *de*" often functions as a predicate as well, as shown in (16) through (18). Here, 的 *de* 'DE' phrase is a nominal phrase. Thus, these kind of sentences, which are generally known as "SHI" construction, are also of the fourth kind.

(16) 这   桌子   是   木头   的。
     zhè   zhuōzǐ   **shì** mùtou   de
     this   table   **be**   wood   DE
     'The table is made of wood.'

(17) 我   是   她   领养   的。（跳舞 140）
     wǒ   **shì** tā   lǐngyǎng de
     1SG   **be**   3SG   wood   DE
     'It is she who adopted me.' (*Tiàowǔ* 140)

(18) 你   的   父母   是   种田   的   吗？（跳舞 14）
     nǐ   de   fùmǔ   **shì** zhòngtián   de   ma
     2SG   DE   parents **be**   till.the.land DE   SFP
     'Are your parents farmers?' (*Tiàowǔ* 14)

More special usages of 是 *shì* 'be' are introduced in Section 5.14.

5.7 Adjectival Predicates

In Singapore Mandarin, bare adjectives as predicates usually indicate comparison and judgement, as in (1) and (2). Sometimes, they are used in parallel, as in (3) through (5).

(1) 内地   天气   **冷,**   不   像   这里,   您
    nèidì   tiānqì   **lěng** bù   xiàng   zhèlǐ   nín
    inland   weather   **cold** NEG   like   here   you

    要   多   披   几   件   衣服。（扶轮 52）
    yào   duō   pī   jǐ   jiàn   yīfu
    should   more   drape   several   CL   clothes
    'The weather inland is colder than here, you'd better put on more clothes.' (*Fúlún* 52)

(2) 油   和   水   重量   不   一样,   油   **轻,**
    yóu   hé   shuǐ   zhòngliàng   bù   yīyàng   yóu   **qīng**
    oil   and   water   weight   NEG   the.same   oil   **light**

(2) 水　　　重，　　所以　　油　　浮　　在　　水面　　　　上。
　　shuǐ　zhòng　suǒyǐ　yóu　fú　zài　shuǐmiàn　shàng
　　water　heavy　so　oil　float　at　water.surface　on

'The weight of oil and water are different: oil is light; water is heavy, so oil can float on the water surface.'

(3) 见闻　　　广博，　　　知识　　　　丰富。（伦理·中三 111）
　　jiànwén　guǎngbó　zhīshí　　fēngfù
　　horizon　extensive　knowledge　abundant

'He is informed and knowledgeable.' (*Lúnlǐ* III 111)

(4) 政治　　　稳定，　　经济　　　繁荣。（华文教材 2A 8）
　　zhèngzhì　wěndìng　jīngjì　fánróng
　　politics　stable　economy　prosperous

'The political system is stable and the economy is prosperous.' (*Huáwénjiàocái* 2A 8)

(5) 新加坡　　是　　一　　个　　蕞尔　　小　　国，　　国土　　小，
　　xīnjiāpō　shì　yī　gè　zuìěr　xiǎo　guó　guótǔ　xiǎo
　　Singapore　be　one　CL　small　small　country　territory　small

　　人口　　　也　　少。（华文教材 4B, 1）
　　rénkǒu　yě　shǎo
　　population　also　small

'Singapore is a very small country with small territory and small population.' (*Huáwénjiàocái* 4B 1)

To indicate meanings other than comparison or contrast, we have to either add other modifying words or complements before or after the adjectives as in (6) through (8), or use coordinate adjective phrases as in (9) through (11).

(6) 这　　本　　书　　太　　厚　　了。（金狮奖 99）
　　zhè　běn　shū　tài　hòu　le
　　this　CL　book　too　thick　LE

'This book is too thick.' (*Jīnshījiǎng* 99)

(7) 车轮　　　特别　　大。（一心 47）
　　chēlún　tèbié　dà
　　wheel　really　big

'The wheels are really big.' (*Yìxīn* 47)

(8) 你　　还　　**忙**　　得　　很　　呢！（微型 56）
　　nǐ　　hái　　**máng**　dé　　hěn　　ne
　　2SG　 still　 busy　　DE　 very　 SFP

'You are still very busy!' (*Wēixíng* 56)

(9) 她　　愚昧　　而　　可怜。（短篇 32）
　　tā　　yúmèi　　ér　　kělián
　　3SG　ignorant　LIG　poor

'She is ignorant and poor.' (*Duǎnpiān* 32)

(10) 气氛　　　热烈　　而　　融洽。（壁虎 50）
　　 qìfēn　　　rèliè　　ér　　róngqià
　　 atmosphere　warm　　LIG　harmonious

'The atmosphere is warm and harmonious.' (*Bìhǔ* 50)

(11) 它　　整洁　　而　　又　　明亮，
　　 tā　　zhěngjié　ér　　yòu　　míngliàng
　　 3SG　neat　　　LIG　and　　bright

　　 雅丽　　而　　又　　恬静。（石头 38）
　　 yǎlì　　ér　　yòu　　tiānjìng
　　 beautiful LIG　and　　quiet

'It is neat and bright, beautiful and quiet.' (*Shítóu* 38)

"Adjective +了 *le* 'LE'" is also a type of commonly seen adjectival predicate, usually indicating changes. For example, 黑了 *hēile* in (12) and 老了 *lǎole* in (13) mean 'getting dark' and 'getting old' respectively.

(12) 天　　黑　　了。（太阳 111）
　　 tiān　hē　　le
　　 heaven　black　LE

'It is getting dark.' (*Tàiyáng* 111)

(13) 我　　老　　了。
　　 wǒ　　lǎo　　le

| 1SG | old | LE |

'I am getting old.'

Such structure sometimes implies an excessive meaning. For example, 贵了 *guìle* 'expensive' in (14) means 'too expensive' and 长了 *chángle* 'long' in (16) means 'way too long'.

(14) 你   买   的   虾   **贵**   了，（我   买
     nǐ   mǎi   de   xiā   **guì**   le   wǒ   mǎi
     2SG buy   DE   shrimp **expensive** LE 1SG buy

    的   便宜。）
    de   piányí
    DE   cheap

'The shrimp you bought were too expensive, mine were cheaper.'

(15) 这   块   木板   **长**   了，（要   锯   掉   些。）
     zhè kuài mùbǎn **cháng** le   yào   jù   diào xiē
     this CL   board **long** LE   need saw off   some

'The board is too long and needs to be sawed off.'

Given that bare adjectival predicates implies contrastive meanings, when we want to simply describe the nature of something without contrast, we ususally add an adverb 很 *hěn* 'very' before the adjective. For instance, when somebody asks you about your opinion of a painting, 'How about this painting?', if you think it is pretty good but not better than other paintings, you may answer 这幅画很好 *zhèfúhuàhěnhǎo* 'This painting is very good'. Note that 很 *hěn* 'very' here does not express a high degree, but a weakened meaning, and it is pronounced lightly.

Influenced by English, in Singapore Mandarin 是 *shì* 'be' is often added before the adjective predicate as shown in the following examples. However, there is no such use in Chinese Mandarin.

(16) 内心   **是**   踏实   与   饱满， 脚步   **是**   健朗
     nèixīn **shì** tāshí yǔ   bǎomǎn jiǎobù **shì** jiànlǎng
     heart   **be**   sure   and   full   footstep **be**   vigorous

    与   轻快。（青青 27）
    yǔ   qīngkuài
    and   light

'The heart is steadfast and full; the footstep is vigorous and light.' (*Qīngqīng* 27)

(17) 五、六十   年代，   市区   中心   的   房屋，   一般上
    wǔliùshí   niándài shìqū   zhōngxīn de   fángwū   yībānshàng
    fifty.or.sixty time downtown centre   DE   buildings commonly

    是   拥挤、   杂乱   和   陈旧。（风筝 139）
    shì   yōngjǐ   záluàn   hé   chénjiù
    be   crowded messy   and   obsolete

    'The buildings in the centre of downtown in the 1950s and 1960s were generally crowded, messy and obsolete.' (*Fēngzhēng* 139)

(18) （我 认为）   这   是   很   不   公平。（报 1995 年 4 月 5 日
                                                      18 版）
    wǒ rènwéi   zhè   shì   hěn   bù   gōngpíng
    1SG think   this be   very   NEG   fair

    'I think it is unfair.' (*Bào*, Apr. 5, 1995, Issue no. 18)

5.8 Stative Word Predicates

Stative words frequently function as predicates on their own.

(1) 脸色   煞白。（跳舞 11）
    liǎnsè   shàbái
    complexion   pale

    '(His) face is pale.' (*Tiàowǔ* 11)

(2) 她   双颊   红红   的。（跳舞 107）
    tā   shuāngjiá   hónghóng   de
    3SG cheeks   red   DE

    'Her cheeks were red.' (*Tiàowǔ* 107)

(3) 全身   红艳艳   的。（冰灯 31）
    quánshēn   hóngyànyàn   de
    from.head.to.foot bright.red   DE

    'He is in bright red from head to foot.' (*Bīngdēng* 31)

Unlike adjectival predicates, stative word predicates do not indicate contrast. The expression 他个子高 *tāgèzigāo* 'he is taller' has an adjective predicate and implies that others are short, while the expression 他个子高高 *tāgèzigāode* 'he is tall' has a stative word predicate and does not indicate comparison with others.

Furthermore, adjective predicates express the speaker's opinions, while stative word predicates are descriptive in nature.

Stative words can be divided into two types, depending on whether or not they are used with 的 *de* 'DE' (see Section 5.4). Generally speaking, stative words with 的 *de* 'DE' are more free when acting as predicates.

In Chinese Mandarin, reduplicated forms of disyllabic adjectives are stative words, which can be predicates on their own (for example, 那房间干干净净 *nàfángjiāngāngānjìngjìng* 'That room is very clean'); whereas, reduplicated forms of monosyllabic adjectives cannot act as predicates. According to the research by Zhu (1961), reduplicated forms of monosyllabic adjectives can be divided into two types according to their syntactic functions: The first type can, and can only, function as adverbial modifiers on their own, and thus they are adverbs, as shown in the following examples.

好好 *hǎohǎo*:

好好	学习		好好	工作		*身体	好好
hǎohǎo	*xuéxí*		*hǎohǎo*	*gōngzuò*		*shēntǐ*	*hǎohǎo*
well	study		well	work		health	well
'study hard'			'work hard'			'in good health'	

高高 *gāogāo*:

高高	举起		高高	翘起		*那	楼房	高高
gāogāo	*jǔqǐ*		*gāogāo*	*qiàoqǐ*		*nà*	*lóufáng*	*gāogāo*
highly	lift		highly	stick.up		that	building	highly
'lift high'			'stick up high'			'That building is high.'		

大大 *dàdà*:

大大	提高	生活	水平		*那	西瓜	大大
dàdà	*tígāo*	*shēnghuó*	*shuǐpíng*		*nà*	*xīguā*	*dàdà*
greatly	improve	life	standard		that	watermelon	big
'greatly improve living standards'					'That watermelon is big.'		

Similarly, 慢慢 *mànmàn* 'slowly', 快快 *kuàikuài* 'quickly', 远远 *yuǎnyuǎn* 'remotely' and 轻轻 *qīngqīng* 'lightly' all belong to the first type. The second type are non-words, which cannot form any syntactic constituent on their own, such as 热热 *rèrè* 'hot', 红红 *hónghóng* 'red', 扁扁 *biǎnbiān* 'flat', 胖胖 *pàngpàng* 'fat', 瘦瘦 *shòushòu* 'thin'.

Significantly, both types of reduplicated forms of monosyllabic adjectives will transform into stative words if they are followed by a *de* 'DE' suffix and thereby can function as adverbials, predicates, complements and attributives. (When used as adverbials, 'DE' is written as 地 *de*, otherwise 的 *de*.) Consider the following examples.

好好 de:　好好　　　地　　学习　　　[状语]
hǎohǎode　hǎohǎo　　de　　xuéxí　　zhuàngyǔ
　　　　　good　　　DE　　study　　[adverbial]
　　　　　'study hard'

　　　　　衣服　　叠　　得　　好好　　[补语]
　　　　　yīfú　　dié　 de　　hǎohǎo　bǔyǔ
　　　　　clothes　fold　DE　　good　　[complement]
　　　　　'The clothes are folded properly.'

　　　　　好好　　　的　　　　衣服　　[定语]
　　　　　hǎohǎo　　de　　　　yīfú　　dìngyǔ
　　　　　good　　　DE　　　　clothes　[attributive]
　　　　　'good clothes'

高高 de:　高高　　　地　　举起　　　[状语]
gāogāode　gāogāo　　de　　jǔqǐ　　 zhuàngyǔ
　　　　　high　　　DE　　raise　　[adverbial]
　　　　　'lift (it) up high'

　　　　　那　　楼房　　　高高　　的　　　[谓语]
　　　　　nà　　lóufáng　　gāogāo　de　　 wèiyǔ
　　　　　that　building　　high　　DE　　[predicate]
　　　　　'That building is tall.'

　　　　　高高　　　的　　　　宝塔　　[定语]
　　　　　gāogāo　　de　　　　bǎotǎ　dìngyǔ
　　　　　high　　　DE　　　　pagoda　[attributive]
　　　　　'tall pagoda'

热热 de:　热热　　地　　喝　　了　　杯　　茶　　[状语]
rèrède　　rèrè　　de　　hē　　le　　bēi　　chá　 zhuàngyǔ
　　　　　hot　　DE　　drink　LE　　CL　　tea　 [adverbial]
　　　　　'drink a cup of hot tea'

	那	茶	热热	的	[谓语]
	nà	chá	rèrè	de	wèiyǔ
	that	tea	hot	DE	[predicate]

'That tea is hot.'

	水	烧	得	热热	的	[补语]
	shuǐ	shāo	de	rèrè	de	bǔyǔ
	water	heat.up	DE	hot	DE	[complement]

'That water is heated hot.'

红红 de:	红红	地	抹	了	一	脸	[状语]
hónghóngde	hónghóng	de	mǒ	le	yī	liǎn	zhuàngyǔ
	red	DE	wipe	LE	one	face	[adverbial]

'wipe his face red'

	那	枫叶	红红	的	[谓语]
	nà	fēngyè	hónghóng	de	wèiyǔ
	that	maple.leaf	red	DE	[predicate]

'That maple leaf is red.'

	红红	的	太阳	[定语]
	hónghóng	de	tàiyáng	dìngyǔ
	red	DE	sun	[attributive]

'red sun'

Thus, in Chinese Mandarin, reduplicated forms of monosyllabic adjectives cannot be directly used as predicates, complements or attributives unless they are transformed into stative words with 'DE'. However, in Singapore Mandarin, they are stative words, similar to reduplicated forms of disyllabic adjectives, and thus can be directly used as predicates.

(4) 他　　鼻梁　**高高**　嘴唇　微　　翘，　像　一　　尊
　　 tā　　bíliáng **gāogāo** zuǐchún wēi　 qiào, xiàng yī　 zūn
　　 3SG　 nose　 **high**　 lip　　 slightly pout　like　one　CL

　　 美丽　　 高雅　 的　　石膏像。（吾土·小说上 156）
　　 měilì　　 gāoyǎ　 de　　 shígāoxiàng
　　 beautiful elegant DE　 plaster.model

'His nose is high and his lips are slightly pouting, like a beautiful and elegant plaster model.' (*Wútǔ·xiǎoshuōshàng* 156)

(5) 她　　眉毛　　**弯弯，**　双　　眸　　**圆圆。**（跳舞 120）
    tā　　méimáo　**wānwān**　shuāng　móu　**yuányuán**
    3SG　 eyebrow　**curved**　 two　　eye　 **round**
    'She has curved eyebrows and round eyes.' (*Tiàowǔ* 120)

(6) 落地　　　　　长　　　　窗　　　　外，　　　天鹅河　　　**长长、**
    luòdì　　　　cháng　　chuāng　　wài　　　tiānéhé　　**chángcháng**
    floor.to.ceiling　long　　　window　　outside　swan.river　**long**

静静。（大胡子 89）
jìngjìng
quiet
'Outside the French window, Swan River lay long and quiet.' (*Dàhúzi* 89)

5.9 Subject-Predicate Predicates

Subject-predicate predicates refer to subject-predicate phrases being the predicates of the sentences, as illustrated in the following example:

那几个人　　我　　已经给安排了工作

nàjǐgèrén　　wǒ　　yǐjīnggěiānpáilegōngzuò

————　————————————
　1　　　　　　　　2　　　　　　　(subject-predicate)
　　　　———　——————
　　　　　3　　　　4　　　　　　　(subject-predicate)

The subject, 那几个人 *nàjǐgèrén* 'those people' of the entire sentence is usually called the main subject. In the subject-predicate phrase, the subject 我 *wǒ* '1SG' and the predicate 已经给安排了工作 *yǐjīnggěiānpáilegōngzuò* 'have already arranged jobs' are called the clause subject and the clause predicate respectively. Here are more examples of subject-predicate phrases serving as predicates.

(1) 漫画　　　我　　最　　欣赏。（笑眼 218）
    mànhuà　　wǒ　　zuì　　xīnshǎng
    comic　　　1SG　 most　appreciate
    'I appreciate comic books most.' (*Xiàoyǎn* 218)

(2) 我　　天性　　　好动。（冰灯 46）
    wǒ　　tiānxìng　　hàodòng
    1SG　 nature　　　active
    'I am active by nature.' (*Bīngdēng* 46)

(3) 八　　个，　一　　个　　也　　没　　剩。（金狮奖 208）
    bā   gè   yī   gè   yě   méi   shèng
    eight CL   one   CL   also NEG   left
    'Eight, not one left.' (*Jīnshījiǎng* 208)

(4) 鸡蛋　一　　块　　钱　　十　　粒。
    jīdàn yī   kuài   qián   shí   lì
    egg   one   CL   money ten   CL
    'Eggs, ten for one Chinese yuan.'

(5) 今晚，　我　　不　　买　　香皂　　了。（风雨 14）
    jīnwǎn   wǒ   bú   mǎi   xiāngzào le
    tonight 1SG   NEG   buy   soap   LE
    'I won't buy soap tonight.' (*Fēngyǔ* 14)

(6) 喜欢　　文学，　那　　是　　我　　选择　　自我　　充实
    xǐhuān wénxué   nà   shì   wǒ   xuǎnzé zìwǒ   chōngshí
    love   literature that be   1SG   choice myself fufill

    与　　自我　　提升　　的　　方式。（渐行 88）
    yǔ   zìwǒ   tíshēng   de   fāngshì
    and   myself promotion DE   way

    'Loving literature, that's my way of self-enrichment and self-improvement.' (*Jiànxíng* 88)

The relation between the clause subject and the main subject is the agent-patient relation in (1); it is of the affiliation relation in (2) and of the part-whole relation in (3). In (4), the main subject refers to an item, the clause subject is a numeral-classifier phrase, and the clause predicate is or includes a numeral-classifier phrase. The entire structure emphasises the value of the item denoted by the main subject. In (5), the main subject indicates time and in (6), the clause subject refers to the same thing as the main subject.

Sometimes, the predicate may be a coordinating subject-predicate phrase.

(7) 她　　人　　小　　声　　大。（金狮奖 135）
    tā   rén   xiǎo   shēng dà
    3SG   body   small voice loud
    'Her body is small but her voice is loud.' (*Jīnshījiǎng* 135)

Sentence (7) may be analysed as follows.

```
她    人  小  声  大。
tā    rén xiǎo shēng dà
―――  ――――――――         (subject-predicate)
 1         2
      ―――  ――――――       (coordinate phrase)
       3      4
      ―  ―  ―  ―        (both 5-6 and 7-8 are subject-predicate phrases)
      5  6  7  8
```

In contrast with English, in Chinese the predicate itself can be a subject-predicate phrase. This is one common grammatical feature of the lingua franca of modern Chinese ethic groups, including of Singapore Mandarin.

5.10 Nominal Predicates

5.10.1 Numeral-Classifier Phrases as Predicates

Among all nominal words, numeral-classifier phrases are the most frequently used nominal predicates. Depending on the properties of the subject phrase, the numeral-classifier phrase predicate may express four types of meanings.

1 The numeral-classifier phrase expresses the quantity of the items denoted by the nominal subject.

(1) 鸭子　　　两　　　只。（微型 5）
    yāzi   liǎng   zhī
    duck   two   CL
    'two ducks' (*Wēixíng* 5)

(2) 妻　　　妾　　　六　　　个。（青青 18）
    qī   qiè   liù   gè
    wife   concubine six   CL
    'There are six wives and concubines.' (*Qīngqīng* 18)

(3) 旧　诗　　四　　首，　散文　两　　篇。（△中国作家 50）
    jiù shī   sì   shǒu   sǎnwén liǎng piān
    old poem four CL   essay two   CL
    'There are four old poems and two essays.' (*Zhōngguózuòjiā* 50)

When the numeral-classifier phrase is about a sum of money, it expresses the price of the item indicated by the subject.

(4) 三文治　　　　三　　　　　　块钱。（梦 101）
　　 sānwénzhì　　**sān**　　　　***kuàiqián***
　　 sandwich　　　**three**　　　**CL**
　　 'Three yuan for a sandwich.' (*Mèng* 101)

2　The numeral-classifier phrase expresses age when the subject is a proper name referring to people or a personal pronoun.

(5) 他　　　　　十四　　　　　岁。（狮子 68）
　　 tā　　　　**shísì**　　　　*suì*
　　 3SG　　　　**14**　　　　　year/CL
　　 'He's 14.' (*Shīzǐ* 68)

(6) 宝晴、　　宝华　　　才　　　十七　　　岁。（金狮奖（四）22）
　　 bǎoqíng　*bǎohuá*　*cái*　　**shíqī**　　*suì*
　　 Baoqing　 Baohua　　only　　**17**　　　year/CL
　　 'Baoqing and Baohua are only 17.' (*Jīnshījiǎng* IV 22)

3　Both the subject and the predicate are numeral-classifier phrases, with the whole construction expressing a corresponding relationship between the things indicated by the two phrases, which could roughly be paraphrased with 'each' or 'every'.

(7) 一　　　晚　　　三　　　四十　　　元　　　吧。（金狮奖 224）
　　 yī　　 *wǎn*　　*sān*　　*sìshí*　　*yuán*　　*ba*
　　 one　　CL　　　three　　forty　　　yuan　　 SFP
　　 'Thirty to forty yuan for one night.' (*Jīnshījiǎng* 224)

(8) 一　　　毛钱　　　　一　　　　碗。（梦 26）
　　 yī　　 *máoqián*　　*yī*　　　*wǎn*
　　 one　　CL　　　　　one　　　CL
　　 'Ten cents for one bowl (of food).' (*Mèng* 26)

(9) 一　　　包　　　一　　　块钱。（华文教材 2A 28）
　　 yī　　 *bāo*　　*yī*　　*kuàiqián*
　　 one　　CL　　　one　　CL
　　 'One yuan for a pack.' (*Huáwénjiàocái* 2A 28)

In (7), 一晚 *yīwǎn* equals to 每晚 *měiwǎn* 'each night', the whole sentence meaning 'each night for thirty to forty yuan'. Here we should draw attention to the difference between (8) and (9). In (8), the numeral-classifier phrase indicating money 一毛钱 *yīmáoqián* 'ten cents' serves as the subject, meaning 'to buy', namely, 'ten cents can buy one bowl (of food)'; while in (9), the numeral-classifier phrase indicating money 一块钱 *yīkuàiqián* 'one yuan' serves as the predicate, meaning 'to sell', namely, 'each pack sells for one yuan'.

Sometimes, the meaning of 'every' can be enhanced when there is an overt 每 *měi* before the numeral-classifier phrase, as shown in (10) and (11).

(10) 每　　　一　　　包　　　二十　　　本。
　　 měi　　 *yī*　　 *bāo*　　 *èrshí*　　 *běn*
　　 every　 one　　 CL　　　 20　　　　 CL
'20 copies per pack.'

(11) 每　　　年　　　两千　　　元。（短篇 10）
　　 měi　　 *nián*　　 *liǎngqiān*　　 *yuán*
　　 every　 CL　　　 2000　　　 CL
'2000 yuan per year.' (*Duǎnpiān* 10)

4 The numeral-classifier phrase expresses a meaning of measurement when the subject is an adjective indicating dimensions. In this case, the adjective chosen is usually the one that expresses a higher degree, for example, 高 *gāo* 'high', 宽 *kuān* 'wide', 重 *zhòng* 'heavy', 长 *cháng* 'long', 深 *shēn* 'deep' and so on.

(12) 高　　　1.45　　　米。（万花筒 33）
　　 gāo　　 *yīdiǎnsìwǔ*　　 *mǐ*
　　 high　 1.45　　　 metre
'1.45 metres high.' (*Wànhuātǒng* 33)

(13) 重　　　三十　　　公斤。
　　 zhòng　　 *sānshí*　　 *gōngjīn*
　　 heavy　 30　　　 kilogram
'It weighs 30 kg.'

(14) 长　　　约　　　一　　　寸。（壁虎 62）
　　 cháng　　 *yuē*　　 *yī*　　 *cùn*
　　 long　 about　 one　 inch
'About an inch long.' (*Bìhǔ* 62)

(15) 深　　　约　　　二　　　　公尺。（晚上 76）
    shēn　*yuē*　*èr*　　*gōngchǐ*
    deep　about　two　metre
    'About two metres deep.' (*Wǎnshàng* 76)

Notably, such usage is only found for numeral-classifier predicates in which the classifer expresses the unit of measurement, such as 米 *mǐ* 'metre', 公斤 *gōngjīn* 'kilogram', 寸 *cùn* 'inch' and 公尺 *gōngchǐ* 'metre', as shown in the preceding examples.

5.10.2 Nominal Phrases as Predicates

Although nominal phrases can serve as predicates too, this is not common in written genre, and most sentences of this kind are descriptive.

(16) 窗　　　外，　　响晴　　　　　　的　　　蓝天。（怀旧 24）
    chuāng　*wài*　*xiǎngqíng*　*de*　*lántiān*
    window　outside　clear.and.bright　DE　blue.sky
    'Outside the window is the clear blue sky.' (*Huáijiù* 24)

(17) 屋　　　外，　　很　　　好　　　的　　　阳光。（太阳 38）
    wū　*wài*　*hěn*　*hǎo*　*de*　*yángguāng*
    house　outside　very　good　DE　sunshine
    'Outside there is bright sunshine.' (*Tàiyáng* 38)

Nominal predicates are more common in spoken genre, but are confined to the following cases.

1   When a nominal phrase that indicates one's birthplace or appearance serves as the predicate, the subject is a personal pronoun or a noun referring to a person.

(18) 他　　　广东　　　　人。
    tā　*guǎngdōng*　*rén*
    3SG　Guangdong　person
    'He is from Guangdong province.'

(19) 杜运燮，　　福建　　　古田　　　人。（△中国作家 143）
    dùyùnxiè　*fújiàn*　*gǔtián*　*rén*
    Du Yunxie　Fujian　Gutian　person
    'Du Yunxie is from Gutian county, Fujian province.' (*Zhōngguózuòjiā* 143)

(20) 那   孩子   黄   头发。
    nà   háizi   huáng   tóufà
    that kid   fair   hair
    'That kid has fair hair.'

2   When a nominal phrase that indicates a date, a festival or weather serves as the predicate, the subject is often a noun that denotes time.

(21) 今天   星期三。
    jīntiān   xīngqīsān
    today   Wednesday
    'Today is Wednesday.'

(22) 八月   十五   中秋节。
    bāyuè   shíwǔ   zhōngqiūjié
    august fifteenth Mid-autumn.Festival
    'August 15th is Mid-autumn Festival.'

(23) 昨天   阴天，   今天   晴天。
    zuótiān   yīntiān   jīntiān   qíngtiān
    yesterday cloudy   today   sunny
    'Yesterday was cloudy but today is sunny.'

3   When a single noun serves as a predicate, the subject often takes the form of a subject-predicate phrase plus 的 *de* 'DE'. The predicate is often semantically interpreted as the patient of the verb in this DE construction.

(24) 我   买   的   榴莲，   他   买   的   山竹。
    wǒ   mǎi   de   liúlián tā   mǎi   de   shānzhú
    1SG   buy   DE   durian   3SG   buy   DE   mangosteen
    'What I bought is the durian and what he bought is the mangosteen.'

(25) 我   说   的   心里   话。
    wǒ   shuō   de   xīnlǐ   huà
    1SG   say   DE   from.the.heart word
    'What I spoke are words from my heart.'

(26) (他   呀！）吃   的   山珍海味，   住   的   高楼大厦。
     tā   ya   chī   de   shānzhēnhǎiwèi zhù   de   gāolóudàshà
     3SG   TOP   eat   DE   delicacies   live   DE   high.building
     'As for him, what he eats are delicacies and what he lives are high buildings.'

If we look at sentence (24) in isolation, 我买的榴莲 *wǒmǎideliúlián* is ambiguous: it can be interpreted as a subject-predicate phrase, which means 'what I bought is durian'; it can also be interpreted as an attribute-head phrase, which means 'the durian I bought' (e.g. 我买的榴莲 *wǒmǎideliúlián* is an attribute-head phrase in 我买的榴莲好吃 *wǒmǎideliúliánhǎochī* 'The durian I bought is delicious'). Likewise, the *de* 'DE' constructions in (25) and (26) are also ambiguous.

4   DE constructions often serve as predicates.

(27) 我   从   山城   来   的。（风雨 36）
     wǒ   cóng   shānchéng   lái   de
     1SG   from   mountain.city come   DE
     'I come from the mountain city.' (*Fēngyǔ* 36)

(28) 这   篇   文章   抄   别人   的。
     zhè   piān   wénzhāng   chāo   biérén   de
     this CL   article   copy   other.people   DE
     'This article is copied from someone else's.'

The meaning of sentence (27) remains the same if we insert 是 *shì* 'be' between 我 *wǒ* '1SG' and 从 *cóng* 'from'. Here 从山城来的 *cóng shānchéng láide* 'from the mountain city' is a DE construction that functions as the predicate of the sentence. Sentence (28) can also be understood in this way.

5.10.3 Subject-Predicate Sentences With Nominal Predicates

A nominal predicate can be regarded as the shortened form of a verbal predicate. The verb being omitted is usually 是 *shì* 'be'. This can be tested by the fact that the insertion of 不是 *búshì* 'not be' is obligatory to obtain the negative form of this sentence, as demonstrated in (1) through (11). Therefore, nominal predicates can also be seen as quasi-nominal predicates.

(1)' 鸭子   两   只。   →   鸭子   不   是   两   只。
      yāzi   liǎng   zhī   yāzi   bù   shì   liǎng   zhī
      duck   two   CL   duck   NEG   be   two   CL
      'two ducks'   'There are not two ducks.'

(2)' 他　　十四　　岁。　→　他　　不　　是　　十四　　岁。
　　　tā　　shísì　　suì　　　tā　　bù　　shì　　shísì　　suì
　　　3SG　14　　　CL　　　3SG　NEG　be　　14　　　CL
　　　'He is 14.'　　　　　　'He is not 14.'

(3)' 一　　晚　　三　　四十　　元。
　　　yī　　wǎn　　sān　　sìshí　　yuán
　　　one　CL　　three　forty　　yuan
　　　'It is thirty to forty yuan for one night.'

　→　一　　晚　　不　　是　　三　　四十　　元。
　　　yī　　wǎn　　bù　　shì　　sān　　sìshí　　yuán
　　　one　CL　　NEG　be　　three　forty　　yuan
　　　'It is not thirty to forty yuan for one night.'

(4)' 每　　一　　包　　二十　　本。
　　　měi　　yī　　bāo　　èrshí　　běn
　　　every　one　CL　　20　　　CL
　　　'20 copies per pack.'

　→　每　　一　　包　　不　　是　　二十　　本。
　　　měi　　yī　　bāo　　bù　　shì　　èrshí　　běn
　　　every　one　CL　　NEG　be　　20　　　CL
　　　'There are not 20 copies in each pack.'

(5)' 高　　1.45　　　米。　　→　高　　不　　是　　1.45　　　米。
　　　gāo　yīdiǎnsìwǔ　mǐ　　　　gāo　bù　　shì　　yīdiǎnsìwǔ　mǐ
　　　high　1.45　　　metre　　high　NEG　be　　1.45　　　metre
　　　'1.45 metres high.'　　　　　'The height is not 1.45 metres.'

(6)' 他　　广东　　　人。　　→　他　　不　　是　　广东　　　人。
　　　tā　　guǎngdōng　rén　　　tā　　bù　　shì　　guǎngdōng　rén
　　　3SG　Guangdong　person　3SG　NEG　be　　Guangdong　person
　　　'He is from Guangdong.'　　'He is not from Guangdong.'

(7)' 那　　孩子　　黄　　头发。
　　　nà　　háizi　　huáng　tóufà
　　　that　kid　　　fair　　hair
　　　'That kid has fair hair.'

→ 那 孩子 不 是 黄 头发。
　　nà háizi **bù** **shì** huáng tóufà
　　that kid **NEG** **be** yellow hair
'That kid does not have fair hair.'

(8)' 今天 星期三。 → 今天 不 是 星期三。
　　jīntiān xīngqīsān　　jīntiān **bù** **shì** xīngqīsān
　　today Wednesday　　today **NEG** **be** Wednesday
　　'Today is Wednesday.'　'Today is not Wednesday.'

(9)' 昨天 阴天。 → 昨天 不 是 阴天。
　　zuótiān yīntiān　　zuótiān **bù** **shì** yīntiān
　　yesterday cloudy　　yesterday **NEG** **be** cloudy
　　'It was cloudy yesterday.'　'It was not cloudy yesterday.'

(10)' 我 买 的 榴莲。 → 我 买 的 不 是 榴莲。
　　wǒ mǎi de liúlián　　wǒ mǎi de **bù** **shì** liúlián
　　1SG buy DE durian　　1SG buy DE **NEG** **be** durian
　　'What I bought is durian.'　'What I bought is not durian.'

(11)' 我 从 山城 来 的。
　　wǒ cóng shānchéng lái de
　　1SG from mountain.city come DE
　　'I come from the mountain city.'

→ 我 不 是 从 山城 来 的。
　　wǒ **bù** **shì** cóng shānchéng lái de
　　1SG **NEG** **be** from mountain.city come DE
　　'I am not from the mountain city.'

5.11 Agent Subject Sentences

In this section, we will introduce the three most common sentence patterns from a semantic perspective. The first type is the agent subject sentence, the most common sentence pattern in verb predicate sentences, with the subject being the agent, or actor, of the verb predicate.

(1) 我   画   了   一   个   球。（△含羞草 49）
    wǒ   huà   le   yī   gè   qiú
    1SG draw LE   one CL   ball
    'I drew a ball.' (*Hánxiūcǎo* 49)

(2) 师傅   又   作   了   一   个   手势。（狮子 4）
    shīfu   yòu   zuò   le   yī   gè   shǒushì
    master.worker again do   LE   one CL   gesture
    'The master worker made another gesture.' (*Shīzǐ* 4)

(3) 她   喜欢   里头   的   蜡烛。（梦 98）
    tā   xǐhuān   lǐtóu   de   làzhú
    3SG like   inside   DE   candle
    'She likes the candle in it.' (*Mèng* 98)

(4) 潘先生   终于   接受   了   我   的   请求。（痕迹 115）
    pānxiānshēng zhōngyú   jiēshòu   le   wǒ   de   qǐngqiú
    Mr. Pan   finally   accept   LE   1SG DE   request
    'Mr. Pan finally accepted my request.' (*Hénjì* 115)

(5) 我们   结婚。（跳舞 42）
    wǒmén   jiéhūn
    1PL   get.married
    "We get married.' (*Tiàowǔ* 42)

The basic pattern of an agent-subject sentence is as follows:

Noun(agent) + Verb + Noun(patient)
    1   2   (subject-predicate)
         3   4   (predicate-object)

If the predicate is a transitive verb, the patient of the verb usually comes after it, as in sentences (1) through (4). If the predicate is an intransitive verb, there is no noun after it, as in sentence (5). However, unlike in English, in Singapore Mandarin the patient can be omitted if it has already been mentioned in the previous context. As is evident in sentence (6), 钢笔 *gāngbǐ* 'pen' is already mentioned in Peijuan's question, therefore it is omitted in Lizhen's answer.

(6) 佩娟： 我 可以 借用 你 的 **钢笔** 吗？
　　 pèijuān *wǒ* *kěyǐ* *jièyòng* *nǐ* *de* ***gāngbǐ*** *mā*
　　 Peijuan 1SG can borrow 2SG DE **pen** SFP
　　 Peijuan: Can I borrow your pen?

丽珍： 我 今天 没 带来。（华文教材 1A 66）
lìzhēn *wǒ* *jīntiān* *méi* *dàilái*
Lizhen 1SG today NEG bring
Lizhen: I didn't bring it today. (*Huáwénjiàocái* 1A 66)

In agent subject sentences, the patient often comes after the predicate verb as shown in sentences (1) through (4). However, if the patient expresses a distributive meaning, it is placed before the predicate verb. In this case, adverbs 都 *dōu* 'all' or 也 *yě* 'also' are added before the predicate verb.

(7) 你 **什么** **都** 不要 想。（独上 81）
　　 nǐ ***shénme*** ***dōu*** *búyào* *xiǎng*
　　 2SG **what** **all** NEG think
　　 'You'd better not think about anything.' (*Dúshàng* 81)

(8) 他 索性 **什么** 也 不 想。（牛车水 31）
　　 tā *suǒxìng* ***shénme*** *yě* *bù* *xiǎng*
　　 3SG simply **what** **also** NEG think
　　 'He simply doesn't think about anything.' (*Niúchēshuǐ* 31)

(9) 他 一 个 字 也 听 不 进。（华韵 46）
　　 tā *yī* *gè* *zì* *yě* *tīng* *bú* *jìn*
　　 3SG one CL word also listen NEG inside
　　 'He could not hear a word.' (*Huáyùn* 46)

In (7) and (8), 什么 *shénme* 'what' indicates 'anything'. In (9), 一个字 *yīgèzì* 'one word' indicates 'all the words'. They all indicate a distributive meaning and all of them are the patients of the following predicate verbs.

If the patient does not express a distributive meaning and can not come after the predicate due to grammatical constraints, we can employ the following two methods to place the patient before the predicate verb.

A   Using prepositions.

(10) 我   把   你   打   得   都   流血   了。（撞墙 67）
     wǒ   bǎ   nǐ   dǎ   de   dōu liúxuè le
     1SG BA   2SG beat DE   even bleed   LE
     'I beat you until you bleed.' (*Zhuàngqiáng* 67)

(11) 妈妈   终于   把   钱   接   了   下来。（太阳 68）
     māmā   zhōngyú   bǎ   qián   jiē   le   xiàlái
     Mom   finally   BA   money   take LE   come.down
     'Mom finally accepted the money.' (*Tàiyáng* 68)

(12) 谁   把   死   猫   死   狗   也   丢
     shuí   bǎ   sǐ   māo   sǐ   gǒu   yě   diū
     who   BA   dead   cat   dead   dog   also   drop

     进   垃圾槽？（万花筒 24）
     jìn   lājīcáo
     into   garbage.chute
     'Who dropped dead cats and dogs into the garbage chute?' (*Wànhuātǒng* 24)

B   Repeating the predicate verb to make the patient as the object of the first predicate verb.

(13) 姐姐   管   她   管   得   好   严。（风雨 15）
     jiějie guǎn   tā   guǎn   de   hǎo   yán
     sister discipline   3SG   discipline   DE   very   strict
     'Her sister is very strict with her.' (*Fēngyǔ* 15)

(14) 你   以前   跳   舞   跳   得   十分   好。（吾土·
                                                                 小说上 89）
     nǐ   yǐqián   tiào   wǔ   tiào   de   shífēn   hǎo
     2SG   before   dance   dance dance   DE   extremely   good
     'You used to dance very well before.' (*Wútǔ·xiǎoshuōshàng* 89)

Sentences like (13) can be analysed as follows:

姐姐　　管　　她　　管得好严。

Jiějiě   guǎn   tā   guǎndéhǎoyán

1	2	(subject-predicate)
	3　　4	(subject-predicate)
	5　6	(predicate-object)

5.12 Patient Subject Sentences

The patient subject sentence also belongs to verb predicate sentences. It is called a patient subject sentence when the subject is semanticaly the patient of the predicate verb. According to whether the agent appears in the sentence or not, we can divide the patient subject sentence into two subclasses:

In one subclass, the agent appears in the sentence, after the subject and before the predicate verb.

(1) 漫画　　　**我**　　　最　　　欣赏。（笑眼 218）
    mànhuà　**wǒ**　　*zuì*　　*xīnshǎng*
    comic　　**1SG**　　most　　appreciate
    'I enjoy comics the most.' (*Xiàoyǎn* 218)

(2) 饭菜　　　**我**　　　弄　　　好　　　了。（狮子 5）
    fàncài　**wǒ**　　*nòng*　*hǎo*　*le*
    food　　　**1SG**　　cook　　finish　LE
    'I have cooked the meal.' (*Shīzǐ* 5)

(3) 这　　一　　点　　**我**　　知道。（万花筒 59）
    zhè　*yī*　*diǎn*　**wǒ**　*zhīdào*
    this　one　CL　　**1SG**　know
    'I know this point.' (*Wànhuātǒng* 59)

(4) 你　　　被　　　**他**　　　欺侮　　　了？（金狮奖 169）
    nǐ　　*bèi*　　**tā**　　*qīwǔ*　　*le*
    2SG　　BEI　　**3SG**　　bully　　LE
    'Were you bullied by him?' (*Jīnshījiǎng* 169)

In the other, the agent doesn't appear in the sentence.

(5) 小河　　不见　　了。（报 1995 年 8 月 17 日副刊 12 版）
    xiǎohé bújiàn   le
    stream disappear LE
    'The stream is gone.' (*Bào*, Aug. 17, 1995, supplement edition no. 12)

(6) 款子　　领　　　了　　　没有？（笑眼 54）
    kuǎnzi lǐng   le   méiyǒu
    money   receive LE   NEG
    'Have you received the money yet?' (*Xiàoyǎn* 54)

(7) 她　　　被　　　推　　　倒。（万花筒 38）
    tā   bèi   tuī   dǎo
    3SG   BEI   push   fall
    'She was pushed over.' (*Wànhuātǒng* 38)

There are two characteristics of the patient subject sentence: First, the subjects are always definite. None of the preceding examples is an exception. Second, the predicates are all complex in the sense that they cannot be single verbs.

In English, active sentences and passive sentences use different voices, which is signified by the different forms of the predicates. By contrast, in Singapore Mandarin, the passive sentence does not nessarily have passive markers, and the patient-subject sentence is a kind of passive sentence. In other words, both active and passive sentences can share the same form. Compare the following two sentences.

(8) 我　　吃　　了。
    wǒ   chī   le
    1SG   eat   LE
    'I have eaten (it).'

(9) 鸡蛋　　吃　　了。
    jīdàn   chī   le
    egg   eat   LE
    'The egg are eaten.'

Example (8) is an active sentence. 我 *wǒ* '1SG' is the agent and 吃 *chī* 'eat' is the action. Example (9) is a passive sentence. 鸡蛋 is the patient and 吃 *chī* 'eat' is the action. Their predicates are completely the same, that is, 吃了 *chīle* 'eat'.

There are sentences with overt passive markers like 被 *bèi* 'BEI', as in sentences (4) and (7). However, they only make up a small proportion of passive sentences in Singapore Mandarin and most of them have an adverse meaning. Let's look at the following two sentences.

(10) 汽车　　　撞　　　坏　　　了。
　　　qìchē　*zhuàng*　*huài*　*le*
　　　car　　　crash　　broken　LE
　　　'The car crashed.'

(11) 汽车　　修　　好　　了。
　　　qìchē　*xiū*　*hǎo*　*le*
　　　car　　repair　well　LE
　　　'The car is repaired.'

Both sentences (10) and (11) are in passive voice. Sentence (10) has an adversive meaning. Thus, 被 *bèi* 'BEI' can be added, as shown here.

(10)' 汽车　　**被**　　撞　　　坏　　　了。
　　　qìchē　***bèi***　*zhuàng*　*huài*　*le*
　　　car　　　**BEI**　crash　　broken　LE
　　　'The car crashed.'

By contrast, sentence (11) has a pleasant meaning, so we cannot insert 被 *bèi* 'BEI' into the sentence. Otherwise, the sentence would sound strange.

(11)' *汽车　　**被**　　修　　好　　了。
　　　qìchē　***bèi***　*xiū*　*hǎo*　*le*
　　　car　　　**BEI**　repair　well　LE
　　　'The car is repaired.'

5.13 Distributive Subject Sentences

Distributive subject sentences are a type of subject-predicate sentence in which the subject, in some forms, emphasises that its referent is distributive in nature. For instance:

(1) **任何**　人　　　都　　要　　遵守　　　国家　　　的　　法令。
　　rènhé　*rén*　*dōu*　*yào*　*zūnshǒu*　*guójiā*　*de*　*fǎlìn*
　　any　　person　all　　need　obey　　　country　DE　law
　　'Everyone must abide by the laws of the country.'

(2) 个个   都   意气风发，   斗志昂扬。
    gègè   **dōu** **yìqìfēngfā** **dòuzhìángyáng**
    everybody **all** **full.of.vigour** **full.of.fighting.spirit**
    'Everybody is full of vigour and fighting spirit.'

In sentences (1) and (2), both 任何人 *rènhérén* 'anyone' and 个个 *gègè* 'everyone' refer to all the people within a certain range. Both of them have a referent of distributive meaning. However, the distributive meaning of sentence (1) is obvious as we can see from the use of a lexical word (任何 *rènhé* 'any'), whereas the distributive meaning of sentence (2) is not obvious as it is expressed by grammatical means (duplicated classifier in this case). In this section we will merely focus on sentences with distributive meanings expressed by grammatical means. This type of sentences can be divided into the following three types:

A   The subject position is occupied by an interrogative pronoun, or by a nominal phrase containing an interrogative pronoun that denotes an arbitrary referent like 'anything', 'anyone'.

(3) 什么   都   要，   什么   都   买   不   成。（牛车水 76）
    shénme **dōu** **yào** **shénme** **dōu** **mǎi** **bù** **chéng**
    what   **all** **want** **what** **all** **buy** **NEG** **finish**
    'One can't want everything and buy everything.' (*Niúchēshuǐ 76*)

(4) 什么   都   不   想   做，   什么   都   不   要   想。（独上 81）
    shénme **dōu** **bù** **xiǎng** **zuò** **shénme** **dōu** **bú** **yào** **xiǎng**
    what   **all** **NEG** **want** **do** **what**   **all** **NEG** **want** **think**
    'If you don't want to do anything, don't think about getting anything either.' (*Dúshàng 81*)

(5) 谁   也   不   能   撤销   死亡   的   注册
    shéi **yě** **bú** **néng** **chèxiāo** **sǐwáng** **de** **zhùcè**
    who   **also** **NEG** **can** **cancel** **death** **DE** **registration**

证。（八方 142）
zhèng
certificate
'No one can revoke the death certificate.' (*Bāfāng 142*)

(6) 谁　　　都　　　不　　　爱　　　听。（笑眼 86）
　　shéi　　dōu　　bú　　ai　　ting
　　who　　all　　NEG　　like　　listen
　　'No one likes to listen to it.' (*Xiàoyǎn 86*)

(7) 做　　什么　　工作　　的　　人　　都　　有。
　　zuò　**shénme**　**gōngzuò**　**de**　**rén**　**dōu**　**yǒu**
　　do　　what　　job　　DE　　people　　all　　have
　　'There are people from every walk of life.'

None of the interrogative pronouns here indicate an interrogative question. They all express a free choice of referents. This type of distributive subject sentence may take affirmative form (as the first clause in (3) and the sentence in (7)), as well as negative form (as the second clause in (3) and the sentences in (4) through (6)). The predicate of these sentences contains the adverb 都 *dōu* 'all' or 也 *yě* 'also'.

B The subject position is occupied by duplicative forms of nouns, or classifiers, or a nominal phrase that contains duplicative forms of nouns or classifiers.

(8) 人人　　都　　中　　了　　彩。（笑颜 10）
　　rénrén　dōu　zhòng　le　cǎi
　　everyone　all　win　LE　lottery
　　'Everyone won the lottery.' (*Xiàoyán 10*)

(9) 个个　　真情流露。（一心 125）
　　gègè　　zhēnqíngliúlù
　　everyone　show.true.feelings
　　'Everyone shows their true feelings.' (*Yìxīn 125*)

(10) 条条　　大　　路　　通　　罗马。
　　tiáotiáo　dà　lù　tōng　luómǎ
　　all　　big　road　lead.to　Rome
　　'All roads lead to Rome.'

This type of distributive subject sentence seldom takes negative form. We can use the adverb 都 *dōu* 'all' in the predicate, but no instance of the adverb 也 *yě* 'also' is found in this case.

C The subject position is occupied by a numeral-classifier phrase in which the numeral word is 一 *yī* 'one'.

(11) 一　　　　点　　　　味道　　　也　　　　没有。（金狮奖 226）
　　　yī　　　*diǎn*　　*wèidào*　*yě*　　　*méiyǒu*
　　　one　　　CL　　　taste　　　also　　　not.have
　　　'It has no taste at all.' (*Jīnshījiǎng* 226)

(12) 一　　　　点儿　　　也　　　　不　　　　知道。（华文教材 1A 85）
　　　yī　　　*diǎner*　　*yě*　　　*bù*　　　*zhīdào*
　　　one　　　CL　　　also　　　NEG　　　know
　　　'I don't know it at all.' (*Huáwénjiàocái* 1A 85)

(13) 一　　　　分　　　　钱　　　　也　　　　没有。（青青 80）
　　　yī　　　*fēn*　　　*qián*　　*yě*　　　*méiyǒu*
　　　one　　　CL　　　money　　also　　　not.have
　　　'I don't have any money.' (*Qīngqīng* 80)

This type of distributive subject sentence always takes a negative, not an affirmative, form. The predicate part often contains the adverb 也 *yě* 'also' or 都 *dōu* 'all'. 也 *yě* 'also' in sentences (11) through (13) can be replaced with 都 *dōu* 'all' without changing the meaning.

5.14 Some Special Types of Subject-Predicate Sentences

5.14.1 Verb (Object) + 的 de 'DE' + Verb (Object)

verb (object) + 的 DE + verb (object)
　　　　　―――――――　　―――――――
　　　　　　　　1　　　　　　　2　　　　(subject-predicate)

In this type of sentence, the subject is a DE construction with a verb phrase plus 的 *de* 'DE'. The verb in the DE construction shares the same form as the verb in the predicate position.

(1) 小　　　　屋　　　　里　　　　的　　　　人，　　　走　　　　的　　　　走，
　　　xiǎo　　*wū*　　　*lǐ*　　　*de*　　　*rén*　　　*zǒu*　　*de*　　　*zǒu*
　　　small　　room　　inside　　DE　　　person　　go　　　DE　　　go

死 的 死……（独上 102）
sǐ de sǐ
die DE die

'People in the small room either left or died.' (*Dúshàng* 102)

(2) 布 上 的 花花草草, 笑 的 笑,
bù shàng de huāhuācǎocǎo xiào de xiào
cloth on DE flower.and.grass smile DE smile

摇 的 摇, 全 都 灵活 起来 了。（独上 107）
yáo de yáo quán dōu línghuó qǐlái le
shake DE shake all entirely flexible up LE

'The flower and grass pattern on the cloth, seemed to be smiling and waving, as if alive.' (*Dúshàng* 107)

(3) 他们 大学 毕业 后, 工作 的 工作
tāmen dàxué bìyè hòu gōngzuò de gōngzuò
3PL college graduate after work DE work

留学 的 留学, 很少 到 书店
liúxué de liúxué hěnshǎo dào shūdiàn
study.abroad DE study.abroad seldom go bookstore

里 来 了。（胜利 43）
lǐ lái le
inside come LE

'After they graduated from the college, they worked or studied abroad and seldom came to the bookstore.' (*Shènglì* 43)

There are two points worth noting: First, semantically, this type of subject-predicate sentence indicates a series of narration, the meaning of which roughly correspondes to the sentence pattern with '有的 *yǒude* 'some'. . ., 有的 *yǒude* 'some' . . .'. Thus, it cannot be used for a single sentence, but at least two sentences are required to express a complete meaning. Second, the verb phrase used in this type of sentence can only be a single verb or a simple predicate-object phrase. Here is an illustrative example:

(4) 人群   继而   起   了   一   阵   骚动，
    rénqún jìér   qǐ   le   yī   zhèn sāodòng
    crowd   then   up   LE   one CL   uproar

    喊   的   喊， 叫   的   叫；   有的   不停   地
    hǎn   de hǎn jiào   de jiào   yǒude   bùtíng   de
    yell DE yell call   DE call   some   unceasingly DE

    挥动   着   拳头，   有的   踮   起   脚跟，   拉
    huīdòng zhe   quántóu yǒude diǎn   qǐ   jiǎogēn lā
    wave   ZHE   fist   some   stand.on.tiptoe up   heel   stretch

    拉   长   了   颈项。（吾土·小说上 183）
    lā   cháng le   jǐngxiàng
    stretch long   LE   neck

'Then, there was uproar among the crowd. Some people were shouting, some were crying; some unceasingly waving their fists, some standing on their tiptoes, stretching out their necks to watch.' (*Wútǔ·xiǎoshuōshàng* 183)

Here, the "verb + 的 *de* 'DE' + verb" structure is used for the single verb 喊 *hǎn* 'yell' and 叫 *jiào* 'shout'. In contrast, 不停地挥动着拳头 *bùtíngdehuīdòngzhequántóu* 'keep shaking fists' and 踮起脚跟，拉长了颈项 *diǎnqǐjiǎogēn, lāchánglejǐngxiàng* 'stand on one's tiptoe and stretch one's neck' are all complicated verb phrases, thus the 有的 . . . , 有的 . . . . . . *yǒude* . . . , *yǒude* . . . 'some . . . some . . .' sentence pattern is adopted.

5.14.2 X 是 *'Be'* X (了 *le 'LE'*)

X   是 *shì* X (了)
—   ————
1   2   (subject-predicate)

In this type of sentence, the same words come before and after 是 *shì* 'be'. The word can be a verb, as shown in (5) and (6), or an adjective, as shown in (7). This type of sentence expresses concession and it is always followed by a clause indicating a contrast.

(5) 有   是   有，   只是，   我   学   的   不
    yǒu   shì yǒu   zhǐshì   wǒ   xué   de   bù
    have be   have   but   1SG learn DE   NEG

是 那些。（微型 2）
shì nàxiē
be those

'Yes, there may well be. But, what I have learned are not those.' (*Wēixíng* 2)

(6) 听 是 听 了， 但是 没 听 懂。
tīng shì tīng le dàn méi tīng dǒng
listen be listen LE but NEG listen understand

'I did listen to it, but I couldn't understand.'

(7) (那 衣服) 漂亮 是 漂亮， 就是 太 贵 了。
nà yīfu piàoliàng shì piàoliàng jiùshì tài guì le
that dress pretty be pretty just too expensive LE

'That dress may be pretty, but it is too expensive.'

5.14.3 Noun + 是 shì 'Be' + Noun

noun + 是 shì + noun
  1   2   (subject-predicate)

In this type of sentence, the nouns before and after 是 *shì* 'be' are also identical. Generally, this type of sentence is not used as a single sentence either. It is common to use two together, usually emphasising the difference between two things.

(8) 嗨呀， 文艺 是 文艺， 生意 是 生意。（吾土・小说上 114）
hēiya wényì shì wényì shēngyì shì shēngyì
hey art be art business be business

'Hey, art is art and business is business.' (*Wútǔ·xiǎoshuōshàng* 114)

(9) 从前 是 从前， 现在 是 现在……（想飞 134）
cóngqián shì cóngqián xiànzài shì xiànzài
past be past now be now

'The past is the past and now is now.' (*Xiǎngfē*, 134)

Sentence (8) emphasises that art and business are two different things and sentence (9) can be understood similarly. Sometimes, this type of sentence is used to describe everything being tidy and in order.

(10) | 书房 | 里， | 书 | 是 | 书， | 报纸 | 是 | 报纸，
| *shūfáng* | *lǐ* | *shū* | *shì* | *shū* | *bàozhǐ* | *shì* | *bàozhǐ*
| study | inside | book | be | book | newspaper | be | newspaper

摆放　　　得　　　整整齐齐。
bǎifàng　*de*　*zhěngzhěngqíqí*
put　　　DE　　neat

'In the study, books and newspapers are neatly arranged.'

Notes

1. In Singapore Mandarin, most of the nouns can serve as subjects, except the noun formed by a monosyllabic morpheme representing action plus a suffix 头 *tóu* 'head'. For example, 吃头 *chītóu* 'reason to eat it', 想头 *xiǎngtóu* 'reason to think about it', 看头 *kàntóu* 'reason to watch it' (like 没有什么吃头 *méiyǒu shénme chītóu* 'no reason to eat', 这有什么看头 *zhè yǒu shénme kàntóu* 'there is no reason to watch it').
2. From a functional perspective, reduplicated forms of adjectives in Singapore Mandarin are also stative words.
3. Translator's note: The original meaning of the verb 是 *shì* is 'be'. However, in different contexts, it might be translated into different words as in the following examples.

6 Predicates and Objects

Lu Jianming

6.1 Predicates and Objects in Singapore Mandarin

6.1.1 Differences in Predicates and Objects Between Singapore Mandarin and English

1 Only nouns and nominal phrases can be used as objects in English, while this restriction does not apply to Singapore Mandarin. Nouns and nominal phrases can certainly serve as objects, as is shown in the following examples.

(1) 学   华文（风筝 61）
    xué   **huáwén**
    learn   **Chinese**
    'learn Chinese' (*Fēngzhēng* 61)

(2) 购买   东西（平心 88）
    gòumǎi   **dōngxi**
    buy   **things**
    'buy things' (*Píngxīn* 88)

(3) 做   其他的   事情（华文 53）
    zuò   **qítāde**   **shìqíng**
    do   **other**   **things**
    'do other things' (*Huáwén* 53)

Numeral-classifier phrases can also serve as objects, as in (4) to (6):

(4) 说   了   一   句（金狮奖 135）
    shuō   *le*   *yī*   *jù*
    say   LE   one   CL/sentence
    'said a few words' (*Jīnshījiǎng* 135)

(5) 笑　　　了　　　一　　　　声（万花筒 51）
    xiào   le   yī   shēng
    laugh   LE   one   CL/sound
    'laughed' (*Wànhuātǒng* 51)

(6) 哭　　　了　　　三　　　天　　　三　　　夜（梦 8）
    kū   le   sān   tiān   sān   yè
    cry   LE   three   CL/days three   CL/nights
    'cried for three days and three nights' (*Mèng* 8)

Predicative phrases can also be used as objects, as illustrated in the following examples:

(7) 想　　　　　　　　　偷看（狮子 73）
    xiǎng   tōukàn
    want   peep
    'want to peep' (*Shīzi* 73)

(8) 感到　　　惊悸　　　与　　　　　沉郁（△含羞草 33）
    gǎndào   jīngjì   yǔ   chényù
    feel   shocked   and   depressed
    'feel shocked and depressed' (△ *Hánxiūcǎo* 33)

(9) （心　　　里）　　觉　　　得　　　热乎乎的
    (xīn   lǐ)   jué   de   rèhūhūde
    (heart   inside) feel   DE   warm
    'feel heart-warming'

(10) 听说　　　寒流　　　　　还　　　有　　　两　　　次　　　过境（寻庙 9）
     tīngshuō hánliú   hái   yǒu   liǎng   cì   guòjìng
     hear   cold.current still   YOU   two   CL   pass.the.border
     'It is said that two more cold currents will pass over the country.' (*Xúnmiào* 9)

The object in example (7) is a verb, while in example (8) an adjective phrase, in example (9) a stative word and in example (10) a subject-predicate phrase.

2   In English, the semantic relation between a verb and an object is relatively simple, usually being an action-patient relation. But in Singapore Mandarin,

the semantic relation between a predicate and an object is much more complicated (see Section 6.2).

3 In English, only transitive verbs can take an object; whereas in Singapore Mandarin, apart from transitive verbs, intransitive verbs and even adjectives can also take an object. This can be seen in the following examples.

(11) "最近   她   的   病情   是   不   是   好转   些？"
     zuìjìn   tā   de   bìngqíng   shì   bú   shì   hǎozhuǎn   xiē
     recently 3SG DE   situation be   NEG be   **better** a.little.bit
     'Has her situation got better recently?'

     "好转   什么,   更   严重   了。"
     hǎozhuǎn   shénme   gèng   yánzhòng   le
     better what   more   serious   LE
     'Not at all. She's got worse.'

(12) 她   神气   她   的   我们   不   理   她
     tā   shénqì   tā   de   wǒmén   bù   lǐ   tā
     3SG arrogant 3SG   DE   1PL   NEG   talk.to 3SG

     就是了。（吾土▪戏剧 159）
     jiùshìle
     it.is.fine

     'She can be as arrogant as she wants to be. We can just ignore her.' (*Wútǔ*▪*xìjù* 159)

In example (11), 好转 *hǎozhuǎn* 'better' is an intransitive verb, yet it is followed by an object 什么 *shénme* 'what'. In example (12), 神气 *shénqì* 'arrogant' is an adjective, yet it is followed by an object 她的 *tāde* '3SG DE'. Apparently, there is a difference between these objects and the objects in examples (1), (2) and (3) (for detailed discussion see Section 6.4).

4 Verb phrases can be used as objects in Singapore Mandarin; therefore, an object of a sentence in Singapore Mandarin can be a number of verb-object phrases embedded in different layers. For example:

(13) (苏哈多   总统)   拒绝   见   他。(报 1995 年 8 月 21 日 6 版)
     (sūhāduō   zǒngtǒng)   jùjué   jiàn   tā
     (Suharto   president)   refuse   meet   3SG
     'President Suharto refused to meet him.' (*Bào*, Aug. 21, 1995, Issue no. 6)

(14) （他）　　想　　　　学习　　　驾驶　　　飞机。
　　　 tā　　　xiǎng　　xuéxí　　jiàshǐ　　fēijī
　　　 3SG　　want.to　learn　　fly　　　　airplane

'He wants to learn to fly an airplane.'

Example (14) can be analysed as follows.

（他）　想　　学习　　驾驶　　飞机
(tā)　　xiǎng　xuéxí　jiàshǐ　fēijī

1	2		(subject-predicate)
3	4		(predicate-object)
	5	6	(predicate-object)
		7 8	(predicate-object)

Clearly the relationship between a predicate and an object in Singapore Mandarin cannot be fully explained with the verb-object concepts in English.

6.1.2 Objects in Singapore Mandarin

1 It should be noted that in Singapore Mandarin, the subject of a sentence tends to be definite (someone or something already known to both the speaker and the listener) while the object of a sentence tends to be indefinite (someone or something yet unknown). Compare the following two pairs.

(15) a　**客人**　　来　　　了。
　　　 kèrén　lái　　　le
　　　 guest　arrive　　LE
　　　 'The guest has arrived.'

(15) b　来　　　**客人**　　了。
　　　 lái　　　**kèrén**　　le
　　　 arrive　**guest**　　LE
　　　 'Here comes a guest.'

(16) a　**书**　　买　　　了。
　　　 shū　mǎi　　　le
　　　 book　buy　　　LE
　　　 'The book has been bought.'

(16) b （我）   买   书   了。
         (wǒ)   mǎi   **shū**   le
         (1SG)   buy   **book**   LE
   'I've bought a book.'

客人 *kèrén* 'guest' in sentence (15a) is in the subject position, and the reference of the guest is definite. 客人 *kèrén* 'guest' in sentence (15b) is in the object position, and the reference is indefinite. If both the speaker and the listener know in advance that a guest is coming, then the speaker will surely use sentence (15a) to express the arrival of the guest. If neither the speaker nor the listener is expecting a guest and somehow a guest has arrived, then sentence (15b) will be appropriate to describe the information. 书 *shū* 'book' in sentence (16a) is used as a subject with a definite reference. 书 *shū* 'book' in sentence (16b) is used as an object, implying an indefinite reference. Sentence (16a) is used only if both the speaker and the listener know in advance what book should be bought, whereas sentence (16b) is appropriate if the listener does not know what book the speaker is buying.

2 Sometimes, the objects can also be definite. In this case, the object nouns usually include the following four types.

   A Proper nouns

(17) 我   同情   拉莫斯   总统。（报 1995 年
                                              8 月 21 日 6 版）
     wǒ   tóngqíng   **lāmòsī**   **zǒngtǒng**
     1SG   sympathise   **Ramos**   **president**
   'I sympathise with President Ramos.' (*Bào*, Aug. 21, 1995, Issue no. 6)

   B Personal pronouns

(18) 他   老是   缠   着   我。（△含羞草 33）
     tā   lǎoshì   chán   zhe   **wǒ**
     3SG   always   pester   ZHE   **1SG**
   'He keeps pestering me.' (△*Hánxiūcǎo* 49)

   C Nouns indicating kinship

(19) 这   一   声，   惊醒   了   母亲。（狮子 73）
     zhè   yī   shēng,   jīngxǐng   le   **mǔqīn**
     this one   CL/sound   awaken   LE   **mother**
   'The sound awakened mother.' (*Shīzi* 73)

D   A modifier-head phrase containing a restrictive attribute

(20) 我   舍不得   这   个   公园。（风雨 8）
      wǒ   shěbùdé   zhè   gè   gōngyuán
      1SG   feel.attached.to this   CL   park

'I feel attached to this park.' (*Fēngyǔ* 8)

The following sections will introduce the objects and the predicates. Verbs will be examined from the perspective of their objects.

6.2   Nominal Objects

As has been discussed earlier, objects in Singapore Mandarin are not restricted to nominal phrases. Predicative phrases can also be used as objects. Hence we can divide objects into two categories, nominal objects and predicative objects (see Section 5.3). This section will focus on nominal objects.

6.2.1 *Nominal Phrases as Objects*

A   Nouns used as objects

(1)   造就   英才（薪传 5）
      zàojiù   yīngcái
      cultivate   talents

'cultivate talents' (*Xīnchuán* 5)

(2)   学习   华文（文艺 6）
      xuéxí   huáwén
      learn   Chinese

'learn Chinese' (*Wényì* 6)

B   Nominal phrases used as objects

(3)   啃   白   面包（青青 90）
      kěn   bái   miànbāo
      eat   white   bread

'eat white bread' (*Qīngqīng* 90)

(4)   作   了   一   个   手势（狮子 4）
      zuò   le   yī   gè   shǒushì
      make   LE   one   CL   gesture

'made a gesture' (*Shīzi* 4)

(5) 买　　　电视机、　　录影机、　　大　　收音机（撞墙 27）
　　 mǎi　　 diànshìjī　　 lùyǐngjī　　 dà　 shōuyīnjī
　　 buy　　 television　　 recorder　　 big　 radio
　　 'buy televisions, tape recorders and big radios' (Zhuàngqiáng 27)

C　Nominal pronouns used as objects

(6) 叫　　　　　住　　　　　他（太阳 29）
　　 jiào　　　　 zhù　　　　 tā
　　 call　　　　 stop　　　　 3SG
　　 'called him' (Tàiyáng 29)

(7) 帮助　　　　我们（晚上 150）
　　 bāngzhù　　 wǒmen
　　 help　　　　 1PL
　　 'help us' (Wǎnshàng 150)

(8) 唱　　　　 什么　　　　呢？（笑眼 142）
　　 chàng　　　 shénme　　　 ne
　　 sing　　　　 what　　　　 SFP
　　 'What are you singing?' (Xiàoyǎn 142)

D　的 de 'DE' phrases used as objects

(9) 还　　 有　　 更　　 好看　　 的（牛车水 48）
　　 hái　　 yǒu　　 gèng　　 hǎokàn　　 de
　　 still　　 have　　 more　　 beautiful　　 DE
　　 'there are things even more beautiful' (Niúchēshuǐ 48)

(10)（你）　 吃　　 我　　 的，　 穿　　 我　　 的......（跳舞 50）
　　 (nǐ)　　 chī　　 wǒ　　 de,　　 chuān　　 wǒ　　 de...
　　 (2SG)　 eat　　 1SG　　 DE　　 wear　　 1SG　　 DE...
　　 '(You) eat my food and wear my clothes...' (Tiàowǔ 50)

的 de 'DE' phrases can be used as objects of the verb 有 yǒu 'have', forming a predicate-object structure 有 yǒu... 的 de... 'people who.../something that ...', which, if used in conjunctions, means narrations of various people or situations. The following is an example.

(11) 这些   投石问路   的， 几乎   全   是   吉普赛人
    zhèxiē tóushíwènlù   de,   jīhū   quán shì   jípǔsàirén
    these   inquire   DE   almost all   be   Gypsies

    ——有   单枪匹马   的， 有   纠朋结党   的，
    ----yǒu dānqiāngpǐmǎ   de,   yǒu   jiūpéngjiédǎng   de,
    ----have work.on.their.own   DE   have   work.in.groups   DE

    也   有   怀抱   着   婴儿   的。（石头 33）
    yě   yǒu   huáibào   zhe   yīngér   de
    also   have   carry   ZHE   babies   DE.

    'Those who inquired were almost all Gypsies. There were people who worked on their own, who worked in groups, and who carried babies in their arms.' (*Shítóu* 33)

6.2.2 Classification of Nominal Objects

The semantic relations between the nominal objects and the predicates are diversified. The following are some common types of nominal objects classified according to their semantic relations with the predicates.

1   Accusative objects (objects being the recipients of the actions described by the predicate verbs)

(12) a   喜欢   《小坡   的   生日》（△中国作家 29）
         xǐhuān   xiǎopō   de   shēngrì
         like   Xiaopo   DE   birthday
         'like *Xiaopo's Birthday*' (△*Zhōngguózuòjiā* 29)

     b   包扎   伤口（沦陷 55 ）
         bāozhā   shāngkǒu
         put.a.bandage.on   wound
         'put a bandage on the wound' (*Lúnxiàn* 55)

(13) a   写   游记（游踪《序》）
         xiě   yóujì
         write   travelling.journal
         'write a travelling journal' (*Yóuzōng* Preface)

b 煮　　　　　粥（再见 27）
　zhǔ　　　　zhōu
　cook　　　 porridge
　'make porridge' (*Zàijiàn* 27)

The objects in examples (12) and (13) are all accusative objects but there are some slight differences between them. The objects in example (12) refer to things that already exist before the action, which can be affected by actions indicated by the predicate verbs, while the object things in example (13) do not exist before the action and they are the results of the actions described by the verbs. The former can be described as target object and the latter result object.

2　Dative objects (objects being the recipients of giving verbs)

(14)　递　　　　给　　　　她（狮子 126）
　　　 dì　　　 gěi　　　 tā
　　　 pass　　 to　　　 3SG
　　　 'pass to her' (*Shīzi* 126)

(15)　告诉　　　不　　　　吸烟者（华文教材 4B 8）
　　　 gàosù　　bù　　　　xīyānzhě
　　　 tell　　　NEG　　　 smokers
　　　 'tell non-smokers' (*Huáwénjiāocái* 4B 8)

3　Agentive objects (objects being the agents of actions described by the predicate verbs)

(16)　（门　　一　　　打开，）冲　　　进来　　　一　　　个
　　　(mén　 yī　　　 dǎkāi,) chōng　 jìnlái　　 yī　　 gè
　　　(door　 once　　open,)　dash　　 come.in　 one　 CL

　　　怒气冲冲的　　　　中年　　　　妇女。（短篇 79）
　　　nùqìchōngchōngde　zhōngnián　 fùnǚ
　　　angry　　　　　　 middle-aged woman
　　　'(Once the door opened,) an angry middle-aged woman dashed in.' (*Duǎnpiān* 79)

(17)　忽然　　　来　　 了　　一　　批　　便衣　　　警探　　　　和
　　　 hūrán　　 lái　　le　　yī　　pī　　biànyī　　 jǐngtàn　　 hé
　　　 suddenly　come　LE　 one　 CL　undercover　detectives　and

警察。（短篇17）
jǐngchá
policemen
'All of a sudden an army of undercover detectives and policemen showed up.' (*Duǎnpiān* 17)

4   Instrument objects (objects being the instruments used to support the actions described by the predicate verbs)

(18) 一同   吃   **饭**   **盒子**（独上79）
     yìtóng   *chī*   *fàn*   *hézi*
     together   eat   **lunch**   **box**
     'have a packed lunch together' (*Dúshàng* 79)

(19) 我   不会   写   **毛笔**,
     wǒ   *búhuì*   *xiě*   *máobǐ*
     1SG   cannot   write   **brush**

     我   只   会   写   **钢笔**   **或**   **圆珠笔**。
     wǒ   *zhǐ*   *huì*   *xiě*   *gāngbǐ*   *huò*   *yuánzhūbǐ*
     1SG   only   can   write   **pen**   **or**   **ballpoint.pen**
     'I cannot write with a brush. I can only write with a pen or a ballpoint pen.'

5   Manner objects (objects indicating manners of the actions described by the predicate verbs)

For example, 走正步 *zǒuzhèngbù* 'walk in parade steps' means to walk in the way of parade steps and 正步 *zhèngbù* 'parade steps' is the manner object of 走 *zǒu* 'walk'.

(20) 他们   在   跳   **迪斯科**。
     tāmen   *zài*   *tiào*   *dísīkē*
     3PL   are   dance   **Disco**
     'They are dancing Disco.'

(21) 那   钱   我   想   存   **定期**。
     nà   *qián*   *wǒ*   *xiǎng*   *cún*   *dìngqī*
     That   money   1SG   want   put   **fixed-term**
     'I want to put that money into a deposit account.'

(22) 练   马步（狮子 3）
     liàn   ***mǎbù***
     practise   **horse stance**
     'practise horse stance' (*Shīzi* 3)

In example (20), 迪斯科 *dísīkē* 'Disco' is the way they dance; in example (21), 定期 *dìngqī* 'fixed-term' specifies the manner of saving money; in example (22), 练马步 *liànmǎbù* means practising Kung Fu according to the gestures of horse stance. Hence, 迪斯科 *dísīkē* 'Disco', 定期 *dìngqī* 'fixed-term' and 马步 *mǎbù* 'horse stance' are all manner objects of the verbs 跳 *tiào* 'dance', 存 *cún* 'save' and 练 *liàn* 'practise' respectively.

6   Place objects (objects being the places of the actions described by the predicate verbs)

(23) 留学   日本（独上 53）
     liúxué   ***rìběn***
     study.abroad   **Japan**
     'study in Japan' (*Dúshàng* 53)

(24) （叫   我）   睡   地上（再见 14）
     (*jiào*   *wǒ*)   *shuì*   ***dìshàng***
     (tell   1SG)   sleep   **on.the.floor**
     '(tell me to) sleep on the floor' (*Zàijiàn* 14)

(25) 离开   书房（独上 46）
     líkāi   ***shūfáng***
     leave   **study**
     'leave the study' (*Dúshàng* 46)

(26) （她   带   着   孩子）   回去   美国。（大胡子 10）
     (*tā*   *dài*   *zhe*   *háizi*)   *huíqù*   ***měiguó***
     (3SG   took   ZHE   children)   return   **America**
     '(She took the children) back to America.' (*Dàhúzi* 101)

In example (23) 日本 *rìběn* 'Japan' indicates where to study; in example (24) 地上 *dìshàng* 'on the floor' indicates the place 我 *wǒ* 'I' sleep; in example (25) 书房 *shūfáng* 'study' is the starting point of departure and in example (26) 美国 *měiguó* 'America' expresses the return destination. Therefore, 日本 *rìběn* 'Japan', 地上 *dìshàng* 'on the floor', 书房 *shūfáng* 'study', 美国 *měiguó*

'America' are the place objects of 留学 *liúxué* 'study abroad', 睡 *shuì* 'sleep', 离开 *líkāi* 'leave', 回去 *huíqù* 'return' respectively.

7 Causative objects

The predicate-object phrase with a causative object denotes a causation, which entails the meaning of making something happen. The "verb + noun" predicate-object phrase actually expresses the meaning of "make + noun + verb". For instance, 方便顾客 *fāngbiàngùkè* expresses the same meaning as 使顾客方便 *shǐgùkèfāngbiàn* 'to make things convienient for customers'. Following are more examples.

(27) 丰富　　你　　的　　知识（独上 47）
　　　fēngfù　*nǐ*　*de*　*zhīshi*
　　　rich　　2SG　DE　knowledge
　　　'enrich your knowledge/make your knowledge rich' (*Dúshàng* 47)

(28) （天气　温暖　得　可以）融化　人　　的　心。（独上 55）
　　　(*tiānqì*　*wēnnuǎn*　*de*　*kěyǐ*)　*rónghuà*　*rén*　*de*　*xīn*
　　　(weather　warm　DE　can)　melt　people　DE　heart
　　　'(The weather is so warm that it can) melt people's heart.' (*Dúshàng* 55)

In example (27), 丰富你的知识 *fēngfù nǐ de zhīshi* literally says "rich your knowledge", meaning the same as "使你的知识丰富 *shǐ nǐ de zhīshi fēngfù* 'to make your knowledge rich'. In example (28), 融化人的心 *rónghuà rén de xīn* literally says "melt people's heart", meaning the same as 使人的心融化 *shǐ rén de xīn rónghuà* 'to make people's heart melt'. Here, 你的知识 *nǐdezhīshi* 'your knowledge' and 人的心 *réndexīn* 'people's heart' are the causative objects of 丰富 *fēngfù* 'enrich' and 融化 *rónghuà* 'melt' respectively.

8 Linked objects

A linked object is the object of a linking verb. The object and the subject, connected by the verb, are either equivalent or of the relationship between class and individual.

(29) 这位　　　是　　　杨铭。（金狮奖 69）
　　　zhèwèi　*shì*　*yángmíng*
　　　This　　　be　　　Yang.Ming
　　　'This is Yang Ming.' (*Jīnshījiǎng* 69)

(30) 我   是   华人！（风雨 104）
    wǒ   shì   **huárén**
    1SG   be   **Chinese**
    'I am Chinese!' (*Fēngyǔ* 104)

In example (29), 杨铭 *yángmíng* 'Yang Ming' is equivalent to 这位 *zhèwèi* 'this'. In example (30), the reference of the object 华人 *huárén* 'Chinese' and that of the subject 我 *wǒ* '1SG' are of class and individual relation. Therefore, 杨铭 *yángmíng* 'Yang Ming' and 华人 *huárén* 'Chinese' are both linked objects. The objects in the following examples are also linked objects.

(31) 朱穆朗   活像   个   小   老头。（金狮奖 69）
    zhūmǔláng   huóxiàng   gè   **xiǎo**   **lǎotóu**
    Zhu.Mulang   just.like   CL   **little** **old.man**
    'Zhu Mulang is just like a little old man.' (*Jīnshījiǎng* 69)

(32) 写词   的   频率   等于   零。（华文 130）
    xiěcí   de   pínlǜ   děngyú   **líng**
    write.poems DE   frequency   equal   **zero**
    'The frequency of writing poems is zero.' (*Huáwén* 130)

(33) 成为   一   个   有道德、   有学问   的   人。（伦理•中三 53）
    chéngwéi yí   gè   yǒudàodé   yǒuxuéwèn   de   rén
    become   a   CL   ethical   knowledgeable   DE   man
    'become an ethical and knowledgeable man' (*Lúnlǐ•zhōngsān* 53)

From what has been discussed so far, it can be concluded that one grammatical structure may represent several different semantic structures.

6.2.3 Insertion of 了 le 'LE' Between a Predictive Verb and a Nominal Object

In general, 了 *le* 'LE' can be inserted between a predictive verb and a nominal object, as is shown in the following two examples.

(34) （在   波兰   旅行，）   发现   了   一   个   很
    (zài   bōlán   lǚxíng)   fāxiàn   **le**   yí   gè   hěn
    (at   Poland   travel)   find   **LE** a   CL   very

奇特的　　　　　　　现象......（石头 73）
qítède　　　　　　　xiànxiàng
strange　　　　　　　phenomenon

'When travelling in Poland, (I) found a very strange phenomenon' (*Shítóu* 73)

(35) （舅舅）　买　　了　　一　　艘　　小　　皮艇。（寻庙 26）
　　　(jiùjiu)　mǎi　**le**　yī　sōu　xiǎo　pítǐng
　　　(uncle)　buy　**LE**　a　CL　small　yacht

'(Uncle) bought a small yacht.' (*Xúnmiào* 26)

However, it should be noted that when 了 *le* 'LE' is inserted between a single verb and a single noun, this predicate-object phrase cannot stand alone as a sentence, even if with a subject. For example, 吃榴莲 *chī liúlián* 'eat durian' is made up of a single verb 吃 *chī* 'eat' and a single noun 榴莲 *liúlián* 'durian' and can be realised as a sentence, as demonstrated in the following example.

(36) 甲：　你　　在　　吃　　什么？
　　　A:　nǐ　　zài　　chī　　shénme
　　　A:　2SG　be　　eat　　what

A: 'What are you eating?'

　　　乙：　吃　　榴莲。
　　　B:　chī　　liúlián
　　　B:　eat　　durian

B: 'Durian.'

But when 了 *le* 'LE' is inserted, the phrase （我）吃了榴莲 (*wǒ*)*chīle liúlián* '(1SG) ate durian' cannot stand alone as a sentence. It can only serve as a clause, usually being followed by other clauses.

(37) 我　　吃　　了　　榴莲，　又　　吃　　了　　山竹。
　　　wǒ　chī　**le**　liúlián　yòu　chī　**le**　shānzhú
　　　1SG　eat　**LE**　durian　and　eat　**LE**　mangosteen

'I ate some durian and then ate some mangosteen.'

(38) 吃　　了　　榴莲，　我　　就　　回　　家　　了。
　　　chī　**le**　liúlián　wǒ　jiù　huí　jiā　le
　　　eat　**LE**　durian　1SG　then　go.back　home　LE

'I ate some durian and then went back home.'

There are three ways to make it into a sentence expressing the meaning of eating durian. The first method is to add a classifier before the noun. See the following examples.

(39) a （我）   吃   了   一   个   榴莲。
        (wǒ)   chī   **le** yí   gè   liúlián
        (1SG)   eat   **LE** one   CL   durian
        '(I) ate a durian.'

(39) b 要   了   一   公斤   鲱鱼。（石头 125）
        yào   **le**   yī   gōngjīn   fēiyú
        ask   **LE**   one   CL/kilogram   herring
        'asked for one kilogram of herring' (*Shítóu* 125)

The second method is to add 了 *le* 'LE' after the noun, that is, after the whole predicate-object phrase.

(40) a （我）   吃   了   榴莲   了。
        (wǒ)   chī   le   liúlián   **le**
        (1SG)   eat   LE   durian   **LE**
        '(I) ate some durian.'

(40) b 调子   转   了   腔调   啦1。（笑眼 155）
        diàozi   zhuǎn   le   qiāngdiào   **lā**
        melody   change   LE   tone   **SFP**
        'The melody changed its tone.' (*Xiàoyǎn* 155)

The third method is to add adverbs like 都 *dōu* 'all/both', 也 *yě* 'also' before the verb, that is, before the whole predicate-object phrase. But in this case, the sentence has to have a subject. See the following two examples.

(41) a 他们   **都**   吃   了   榴莲。
        tāmen   **dōu**   chī   le   liúlián
        3PL   **all**   eat   LE   durian
        'They all ate durian.'

(41) b 人人   **都**   中   了   彩，   发   了   财。（笑眼 10）
        rénrén   **dōu**   zhòng   le   cǎi   fā   le   cái
        people   **all**   win   LE   lottery make   LE   fortune
        'All the people won lotteries and made a fortune.' (*Xiàoyǎn* 10)

(42) a 我   也   吃   了   榴莲。
        wǒ   yě   chī   le   liúlián
        1SG   also   eat   LE   durian
        'I also ate durian.'

(42) b 正平   也   使   了   眼色。（金狮奖 252）
        Zhèngpíng   yě   shǐ   le   yǎnsè
        Zhengping   also   give   LE   wink
        'Zhengping also winked.' (Jīnshījiǎng 252)

In addition, if 都 dōu 'all/both' is added, the subject of the sentence has to be a plural personal pronoun or a common noun with plural meanings.

6.2.4 Omission of the Numeral 一 yī 'One' in a Numeral-Classifier-Noun Object Phrase

In a numeral-classifier-noun object phrase, if the numeral is 一 yī 'one' and the speaker does not want to emphasise the quantity, then it is often omitted, especially in spoken language. See the following example.

(43) 我   妈   以前   生   了   个   孩子
     wǒ   mā   yǐqián   shēng   le   gè   háizi
     1SG   mother   long.ago   give.birth.to   LE   CL   child

     ——   不   是   怪胎......（笑眼 195）
     ----   bú   shì   guàitāi
     ----   NEG   be   weirdo
     'My mother gave birth to a child – not a weirdo.' (Xiàoyǎn 195)

In the preceding example, 生了个孩子 shēng le gè háizi 'gave birth to child' is a simplified way of saying 生了一个孩子 shēng le yī gè háizi 'gave birth to one child'. Other examples follow.

(44) 我们   去   吃   碗   猪肉   粥。（风雨 25）
     wǒmen   qù   chī   wǎn   zhūròu   zhōu
     1PL   go   eat   bowl   pork   porridge
     'Let's go and have some pork porridge.' (Fēngyǔ 25)

(45) 临睡   前，   做   点   运动，   喝   点   牛奶
     línshuì   qián,   zuò   diǎn   yùndòng   hē   diǎn   niúnǎi
     sleep   before   do   some   exercise   drink   some   milk

	能	帮助	你	入睡，	试试看，	好吗？（狮子 37）
	néng	bāngzhù	nǐ	rùshuì	shìshikàn	hǎoma
	can	help	2SG	sleep	have.a.try	okay

'Do some exercise and drink some milk before you go to sleep. It can help you fall asleep. Have a try, won't you?' (*Shīzi* 37)

(46) 杨铭　　用　　手　　比　　了　　个　　好不辛苦的
　　　Yángmíng yòng shǒu bǐ le ge hǎobùxīnkǔde
　　　Yang Ming use hand make LE CL tired

表情。（金狮奖 106）
biǎoqíng
expression

'Yang Ming made a gesture with his hand to show he was very tired.' (*Jīnshījiǎng* 106)

(47) 索性　　做　　个　　顺水人情　　　吧。（追云 114）
　　　suǒxìng zuò ge shùnshuǐrénqíng ba
　　　Just do CL favour SFP

'Just do a favour.' (*Zhuīyún* 114)

In examples (44) through (47), 一 *yī* 'one' can be added before 碗 *wǎn* 'bowl', 点 *diǎn* 'some' and 个 *gè* 'CL' while the meaning of each sentence remains unchanged.

6.3 Predicative Objects

Predicative objects refer to objects that are made up of predicative phrases. Types of predicative objects are as follows.

A   Verb phrases are used as objects.

(1)　（我）　　　　想　　　　　洗澡。（女儿 99）
　　　(wǒ)　　　　xiǎng　　　　xǐzǎo
　　　(1SG)　　　　want　　　　 take.a.bath

'(I) want to take a bath.' (*Nǚér* 99)

(2) 怕　　得罪　　了　　这　　个　　媳妇。（追云 26）
　　pà dézuì le zhè ge xífù
　　afraid offend LE this CL daughter-in-law

'afraid of offending the daughter-in-law' (*Zhuīyún* 26)

(3) 不　　　肯　　　放　　我　　回　　新加坡。（风雨 31）
　　bù　　*kěn*　　*fàng*　*wǒ*　*huí*　*xīnjiāpō*
　　NEG　willing　let　1SG　return　Singapore
　'not willing to let me return to Singapore' (*Fēngyǔ* 31)

B　Adjective phrases are used as objects.

(4) 觉得　　　　　饿（风雨 25）
　　juéde　　　　*è*
　　feel　　　　　hungry
　'feel hungry' (*Fēngyǔ* 25)

(5) （心中　　的　　期待）　夹杂　　着　　不安。（女儿 12）
　　(*xīnzhōng*　*de*　*qīdài*)　*jiāzá*　*zhe*　*bùān*
　　(in.heart　DE　anticipation)　mixed　ZHE　uneasiness
　'(mixed with anticipation) was a sense of uneasiness' (*Nǚér* 12)

(6) 感到　　　　不　　　　舒服（风雨 27）
　　gǎndào　　*bù*　　　*shūfu*
　　feel　　　　NEG　　　comfortable
　'feel uncomfortable' (*Fēngyǔ* 27)

(7) 更　　　　显得　　　宁静（太阳 3）
　　gèng　　*xiǎnde*　*níngjìng*
　　more　　seem　　　tranquil
　'seems more tranquil' (*Tàiyáng* 3)

C　Stative words are used as objects. This usually occurs in spoken language.

(8) （她）　　　喜欢　　　热热闹闹的。
　　(*tā*)　　　*xǐhuān*　*rèrènàonàode*
　　(3SG)　　like　　　noisy
　'She likes to be in a place bustling with noise and excitement.'

(9) （心　　　里）　　觉得　　　热乎乎的。
　　(*xīn*　　*lǐ*)　　*juéde*　　*rèhūhūde*
　　(heart　inside)　feel　　　warm
　'feel warm (inside the heart)'

Predicates and Objects

D Subject-predicate phrases are used as objects.

(10) 看见　　　　麦先生　　　　疾步　　　　　走来（追云 18）
　　　kànjiàn　　màixiānshēng　jíbù　　　　　zǒulái
　　　see　　　　Mr. Mai　　　　fast　　　　　walk.over

　　'see Mr. Mai walking over quickly' (*Zhuīyún* 18)

(11) 知道　　你　　　在　　大学　　里　　　馋坏　　　了（太阳 20）
　　　zhīdào　nǐ　　　zài　dàxué　lǐ　　　chánhuài le
　　　know　　2SG　　in　　college　inside　tempted　LE

　　'know you are tempted by the food in college' (*Tàiyáng* 20)

(12)（我）　　觉得　　我　　　受　　　　的　　委屈　　　　实在
　　　(wǒ)　　juéde　wǒ　　shòu　　　de　　wěiqu　　　shízài
　　　(1SG)　　feel　　1SG　experience　DE　injustice　　really

　　太　　　　　大　　　　　　了。（万花筒 51）
　　tài　　　　dà　　　　　　le
　　too　　　　much　　　　　LE

　　'(I) felt I had been so wronged.' (*Wànhuātǒng* 51)

Predicative objects describe the specific contents or details of the actions, feelings or aspirations expressed by the predicate verbs. So semantically speaking, predicative objects describe contents or propositions.

了 *le* 'LE' cannot be inserted between a predicate verb and a predicative object. For example, we do not say:

(1)　*（我）　　想　　　　了　　　　洗澡
　　　* (wǒ)　　xiǎng　　　le　　　　xǐzǎo
　　　* (1SG)　　want　　　LE　　　　take.a.bath

(2)　*觉得　　　了　　　　饿
　　　* juéde　　le　　　　è
　　　* feel　　　LE　　　　hungry

(8)　*喜欢　　　了　　　　热热闹闹的
　　　* xǐhuān　　le　　　　rèrènàonàode
　　　* like　　　LE　　　　noisy

(10) | *看见 | 了 | 麦先生 | 疾步 | 走来
| * kànjiàn | le | màixiānshēng | jíbù | zǒulái
| * see | LE | Mr. Mai | fast | walk

6.4 Objects and Quasi-objects

The objects in Singapore Mandarin can be classified into two types, objects (or regular objects) and quasi-objects, as is the case in Chinese Mandarin. The nominal objects and predicative objects discussed in previous sections are both regular objects. In this section we will first introduce quasi-objects and then compare them with regular objects.

6.4.1 Quasi-objects

The following three types of quasi-objects are most commonly seen in Singapore Mandarin.

1 什么 *shénme* 'what' can be used as a quasi-object, and in this case it does not have a particular reference. Compare the following two examples.

(1) | 有 | 了 | 一 | 百万， | 可以 | 做 | **什么**？（再见 55）
| *yǒu* | *le* | *yī* | *bǎiwàn* | *kěyǐ* | *zuò* | ***shénme***
| have | LE | one | million | can | do | what

'With one million, what can we do?' (*Zàijiàn* 55)

(2) | 看 | **什么** | 看！ | 老家 | 上星期 | 就拆掉了，
| *kàn* | ***shénme*** | *kàn* | *Lǎojiā* | *shàngxīngqī* | *jiùchāidiàole,*
| look | what | look | the.old.house | last.week | has.been.pulled.down

| 所有 | 的 | 邻居 | 也 | 都 | 搬走 | 了啦！（再见 29）
| *suǒyǒu* | *de* | *línjū* | *yě* | *dōu* | *bānzǒu* | *lelā*
| all | DE | neighbours | also | all | move | SFP

'What are you looking at? The old house has been pulled down last week and all the neighbours have moved away.' (*Zàijiàn* 29)

The interrogative pronoun 什么 *shénme* 'what' is the object of verb 做 *zuò* 'do' in example (1) and the object of verb 看 *kàn* 'look' in example (2). However, what merits our attention is that 什么 *shénme* 'what' indicates a real inquiry and has specific reference in example (1), but not in example (2). The whole predicative-object phrase 看什么 *kànshénme* 'look at what' implies a negative denotation, meaning 'stop looking' or 'no need to look around'. Thus, 什么 *shénme* 'what' is a regular object in (1), a quasi-object in (2). Other examples of quasi-objects are as follows.

(3) 去   **什么**！   回家   吧！（再见 71）
    qù   **shénme**   huíjiā   ba
    go   **where**   go.home   SFP
    'Do not go there! Go home!' (*Zàijiàn* 71)

(4) 怕   **什么**！   路   有   的   是！（金狮奖 261）
    Pà   **shénme**   lù   yǒu   de   shì
    afraid.of **what** roads have   DE   be
    'Don't be afraid. There are lots of roads.' (*Jīnshījiǎng* 261)

2 它 *tā* 'it' (sometimes written as 他 *tā* 'he') without a particular reference, is used as a quasi-object. Compare the following two examples.

(5) 长大   以后，   越来越   觉得   钥匙   这   玩意儿
    zhǎngdà   yǐhòu,   yuèláiyuè   juéde   yàoshi   zhè   wányir
    grow.up   later,   more.and.more   feel   key   this   small.thing

    不   讨人怜了......   一旦   忘   了   带   **它**   出门，
    bù   tǎorénliánle   yīdàn   wàng   le   dài   **tā**   chūmén
    NEG   lovely   once   forget   LE   take   **3SG** go.out

    或是   遗失   了   **它**，   一   整   天   的   生活规律
    huòshì   yíshī   le   **tā**,   yī   zhěng   tiān   de   shēnghuóguīlǜ
    or   lose   LE   **3SG**   a   whole   day   DE   plan

    就   大大地   受到   破坏   了。（牛车水 112）
    jiù   dàdàde   shòudào   pòhuài   le
    then   greatly   get   destroyed   LE

    'As I grow older, I have this increasingly strong feeling that keys are kind of annoying. Once you forget to take them with you or you lose them, your whole day will be almost ruined.' (*Niúchēshuǐ* 12)

(6) 兴许，   今晚   真该   喝上   几   盅   了，   他   想。
    xīngxǔ, jīnwǎn   zhēngāi   hēshàng   jǐ   zhōng   le,   tā   xiǎng
    maybe   tonight   should   drink   several   cups   LE   3SG   think

    对呐，   干脆   就   喝   **它**   个   迷迷糊糊......（太阳11）
    duìnà,   gāncuì   jiù   hē   **tā**   gè   mímíhuhú...
    yes   just   then   drink   **3SG** CL   feel.drowsy

    'Maybe I should really drink several cups tonight, he thinks. Yes, I can just drink until I feel drowsy.' (*Tàiyáng* 11)

In example (5), the object 它 *tā* 'it' following the verb 带 *dài* 'take' and the verb 遗失 *yíshī* 'lose' both refer to the 'key', something real and mentioned before, and thus they are regular objects. In contrast, the object 它 *tā* 'it' following the verb 喝 *hē* 'drink' in example (6) does not refer to anything specific. This 它 *tā* 'it' only adds a playful, light, indifferent or casual tone to the expression and thus is a quasi-object. Please note that a numeral-classifier phrase will be followed directly after this kind of quasi-object. For instance, in example (6), 个迷迷糊糊 *gèmímíhuhú* is the same as 一个迷迷糊糊 *yígèmímíhuhú*. Here is another example.

(7) 这 一 次 是 跑 不 掉 了，
zhè *yí* *cì* *shì* *pǎo* *bù* *diào* *le,*
This one time SHI run NEG away LE

就 拼 **他** 一 拼。（金狮奖 260）
jiù *pīn* ***tā*** *yī* *pīn*
just try.best **3SG** one CL-time

'I won't be able to get off this time. So I'll just do my best.' (*Jīnshījiǎng* 260)

3 "Personal pronoun + 的 *de* 'DE' construction" can be used as a quasi-object when it does not refer to any particular object. Compare the following two examples.

(8) 我 今天 面包 带 得 多， 你
wǒ *jīntiān* *miànbāo* *dài* *de* *duō,* *nǐ*
1SG today bread bring DE much 2SG

就 吃 **我** **的** 吧。
jiù *chī* ***wǒ*** ***de*** *ba*
just eat **1SG** **DE** SFP

'I've brought a lot of bread today. You can just eat mine.'

(9) 人 各 有 志，
rén *gè* *yǒu* *zhì,*
people each have aspirations

他 捞 **他** **的，** 我 做 **我** **的**。（胜利 101）
tā *lāo* ***tā*** ***de,*** *wǒ* *zuò* ***wǒ*** ***de***
3SG reap **3SG** **DE** 1SG do **1SG** **DE**

'Each individual has his aspirations. He reaps his benefits and I do my own work.' (*Shènglì* 101)

Both example (8) and example (9) include a "personal pronoun + 的 *de* 'DE'" construction, namely 我的 *wǒde* 'mine'. It is the object of the verb 吃 *chī* 'eat' and the verb 做 *zuò* 'do' in (8) and (9) respectively. But there is an obvious difference in the reference. 我的 *wǒde* 'mine' in example (8) refers to something specific, "my bread". Yet, it does not refer to anything specific in example (9), where the whole predicate-object phrase means "to mind my own business". Therefore, 我的 *wǒde* 'mine' in example (8) is a regular object while 我的 *wǒde* 'mine' (as well as 他的 *tāde* 'his') in example (9) is a quasi-object. Here is one more example of quasi-object.

(10) 没关系， 让 她 忙 **她** 的 吧！ （吾土·戏剧 103）
　　 méiguānxi *ràng* *tā* *máng* ***tā*** *de* *ba*
　　 that's.fine let 3SG busy **3SG** DE SFP
　　 'That's fine. Leave her alone.' (*Wútǔ·xìjù* 103)

她的 *tāde* 'hers' in example (10) is the object of 忙 *máng* 'busy' and is also a quasi-object.

6.4.2 Distinction Between Regular Objects and Quasi-objects

1 Semantically speaking, regular objects refer to concrete, specific things while quasi-objects do not refer to anything in particular.
2 Regular objects follow only transitive verbs, whereas quasi-objects follow both transitive verbs (as in examples (2), (4), (6) and (9)) and intransitive verbs as well, as can be seen in the following examples.

(11) "老太婆！ 老太婆！ 我 要 吃 粥，
　　 lǎotàipó *lǎotàipó* *wǒ* *yào* *chī* *zhōu*
　　 old.lady old.lady 1SG want.to eat porridge

　　 快 给 我 煮 粥！"
　　 kuài *gěi* *wǒ* *zhǔ* *zhōu*
　　 fast GEI 1SG make porridge
　　 'Old lady! Old lady! I want to have porridge. Make me some porridge! Quick!'

　　 "七早八早的， 吵 **什么** 吵！" （再见 27）
　　 qīzǎobāzǎode *chǎo* ***shénme*** *chǎo*
　　 this.and.that noise **what** noise
　　 'What are you yelling about? There's no need to make such a fuss!' (*Zàijiàn* 27)

(12) "既然   进   大学   无望,   倒不如   轰轰烈烈地
     jìrán   jìn   dàxué   wúwàng   dàobùrú   hōnghōnglièliède
     since   get.into college   hopeless   better   passionately

     玩   它   三   年。"（撞墙 3）
     wán   tā   sān   nián
     play   3SG   three   years

     'Since it seems hopeless to get admitted to college, we might just as well totally enjoy ourselves for three years.' (*Zhuàngqiáng* 3)

(13) 她   哭   她   的,   你   理   她   呢!
     tā   kū   tā   de   nǐ   lǐ   tā   ne!
     3SG   cry   3SG   DE   2SG   care   3SG   SFP

     'Let her cry. Ignore her.'

In examples (11), (12) and (13), 吵 *chǎo* 'make noise', 玩 *wán* 'play', 哭 *kū* 'cry' are all intransitive verbs and 什么 *shénme* 'what', 它 *tā* 'it', 她的 *tāde* 'hers' are their quasi-objects. Moreover, quasi-objects can follow adjectives as well, such as the adjective 忙 *máng* 'busy' in example (10). Other examples are:

(14) 这   房子   好   什么   呀,
     zhè   fángzi   hǎo   shénme   ya
     this   house   good   what   SFP

     你   去   看看   她   家   的   房子!
     nǐ   qù   kànkàn   tā   jiā   de   fángzi
     2SG   go   see-see   3SG   family   DE   house

     'This house is nothing fancy. You should see her house!'

(15) 妈,   等   您   儿子   挣   了   大钱,
     mā   děng   nín   érzi   zhèng   le   dàqián
     mum   when   2SG   son   make   LE   a.lot.of.money

     也   带   您   到   国外   风光   它   几   天。
     yě   dài   nín   dào   guówài   fēngguāng   tā   jǐ   tiān
     also   take   2SG   to   abroad   splendid   3SG   several   days

     'Mum, when your son makes a lot of money, I'll take you abroad to see the splendid world for a couple of days.'

(16) 她   神气   她   的   我们   不   理   她
    tā   shénqì tā   de   wǒmen bù   lǐ   tā
    3SG arrogant 3SG DE   1PL   NEG   talk.to 3SG

就是了。（吾土·戏剧 159）
jiùshìle
it.is.fine

'She can be as arrogant as she wants to be. We can just ignore her.'
(*Wútǔ* ▪*xìjù* 159)

In examples (14), (15) and (16), 好 *hǎo* 'good', 风光 *fēngguāng* 'splendid', 神气 *shénqì* 'arrogant' are all adjectives and 什么 *shénme* 'what', 它 *tā* 'it', 她的 *tāde* 'hers' following them are all quasi-objects.

We regard these words and phrases (e.g. 什么 *shénme* 'what', 它 *tā* 'it', pronoun + 的 *de* 'DE' construction) after verbs or adjectives as objects, because they are no different from other objects in form. But, they do not refer to anything in particular, and the whole predicate-object phrase has a special grammatical meaning. Therefore, we name these objects quasi-objects.

6.5 Numeral-Classifier Phrases as Objects

6.5.1 *Types of Numeral-Classifier Phrases*

The numeral-classifier phrases can serve as the objects. They can be divided into three subclasses according to the properties of the classifier.

1   Numeral-nominal classifier phrases as objects. Examples are as follows.

(1) 她   戴   耳环，   只   戴   一   只。（狮子 36）
    tā   dài   ěrhuán   zhǐ   dài   yī   zhī
    3SG wear   earrings   only   wear   one   CL

'She wears earrings, but only one.' (*Shīzi* 36)

(2) 朵朵   用   手   将   五十元   的   钞票   拈出来，
    duǒduǒ   yòng   shǒu   jiāng   wǔshíyuán   de   chāopiào   niānchūlái
    Duoduo   use   hand   to   fifty.yuan   DE   money   take.out

    一、   二、   三，   总共   拿   了   三   张。（跳舞 23）
    yī,   èr,   sān,   zǒnggòng   ná   le   sān   zhāng
    one   two   three   altogether   take   LE   three   CL

'Duoduo took out several fifty-yuan notes with her hand. One, two, three. She took out three notes altogether.' (*Tiàowǔ* 23)

(3) 行李　　只　　有　　一　　件。（石头 180）
xíngli　zhǐ　yǒu　yí　jiàn
baggage　only　have　one　CL

'There is only one piece of baggage.' (*Shítóu* 180)

(4) 临海处　　有　　许多　　餐馆，　我们　　随意
Línhǎichù　yǒu　xǔduō　cānguǎn　wǒmen　suíyì
near.the.sea　have　many　restaurants　1PL　randomly

选　　了　　一　　间。（石头 210）
xuǎn　le　yī　jiān
choose　LE　one　CL

'There are many restaurants near the sea. We chose one at random.' (*Shítóu* 210)

The numeral-nominal classifier phrases in the object position are to describe the quantity of things following what is expressed by predicate verbs. In example (1), 一只 *yìzhī* 'one CL' describes the number of earrings worn; in example (2), 三张 *sānzhāng* 'three CL' specifies the number of the fifty-yuan notes; in example (3), 一件 *yíjiàn* 'one CL' indicates the quantity of the baggage; and in example (4), 一间 *yījiān* 'one CL' expresses the number of selected restaurants.

2　Numeral-verb classifier phrases as objects. Examples are as follows.

(5) 考　　了　　三　　次。（梦 104）
kǎo　le　sān　cì
take.exam　LE　three　CL/times

'... took the exam three times' (*Mèng* 104)

(6) 我　　沙哑　　着　　嗓子　　喊　　了　　一　　声。（风雨 40）
wǒ　shāyǎ　zhe　sǎngzi　hǎn　le　yī　shēng
1SG　hoarse　ZHE　voice　let.out　LE　a　CL/sound

'I let out a hoarse shout.' (*Fēngyǔ* 40)

(7) 轻轻地　　敲　　了　　三　　下（青青 67）
qīngqīngde　qiāo　le　sān　xià
gently　knock　LE　three　CL/times

'... gently knocked three times' (*Qīngqīng* 67)

(8) 向　　他们　　瞟　　了　　一　　眼。（金狮奖 29）
xiàng　tāmen　piǎo　le　yī　yǎn
to　3PL　glance　LE　one　CL/eye

'... cast a sidelong glance at them' (*Jīnshījiǎng* 29)

Predicates and Objects 177

(9) 很　　想　　到　　楼下　　走　　一　　趟。（扶轮 26）
　　hěn　xiǎng　dào　lóuxià　zǒu　yí　tàng
　　very　want　go　downstairs　walk　**a**　**CL/walk**
　　'. . . really want to go downstairs to have a walk' (*Fúlún* 26)

These numeral-verb classifier phrases in the object position usually describe the quantity of actions or events expressed by the predicate verbs.

3　Numeral-temporal classifier phrases as objects. Examples are as follows.

(10) 我们　在　马丁　家　住　了　三　天。（大胡子 11）
　　wǒmen　zài　mǎdīng　jiā　zhù　le　sān　tiān
　　1PL　at　Martin　home　stay　LE　**three**　**CL/days**
　　'We stayed at Martin's home for three days.' (*Dàhúzi* 11)

(11) 我　又　陪　她　出外　逛　了　几　天。（大胡子 32）
　　wǒ　yòu　péi　tā　chūwài　guàng　le　jǐ　tiān
　　1SG　again　with　3SG　out　hang　LE　**a.few**　**CL/days**
　　'I spent a few more days hanging out with her.' (*Dàhúzi* 32)

(12) 需要　连　服　四、五　日。（金狮奖 45）
　　xūyào　lián　fú　sì　wǔ　rì
　　need.to　continuously　take　**four**　**five**　**CL/days**
　　'. . . need to take it for four or five days in a row' (*Jīnshījiǎng* 45)

(13) 死　了　十　年　了。（风雨 8）
　　sǐ　le　shí　nián　le
　　die　LE　**ten**　**CL/years**　LE
　　'. . . has been dead for ten years' (*Fēngyǔ* 8)

(14) 阔别　七　年（金狮奖 61）
　　kuòbié　qī　nián
　　part.from.each.other　**seven**　**CL/years**
　　'haven't seen each other for seven years' (*Jīnshījiǎng* 61)

The numeral-temporal classifier phrases in the object position explain the duration of the action described by the predicate verb (see examples (10) through (12)) or to explain the length of time starting from completion of the action to the speaking time or to the time when something else happened (see examples (13) and (14)).

Among these three subclasses of objects, numeral-nominal classifier object phrase is a regular object for it can only follow transitive verbs. Numeral-verb classifier object phrase and numeral-temporal classifier phrases are quasi-objects, as they can follow both transitive and intransitive verbs, as shown in examples (9), (13) and (14), and the following examples.

(15) （她　　　拉　　　了　　　拉　　　缰绳，）　　呼啸　　　一
　　　(tā　　　lā　　　le　　　lā　　　jiāngshéng)　hūxiào　　yī
　　　(3SG　　pull　　LE　　pull　　reins)　　　cry.out　　one

　　　声,　　　（黑马　　　起步　　　跑　　　了）。（大胡子 9）
　　　shēng　　(hēimǎ　　qǐbù　　　pǎo　　le)
　　　CL/sound　(black.horse　start　　run　　LE)
　　　'(She pulled the reins) and let out a cry, (and the black horse started to run).' (*Dàhúzi* 9)

(16) （母亲　　也　　　不　　　知　　　和　　　他）　　唠叨
　　　(mǔqin　yě　　　bù　　　zhī　　　hé　　　tā)　　lāodao
　　　(mother　yet　　NEG　　know　　with　　him)　　nag

　　　了　　　多少　　　　　次。（变调 63）
　　　le　　　duōshǎo　　　cì
　　　LE　　how.many　　　CL/times
　　　'(The mother) nagged (him) many times.' (*Biàndiào* 63)

(17) 工作　　　了　　　二十　　　天。（短篇 36）
　　　gōngzuò　le　　　èrshi　　　tiān
　　　work　　LE　　　twenty　　CL/days
　　　'worked for twenty days' (*Duǎnpiān* 36)

(18) 请假　　　　　三　　　　天（再见 24）
　　　qǐngjià　　　sān　　　tiān
　　　ask.for.leave　three　　CL/days
　　　'ask for three days' leave' (*Zàijiàn* 24)

As just shown, intransitive verbs can take numeral-verb classifier object phrases in examples (15) and (16), and numeral-temporal classifier object phrases in examples (17) and (18).

Such numeral-verb classifier phrases and numeral-temporal classifier phrases can follow adjectives as well, as illustrated in the following examples.

(19) （壁上 的 时钟 "当！当！当！"地）
 (*bìshàng* *de* *shízhōng* *dāngdāngdāngde*)
 (on.the.wall DE clock clang.clang.clang)

 响 了 三 下。（短篇 95）
 xiǎng *le* **sān** *xià*
 sound LE three CL/times

 '(The clock on the wall) Struck three times.' (*Duǎnpiān* 95)

(20) 电话 里 静 了 一 下（大胡子 38）
 diànhuà *lǐ* *jìng* *le* **yī** *xià*
 phone inside quiet LE a CL/time

 'There was a moment's silence on the phone.' (*Dàhúzi* 38)

(21) 她 在 歌坛上 也 红 了 几 年。
 tā *zài* *gētánshàng* *yě* *hóng* *le* **jǐ** *nián*
 3SG in the.music.world also red LE several CL/years

 'For several years, she was very popular in the music world.'

6.5.2 Verb Reduplications Taking Numeral-Verb Classifier Phrases as Objects

One phenomenon that merits attention in Singapore Mandarin is that verb reduplication can be followed by numeral-verb classifier phrases, especially 一下 *yīxià* 'one CL/bit'. Look at the following examples.

(22) 然后 找 一天 和 舒小姐 谈 怎么 拍照。
 ránhòu *zhǎo* *yītiān* *hé* *shūxiǎojiě* *tán* *zěnme* *pāizhào*
 then find a.day with Miss.Shu talk how.to take.photos

 'Then find a day to talk to Miss Shu about how to take photos.'

 谈谈 几 次, 就 可以 约 她 去
 tántán *jǐ* *cì* *jiù* *kěyǐ* *yuē* *tā* *qù*
 talk-talk several CL/times then can ask 3SG go

 拍照。（劳达剧作 23）
 pāizhào
 take.photos

 'After several times, you can ask her out to take photos.' (*Láodájùzuò* 23)

(23) 要   念   大学   嘛， 得   **考虑考虑**   一   下。（短篇4）
    yào   niàn   dàxué   ma   děi   **kǎolǜkǎolǜ**   yī   xià
    will study college SFP   must think-think   one   CL/bit

'If (I) want to go to college, (I) will have to think about it.' (*Duǎnpiān* 4)

(24) 你   和   同学们   可以   彼此   先   **认识认识**
    nǐ   hé   tóngxuémen   kěyǐ   bǐcǐ   xiān   **rènshirènshi**
    2SG   and classmates   can   each.other   first   know-know

一   下。（追云16）
yī   xià
one   CL/bit

'You can get to know your classmates first.' (*Zhuīyún* 16)

(25) 其实   给   父亲   **骂骂**   一   下   又   有
    qíshí   gěi   fùqin   **màmà**   yī   xià   yòu   yǒu
    in.fact GEI   father   scold-scold   one   CL/bit then   have

什么   关系……（追云88）
shénme   guānxì
what   importance

'In fact it is no big deal being scolded by one's father.' (*Zhuīyún* 88)

In Chinese Mandarin, verb reduplication can never take such objects as numeral-verb classifier phrases (Zhang 1994).

6.6 Agentive Objects

Starting from this section, three types of objects will be introduced from the semantic perspective. Let's begin with agentive objects.

6.6.1 Agentive Objects

Objects that indicate the agent of the action described by the predicate verbs are called agentive objects. For example, in the sentence 我们家来客人了 *wǒmen jiā lái kèrén le* 'We've got a guest', 客人 *kèrén* 'guest' is the agentive object.

In contrast to English, objects can be used to indicate the agent of the action described by the predicate verbs. It is one of the grammatical features shared by all Chinese languages, including Singapore Mandarin.

Subject-predicate sentences with agentive objects are generally called agentive object sentences.

(1) 这里 住 着 两 个 中国人。
    zhèlǐ zhù zhe liǎng gè zhōngguórén
    here live ZHE two CL Chinese
    'Two Chinese live here.'

(2) 窗口 边 坐 着 一 位 身著 初院
    chuāngkǒu biān zuò zhe yí wèi shēnzhuó chūyuàn
    window side sit ZHE one CL dressed junior.college

    制服 的 男 学生。（有缘 11）
    zhìfú de nán xuéshēng
    uniform DE male student
    'A male student dressed in junior college uniform sits by the window.'
    (Yǒuyuán 11)

In sentences (1) and (2), 两个中国人 liǎng gè zhōngguó rén 'two Chinese' and 一位身着初院制服的男学生 yí wèi shēnzhuó chūyuàn zhìfú de nán xuéshēng 'a male student dressed in junior college uniform' are agentive objects, and these two sentences are called agentive object sentences.

6.6.2 Two Grammatical Meanings of Agentive Object Sentences

Agentive object sentences in Singapore Mandarin represent two grammatical meanings.

1 To express existence, as shown by the following examples:

(3) 对面 坐 着 一 个 中年 妇人。（金狮奖 181）
    duìmiàn zuò zhe yí gè zhōngnián fùrén
    opposite sit ZHE one CL middle-aged woman
    'A middle-aged woman sits opposite (me/him/her).' (Jīnshījiǎng 138)

(4) 门口 站 着 一 个 男孩子。（追云（44）
    ménkǒu zhàn zhe yí gè nánháizǐ
    doorway stand ZHE one CL boy
    'A boy is standing in the doorway.' (Zhuīyún 44)

(5) 车旁 倚 着 一 名 华籍 妇女。（石头 1）
    chēpáng yǐ zhe yī míng huájí fùnǚ
    beside.the.car lean ZHE one CL Chinese woman
    'A Chinese woman leaned against the car.' (Shítóu 1)

(6) 公寓　　　旁边　　　的　　石墩　　　　上，　坐　　了　　几
　　 gōngyù　　pángbiān　de　　shídūn　　 shàng　zuò　 le　　jǐ
　　 flat　　　beside　　 DE　 stone.mounds on　　 sit　 LE　several

名　　　粗壮的　　　　汉子。（石头 183）
míng　　cūzhuàngde　　hànzi
CL　　　stout　　　　　man

'Several stout men sat on the stone mounds beside the flat.' (*Shítóu* 183)

(7) 旅馆　　　门口　　 站　　了　　一　　名　　 中年　　　　汉子。（石头 41）
　　 lǚguǎn　　ménkǒu　zhàn　le　　yī　　míng　zhōngnián　hànzi
　　 hotel　　 doorway　stand LE　 one　CL　 middle-aged　man

'A middle-aged man stood in the doorway of the hotel.' (*Shítóu* 41)

　　In an agentive object sentence which indicates existence, the predicate verb (with agentive objects) is often added with the dynamic auxiliary 着 *zhe* 'ZHE', as can be seen in examples (3) through (5); sometimes 了 *le* 'LE', as in examples (6) and (7).

　　In principle, the subjects cannot be omitted in agentive object sentences indicating existence.

2　To express appearance. Some examples follow:

(8) 幕后　　　出来　　　一　　团　　 表演　　　杂技　　　的。（石头 109）
　　 mùhòu　　chūlái　　 yī　 tuán　biǎoyǎn　zájì　　　de
　　 backstage come.out　one　team　act　　　acrobatics DE

'A team of acrobatic actors came out from backstage.' (*Shítóu* 109)

(9) 门　　 外　　　来　　了　　三　　个　　好　　　兄弟。（撞墙 63）
　　 mén　 wài　　 lái　 le　　sān　 gè　 hǎo　　xiōngdì
　　 door　outside　come　LE　three　CL　 good　 brother

'Three good brothers came from outside the door.' (*Zhuàngqiáng* 63)

(10) 远处　　　走来　　　了　　一　　位　　 "老来娇"　　　　　的
　　 yuǎnchù　zǒulái　　 le　　yí　　wèi　 lǎoláijiāo　　　　　de
　　 faraway　walk　　　 LE　 one　 CL　 dressed.like.a.girl　DE

SP 太太。（△含羞草 29）
*SP*tàitài
Mrs. SP

'Mrs. SP, who was dressed like a young girl, walked from afar.' (*Hánxiūcǎo* 29)

In agentive object sentences indicating appearance, the predicate verbs are either directional verbs (examples (8) and (9)) or verbs with directional complements (example (10)). (For more information about directional verbs and directional complements, see Section 7.3.)

The subjects can be omitted in such agentive object sentences indicating appearance, as is shown in the following examples.

(11) 迎面　　走来　了　一　位　举止优雅的　妇人。（石头 145）
   yíngmiàn zǒulái   le   yí wèi jǔzhǐyōuyǎde fūrén
   head.on   walk   LE   a   CL   elegant   lady
   'An elegant lady was walking over.' (*Shítóu* 145)

(12) 忽然　　来　了　一　批　便衣　　警探　　和
   hūrán   lái le   yī pī   biànyī   jǐngtàn   hé
   suddenly come LE   a   CL   undercover detectives and

   警察。（短篇 17）
   jǐngchá
   policemen
   'All of a sudden an army of undercover detectives and policemen showed up.' (*Duǎnpiān* 17)

In examples (11) and (12), the adverbs 迎面 *yíngmiàn* 'head on' and 忽然 *hūrán* 'suddenly' at the sentence initial position are not subjects but adverbial modifiers.

6.6.3 *Two Characteristics of Agentive Object Sentences*

1 The subjects are usually words that indicate directions or places. In the corpus we have collected, no other type of words used as subjects are found.
2 The objects, without exception, refer to something indefinite, things that are uncertain or unknown.

6.7 Place Objects

6.7.1 *Classification of Place Objects*

Generally speaking, place objects specify the place where the action is performed. Strictly speaking, there are three types of place objects as explained in the following.

1 The object refers to the position or place where the person or thing exists. The role of the predicate verb is simply to indicate in what way or state the person or thing exists. This can be further subdivided into two cases:

A   The object indicates a static position or place of existence. For example:

(1) | 妈妈 | 在 | 房 | 里。 |
    |------|------|------|------|
    | *māmā* | *zài* | *fáng* | *lǐ* |
    | mother | at | house | inside |

'Mother is in the house.'

(2) | 我 | 住 | 东海岸道 | 3 号， |
    |------|------|------|------|
    | *wǒ* | *zhù* | *dōnghǎiàndào* | *sānhào,* |
    | 1SG | live | East.Coast.Road | No. 3 |

他	住	淡滨尼	11 街	6 号。
tā	*zhù*	*dànbīnní*	*shíyījiē*	*liùhào*
3SG	live	Tampines	11th Street	No. 6

'I live at No. 3 East Coast Road, and he lives at No. 6, 11th Street, Tampines.'

Example (2) contains two clauses, with a contrastive meaning. The two clauses could also be two sentences, if a full stop instead of a comma is used after the first clause.[2]

B   The object indicates the position or place where a person or thing is located, usually implying that the person or thing has undergone a change of position first. This usage only occurs in spoken language. For example:

(3) | 你 | 睡 | 床上， | 我 | 睡 | 沙发上。 |
    |------|------|------|------|------|------|
    | *nǐ* | *shuì* | *chuángshàng* | *wǒ* | *shuì* | *shāfāshàng* |
    | 2SG | sleep | in.the.bed | 1SG | sleep | on.the.sofa |

'You sleep in the bed and I sleep on the sofa.'

(4) | 那 | 衣服 | 放 | 柜子 | 里。 |
    |------|------|------|------|------|
    | *nà* | *yīfú* | *fàng* | *guìzǐ* | *lǐ* |
    | that | clothes | put | closet | in |

'Put those clothes in the closet.'

2 The object refers to the starting point, ending point or the point where a person or thing passes by. For example:

(5) | 离开 | 书房（独上 46） |
    |------|------|
    | *líkāi* | *shūfáng* |
    | leave | study |

'Leave the study.' (*Dúshàng* 46)

(6) 跨　　　出　　　**教室**
　　 kuà　　 chū　　 ***jiàoshì***
　　 step　　out　　 **classroom**
　　 'Step out of the classroom.'

(7) 来　　　**学校**（撞墙 49）
　　 lái　　 ***xuéxiào***
　　 come　 **school**
　　 'Come to school.' (*Zhuàngqiáng* 49)

(8) 去　　　**工厂**（变调 15）
　　 qù　　 ***gōngchǎng***
　　 go　　 **factory**
　　 'Go to the factory.' (*Biàndiào* 15)

(9) 冲　　　进　　　**房间**（华韵 45）
　　 chōng　 jìn　　 ***fángjiān***
　　 rush　　into　　**room**
　　 'Rush into the room.' (*Huáyùn* 45)

(10) 他　　 将　　 书包　　 丢　　 进　　 **抽屉**　　 **里**（变调 14）
　　　tā　　jiāng　 shūbāo　 diū　　jìn　　***chōutì***　　***lǐ***
　　　3SG　 BA　　schoolbag　throw　into　**drawer**　　**inside**
　　　'He threw his schoolbag into the drawer.' (*Biàndiào* 14)

(11) 从　　　 裕廊西　　　乘　　　巴士　　 到　　国大，
　　　cóng　　yùlángxī　　 chéng　 bāshì　 dào　 guódà,
　　　from　　Jurong.West　take　　bus　　 to　　National.University.of.Singapore

　　　中间　　　　 要　　　　 经过　　　　**金文泰**。
　　　zhōngjiān　　yào　　　　jīngguò　　 ***jīnwéntài***
　　　middle　　　will　　　　pass　　　　**Clementi**
　　　'If you take a bus from Jurong West to NUS, you'll pass Clementi.'

　　The place object in either example (5) or (6) specifies the starting point of a movement. In examples (7) through (10), all the place objects specify the ending points. The place object 金文泰 *jīnwéntài* 'Clementi' in example (11) refers to a place by which the movement passes.

3 The object refers to range of the motion or influence of the activity indicated by the predicate verb. For example:

(12) 昨天   我们   游览   了   **夜间**   **动物园**。
     zuótiān wǒmen yóulǎn le   **yèjiān** **dòngwùyuán**
     yesterday 1PL   visit   LE   **night**   **zoo**
     'Yesterday we visited the night zoo.'

(13) （我   决定   自己）   闯   **天下**。（撞墙 43）
     (wǒ   juédìng zìjǐ)   chuǎng **tiānxià**
     1SG   decide   myself   travel **world**
     'I decided to travel around by myself.' (Zhuàngqiáng 43)

(14) 逛   **夜市**（跳舞 140）
     guàng   **yèshì**
     shop   **night.market**
     'go shopping at the night market' (Tiàowǔ 140)

(15) 走红   **时装**   **界**（变调 9）
     zǒuhóng   **shízhuāng**   **jiè**
     become.popular   **fashion**   **industry**
     'become popular in the fashion industry' (Biàndiào 9)

Please note that not every word indicating a place will be a place object. Compare the following two examples.

(16) 我   去   **牛车水**。
     wǒ   qù   **niúchēshuǐ**
     1SG   go   **Chinatown**
     'I'll go to Chinatown.'

(17) 我   爱   **牛车水**。
     wǒ   ài   **niúchēshuǐ**
     1SG   love **Chinatown**
     'I love Chinatown.'

Here 牛车水 niúchēshuǐ 'Chinatown' acts as an object in either example (16) or (17), but each with a different semantic role. In example (16) it is a place object which specifies the ending point of the subject's movement, while in example (17) it is the object of 爱 ài 'love'. wǒ ài niúchēshuǐ 'I love Chinatown' is grammatically similar to 我爱妈妈 wǒ ài māma 'I love Mum', in that 牛车水 niúchēshuǐ 'Chinatown' is an accusative object. Likewise, 门口 ménkǒu 'doorway' is a place object in the sentence 他快步跨出门口 *tā kuàibù kuàchū ménkǒu* 'He stepped quickly out of the doorway', but an accusative object in the sentence 他一直注视着门口 *tā yìzhí zhùshì zhe ménkǒu* 'He kept watching the doorway'.

6.7.2 Place Objects Following Compound Directional Verbs

Both compound directional verbs and predicate-complement constructions with compound directional verbs acting as complements may take place objects. It is important to note that in Singapore Mandarin, there are two possible positions for these two types of constructions.

1   The place object may be placed right after the compound directional verb. For example:

(18) 听   祖父   说，   他们   已经   **回去**   **印度**
     tīng *zǔfù* *shuō* *tāmen* *yǐjīng* ***huíqù*** ***yìndù***
     hear   grandpa say   3PL   already **return** **India**

了。（吾土·小说上 223）
le
LE

'I heard from my grandpa that they had gone back to India.' (*Wútǔ·xiǎoshuōshàng* 223)

(19) 两   人   分手   后，   她   带   着
     liǎng *rén*   *fēnshǒu* *hòu*   *tā*   *dài*   *zhe*
     two   people   break.up   after   3SG   take   ZHE

孩子   **回去**   **美国**。（大胡子 101）
háizi   ***huíqù***   ***měiguó***
children   **return**   **America**

'After they broke up, she went back to America with her children.' (*Dàhúzi* 101)

(20) 她   是   在   南洋   出生   的，
     tā   *shì*   *zài*   *nányáng*   *chūshēng*   *de*
     3SG   SHI   in   Southeast.Asia born   DE

她   没有   **回去**   过   唐山。（报 1995 年 6 月 18 日副刊 9 版）
tā   *méiyǒu* ***huíqù*** *guò*   *tángshān*
3SG   NEG   **return**   GUO   Tangshan

'She was born in Southeast Asia, and has not gone back to Tangshan.' (*Bào*, June 18, 1995, Issue no. 9, supplementary edition)

(21) 新加坡　　　已　　　通知　　　陈成财　　　　大使
　　　xīnjiāpō　　yǐ　　　tōngzhī　　chénchéngcái　dàshǐ
　　　Singapore　already　inform　　Chen.Chengcai　ambassador

回来　　　　新加坡。（报 1995 年 4 月 12 日 1 版）
huílái　　　xīnjiāpō
come.back　Singapore

'Singapore has already informed ambassador Chen Chengcai that he should come back to Singapore.' (*Bào*, Apr. 12, 1995, Issue no. 1)

(22) 他　　想　　　父母亲　　这　　一　　　去　　就　　　永远
　　　tā　　xiǎng　　fùmǔqīn　zhè　yí　　qù　　jiù　　yǒngyuǎn
　　　3SG　think　　parents　this　once　go　　then　forever

　　　留　　在　　唐山，　　可能　　不会　　再　　　**回来**
　　　liú　　zài　　tángshān　kěnéng　búhuì　zài　　**huílái**
　　　stay　at　　Tangshan　maybe　NEG　　again　**return**

南洋。（报 1995 年 6 月 18 日副刊 9 版）
nányáng
Southeast.Asia

'He thought his parents would stay in Tangshan forever, and might not come back to Southeast Asia anymore.' (*Bào*, June 18, 1995, Issue no. 9, supplementary edition)

The aforementioned are examples of place objects following compound directional verbs. Next are examples of place objects following predicate-complement constructions with complements of compound directional verbs.

(23) 想不到　　　　过　　了　　半　　个　　钟头　　后，　同　　一
　　　xiǎngbúdào　guò　le　　bàn　gè　　zhōngtóu　hòu　tóng　yí
　　　unexpectedly　pass　LE　half　CL　hour　　　later　same　one

　　　辆　　车　　又　　　**驾　　回来**　　我们　　这里。（风筝 186）
　　　liàng　chē　yòu　　**jià　　huílái**　wǒmen　zhèlǐ
　　　CL　　car　again　**drive　back**　1PL　　here

'I did not expect that half an hour later, the same car would come back to us again.' (*Fēngzhēng* 186)

(24) 有些　　人．．．．．还　　时常　　**跑**　**回来**　**巴刹**　买
　　　yǒuxiē　rén　　　　　hái　　shícháng　**pǎo**　**huílái**　**bāchà**　mǎi
　　　some　　people　　　still　sometimes　**run**　**back**　**Pasha**　buy

东西。（回忆 43）
dōngxi
things

'Some people still come back to Pasha to buy things from time to time.' (*Huíyì* 186)

(25) 当初　　　也　　是　　你　　自己　　把　　他
　　　dāngchū　yě　　shì　 nǐ　　zìjǐ　　 bǎ　　tā
　　　at.first　 also　be　 2SG　yourself　BA　　3SG

带　　进来　　这　　厂　　里　　的。（吾土·小说上 44）
dài　 jìnlái　 zhè　 chǎng lǐ　　de
take　inside　this　factory inside　DE

'It is you who took him to this factory first.' (*Wútǔ·xiǎoshuōshàng* 44)

(26) 你　　如果　　逼　　我　　回去，　我　　就
　　　nǐ　　rúguǒ　bī　　wǒ　　huíqù　　wǒ　　jiù
　　　2SG　if　　　force　1 SG　return　　1SG　will

立刻　　　　**飞**　　　回去　　　澳洲。（大胡子 47）
lìkè　　　　**fēi**　　 huíqù　　 àozhōu
immediately　**fly**　　return　　Australia

'If you force me to go back, I will fly back to Australia immediately.' (*Dàhúzi* 47)

(27) 没有　　想到，　他　　今天　　晚上　　　就　　　把
　　　méiyǒu　xiǎngdào　tā　　jīntiān　　wǎnshàng　jiù　　bǎ
　　　NEG　　 expect　　3SG　today　　　evening　　then　BA

她　　**带**　　过来　　我们　　家　　了。（大胡子 25）
tā　　**dài**　guòlái　 wǒmen　jiā　　le
3SG　**take**　back　　1PL　　home　LE

'I did not expect that he'd take her to our home tonight.' (*Dàhúzi* 25)

2 The place object may also occur in the middle of a compound directional verb phrase. For example:

(28) 他   总是   那么   可怜兮兮的   问   我   什么时候
     tā   zǒngshì   nàme   kěliánxīxīde   wèn   wǒ   shénmeshíhou
     3SG   always   so   pathetically   ask   1SG   when

可以   回   "家"   去？（风雨 38）
kěyǐ   huí   jiā   qù
can   return   home   to

'He always asked me pathetically when he could go back home.' (Fēngyǔ 38)

(29) 过   了   几   分钟,   乙   和尚   气愤愤地
     guò   le   jǐ   fēnzhōng   yǐ   héshàng   qìfènfende
     pass   LE   a. few   minutes   B   monk   angrily

跑   进   房   来,......（八方 37）
pǎo   jìn   fáng   lái
run   into   house   come

'After several minutes, Monk B angrily ran into the house....' (Bāfāng 37)

(30) 她   抱   着   录音机,   几乎   是   **飞奔**   **进**
     tā   bào   zhe   lùyīnjī,   jīhū   shì   **fēibēn**   **jìn**
     3SG   carry   ZHE   recorder   nearly be   **dart**   **into**

房   里   去。（微型 68）
fáng   lǐ   qù
house   inside   go

'She carried a recorder and nearly darted into the house.' (Wēixíng 68)

In Singapore Mandarin, the place object is more commonly seen put right after the compound directional verb. However, in Chinese Mandarin, neither compound directional verbs nor predicate-complement constructions with compound directional verb complements can directly carry place objects. A place object must be put in the middle of a compound directional verb phrase, as demonstrated in the second type (examples 28–30) (Lü 1980; Zhu 1982; see Section 7.3).

6.8 Dative Objects

Please look at the following examples.

(1) 给　　我，　给　　我。（石头 29）
　　 gěi　 wǒ　　gěi　 wǒ
　　 give　1SG　 give　1SG

'Give it to me. Give it to me.' (*Shítóu* 29)

(2) 请　　　你　　相信　　　我！（追云 66）
　　 qǐng　　nǐ　　xiāngxìn　 wǒ
　　 please　2SG　 trust　　　1SG

'Please trust me!' (*Zhuīyún* 66)

The word 我 *wǒ* '1SG' serves as an object in both example (1) and example (2), but each with a different semantic role. 我 *wǒ* '1SG' in example (2) is the direct object of the verb 相信 *xiāngxìn* 'believe' and is an accusative object. 我 *wǒ* '1SG' in example (1) is the indirect object of the verb 给 *gěi* 'give', the recipient of the giving action. Objects of this kind are dative objects. In the following examples, the objects after verbs are all dative objects.

(3) a　告诉　　　你（追云 61）
　　　 gàosù　　 nǐ
　　　 tell　　　 2SG

　　　'Let me tell you.' (*Zhuīyún* 61)

　　b　送　　　给　　李老师
　　　 sòng　　 gěi　 lǐlǎoshī
　　　 give　　 to　　Teacher.Li

　　　'Give it to Teacher Li.'

　　c　卖　　给　　你
　　　 mài　 gěi　 nǐ
　　　 sell　to　　2SG

　　　'Sell it to you.'

　　d　还　　　给　　你（金狮奖 222）
　　　 huán　　 gěi　 nǐ
　　　 return　 to　　2SG

　　　'Return it to you.' (*Jīnshījiǎng* 222)

All verbs with dative objects contain the semantic meaning of transfer, referring to the transfer of possession in most cases. These verbs often take an accusative object, that is the object being transferred, along with the dative object, thus forming a double-object construction (see Section 6.9). For example:

(4) （你）　　给　　他　　一　　杯　　酒。（石头 29）
　　 (nǐ)　　 gěi　 tā　　yī　　bēi　 jiǔ
　　 (2SG)　 give　3SG　 a　　CL/glass wine
　　 'Give him a glass of wine.' (*Shítóu* 29)

(5) 爹　　就　　只　　留给　　我　　娘　　一　　枚　　戒指。（金狮奖（四）9）
　　 diē　 jiù　 zhǐ　 liúgěi　wǒ　 niáng　yī　 méi　 jièzhǐ
　　 dad　just　only　leave　 1SG　 mom　 a　　CL　 ring
　　 'Dad only left my mum a ring.' (*Jīnshījiǎng* IV 9)

(6) 我　　借　　你　　两　　把　　伞，
　　 wǒ　 jiè　 nǐ　　liǎng　bǎ　　sǎn
　　 1SG　lend　2SG　 two　 CL　 umbrellas

　　 你　　　放心　　　　去　　　　玩。（石头 130）
　　 nǐ　　 fàngxīn　　　 qù　　　 wán
　　 2SG　 be.at.ease　　 go　　　 play
　　 'I'll lend you two umbrellas. Feel free to play.' (*Shítóu* 130)

(7) 告诉　　你　　一　　件　　事（撞墙 58）
　　 gàosù　 nǐ　　yī　　jiàn　 shì
　　 tell　　2SG　 one　 CL　　thing
　　 'Let me tell you something.' (*Zhuàngqiáng* 58)

In example (4), both 他 *tā* '3SG' and 一杯酒 *yī bēi jiǔ* 'a glass of wine' are objects of the verb 给 *gěi* 'give', with 他 *tā* '3SG' being the dative object and 一杯酒 *yī bēi jiǔ* 'a glass of wine' being the accusative object. The ownership of 酒 *jiǔ* 'wine' is transferred from "you" to "him". The same logic applies to examples (5) and (6). The ownership of 一枚戒指 *yī méi jièzhi* 'a ring' is transferred from "dad" to "my mum" in example (5), while the ownership of 伞 *sǎn* 'umbrella' is transferred from "me" to "you". Though there is no actual transfer of ownership in example (7), it still involves an abstract transfer of information.

6.9 Double Objects

6.9.1 Double Objects and Double Object Phrases

"Double object" is a traditional term. When a verb carries two objects at the same time, those two objects are generally referred to as double objects and the whole predicate-object phrase is called a double object phrase. For example:

(1) 给   他   一   杯   汽水（风雨 115）
    gěi   tā   yī   bēi   qìshuǐ
    give 3SG   a   glass soda.water
    'Give him a glass of soda water.' (*Fēngyǔ* 115)

Here 他 *tā* '3SG' is the object of the verb 给 *gěi* 'give', and so is 一杯汽水 *yī bēi qìshuǐ* 'a glass of soda water'. In traditional grammar books, these two objects are known as double objects. 他 *tā* '3SG' is called the indirect object, which usually refers to people. 一杯汽水 *yī bēi qìshuǐ* 'a glass of soda water' is called the direct object, which usually refers to things.

A double object phrase, in terms of structural analysis, could be regarded as a special kind of predicate-object phrase embedded in another predicate-object phrase. Example (1) could be analysed as follows:

给   他   一杯汽水

gěi tā   yī bēi qìshuǐ

  1   2   (predicate-object relation)
  ─────────
  3 4   (predicate-object relation)

6.9.2 Classification of Double Object Phrases

According to the characteristics of the objects followed, double object phrases in Singapore Mandarin can be divided into two types:

1   Both objects are regular objects, one being a dative object, the other being an accusative object. This is the case for example (1). Here are more examples.

(2) 给   我   一   盒   双黄   月饼。（微型 16）
    gěi   wǒ   yī   hé   shuānghuáng   yuèbǐng
    give 1SG   a   Cl/box double.yolks   mooncake
    'Give me a box of mooncakes with double yolks.' (*Wēixíng* 16)

(3) （我   的   邻居）   送   了   我   一
    (wǒ   de   línjū)   sòng   le   wǒ   yī
    (1SG DE   neighbour) give   LE   1SG   a

只   猫。（报 1995 年 3 月 5 日副刊 11 版）
zhī   **māo**
CL   **cat**

'My neighbour gave me a cat as a present.' (*Bào,* Mar. 5, 1995, Issue no. 11, supplementary edition)

(4) a   告诉   你   一   个   好   消息。（跳舞 107）
        gàosù   nǐ   yī   gè   hǎo   xiāoxi
        tell   2SG   a   CL   good news

'Tell you some good news.' (*Tiàowǔ* 107)

(4) b   告诉   你   一   个   笑话。（石头 118）
        gàosù   nǐ   yī   gè   xiàohua
        tell   2SG   a   CL   joke

'Tell you a joke.' (*Shítóu* 118)

(5) （您）   借   了   我   一   本   书。（青青 103）
    (nín)   jiè   le   wǒ   yī   běn   shū
    2SG   lend LE   1SG   a   CL   book

'You lent me a book.' (*Qīngqīng* 103)

(6) （他们   只）   收   我   五   元。（怀旧 103）
    (tāmen   zhī)   shōu   wǒ   wǔ   yuán
    (3PL   only)   charge 1SG   five yuan

'They only charged me five yuan.' (*Huáijiù* 103)

There are also instances where one object is an accusative object while the other is a linked object which is used for addressing. For example:

(7) 叫   我   美玲。（金狮奖（四）124）
    jiào   wǒ   měilíng
    call   1SG   Meiling

'Call me Meiling.' (*Jīnshījiǎng* IV 124)

In example (7), 我 *wǒ* '1SG' is an accusative object and 美玲 *měilíng* 'Meiling' is a linked object. More examples follow.

(8) 骂　　　　他　　　　蠢　　　　猪。
　　 mà　　　 tā　　　 chǔn　　　zhū
　　 curse　　3SG　　 stupid　　 pig
　　 'Call him a stupid pig.'

(9) （大家）　　称呼　　　他　　　老　　　校长。
　　 (dàjiā)　　 chēnghu　 tā　　 lǎo　　 xiàozhǎng
　　 (everyone)　call　　　3SG　　old　　 headmaster
　　 'Everyone called him the old headmaster.'

2　Of the two objects, one is a true object and the other is a quasi-object. For example:

(10) 训诫　　　了　　　我　　　一　　　顿。（万花筒 51）
　　 xùnjiè　　 le　　　wǒ　　　yī　　　dùn
　　 admonish　LE　　　1SG　　 a　　　 CL
　　 'Gave me a lecture.' (*Wànhuātǒng* 51)

In example (10), 我 *wǒ* '1SG' is a regular object while 一顿 *yīdùn* 'a lecture' is a quasi-object. More examples are as follows.

(11) a　咬　　　你　　　一　　　口（八方 58）
　　　 yǎo　　 nǐ　　　yì　　　kǒu
　　　 bite　　 2SG　　one　　 CL/bite
　　　 'bite you' (*Bāfāng* 58)

　　 b　看　　　她　　　一　　　眼（梦 24）
　　　 kàn　　 tā　　　yī　　　yǎn
　　　 look　　3SG　　 one　　 CL/glance
　　　 'glance at her' (*Mèng* 24)

(12) 认识　　　她　　　八　　　年（风雨 98）
　　 rènshi　　 tā　　　bā　　　nián
　　 know　　　3SG　　 eight　　CL/years
　　 'having known her for eight years' (*Fēngyǔ* 98)

(13) a　碰　　　了　　　两　　　次　　　钉子（浮萍 71）
　　　 pèng　　le　　　liǎng　　cì　　　dīngzi
　　　 hit　　　LE　　　two　　 CL/times　nail
　　　 'be rejected twice' (*Fúpíng* 71)

	b	点	了	一	下	头（狮子 34）
		diǎn	le	yī	xià	tóu
		nod	LE	one	CL/time	head

'nodded the head' (*Shīzi* 34)

In examples (11) and (12), the regular object precedes the quasi-object, whereas in example (13), it is vice versa.

There are also cases where both objects are quasi-objects. For example:

(14) "既然 进 大学 无望， 倒不如 轰轰烈烈地
　　　jìrán jìn dàxué wúwàng dàobùrú hōnghōnglièliède
　　　since get.into college hopeless better passionately

　　　玩 它 三 年。"（撞墙 3）
　　　wán tā sān nián
　　　play 3SG three CL/years

'Since it seems hopeless to get admitted to college, we might just as well totally enjoy ourselves for three years.' (*Zhuàngqiáng* 3)

In example (14), 它 *tā* '3SG' and 三年 *sānnián* 'three years' are both quasi-objects of the verb 玩 *wán* 'play'. This kind of double object phrase with two quasi-objects is not commonly seen and is mostly found in spoken language.

6.9.3 Order of Direct Objects and Indirect Objects in Singapore Mandarin

What merits our attention about double objects is that in Chinese Mandarin, a dative object, that is an indirect object, always precedes a direct object. But in Singapore Mandarin, a dative object may either precede or follow a direct object. For example, 我给他钱 *wǒ gěi tā qián* 'I gave him money' and 我给钱他 *wǒ gěi qián tā* 'I gave money to him' work equally fine. Following is another example.

(15) 他 刚才 给 这 本 书 我。
　　　tā gāngcái gěi zhè běn shū wǒ
　　　3SG just.now give this CL book 1SG

'He gave me this book just now.'

However, this kind of expression is mostly seen in spoken language and is restricted to the verb 给 *gěi* 'give'.

6.10 Classification of Verbs From the Perspective of Their Objects

The preceding is a general introduction to objects in Singapore Mandarin. We have mentioned that from a grammatical point of view, objects can be divided into regular objects and quasi-objects, and regular objects can be further divided into nominal objects and predicative objects. As for quasi-objects, there is no need for further discussion, since they can even follow adjectives. The relevant point is regular objects, because not all verbs can carry regular objects. The verb 合作 *hézuò* 'cooperate' is a typical example of not being able to take an object, and it is ungrammatical to say 合作他 *hézuòtā* 'cooperate him'. We can only use a prepositional phrase to introduce the entity involved, saying 跟他合作 *gēntāhézuò* 'with him cooperate'. In addition, verbs which do take objects also differ in what kind of objects they take. For instance, the verb 吃 *chī* 'eat' can only take nominal objects, while the verb 打算 *dǎsuàn* 'intend' can only take predicative objects. The fact that different verbs take different kinds of objects reflects the versatility of verbs. Given that the verb is the core of a sentence, it is of significance to study verbs by examining the types of objects they carry, which will be carried out from the next section.

6.11 Transitive Verbs and Intransitive Verbs

Depending on whether or not they can take an object (either a nominal object or a predicative object), verbs can first be divided into two subgroups: transitive and intransitive verbs.

6.11.1 Transitive Verbs

Let's talk about transitive verbs first. A verb that can take an object is a transitive verb. The following verbs are all transitive verbs.

喝 *hē* 'drink': **喝** 米酒（狮子 26）
　　　　　　　　 hē　 *mǐjiǔ*
　　　　　　　　 drink　rice.wine
　　　　　　　　 'drink rice wine' (*Shīzi* 26)

买 *mǎi* 'buy':　**买**　　一点　　小　　　礼物（大胡子 18）
　　　　　　　　 mǎi　*yīdiǎn*　*xiǎo*　　*lǐwù*
　　　　　　　　 buy　some　　small　　present
　　　　　　　　 'buy some small presents' (*Dàhúzi* 18)

吃 chī 'eat': 吃   同样的   食物（△南风 12）
              chī   tóngyàngde   shíwù
              eat   same   food
              'eat the same food' (△Nánfēng 12)

保护 bǎohù 'protect': 保护   你（华韵 95）
                      bǎohù   nǐ
                      protect   you
                      'protect you' (Huáyùn 95)

寻找 xúnzhǎo 'search': 寻找   小猫（科学 76）
                       xúnzhǎo   xiǎomāo
                       search   kitten
                       'search for the kitten' (Kēxué 76)

希望 xīwàng 'hope': 希望   这   个   传说   是   真的（太阳 85）
                    xīwàng   zhè   gè   chuánshuō shì zhēnde
                    hope   this CL   legend   be   true
                    'hope this legend is true' (Tàiyáng 85)

受到 shòudào 'receive': 受到   重视（文艺 73）
                        shòudào   zhòngshì
                        receive   much.attention
                        'receive much attention' (Wényì 73)

值得 zhídé 'deserve': 值得   一看再看（青青 36）
                      zhídé   yīkànzàikàn
                      deserve   read.over.and.over.again
                      'worth reading over and over again' (Qīngqīng 36)

愿意 yuànyì 'willing': 愿意   作   政治   或   工商   领袖
                       yuànyì   zuò   zhèngzhì huò gōngshāng lǐngxiù
                       willing be   political or   business   leader

                       的   支持者（风筝 27）
                       de   zhīchízhě
                       DE   supporter
                       'willing to be a supporter of the political or business leaders' (Fēngzhēng 27)

Three points need to be made clear about transitive verbs.

1. A transitive verb is a verb with an object, but it may appear in a sentence without an object. Please see the following.

(1) "老师！ 我 是 个 粗人， 不会 说话， 但是......"
　　lǎoshī wǒ shì gè cūrén búhuì shuōhuà dànshì
　　teacher 1SG be CL rough.man NEG talk but
　　'Sir! I am a rough man and can't talk well, but...'

徐戚安 说 着， 伸出 了 双手： "你 **看** 你 **看**！"
xúqiān shuō zhe shēnchū le shuāgnshǒu nǐ **kàn** nǐ **kàn**
Xu Qian say ZHE reach.out LE both.hands 2SG **look** 2SG **look**
'said Xu Qian, reaching out both his hands, "Look! Look!"'

邓文茵　　　　**看**。
dèngwényīn　　**kàn**
Deng.Wenyin　**look**
'Deng Wenyin looked.'

那 是 一 双 饱经沧桑的 手，
nà shì yī shuāng bǎojīngcāngsāngde shǒu
those be a pair weathered hands

非常 粗糙、 非常 苍老。（跳舞 88）
fēicháng cūcāo fēicháng cānglǎo
very rough very old
'They were weathered hands, very rough and very old.' (*Tiàowǔ* 88)

In example (1), 看 *kàn* 'look' is a transitive verb. But either in the imperative sentence 你看，你看！ *nǐkàn, nǐkàn!* 'Look! Look!' or in the declarative sentence 邓文茵看 *dèngwényīn kàn* 'Deng Wenyin looked', the object of the verb 看 *kàn* 'look', which could be understood from the previous context, is omitted.

2. Some verbs that do not semantically involve an inherent patient can take an object in the discourse as well and thus are regarded as transitive verbs. 来 *lái* 'come' is such a verb. Semantically speaking, 来 *lái* 'come' can only have an agent, not an object. But in the sentence it can take an object, as shown in the following example.

(2) 门　　外　　**来**　　了　　三　　个　　好　　兄弟。（撞墙 63）
　　 mén   wài   **lái**   le   sān   gè   hǎo   xiōngdì
　　 door outside **come** LE three CL   good brother
'Three good brothers came from outside the door.' (*Zhuàngqiáng* 63)

(3) 来　　　　学校（撞墙 49）
　　 lái　　 xuéxiào
　　 come　 school
'come to school' (*Zhuàngqiáng* 49)

In example (2), 来 *lái* 'come' is followed by an agentive object, that is to say the object can be semantically interpreted as the agent of the verb. In example (3), 来 *lái* 'come' is followed by a place object. Other similar verbs such as 去 *qù* 'go', 坐 *zuò* 'sit', 站 *zhàn* 'stand', 睡 *shuì* 'sleep', 住 *zhù* 'stay', 飞 *fēi* 'fly' are also such transitive verbs.

3   Adjectives are more widely used as transitive verbs in Singapore Mandarin than in Chinese Mandarin. But in recent years, more and more adjectives can take objects in Chinese Mandarin, all denoting a causative meaning. For example:

方便	顾客	=	使	顾客	方便
fāngbiàn	*gùkè*	=	*shǐ*	*gùkè*	*fāngbiàn*
convenient	customer	=	make	customer	convenient
清醒	头脑	=	使	头脑	清醒
qīngxǐng	*tóunǎo*	=	*shǐ*	*tóunǎo*	*qīngxǐng*
clear	mind	=	make	mind	clear
清洁	环境	=	使	环境	清洁
qīngjié	*huánjìng*	=	*shǐ*	*huánjìng*	*qīngjié*
clean	environment	=	make	environment	clean
熟练	技术	=	使	技术	熟练
shúliàn	*jìshù*	=	*shǐ*	*jìshù*	*shúliàn*
perfect	skills	=	make	skills	perfect

There are similar usages in Singapore Mandarin. Examples are:

(4) 丰富　　 你　　 的　　 知识（独 47）
　　 fēngfù　 nǐ　　 de　　 zhīshí
　　 rich　　 2SG　　 DE　　 knowledge
'enrich your knowledge' (*dú* 47)

(5) 充实   人   的   精神   粮食（薪传 130）
    chōngshí rén   de   jīngshén liángshí
    rich   people DE   spirit   food
    'enrich people's spiritual food' (*Xīnchuán* 130)

But in Singapore Mandarin, there are even usages of adjectives taking objects without causative meanings, like the following.

(6) 用   外国   学籍   和   地位   来   **骄傲**
    yòng wàiguó xuéjí   hé   dìwèi lái   **jiāoào**
    use   foreign school.registration and status to   **proud**

国人（金狮奖 76）
guórén
fellow.countrymen

'They use foreign school registration and status to show their pride in front of their fellow countrymen' (*Jīnshījiǎng* 76)

(7) 平,   你   **生气**   妈妈？（新马·剧本 19）
    píng nǐ   **shēngqì** māma
    Ping 2SG **mad**   mum
    'Ping, are you angry with Mum?' (*Xīnmǎ·jùběn* 19)

(8) 亲爱   父母   和   兄弟   姐妹,
    qīnài fùmǔ   hé   xiōngdì jiěmèi
    dear   parents and brothers sisters

    就   是   仁   的   表现。（伦理·中四 4）
    jiù   shì   rén   de   biǎoxiàn
    just be   benevolence DE   manifestation

    'To love parents, brothers and sisters is a manifestation of benevolence.' (*Lúnlǐ·zhōngsì* 4)

(9) 佛经   有   一   则   故事, 说   有   一   个   人,
    fójīng   yǒu   yī   zé   gùshì shuō yǒu   yī   gè   rén
    Buddhist.scriptures have a   CL   story say   have   a   CL   man

    为了   恐惧   自己   会   老死,   便   去
    wèile   kǒngjù zìjǐ   huì   lǎosǐ   biàn qù
    in.order.to   fear   himself will   die.of.old.age so   go

修行。（八方 142）
xiūxíng
practise

'There is a story in Buddhist scriptures about a man who went to practise for fear of dying of old age.' (*Bāfāng* 142)

(10) 我   应该   **恼怒**   你   的   **直率**   抑或
    wǒ   yīnggāi   nǎonù   nǐ   de   zhíshuài   yìhuò
    1SG   should   annoyed   2SG   DE   frankness   or

   感谢   你   的   提醒？（牛车水 94）
   gǎnxiè   nǐ   de   tíxǐng
   thank   2SG DE   reminder

'Should I be annoyed by your frankness or should I thank you for your reminder?' (*Niúchēshuǐ* 94)

In examples (6) through (10), adjectives used as verbs do not indicate a causative meaning. 骄傲国人 *jiāoào guórén* means to show their proud in front of their fellow countrymen. 生气妈妈 *shēngqì māma* means to be mad at Mum. 亲爱父母和兄弟姐妹 *qīnài fùmǔ hé xiōngdìjiěmèi* means to love one's parents, brothers and sisters. 恐惧自己会老死 *kǒngjù zìjǐ huì lǎosǐ* means to feel frightened at the thought of dying of old age. 恼怒你的直率 *nǎonù nǐ de zhíshuài* means to be annoyed by "your" frankness. There are no such usages in Chinese Mandarin.

6.11.2 Intransitive Verbs

Now let's discuss intransitive verbs. A verb that never takes an object is an intransitive verb. Here are some examples of intransitive verbs.

Monosyllables

败 *bài* 'fail'   滚 *gǔn* 'roll'   鸣 *míng* 'tweet'   疯 *fēng* 'go mad'   枯 *kū* 'droop'

Disyllables

Predicate-object compounds:

安家 *ānjiā* 'settle down at a place'   罢工 *bàgōng* 'go on strike'
办公 *bàngōng* 'do officework'   保密 *bǎomì* 'keep secrets'
道歉 *dàoqiàn* 'make an apology'   拜年 *bàinián* 'pay a new year's greeting'

Juxtaposition compounds:

奔走 *bēnzǒu* 'run around' 崩溃 *bēngkuì* 'collapse'
出发 *chūfā* 'depart' 等同 *děngtóng* 'equate'
失败 *shībài* 'fail' 考试 *kǎoshì* 'take a test'

Modifier-head compounds:

好转 *hǎozhuǎn* 'turn better' 惨败 *cǎnbài* 'suffer a crushing defeat'
安息 *ānxī* 'rest in peace' 丰收 *fēngshōu* 'harvest'

subject-predicate compounds:

地震 *dìzhèn* 'earthquake' 声张 *shēngzhāng* 'claim'
政变 *zhèngbiàn* 'overthrow' 便秘 *biànmì* 'constipate'

Some intransitive verbs are also semantically related with an entity, but the noun phrase denoting this entity never occurs in the object position; thus these verbs cannot be regarded as transitive verbs. There are three possible positions for this noun phrase, the so-called semantic patient, if it is seen with verbs in sentences.

1 Being placed at the beginning of a sentence as the subject. For example:

(11) 定稿 *dìnggǎo* 'finalise':

那	篇	文章	他	已经	定稿	了。
nà	*piān*	*wénzhāng*	*tā*	*yǐjīng*	**dìnggǎo**	le
that	CL	article	3SG	already	**finalise**	LE

'He has finalised that article.'

(12) 丰收 *fēngshōu* 'harvest':

榴莲	我们	今年	又	丰收	了。
liúlián	*wǒmēn*	*jīnnián*	*yòu*	**fēngshōu**	le
durian	1PL	this.year	again	**harvest**	LE

'We have another bumper harvest of durian this year.'

2 Being placed at the preverbal position with a preposition. For example:

(13) 道歉 *dàoqiàn* 'apologise':

我	向	他	道歉。
wǒ	*xiàng*	*tā*	*dàoqiàn*
1SG	to	3SG	apologise

'I apologised to him.'

(14) 拜年 *bàinán* 'pay a new year's greeting':

明天	上午，	冯先生	会	**给**	**您**
míngtiān	shàngwǔ	féngxiānshēng	huì	**gěi**	**nín**
tomorrow	morning	Mr. Feng	will	**GEI**	**2SG**

拜年
bàinián
pay.a.new.year's.greeting

'Tomorrow morning, Mr. Feng will pay you a new year's greeting.' (*Dàxǐ* 162)

3 Being embedded inside a predicate-object verb phrase. For example:

(15) 拆台 *chāitái* 'embarrass'

你	别	**拆**	他	的	**台**。
nǐ	bié	**chāi**	tā	de	**tái**
2SG	NEG	**embarrass**	3SG	DE	**stage**

'Do not embarrass him in public.'

(16) 盯梢 *dīngshāo* 'shadow'

他	居然	派	人	**盯**	我	的	**梢**。
tā	jūrán	pài	rén	**dīng**	wǒ	de	**shāo**
3SG	unexpectedly	send	people	**stare**	1SG	DE	**shadow**

'Unexpectedly he sent someone to shadow me.'

6.11.3 *Unique Properties of Transitive and Intransitive Verbs in Singapore Mandarin*

It is evident from the preceding that the distinction between transitive and intransitive verbs does not depend on meaning but on the grammatical function, namely, the ability to carry an object. A verb that can carry an object is a transitive verb, and a verb that never carries an object is an intransitive verb. It is for this reason that Singapore Mandarin is not entirely consistent with Chinese Mandarin in terms of the distinction between transitive and intransitive verbs. Most notably, many intransitive verbs in Chinese Mandarin are transitive in Singapore Mandarin. For example:

(17)

不断地	**修养**	自己。（伦理·中四 5）
búduànde	**xiūyǎng**	zìjǐ
continuously	**improve**	oneself

'keep on improving himself' (*Lúnlǐ·zhōngsì* 5)

(18) 只   和   他   见   了   一   次   面   的   陈老师，
    zhǐ hé tā jiàn le yī cì miàn de chénlǎoshī
    only with 3SG see LE one CL face DE Mr. Chen

    竟   这么的   关心   他， **帮忙**   他，
    jìng   zhèmede guānxīn   tā   **bāngmáng** tā
    unexpectedly so   concern   3SG **help**   3SG

    他   怎么   不   感动   呢？ （恶梦 44）
    tā   zěnme   bù   gǎndòng   ne
    3SG how   NEG moved   SFP

'Mr. Chen has just met him once but is so concerned about him and helps him a lot. How can he not be moved?' (*Èmèng* 44)

In the preceding examples, 修养 *xiūyǎng* 'improve' and 帮忙 *bāngmáng* 'help' should both be seen as transitive verbs in Singapore Mandarin as they can carry objects, whereas in Chinese Mandarin, they never carry objects and thus are intransitive.

Singapore Mandarin and Chinese Mandarin have the same origin, but how is it that these verbs that are intransitive in Chinese Mandarin can carry objects in Singapore Mandarin? There may be several reasons. Some of them (e.g. 挑衅 *tiǎoxìn* 'provoke', 挑战 *tiǎozhàn* 'challenge') are apparently influenced by English. We know that the English verbs "provoke" and "challenge" can both carry objects, as can be seen in the following examples.

He deliberately **provoked** us.

He **challenged** me.

It is true that some intransitive verbs in Singapore Mandarin have shifted into transitive verbs due to the influence of English. However, this is only an external cause, which works through the internal principles of language evolution, namely the language simplicity and economy principle.

The same is true for the distinction between transitive and intransitive verbs in English, which is also based on whether the verb can be followed by an object. Transitive verbs can carry objects, while intransitive verbs cannot. It is for this reason that Singapore Mandarin and English have both similarities and differences in the distinction between transitive and intransitive verbs.

Let's first look at the similarities.

Transitive verbs:

	Singapore Mandarin	English
研究 yánjiū 'study'	研究自然规律 yánjiū zìrán guīlǜ	to **study** the laws of nature
学习 xuéxí 'learn'	学习英语 xuéxí yīngyǔ	to **learn** English
保卫 bǎowèi 'defend'	保卫我们的祖国 bǎowèi wǒmen de zǔguó	to **defend** our country
吃 chī 'eat'	吃苹果 chī píngguǒ	to **eat** an apple

Intransitive verbs:

Singapore Mandarin	English
示威 shìwēi	**demonstrate**
合作 hézuò	**cooperate**
造反 zàofǎn	**rebel**
道歉 dàoqiàn	**apologize**

Then let's look at the differences.
The following are transitive verbs in Singapore Mandarin but intransitive verbs in English.

	Singapore Mandarin(transitive)	English(intransitive)
听 tīng 'listen'	听报告 tīng bàogào	to **listen** to a report
等 děng 'wait'	等我爸爸 děng wǒbàba	to **wait** for my father
同意 tóngyì 'agree'	同意这个计划 tóngyì zhègejìhuà	to **agree** to the plan
照料 zhàoliào 'look after'	照料孩子们 zhàoliào háizimen	to **look** after the children

The following are intransitive verbs in Singapore Mandarin but transitive verbs in English.

	Singapore Mandarin(intransitive)	English(transitive)
看齐 kànqí 'emulate'	向他看齐 xiàngtā kànqí	to **emulate** him
盯梢 dīngshāo 'shadow'	对他盯梢 duìtā dīngshāo	to **shadow** him

6.12 Verbs Taking Nominal Objects and Verbs Taking Predicative Objects

Transitive verbs can be further classified into two subclasses according to the lexical nature of the objects that follow them: Verbs taking nominal objects and verbs taking predicative objects.

Verbs taking nominal objects refer to transitive verbs such as 喝 hē 'drink', 买 mǎi 'buy', 吃 chī 'eat', 保护 bǎohù 'protect', 寻找 xúnzhǎo 'search' in Section 6.11. Here are more examples.

穿 *chuān* 'wear':

穿	着	纯白的	校服（独上 93）
chuān	zhe	chúnbáide	xiàofú
wear	ZHE	pure.white	school.uniform

'wearing pure white school uniform' (*Dúshàng* 93)

拣 *jiǎn* 'pick':

拣	小	石子（风雨 2）
jiǎn	xiǎo	shízi
pick	small	stones

'pick small stones' (*Fēngyǔ*, 2)

画 *huà* 'draw':

画	妈妈	的	脸（△含羞草 65）
huà	māmā	de	liǎn
draw	mum	DE	face

'draw mum's face' (△*Hánxiūcǎo* 65)

同情 *tóngqíng* 'sympathise':

同情	她（金狮奖 127）
tóngqíng	tā
sympathize	3SG

'show sympathy for her' (*Jīnshījiǎng* 127)

具备 *jùbèi* 'possess':

具备	两	个	因素（话剧 12）
jùbèi	liǎng	gè	yīnsù
possess	two	CL	factors

'have two factors' (*Huàjù* 12)

爱惜 *àixī* 'treasure':

爱惜	自己	的	骨肉（晚上 42）
àixī	zìjǐ	de	gǔròu
treasure	own	DE	flesh.and.blood

'love one's own children' (*Wǎnshàng* 42)

Verbs taking predicative objects refer to transitive verbs such as 希望 *xīwàng* 'hope', 受到 *shòudào* 'receive', 值得 *zhídé* 'deserve', 愿意 *yuànyì* 'be willing to' as mentioned in Section 6.11. Here are more examples.

以为 *yǐwéi* 'think':

（我	还）	以为	她	非	重写	不可。（金狮奖 126）
wǒ	hái	**yǐwéi**	tā	fēi	chóngxiě	bùkě
1SG	still	**think**	3SG	NEG	rewrite	NEG

'I thought she had to rewrite it.' (*Jīnshījiǎng* 126)

打算 *dǎsuàn* 'plan': **打算**　　　写成　　　一　　　"秘笈"。（八方 18）
　　　　　　　　　　　dǎsuàn　　*xiěchéng*　*yī*　　*mìjí*
　　　　　　　　　　　plan　　　write　　　a　　　secret.book
　　　　　　　　　　　'plan to write it as a "secret book"' (*Bāfāng* 18)

企图 *qǐtú* 'attempt': **企图**　　突破　　　传统的　　　　创作　　　　框框（至性 154）
　　　　　　　　　　　qǐtú　　　*tūpò*　　*chuántǒngde*　*chuàngzuò*　*kuàngkuang*
　　　　　　　　　　　attempt　break　　traditional　　create　　　limitation
　　　　　　　　　　　'attempt to break out of the traditional creative box' (*Zhìxìng* 154)

可以 *kěyǐ* 'may': **可以**　　　不　　　必　　　　　工作　　　　太久（渐行 64）
　　　　　　　　　　kěyǐ　　　*bú*　　*bì*　　　　*gōngzuò*　*tàijiǔ*
　　　　　　　　　　may　　　NEG　　have.to　　work　　　　too.long
　　　　　　　　　　'do not have to work too long' (*Jiànxíng* 64)

进行 *jìnxíng* 'perform': **进行**　　　　创作（科学 12）
　　　　　　　　　　　　　jìnxíng　　*chuàngzuò*
　　　　　　　　　　　　　perform　　create
　　　　　　　　　　　　　'perform creative work' (*Kēxué* 12)

加以 *jiāyǐ* 'do': **加以**　　　重视（华文 24）
　　　　　　　　　　jiāyǐ　　　pay.attention.to
　　　　　　　　　　do　　　*zhòngshì*
　　　　　　　　　　'pay much attention' (*Huáwén* 24)

Some verbs can take both nominal objects and predicative objects. They are still classified into the type of verbs taking predicative objects. For example:

看 *kàn*: **看**　　　戏（△含羞草 69）（带体宾）
　　　　　kàn　　*xì*
　　　　　watch　show
　　　　　'watch the show' (△*Hánxiūcǎo* 69) (with a nominal object)

　　　　　　看　　　有　　　　没　　　有　　　　狗（△含羞草 74）（带谓宾）
　　　　　　kàn　　*yǒu*　　　*méi*　　*yǒu*　　　*gǒu*
　　　　　　see　　have　　　NEG　　have　　　dog
　　　　　　'see if there is a dog' (△*Hánxiūcǎo* 74) (with a predicative object)

需要 xūyào: **需要** 更多的 真正的 双语 人才（风筝 41）
　　　　　　　　　　　　　　　　　　　（带体宾）
　　　　　　xūyào gèngduōde zhēnzhèngde shuāngyǔ réncái
　　　　　　need more real bilingual talent
　　　　　　'need more real bilingual talent' (*Fēngzhēng* 41) (with a nominal object)

　　　　　　需要 改善（华文 2）（带谓宾）
　　　　　　xūyào gǎishàn
　　　　　　need improvement
　　　　　　'need improvement' (*Huáwén* 2) (with a predicative object)

重视 zhòngshì: **重视** 自己的 传统 文化（华文 7）（带体宾）
　　　　　　zhòngshì zìjǐde chuántǒng wénhuà
　　　　　　value own traditional culture
　　　　　　'value our own traditional culture' (*Huáwén* 7) (with a nominal object)

　　　　　　重视 培养 学生 的 阅读 习惯（华文 6）
　　　　　　　　　　　　　　　　　　　　　　　（带谓宾）
　　　　　　zhòngshì péiyǎng xuéshēng de yuèdú xíguàn
　　　　　　value develop students DE reading habits
　　　　　　'attach importance to developing students' reading habits'
　　　　　　(*Huáwén* 6) (with a predicative object)

接受 jiēshòu: **接受** 这些 新 事物（风筝 29）（带体宾）
　　　　　　jiēshòu zhèxiē xīn shìwù
　　　　　　accept these new things
　　　　　　'accept these news things' (*Fēngzhēng* 29) (with a nominal object)

　　　　　　接受 训练（风筝 41）（带谓宾）
　　　　　　jiēshòu xùnliàn
　　　　　　receive train
　　　　　　'receive training' (*Fēngzhēng* 41) (with a predicative object)

6.13 Verbs Taking Predicative Objects and Verbs Taking Quasi-predicative Objects

Within the group of verbs taking predicative objects, a further division can be made according to the properties of objects: Verbs taking predicative objects and verbs taking quasi-predicative objects.

It is observed that when verbs carry predicative objects, there exist two paradigms:

A Some verbs may take either a single verb or adjective, or a verb phrase, as in the case of 希望 *xīwàng*, 'hope' and 感到 *gǎndào*, 'feel'.

(a) The object is a single verb or adjective:

希望	参加
xīwàng	*cānjiā*
hope	join

'hope to join'

感到	舒服
gǎndào	*shūfú*
feel	comfortable

'feel comfortable'

(b) The object is a modifier-head phrase:

希望	马上	参加
xīwàng	*mǎshàng*	*cānjiā*
hope	immediately	join

'hope to join immediately'

感到	十分	舒服
gǎndào	*shífēn*	*shūfú*
feel	extremely	comfortable

'feel extremely comfortable'

(c) The object is a predicate-object phrase:

希望	参加	开幕	典礼
xīwàng	*cānjiā*	*kāimù*	*diǎnlǐ*
hope	attend	opening	ceremony

'hope to attend the opening ceremony'

感到	舒服	一些
gǎndào	*shūfú*	*yīxiē*
feel	comfortable	a.bit

'feel a bit more comfortable'

(d) The object is a predicate-complement phrase:

希望	参加	得	早	一些
xīwàng	cānjiā	de	zǎo	yīxiē
hope	attend	DE	early	a.bit

'hope to be there a bit earlier'

感到	舒服	得	很
gǎndào	shūfú	de	hěn
feel	comfortable	DE	much

'feel very comfortable'

(e) The object is a subject-predicate phrase:

希望	他	也	参加
xīwàng	tā	yě	cānjiā
hope	he	also	join

'hope he will also join'

感到	身体	很	舒服
gǎndào	shēntǐ	hěn	shūfú
feel	body	very	comfortable

'feel my body is very comfortable'

It is evident that the objects of the verb 希望 *xīwàng* 'hope' and 感到 *gǎndào* 'feel' are predicative objects in every sense.

B Some other verbs can only take a single two-syllable verb, not a verb phrase, as their objects. 进行 *jìnxíng*, 'conduct' is a case in point, as illustrated by the following example phrases.

进行	研究
jìnxíng	yánjiū
conduct	research

'conduct research' (The object is a single two-syllable verb.)

> * | 进行 | 马上 | 研究 |
> |---|---|---|
> | jìnxíng | mǎshàng | yánjiū |
> | conduct | immediately | research |
>
> Intended meaning: 'conduct research immediately' (The object cannot be a modifier-head phrase.)

* 进行　　　研究　　　华语　　　　　　　语法
  jìnxíng　*yánjiū*　*huáyǔ*　　　　　*yǔfǎ*
  conduct　research　Singapore.Mandarin　grammar
  Intended meaning: 'conduct research on Singapore Mandarin' (The object cannot be a predicate-object phrase.)

* 进行　　　研究　　　得　　深　　　一些
  jìnxíng　*yánjiū*　*de*　*shēn*　*yīxiē*
  conduct　research　DE　deep　a.bit
  Intended meaning: 'conduct deeper research' (The object cannot be a predicate-complement phrase.)

* 进行　　　大家　　都　　研究
  jìnxíng　*dàjiā*　*dōu*　*yánjiū*
  conduct　everybody　all　research
  Intended meaning: 'everybody conducts research' (The object cannot be a subject-predicate phrase.)

* 进行　　　学
  jìnxíng　*xué*
  conduct　learn
  Intended meaning: 'learn' (The object cannot be a monosyllable verb.)

These examples show that 研究 *yánjiū* 'research' loses some verbal properties once it becomes the object of 进行 *jìnxíng* 'conduct', but acquires some nominal properties, such as being modified by attributes. For example:

(1) 进行　　　课室　　　研究（华文 34）
　　jìnxíng　*kèshì*　*yánjiū*
　　conduct　classroom　research
　　'conduct classroom research' (*Huáwén* 34)

(2) 进行　　　华文　　　教学（华文 19）
　　jìnxíng　*huáwén*　*jiàoxué*
　　conduct　Chinese　education
　　'carry out Chinese education' (*Huáwén* 19)

(3) 进行   了   一   次   阅读   能力   调查（华文 23）
    jìnxíng le   yí   cì   yuèdú   nénglì   diàochá
    conduct LE   a   CL   reading ability   investigation
    'conducted an investigation into reading ability' (*Huáwén* 23)

It is apparent that the objects of 进行 *jìnxíng* 'conduct' are not authentic predicative objects.

To make a distinction between them, predicative objects following 希望 *xīwàng* 'hope' and 感到 *gǎndào* 'feel' are referred to as predicative objects while those following 进行 *jìnxíng* 'conduct' are referred to as quasi-predicative objects. Correspondingly, the verbs are thereby classified into two groups, those taking predicative objects and those taking quasi-predicative objects. Verbs mentioned in this section and Section 6.1.2, such as 觉得 *juéde* 'feel', 希望 *xīwàng* 'hope', 认为 *rènwéi* 'think', 值得 *zhídé* 'worth of', 愿意 *yuànyì* 'be willing', 以为 *yǐwéi* 'thought', 打算 *dǎsuàn* 'plan', 企图 *qǐtú* 'attempt', 妄想 *wàngxiǎng* 'vainly think', 主张 *zhǔzhāng* 'state', 感到 *gǎndào* 'feel', 显得 *xiǎnde* 'look', 应该 *yīnggāi* 'should', 可以 *kěyǐ* 'can', 看 *kàn* 'see', 需要 *xūyào* 'need', 喜欢 *xǐhuān* 'like' are all verbs taking predicative objects. More examples are:

想 *xiǎng* 'want':   **想**   上学 (女儿 167)
                   xiǎng   shàngxué
                   want   go.to.school
                   'want to go to school' (*Nǚér* 167)

敢 *gǎn* 'dare':   不   **敢**   看   他（青青 115）
                   bù   ***gǎn***   kàn   tā
                   NEG   **dare**   look   3SG
                   'don't dare to look at him' (*Qīngqīng* 115)

爱 *ài* 'love':   **爱**   种   花（壁虎 23）
                   ài   zhòng   huā
                   love   plant   flowers
                   'love planting flowers' (*Bìhǔ* 23)

知道 *zhīdào* 'know': **知道**   如何   待人接物（风筝 10）
                     zhīdào   rúhé   dàirénjiēwù
                     know   how   get.along.with.people
                     'know how to get along with people' (*Fēngzhēng* 10)

相信 xiāngxìn 'believe': 相信　　　儿童　　　文学　　　是　有前途的（风筝 19）
　　　　　　　　　　　　xiāngxìn　értóng　wénxué　shì　yǒuqiántúde
　　　　　　　　　　　　believe　children　literature　be　promising
　　　　　　　　　　　　'believe that children's literature is promising'
　　　　　　　　　　　　(*Fēngzhēng* 19)

看见 kànjiàn 'see':　　　看见　　　麦先生　　　疾步　　　走来（追云 18）
　　　　　　　　　　　　kànjiàn　màixiānshēng　jíbù　zǒulái
　　　　　　　　　　　　see　　Mr. Mai　　fast　　walk
　　　　　　　　　　　　'see Mr. Mai walking over quickly' (*Zhuīyún* 18)

准备 zhǔnbèi 'prepare':　准备　　　下　　　车（有缘 11）
　　　　　　　　　　　　zhǔnbèi　xià　　chē
　　　　　　　　　　　　prepare　get.off　car
　　　　　　　　　　　　'prepare to get out of the car' (*Yǒuyuán* 11)

乐得 lède 'happy':　　　乐得　　　送　　　人（壁虎 23）
　　　　　　　　　　　　lède　　sòng　　rén
　　　　　　　　　　　　happy　give　someone
　　　　　　　　　　　　'happy to give it to someone' (*Bìhǔ* 23)

准许 zhǔnxǔ 'permit':　准许　　　进入　　　市区（有缘 20）
　　　　　　　　　　　　zhǔnxǔ　jìnrù　shìqū
　　　　　　　　　　　　permit　enter　urban.area
　　　　　　　　　　　　'permit to enter urban areas' (*Yǒuyuán* 20)

In contrast, verbs like 受到 *shòudào* 'get', 进行 *jìnxíng* 'conduct', 加以 *jiāyǐ* 'do', 有 *yǒu* 'have', 接受 *jiēshòu* 'receive' are verbs taking quasi-predicative objects. More examples are 作 *zuò* 'do' and 得到 *dédào* 'get'.

作　a　　作　　　　了　　　研究（报 1995 年 8 月 21 日 6 版）
　　　　　zuò　　le　　yánjiū
　　　　　do　　LE　　research
　　　　　'did research' (*Bào*, Aug. 21, 1995, Issue no. 6)

　　b　　作　　　　了　　　下列　　的　　调整（华文 11）
　　　　　zuò　　le　　xiàliè　de　tiáozhěng
　　　　　make　LE　following　DE　adjustment
　　　　　'made adjustments as follows' (*Huáwén* 11)

得到 a	**得到**	帮助		
	dédào	*bāngzhù*		
	get	help		
	'get help'			

b	**得到**	了	很	大的	休息（女儿 164）
	dédào	*le*	*hěn*	*dàde*	*xiūxī*
	get	LE	very	big	rest
	'got a very nice rest' (*Nǚér* 164)				

Verbs taking quasi-predicative objects are not many in number but are used quite frequently, especially in written language.

6.14 Modal Verbs

6.14.1 Modal Verbs and Their Properties

Modal verbs refer to the following:

能 *néng* 'can'	能够 *nénggòu* 'can'	可 *kě* 'can'
可以 *kěyǐ* 'may'	可能 *kěnéng* 'may'	要 *yào* 'want'
会 *huì* 'be able to'	应 *yīng* 'should'	应该 *yīnggāi* 'should'
该 *gāi* 'ought to'	应当 *yīngdāng* 'should'	愿 *yuàn* 'wish'
愿意 *yuànyì* 'will'	情愿 *qíngyuàn* 'be willing to'	乐意 *lèyì* 'be willing to'
肯 *kěn* 'be ready to'	敢 *gǎn* 'dare'	值得 *zhídé* 'deserve'
配 *pèi* 'deserve'	许 *xǔ* 'allow'	准 *zhǔn* 'permit'
准许 *zhǔnxǔ* 'allow'		

In China, some people call these words auxiliary verbs (Ding Shenshu etc. 1961; Zhu 1982). Not to be confused with auxiliary verbs in English, we are not going to use this term, but use modal verbs instead.

Modal verbs are a subcategory of verbs taking predicative objects. They are defined as follows:

1 Modal verbs can only carry predicative objects, but not nominal objects.
2 Modal verbs cannot be followed by dynamic auxiliary such as 了 *le* 'LE', 着 *zhe* 'ZHE', 过 *guò* 'GUO'.
3 Modal verbs can be reduplicated in the form of ~不~~*bù*~ 'V NEG V', such as 能不能 *néng bù néng* 'can or cannot', 可以不可以 *kě bù kěyǐ* 'may or may not', 该不该 *gāi bù gāi* 'ought to or ought not to', 应当不应当 *yīng bù yīngdāng* 'should or should not', 值得不值得 *zhídé bù zhídé* 'deserve or not', 准不准 *zhǔn bù zhǔn* 'allow or not'.

4   Modal verbs can be used alone, with no objects. For example:

(1) "你   可以   不   可以   挪进   一点,   让   我   分享?"
    nǐ   kěyǐ   bù   kěyǐ   nuójìn   yìdiǎn   ràng   wǒ   fēnxiǎng
    2SG   can   NEG   can   move   a.little   let   1SG   share
    'Can you move a little to share with me?'

    "当然   可以。"（金狮奖 135）
    dāngrán   kěyǐ
    of.course   can
    'Of course, I can.' (*Jīnshījiǎng* 135)

(2) 乙: 你   能   唱?
    yǐ: nǐ   **néng**   chàng
    B: 2SG   can   sing
    'B: Can you sing?'

    甲: 能!   （笑眼47）
    jiǎ: **néng**
    A: can
    'A: I can!' (*Xiàoyǎn* 47)

According to the preceding four criteria, some verbs taking predicative objects such as 喜欢 *xǐhuān* 'like', 得 *de* 'allow' (as in 不得随地吐痰 *bùdé suídì tǔtán* 'no spitting'), 打算 *dǎsuàn* 'plan' are not modal verbs. 喜欢 *xǐhuān* 'like' can carry both predicative objects and nominal objects (as in 喜欢孩子 *xǐhuān háizi* 'like kids'). 得 *de* 'allow' can only carry predicative objects, but it cannot be used in the question form of ~不~ ~*bù*~ 'V NEG V'. Although 打算 *dǎsuàn* 'plan' can carry predicative objects and be used in the question form of ~不~ ~*bù*~ 'V NEG V', it cannot be used alone without an object. Thus these words are verbs taking predicative objects, but not modal verbs.

6.14.2 要 yào 'Should', 会 huì 'Can', 配 pèi 'Deserve'

Among the aforementioned modal verbs, 要 *yào* 'should', 会 *huì* 'can', 配 *pèi* 'deserve' can carry nominal objects. They do not seem to agree with the grammatical features of modal verbs. In fact, these three words have different meanings when being used as modal verbs and verbs taking nominal objects. Grammatically they should be seen as two different words in the same form. Compare the following examples.

要 yào

a should, must (as a modal verb)

你	要	努力		学习
nǐ	yào	nǔlì		xuéxí
2SG	**should**	make.great.efforts		study

'You should study hard.'

b want or to retain (as a verb taking a nominal object)

我	要	这	本	书
wǒ	yào	zhè	běn	shū
1SG	**want**	this	CL	book

'I want this book.'

这些	衣服	我	还	要	呢
zhèxiē	yīfú	wǒ	hái	yào	ne
these	clothes	1SG	still	**retain**	SFP

'I will retain these clothes.'

会 huì

a can, be able to (as a modal verb)

他	很	会	说话
tā	hěn	huì	shuōhuà
3SG	very	**can**	talk

'He is a good talker.'

他	不	会	打	球
tā	bú	huì	dǎ	qiú
3SG	NEG	**can**	play	ball

'He cannot play ball.'

b be familiar with, understand, know (as a verb taking a nominal object)

他	会	英语	也	会	华语
tā	huì	yīngyǔ	yě	huì	huáyǔ
3SG	**know**	English	also	**know**	Chinese

'He knows both English and Chinese.'

配 *pèi*

a deserve (as a modal verb)

他	不	配	做	教师
tā	*bú*	***pèi***	*zuò*	*jiàoshī*
3SG	NEG	**deserve**	be	teacher

'He doesn't deserve to be a teacher.'

b to make up for (as a verb taking a nominal object)

我	要	配	一	个	钮扣
wǒ	*yào*	***pèi***	*yí*	*gè*	*niǔkòu*
1SG	want	**fix**	a	CL	button

'I'd like to have a button (to make up for the missing one).'

6.14.3 Grammatical Meanings of Modal Verbs

Grammatically, modal verbs express the following meanings.

1 To talk about possibility. This can be further divided into three types.

　A To express subjective possibility or subjective ability. Commonly used modal verbs include 能 *néng* 'can', 能够 *nénggòu* 'can', 可 *kě* 'can', 可以 *kěyǐ* 'may', 会 *huì* 'will'. For example:

(3)

我	能	为	她	解开	心	中	的	结。（短篇 30）
wǒ	***néng***	*wèi*	*tā*	*jiěkāi*	*xīn*	*zhōng*	*de*	*jié*
1SG	**can**	for	3SG	untie	heart	inside	DE	knot

'I can ease her mind.' (*Duǎnpiān* 30)

(4)

我	并不	是	医生，	不	能	帮	你	什么
wǒ	*bìngbú*	*shì*	*yīshēng*	*bù*	***néng***	*bāng*	*nǐ*	*shénme*
1SG	NEG	be	doctor	NEG	**can**	help	2SG	what

忙……（有缘49）
máng
help

'I am not a doctor. I cannot help you.' (*Yǒuyuán* 49)

(5)

通过	想象	之	窗，	我们	能够	想象
tōngguò	*xiǎngxiàng*	*zhī*	*chuāng*	*wǒmen*	***nénggòu***	*xiǎngxiàng*
through	imagination	of	window	1PL	**can**	imagine

窗	内	的	人	和	物。（独上 24－25）
chuāng	nèi	de	rén	hé	wù
window	inside	DE	people	and	objects

'Through the window of imagination, we can imagine the people and things inside the window.' (*Dúshàng* 24–25)

(6)
什么	都	不	看	是	最	幸福的,
shénme	dōu	bú	kàn	shì	zuì	xìngfúde
anything	altogether	NEG	look	SHI	most	happy

可是	我	不	**能够,**	也	不	愿意。（独上 2）
kěshì	wǒ	bù	**nénggòu**	yě	bú	yuànyì
but	1SG	NEG	**can**	also	NEG	want

'Looking at nothing would make me happiest, but I can't and don't want to do that.' (*Dúshàng* 2)

(7)
有	了	一百万,	**可以**	买	房子,	买	汽车……（再见 55）
yǒu	le	yībǎiwàn	**kěyǐ**	mǎi	fángzi	mǎi	qìchē
have	LE	one.million	**can**	buy	house	buy	car

'With one million you can buy houses and cars.' (*Zàijiàn* 55)

(8)
我	**会**	下田	帮	我	父母	耕种。（跳舞 16）
wǒ	**huì**	xiàtián	bāng	wǒ	fùmǔ	gēngzhòng
1SG	**will**	go.to.the.field	help	1SG	parents	farming

'I will go to the field and help my parents with the farming.' (*Tiàowǔ* 16)

Please note: 能 *néng*, 能够 *nénggòu* and 可 *kě*, 可以 *kěyǐ* can express subjective possibility, but there are differences in between. 能 *néng* and 能够 *nénggòu* can be used in both positive and negative forms, while 可 *kě* and 可以 *kěyǐ* can only be used in positive forms (不可 *bùkě* and 不可以 *bùkěyǐ* do not denote negative subjective possibility). Therefore, 能 *néng*, 能够 *nénggòu* in examples (3) and (5) and 可以 *kěyǐ* in example (7) are interchangeable. Nevertheless, 不能 *bùnéng* and 不能够 *bùnénggòu* in examples (4) and (6) cannot be replaced by 不可 *bùkě* or 不可以 *bùkěyǐ*. 会 *huì* also differs from 能 *néng* and 能够 *nénggòu*, in that the former usually describes the ability gained through learning or training while the latter do not have this limitation. So 会 *huì* in any sentences can be replaced by 能 *néng* or 能够 *nénggòu* but not vice versa. For example, 他**能**喝三瓶啤酒 *tā néng hē sān píng píjiǔ* 'He can drink three bottles of beer' cannot be expressed as 他**会**喝三瓶啤酒 *tā huì hē sān píng píjiǔ*.

B To express objective possibility. Commonly used modal verbs include 会 *huì* 'will', 能 *néng* 'can', 可能 *kěnéng* 'maybe'. For example:

(9) 念　　　大学　　就　　一定　　**会**　　找到　　　　好的　　对象。（大喜 191）
    niàn　　dàxué　 jiù　 yídìng　**huì**　zhǎodào　hǎode　duìxiàng
    study　 college　thus　certainly　will　 find　　 good　 partner
    'If you go to college, you will find a good life partner.' (*Dàxǐ* 191)

(10) 肯定　　　　不　　 **会**　　发现　　　　的。（金狮奖 100）
    kěndìng　　 bú　　**huì**　 fāxiàn　　　de
    certainly　 NEG　 **will**　find.out　　DE
    'It certainly won't be found out.' (*Jīnshījiǎng* 100)

(11) 我　　　想：　任何人　　　拜读　　　　　　　　　　过　　　大札，
    wǒ　　xiǎng　rènhérén　 bàidú　　　　　　　　　　guò　　dàzhá
    1SG　 think　anybody　 have.the.honour.to.read　GUO　 DaZha

    必定　　 都　　希望　　**能**　　和　　　你　　　做　　　朋友。
    　　　　　　　　　　　　　　　　　　　　　　　　　　　　　　（短篇14）
    bìdìng　dōu　 xīwàng　**néng**　hé　　　 nǐ　　　zuò　　péngyǒu
    surely　all　 wish　　**can**　with　　2SG　　　make　 friends
    'I think anybody who has the honour to read *Da Zha* would certainly like to be friends with you.' (*Duǎnpiān* 14)

(12) 照　　　　　 她　　 的　 一举一动，　　 还有　　 她　　 的　　谈吐，
    zhào　　　　tā　　 de　 yìjǔyídòng　　 háiyǒu　 tā　　 de　　tántǔ
    according.to　3SG　 DE　behaviour　　 also　　 3SG　 DE　 manners

    她　　　很　　**可能**　　是　　 一　　位　　吃过教育饭的　　　　人。（一心 8－9）
    tā　　　hěn　 **kěnéng**　shì　 yí　　wèi　chīguòjiàoyùfànde　 rén
    3SG　 very　 **maybe**　 be　　a　　 CL　 educated　　　　　 person
    'Judging from her behaviour and manners, she is very likely to be an educated person.' (*Yixin* 8–9)

C To express permission. Commonly used modal verbs are as follows.

能 *néng* 'can'　　　　能够 *nénggòu* 'can'　　　　可以 *kěyǐ* 'may'
许 *xǔ* 'permit'　　　 准 *zhǔn* 'permit'　　　　　 准许 *zhǔnxǔ* 'allow'

For example:

(13) a 愿意 去 的 都 **能** 去。
       yuànyì qù de dōu **néng** qù
       willing go DE all **can** go
       'Anyone who wants to go can go.'

   b 你 的 报告 是否 **能** 借 我 看看？（金狮奖 99）
       nǐ de bàogào shìfǒu **néng** jiè wǒ kànkàn
       2SG DE report whether **can** borrow 1SG look-look
       'Can I borrow your report to have a look?' (*Jīnshīijiǎng* 99)

(14) a 教室 里 不 **能** 抽烟。
       jiàoshì lǐ bù **néng** chōuyān
       classroom inside NEG **permit** smoke
       'Smoking is not allowed in the classroom.'

   b 被 传讯 的 是 孩子，家长 绝 不 **能**
       bèi chuánxùn de shì háizi jiāzhǎng jué bù **néng**
       BEI summon DE be child parents must NEG **permit**

       插手。（女儿 38）
       chāshǒu
       interfere

       'It is the child who is summoned. The parents are not allowed to interfere.' (*Nǚér* 38)

(15) 女孩子 不 **能够** 在 外面 过 夜！
       nǚháizi bù **nénggòu** zài wàimiàn guò yè
       Girls NEG **can** at outside spend night
       'Girls mustn't spend the night outside!'

(16) 我 等 一 下 来 领，**可以** 吗？（跳舞 3）
       wǒ děng yí xià lái lǐng, **kěyǐ** ma
       1SG wait a moment come get, **may** SFP
       'I'll get it later, may I?' (*Tiàowǔ* 3)

(17) 妈妈   终于   答应   了，   条件   是   不   **许**   吵到
     māmā   zhōngyú   dāyìng   le,   tiáojiàn shì   bù   **xǔ**   chǎodào
     mum   finally   agree   LE,   condition be   NEG   **permit** disturb

   邻居，   不   **许**   弄脏   地方，   不   **许**   玩
   línjū   bù   **xǔ**   nòngzāng   dìfāng   bù   **xǔ**   wán
   neighbours NEG   **permit** mess   place   NEG   **permit** play

   得   太   迟，   在   午夜   之前   必须   结束   舞会。（牛车水 73）
   de   tài   chí   zài   wǔyè   zhīqián   bìxū   jiéshù   wǔhuì
   DE   too   late   at   midnight before   must   finish   ball.
   'Mum finally agreed on the following conditions. No disturbing the neighbours. No messing up the place. No staying up too late. Finish the ball before midnight.' (*Niúchēshuǐ* 73)

(18) 以后   不   **准**   再   提起   养   狗   的   事
     yǐhòu   bù   **zhǔn**   zài   tíqǐ   yǎng   gǒu   de   shì
     later   NEG   **permit**   again   mention keep   dog   DE   thing

   呵！（追云7）
   he
   SFP
   'Don't talk about keeping a dog anymore!' (*Zhuīyún* 7)

(19) **准许**   进入   市区（有缘 20）
     zhǔnxǔ   jìnrù   shìqū
     permit   enter   urban.district
     'Permit them to enter the city.' (*Yǒuyuán* 20)

2 To express obligation. Commonly used modal verbs are as follows.

应 *yīng* 'should'   该 *gāi* 'should'   应该 *yīnggāi* 'should'
应当 *yīngdāng* 'should'   要 *yào* 'must'

   For example:

(20) 你   **应**   如实   告诉   他。
     nǐ   **yīng**   rúshí   gàosù   tā
     2SG   **should**   things.as.they.really.are tell   3SG
     'You should tell him exactly what happened.'

(21) a 你 该 吃 药 了。
  nǐ **gāi** chī yào le
  2SG **should** take medication LE
  'You should take medicine now.'

 b 该 回去 了（金狮奖 240）
  gāi huíqù le
  should go.back LE
  'It is time to go back.' (*Jīnshījiǎng* 240)

(22) 你们 身为 师表, **应该** 走 得 正,
  nǐmen shēnwéi shībiǎo, **yīnggāi** zǒu de zhèng
  2PL as teachers **should** walk DE upright.

 行 得 正, 坐 得 正。（一心 7）
 xíng de zhèng, zuò de zhèng.
 act DE upright, sit DE upright.
 'As teachers you should be upright and behave in a moral way.' (*Yixin* 7)

(23) a 你 **应当** 向 他 赔礼道歉。
  nǐ **yīngdāng** xiàng tā péilǐdàoqiàn
  2SG **should** towards 3SG apologise
  'You should apologise to him.'

 b 你 是 他 娘, 你 **应当** 知道 的!（大胡子 137）
  nǐ shì tā niáng, nǐ **yīngdāng** zhīdào de
  2SG be his mother 2SG **should** know DE
  'You are his mother, you ought to know.'

(24) a 你 **要** 听 老师 的 话。
  nǐ **yào** tīng lǎoshī de huà
  2SG **should** listen teacher DE words
  'You should listen to the teacher.'

 b 现在 钟依琳 既然 有喜在身,
  xiànzài zhōngyīlín jìrán yǒuxǐzàishēn,
  now Zhongyilin now.that pregnant,

少不得	要	顺	着	她	些儿。（追云 33）
shǎobùdé	yào	shùn	zhe	tā	xiēér
necessary	must	follow	ZHE	3SG	a.bit

'Now that Zhongyilin is pregnant, we might as well be nice to her.' (*Zhuīyún* 33)

3   To express volition. Commonly used modal verbs include:

愿 *yuàn* 'want'　　　　　愿意 *yuànyì* 'wish'　　　情愿 *qíngyuàn* 'be willing to'
乐意 *lèyì* 'be happy to'　　肯 *kěn* 'will'　　　　　敢 *gǎn* 'dare'
要 *yào* 'want'

For example:

(25)
我	不	愿	伤害	她。（短篇 70）
wǒ	bú	yuàn	shānghài	tā
1SG	NEG	want	hurt	3SG

'I don't want to hurt her.' (*Duǎnpiān* 70)

(26)
老二	当时	心里头	压根儿	不	愿意	回来。（风雨 38）
lǎoèr	dāngshí	xīnlǐtóu	yāgēner	bú	yuànyì	huílái
No. 2	at.that.time	heart.inside	indeed	NEG	want	return

'The second child at that time didn't want to come back at all.' (*Fēngyǔ* 38)

(27) a
他	自己	情愿	当	的士	司机。
tā	zìjǐ	qíngyuàn	dāng	dīshì	sījī
3SG	himself	want	work.as	taxi	driver

'He would rather be a taxi driver.'

b
你	自己	情愿	摆摊子？（大喜29）
nǐ	zìjǐ	qíngyuàn	bǎitānzi
2SG	yourself	want	set.up.a. stall

'Would you rather set up your own stall?' (*Dàxǐ* 29)

(28)
他们	乐意	伸出	热诚之手	去	援助	别人（一心 48）
tāmen	lèyì	shēnchū	rèchénzhīshǒu	qù	yuánzhù	biérén
3PL	be.happy.to	stretch.out	a warm hand	to	help	others

'They are happy to lend a warm hand to help others.' (*Yixin* 48)

(29) a 他 肯 原谅 姑母 吗？（大胡子 90）
    tā **kěn** yuánliàng gūmǔ ma
    3SG **will** forgive aunt SFP
    'Will he forgive his aunt?' (*Dàhúzi* 90)

   b 爸爸 不 肯 去（有缘7）
    bàbà bù **kěn** qù
    dad NEG **will** go
    'Dad won't go.' (*Yǒuyuán* 7)

(30) a 我 不 想 说，而 她，不 敢 说。（大胡子 84）
    wǒ bù xiǎng shuō ér tā bù **gǎn** shuō
    1SG NEG want say whereas 3SG NEG **dare** say
    'I don't want to say but she doesn't dare to say.' (*Dàhúzi* 84)

   b 你 敢 保证？（金狮奖94）
    nǐ **gǎn** bǎozhèng
    2SG **dare** promise
    'Dare you promise?' (*Jīnshījiǎng* 94)

(31) 我 要 吃 粥。（有缘27）
    wǒ **yào** chī zhōu
    1SG **want** eat porridge
    'I want to have some porridge.' (*Yǒuyuán* 27)

4 To express value or qualification. Commonly used modal verbs are 值得 *zhídé* 'deserve' and 配 *pèi* 'deserve'. For example:

(32) 值得 一看再看。（青青 36）
    zhídé yíkànzàikàn
    worth reading.over.and.over
    'It is worth reading over and over again.' (*Qīngqīng* 36)

(33) a 你 不 配 当 我 的 爸爸。（有缘 33）
    nǐ bú **pèi** dāng wǒ de bàbà
    2SG NEG **deserve** be 1SG DE dad
    'You don't deserve to be my dad.' (*Yǒuyuán* 33)

(33) b

我	不	**配**	爱	你？（△浮萍 82）
wǒ	bú	***pèi***	ài	nǐ
1SG	NEG	deserve	love	2SG

'I don't deserve to love you?' (△*Fúpíng* 82)

c

你们	现在	这些	新闻记者，
nǐmen	xiànzài	zhèxiē	xīnwénjìzhě
2PL	nowadays	these	reporter

根本	不	**配**	称	无冕之王。（变调 11）
gēnběn	bú	***pèi***	chēng	wúmiǎnzhīwáng
simply	NEG	deserve	called	uncrowned.king

'You reporters don't deserve to be called uncrowned kings.' (*Biàndiào* 11)

Notes

1 啦 *lā* 'SFP' is the abbreviated form of 了 *le* 'SFP' plus 啊 *a* 'SFP'.
2 Translator's note: in this case of two sentences, there will be no contrastive meaning.

7 Predicates and Complements

Lu Jianming

7.1 Predicate-Complement Phrases in Singapore Mandarin

7.1.1 Predicate-Complement Phrases and Their Unique Features

Predicate-complement phrases usually consist of a verb or an adjective followed by a constituent that complements the predicate. For example, 洗干净 *xǐ gānjìng* 'wash clean' is a predicate-complement phrase in which the verb 洗 *xǐ* 'wash' is the predicate and 干净 *gānjìng* 'clean' is the complement attached to the predicate.

Predicate-complement phrases represent a special syntactic structure peculiar to the lingua franca of the Han people, including Singapore Mandarin. Different from the aforementioned subject-predicate phrases and predicate-object phrases, they can be viewed as an abbreviated structure of two sentences combined together.[1] This is most clearly seen when the predicate-complement phrase functions as the predicate, in which case the resulting subject predicate sentence is actually an abbreviated form of two sentences, as shown here.

(1) 我   走   累   了   ←   我   走   +   我   累   了
    wǒ   zǒu lèi   le   wǒ   zǒu   wǒ   lèi   le
    1SG walk tired LE   1SG walk   1SG tired LE
    'I walked until I am tired.'   'I walk.'   'I am tired.'

(2) 衣服   洗   干净   了   ←   衣服   洗   了   +
    yīfú   xǐ   gānjìng le   yīfú   xǐ   le
    clothes wash clean   LE   clothes wash LE
    'Clothes were washed clean.'   'Clothes were washed.'

    衣服   干净   了
    yīfú   gānjìng le
    clothes clean   LE
    'Clothes are clean.'

DOI: 10.4324/b23129-7

(3) 我   把   黑板   **擦**   **干净**   了   ←   我   **擦**   黑板
    wǒ   bǎ   hēibǎn   cā   gānjìng   le   wǒ   cā   hēibǎn
    1S   BAG blackboard scrub clean   LE   1SG scrub blackboard
    'I scrubbed the blackboard (until it was) clean.'   'I scrubbed the blackboard.'

    +   黑板   **干净**   了
        hēibǎn   gānjìng   le
        blackboard clean   LE
        'The blackboard was clean.'

Many foreign students who have just begun their study of Singapore Mandarin often find it difficult to master predicate-complement phrases because they don't know how these phrases are formed. Thus, it is necessary to give enough attention to the features of these phrases in our teaching.

7.1.2 *Semantic Orientation of the Complements*

A complement is a grammatical constituent that provides supplementary information to the predicate. But the semantic orientation of the complement (i.e. which constituent does the complement predicate semantically?) is a complicated issue because there are at least five possibilities. They are shown next with examples.

1   The complement semantically points to the predicate.

(4) 飞   得   快快。（独上 74）
    fēi   de   kuài-kuài
    fly   DE   very.fast
    'Fly very fast.' (*Dúshàng* 74)

(5) 美观   极   了！（晚上 15）
    měiguān   jí   le
    beautiful extremely LE
    'Very beautiful!' (*Wǎnshàng* 15)

In sentence (4), the complement 快快 *kuàikuài* 'very fast' states the speed of the action verb 飞 *fēi* 'fly' (a duplication of monosyllabic adjective being the complement will be elaborated in Section 7.6), while in sentence (5) the complement 极了 *jíle* 'extremely' indicates the degree of the property denoted by the adjective predicate 美观 *měiguān* 'beautiful'.

2 The complement semantically points to the agent (the actor) of the action verb.

(6) 他　　　走　　　累　　　了。（梦 45）
    tā   zǒu   lèi   le
    3SG   walk   tired   LE
    'He walked until he is tired.' (*Mèng* 45)

(7) （我）　　听　　　不　　　懂。（石头 111）
    wǒ   tīng   bù   dǒng
    1SG   listen   NEG   understand
    'I don't understand.' (*Shítou* 111)

The complement 累 *lèi* 'tired' in sentence (6) states 他 *tā* 'he', the agent of the verb 走 *zǒu* 'walk', was tired and the complement 不懂 *bùdǒng* 'not understand' in sentence (7) is about 我 *wǒ* 'I', the agent of the verb 听 *tīng* 'listen'.

3 The complement semantically points to the patient (the undergoer) of the action verb.

(8) 把　　整个　　　模型　　　染　　　红。（△一壶 101）
    bǎ   zhěnggè   móxíng   rǎn   hóng
    BA   whole   model   dye   red
    'Dye the whole model red.' (*Yìhú* 101)

(9) 花啊　　草啊　　树啊，　剪　　得　　整整齐齐的。（撞墙 65）
    huā'a   cǎo'a   shù'a,   jiǎn   de   zhěngzhěngqíqíde
    flowers grass   trees   trim   DE   tidy
    'The flowers, grass and trees are trimmed tidily.' (*Zhuàngqiáng* 65)

In sentence (8), the complement 红 *hóng* 'red' states that 模型 *móxíng* 'model', the patient of the verb 染 *rǎn* 'dye', is red; in sentence (9), the complement 整整齐齐 *zhěngzhěngqíqí* 'tidy' describes that 花、草、树 *huācǎoshù* 'flowers, grass and trees', the patient of the verb 剪 *jiǎn* 'trim', are tidy.

4 The complement semantically points to the instrument of the action verb.

(10) 砍　了　一　下午　　　竹子，　把　刀　　都　　砍　　钝　　了。
     kǎn   le   yī   xiàwǔ   zhúzi   bǎ   dāo   dōu   kǎn   dùn   le
     cut   LE   one afternoon bamboo   BA   knife all   cut   blunt LE
     'Having been used for cutting bamboo for an afternoon, the knife was all blunt.'

(11) 他   把   我   的   **钢笔**   都   写   **坏**   了。
     tā   bǎ   wǒ de **gāngbǐ** dōu xiě **huài** le
     3SG   BA   1SG DE **pen**   all write **broken** LE
     'He wrote with my pen and has broken it.'

In sentence (10), the complement 钝 *dùn* 'blunt' indicates that the tool of the cutting action, that is the 刀 *dāo* 'knife', becomes blunt; in sentence (11), the complement 坏 *huài* 'broken' indicates that 钢笔 *gāngbǐ* 'pen', the tool of the writing action, is broken.

5 The complement semantically points to the location where the predicate verb performs.

(12) **法院里**   坐   **满**   了   人。（有缘 66）
     fǎyuànlǐ   zuò   **mǎn**   le   rén
     court   sit   **full**   LE   people
     'The court was full of people.' (*Yǒuyuán* 66)

(13) 我   几乎   跑   **遍**   了   新加坡。
     wǒ   jīhū   pǎo   **biàn**   le   xīnjiāpō
     1SG almost run   **all.over** LE   Singapore
     'I almost ran all over Singapore.'

In sentence (12), the complement 满 *mǎn* 'full' describes the location 法院里 *fǎyuànlǐ* 'in the court'; in sentence (13), the complement 遍 *biàn* 'all over' describes the region 新加坡 *Xīnjiāpō* 'Singapore'.

7.1.3 Predicates in the Predicate-Complement Phrases

It is obvious that the predicate in a predicate-complement phrase is quite simple, usually a single verb or an adjective, occasionally a coordinate verb phrase as 冲洗 *chōngxǐ* 'wash and shower', 打扫整理 *dǎsǎo zhěnglǐ* 'clean and tidy' illustrated in sentences (14) and (15) respectively.

(14) 使用   再   好   的   洗发乳   都   必须   将   头发
     shǐyòng zài   hǎo   de   xǐfàrǔ   dōu   bìxū   jiāng tóufà
     use   even good   DE   shampoo   still necessary BA   hair

     冲洗   干净。（报 1995 年 3 月 15 日副刊 2 版）
     chōngxǐ   gānjìng

wash.shower clean

'No matter how good the shampoo you are using,' 'it's necessary to clean the hair by washing and showering.' (*Bào*, Mar. 15, 1995, Issue no. 2, supplementary edition)

(15) 屋子 给 **打扫整理** 得 井井有条。（△大喜 174）
  wūzi *gěi* ***dǎsǎozhěnglǐ*** *de* *jǐngjǐngyǒutiáo*
  house GEI **clean.tidy** DE in.perfect.order

'The house was cleaned and tidied up in perfect order.' (*Dàxǐ* 174)

Such cases are, after all, rare. Note that the predicate in a predicate-complement phrase cannot be a stative word. In other words, a stative word cannot take a complement (see Section 3.6).

7.1.4 Complement Types

The complement is quite complicated in Singapore Mandarin. It can be divided into six types as shown next.

1 Resultative complement

  染 红（青青 31） 冻 死（△天长 120）
  rǎn *hóng*   *dòng* *sǐ*
  dye red   freeze dead
  'dye it red' (*Qīngqīng* 31) 'be frozen to death' (*Tiāncháng* 120)

2 Directional complement

  走 过来（牛车水 106） 拖 下去（再见 19）
  zǒu *guòlái*   *tuō* *xiàqù*
  walk come   drag away
  'come here' (*Niúchēshuǐ* 106) 'drag him away' (*Zàijiàn* 19)

3 Potential complement

  提 得 起， 放 得 下（△浮萍 84）
  tí *de* *qǐ* *fàng* *de* *xià*
  lift DE up put DE down
  'be able to raise it and put it down' (*Fúpíng* 84)

讲　　不　　出　　忍　　不　　住（追云 107）
jiǎng　bù　　chū　　rěn　　bú　　zhù
speak　NEG　out　　hold　NEG　stop
'can neither speak it out nor hold (it)' (*Zhuīyún* 107)

4　Degree complement

精致　极　　了（牛车水 85）　　乖　　得　　很（追云 79）
jīngzhì　jí　　le　　　　　　　guāi　de　　hěn
delicate　extremely　LE　　　obedient　DE　very
'extremely delicate' (*Niúchēshuǐ* 85)　'very obedient' (*Zhuīyún* 79)

5　State complement

绑　　得　　紧紧的（有缘 37）　　问　　个　　清楚（风雨 15）
bang　de　　jǐnjǐnde　　　　　　wèn　gè　　qīngchǔ
tie　　DE　very.tight　　　　　　ask　　CL　clear
'be tied very tightly' (*Yǒuyuán* 37)　'figure it out' (*Fēngyǔ* 15)

6　Temporal and locative complement

作　　于　　1933　年　　11　月　　1　日（△中国作家 30）
zuò　　yú　　1933　nián　11　yuè　1　rì
written　in　1933　year　11　month　1　day
'written on November 1st in 1933' (*Zhōngguózuòjiā* 30)

坐　　在　　课室　　　里（伦理·中三 21－22）
zuò　zài　　kèshì　　lǐ
sit　　at　　classroom　in
'sit in the classroom' (*Lúnlǐ* III 21–22)

In the following sections we will describe and explain the predicate and the complement in Singapore Mandarin based on the classification of complements.

7.2 Resultative Complements

Following are some examples of predicate-complement phrases with resultative complements.

看懂　　*kàndǒng*　read-understand　　学会　　*xuéhuì*　　learn-master
洗干净　*xǐgānjìng*　wash-clean　　　　说清楚　*shuōqīngchǔ*　say-clear

冻伤	*dòngshāng*	freeze-injury		冷死	*lěngsǐ*	cold-dead
热晕了	*rèyūnle*	hot-faint-LE		急瞎了	*jíxiāle*	anxious-blind-LE

In these examples, the predicate expresses a specific manner or cause while the complement indicates a result. For instance, in the phrase 看懂 *kàndǒng* 'read and understand', the predicate 看 *kàn* 'read' expresses the manner and the complement 懂 *dǒng* 'understand' indicates the result. In the phrase 冻伤 *dòngshāng* 'suffer from frostbite', the predicate 冻 *dòng* 'freeze' describes the cause of the result indicated by the complement 伤 *shāng* 'injury'. This kind of complement is called a resultative complement.

7.2.1 Characteristics of Resultative Complement Phrases

The predicate-complement phrases with resultative complements have several characteristics:

1 The complement and predicate are combined directly without auxiliary words (such as 得 *dé* 'DE') in-between. For example, the predicate 看 *kàn* 'read' and the complement 懂 *dǒng* 'understand' are directly combined.
2 The predicate is usually a verb. There are only a few adjectival predicates that can take resultative complements. They are all monosyllabic adjectival predicates.

热 *rè* 'hot': 热死 *rèsǐ* 'hot-dead' 　　冷 *lěng* 'cold': 冷死 *lěngsǐ* 'cold-dead'

胀 *zhàng* 'distent': 胀坏 *zhànghuài* 'distend-broken' 　　累 *lèi* 'tired': 累坏 *lèihuài* 'tired-broken'

闷 *mēn* 'sealed': 闷死 *mēnsǐ* 'sealed-dead' 　　急 *jí* 'anxious': 急瞎 *jíxiā* 'anxious-blind'

气 *qì* 'angry': 气坏 *qìhuài* 'angry-broken' 　　枯 *kū* 'withered': 枯死 *kūsǐ* 'scorch-dead'

Let's see how they are used in a sentence.

(1) 给² 压 困 在 废墟 里 的 人，
　　gěi *yā* *kùn* *zài* *fèixū* *lǐ* *de* *rén*
　　GEI crush trapped in ruins inside DE people

不 给 压 死 也会 给 **闷 死**，......
　　　　　　　　　　　　　　　　　　（△大喜 255）
bù *gěi* *yā* *sǐ* *yěhuì* *gěi* ***mēn*** ***sǐ***
NEG GEI crush die also GEI **suffocated** **die**

'People who are trapped in the ruins will be suffocated even if they are not crushed to death...' (*Dàxǐ* 255)

(2) 我　　差点　　被　　她　　**气**　　**死**。（变调 27）
　　wǒ　chādiǎn　bèi　tā　**qì**　**sǐ**
　　1SG　almost　BEI　3SG　**angry**　**die**
　　'I almost died of anger because of her.' (*Biàndiào* 27)

(3) 不　　饿　　死，　　气　　也　　**气**　　**死**　　了。（金狮奖 194）
　　bú　è　sǐ　qì　yě　**qì**　**sǐ**　le
　　NEG　starve　dead　angry　also　**angry**　**die**　LE
　　'I was so angry that I was almost pissed off even if I didn't starve to death.'
　　(*Jīngshījiǎng* 194)

As can be seen from sentences (1) through (3), the resultative complements of adjectives all express unpleasant results.

3　Unlike the predicate, the complement is usually an adjective. Only a few verbs can serve as a complement. They are all monosyllabic verbs.

动：　　开　　　　动　　　　引擎（晚上 112）
dòng　　kāi　　　dòng　　　yǐnqín
move　　start　　move　　　engine
'start the engine' (*Wǎnshàng* 112)

完：　　念　　　完　　　　小学（△ 中国作家 143）
wán　　niàn　　wán　　　xiǎoxué
finish　read　　finish　　primary.school
'finish primary school' (*Zhōngguózuòjiā* 143)

翻 *fān* 'flip': 闹翻了 *nàofānle* 'sulk-flip-LE'（△大喜 6）(△*Dàxǐ* 6)
成 *chéng* 'achieve': 做成 *zuòchéng* 'do-achieve'（△天长 4）(*Tiāncháng* 4)
懂 *dǒng* 'understand': 听懂 *tīngdǒng* 'listen-understand'（笑眼 13）
　　(*Xiàoyǎn* 13)
会 *huì* 'master': 学会 *xuéhuì* 'learn-master'
走 *zǒu* 'go': 移走 *yízǒu* 'move-go'（青青 59）(*Qīngqīng* 59)
住 *zhù* 'hold': 捉住 *zhuōzhù* 'catch-hold'（一心 108）(*Yīxīn* 108)
死 *sǐ* 'dead': 打死 *dǎsǐ* 'beat-die'（狮子 87）(*Shīzi* 87)
到 *dào* 'reach': 看到 *kàndào* 'see-reach'（南北 2）(*Nánběi* 2)
倒 *dǎo* 'fall': 扑倒 *pūdǎo* 'pounce-fall'（△浮萍 71）(*Fúpíng* 71)
见 *jiàn* 'perceive': 听见 *tīngjiàn* 'listen-perceive'（追云 15）(*Zhuīyún* 15)
醒 *xǐng* 'wake': 吵醒 *chǎoxǐng* 'disturb-wake'（△大喜 1）(*Dàxǐ* 1)
丢 *diū* 'lose': 弄丢了 *nòngdiūle* 'do-lose-LE'
着 *zháo* 'attach': 睡着了 *shuìzháole* 'sleep-attach-LE'（大胡子 145）
　　(*Dàhúzi* 145)

中 *zhòng* 'hit': 看中 *kànzhòng* 'see-hit'（南北 1）(*Nánběi* 1)
掉 *diào* 'off': 关掉（水喉）*guāndiào(shuǐhóu)* 'close-off (the tap)'（话剧 60）(*Huàjù* 60)

7.2.2 Resultative Complement Phrase Taking Objects

Most resultative complement phrases can take objects, as shown in examples (4) through (6).

(4) 记　　　　住　　　　她　　　　的　　　　名字（笑眼 210）
    jì　　　　*zhù*　　　　*tā*　　　　*de*　　　　*míngzì*
    remember　　hold　　　　3SG　　　　DE　　　　name
    'remember her name' (*Xiàoyǎn* 210)

(5) 卖　　　　掉　　　　她　　　　的　　　　汽车（梦 34）
    mài　　　　*diào*　　　　*tā*　　　　*de*　　　　*qìchē*
    sell　　　　out　　　　3SG　　　　DE　　　　car
    'sell her car' (*Mèng* 210)

(6) 每　　一　　次　　跑步，　总会　　碰　　见　　这　　一　　对
    měi　*yī*　*cì*　*pǎobù*　*zǒnghuì*　*pèng*　*jiàn*　*zhè*　*yī*　*duì*
    every　one　CL　run　　always　　meet　see　this　one　CL

    中年　　　　的　　　欧籍　　　　　　　　夫妇。（壁虎 59）
    zhōngnián　*de*　　*ōují*　　　　　　　　*fūfù*
    middle-aged　DE　　European.nationality　couple
    'Every time I go jogging, I come across that middle-aged European couple.' (*Bìhǔ* 59)

7.3 Directional Complements

We now look at some with directional complement phrases.

跑来 *pǎolái* 'run-come'　　　爬上去 *páshàngqù* 'climb-go.up'
拿来 *nálái* 'take-come'　　　递上去 *dìshàngqù* 'pass-go.up'
走进 *zǒujìn* 'walk-enter'　　　拔出来 *báchūlái* 'pull-get.out.of'
扔进 *rēngjìn* 'throw-enter'　　钻出来 *zuānchūlái* 'crawl-get.out.of'

The preceding examples show that the predicate and the complement are closely related in meaning and directly combined without the auxiliary 得 *de* 'DE'[3] in-between. The defining feature of this type of predicate-complement phrase lies in the complements, which are only verbs of direction and thereby are called directional complements.

7.3.1 Verbs of Direction

There are only 24 verbs of direction in modern Singapore Mandarin. They can be categorised into three groups:

1. 来 *lái* 'come' and 去 *qù* 'go' express the movement direction from the perspective of the speaker. 来 *lái* 'come' indicates movement towards the speaker, while 去 *qù* 'go' means moving away from the speaker.
2. 上 *shàng* 'up', 下 *xià* 'down', 进 *jìn* 'enter', 出 *chū* 'out', 回 *huí* 'back', 过 *guò* 'through', 起 *qǐ* 'rise' and 开 *kāi* 'open'. This group of verbs indicate the direction of movement based on the original position of the moving object itself. 上 *shàng* 'up' means moving upward; conversely, 下 *xià* 'down' means moving downward. 进 *jìn* 'enter' means moving inward and 出 *chū* 'out' means moving outward. 回 *huí* 'back' means the returning movement; 过 *guò* 'pass' means passing by somewhere; 起 *qǐ* 'rise' means the rising movement; 开 *kāi* 'away' indicates moving away from the things they originally attach to.
3. 上来 *shànglái* 'come up', 上去 *shàngqù* 'go up', 下来 *xiàlái* 'come down', 下去 *xiàqu* 'go down', 进来 *jìnlái* 'come in', 进去 *jìnqù* 'go in', 回来 *huílái* 'come back', 回去 *huíqù* 'go back', 过来 *guòlái* 'come over', *guòqù* 'go over', 开来 *kāilái* 'spread out'. For this group of verbs, the reference point relates to both the speaker's position and moving direction of the objects. For example, 上来 *shànglái* 'come up' denotes that the object is moving toward the speaker as well as moving from the bottom to the top, as in the sentence 他从楼下走上来 *tā cóng lóuxià zǒu shànglái* 'He comes up from downstairs'. The same is true of the other complements.

The preceding 24 verbs of direction are illustrated in the following table.

	上 shàng	下 xià	进 jìn	出 chū	回 huí	过 guò	起 qǐ	开 kāi
来 lái	上来 shànglái come up	下来 shàngqù come down	进来 jìnlái come in	出来 chūlái come out	回来 huílái come back	过来 guòlái come over	起来 qǐlái get up	开来[4] kāilái spread out
去 qù	上去 shàngqù go up	下去 xiàqu go down	进去 jìnqù go in	出去 chūqù go out	回去 huíqù go back	过去 guòqù go over	——	——[5]

7.3.2 Directional Complements and Quasi-Directional Complements

According to the grammatical meanings expressed, directional complements can be divided into two types: directional complements and quasi-directional

Predicates and Complements 237

complements. Directional complements denote the moving direction of an object, more specifically, the moving direction of the agent or the patient of the action verb.

(1) 听说 **百利** 这几天 将会 **飞** **来** 新加坡......
（大胡子54）
  tīngshuō **bǎilì** zhèjǐtiān jiānghuì **fēi** **lái** xīnjiāpō
  heard **Baili** these.days will **fly** **come** Singapore
  'I heard that Bailey will come to Singapore by plane in the next few days...'
  (*Dàhúzi* 54)

(2) 罗涵珊...... 吁 了 一口气 这 才 往 大门
  luóhánshān xū le yìkǒuqì zhè cái wǎng dàmén
  Luohanshan sigh LE one.breath this just toward big.gate

走 去。（跳舞2）
zǒu *qù*
walk **go**
'Luo Hanshan sighed and then went to the gate.' (*Tiàowǔ* 2)

The directional complement 来 *lái* 'come' in example (1) denotes the moving direction of 百利 *bǎilì* 'Bailey', the agent of the action 飞 *fēi* 'fly'. 去 *qù* 'go' in example (2) denotes the moving direction of 罗涵珊 *luóhánshān* 'Luohanshan', the agent of the action 走 *zǒu* 'walk'. Examples of directional complements indicating movement of the objects denoted by the patient are given in (3) and (4).

(3) 见 陶陶 真的 把 **药丸** 吞 **下**， 他 急 得......
..[金狮奖（四）65]
  jiàn táotáo zhēnde bǎ **yàowán** tūn **xià** tā jí dé
  see Taotao really BA **pill** swallow **down** 3SG hurry DE
  'Seeing Taotao really swallow down the pills, he was so worried that...'
  (*Jīnshījiǎng* IV, 65)

(4) 涵珊 拿 **出** 针 线 盒子,... （跳舞2）
  hánshān ná **chū** zhēn xiàn hézi
  Hanshan take **out** needle thread box
  'Hanshan took out the sewing kit...' (*Tiàowǔ* 2)

The directional complement 下 *xià* 'down' denotes the moving direction of 药丸 *yàowán* 'pill', the patient of the verb 吞 *tūn* 'swallow' in example (3). Similarly, the directional complement 出 *chū* 'out' denotes the moving direction of 针线盒子 zhēnxiànhézi 'sewing kit', the patient of the verb 拿 ná 'take' in example (4).

However, the quasi-directional complement does not refer to the physical moving path, but only expresses extended meanings. For instance, 来 lái 'come' doesn't refer to the actual movement, but means "focusing on a certain aspect" when it complements 看 kàn 'look', 想 xiǎng 'think', 听 tīng 'hear', 算 suàn 'calculate', 说 shuō 'speak' in phrases 看来 kànlái 'look', 想来 xiǎnglái 'think', 算来 suànlái 'calculate', 说来 shuōlái 'speak' and so on. This is illustrated in the following example:

(5) 从   教育   背景   看来,   华文   教师   比
    cóng jiàoyù bèijǐng   kàn lái huáwén jiàoshī bǐ
    from education background look come Chinese teacher than

英文   教师   更   有   成为   双语   人才   的 希望。
                                                    （风筝 41）
yīngwén jiàoshī gèng yǒu chéngwéi shuāngyǔ réncái de xīwàng
English teacher more have become bilingual talent DE hope

'In terms of educational background, Chinese teachers are more likely to be bilingual talents than English teachers.' (Fēngzhēng 41)

(6) 我   上月   给   你   的   信,   想   来   你   早已
    wǒ   shàngyuè gěi   nǐ   de   xìn   xiǎng lái   nǐ   zǎoyǐ
    1SG last.month give 2SG DE   letter think come 2SG   already

收到。
shōudào
receive

'As for the letter I sent you last month, I think you've already received it.'

(7) 算   来   他   走   了   也   有   八   天   了。
    suàn   lái   tā   zǒu   le   yě   yǒu   bā   tiān   le
    calculate come 3SG   walk   LE   also   have   eight day   LE

'Counting the days, it's eight days since he left.'

(8) 关于   他   的   婚姻   问题,   说   来   话长。
    guānyú tā   de   hūnyīn   wèntí   shuō   lái   huàcháng
    about   3SG   DE   marriage problem speak   come a.long.story

'It's a long story when talking about the problems in his marriage.'

Predicates and Complements 239

Another example is 下去 *xiàqu* 'go down', which often indicates the continuation of the action, as shown in sentences (9) and (10).

(9) 她　　　既然　　　是　　无心向学，　　　　勉强　　　　**读**　　**下去**　　也
　　 tā　　　*jìrán*　　 *shì*　*wúxīnxiàngxué*　*miǎnqiǎng*　**dú**　**xiàqù**　*yě*
　　 3SG　　now.that　be　not.want.to.study　unwilling　**read**　**on**　also

没有　　　　　用处。（追云 81）
méiyǒu　　　*yòngchù*
not.have　　　usage

'Now that she is unwilling to carry on studying, there is no point forcing her.' (*Zhuīyún* 81)

(10) 坚持　　　　下去　　　吧！（青青 16）
　　　jiānchí　　*xiàqù*　　*ba*
　　　insist　　　on　　　　SFP

'Keep going!' (*Qīngqīng* 16)

Here are more examples of quasi-directional complements with extended meanings instead of stating an actual moving direction.

(11) 她　　　**爱**　　　**上**　　　了　　　中学　　　　　生活。（女儿 5）
　　　tā　　　**ài**　　　**shàng**　　*le*　　*zhōngxué*　　*shēnghuó*
　　　3SG　　**love**　　**up**　　　LE　　middle.school　life

'She loves her middle school life.' (*Nǚér* 5)

(12) 校服　　　　最　　　上面　　　　的　　两　　　颗　　纽扣　　　没
　　　xiàofú　　*zuì*　　*shàngmiàn*　*de*　*liǎng*　*kē*　*niǔkòu*　*méi*
　　　uniform　most　top　　　　　　DE　two　　CL　button　　NEG

扣　　　上，......（狮子 34）
kòu　　*shàng*
fasten　　up

'The top two buttons of the school uniform are not fastened, . . .' (*Shīzi* 34)

(13) ...**停**　　**下**　　　脚步　　　来　　　看。（狮子 38）
　　　　tíng　**xià**　　*jiǎbù*　　*lái*　　*kàn*
　　　　stop　**off**　　step　　　come　see

'. . . then he stopped to see (what happened)' (*Shīzi* 38)

(14) . . . 就 **作** **出** 一 个 决定：. . .（追云 39）
　　　jiù **zuò** **chū** yī gè juédìng
　　　then **make** **out** one CL decision
　　　'. . . therefore made a decision that . . .' (*Zhuīyún* 39)

(15) 我　不禁　**想 起**　第一 次　你　不　理睬 我
　　　wǒ bùjìn **xiǎng qǐ** dìyī cì nǐ bù lǐcǎi wǒ
　　　1SG cannot.help **think up** first time 2SG NEG reply 1SG

　　　的　情形。（青青 93）
　　　de qíngxíng
　　　DE situation
　　　'I can't help thinking about how you ignored me the first time we met.' (*Qīngqīng* 93)

(16) 浑身　都　**热**　**起来**　了。（大胡子 5）
　　　húnshēn dōu **rè** **qǐlái** le
　　　all.body all **hot** **rise.up** LE
　　　'The whole body is getting warm.' (*Dàhúzǐ* 5)

In (11), the directional complement 上 *shàng* 'up' indicates "to begin and continue"; in (12), it means "separated things are put together"; 下 *xià* 'down' in (13) implies completion of the action; 出 *chū* 'out' in (14) means "completion of something newly started"; 起 *qǐ* 'rise' in (15) means "getting into ce state" (here it means enter the state of thinking); 起来 *qǐlái* 'rise up' in (16) means "to start and keep going".

In Singapore Mandarin, 回 *huí* 'back' also has some extended meanings when it acts as the complement of a common verb instead of a verb of movement, as can be seen in the following sentences (17) through (20).

(17) "天　冷，　快些　演好，　**穿**　**回**
　　　tiān lěng kuàixiē yǎnhǎo **chuān** **huí**
　　　weather cold fast act **dress** **back**

　　　大衣。"（报 1995 年 3 月 22 日副刊 5 版）
　　　dàyī
　　　coat
　　　'It's cold, hurry up and put your coat back on.' (*Bào*, Mar. 22, 1995, Issue no. 5, supplementary edition)

(18) "快,   快,   **给**   回   我!" "不   给!" (金狮奖 220)
    kuài   kuài **gěi** huí   wǒ   bù   gěi
    fast   fast **give** back   1SG   NEG   give
    'Come on, give it back to me!' 'No! I will not!' (*Jīnshījiǎng* 220)

(19) 我   爱   人家   多少,   我   一定要   **得**   回
    wǒ   ài   rénjiā   duōshǎo   wǒ   yīdìngyào   **de**   huí
    1SG   love   others   how.much   1SG   must   **obtain** back

    相等的   爱。   (年岁 27)
    xiāngděngde   ài
    equal   love
    'If I love a person, I want equal love from him/her.' (*Niánsuì* 27)

(20) **说**   **回**   德士   司机   德士   是   旅游业   里   重要的   一环,
    shuō **huí**   déshì   sījī   déshì   shì   lǚyóuyè   lǐ   zhòngyàode   yīhuán
    speak **back** taxi   drivers   taxi   be   tourism   in   important   part

    对   我   国   的   经济   活动   扮演   积极的   角色。
                                                                          (平心 73)
    duì   wǒ   guó   de   jīngjì   huódòng   banyan   jījíde   juésè
    to   1SG   country DE   economy   activity   play   positive   role
    'Let's get back to the topic of taxi drivers. Taxis are an important part of the tourism industry and play an active role in our economic activity.' (*Píngxīn* 73)

These examples show that the predicate-complement phrase is a way to describe things economically and vividly. In some of the examples, it seems possible to translate 回 *huí* 'back' into Chinese Mandarin.

(18)' 快,   快,   **还**   **给**   我!
     kuài   kuài   **huán**   **gěi**   wǒ
     quick quick **return** **give**   1SG
     'Come on, give it back to me!'

(19)' 我   一定也要   从   人家   那儿   得到   相等的   爱。
     wǒ   yīdìngyěyào   cóng   rénjiā   nàer   **dedào**   xiāngděngde   ài
     1SG   also.must   from   others   there   **obtain**   equal   love
     'I must get equal love from him/her.'

However, other cases are difficult to translate into Chinese Mandarin with simple words. For example, 穿回大衣 *chuānhuí dàyī* means "to put your coat back on" in (17), and 说回德士司机 *shuōhuí déshì sījī* means "now we return to the topic about taxi drivers". Both of these examples are hard to express using only a few words in Chinese Mandarin, for the directional complement verb 回 *huí* 'back' in Chinese Mandarin does not have similar extended meanings.

Directional complements always follow verbs meaning "physical movement" (for example, 走 *zǒu* 'walk', 跑 *pǎo* 'run', 爬 *pá* 'crawl', 跳 *tiào* 'jump' and 飞 *fēi* 'fly', etc.) or action verbs that may cause movement (for example, 踢 *tī* 'kick', 扔 *rēng* 'throw', 拉 *lā* 'pull', 推 *tuī* 'push', 拿 *ná* 'take', 扛 *káng* 'carry', 搬 *bān* 'move', 吞 *tūn* 'swallow' and 吐 *tǔ* 'spit', etc.). On the contrary, quasi-directional complements have no such restrictions and they can even be complements of adjectives, as in sentence (16) and the following examples:

(21) 摄影棚　　里面　**响**　**起**　了　　庄严　　的　　结婚
　　　*shèyǐngpéng lǐmiàn **xiǎng qǐ** le zhuāngyán de jiéhūn*
　　　film.booth　inside　**sound up**　LE　solemn　　DE　wedding

进行曲，（金狮奖（四）38–39）
jìnxíngqǔ
march

'A solemn wedding march was played inside the film studio. . . .'
(*Jīnshījiǎn* IV 38–39)

(22) 也　　不　　知　　什么时候　　能　　真正　　**好**
　　　*yě　bú　zhī　shénmeshíhòu　néng　zhēnzhèng **hǎo***
　　　also NEG know when　　　could really　　**good**

起来。（金狮奖（四）40）
qǐlái
up

'I don't know when it will really get better.' (*Jīnshījiǎn* IV 40)

(23) 你　　难道就　　忍心　　　　让　　咱们　的　　儿子
　　　nǐ　nándào jiù rěnxīn　　　rang zánmen de érzǐ
　　　2SG how then have.the.heart.to let　1PL　DE　son

这样　　**荒唐**　　　**下去**？（△大喜 215）
*zhèyàng **huāngtáng　xiàqù***
so　　　**ridiculous　on**

'How can you bear to let our son go on like this?' (*Dàxǐ* 215)

7.3.3 Objects of Predicate-Directional Complement Phrases

Predicate-complement phrases with directional complements, or quasi-directional complements, can take objects, which can be categorised into three groups.

1. The object is the agent of the predicate-complement phrase, as shown in sentences (22) and (25).

(24) 冲   进   一个   怒气冲冲的   中年   妇女。（短篇 79）
     chōng jìn yī gè   nùqìchōngchōngde zhōngnián fùnǚ
     rush   in   one CL enraged   middle-aged woman

'An angry middle-aged woman rushed in.' (*Duǎnpiān* 79)

(25) 迎面   走   来   了 一 位   举止   优雅的   妇人。
                                                    （石头 145）
     yíngmiàn zǒu   lái   le yī wèi jǔzhǐ   yōuyǎde   fùrén
     oncoming walk come LE one CL   manner elegant   woman

'An elegant woman came up.' (*Shítou* 145)

2. The object is the patient of the predicate-complement phrase, as illustrated in sentences (26) through (28).

(26) 老人   狠狠地   吐   出   了 一 口   烟，......（追云 30）
     lǎorén   hěnhěnde   tǔ   chū   le yī kǒu yān
     old.man hardly   spit   out   LE one CL   smoke

'The old man spat out a mouthful of smoke . . .' (*Zhuīyún* 30)

(27) 我... 取   出   那   封   已经   拆   阅   过
     wǒ   qǔ   chū   nà   fēng yǐjīng   chāi yuè   guò
     1SG   take out   that CL   already   open read GUO

     的   遗书。（变调 31）
     de yíshū
     DE   suicide.note

'I took out that suicide note which has already been opened and read.' (*Biàndiào* 31)

(28) 玻璃市   队   踢   进   了 一 粒   好
     bōlíshì   duì   tī   jìn   le yī lì   hǎo
     Glass.City team kick   in   LE one CL good

球。（报 1995 年 3 月 14 日 13 版）
qiú
ball

'The Glass City Team scored a good goal.' (*Bào*, Mar. 14, 1995, Issue no. 13)

3   The object indicates the place related to the predicate-complement phrase, as exemplified in sentences (29) through (31).

(29) 使者　　飞快地　　**跑**　　**进**　　了　　厨房。（石头 111）
　　 shǐzhě　fēikuàide　pǎo　　jìn　　le　　chúfáng
　　 envoy　 rapidly　　run　　in　　 LE　　kitchen

'The envoy rushed rapidly into the kitchen.' (*Shítou* 111)

(30) 他们　　一起　　**走**　　**出**　　图书馆。（梦 52）
　　 tāmen　yìqǐ　　zǒu　　chū　　túshūguǎn
　　 3PL　　together　walk　　out　　library

'They walked out of the library together.' (*Mèng* 52)

(31) 进　　门　　后，阿妈　帮　　我　　把　　行李　　**搬**　　**进**
　　 Jìn　　mén　hòu　āmā　bang　wǒ　　bǎ　　xíngli　bān　　jìn
　　 enter　door　after　mum　help　1SG　BA　　luggage　move　in

房子，……（微型 13）
fángzǐ
house

'After entering the house, mum helped me carry my luggage into the house . . .' (*Wēixíng* 13)

There is a slight difference between Singapore Mandarin and Chinese Mandarin in respect of whether or not the predicate directional complement phrase can take a place object. In Chinese Mandarin, when the complement is a compound directional verb like 回去 *huíqù* 'go back' or 进来 *jìnlái* 'come in', the predicate-complement phrase can no longer take a place object. For instance, it is ungrammatical to say *走进来屋里 *zǒu jìnláiwūlǐ* 'walk into the room' or *拿出去图书馆 *ná chūqù túshūguǎn* 'take out from the library' (Lü 1980, Zhu 1982). However, these expressions are grammatical in Singapore Mandarin, as shown in sentences (32) and (33).

(32) 想不到　　　　过　　了　　半　　个　　钟头　　后，同　　一　　辆　　车
　　 xiǎngbúdào　guò　le　　bàn　　gè　　zhōngtóu　hòu，tóng　yī　　liàng　chē
　　 unexpected　GUO　LE　half　CL　hour　　　　after　same　one　CL　　car

又	驾	回	来	我们	这里。（风筝 186）
yòu	jià	huí	lái	wǒmen	zhèlǐ
again	drive	back	come	1PL	here

'Unexpectedly, the same car drove back to us half an hour later.' (*Fēngzhēng* 186)

(33)
有些	人……	还	时常	跑	回	来	巴刹	买
yǒuxiē	rén…	hái	shícháng	pǎo	huí	lái	bāshā	mǎi
some	people	still	often	run	back	come	bazaar	buy

东西。（回忆 43）
dōngxī
thing

'Some people still often come back to the bazaar to buy something.' (*Huíyì* 43)

Two points are noteworthy regarding the predicate-directional complement phrase:

1 It is no longer a predicate-complement phrase if 了 *le* 'LE' is inserted in the middle of the phrase. For example, 飞过来 *fēi guòlái* 'fly over here' is a predicate-complement phrase with a directional complement, while 飞了过来 *fēi le guòlái* 'flew over here' (Shīzi, 29) is a complex predicate phrase, which will be introduced in Chapter 9.
2 The insertion of an object also changes the predicate directional phrase into a complex predicate phrase. For example, 带来 *dàilái* 'bring' is a predicate-complement phrase with a directional complement, while 带你来 *dài nǐ lái* 'bring you here' (Zhuīyún, 45) is a complex predicate phrase. Again, this will be elaborated in Chapter 9.

7.4 Potential Complements

7.4.1 Potential Complements and Negation

The predicate-complement phrase with a resultative complement and the one with a directional complement will become a predicate-complement phrase with a potential complement by inserting 得 *de* 'DE' or 不 *bù* 'NEG'.

		Inserting 得 *de* 'DE'	Inserting 不 *bù* 'NEG'
A	看懂 *kàndǒng* →	看得懂 *kàn-de-dǒng*	看不懂 *kàn-bù-dǒng*
	'understand'	'can understand'	'can't understand'

学会 xuéhuì 'learn'	→ 学得会 xué-de-huì 'can learn well'	学不会 xué-bú-huì 'can't learn well'
洗干净 xǐgānjìng 'wash clean'	→ 洗得干净 xǐ-de-gànjìng 'can wash clean'	洗不干净 xǐ-bù-gànjìng 'can't wash clean'
说清楚 shuōqīngchǔ 'make clear'	→ 说得清楚 shuō-de-qīngchǔ 'can make clear'	说不清楚 shuō-bù-qīngchǔ 'can't make clear'
B 走开 zǒukāi 'walk away'	→ 走得开 zǒu-dé-kāi 'sb. is available'	走不开 zǒu-bù-kāi 'sb. is not available'
拿出 náchū 'take'	→ 拿得出 ná-de-chū 'can take out'	拿不出 ná-bù-chū 'can't take out'
爬上去 páshàngqù 'climb up'	→ 爬得上去 pá-de-shàngqù 'can climb up'	爬不上去 pá-bú-shàngqù 'can't climb up'
取出来 qǔchūlái 'bring out'	→ 取得出来 qǔ-de-chūlái 'can bring out'	取不出来 qǔ-bù-chūlái 'can't bring out'

Both Group A and Group B are predicate-complement phrases with potential complements. Group A derives from the predicate-resultative complement phrases inserted by 得 de 'DE' or 不 bù 'NEG'; Group B derives from the predicate-directional complement phrases inserted by 得 de 'DE' or 不 bù 'NEG'. 得 de 'DE' indicates an affirmative statement, while 不 bù 'NEG' indicates a negative statement. Literally, the predicate-complement phrases with potential complements, as the name implies, denote possibility. The affirmative statement means 'can' or 'may', for example, 看得懂 kàndédǒng indicates that one can understand and 走得开 zǒudekāi indicates that one can walk away from his work and thus is available. The negative statement means 'can't', for example, 看不懂 kànbùdǒng denotes that one can't understand and 走不开 zǒubùkāi denotes that one is too busy to walk away. The same logic applies to the other examples. In summary, these kind of complements are called potential complements.

Although there are both affirmative and negative forms for this type of predicate-complement phrase, in the actual discourse, the frequency of the negative form is much higher than that of the affirmative one. We counted the occurrence of the predicate-potential complement phrases in Tian Liu's collection of short stories 《大喜临门》 dàxǐlínmén 'Arrival of Great Joy' (published by Dadi Culture Co., Ltd., Singapore, 1989, p. 280). We found that out of a total of 151 predicate-complement phrases, there were only 21 affirmative forms (14%), compared to 130 negative forms (86%). It suggests that we generally do not use the affirmative form of potential complements, since the same meaning can be expressed by the modal verb 能（够）*néng(gòu)* 'can' or 可以 *kěyǐ* 'can'. For example, 能（够）/可以看懂 *néng(gòu)/kěyǐ kàndǒng* rather than 看得懂 *kàndedǒng* are often used to indicate 'can understand'.

(1) 我们　　常常　　　坐　在　凉凳　　上，　天真地　　　　谈　我们
    wǒmen   chángcháng zuò zài liángdèng shàng tiānzhēnde   tán   wǒmen
    1PL   often   sit in   cool.bench up   naively   talk 1PL

    年龄　　所　**能**　**理解**　　到　　的　想法，……（梦 2）
    *niánlíng suǒ **néng** **lǐjiě**   dào   de   xiǎngfǎ*
    age   SUO **can**   **understand** reach DE idea

    'We often sit on the cool bench and talk naively about the ideas that we can understand at that age…' (*Mèng* 2)

(2) 他　　只　　盼望　　　有朝一日，　　　　**能够**　　**还　清**
    *tā   zhǐ   pànwàng   yǒuzhāoyīrì   **nénggòu** **huán qīng**
    3SG only expect   some.day.in.the.future **can**   **return all**

    那　一　　笔　可以　要　　他　　老命　　的　高利贷！
    　　　　　　　　　　　　　　　　　　　　　　　（△大喜 151）
    nà   yī   bǐ   kěyǐ yào   tā   lǎomìng   de gāolìdài
    that one CL   can   ask.for 3SG old.life   DE high.interest.loan

    'He only hopes that one day, he can pay off the damned hight interest loan!' (*Dàxǐ* 151)

(3) 说到　　　园丁　　　阿木，　长得　　　一　　副　　傻相，　　气力
    shuōdào   yuándīng   āmù   zhǎngde   yī   fù   shǎxiàng   qìlì
    speak.of   gardener   Amu   look   one   CL   stupid.face strength

    是　　不　　小，　脑筋　　却　　很　　迟钝；　这　　在
    shì bú   xiǎo   nǎojīn   què   hěn   chídùn   zhè   zài
    is   NEG   small brain   but   very slow   this in

    案发　　　　　　　　　的　那　一　天，　王探长
    ànfā   de nà yī tiān   wángtànzhǎng
    at.the.scene.of.the.crime DE that one CL Detective.Wang

只须	三两		句	话	就	**可以**
zhīxū	sānliǎng		jù	huà	jiù	**kěyǐ**
only.need	three.two.several		CL	words	then	**can**

看出来。（△大喜 105）

kànchūlái

see

'When it comes to the gardener Amu, he looks like a fool. He has a lot of strength, but a slow brain. About the day of the crime, detective Wang tells the fact in only several words.' (*Dàxǐ* 105)

   It is evident from sentences (1) through (3) that the authors use 能理解到 *néng lǐjiědào* rather than 理解得到 *lǐjiě de dào*, use 能够还清 *nénggòu háiqīng* rather than 还得清 *huán de qīng* and use 可以看出来 *kěyǐ kàn chūlái* rather than 看得出来 *kàn de chūlái* to express the meaning of "can understand", "can pay off", "can tell", respectively.

7.4.2 Objects of Predicate-Potential Complement Phrases

The predicate-complement phrase with the potential complement may take an object as well, such as 吃得/不下饭 *chīde/búxiàfàn* 'can/can't eat'. In Singapore Mandarin, there are two possible word orders of the predicate, the potential complement, and the object, as shown here.

1   V 得 *de* 'DE'/不 *bù* 'NEG' C + object (hereafter V for verb, C for complement).

(4)	那	动辄	千万	元	的	合同，	他	**放**	**得**
	nà	dòngzhé	qiānwàn	yuan	de	hétóng	tā	**fàng**	**de**
	that	easily	ten.million	yuan	DE	contract	3SG	**put**	**DE**

下	心？（想飞 89）
xià	**xīn**
down	**heart**

'Can he feel at ease when it comes to the contract worth at least ten million?' (*Xiǎngfēi* 89)

(5)	我们	斗	不	过	他们。（金狮奖 18）
	wǒmen	**dòu**	**bú**	**guò**	tāmen
	we	**fight**	**NEG**	**pass**	3PL

'We can't beat them.' (*Jīnshījiǎng* 18)

(6) 心里　　　兀自　　放　　不　　下　　那　　口　　乌气。（噩梦 118）
　　 xīnlǐ　　　wùzì　　fàng　bú　xià　nà　kǒu　wūqì
　　 in.the.heart　still　put　NEG　down　that　CL　wūqì

　　 'I can't let go of that anger.' (Èmèng 118)

2　V + object + 不 bù 'NEG' + C. This form is most commonly seen in spoken Singapore Mandarin and can only be used in a negative form.

(7) 小黑子　　向来　　就　　瞧　　他　　不　　起。（噩梦 37）
　　 xiǎohēizi　xiànglái　jiù　qiáo　tā　bú　qǐ
　　 xiaoheizi　always　just　look　3SG　NEG　up

　　 'Little Heizi always looks down on him.' (Èmèng 37)

(8) 我　　实在　　放心　　不　　下。
　　 wǒ　shízài　fàngxīn　bú　xià
　　 1SG　really　be.at.ease　NEG　down

　　 'I can't rest assured.'

(9) 生活　　里　　的　　惊涛骇浪　　击　　它　　不
　　 shēnghuó　lǐ　de　jīngtāohàilàng　jī　tā　bú
　　 life　inside　DE　tempestuous.waves　hit　3SG　NEG

　　 碎，砍　　它　　不　　断。（大胡子·序）
　　 suì　kǎn　tā　bú　duàn
　　 smashed　chop　3SG　NEG　broken

　　 'It will not be smashed or broken by the tempestuous waves of life.'
　　 (Dàhúzi Xù)

Only the first word order is used in Chinese Mandarin. The second type is used in early vernacular, which is reserved in some dialects, but no longer in Chinese Mandarin.

7.4.3 V 得了 deliǎo 'V Able' and V 不了 bùliǎo 'V Not Able'

V 得了 deliǎo 'V able'[6] and V 不了 bùliǎo 'V not able' are predicate-potential complement phrases, but they have become fixed expressions.[7]

(10) 同学们　　帮　　得了　　我，可是　　帮　　不了
　　 tóngxuémen　bāng　de-liǎo　wǒ　kěshì　bāng　bù-liǎo
　　 3PL　help　able　1SG　but　help　not.able

我   的   家庭。（△大喜 21）
wǒ   de   jiātíng
1SG   DE   family

'The students can help me, but they can't help my family.' (*Dàxǐ* 21)

(11) 论文   没法   写完，   还是   回   不了   家。（金狮奖 152）

lùnwén   méifǎ   xiěwán   háishì   huí   bù-liǎo   jiā

paper   not.be.able.to write.   still   return not.able   home
                        finish

'I can't go home until I finish my paper.' (*Jīnshījiǎng* 152)

(12) 这下   他   可   逃   不了   了！（△大喜 13）

zhèxià   tā   kě   táo   bù-liǎo   le

this.time 3SG whatever escape not.able   LE

'This time he can't escape!' (*Dàxǐ* 13)

The original meaning of 了 *liǎo* is "finish". In some verbal complement phrases of V 得了 *deliǎo* 'V able' and V 不了 *bùliǎo* 'V not able' 了 *liǎo* still retains its original meaning. For example, in the sentence 这一大碗饭你吃得了吃不了 *zhè yī dàwǎn fàn nǐ chī deliǎo chī bùliǎo* 'can you finish this huge bowl of rice or not?', here 吃得了吃不了 *chī deliǎo chībùliǎo* means "can you finish or not". However, when V 得了 *deliǎo* 'V able' and V 不了 *bùliǎo* 'V not able' become conventionalised expressions, as in sentences (10) through (14), 了 *liǎo* has lost its original meaning. Therefore, V 得了 *deliǎo* 'V able' and V 不了 *bùliǎo* 'V not able' are different from other predicate-potential complement phrases in meaning. In general, a predicate potential complement indicates whether or not the result of the action represented by the predicate verb is likely to occur, while V 得了 *deliǎo* 'V able' and V 不了 *bùliǎo* 'V not able' mean whether or not the action represented by the predicate verb itself can be carried out. The meaning contrast is illustrated by the following examples (the predicate-potential complement phrase is represented by V 得 *de* /不 *bù* C, C for complement):

V 得/不 C

洗   得   干净   =   能   洗   干净

xǐ   de   gānjìng   néng   xǐ   gānjìng

wash   DE   clean   can   wash   clean

'(I) can wash (it) clean.'

Predicates and Complements

洗	不	干净	=	不能	洗	干净	/没法	洗	干净
xǐ	bù	gānjìng		bùnéng xǐ		gānjìng	/méifǎ	xǐ	gānjìng
wash	NEG	clean		cannot wash		clean	/have.no.way	wash	clean

'(I) cannot/am not able to wash (it) clean.'

看	得	懂	=	能	看	懂
kàn	de	dǒng		néng	kàn	dǒng
watch	DE	understand		can	watch	understand

'(I) can understand (it).'

看	不	懂	=	不能	看	懂	/没法	看	懂
kàn	bù	dǒng		bùnéng kàn		dǒng	/méifǎ	kàn	dǒng
watch	NEG	understand		cannot watch		understand	/have.no.way	watch	understand

'(I) cannot/am not able to understand (it).'

V 得/不了

洗	得了	=	能	洗
xǐ	de-liǎo		néng	xǐ
wash	able		can	wash

'(I) can wash (it).'

洗	不了	=	不能	洗	/没法	洗
xǐ	bù-liǎo		bùnéng	xǐ	/méifǎ	xǐ
wash	not.able		cannot	wash	/have.no.way	wash

'(I) cannot wash (it).'

看	得了	=	能	看
kàn	de-liǎo		néng	kàn
see	able		can	see

'(I) can read (it).'

看	不了	=	不能	看	/没法	看
kàn	bù-liǎo		bùnéng	kàn	/méifǎ	kàn
see	not.able		cannot	see	/have.no.way	see

'(I) cannot read (it).'

There is another fixed predicate-potential complement phrase in Chinese Mandarin. Its form is V 得 [8] *de* (affirmative) 'V may' or V 不得 *bùdé* (negative) 'V may not'. This kind of phrase is very common, such as 洗得 *xǐdé* 'may wash' and 洗不得 *xǐbùdé* 'may not wash', 看得 *kàndé* 'may watch' and 看不得 *kànbùdé* 'may not watch'. It also indicates whether or not the action can be carried out. But its meaning is different from V 得了 *deliǎo* 'V able' and V 不了 *bùliǎo* 'V not able': V 得/不了 *de/bùliǎo* 'V able/not able' emphasises subjective possibility, whereas V 得 *dé* 'V may'/不得 *bùdé* 'V may not' emphasises objective possibility. Let's compare these two expressions:

V 得 *de* /不了 *bù-liǎo*

洗	得了	=	能	洗
xǐ	de-liǎo		néng	xǐ
wash	able		can	wash

'(I) can wash (it).'

洗	不了	=	不能	洗
xǐ	de-liǎo		bùnéng	xǐ
wash	not.able		cannot	wash

'(I) cannot wash (it).'

去	得了	=	能	去
qù	de-liǎo		néng	qù
go	able		can	go

'(I) can go.'

去	不了	=	不能	去
qù	bù-liǎo		bùnéng	qù
go	not.able		cannot	go

'(I) cannot go.'

V（得 *de*）/不得 *bù-dé*

洗	得	=	可以	洗
xǐ	dé		kěyǐ	xǐ
wash	DE		can	wash

'(I) may wash (it).'

洗	不得	=	不可以	洗
xǐ	bù-dé		bùkěyǐ	xǐ
wash	not-DE		may not	wash

'(I) may not wash (it).'

去	得	=	可以	去
qù	dé		kěyǐ	qù
go	DE		may	go

'(I) may go.'

去	不得	=	不可以	去
qù	bù-dé		bùkěyǐ	qù
go	not-De		may.not	go

'(I) may not go.'

The expressions of V 得 *dé* 'V DE' and V 不得 *bùdé* 'V not DE' are rarely used in Singapore Mandarin. Only a few examples were found in the written corpus we were able to access, and they were all negatives, as in sentences (13) and (14).

(13) 有一回, 父子 对奕, 老父 进行 封锁,
yǒuyīhuí fùzǐ duìyì lǎofù jinxing fēngsuǒ
once father.and.son play.chess father going block

令	我	丝毫	动弹	不得。(无 57)
lìng	wǒ	sīháo	**dòngtan**	**bù-dé**
make	me	a.bit	move	not-DE

'Once, when I played chess with my father, he blocked me completely, and I couldn't move.' (*Wú* 57)

(14) 就　因为　得到　如此　的　优酬，因此　道士们
jiù　yīnwéi　dédào　rúcǐ　de　yōuchóu　yīncǐ　dàoshimen
just　because　get　such　DE　bones　so　taoists

办起事来，分外　有神，**马虎　不得**。（金狮奖 181）
bàqǐshìlái　fènwài　yǒushén　**mǎhu　bù-dé**
do.a.job　very　earnest　careless　not-DE

'Because of such a huge reward, the Taoists are very earnest and careful in their work.' (*Jīnshījiǎng* 181)

7.5 Degree Complements

Predicate-complement phrases with degree complements, in which the predicates are usually adjectives and the complements indicate degree, can be divided into two types: One with the auxiliary 得 *de* 'DE' and the other without. For both types of phrases, the complement position can only be filled by a limited number of words, all of which are used in fixed forms.

7.5.1 Degree Complements With 得 de 'DE'

Degree complements with 得 *de* 'DE' are mainly used as fixed forms, which include the following forms:

1　~得很 *dehěn* 'DE-much'.

(1) 也许　有人　并不　**高兴**，可是　我　自己
yěxǔ　yǒurén　bìngbù　**gāoxìng**　kěshì　wǒ　zìjǐ
maybe　someone　NEG　happy　but　1SG　self

可　**高兴　得很**。（笑眼 83）
kě　**gāoxìng　de-hěn**
but　happy　DE-much

'Some may feel upset, but I am very happy.' (*Xiàoyǎn* 83)

(2) 幺七   这次   输   了   这么多   钱，   心里   也   是
    yāoqī   zhècì   shū   le   zhèmeduō   qián,   xīnlǐ   yě   shì
    Yaoqi   this.time lose LE   so.much   money   heart   also   be

   难过   得很。（金狮奖 195）
   nánguò   de-hěn
   sad   DE-much

   'Having lost so much money this time, Yaoqi is very upset.' (*Jīnshījiǎng* 195)

(3) 这一回，   李月娟   倒是   冷静   得很。（胜利 84）
    zhèyīhuí lǐyuèjuān dǎoshì   lěngjìng   de-hěn
    this.time Liyuejuan unexpectedly calm   DE-much

   'Li Yuejuan is unexpectedly very calm this time.' (*Shènglì* 84)

(4) 这回   她   倒是   乖   得很。   快   去   快   来。
                                                                    （追云 79）
    zhèhuí   tā   dǎoshì   guāi   de-hěn   kuài   qù   kuài   lái
    this.time 3SG unexpectedly obedient DE-much   quick go   quick come

   'This time she is unexpectedly very obedient and comes back very quickly.'
   (*Zhuīyún* 79)

2 ~得不得了 debùdéliǎo 'DE-extreme'.

(5) 大家   一   见面，   高兴   得不得了，……（冰灯 12）
    dàjiā   yī   jiànmiàn,   gāoxìng   de-bù-dé-liǎo
    everyone once meet   happy   DE-extreme

   'Everyone is extremely happy upon meeting each other.' (*Bīngdēng* 12)

(6) 哇，   人   多   得不得了！（微型 219）
    wa,   rén   duō   de-bù-dé-liǎo
    wow   people many   DE-extreme

   'Wow, so many people!' (*Wēixíng* 219)

(7) 我   的   神经，   这   时候   紧张   得不得了，……（△大
                                                                    喜 12）
    wǒ   de   shénjīng zhè   shíhòu   jǐnzhāng   de-bù-dé-liǎo
    1SG   DE   neuro   this time   nervous   DE-extreme

   'At this moment, I was extremely nervous.' (*Dàxǐ* 12)

Predicates and Complements

3   ~得要命/要死 *deyàomìng* 'DE-as hell'.

(8) 其实， 肚子里 是 **饿** **得要命**！（笑眼 81）
    qíshí dùzǐlǐ shì è de-yào-mìng
    actually belly be hungry DE-as hell
    'Actually I am hungry as hell!' (*Xiàoyǎn* 81)

(9) 他 这个 人 哪， **懒** **得要命**！
    tā zhègè rén na lǎn de-yào-mìng
    2SG this person TOP lazy DE-as hell
    'Oh he is lazy as hell!'

(10) 起初 还好， 现在 越来越 难 服侍 了，
     qǐchū háihǎo xiànzài yuèláiyuè nán fúshì le
     at.first alright now more.and.more hard attend LE

   大小便 都 不 会， **脏** **得要死**，......（追云 26）
   dàxiǎobiàn dōu bú huì zāng de-yào-sǐ
   poop.pee all NEG can dirty DE-as hell
   'At first, it was alright. Now it is harder and harder to manage. (He) is incontinent and extremely dirty!' (*Zhuīyún* 26)

(11) 我 最近 **忙** **得要死**， 哪有 时间 看 电影
     wǒ zuìjìn máng de-yào-sǐ nǎyǒu shíjiān kàn diànyǐng
     1SG lately busy DE-as hell how.have time watch movie

   电影 啊！
   diànyǐng ā
   movie SFP
   'I have been terribly busy lately. How am I supposed to find time to watch movies!'

4   ~得厉害 *delìhài* 'DE-so much'.

(12) 一 觉 醒来， 喉咙 **干渴** **得厉害**，......（金狮奖 136）
     yī jiào xǐnglái hóulóng gānkě de-lì-hài
     one sleep wake throat thirsty DE-so much
     'After I woke up I felf so thirsty.' (*Jīnshījiǎng* 136)

(13) 老人   的   记忆力   已   日渐   衰退，   **眼花**
    lǎorén   de   jìyìlì   yǐ   rìjiàn   shuāituì **yǎnhuā**
    old.man DE   memory   has   gradually weaken   **dim.sighted**

   得厉害，   听觉   也   不   太   灵敏   了，……
                                                                 （追云 27）
   de-lì-hài tīngjué   yě   bú   tài   língmǐn   le
   DE-so much hearing   also   NEG   very   acute   LE

   'The old man's memory is gradually failing, and his sight and hearing is also degenerating.' (*Zhuīyún* 27)

(14) 由于   不   简单，   心绪   **烦**   得厉害！（△断情剪 38）
    yóuyú   bù   jiǎndān   xīnxù   **fán**   **de-lì-hài**
    due.to   NEG   easy   mind   **annoyed** **DE-so much**

   'I was so annoyed because it's not an easy task.' (*Duànqíngjiǎn* 38)

5 ~得多 *deduō* 'DE-much more'.

(15) 总   比   我   好   得多。（金狮奖 170）
    zǒng   bǐ   wǒ   hǎo   de-duō
    always than   1SG   good   DE-much more

   'Far better than me after all.' (*Jīnshījiǎng* 170)

(16) 拆毁   比   建设   要   容易   得多。（牛车水 128）
    chāihuǐ   bǐ   jiànshè   yào   róngyì   de-duō
    demolish than   construct   will   easy   DE-much more

   'Demolition is much easier than construction.' (*Niúchēshuǐ* 128)

Among the preceding five expressions, the first form is used the most frequently. Forms 2, 3 and 4 all convey an exaggerated tone while form 5 contains comparative meanings, usually used in 比 *bǐ* 'than' phrases, as shown in sentences (15) and (16). One more example is given in sentence (17).

(17) 以   这种   方式   成名，   究竟   比   辛辛苦苦
    yǐ   zhèzhǒng   fāngshì   chéngmíng   jiūjìng   bǐ   xīnxīnkǔkǔ
    by   this   way   famous   after.all   than   arduously

   投稿   容易   得多。（八方 23）
   tóugǎo   róngyì   de-duō

	contribute	**easy**		**DE-much more**

'Coming to fame by this way is after all far easier than being a contributor.' (*Bāfāng* 23)

There are three other fixed forms in Chinese Mandarin. The first one is ~得慌 *dehuāng* 'unbearably' as in 闷得慌 *mèndehuāng* 'unbearably boring' and 累得慌 *lèidehuāng* 'unbearably tired'. The second one is ~得了不得 *déliǎobùdé*, which is semantically similar with ~得不得了 *debùdéliǎo* 'can't be more...', such as 好/气得了不得 *hǎo/qìdeliǎobùdé* 'can't be better/can't be more angry'. The last one is ~得不成 *debùchéng* 'so much' as in 累/脏得不成 *lèi/zāngdebùchéng* '(I'm) so tired/(It's) so dirty'. However, there seems to be no such expressions in Singapore Mandarin, as we did not find these three forms in our written corpus.

Structurally, the auxiliary word 得 *de* 'DE' in all five forms should be regarded as part of the predicate. For example, the phrase 好得很 *hǎodehěn* 'very good' can be analysed as follows:

好	得	很
hǎo	dé	hěn

```
 _____
  1      2     (predicate-complement phrase)
 _____
  3  4         (auxiliary phrase)
```

7.5.2 Degree Complements Without 得 *de* 'DE'

Degree complements without 得 *de* 'DE' all end with 了 *le* 'LE' and are used as fixed forms as well.

1 ~极了 *jíle* 'exceeding-LE'.

(18) 巧　　　极了，　　妙　　极了，　　　有趣　　　极了。(笑眼 171)
　　 qiǎo　　jí-le　　　miào　jí-le　　　　yǒuqù　　jí-le
　　 artful　exceeding-LE　nice　exceeding-LE　interesting　exceeding-LE

'It was exceedingly artful, wonderful and interesting.' (*Xiàoyǎn* 171)

(19) 美观　　　极了！（晚上 15）
　　 měiguān　　jí-le
　　 beautiful　exceeding-LE

'It's exceedingly beautiful!' (*Wǎnshàng* 15)

(20) 真是　　混账　　　　极了，　　　　可恶　　　　极了！（追云 30）
　　　zhēnshì　hùnzhàng　　jí-le　　　　　kěwù　　　　jí-le
　　　truly　　scoundrel　　exceeding-LE　obnoxious　　exceeding-LE
　　　'He was exceedingly scoundrel and obnoxious!' (*Zhuīyún* 30)

2　~死了 *sǐle* 'dead-LE'.

(21) 这么好的　　　工作，　　乐　　　死了！（恶梦 38）
　　　zhèmehǎode　gōngzuò　　lè　　　sǐ-le
　　　perfect　　　job　　　　happy　dead-LE
　　　'Getting such a good job, (one) couldn't be happier!' (*Èmèng* 38)

(22) 看看　　你　　的　　校服，　脏　　　死了！（狮子 65）
　　　kànkàn　nǐ　　de　　xiàofú　　zāng　　sǐ-le
　　　look　　2SG　DE　　uniform　　dirty　dead-LE
　　　'Look at your uniform, it's really dirty!' (*Shīzi* 65)

(23) 什么　　鸟　　　　河　　　嘛！　臭　　　　死了！（扶轮 67）
　　　shénme　niǎo　　　hé　　　ma　　　chòu　　　sǐ-le
　　　what　　damned　　river　　SFP　　stinky　　dead-LE
　　　'That damned river! It stinks to high heavy!' (*Fúlún* 67)

3　~透了 *tòule* 'complete-LE'.

(24) 这个　　下午　　　　的　演讲　　　糟　　　透了。（金狮奖 136）
　　　zhègè　　xiàwǔ　　　de　yǎnjiǎng　　zāo　　tòu-le
　　　this　　afternoon　　DE　speech　　　awful　complete-LE
　　　'This afternoon's speech sucks.' (*Jīnshījiǎng* 136)

(25) 乡愁，　　　　解　　　不　　　开　　　的　　感情　　　死结，
　　　xiāngchóu　　jiě　　bú　　kāi　　de　　gǎnqíng　　sǐjié
　　　homesickness　undo　NEG　open　DE　emotion　　fast.knot

　　　已　　叫　　　人　　　　烦　　　　透了。（金狮奖 323）
　　　yǐ　　jiào　　rén　　　　fán　　　　tòu-le
　　　already　make　people　　annoyed　　complete-LE
　　　'Homesickness, like a fast knot that can never be undone, is already so annoying.' (*Jīnshījiǎng* 323)

(26) 农人们　　可　　苦　　　透了。（金狮奖 352）
　　 nóngrénmen　kě　 kǔ　　 tòu-le
　　 farmers　　really　miserable　complete-LE
　　 'Farmers are extremely miserable.' (*Jīnshījiǎng* 352)

4　~坏了 *huàile* 'broken-LE'.

(27) 连　 公安局　　　也　　忙　　坏了。（怀旧 102）
　　 lián　gōngānjú　　yě　 máng　huài-le
　　 even　police.station　also　busy　 broken-LE
　　 'Even the police station was exceptionally busy.' (*Huáijiù* 102)

(28) 林主任　　　急　　　　坏了。（有缘 19）
　　 línzhǔrèn　　jí　　　　huài-le
　　 Lin.director　worried　 broken-LE
　　 'Director Lin was worried to death.' (*Yǒuyuán* 19)

(29) 这下　　可　　把　偷　　东西　　的　乐　　坏了。（△大喜 16）
　　 zhèxià　 kě　　bǎ　tōu　 dōngxī　de　 lè　　huài-le
　　 now　　 really　BA　steal　things　 DE　happy　broken-LE
　　 'Now the thief will be more than happy.' (*Dàxǐ* 16)

5　~多了 *duōle* 'much more-LE'.

(30) 您　　 现在　　　瘦　　 多了。（△南风 32）
　　 nín　　xiànzài　　shòu　 duō-le
　　 2SG　now　　　thin　　much more-LE
　　 'You are much thinner now.' (*Nánfēng* 32)

(31) "好久　　没　　见，　你　　发福　　多了！"
　　 hǎojiǔ　 méi　 jiàn　　 nǐ　　fāfú　　 duō-le
　　 long　　NEG　see　　 2SG　 fat　　 much more-LE
　　 'Have not seen you for such a long time, you have put on weight now!'

　　 "哪里　　哪里！"（△大喜 24）
　　 nǎlǐ　　 nǎlǐ
　　 where　where
　　 'Oh really!' (*Dàxǐ* 24)

(32) 态度   也   温和   多了。（金狮奖 186）
    tàidù   yě   wēnhé   duō-le
    attitude also gentle   much more-LE
    'The attitude is also much gentler.' (*Jīnshījiǎng* 186)

Among the five conventional forms mentioned earlier, form 5 is the only one that contains comparative meaning and thus can be used in 比 *bǐ* 'than' comparative sentences (while other forms cannot), as shown in examples (33) and (34).

(33) 相思草   就   不   怕   蚂蚁   和   蚱蜢，
    xiàngsīcǎo jiù   bú   pà   mǎyǐ   hé   zhàměng
    begonia   just   NEG   afraid ant   and   grasshopper

    只是   这   一   点，   相思草   就   比   爸爸   的
    zhǐshì   zhè   yī   diǎn   xiàngsīcǎo jiù   bǐ   bàba   de
    just   this   one   point   begonia   thus   than   daddy   DE

    玫瑰   和   芍药   "厉害"   多了！（△含羞草 77）
    méiguī   hé   sháoyào   lìhài   duō-le
    rose   and   peony   strong   much more-LE
    'Begonia is not afraid of ants and grasshoppers. In this respect, it's much stronger than daddy's roses and peonies!' (*Hánxiūcǎo* 77)

(34) 这一来，   我   和   家   里   的   联系   自然   比
    zhèyīlái   wǒ   hé   jiā   lǐ   de   liánxì   zìrán   bǐ
    thus   1SG   and   home   in   DE   connection naturally than

    以往   松弛   多了。（短篇 7）
    yǐwǎng   sōngchí   duō-le
    past   loose   much more-LE
    'Thus, my connection with my family has naturally become much more estranged.' (*Duǎnpiān* 7)

Contrasted with the usage in Chinese Mandarin, the first form in Singapore Mandarin, that is, the verbal predicate plus 极了 *jíle* 'exceeding-LE' can take an object, as in (35) and (36). Such usage has not been observed in Chinese Mandarin.

(35) 他   恨   极了   酒鬼。（金狮奖 228）
    tā   hèn   jí-le   jiǔguǐ

	2SG	hate	exceeding-LE	drunkard			

'He hates drunkards exceedingly.' (*Jīnshíjiǎng* 228)

(36) 我　　默默地　　打量　　他：　　乍看　　像　　极了

wǒ　　mòmòde　　dǎliàng　　tā　　zhàkàn　　xiàng　　jí-le

1SG　　silently　　look.at　　3SG　　once.look　　like　　exceeding-LE

电影　　明星　　岳华。（梦 81）

diànyǐng　　míngxīng　　yuèhuá

movie　　stars　　Yuehua

'I looked at him in silence, thinking that he is very much like the movie star Yue Hua.' (*Mèng* 81)

For the aforementioned phrases without 得 *de* 'DE', be it ~极 *jíle* 'exceeding-LE', ~死了 *sǐle* 'dead-LE', ~透了 *tòule* 'complete-LE', or ~坏了 *huàile* 'broken-LE' and ~多了 *duōle* 'much more-LE', the auxiliary word 了 *le* 'LE' is part of the complement, for example, 好极了 *hǎojíle* 'excellent-LE' can be analysed in the following way.

好　　极　　了

hǎo　　jí　　le

$\overline{1\quad\quad 2}$　　　　(predicate-complement phrase)

$\overline{3\quad 4}$　　　　(sentence-final particle phrase)

7.6 State Complements

Let's start with examples (1) and (2).

(1) 今年　　我　　和　　家人　　一起　　大扫除，　　把　　家里

jīnnián　　wǒ　　hé　　jiārén　　yīqǐ　　dàsǎochú　　bǎ　　jiālǐ

this.year　　1SG　　and　　family　　together　　sweep　　BA　　house

收拾　　得　　整整齐齐、　　干干净净。（课本 1A 18）

shōushí　　de　　zhěngzhěngqíqí　　gāngānjìngjìng

tidy.up　　DE　　neat　　clean

'My family and I did a spring-cleaning this year, making our house neat and clean.' (*Kèběn* 1 A 18)

(2) 两   父女   亲热   得   叫人妒忌。（报 1995
                                              年 7 月 27 日副刊 4 版）
    liǎng   fùnǚ   qīnrè   de   jiàoréndùjì
    two   father.and.daughter close   DE   make.others.jealous
    'The father and daughter are so close that it makes others jealous.' (*Bào*,
    July 27, 1995, Issue no. 4, supplementary edition)

In the first example, the complement 整整齐齐、干干净净 *zhěngzhěngqíqí gāngānjìngjìng* 'neat and clean' seems to address the result of the actions denoted by the verb 收拾 *shōushí* 'tidy up'. In the second example, the complement 叫人妒忌 *jiàoréndùjì* 'make others jealous' seems to denote the degree of the state indicated by the word 亲热 *qīnrè* 'close'. However, we do not regard the complements in these examples as resultative complements or degree complements, because they have distinct differences from the other two in both form and meaning. First, these complements are not directly attached to the verb or adjective predicate. Second, these complements are not in fixed forms. Third, they generally describe a state to complement the predicates. Consequently, "state complement" is used particularly for this kind of complement so as to be distinguished from resultative complements and degree complements.

In Singapore Mandarin, there are three forms of predicate-state complement phrases: one with 得 *de* 'DE', one with 到 *dào* 'until' and one with 个 *gè* 'CL', as exemplified here.

跑   得   直   喘气
pǎo   *de*   *zhí*   *chuǎnqì*
run   DE   always   pant
'running untill panting heavily'

（把   孩子）   打   到   昏沉沉的
bǎ   *háizi*   *dǎ*   *dào*   *hūnchénchénde*
BA   child   beat   until   senseless
'beat (a child) until he is senseless'

看   个   清楚
kàn   *gè*   *qīngchǔ*
see   GE   clear
'observe until (one) see clearly'

Next, we will introduce these three forms in Sections 7.6.1 through 7.6.3, respectively.

7.6.1 State Complements With 得 de 'DE'

In most cases, the predicates that take state complements with 得 de 'DE' are verbs, as in sentences (3) and (4), or adjectives, as in sentence (5).

(3) 文笔　　　好　的　人　　　通常　　　历史　　考　　　　得　不
　　 wénbǐ　　 hǎo de rén　　 tōngcháng　 lìshǐ　 kǎo　　　 de bù
　　 writing.style good DE people usually　 history take.exams DE NEG

好。（牛车水 119）
hǎo

'People who can write a good essay usually do badly in history exams.' (*Niúchēshuǐ* 119)

(4) 不要　　卖　　　得　　太　　夜。（恶梦 120）
　　 búyào　 mài　　 de　 tài　 yè
　　 NEG　　 sell　　 DE　 too　 night

'Don't sell far into the night.' (*Èmèng* 120)

(5) 学校　　　开　　课　　以后，　我　　自己　　忙　　　得
　　 xuéxiào　 kāi　 kè　 yǐhòu　 wǒ　 zìjǐ　　 máng　 de
　　 school　 start course after　 1SG　 self　 busy　 DE

分身乏术，． ． ． ． ． ．（大胡子 33）
fēnshēnfáshù
can't.be.in.two.places.at.once

'After the school started, I was too busy to care about other things.' (*Dàhúzǐ* 33)

Be it a verb predicate or an adjective predicate, the complement can be a single adjective, as in sentences (6) and (7), a single stative word, as in sentences (8) through (10), or more commonly a predicate phrase, as in sentences (11) through (13).

(6) 让　　儿　女　　　吃　得　饱，　穿　　　得　暖．．．（变调 21）
　　 ràng　 ér　 nǚ　　 chī　 de　 bǎo　 chuān　 de　 nuǎn
　　 let　 son daughter eat　 DE　 full　 wear　 DE　 warm

'Let children have access to enough food and warm clothes in order not to be hungry and cold . . .' (*Biàndiào* 21)

(7) 华文　　　知识分子　　以为　　自己　　有　　　了
　　huáwén　　zhīshífènzǐ　yǐwéi　　zìjǐ　　yǒu　　le
　　Chinese　　intellectual　think　　self　　have　　LE

　　知识　　和　　　学问，　　便　　比　　　一般　　人
　　zhīshí　　hé　　xuéwèn　　biàn　　bǐ　　　yībān　　rén
　　knowledge and　knowledge thereupon than　 average people

　　看　　得　　透，　　想　　得　　深，　　所以…（风筝 23）
　　kàn　　de　　tòu　　　xiǎng　de　　shēn　　suǒyǐ
　　look　DE　thoroughly　think　DE　deeply　so

　　'Chinese intellectuals believe that, after acquiring knowledge, they can think
　　about things more thoroughly and deeply than average people and so …'
　　(*Fēngzhēng* 23)

(8) 每　　次　　都　　　输　　得　　精光。（△大喜 39）
　　měi　　cì　　dōu　　shū　　de　　jīngguāng
　　every　time　all　　lose　　DE　with.nothing.left
　　'Every time (he) loses everything.' (*Dàxǐ* 39)

(9) 现在　　　街道　　　变　　　得　　冷清清的。（风筝 141）
　　xiànzài　　jiēdào　　biàn　　de　　lěngqīngqīngde
　　now　　　street　　change　DE　deserted
　　'The street became deserted now.' (*Fēngzhēng* 141)

(10) 他　　的　　头发　　梳　　得　　服服贴贴，　校服　　　　穿　　　得
　　 tā　　de　　tóufā　　shū　　de　　fúfútiētiē　　xiàofú　　　　chuān　de
　　 3SG　DE　hair　　comb　DE　smooth　　　school.uniform　wear　DE

　　整整齐齐。（狮子 51）
　　zhěngzhěngqíqí
　　neat
　　'He hair was well combed and his school uniform was neat.' (*Shīzi* 51)

(11) 儒家　　　　重视　　　　仁德，　　把　　仁德　　看　　得　　比
　　 rújiā　　　zhòngshì　　réndé　　　bǎ　　réndé　　kàn　　de　　bǐ
　　 Confucianism emphasise　virtue　　BA　　virtue　　see　　DE　than

生命　　　　　还　　　　　重要。（伦理·中四 6）
shēngmìng　　hái　　　　zhòngyào
life　　　　　more　　　important

'The Confucianists attach great importance to the virtues, considering it more important than their lives.' (*Lúnlǐ* IV 6)

(12) 他　　贴身　　　在　　垒壁上，　炮火　　　照耀　　　得　　他
　　　tā　　tiēshēn　　zài　　lěibìshàng　pàohuǒ　zhàoyào　de　　tā
　　　3SG　lean.closely　at　　rampart　　gunfire　　blaze　　DE　　3SG

无处可遁。（金狮奖 4）
wúchùkědùn
have.no.place.to.hide

'He leaned closely on the rampart and the gunfire blazed so that he could scarcely find a place to hide.' (*Jīnshījiǎng* 4)

(13) 她　　回答　　得　　很　　冷淡。（△大喜 126）
　　　tā　　huídá　　de　　hěn　　lěngdàn
　　　3SG　answer　　DE　　very　　nonchalant

'She answered nonchalantly.' (*Dàxǐ* 126)

If the state complement is a single adjective, the resulting predicate-state complement phrase may be ambiguous, as they look the same as predicate-potential complement phrases. For instance, 唱得好 *chàngdehǎo* has two interpretations: *one* meaning is "sing well" and 好 *hǎo* is a state complement, the other meaning is "one can sing well" and here 好 *hǎo* is a potential complement. The difference is evident if we compare these two in terms of the position of the stress, negative form and extensibility.

	stress position	negative form	extendibility
唱得好 *chàngdehǎo* 'sing well'(state)	好 *hǎo* 'nicely'	唱得不好 *chàngdebùhǎo* 'sing badly'	唱得很好 *chàngdéhěnhǎo* 'sing very well'
唱得好 *chàngdehǎo* 'can sing well' (potentiality)	唱 *chàng* 'sing'	唱不好 *chàngbùhǎo* 'can't sing well'	not extensible

As we have mentioned before, the reduplicated form of monosyllabic adjectives can't function as a predicate in Chinese Mandarin whereas it can do so in Singapore Mandarin (see Section 5.8). Similarly, it cannot act as a state complement in Chinese Mandarin whereas it can serve as a state complement in Singapore Mandarin, as exemplified by the following sentences.

(14) 驾驶员   眼睛   睁   得   大大,   脸色   也   发
     jiàshǐyuán yǎnjīng zhēng de   dàdà   liǎnsè   yě   fā
     driver   eye   open   DE   big   complexion also become

     白   了。（一心 54）
     bái   le
     white   Le

     'The driver's eyes widened and his face turned white.' (Yīxīn 54)

(15) 问   他   又   不   答,   只   把   头   压   得
     wèn   tā   yòu   bù   dá   zhǐ   bǎ   tóu   yā   de
     ask   3SG   yet   NEG   answer   only BA   head hold DE

     低低。（胜利 23）
     dīdī
     low

     'He did not answer the questions. He just kept his head down.' (Shènglì 23)

(16) 大门   一概   都   关   得   严严。（独上 27）
     dàmén   yīgài   dōu   guān   de   yányán
     gate   always   all   close   DE   tight

     'All gates are always tightly closed.' (Dúshàng 27)

7.6.2 State Complements With 到 dào 'DAO'

In Singapore Mandarin, there is an auxiliary word 到 dào 'DAO', which can be attached to a verb or an adjective and then followed by a state complement. The examples are given here.

(17) 还是   死   了   的   好。   真的!   我   做人   都   做
     háishì   sǐ   le   de   hǎo   zhēnde   wǒ   zuòrén   dōu   zuò
     still   die   LE   DE   good   seriously 1SG   be.human   already do

     到   厌   了。（吾土·小说上 193）
     dào   yàn   le
     DAO   tired LE

     'It's better to die. Seriously! I am already tired of being a person.' (WútǔXiǎoshuōshàng 193)

(18) "你   今天   **玩**   **到**   **好**   **高兴**   呀！" 小倩   说。
　　　　　　　　　　　　　　　　　　　　　　　　　（年岁 54）
　　　nǐ   jīntiān   **wán**   **dào**   **hǎo**   **gāoxìng**   ya   xiǎoqiàn   shuō
　　　2SG   today   **play**   **DAO**   **very**   **happy**   SFP   Xiaoqian   say
　　　'"Today you really had a good time!" said Xiaoqian.' (*Niánsuì* 54)

(19) 黄先生   　　　本来   邀   你   一起   去，   看   你   **睡**
　　　huángxiānshēng   běnlái   yāo   nǐ   yīqǐ   qù   kàn   nǐ   **shuì**
　　　Mr. Huang   at.first   invite   2SG   together   go   see   2SG   **sleep**

　　　到   **那么 甜**，   不   忍心   　　　　　叫醒   你。（金狮奖 101）
　　　dào   **nàme tián**   bù   rěnxīn   　　　　jiàoxǐng   nǐ
　　　DAO   **that   sweet**   NEG   have.the.heart.to   wake.up   2SG
　　　'At first Mr. Huang wanted to invite you to come together, but you were sleeping so well that he didn't have the heart to wake you up.' (*Jīnshījiǎng* 101)

The auxiliary word 到 *dào* 'DAO' is grammaticalised from the verb 到 *dào* 'reach'. Its function is equivalent to the auxiliary word 得 *de* 'DE'. However, there are still subtle differences between them. The state complement following 得 *de* 'DE' can be a single adjective, as in (6) and (7), also in (20).

(20) 飞   得   远，   飞   得   近，   都   没关系（青青 64）
　　　fēi   de   yuǎn   fēi   de   jìn   dōu   méiguānxì
　　　fly   DE   far   fly   DE   near   all   don't.matter
　　　'It doesn't matter whether it flies far or near.' (*Qīngqīng* 64)

However, the state complement following 到 *dào* 'until' can't be a single adjective. 得 *de* 'DE' in (20) can't be substituted with 到 *dào* 'DAO'. *飞到远，飞到近 *fēi dàoyuǎn fēi dàojìn* 'fly far, fly near' are ungrammatical.

In Singapore Mandarin, 到 *dào* 'DAO' is much more frequently used than 得 *de* 'DE'. This may explain why 使得 *shǐdé* 'make' rather than 使到 *shǐdào* 'make' is often used in Singapore Mandarin. Here are some examples.

(21) 江浪   　　笔锋   　　锐利，   文艺理论   　　　　　修养
　　　jiānglàng   bǐfēng   ruìlì   wényìlǐlùn   　　　　　xiūyǎng
　　　Jianglang   brushstroke   sharp   literary.and.artistic.   accomplishments
　　　　　　　　　　　　　　　　　　theories

　　　高，   为人   又   正直，   敢   评   敢   言，   **使到**
　　　gāo   wéirén   yòu   zhèngzhí   gǎn   píng   gǎn   yán   **shǐdào**
　　　high   behaviour   again   upright   dare   remark   dare   say   **make**

写作　的　人　出　书　时　都　战战兢兢。
xiězuò de rén chū shū shí dōu zhànzhànjīngjīng
write DE person release book time all tremble with fear

'Jiang Lang's sharp writing style, high accomplishments in literary and artistic theory and upright personality, together with his courage to comment and criticize, all make the writers quite nervous when their books are published.' (*Shènglì* 102)

(22)　现在　姐姐　已婚，　但　婚姻　生活　并　不
xiànzài jiějiě yǐhūn dàn hūnyīn shēnghuó bìng bù
now elder.sister married but marriage life yet NEG

愉快，　常　吵着　要　离婚，　**使到**　我　的　情绪
yúkuài cháng chǎozhe yào líhūn **shǐdào** wǒ de qíngxù
happy often quarrel want divorce **make** 1SG DE emtion

大　受　影响。（华文教材 3A133）
dà shòu yǐngxiǎng
greatly receive influence

'Now my sister is married, but her marriage is not a happy one. She often quarrels about divorce, which also influences me.' (*Huáwénjiàocái* 3A 133)

In Chinese Mandarin, there is no auxiliary 到 *dào* 'DAO'. So only 得 *de* 'DE' is used in predicate-state complement phrases. Certainly, there is no such expression as 使到 *shǐdào* 'make'.

7.6.3 *State Complements With* 个 *gè 'GE'*

Singapore Mandarin has an auxiliary word 个 *gè* 'GE' like Chinese Mandarin, which is derived from the classifier 个 *gè* 'CL'. Following the auxiliary 个 *gè* 'GE', there are often three types of constituents serving as state complements.

1　Single adjectives.

(23)　"她　的　父母　呢?　为什么　只　姐姐　管　她?"
tā de fùmǔ ne wèishénme zhī jiějiě guǎn tā
3SG DE parents SFP why only sister care 3SG

我　要　**问**　**个**　**清楚**。（风雨 15）
wǒ yào **wèn** **gè** **qīngchǔ**

Predicates and Complements 269

| | 1SG | want | **ask** | **GE** | **clear** |

'Where are her parents? Why is it that only her sister takes care of her? I want to be clear about it.' (*Fēngyǔ* 15)

(24) 今天 我 非 得 弄 个 明白 不可。（吾土·戏剧 55）
jīntiān wǒ fēi děi **nòng** **gè** **míngbái** bùkě
today 1SG must DE **make** **GE** **clear** must

'I have to figure it out today.' (*WútǔXìjù* 55)

(25) 今晚 你 要 陪 我 玩 个
jīnwǎn nǐ yào péi wǒ **wán** **gè**
tonight 2SG must accompany 1SG **play** **GE**

痛快。（吾土·小说上 187）
tòngkuài
happy

'Tonight you must give me a good time.' (*Wútǔ Xiǎoshuōshàng* 187)

(26) 有时 看到 她 所 喜欢 的 东西， 她 也
yǒushí kàndào tā suǒ xǐhuān de dōngxī tā yě
sometimes see 3SG SUO like DE thing 3SG also

会 毫不顾忌地 拉 我 一 把， 要 我
huì háobùgùjìde lā wǒ yī bǎ yào wǒ
will without consideration pull 1SG one CL want 1SG

看 个 仔细。(吾土·小说上 177)
kàn **gè** **zǐxì**
see **GE** **clearly**

'Sometimes when she sees something she likes, she will pull me over to look at it clearly without consideration.' (*WútǔXiǎoshuōshàng* 177)

2   Idioms or quadrisyllabic words.

(27) 总 要 拼 个 你死我活。（金狮奖 104）
zǒng yào **pīn** **gè** **nǐ-sǐ-wǒ-huó**
always want **battle** **GE** **fight.at.outrance**

'We always fight hard.' (*Jīnshījiǎng* 104)

(28) 立时，   过   路   的   群众   把   那个   小偷
    lìshí   guò   lù   de   qúnzhòng   bǎ   nàge   xiǎotōu
    immediately pass road DE the.masses BA   that   thief

围了   个   水泄不通。（报 1995 年 6 月 24 日 11 版）
wéile   gè   shuǐ-xiè-bú-tōng
surround   GE   to.be.jammed

'Immediately, the passers-by tightly surrounded the thief.' (*Bào*, June 24, 1995, Issue no. 11)

(29) 朱熹   甚至   认为   有   怀疑   精神，   读书   才
    zhūxī   shènzhì   rènwéi   yǒu   huáiyí   jīngshén   dúshū   cái
    Zhuxi   even   think   have   wonder   spirit   read   only

会   进步；   因为   "一   有   怀疑，   便   会   想
huì   jìnbù   yīnwéi   yī   yǒu   huáiyí   biàn   huì   xiǎng
can   improve   because   once   have   wonder   then   can   think

弄   个   水落石出。"（伦理·中三 51）
nòng   gè   shuǐ-luò-shí-chū
figure   GE   find.out.the.truth

'Zhuxi even thinks that only with the spirit of doubt can we make progress in reading. Because once we have questions about things, we will try to work it out.' (*Lúnlǐ* III 51)

3   Some fixed form of negations. For example, 不停 *bùtíng* 'without stop', 不休 *bùxiū* 'without stop', 不住 *búzhù* 'without stop', 不止 *bùzhǐ* 'without stop', 没完 *méiwán* 'endless' and 没完没了 *méiwánméiliǎo* 'endless'.

(30) 大学   学费   靠   的   都   是   她   自己   的   一双
    dàxué   xuéfèi   kào   de   dōu   shì   tā   zìjǐ   de   yīshuāng
    college   fee   rely   DE   all   be   3SG   self   DE   a.pair

手；   暑假   寒假   都   做   个   不停。（想飞 35）
shǒu   shǔjià   hánjià   dōu   zuò   gè   bú-tíng
hands   summer.   winter.   all   do   GE   without.stop
        vacation   vacation

'She relies on her own hard work to earn her college tuition. She has been working around the clock during the summer and winter vacations.' (*Xiǎngfēi* 35)

(31) 大家　　一个劲儿　地　　劝　　　她，　可是　她　　还是
     dàjiā   yīgèjìnér de   quàn   tā   kěshì tā   háishì
     everyone keep.on   DE   comfort   3SG but   3SG   still

哭　　个　　不住。
kū   gè   bú-zhù
cry   GE   without.stop

'Everyone tried to comfort her, but she kept on crying without stop.'

(32) 他　　很　　会　　说　　笑话，　一　　说起来，　　总是
     tā   hěn   huì   shuō xiàohuà   yī   shuōqǐlái   zǒngshì
     3SG   very can   tell joke   once speak.up   always

逗　　得　　大家　　笑　　个　　不止。
dòu   dé   dàjiā   xiào gè   bú-zhǐ
tease DE   everyone laugh GE   without.stop

'He is good at telling jokes. Every time he tells a joke, everyone laughs non-stop.'

(33) 他　　一　　坐　　下来　　就　　写　　个　　没完。
     tā   yī   zuò   xiàlái   jiù   xiě   gè   méi-wán
     3SG   once sit   down   then write GE   without.stop

'As soon as he sat down, he wrote without stopping.'

Sometimes the state complement phrases take both 得 *dé* 'DE' and 个 *gè* 'GE', for example:

(34) 人　　　的　　感情，　　哪　　是　　一　　纸　　离婚　　　证书
     rén   de   gǎnqíng   nǎ   shì   yī   zhǐ   líhūn   zhèngshū
     human   DE   emotion   PRT   is   one paper divorce   certificate

便　　能　　**断**　　**得**　　**个**　　**干干净净**　　的。（大胡子 39）
biàn   néng   **duàn**   **de**   **gè**   **gāngānjìngjìng**   de
then   can   **cut**   **DE**   **GE**   **clean**   DE

'People's feelings cannot be broken completely by a divorce certificate.' (*Dàhúzǐ* 39)

(35) 伸　　手　　向　　母亲　　要来　　的　　钱，　转眼间
     shēn   shǒu   xiàng   mǔqīn   yàolái   de   qián   zhuǎnyǎnjiān
     stretch hand to   mother ask   DE   money in.a.flash

便	在	"手舞足蹈"	中	花	得	个
biàn	zài	shǒuwǔzúdǎo	zhōng	**huā**	**de**	**gè**
then	in	dance.with.joy	in	**spend**	**DE**	**GE**

干干净净。（狮子 128）
gāngānjìngjìng
clean

'The money I asked for from my mother ran out in a flash.' (*Shīzi* 128)

(36)
不	一会儿	功夫，	花布上	的	辣椒，	便
bú	yīhuìér	gōngfū	huābùshàng	de	làjiāo	biàn
NEG	a.while	time	cloth	DE	chilly	then

售	得	个	清清光光。（石头 94）
shòu	de	gè	qīng-qīng-guāng-guāng
sell	DE	GE	with.nothing.left

'After a while, the chillies on the cloth were all sold out.' (*Shítou* 94)

In terms of grammatical structure, the auxiliary words 得 *dé* 'DE', 到 *dào* 'DAO' or 个 *gè* 'GE' are all the part of the predicates, as shown here.

洗　得　一干二净

xǐ　de　yìgānèrjìng

——1—— ——2——　(predicate-complement phrase)

——3—— ——4——　(auxiliary phrase)

洗　到　一干二净

xǐ　dào　yìgānèrjìng

——1—— ——2——　(predicate-complement phrase)

——3—— ——4——　(auxiliary phrase)

洗　个　一干二净

xǐ　gè　yìgānèrjìng

——1—— ——2——　(predicate-complement phrase)

——3—— ——4——　(auxiliary phrase)

7.7 Temporal and Locative Complements

The temporal and locative complements are composed of prepositional phrases, such as 出生在新加坡 *chūshēng zài xīnjiāpō* 'born in Singapore', and its structure is shown here.

```
出生        在    新加坡
chūshēng    zài   xīnjiāpō
―――――       ―――――――――――
  1              2           (predicate-complement phrase)
            ―――   ―――――
             3       4       (prepositional phrase)
```

In the temporal and locative complements, there are only five prepositions used: 在 *zài* 'in/on', 到 *dào* 'until', 自 *zì* 'from', 向 *xiàng* 'to/towards', 于 *yú* 'at/in/than'. We will introduce them one by one in Sections 7.7.1 through 7.7.5.

7.7.1 在 *zài* 'In/On' Phrases as Complements

Of these five prepositions, 在 *zài* 'in/on' is the most commonly used. Prepostional phrases introduced by 在 *zài* 'in/on' as the complement generally express places, as shown in sentences (1) through (5).

(1) 住   在   哪儿？（有缘 44）
     zhù   *zài* *nǎér*
     live   in   where
     'Where do you live?' (*Yǒuyuán* 44)

(2) 他   搓   了   搓   手，   端端正正   地
     tā *cuō*   *le* *cuō*   *shǒu* *duānduānzhèngzhèng*   *de*
     3SG   twist   LE   twist   hand   straight   DE

     坐   在   椅子上。（胜利 92）
     zuò   *zài* *yǐzishàng*
     sit   on   chair
     'He rubbed his hands and sat upright on the chair.' (*Shènglì* 92)

(3) 我们   总   不   能   一直   站   在   这里。（想飞 63）
     wǒmen *zǒng*   *bú*   *néng* *yīzhí*   *zhàn*   *zài* *zhèlǐ*
     1PL   always   NEG   can   still   stand   in   here
     'We can't stand here forever.' (*Xiǎngfēi* 63)

(4) 她　把　火柴盒　**放**　**在**　桌子上。（△断情剪 161）
    tā   bǎ   huǒcháihé **fàng** **zài** zhuōzǐshàng
    3SG BA   match.box   put   on   table
    'She put the matchbox on the table.' (*Duànqíngjiǎn* 161)

(5) 童心　　　未泯　　的　我们，　会　**躲**　**在**　楼梯
    tóngxīn   wèimǐn de wǒmen   huì **duǒ** **zài** lóutī
    childishness remian DE 1PL   will   hide   in   downstair

    拐弯处，　　　想　　吓　一　吓　　老刘。（牛水车 44）
    guǎiwānchù   xiǎng xià yī xià lǎoliú
    turning.point want scare one scare LaoLiu
    'Childishly, we would hide in the corner of the stairs and try to scare Mr. Liu.' (*Niúchēshuǐ* 44)

在 *zài* 'in/on' can also express time, but this usage is much less.

(6) 今天，　我们　是　**生活**　**在**　九十　年代，　我们　的
    jīntiān wǒmen shì **shēnghuó** **zài** jiǔshí niándài wǒmen de
    today   1PL   are   live   in   ninety years   1PL   DE

    思想　　不　　能　**停留**　**在**　过去，　要　跟　　上
    sīxiǎng bú   néng **tíngliú** **zài** guòqù yào gēn shàng
    thinking NEG can   stop   in   the.past want follow up

    时代　　的　步伐。（报 1995 年 4 月 18 日 11 版）
    shídài   de bùfá
    times   DE pace
    'Today, we are living in the 1990s. Our mindset should not remain in the past, but keep pace with the times.' (*Bào*, Apr. 8, 1995, Issue no. 11)

7.7.2 到 dào *'To/Until...' Phrases as Complements*

Complements with the prepositional phrases 到 *dào* 'to/until' mainly have three functions, which are illustrated in the following with examples respectively.

1 Indicating places, that is, the destination of movement.

(7) 浴嫂　　忽然　　站起来，　走　　到　　右边　　的
    yùsǎo   hūrán   zhànqǐlái zǒu   dào   yòubiān   de
    caregiver suddenly stand.up   walk to   right   DE

    房间里　　　　去。(断情剪 160)
    fángjiānlǐ   qù
    room   go

    'The caregiver suddenly stood up and walked into the room on the right.' (*Duànqíngjiǎn* 160)

(8) 大概　　走　　到　　哪里，　　老虎　　总是　　老虎，
    dàgài   zǒu   dào   nǎlǐ   lǎohǔ   zǒngshì lǎohǔ
    perhaps walk to   anywhere tiger   always   tiger

    猴子　　总是　　猴子。（金狮奖 64）
    hóuzǐ   zǒngshì hóuzǐ
    monkey always   monkey

    'Perhaps no matter where you go, tiger is always tiger and monkey is just monkey.' (*Jīnshījiǎng* 64)

2 Indicating time.

(9) 我　　一直　　　　等　　到　　下午　　　两点,
    wǒ   yīzhí   děng dào   xiàwǔ   liǎngdiǎn
    1SG all.the.time wait until afternoon two.o'clock

    她　　还　　没有　　　来，　我　　真　　　有点　　　急　　　了。
    tā   hái   méiyǒulái lái   wǒ   zhēn   yǒudiǎn   jí   le
    3SG   still NEG   come 1SG   really a.little anxious LE

    'I kept waiting for her until two o'clock in the afternoon but she still didn't show up, which made me a little anxious.'

(10) 谈　　　到　　　不能　　　不　　　分手　　　的　　　时候
　　　 tán　　dào　　búnéng　　bú　　fēnshǒu　　de　　shíhòu
　　　 talk　until　 can't　　NEG　 separate　　DE　　time

离开。（吾土·小说 159）
líkāi
leave

'(They) kept talking until they have to leave.' (*Wútǔ Xiǎoshuō* 159)

3   Indicating limitations.

(11) 华文　　　减　　　到　　　学　　　语言　　　最低
　　　 huáwén　jiǎn　　dào　　xué　　yǔyán　　zuìdī
　　　 Chinese　reduce　to　 learn　language　lowest

要求　　　的　　　时数　　　以下,......（风筝 67）
yāoqiú　　de　　shíshù　　yǐxià
requirement　DE　 hour　　below

'The learning hour for Chinese was reduced to below the minimum language requirement, . . .' (*Fēngzhēng* 67)

(12) 逾期　　　未　　　呈报　　　所得税　　　估税　　　表格，
　　　 yúqī　　wèi　　chéngbào　suǒdéshuì　gūshuì　biǎogé
　　　 overdue　NEG　declare　 income.tax　assessment　chart

最低　　罚款　　从　　50　　元　　提高　　到　　100
zuìdī　　fákuǎn　cóng　wǔshí　yuán　tígāo　　dào　yìbǎi
lowest　fine　　from　fifty　yuan　improve　to　one.hundred

元，　最高　　罚款　　则　　从　　千　　元，　减
yuán　zuìgāo　fákuǎn　zé　　cóng　qiān　yuán　jiǎn
yuan　highest　fine　　then　from　thousand　yuan　reduce

到　　800　　　　　　　元。（报 1995 年 4 月 5 日 3 版）
dào　bābǎi　　　　　　 yuán
to　 eight.hundred　　yuan

'The minimum fine for failing to file an income tax assessment form on time has been raised from 50 to 100 yuan, while the maximum fine has been reduced from 1,000 to 800 yuan.' (*Bào*, Apr. 5, 1995, Issue no. 3)

7.7.3 自 zì 'From' Phrases as Complements

The complements of the prepositional phrase 自 *zì* 'from' can imply one of the two meanings:

1. The complement expresses location, that is, the starting point of movement. In this case, the predicate can only be the verb 来 *lái* 'come'.

(13) 娇小 的 她 今年 26岁, 来 自 中国
 jiāoxiǎo de tā jīnnián èrshíliùsuì **lái zì** zhōngguó
 petite DE 3SG this.year 26.year **come from** China

 海南 省。(报 1995 年 3 月 10 日 20 版)
 hǎinán shěng
 Hainan province

 'The petite 26-year-old girl comes from Hainan Province, China.' (*Bào*, Mar. 10, 1995, Issue no. 20)

(14) 医院 设备 良好 的 大 讲堂 里,
 yīyuàn shèbèi liánghǎo de dà jiǎngtáng lǐ
 hospital equipment fine DE big lecture.hall inside

 密密 地 坐 满 了 来 自 他国
 mìmì de zuò mǎn le **lái zì** tāguó
 rather.dense DE sit full LE **come from** other.country

 的 游客。(天长 24)
 de yóukè
 DE tourist

 'The well-equipped lecture hall of the hospital is crowded with tourists from other countries.' (*Tiāncháng* 24)

(15) 几 名 来 自 澳洲 的 游客 去 向
 jǐ míng **lái zì** àozhōu de yóukè qù xiàng
 several CL **come from** Australia DE tourist go toward

 有关 的 职员 交涉, ...(石头 223)
 yǒuguān de zhíyuán jiāoshè
 relevant DE staff negotiate

 'Several tourists from Australia went to negotiate with the relevant staff...' (*Shítou* 223)

278 Lu Jianming

2 The complement can also indicate the origin of something.

(16) 别人   一   听到   我   毕业   自
     biérén   yī   tīngdào   wǒ   **bìyè**   **zì**
     others   once   hear   1SG   graduate from

光华（中学）   他们   的   直觉   一定   是：
guānghuá(zhōngxué)   tāmen   de   zhíjué   yīdìng   shì
Guanghua.Middle.School   3PL   DE   intuition must   be

他   是   从小   练   乒乓球，
tā   shì   cóngxiǎo   liàn   pīngpāngqiú
3SG   be   from.childhood   practice   table.tennis

不   是   中学   才   开始   的。（薪传 57）
bú   shì   zhōngxué   cái   kāishǐ   de
NEG   be   middle   just   begin   DE

'When people hear that I graduated from Guanghua middle school, their intuition must be that I have been practising table tennis since childhood, not from middle school.' (*Xīnchuán* 57)

(17) "筚路蓝缕"   这   个   成语   出
     bìlùlánlǚ   zhè   Gè   chéngyǔ   **chū**
     endure.great.hardships.in.pioneer.work this   CL   idiom   come

自   《左传·宣公十三年》。
zì   zuǒzhuàn-xuāngōngshísānnián
from   13th.year.of.DukeXuan's.reign.in.Zuozhuan

'The idiom 筚路蓝缕 *bìlùlánlǚ* "to endure great hardships in pioneer work" is from *13th year of Duke Xuan's reign in Zuozhuan*（*The Spring and Autumn Annals*）.'

(18) 警署   行动   中心   所   接到   的
     jǐngshǔ   xíngdòng   zhōngxīn   suǒ   jiēdào   de
     police.station   action   centre   SUO   receive   DE

100   起   无聊   电话   当中，   80   多
yībǎi   qǐ   wúliáo   diànhuà   dāngzhōng bāshí   duō
one.hundred   CL   boring   call   middle   eighty   over

起	来	自	儿童。（报 1995 年 3 月 9 日 5 版）
qǐ	lái	zì	Értóng
CL	come	from	Children

'Among the 100 boring calls received by the Police Action Centre, more than 80 of them are from children.' (*Bào*, Mar. 9, 1995, Issue no. 5)

7.7.4 向 *xiàng* 'To' Phrases as Complements

When the 向 *xiàng* 'to' prepositional phrase functions as the complement, it always indicates the direction of the action. In such cases, the predicate is restricted to a few monosyllabic verbs, as in (19) through (21).

(19)
这样	一	个	国家	的	文学	才	能	算	是
zhèyàng	yí	gè	guójiā	de	wénxué	cái	néng	suàn	shì
this.way	one	CL	country	DE	literature	then	can	to.be	is

成长，	可以	走	向	世界。（△新华文学 245）
chéngzhǎng	kěyǐ	zǒu	xiàng	Shìjiè
develop	can	go	to	world

'Only in this way can a country's literature be developed and go global.' (*Xīnhuáwénxué* 245)

(20)
这	条	水沟	宽	二十尺，	也	不	知	流
zhè	tiáo	shuǐgōu	kuān	èrshí chǐ	yě	bù	zhī	liú
this	CL	ditch	width	twenty.foot	also	NEG	know	flow

向	何方。（壁虎 61）
xiàng	Héfāng
to	where

'Nobody knows where this ditch, with a width of 20, flows to.' (*Bìhǔ* 61)

(21)
一	股	又	浓	又	浊	的	气味，	直直	地
yì	gǔ	yòu	nóng	yòu	zhuó	de	qìwèi	zhízhí	de
one	CL	also	dense	also	pungent	DE	smell	directly	DE

冲	向	脑门，……（△天长 30）
chōng	xiàng	Nǎomén
rush	to	forehead

'A dense and pungent smell went straight to my face.' (*Tiānzhǎng* 30)

7.7.5 于 *yú* 'At/In/Than' Phrases as Complements

When the 于 *yú* 'at/in/than' prepositional phrase serves as the complement, it has three functions:

1   Introducing location.

(22) 流冰　　一九一四年　　出生　　于　新加坡，......（△新华文学 61）
　　 liúbīng　yījiǔyīsìnián　chūshēng yú　xīnjiāpō
　　 LiuBing　1914　　　　　born　 in Singapore
　　 'Liu Bing was born in Singapore in 1914.' (*Xīnhuáwénxué* 61)

(23) 龙　　的　家　　坐落　　于　离　　多瑙河　　　不　　远
　　 lóng de jiā   zuòluò yú lí   duōnǎohé   bù   yuǎn
　　 Long DE house locate at away Danube.River NEG   far

　　 的　　一　　间　　公寓　　　　里。（南北 44）
　　 de   yī   jiān gōngyù   Lǐ
　　 DE   one CL   apartment   Within
　　 'Long's (the name of a tour guide) home is located in an apartment building not far away from the Danube River.' (*Nánběi* 44)

(24) 苦苦　　挣扎　　　于　　生活线上。（△天长 25）
　　 kǔkǔ   zhēngzhá yú   Shēnghuóxiànshàng
　　 bitterly struggle at   living standard
　　 '(He) is struggling hard at a basic standard of living.' (*Tiāncháng* 25)

2   Introducing time.

(25) 方修　　　的　　《马华新文学简史》　　　　　　　出版
　　 fāngxiū   de   Mǎhuáxīnwénxuéjiǎnshǐ   chūbǎn
　　 FangXiu   DE   *A Brief History of New Malaysian Chinese Literature* publish

　　 于　　一九七四年，......（△新华文学 75）
　　 yú   Yījiǔqīsìnián
　　 in   1974
　　 'Fang Xiu's book, *A Brief History of New Malaysian Chinese Literature*, was published in 1974.' (*Xīnhuáwénxué* 75)

(26) | 艾芜 | 的 | 《南行记》 | 作 | 于 | 1993年
| àiwú | de | nánxíngjì | zuò | Yú | 1933nián
| AiWu | DE | Journey to the South | written | on | 1993.year

△ 11月　　　1日。(△ 中国作家 30–31)
11yuè　　　1rì
November　　1th

'Ai Wu finished the book *Journey to the South* on Nov. 1st, 1993.' (*Zhōngguózuòjiā* 30−31)

(27) | 龙 | 生 | 于 | 龙年，......（南北 43）
| long | shēng | yú | Lóngnián
| Long | born | in | the.year.of.dragon

'Long (the name of a tour guide) was born in the Chinese lunar year of dragon.' (*Nánběi* 43)

3   Introducing the things to be compared in comparative sentences. In this case, only adjectives can be the predicate, such as 多于 *duōyú* 'more than' and 高于 *gāoyú* 'higher than'.

(28) | 新加坡 | 中产阶级 | 的 | 政治 | 倾向 | 是
| xīnjiāpō | zhōngchǎnjiējí | de | zhèngzhì | qīngxiàng | shì
| Singapore | middle class | DE | political | inclination | is

| 冷漠 | 多 | 于 | 热诚， | 对 | 现有 | 的
| lěngmò | duō | yú | rèchéng | Duì | xiànyǒu | de
| unconcerned | more | than | passionate | to | present | DE

| 体制 | 是 | 拥护 | 多 | 于 | 反对， | 甚至
| tǐzhì | shì | yōnghù | duō | yú | fǎnduì | shènzhì
| mechanism | is | promotion | more | than | objection | even

| 是 | "保守" | 多 | 于 | "自由化"。（报 1995 年 4 月
| | | | | | 19 日 4 版）
| shì | bǎoshǒu | duō | yú | zìyóuhuà
| is | conventionalism | more | than | liberalisation

'As for the political preference of the Singaporean middle class, they are more indifferent than passionate, more supportive of the present mechanism than objective, with even more support for "convention" than for "liberalisation."' (Bào, Apr. 19, 1995, Issue no. 4)

(29) 新加坡   的   年   工资   增长   率   **高**   **于**
    xīnjiāpō   *de*   *nián* *gōngzī* *zēngzhǎng* *lǜ*   ***gāo***   ***yú***
    Singapore   DE   annual salary   increase   rate   **higher** **than**

通货膨胀   率。
tōnghuòpéngzhàng   *lǜ*
inflation   rate

'The rate of annual wage growth of Singapore is higher than its inflation rate.'

As a functional word in classical Chinese, 于 *yú* 'at/in/than' is only used in written language today. It acts in a similar way with 在 *zài* 'in/on' when it expresses location or time.

As illustrated earlier, it is obvious that prepositional complement phrases mainly denote time or location. Therefore, they are called temporal and locative complements in Singapore Mandarin.

Notes

1 See Ma, Z. (1991). Nanchonghua Li de Fanfu Wenju yu "Meide" He "Meiyou" [VP-Neg Interrogatives and 'Meide' and 'Meiyou' in Nanchong Dialect]. *Yuyanxue Luncong* [Essays on Linguistics], (16), 99–111.
2 Translator's note: 给 *gěi* 'GEI' is used as a passive marker here. Its function is like 被 *bèi* 'BEI'.
3 Translator's note: 得 *de* 'DE' is an auxiliary word, usually used to connect the predicate and the degree complement, as in sentence (10) in Section 7.1.2; also see Section 7.4.
4 开来 *kāilái* 'spread out' can only serve as a complement.
5 起 *qǐ* 'rise' and 开 *kāi* 'open' can't be combined with 去 *qù* 'go'.
6 Translator's note: 了 is a polyphonic character which has two different pronunciations: *le* and *liǎo*. When it is used with 得 *de* 'DE' or 不 *bù* 'NEG', it means "can" or "cannot", and is pronounced as *liǎo*.
7 Translator's note: These two fixed forms are post-verbal complements, the meaning of 得了 *deliǎo* is similar to 'can' or 'be able to', and the meaning of 不了 *bùliǎo* is similar to 'cannot' or 'not be able to'. But they are not modal verbs which precede the main verb.
8 V 得 *de* is actually the omitted form of V 得得 *dede* (it can be compared with the negative form of V 得 *de*,—V 不得 *bùde*). The first 得 *de* is an auxiliary verb and the second 得 *de* is a verb, serving as a complement. Because the phonetic form of the two 得 *de* is the same, the auxiliary 得 *de* is omitted.
9 Translator's note: 哪里 *nǎlǐ* 'where' is a humble address in Chinese Mandarin and Singapore Mandarin. It literally means "where", but is used to express an attitude of humility in daily communication.

8 Attributes and Adverbials

Lu Jianming

8.1 Two Types of Modifier-Head Phrases in Singapore Mandarin

Let's have a look at the following two groups of phrases:

A
纸	飞机（青青 62）	华文	文学（文艺 139）
zhǐ	fēijī	huáwén	wénxué
paper	plane	Chinese	literature

'paper plane' (*Qīngqīng* 62)   'Chinese literature' (*Wényì* 139)

小莉	的	妈妈（金狮奖（四）88）	大	房子（追云 27）
xiǎolì	de	māma	dà	fángzi
Xiaoli	DE	mother	big	house

'Xiaoli's mother' (*Jīnshījiǎng* IV 88)   'big house' (*Zhuīyún* 27)

细细	的	双眼（金狮奖 222）	两	封	信（△浮萍 73）
xìxì	de	shuāngyǎn	liǎng	fēng	xìn
narrow	DE	eyes	two	CL	letter

'narrow eyes' (*Jīnshījiǎng* 222)   'two letters' (*Fúpíng* 73)

B
悄悄地	问	你（青青 55）	经常	去	光顾（文艺 87）
qiāoqiāode	wèn	nǐ	jīngcháng	qù	guānggù
gently	ask	2SG	often	go	visit

'ask you gently' (*Qīngqīng* 55)   'often pay a visit there' (*Wényì* 87)

DOI: 10.4324/b23129-8

相当	喜欢（金狮奖（四）150）	非常	好（金狮奖 166）
xiāngdāng	*xǐhuān*	*Fēicháng*	*hǎo*
quite	like	very	good

'quite like it' (*Jīnshījiǎng* IV *150*)   'very good' (*Jīnshījiǎng* 166)

特别	要紧（△浮萍 129）	急忙忙地	跑	出来（追云 6）
tèbié	*yàojǐn*	*Jímángmángde*	*pǎo*	*chūlái*
especially	important	hurriedly	run	out

'especially important' (*Fúpíng* 129)   'hurriedly run out' (*Zhuīyún* 6)

The phrases in Group A and Group B are referred to as modifier-head phrases (see Section 2.2) in Chapter 2. For all these phrases, regardless of the specific meanings expressed, the first part of the phrase always modifies the second part; thus the former part is called the modifier and the latter part is called the head.

However, if we take into account the grammatical meanings of these phrases and their roles in sentence formation (i.e. grammatical functions), the modifier-head phrases can be divided into two types: The first type is nominal, which denotes things; the second type is predicative, which denotes actions or atributes. In order to differentiate one from another, the modifier in the first type is called an attribute and the whole phrase an attribute-head endocentric phrase; the modifier in the second type is called an adverbial, and the whole phrase an adverbial-head phrase.

8.2   Differences Between Attributes and Adverbials

In English, it is easy to distinguish an attribute from an adverbial, for it depends on its head. If the head is a noun, the modifier before or after it is an attribute; if the head is a verb or an adjective, the modifier before or after it is an adverbial. However, due to the lack of morphological inflections in Singapore Mandarin, attributes and adverbials are not as easily distinguishable as those in English.

In Singapore Mandarin, if the head is a noun, the modifier before it is usually an attribute, but sometimes it may be an adverbial when the modifier is an adverb. Please consider the following examples.

(1) 足足   一   个   礼拜   了。（变调 8）
    zúzú   yí   gè   lǐbài   le
    full   one   CL   week   LE
    'It has been a full week.' (*Biàndiào* 8)

Attributes and Adverbials 285

(2) 才　　五　　毛　　钱。（石头 29）
    cái　 *wǔ*　 *máo*　 *qián*
    only　 five　 ten.cents yuan
    'It's only fifty cents.' (*Shítou* 29)

(3) 今天　　才　　星期三。
    jīntiān　 *cái*　 *xīngqīsān*
    today　　 only　 Wednesday
    'It's only Wednesday today.'

(4) 你　已经　　大学生　　　了，还　　那么　不　　懂事。
    nǐ　 *yǐjīng*　 *dàxuéshēng*　 *le*　 *hái*　 *nàme*　 *bù*　 *dǒngshì*
    2SG　already　college.student　LE　still　such　NEG　mature
    'You are a college student now, but you're still so naive.'

In sentences (1) through (4), the nominal phrases 一个礼拜 *yīgèlǐbài* 'one week', 五毛钱 *wǔmáoqián* 'fifty cents', 星期三 *xīngqīsān* 'Wednesday' and 大学生 *dàxuéshēng* 'college student' are modified by 足足 *zúzú* 'full', 才 *cái* 'only' and 已经 *yǐjīng* 'already', which are all adverbs and thus are adverbials, not attributes.

Usually, if the head is a verb or an adjective, the modifier will be an adverbial, but it could also be an attribute when the modifier position is filled by a noun, as shown in the following examples:

(5) 舞蹈　　演出（追云 110）
    wǔdǎo　 *yǎnchū*
    dance　　perform
    'dance performance' (*Zhuīyún* 110)

(6) 心理　　准备（寻庙 74）
    xīnlǐ　 *zhǔnbèi*
    mentality　prepare
    'mental preparation' (*Xúnmiào* 74)

(7) （等待　着）　半夜　　的　　到来（壁虎 55）
    děngdài　 *zhe*　 *bànyè*　 *de*　 *dàolái*
    wait　　　 ZHE　 midnight DE　come
    'wait for midnight to come' (*Bìhǔ* 55)

(8) 科学   技术   方面   的   创新   与   突破（何 130）
    kēxué   jìshù   fāngmiàn   de   chuàngxīn yǔ   tūpò
    science technology field   DE   innovate and break.through

'innovation and breakthrough in science and technology' (*Hé* 130)

(9) 大学生   的   悲哀（寻庙 80）
    dàxuéshēng   de   bēiāi
    college.student   DE   sad

'college student's sadness' (*Xúnmiào* 80)

(10) 科技   的   发达（△天长 58）
    kējì   de   fādá
    science.and.technology DE   developed

'development of science and technology' (*Tiāncháng* 58)

(11) 大哥   的   聪明（变调 18）
    dàgē   de   cōngmíng
    older.brother   DE   intelligent

'older brother's intelligence' (*Biàndiào* 18)

(12) 绿叶   的   茂盛肥美（心情 138）
    lǜyè   de   màoshèngféiměi
    green.leaves   DE   lush

'lushness of leaves' (*Xīnqíng* 138)

The verbs 演出 *yǎnchū* 'perform', 准备 *zhǔnbèi* 'prepare', 到来 *dàolái* 'come', 创新与突破 *chuàngxīnyǔtūpò* 'innovate and break through' and the adjectives 悲伤 *bēishāng* 'sad', 发达 *fādá* 'developed', 聪明 *cōngmíng* 'intelligent', 茂盛肥美 *màoshèngféiměi* 'lush' in the preceding phrases are modified by nouns, which are attributes, not adverbial modifiers.

In brief, in Singapore Mandarin, we cannot judge whether the modifier is an attribute or an adverbial only by the nature of the head. As can be seen from sentences (13) and (14), the same adjective modifier may either be an attribute or an adverbial.

(13) 这些   **具体**   问题，   必须   尽快   解决。
     zhèxiē   jùtǐ   wèntí   bìxū   jìnkuài   jiějué
     these   specific   problem must   soon   solve

'These specific problems must be solved as soon as possible.'

(14) 这些   问题   你们   再   **具体**   讨论   一下。
    zhèxiē wèntí   nǐmen   zài   **jùtǐ**   tǎolùn   yíxià
    these   problem 2PL   again **specific** discuss a.bit
    'You should discuss these issues specifically again.'

具体 *jùtǐ* 'specific' is an adjective modifier in both sentences. However, in sentence (13), it is an attribute, while in sentence (14), it is an adverbial. Why are they different? It seems that we can find the answer from the head: in sentence (13), 具体 *jùtǐ* 'specific' modifies the noun 问题 *wèntí* 'problem'; in sentence (14), it modifies the verb 讨论 *tǎolùn* 'discuss'. So far, this explanation seems very reasonable, but this does not work out for the following sentences.

(15) 对于   这些   问题   不   能   一概而论,
    duìyú   zhèxiē wèntí   bù   néng   yígàiérlùn
    about   these   problem NEG   can   generalise

    我们   应该   **具体**   分析。
    wǒmen   yīnggāi   **jùtǐ**   fēnxī
    1PL   should   **specific** analyse
    'We should not generalise these issues, but analyse them specifically.'

(16) 对于   他们   所   提   的   意见,   我们   必须   **做**
    duìyú   tāmen   suǒ   tí   de   yìjiàn   wǒmen   bìxū   **zuò**
    about   3PL   SUO   raise   DE   suggestion 1PL   must   **make**

    具体   分析,   不能   什么   都   接受。
    jùtǐ   fēnxī   bùnéng   shénme dōu   jiēshòu
    specific analyse NEG   what   all   accept
    'We must make a specific analysis of their suggestions, but cannot accept them all.'

Both sentences (15) and (16) have the same modifier-head phrase 具体分析 *jùtǐfēnxī* 'analyse them specifically/make a specific analysis'. In terms of word class, in both sentences 具体 *jùtǐ* 'specific' is an adjective and 分析 *fēnxī* 'analyse' is a verb. However, *jùtǐ* 'specific' in sentence (15) is an adverbial, whereas in sentence (16), it is an attributive. Why? Because 具体分析 *jùtǐfēnxī* 'analyse them specifically' in sentence (15) is the object of the predicative-object-taking-verb 应该 *yīnggāi* 'should', and it is a predicative. Thus the modifier 具体 *jùtǐ* 'specific' is an adverbial. By contast, 具体分析 *jùtǐfēnxī* 'specific analysis' in sentence (16) is the object of the quasi-predicate-object-taking-verb 做 *zuò* 'make', and it is nominal. Thus the modifier 具体 *jùtǐ* 'specific' is an attribute (for predicative-object-taking-verbs and quasi-predicate-object-taking-verbs, please refer to Section 6.13).

It can be seen from the preceding that we must look carefully into the nature of the whole modifier-head phrase in order to distinguish attributes and adverbials in Singapore Mandarin. If the modifier-head phrase is nominal, the modifier is an attribute; if the modifier-head phrase is predicative, the modifier is an adverbial. Therefore, the adverb in a modifier-head phrase of "adverb + noun" is an adverbial due to the predicative nature of the phrase; the noun in a modifier-head phrase of "noun + verb/an adjective" is an attribute due to the nominal nature of the phrase. Thus, the reason we regard 具体 *jùtǐ* 'specific' in the phrase 具体问题 *jùtǐwèntí* 'specific problem' in sentence (13) as an attribute is not that the head 问题 *wèntí* 'problem' is a noun, but that the whole modifier-head is nominal; likewise, we regard 具体 *jùtǐ* 'specific' in 具体讨论一下 *jùtǐtǎolùnyíxià* 'discuss specifically' in sentence (14) as an adverbial not because the head 讨论一下 *tǎolùnyíxià* 'discuss' is verbal, but because the modifier-head phrase is predicative.

To sum up, attributes and adverbials in Singapore Mandarin are defined in terms of the nature of the modifier-head phrase as a whole: The modifier in the nominal modifier-head phrase is an attribute; the modifier in the predicative modifier-head phrase is an adverbial.

Within the two types of modifier-head phrases, attribute-head phrases are used more frequently and more complex than adverbial-head phrases, and thus need more attention. In the following sections, we will introduce attribute-head phrases in more detail.

8.3 Different Types of Heads and Their Attributes

In this section, we will discuss the type of words that can be modified by attributes and the restrictions on the form of the attributes.

8.3.1 Nouns Taking Attributes

All nouns can take attributes, and the resulting phrase is the most typical type of attribute-head endocentric phrase. The various cases of nouns taking attributes are discussed in Sections 8.4 through 8.11.

8.3.2 Verbs and Adjectives Taking Attributes

Verbs and adjectives can take attributes, usually with 的 *de* 'DE', as shown in the following examples.

(1) 学业　　的　　终止（短篇 53）
　　xuéyè　*de*　*zhōngzhǐ*
　　study　DE　terminate

'termination of one's studies' (*Duǎnpiān* 53)

(2) 红花 的 凋谢（青青 39）
　　hónghuā de diāoxiè
　　red.flower DE wither
　　'withering of red flowers' (*Qīngqīng* 39)

(3) 远方 的 祝福（△天长 57）
　　yuǎnfāng de zhùfú
　　distant.place DE bless
　　'blessing from a distant place' (*Tiāncháng* 57)

(4) 少年 的 苦闷（寻庙 74）
　　shàonián de Kǔmèn
　　teenage DE depress
　　'teenage depression' (*Xúnmiào* 74)

(5) 表面 的 冷漠（壁虎 77）
　　biǎomiàn de Lěngmò
　　surface DE indifferent
　　'superficial indifference' (*Bìhǔ* 77)

Examples (1) through (3) are verbs taking attributes and examples (4) and (5) are adjectives taking attributes, all of which contain the auxiliary word 的 *de* 'DE'. Nevertheless, there are two cases in which 的 *de* 'DE' can be omitted:

1 A few disyllabic verbs can accept noun attributes without 的 *de* 'DE'.

(6) 心理 **准备**（寻庙 74）
　　xīnlǐ **zhǔnbèi**
　　mentality **prepare**
　　'mental preparation' (*Xúnmiào* 74)

(7) 经济 **帮助**（短篇 54）
　　jīngjì **bāngzhù**
　　economy **help**
　　'economic help' (*Duǎnpiān* 54)

(8) 语文　　　　**教学**（华文教学 135）
　　 yǔwén　　　**jiàoxué**
　　 Chinese　　 teach

'Chinese teaching' (*Huáwénjiàoxué* 135)

These verbs, which accept noun attributes directly without 的 *de* 'DE', have some special features. We will discuss these later in Section 8.12.

2　A few monosyllabic adjectives can take numeral-classifier phrases as attributes.

(9)　八　　　尺　　　宽，　　十二　　尺　　　长（怀旧 11）
　　 bā　　　chǐ　　 kuān　　 shíèr　　chǐ　　 cháng
　　 eight　　feet　　wide　　 twelve　 feet　　long

'eight feet wide, twelve feet long' (*Huáijiù* 11)

(10)　三　　　尺　　　深（一心 3）
　　　sān　　 chǐ　　 shēn
　　　three　　feet　　deep

'three feet deep' (*Yīxīn* 3)

(11)　一　　　点　　　八　　　米　　　高（再见 2）
　　　yī　　　diǎn　　bā　　　mǐ　　　gāo
　　　one　　 point　　eight　 metre　 high

'1.8 metres high' (*Zàijiàn* 2)

This type of attribute-head endocentric phrase is special in that both the adjective and the numeral-classifier phrase in it are limited in number. The adjective heads are only limited to some conventional measuring adjectives, such as 宽 *kuān* 'wide', 长 *cháng* 'long', 深 *shēn* 'deep' 高 *gāo* 'high' and 重 *zhòng* 'heavy', 远 *yuǎn* 'distant'(for example, 六里远 *liùlǐyuǎn* 'six miles away'), 厚 *hòu* 'thick' (for example, 三公寸厚 *sāngōngcùnhòu* 'three decimetres thick') and so on. The classifiers in the attribute phrase are only limited to units of weights and measures, such as 尺 *chǐ* 'feet', 寸 *cùn* 'inch', 米 *mǐ* 'metre', 斤 *jīn* 'jin/half-kilogram', 公分 *gōngfēn* 'centimetre', 公斤 *gōngjīn* 'kilogram', 公里 *gōnglǐ* 'kilometre' and so on.

8.3.3 Personal Pronouns Taking Attributes

Personal pronouns can take attributes, all by adding 的 *de* 'DE', as shown in examples (12) through (15).

(12) 火车   最终   还是   走   了，   泪眼   模糊中
     huǒchē zuìzhōng   háishì   zǒu   le   lèiyǎn   móhúzhōng
     train   finally   still   go   LE   tearful.eyes obscurely

    我   向   下   了   车、   在   月台上   的
    wǒ   xiàng   xià   le   chē   zài   yuètáishàng   de
    1SG   toward   get.off   LE   train   at   platform   DE

    你   挥手。（青青 56）
    nǐ   huīshǒu
    2SG   wave.hands

'The train finally pulled out and with tears in my eyes, I waved to you who have got off the train and was standing on the platform.' (*Qīngqīng* 56)

(13) 作为   义顺   中组屋区   居民   的   我，
     zuòwéi   yìshún   zhōngzǔwūqū   jūmín   de   wǒ
     as   Yishun   middle.public.house.zone   resident DE   1SG

    向   这些   荣获   最佳   安全住家   称号   的
    xiàng   zhèxiē   rónghuò   zuìjiā   ānquánzhùjiā   chēnghào   de
    toward   these   win   best   safe.home   title   DE

    住户   表示   敬意。（报 1995 年 4 月 19 日 8 版）
    zhùhù   biǎoshì   jìngyì
    resident show   respect

'As a resident living in Yishun block, I'd like to show my respect to these residents who won the title of Best Safe Home.' (*Bào*, Apr. 19, 1995, Issue no. 8)

(14) 饿   得   肚子   呱呱叫   的   他，   只   那么   几
     è   dé   dùzi   guāguājiào   de   tā   zhǐ   nàme   jǐ
     hungry   DE   stomach   rumble   DE   3SG   only   that   a.few

    口   就   吃   完   了。（恶梦 44）
    kǒu   jiù   chī   wán   le
    CL   then   eat   up   LE

'His stomach rumbling with hunger, and he finished the meal in a few mouthfuls.' (*È mèng* 44)

(15) 目前　　育有　　一　　个　　3　　岁　　女儿
　　　mùqián　yùyǒu　yī　gè　sān　suì　nǚér
　　　now　　have　　a　　CL　three　year.old　daughter

　　　的　　他　　说：" . . ."　　（报 1995 年 3 月 10 日 6 版）
　　　de　　tā　　shuō
　　　DE　　3SG　say

'Now the father of a 3-year-old daughter, he said . . .' (*Bào*, Mar. 10, 1995, Issue no. 6)

Sometimes, stative words can also serve as attributes via 的 *de* 'DE'. In sentence (16), 我 *wǒ* '1SG' is modified by the stative word 气冲冲 *qìchōngchōng* 'angry'.

(16) 他　　气冲冲地　　　　走　　了，
　　　tā　　qìchōngchōngde　zǒu　le
　　　3SG　angrily　　　　　leave　LE

　　　留下　　气冲冲　　　　的　　我。（△一壶 3）
　　　liúxià　qìchōngchōng　de　wǒ
　　　leave　angry　　　　　DE　1SG

'He left away angrily, leaving me feel angry.' (*Yīhú* 3)

Personal pronouns with attributes, a westernised sentence pattern, are occasionally found in Chinese Mandarin. However, due to greater influence of English, this usage is much more frequent in Singapore Mandarin than in Chinese Mandarin.

Some personal pronouns don't take modifiers, including 别人 *biérén* 'others', 人家 *rénjiā* 'others', 大家 *dàjiā* 'everybody' and 自己 *zìjǐ* 'oneself'.

8.3.4 Stative Words Taking Attributes

Stative words with 的 *de* 'DE' can also take attributes, however this is only used in spoken language. The only possible attributes for them are demonstrative pronouns 这 *zhè* 'this' and 那 *nà* 'that'.

(17) 这　　黑乎乎　　的　　（是　　什么？）
　　　zhè　hēihūhu　　de　　shì　　shénme
　　　this　black　　　DE　　be　　what

'(What is) this black thing?'

(18)	那	红红	的	（是	牡丹花）
	nà	hónghóng	de	shì	mǔdānhuā
	that	red	DE	be	peony

'That red thing (is a peony).'

This type of attribute-head endocentric phrases is referential. For instance, 这黑乎乎的 *zhèhēihūhūde* 'this black thing' and 那红红的 *nàhónghóngde* 'that red thing' both denote things.

Stative words without 的 *de* 'DE' cannot be modified by attributes.

8.3.5 DE Constructions Taking Attributes

1 Numeral-classifier phrases serve as attributes.

(19)	我	还	要	圣诞树	呢,	至少	要	一
	wǒ	hái	yào	shèngdànshù	ne	zhìshǎo	yào	yī
	1SG	still	want	Christmas.tree	SFP	at.least	want	one

	棵	小	的。（牛车水 76）
	kē	xiǎo	de
	CL	small	DE

'I want a Christmas tree, at least a small one.' (*Niúchēshuǐ* 76)

(20)	想起	两	个	小	的,	我	的	干劲	就
	xiǎngqǐ	liǎng	gè	xiǎo	de	wǒ	de	gànjìn	jiù
	think.about	two	CL	small	DE	1SG	DE	enthusiasm	thus

	来	了！（有缘 34）
	lái	le
	come	LE

'Thinking about the two little ones, I feel enthusiastic.' (*Yǒuyuán* 34)

(21)	先	给	你	唱	一	段	日本	的。（笑眼 46）
	xiān	gěi	nǐ	chàng	yī	duàn	rìběn	de
	first	give	2SG	sing	one	CL	Japan	DE

'First, I will sing you a Japanese song.' (*Xiàoyǎn* 46)

2 Demonstrative pronouns 这 *zhè* 'this' and 那 *nà* 'that' as well as demonstrative-classifier compounds serve as attributes.

(22) 这   红   的   （是   她   的。）
    zhè   hóng de   shì   tā   de
    this red   DE   be   3SG   DE
    'This red one (is hers).'

(23) 我   要   那   蓝   的。
    wǒ   yào   nà   lán   de
    1SG   want that blue DE
    '(I want) that blue one.'

(24) 那个   男   的   （借助于   手杖，   吃力   万分地
    nàgè nán   de   jièzhùyú   shǒuzhàng chīlì   wànfēnde
    that man   DE   with.the.aid.of stick   struggle extremely

    站   了   起来。）（石头 88）
    zhàn   le   qǐlái
    stand LE   up

    'That man struggled to stand up with the aid of stick.' (*Shítou* 88)

8.3.6 Numerals Never Take Attributes

See Chapter 1 of Volume II.

8.3.7 Classifiers Taking Attributes

Classifiers can take numerals or demonstrative pronouns as attributes.

1 Classifiers can be modified by numerals, and the phrases thus formed, namely 'numeral + classifier' are often called numeral-classifier compounds.

(25) 一   个   衣厨（△断情剪203）   五   块   钱（笑眼 55）
    yí   gè   yīchú   wǔ   kuài   qián
    one   CL   wardrobe   five CL   money
    'a wardrobe' (*Duànqíngjiǎn* 203)   'five yuan' (*Xiàoyǎn* 55)

    一   件   外衣（平心 124）   一   把   太极   剑（话剧 77）
    yí   jiàn   yīchú   yī   bǎ   tàijí   jiàn
    one   CL   wardrobe   one   CL   Tai Chi sword
    'a wardrobe' (*Píngxīn* 124)   'a Tai Chi sword' (*Huàjù* 77)

一   首   诗（△新华文学 195）
yī   shǒu   shī
one   CL   poem

'a poem' (*Xīnhuáwénxué* 195)

(26) 第一   次（寻庙 27）   第二   天（金狮奖 197）
     dìyī   cì   dìèr   tiān
     first   time   second   day

     'the first time' (*Xúnmiào*, 27)   'the second day' (*Jīnshījiǎng* 197)

2   Classifiers can also be modified by demonstrative pronouns and the phrases thus formed, namely '这 zhè 'this'/那 nà 'that' + classifier' are often called demonstrative-classifier compounds.

(27) 这   个   小   岛（牛车水 95）   这   次（怀旧 108）
     zhè   gè   xiǎo   dǎo   zhè   cì
     this   CL   small   island   this   CL

     'this small island' (*Niúchēshuǐ* 95)   'this time' (*Huáijiù* 108)

     这   种   人（华文教材 2A12）   那   个   孙女（△含羞草 22）
     zhè   zhǒng   rén   nà   gè   sūnnǚ
     this   CL   person   that   CL   granddaughter

     'these kind of people'   'that granddaughter'
     (*Huáwénjiàocái* 2A 12)   (*Hánxiūcǎo* 22)

     那   个   女子（太阳 61）
     nà   gè   nǚzǐ
     that   CL   woman

     'that woman' (*Tàiyáng* 61)

Taking 一个衣厨 *yígèyīchú* 'a wardrobe', 这个小岛 *zhègè xiǎodǎo* 'this small island' and 那个女子 *nàgènǚzǐ* 'that woman' as examples, their internal structure layers are shown as follows.

一 个	衣厨	这 个	小岛	那 个	女子	
yī gè	yīchú	zhè gè	xiǎodǎo	nà gè	nǚzǐ	
1	2	1	2	1	2	(attribute-head endocentric phrase)
3 4		3 4		3 4		(attribute-head endocentric phrase)

That is to say, the classifier 个 gè 'CL' does not directly modify the head noun. It is first modified by the numeral 一 yī 'one' or the demonstrative pronoun '这 zhè 'this'/那 nà 'that' + classifier' to form a numeral/demonstrative-classifier phrase, which then modifies the head noun that follows.

8.4 Adjectives as Attributes

From Sections 8.4 to 8.11, we will focus on nouns with attributes, and while doing so we describe various attributes in Singapore Mandarin.

When we say that adjectives can function as attributes, we are referring to cases in which adjectives directly modify nouns without 的 de 'DE'.

(1) a 热   茶（牛车水 43）   b 热   的   茶
       rè   chá   rè   de   chá
       hot   tea   hot   DE   tea
       'hot tea' (Niúchēshuǐ 43)   'hot tea'

(2) a 小   毛巾（狮子 3）   b 小   的   毛巾
       xiǎo   máojīn   xiǎo   de   máojīn
       small   towel   small DE   towel
       'small towel' (Shīzi 3)   'small towel'

Note that (1a) and (1b), (2a) and (2b) are grammatically and semantically different.

Grammatically, in (1a-2a), adjectives 热 rè 'hot' and 小 xiǎo 'small' directly serve as the attributes of 茶 chá 'tea' and 毛巾 máojīn 'towel', while in (1b-2b), they are linked by 的 de 'DE'. Because of this difference, the head nouns 茶 chá 'tea' and 毛巾 máojīn 'towel' in (1b-2b) can be omitted in a certain context. However, the head nouns in (1a-2a) cannot be omitted under any circumstances. Let's compare the following examples.

一   杯   热   茶   ≠   *一   杯   热
yī   bēi   rè   chá   yī   bēi   rè
one   CL   hot   tea   one   CL   hot
'a cup of hot tea'   * 'a cup hot'

一   杯   热   的   茶   =   一   杯   热   的
yī   bēi   rè   de   chá   yī   bēi   rè   de
one   CL   hot   DE   tea   one   CL   hot   DE
'a cup of hot tea'   'a cup of hot (tea)'

一 yī one	条 tiáo CL	小 xiǎo small	毛巾 máojīn towel	≠	*一 yī one	条 tiáo CL	小 xiǎo small		
'a small towel'					*'one small'				

一 yī one	条 tiáo CL	小 xiǎo small	的 de DE	毛巾 máojīn towel	=	一 yī one	条 tiáo CL	小 xiǎo small	的 de DE
'a small towel'						'a small (towel)'			

我 wǒ 1SG	喝 hē drink	热 rè hot	茶 chá tea	≠	*我 wǒ 1SG	喝 hē drink	热 rè hot		
'I drink hot tea.'					*'I drink hot'				

我 wǒ 1SG	喝 hē drink	热 rè hot	的 de DE	茶 chá tea	=	我 wǒ 1SG	喝 hē drink	热 rè hot	的 de DE
'I drink hot tea.'						'I drink hot (tea).'			

买 mǎi buy	一 yī one	条 tiáo CL	小 xiǎo small	毛巾 máojīn towel	≠	*买 mǎi buy	一 yī one	条 tiáo CL	小 xiǎo small
'buy a small towel'						*'buy a small'			

买 mǎi buy	一 yī one	条 tiáo CL	小 xiǎo small	的 de DE	毛巾 máojīn towel	=	买 mǎi buy	一 yī one	条 tiáo CL	小 xiǎo small	的 de DE
'buy a small towel'							'buy a small (towel)'				

The semantic relation between the attributes and the heads are closely related in the modifier-head phrases without 的 de 'DE' and are comparatively loose in the ones with 的 de 'DE'. This contrast can be seen in the differences between the meanings of these two types of phrases, as shown in the following examples.

小鸟	—	小	的	鸟	
xiǎoniǎo		*xiǎo*	*de*	*niǎo*	
little.bird		little	DE	bird	
'little bird'		'little bird/birds that are small'			
咸鱼	—	咸	的	鱼	
xiányú		*xián*	*de*	*yú*	
salty.fish		salty	DE	fish	
'salted fish'		'salted fish/fish that tastes salty'			
乖孩子	—	乖	的	孩子	
guāiháizi		*guāi*	*de*	*háizi*	
good.child		good	DE	child	
'good child'		'good child/child that is well-behaved'			

小鸟 *xiǎoniǎo* 'little bird' can sometimes refer to birds in general (as in 小鸟在歌唱 *xiǎoniǎozāigēchàng* 'the bird is singing'), while 小的鸟 *xiǎodeniǎo* 'little bird' does not have the generic meaning but refers to smaller birds in comparison. 咸鱼 *xiányú* 'salted fish' refers to the pickled fish that has a strong flavour, while 咸的鱼 *xiándeyú* 'salted fish' generally refers to the fish that tastes salty when there are multiple fish. 乖孩子 *guāiháizi* 'good child' is a term of endearment for a child, even when the child is making a noise, as in the following sentence. However, 乖的孩子 *guāidehá izi* 'good child' specifically refers to a child who is well-behaved in contrast to other children.

(3) "乖孩子, 别 吵, 别 闹。"
    guāiháizi *bié* *chǎo* *bié* *nào*
    good.child not make.noise not make.trouble
    'My dear child, don't make a noise.'

There are two points worth noting about adjective attributes. First, not all adjectives can directly modify nouns without 的 *de* 'DE'. The adjective 美丽 *měilì* 'beautiful' is a case in point. What we see in Liang Yongfu's collection of essays 《最后的牛车水》 *zuìhòu de niúchēshuǐ The Last Chinatown* is 美丽的 *měilìde* 'beautiful' functioning as an attribute, without even a single case of 美丽 *měilì* 'beautiful' as a direct attribute of nouns.

(4) 美丽 的 细纹   美丽 的 方块字
    měilì *de* *xìwén*   *měilì* *de* *fāngkuàizì*
    beautiful DE fine.line   beautiful DE characters

'beautiful fine lines' (49)   'beautiful characters' (55)

美丽	的	穴位	名字	美丽	的	梦
měilì	*de*	*xuèwèi*	*míngzì*	*měilì*	*de*	*mèng*
beautiful	DE	acupoint	name	beautiful	DE	dream

'beautiful acupoint names' (86)   'beautiful dreams' (117)

美丽	的	文字		美丽	的	圈套
měilì	*de*	*wénzì*		*měilì*	*de*	*quāntào*
beautiful	DE	word		beautiful	DE	trap

'beautiful words' (91)   'beautiful traps' (119)

There are quite a few adjectives that resemble 美丽 *měilì* 'beautiful' in the sense that they cannot modify nouns directly. Our statistics reveal that these account for about 36% of the total adjectives. Here are more examples:

Monosyllabic adjectives:

迟 *chí* 'late'	脆 *cuì* 'crisp'	对 *duì* 'right'	乏 *fá* 'tired'
烦 *fán* 'upset'	横 *hèng* 'rude'	紧 *jǐn* 'tight'	灵 *líng* 'flexible'
麻 *má* 'numb'	密 *mì* 'thick'	松 *sōng* 'loose'	烫 *tàng* 'scalding'
晚 *wǎn* 'late'	早 *zǎo* 'early'	准 *zhǔn* 'accurate'	

Disyllabic adjectives:

呆板 *dāibǎn* 'stiff'	肮脏 *āngzāng* 'dirty'	卑贱 *bēijiàn* 'ignoble'
逼真 *bīzhēn* 'vivid'	不错 *búcuò* 'good'	吃香 *chīxiāng* 'popular'
充沛 *chōngpèi* 'abundant'	慈祥 *cíxiáng* 'benign'	匆忙 *cōngmáng* 'rushed'
大方 *dàfāng* 'generous'	肥大 *féidà* 'loose'	分明 *fēnmíng* 'distinct'
工整 *gōngzhěng* 'neat'	光滑 *guānghuá* 'sleek'	好看 *hǎokàn* 'good-looking'
慌忙 *huāngmáng* 'rushed'	精巧 *jīngqiǎo* 'delicate'	开朗 *kāilǎng* 'outgoing'
苦恼 *kǔnǎo* 'upset'	冷静 *lěngjìng* 'calm'	流利 *liúlì* 'fluent'
美观 *měiguān* 'beautiful'	敏锐 *mǐnruì* 'keen'	耐心 *nàixīn* 'patient'
朴实 *pǔshí* 'simple'	勤奋 *qínfèn* 'hard-working'	清楚 *qīngchǔ* 'clear'
容易 *róngyì* 'easy'	瘦弱 *shòuruò* 'emaciated'	肃静 *sùjìng* 'solemn'

坦率 *tǎnshuài* 'frank'   通顺 *tōngshùn* 'smooth'   透彻 *tòuchè* 'thorough'
稀少 *xīshǎo* 'rare'   辛勤 *xīnqín* 'industrious'   迅速 *xùnsù* 'rapid'
整齐 *zhěngqí* 'trim'   庄重 *zhuāngzhòng* 'serious'

Second, even adjectives that can be used directly as attributes cannot be used with just any noun. For example, we can say 小狗（追云 6） *xiǎogǒu* 'little dog' (*Zhuīyún*, 6), 小鸟（再见 46） *xiǎoniǎo* 'little bird' (*Zàijiàn*, 46) and 小燕子（华文教材 3A 201） *xiǎoyànzi* 'little swallow' (*Huáwénjiàocái* 3A 201), but we cannot say *小长颈鹿 *xiǎochángjǐnglù* 'little giraffe' and *小水鸟 *xiǎoshuǐniǎo* 'little waterfowl'. We have to say 小的长颈鹿 *xiǎoxiǎodechángjǐnglù* 'little giraffe' and 小小的水鸟（牛车水 49） *xiǎoxiǎodeshuǐniǎo* 'little waterfowl' (*Niúchēshuǐ* 49). Here are some more examples to illustrate the selectivity of adjectives as attributes of nouns.

薄板 *báobǎn* 'thin books'	*薄书 *báoshū* 'thin books'	薄的书 *báo de shū* 'thin books'
薄纸 *báozhǐ* 'thin paper'	*薄灰尘 *báo huīchén* 'thin dust'	薄薄的灰尘 *báobáo de huīchén* 'thin dust'
短裙子 *duǎn qúnzi* 'short skirts'	*短衣服 *duǎn yīfu* 'short shirts'	短的衣服 *duǎn de yīfu* 'short shirts'
短距离 *duǎn jùlí* 'short distance'	*短路程 *duǎn lùchéng* 'short distance'	短短的路程 *duǎn de lùchéng* 'short distance'
绿叶子 *lǜ yèzi* 'green leaves'	*绿羽毛 *lǜ yǔmáo* 'green feathers'	绿的羽毛 *lǜ deyǔmáo* 'green feathers'
绿绸子 *lǜ chóuzi* 'green silk'	*绿庄稼 *lǜ zhuāngjià* 'green crops'	绿油油的庄稼 *lǜyóuyóu de zhuāngjià* 'green crops'

Through conducting a statistic analysis of the modifier-head phrases in the prose collection *The Last Chinatown* (about 76,000 words) written by the influential young Singaporean writer Liang Wenfu, we have found that there are 51 cases of "adjective + noun", 117 cases of "adjective + DE + noun" and 51 cases of "stative adjective with DE + noun". It is further evidenced that the direct use of adjectives as the attributes of nouns in Singapore Mandarin is rather limited. In the lingua franca of modern Chinese nationalities, including Sinagpore Mandarin, the modifier-head phrases in which adjectives directly modify nouns tend to be lexicalised, such as 小鸟 *xiǎoniǎo* 'lttile bird', 咸鱼 *xiányú* 'salted fish', 新兵 *xīnbīn* 'recruit', 新同学 *xīntóngxué* 'new classmate', 老朋友 *lǎopéngyǒu* 'old friend', 小男孩 *xiǎonánhái* 'little boy', 寒风 *hánfēng* 'cold wind' and 老实人 *lǎoshírén* 'honest people'. These phrases may be regarded as one word. Thus, there are fewer attribute-head endocentric phrases with adjectives directly modifying nouns.

In addition, adjective phrases have to take 的 *de* 'DE' when used as the attributes of nouns.

(5) 展现   在   眼前   的,   是   一   幅
    zhǎnxiàn zài   yǎnqián   de   shì   yī   fú
    unfold   at   before.   DE   be   one CL
                    eyes

    美丽   而   实在   的   图景。（牛车水 29）
    měilì   er   shízài   de   tújǐng
    beautiful LIG   real   DE   picture

    'What unfolded before us is a beautiful and real picture.' (Niúchēshuǐ 29)

(6) 人，   永远   是   最   残酷   的   动物…（牛车水 30）
    rén   yǒngyuǎn   shì   zuì   cánkù   de   dòngwù
    people   forever   be   most   cruel   DE   animal

    'People have foreven been the cruelest animal …' (Niúchēshuǐ 30)

(7) 原来   不   吃   东西   也   不是   太   难受   的
    yuánlái   bù   chī   dōngxī   yě   bùshì   tài   nánshòu   de
    original NEG   eat   thing   also   NEG   too   uncomfortable DE

    事。（撞墙 13）
    shì
    matter

    'It turns out that not eating is not that uncomfortable.' (Zhuàngqiáng 13)

(8) 你   是   个   不   健全   的   人，…（太阳 13）
    nǐ   shì   gè   bù   jiànquán   de   rén
    2SG   be   CL   NEG   sound   DE   person

    'You are not a sound person …' (Tàiyáng 13)

(9) 蓝   得   极其   妩媚   的   天空   底下,   是
    lán   de   jíqí   wǔmèi   de   tiānkōng   dǐxià   shì
    blue DE   extremely   enchanting   DE   sky   under   be

    许许多多   株   灿美   绽放   的   玉兰花。（天长 57）
    xǔxǔduōduō   zhū   cànměi   zhànfàng   de   yùlánhuā
    many   CL   beautiful   blossom   DE   magnolia

    'Under the extremely enchanting blue sky are many beautiful magnolias in full bloom.' (Tiāncháng 57)

In sentence (5), the adjective coordinative phrase 美丽而实在 *měilìershízài* 'beautiful and real' in the attribute position has to take 的 *de* 'DE'. In sentences (6) through (8), the adjective modifier-head phrases 最残酷 *zuìcánkù* 'the cruelest', 太难受 *tàinānshòu* 'too ill' and 不健全 *bùjiànquán* 'not sound' are all followed by 的 *de* 'DE'. In sentence (9), the predicate-complement phrase 蓝得极其妩媚 *lándejíqíwǔmèi* 'extremely enchanting blue' with 的 *de* 'DE' serves as the attribute. If 的 *de* 'DE' is removed, none of these sentences are grammatical.

8.5 Stative Words as Attributes

As we mentioned in Chapter 5, stative adjectives can be divided into two types: Those used without 的 *de* 'DE' and those used with 的 *de* 'DE'. In Chinese Mandarin, only stative words with 的 *de* 'DE' can be used as the attributes of nouns directly, while those without 的 *de* 'DE' can only be used as attributes of "numeral + classifier + noun" phrases. Here are some examples.

(1) 雪白　　　　一　　　双　　　鞋　　　　黑乎乎　　　一　　　堆　　　东西
    xuěbái　　 *yī*　 *shuāng*　*xié*　　 *hēihūhū*　　 *yī*　　*duī*　*dōngxī*
    snow.white　one　 pair　　 shoe　　 black　　　　one　　CL　　thing
    'a pair of snow-white shoes'　　　　　　　　　'a pile of black things'

In Singapore Mandarin, stative adjectives with 的 *de* 'DE' can certainly be used as attributes of nouns, as shown in the following examples.

(2) 风　　　从　　　湖面，　　　轻轻　　　的　　　缓缓　　　掠　　　过，
    fēng　*cóng*　*húmiàn*　　*qīngqīng*　*de*　*huǎnhuǎn*　*lüè*　*guò*
    wind　 from　 lake.surface　gently　　　DE　 slowly　　　skim　GUO

   形成　　　　一　　　层层　　　　皱皱　　　的　　　水纹。（晚上 59）
   xíngchéng　*yī*　*céngcéng*　*zhòuzhòu*　*de*　*shuǐwén*
   form　　　　one　 CL　　　　 wrinkled　　DE　 water.wave
   'The wind skimmed the lake gently and slowly, forming wrinkled waves.' (*Wǎnshang* 59)

(3) 水果摊　　　　前　　　排　　　了　　　长长　　　　的　　　人龙。（石头 27）
    shuǐguǒtān　*qián*　*pái*　*le*　*chǎngchǎng*　*de*　*rénlóng*
    fruit.stand　　front　 line　 LE　 long　　　　　DE　 people
    'People lined up in front of the fruit stand.' (*Shítou* 27)

Attributes and Adverbials 303

(4) 我们　　都　　是　　平平凡凡　　的　　人，...(△浮萍 83)
    wǒmen　dōu　shì　píngpíngfánfán　de　rén
    1PL　　all　　be　　ordinary　　　　DE　people
    'We are all ordinary people ...' (*Fúpíng* 83)

Stative words without 的 *de* 'DE' can also be used as attributes of nouns directly, but they are not as common.

(5) 做不了　　　轰轰烈烈　　　　大事。（晚上 28）
    zuòbùliǎo　hōnghōnglièliè　dàshì
    cannot　　 briliant　　　　great.thing
    'Can't do a brilliant great thing.' (*Wǎnshang* 28)

(6) 桌面　　　　的　　右缘处，　　　长期　　　摆　　着　　的　　黝黑
    zhuōmiàn　　de　　yòuyuánchù　chángqī　bǎi　zhe　de　yǒuhēi
    table.surface　DE　right.edge　　long.time　put　ZHE　DE　black

    瓷瓶　　　　　里，　突兀地　　　挺立　　着　　一　　株　　玫瑰。（再见 69）
    cípíng　　　　 lǐ　　 tūwùde　　 tǐnglì　　 zhe　yī　　zhū　méiguī
    porcelain.vase　inside　abruptly　stand　ZHE　one　CL　rose

    'On the right-hand edge of the table, inside a black porcelain vase that had been there for a long time, suddenly stood a single rose.' (*Zàijiàn* 69)

It should be noted that in Singapore Mandarin, reduplicated forms of monosyllabic adjectives can be used as attributes of nouns freely and are used frequently, just as they are used as predicates (see Section 5.8) and complements (see Section 7.6). Here are a couple of examples.

(7) 走　　过　　　青青　　　　墓山...（青春 15）
    zǒu　guò　　 qīngqīng　　 mùshān
    go　 GUO　　 green　　　　tomb.hill
    'walk through a green graveyard ...' (*Qīngchūn* 15)

(8) 现在　　　吃　　的　　是　　白白　　　大米...（金狮奖（四）9）
    xiànzài　chī　de　shì　báibái　dàmǐ
    now　　　eat　DE　be　white　rice
    'Now (people) are eating white rice ...' (*Jīnshījiǎng* IV 9)

As mentioned earlier, the use of adjectives directly modifying nouns is highly restricted. For example, we can say 蓝墨水 *lánmòshuǐ* 'blue ink' but cannot say *蓝天空 *lántiānkōng* 'blue sky'; we can say 绿绸子 *lǜchóuzi* 'green silk' but cannot say *绿庄稼 *lǜzhuāngjia* 'green crops'. This is not because that "blue" and "sky", "green" and "crops" do not match semantically. They will become acceptable if we replace the adjectives with corresponding stative words, such as 蓝蓝的天空 *lánlándetiānkōng* 'blue sky', 绿油油的庄稼 *lǜyóuyóudezhuāngjia* 'green crops'. This indicates that stative words as the attributes of nouns are grammatically less restricted than adjectives.

8.6 Nouns as Attributes

Generally speaking, nouns can be used as attributes of nouns, but whether 的 *de* 'DE' is added or not is related to the semantic relations between the attributes and the head nouns and the properties of the two words as well. In this section, we first outline the semantic relations between the attribute and the head, and then give brief explanations.

8.6.1 Material Relation

For this type of relation, the attribute refers to the material of the things denoted by the head noun. Both nouns are about concrete things. Among the written data we have observed, there are occurrences of 的 *de* 'DE'. Here are some examples.

(1) 粗布　　　　长裤（风雨 12）　　　石头　　屋子（石头 204）
　　cūbù　　　*chángkù*　　　　　　*shítou*　　*wūzi*
　　coarse.cloth　trousers　　　　　　stone　　　house
　　'trousers of coarse cloth' (*Fēngyǔ* 12)　'stone house' (*Shítou* 204)

　　玻璃　　　门（大胡子 126）　　　　木　　　楼梯（怀旧 13）
　　bōli　　　*mén*　　　　　　　　　*mù*　　*lóutī*
　　glass　　　door　　　　　　　　　wood　　stairs
　　'glass door' (*Dàhúzi* 126)　　　　'wooden stairs' (*Huáijiù* 13)

However, according to the linguistic intuitions of Singaporean speakers, most of the preceding attributes can also take 的 *de* 'DE', such as 粗布的长裤 *cūbùdechángkù* 'coarse trousers', 石头的屋子 *shítoudewūzi* 'stone house', 玻璃的门 *bōlídemén* 'glass door', 木的楼梯 *mùlóutī* 'wooden stairs'. Such expressions with 的 *de* 'DE' show more emphasis on the noun indicating materials.

8.6.2 Kinship Relation

In addition to the kinship generally understood (such as 'Wang Gang's younger brother' and 'Xiao Zhang's mother'), the kinship mentioned here also includes the relationships

Attributes and Adverbials 305

between teachers and students, friends and colleagues, and so on. The attribute is a noun that refers to people, and the head is a noun denoting kinship relations. In this case, it is acceptable to use attributes both with or without 的 *de* 'DE', however, the one using 的 *de* 'DE' is more common, as shown in examples (2) and (3).

(2) 杨成　　　的　　母亲（梦 64）
　　yángchéng　de　 mǔqīn
　　Yang Cheng　DE　mother
　　'Yang Cheng's mother' (*Mèng* 64)

　　小雯　　的　　爸爸（再见 55）
　　xiǎowén　de　 bàba
　　Xiaowen　DE　father
　　'Xiaowen's father' (*Zàijiàn* 55)

　　王志平　　的　　老师　　母亲　　的　　朋友（△南风 13）
　　wángzhìpíng　de　lǎoshī　mǔqīn　de　péngyǒu
　　Wang Zhiping　DE　teacher　mother　DE　friend
　　'Wang Zhiping's teacher'　　　'mother's friend' (*Nánfēng* 13)

(3) 何君　妹妹（一心 36）　　卓先生　　　　岳母（一心 210）
　　héjūn　mèimei　　　　 zhuóxiānsheng　yuèmǔ
　　He Jun　sister　　　　 Mr. Zhuo　　　 mother-in-law
　　'He Jun's sister' (*Yīxīn* 36)　'Mr. Zhuo's mother-in-law' (*Yīxīn* 210)

The attributes in (2) are used alongside 的 *de* 'DE', while those in (3) are not. In the written corpus we have observed, there are more examples of attributive nouns used alongside 的 *de* 'DE' than ones that aren't.

8.6.3 *Possession Relation*

The possession relationship indicates ownership. The attributive noun, usually referring to human beings, and the head noun, denoting a specific thing or things, are in an ownership relation. In possession relations, attributes are usually followed by 的 *de* 'DE', as shown in example (4).

(4) 大伯公　　的　　香炉（胜利 36）　　老张　　的　　车（太阳 25）
　　dàbógōng　de　xiānglú　　　　　 lǎozhāng　de　chē
　　elder.uncle　DE　censer　　　　　 Mr. Zhang　DE　car
　　'elder uncle's censer' (*Shènglì* 36)　'Mr. Zhang's car' (*Tàiyáng* 25)

父亲   的   医药费（短篇 36）
fùqīn   de   yīyàofèi
father   DE   medical.fee
'father's medical bills' (Duǎnpiān 36)

Notably, in certain contexts, 老张的车 lǎozhāngdechē 'Mr. Zhang's car' can also be said as 老张车 lǎozhāngchē 'Mr. Zhang's car'. Nevertheless, such modifier-head phrases always appear in sentence internal positions, as shown in sentence (5).

(5) 我   看见   陈经理   把   老张   车   开走   了。
    wǒ   kànjiàn chénjīnlǐ   bǎ   lǎozhāng   chē   kāizǒu   le
    1SG   see   Manager.Chen BA   Mr. Zhang car   drive.away LE
    'I saw Manager Chen drive Mr. Zhang's car away.'

8.6.4 Affiliated Relation

Affiliation means the relation between the whole and the part. For instance, in the phrase 桌子的腿 zhuōzidetuǐ 'the legs of the table', 'the legs' belongs to 'the table' and they form a whole-part relation. The attribute is usually filled by nouns denoting people or things, and the head is usually a noun representing body parts or specific parts of things. The attribute can either be followed by 的 de 'DE' as in example (6), or not, as in example (7).

(6) 妈妈   的   脚指头（追云 6）   海华   的   头发（跳舞 101）
    māma   de   jiǎozhǐtóu   hǎihuá   de   tóufà
    mother DE   toe   Hai Hua   DE   hair
    'mother's toes' (Zhuīyún 6)   'Hai Hua's hair' (Tiàowǔ 101)

    小狗   的   眼睛（追云 6）   鸽子   的   翅膀（风雨 7）
    xiǎogǒu de   yǎnjīng   gēzi   de   chìbǎng
    puppy   DE   eye   pigeon   DE   wings
    'puppy's eyes' (Zhuīyún 6)   'pigeon's wings' (Fēngyǔ 7)

(7) 小黑子   眼睛（恶梦 38）   机场   大厦（风雨 10）
    xiǎohēizi yǎnjīng   jīchǎng   dàshà
    Xiaoheizi eye   airport   building
    'Xiaoheizi's eyes' (Èmèng 38)   'airport building' (Fēngyǔ 10)

骆驼　　皮（一壶 69）
luòtuó　pí
camel　skin
'camel's skin' (*Yīhú* 69)

But, if the attribute is a monosyllabic noun, 的 *de* 'DE' is obligatory. Let's compare (8) and (9).

(8)　杂志　　　（的）　　封面
　　zázhì　　*de*　　*fēngmiàn*
　　magazine　DE　　cover
　　'the magazine cover'

(9)　书　　　的　　　封面　　　　*书　　封面
　　shū　　*de*　　*fēngmiàn*　　　*shū*　　*fēngmiàn*
　　book　　DE　　cover　　　　　book　　cover
　　'the book cover'　　　　　　　*'the book cover'

Both 杂志 *zázhì* 'magazine' and 书 *shū* 'book' modify 封面 *fēngmiàn* 'cover'. 的 *de* 'DE' is optional in (8) and obligatory in (9), as 杂志 *zázhì* 'magazine' is a disyllabic noun and 书 *shū* 'book' is a monosyllablic noun. However, if the modifier-head phrase of affiliated relation has the tendency of being lexicalised, 的 *de* 'DE' may be absent even when the attribute is a monosyllable noun, as shown in the following examples.

(10)　牛皮　　　　　　猪耳朵　　　　　　羊皮（△一壶 69）
　　　niúpí　　　　　*zhūěrduo*　　　　*yángpí*
　　　cattle.hide　　　pig.ear　　　　　　sheep.skin
　　　'cattle hide'　　 'pig ear'　　　　　'sheep skin' (*Yīhú* 69)

　　　鱼尾巴　　　　　象鼻子　　　　　　树叶（独上 56）
　　　yúwěiba　　　 *xiàngbízi*　　　　*shùyè*
　　　fish.tail　　　　elephant.nose　　　tree.leaf
　　　'fish tail'　　　　'elephant trunk'　　'tree leaf' (*Dúshàng* 56)

　　　羊毛（△一壶 67）
　　　yángmáo
　　　wool
　　　'wool' (*Yīhú* 67)

Note that we cannot say *人脚 *rénjiǎo* 'people feet', *人耳朵 *rénérduō* 'people ear', *猪嘴巴 *zhūzuǐbā* 'pig' mouth' and *象尾巴 *xiàngwěiba* 'elephant tail', for they are not lexicalised. For these cases, we have to say 人的脚 *réndejiǎo* 'people's feet', 人的耳朵 *réndeěrduo* 'people's ears', 猪的嘴巴 *zhūzuǐbā* 'pig's mouth' and 象的尾巴 *xiàngdewěiba* 'elephant's tail' as 的 *de* 'DE' cannot be left out.

8.6.5 Attribute Relation

The attributive noun refers to people or things, while the head noun expresses abstract notions., indicating some properties of the people or the things. Such modifier-head phrase implies an attribute relation. The attribute is usually followed by 的 *de* 'DE', but it doesn't always have to be.

(11) 父亲　　　的　　　性格（青春 116）
　　　fùqīn　　*de*　　*xìnggé*
　　　father　　DE　　character
　　　'father's character' (*Qīngchūn* 116)

　　　知识分子　　的　　　缺点（吾土·戏剧 31）
　　　zhīshífènzǐ　*de*　　*quēdiǎn*
　　　intellectual　　DE　　defect
　　　'intellectuals' defects' (*Wútǔ*(drama) 31)

　　　后娘　　　的　　　心眼（太阳 9）
　　　hòuniáng　*de*　　*xīnyǎn*
　　　stepmother　DE　　mind
　　　'(my) stepmother's mind' (*Tàiyáng* 9)

　　　妈妈　　　的　　　脸色（追云 7）
　　　māma　　*de*　　*liǎnsè*
　　　mother　　DE　　complexion
　　　'mother's complexion' (*Zhuīyún* 7)

　　　选手　　　的　　　身材（报 1995 76 月 7 日4 版）
　　　xuǎnshǒu　*de*　　*shēncái*
　　　player　　DE　　figure
　　　'the player' figure' (*Bào*, June 7, 1995, Issue no. 4)

蜡烛	的	亮光（风雨 17）
làzhú	de	liàngguāng
candle	DE	light

'the light of the candle' (*Fēngyǔ* 17)

The modifier-head phrases in (11) are all grammatical if 的 *de* 'DE' is omitted. But if the attribute is a monosyllabic noun, 的 *de* 'DE' is obligatory. For instance, 白糖的价格 *báitángdejiàgé* 'the price of white sugar' can be said as 白糖价格 *báitángjiàgé* 'the price of white sugar', while 糖的价格 *tángdejiàgé* 'the price of sugar' cannot be said as *糖价格 *tángjiàgé*. More examples are given in (12). These modifier-head phrases would be ungrammatical if 的 *de* 'DE' is removed.

(12)
人	的	感情（大胡子 39）	水	的	密度
rén	de	gǎnqíng	shuǐ	de	mìdù
people	DE	feeling	water	DE	density

'people' feeling' (*Dahuzi* 39)   'the density of water'

鱼	的	颜色（报 1995 年 4 月 19 日 7 版）
yú	de	yánsè
fish	DE	colour

'the colour of the fish' (*Bào*, Apr. 19, 1995, Issue no. 7)

鞋	的	质量	人	的	高度
xié	de	zhìliàng	rén	de	gāodù
shoe	DE	quality	people	DE	height

'the quality of shoes'   'people's height'

8.6.6 Categorical Relation

The head noun refers to people or things both concrete and abstract, while the attribute noun denotes the categories that people or things belong to. In this case, the attribute is not followed by 的 *de* 'DE'.

(13)
缅甸	朋友（△一壶 95）	大衣	扣子
miǎndiàn	péngyǒu	dàyī	kòuzi
Myanmar	friend	over coat	button

'a friend from Myanmar' (*Yīhú* 95)   'overcoat buttons'

华文	教材（华文 65）	狐狸	尾巴
huáwén	*jiàocái*	*húli*	*wěibā*
Chinese	textbook	fox	tail

'Chinese textbook (*Huáwén*, 65)' 'fox tail/evil intention'

缅甸朋友 *miǎndiàn péngyǒu* means that the friend is from Myanmar and in this sense it cannot be said as 缅甸的朋友 *miǎndiàn de péngyǒu*, which refers to a country that is friendly with the country Myanmar. 大衣扣子 *dàyī kòuzi* 'overcoat buttons' specifies a big button used only for overcoats, which is different from 大衣的扣子 *dàyī de kòuzi*, which generally refers to the buttons on over coats, including big coat buttons and small buttons pinned to the cuffs. The expression 华文教材 *huáwén jiàocái* has two readings: The first is the textbooks for teaching Chinese language, which are similar to those textbooks for math, chemistry and physics. In this sense, it can never be said as 华文的教材 *huáwén de jiàocái*. The other reading is teaching materials written in Chinese. In this case, it is interchangeable with 华文的教材 *huáwén de jiàocái* 'textbook in Chinese'. When 狐狸尾巴 *húli wěibā* in (13) is a metaphor used for an evil intention or behaviour, it can never be said as 狐狸的尾巴 *húli de wěibā* 'fox's tail'; when 狐狸尾巴 *húli wěibā* literally means the tail of a fox, it can be called 狐狸的尾巴 *húli de wěibā* 'fox's tail'.

8.6.7 *Metaphorical Relation*

The head noun refers to a person or a thing both concrete and abstract, while the attribute noun expresses a metaphor. In such modifier-head phrases, whether the attribute is followed by 的 *de* 'DE' or not depends on the nature of the head noun. If the head is a noun which refers to meanings of a person or thing, the attribute cannot take 的 *de* 'DE'.

(14) （你 呀, 真 是 个） 木头 人儿。
nǐ *ya* *zhēn* *shì* *gè* *mùtóu* *rénr*
2SG TOP really be CL wood person
'You really are a dull person.'

(15) 玻璃 色纸（微型 18）
bōli *sèzhǐ*
glass coloured.paper
'cellophane paper' (*Wēixíng* 18)

瓜子 脸儿 (风雨 11)

guāzǐ	*liǎner*
melon.seed	face

'oval face' (*Fēngyǔ* 11)

花园	城市 (报 1995 年3月3日 17 版)
huāyuán	*chéngshì*
garden	city

'garden city' (*Bào*, Mar. 3, 1995, Issue no. 17)

木头人儿 *mùtóurénr* 'a dull person' refers to a stupid and dull person, and it cannot be said as *木头的人儿 *mùtóuderénr*. The same holds for examples in (15).

If the head noun is an abstract one, the attribute needs to be followed by 的 *de* 'DE'. For instance, in the following example, 铁的纪律 *tiědejìlǜ* 'ruthless discipline' cannot be said as *铁纪律 *tiějìlǜ*.

(16) 铁   的   纪律 (无 55)
     tiě   *de*   *jìlǜ*
     iron   DE   discipline

'ruthless discipline' (*Wú* 55)

8.7 Pronouns as Attributes

8.7.1 Personal Pronouns as Attributes

When personal pronouns are used as attributes, they can indicate kinship, affiliation, possession or attribute relation.

1   When denoting kinship, the attribute can either be followed by 的 *de* 'DE' or not.

(1) " 她   的   父母   呢?   为什么   只   姐姐   管
    tā   *de*   *fùmǔ*   *ne*   *wèishénme*   *zhǐ*   *jiějie*   *guǎn*
    3SG   DE   parent   SFP   why   just   sister   supervise

    她?"   我   要   问个清楚。
    tā   *wǒ*   *yào*   *wèngèqīngchǔ*
    3SG   1SG   will   make.it.clear

' "Where are her parents? Why is her sister the only one to support her?" I want to be clear.'

"她   父母   早   死   了，   姐姐   当   售货员
 tā   fùmǔ   zǎo   sǐ   le   jiějie dāng   shòuhuòyuán
 3SG   parent early die   LE   sister serve   salesperson

 扶养   她…"   王大嫂   说。   （风雨 15）
 fúyǎng   tā   wángdàsǎo   shuō
 raise   3SG   aunt.Wang   say

'"Her parents died a long time ago, and her elder sister worked as a salesperson to bring her up . . ." said Aunt Wang.' (*Fēngyǔ* 15)

Sentences in (1) are quoted from the same dialogue of the essay "The Girl Who Sells Soap" in the book 风雨 *Fēngyǔ The Wind and Rain*, Baihe's collection of essays. Both occurrences of 她 *tā* '3SG' are used as the attribute of 父母 *fùmǔ* 'parent', one with 的 *de* 'DE', the other without, with basically the same meaning. The following are more examples with 的 *de* 'DE' in (2) and without 的 *de* 'DE' in (3):

(2) 您   的   家人（风雨 8）   你   的   男朋友（吾土·戏剧 158）
    nín   de   jiārén   nǐ   de   nánpéngyǒu
    2SG   DE   family   2SG   DE   boyfriend
    'your family' (*Fēngyǔ* 8)   'your boyfriend' (*Wútǔ*(drama) 158)

    你   的   校长（吾土·小说上 125）   我   的   父亲（△南风 31）
    nǐ   de   xiàozhǎng   wǒ   de   fùqīn
    2SG   DE   principal   1SG   DE   father
    'your principal' (*Wútǔ*(novel) 125)   'my father' (*Nánfēng* 31)

    我们   的   孩子（建屋 14）   他   的   妻子（太阳 7）
    wǒmen de   háizi   tā   de   qīzi
    1PL   DE   child   3SG   DE   wife
    'our child' (*Jiànwū* 14)   'his wife' (*Tàiyáng* 7)

(3) 你   爸爸（微型 50）   我   先生（今后 116）
    nǐ   bàba   wǒ   xiānsheng
    2SG   father   1SG   husband
    'your father' (*Wēixíng* 50)   'my husband' (*Jīnhòu* 116)

我	儿女（回忆 70）		他	妻子（太阳 7）
wǒ	érnǚ		tā	qīzi
1SG	children		3SG	wife

'my children' (*Huíyì* 70)   'his wife' (*Tàiyáng* 7)

我们	校长（恶梦 24）
wǒmen	xiàozhǎng
1PL	principal

'our principal' (*Èmèng* 24)

2 When expressing an affiliated relation, the attribute can be either with 的 *de* 'DE' or without, but the ones with 的 *de* 'DE' are more common.

(4)
你	的	大	嘴巴（金狮奖 252）		他	的	手（太阳 8）
nǐ	de	dà	zuǐba		tā	de	shǒu
2SG	DE	big	mouth		3SG	DE	hand

'your big mouth' (*Jīnshījiǎng* 252)   'his hands' (*Tàiyáng* 8)

我	肚子（恶梦 102）
wǒ	dùzi
1SG	belly

'my belly' (*Èmèng* 102)

3 When there is a possession or an attribute relation between the attribute pronoun and the head noun, the attribute will take 的 *de* 'DE', as shown in the following examples in (5) and (6) respectively.

(5)
你	的	功课（想飞 145）		我	的	颜色笔（何 78）
nǐ	de	gōngkè		wǒ	de	yánsèbǐ
2SG	DE	homework		1SG	DE	colour.pen

'your homework' (*Xiǎngfēi* 145)   'my colour pen' (*Hé* 78)

他	的	房间（醒醒 75）		我们	的	摊子（吾土·戏剧 82）
tā	de	fángjiān		wǒmen	de	tānzi
3SG	DE	room		1PL	DE	stall

'his room' (*Xīngxīng* 75)   'our stall' (*Wútǔ*(drama) 82)

(6) 我   的   身份（风雨 22）   他   的   脸色（太阳 30）
    wǒ   de   shēnfèn   tā   de   liǎnsè
    1SG   DE   identity   3SG   DE   complexion
    'my identity' (Fēngyǔ 22)   'his complexion' (Tàiyáng 30)

    她   的   仪表（一心 8）   他们   的   视野（△南风 7）
    tā   de   yíbiǎo   tāmen   de   shìyě
    3SG   DE   appearance   3PL   DE   vision
    'her appearance' (Yīxīn 8)   'their vision' (Nánfēng 7)

8.7.2 Demonstrative Pronouns as Attributes

1 When demonstrative pronouns 这 zhè 'this', 那 nà 'that' and 这些 zhèxiē 'these' and 那些 nàxiē 'those' are used as attributes, 的 de 'DE' is not needed.

(7) 这   话   有   什么   毛病？（笑眼 4）
    zhè   huà   yǒu   shénme   máobìng
    this   word   have   what   mistake
    'What's wrong with this statement?' (Xiàoyǎn 4)

(8) 我们   一行   三   人   来到   那   入口处，
    wǒmen   yīxíng   sān   rén   láidào   nà   rùkǒuchù
    1PL   together three   person   come.at   that   entrance

    那   守门   的   收票员   说：
    nà   shǒumén   de   shōupiàoyuán   shuō
    that   guard   DE   ticket.seller   say

    "两   张   票   就   够   了。"（怀旧 103）
    liǎng   zhāng   piào   jiù   gòu   le
    two   CL   ticket   then   enough   LE
    'We three together came to the entrance and the ticket seller told us, "two tickets are enough."' (Huáijiù 103)

(9) 这些   建筑   都   是   经过   专家   认真   考据
    zhèxiē   jiànzhù   dōu   shì   jīngguò   zhuānjiā   rènzhēn   kǎojù
    these   building   all   be   through   expert   carefully   research

聘请　　山地人　　共同筹划　　　建成　　　的，...（怀旧 109）
pìnqǐng　shāndìrén　gòngtóngchóuhuà　jiànchéng　de
hire　　villagers　plan.together　　build　　　DE

'These buildings were built by experts who had done much research carefully and hired villagers to make plans and build together . . .' (*Huáijiù* 109)

(10) 其实　　那些　　地方　　我们　　多　　位　　以前　　也　　未曾
　　　qíshí　　nàxiē　　dìfāng　wǒmen　duō　　wèi　　yǐqián　yě　　wèicéng
　　　in.fact　those　　place　　1PL　　many　CL　　before　also　never

　　　到　　过。（痕迹 152）
　　　dào　　guò
　　　arrive　GUO

'In fact, many of us have never been to those places before.' (*Hénjì* 152)

这话 zhèhuà 'this word' in (7), 那入口处 nàrùkǒuchù 'that entrance' and 那守门的收票员 nàshǒuméndeshōupiàoyuán 'the ticket seller guarding the door' in (8), 这些建筑 zhèxiējiànzhù 'these buildings' in (9) and 那些地方 nàxiēdìfāng 'those places' in (10) are ungrammatical if 的 *de* 'DE' is used, that is, we cannot say *这的话 zhèdehuà, *那的入口处 nàderùkǒuchù, *那的守门的收票员 nàdeshǒuméndeshōupiàoyuán, *这些的建筑 zhèxiēdejiànzhù and *那些的地方 nàxiēdedìfāng.

2　When demonstrative pronouns 这里 zhèlǐ 'here' and 那里 nàlǐ 'there' are used as attributes, 的 *de* 'DE' has to be used.

(11) 这里　　的　　组屋　　全　　是　　三房　　式。
　　　zhèlǐ　　de　　zǔwū　　quán　shì　　sānfáng　shì
　　　here　　DE　　HDB flat　all　　be　　three.room　type

'The HDB (public) flat here are all three-room types.'

(12) 那里　　的　　小学　　　　　　一直　　重视　　乒乓球
　　　nàlǐ　　de　　xiǎoxué　　　　yìzhí　　zhòngshì　pīngpāngqiú
　　　there　DE　　elementary.school　always　emphasise　table.tennis

运动。
yùndòng
sport

'Elementary schools there have always paid attention to table tennis.'

In sentence (11), 的 *de* 'DE' cannot be omitted. 这里的组屋 *zhèlǐdezǔwū* 'the HDB flat' here cannot be expressed as *这里组屋 *zhèlǐzwū*. Likewise, sentence (12) cannot be said as *那里小学 *nàlǐxiǎoxué*.

8.8 Distinguishing Words as Attributes

The defining feature of distinguishing words is that they can act as attributes (see Section 3.7). Thus all distinguishing words may be used as attributes, usually without adding 的 *de* 'DE'.

(1) 女　　　朋友（金狮奖 220）　　　　微型　　小说（胜利·序）
　　nǚ　　*péngyǒu*　　　　　　　　　*wēixíng*　*xiǎoshuō*
　　female　friend　　　　　　　　　　miniature　novel
　　'girlfriend' (*Jīnshīijǎng* 220)　　　　'mini novel' (Preface of *Shènglì*)

　　大型　　百货公司（风筝 167）　　　高速　　公路（至 29）
　　dàxíng　*bǎihuògōngsī*　　　　　*gāosù*　*gōnglù*
　　large　　department.store　　　　　high.speed　road
　　'large department store' (*Fēngzheng* 167)　'expressway' (*Zhì* 29)

If a distinguishing word is followed by 的 *de* 'DE', then it is emphasising the difference, as shown in the following sentence:

(2) **大型**　　**的**　　百货公司　　　　有　　它　　经济　　上
　　dàxíng　***de***　*bǎihuògōngsī*　*yǒu*　*tā*　*jīngjì*　*shàng*
　　large　　**DE**　department.store　have　3SG　economy　on

　　的　　优势，　　但　　也　　有　　它　　经营　　上
　　de　*yōushì*　*dàn*　*yě*　*yǒu*　*tā*　*jīngyíng*　*shàng*
　　DE　advantage　but　also　**have**　3SG　operation　on

　　的　　弱点。（报 1995 年 7 月 23 日 7 版）
　　de　*ruòdiǎn*
　　DE　weakness

'Large department stores have their economic advantages, but they also have their operating weaknesses.' (*Bào*, July 23, 1995, Issue no. 7)

8.9 Numeral-Classifier Phrases as Attributes

In the common language of modern Chinese nationalities, including Singapore Mandarin, numerals cannot modify nouns directly to signify the number of things. In this case, classifiers are inserted between the numerals and the head nouns. For example, we say 三本书 *sānběnshū* 'three books', 四支笔 *sìzhībǐ* 'four pens' and 十粒鸡蛋 *shílìjīdàn* 'ten eggs' instead of *三书 *sānshū*, *四笔 *sìbǐ* or *十鸡蛋 *shíjīdàn*. This is a difference between Singapore Mandarin Chinese and English (see Section 3.8).

"Numeral + classifier" is also one kind of attribute-head endocentric phrase, but it is usually called numeral-classifier compound. They can be attributes of nouns, describing the quantity of things, without taking 的 *de* 'DE'. For example, 三个人 *sāngèrén* 'three people' cannot be said as *三个的人 *sāngèderén* 'three DE people'. Here are more examples.

(1) 你 今天 忘 了 带 两 样 东西：
    nǐ *jīntiān* *wàng* *le* *dài* **liǎng** **yàng** *dōngxī*
    2SG today forget LE bring two CL thing

    一 把 伞， 一 盒 录音带。（太阳 92）
    yì *bǎ* *sǎn* *yì* *hé* *lùyīndài*
    one CL umbrella one CL audio.cassette

    'You forgot to bring two things today: an umbrella and a cassette.' (*Tàiyáng* 92)

(2) 盒子里 盛 着 一 个 方形 蛋糕。（何 61）
    hézilǐ *chéng* *zhe* *yí* *gè* *fāngxíng* *dàngāo*
    box.inside fill ZHE one CL square cake

    'There is a square cake in the box.' (*Hé* 61)

(3) 教育部 从 台湾 邀请 了 四 位
    jiàoyùbù *cóng* *táiwān* *yāoqǐng* *le* **sì** **wèi**
    education.ministry from Taiwan invite LE four CL

    华文 学者， 先后 到 本国
    huáwén **xuézhě** *xiānhòu* *dào* *běnguó*
    Chinese scholar successively arrive home.country

    考察 华文 教学 情况。（风筝 54–55）
    kǎochá *huáwén* *jiàoxué* *qíngkuàng*
    inspect Chinese teaching situation

    'The Ministry of Education has invited four Chinese scholars from Taiwan to inspect the teaching of Chinese language in our countries.' (*Fēngzhēng* 54–55)

Numeral-classifier phrases in sentences (1) through (3) all describe the number of things, such as the number of items, umbrellas, square cakes, audio cassettes and Chinese scholars respectively, none of which can be followed by 的 *de* 'DE'.

Note that if the attributive numeral-classifier phrases do take 的 *de* 'DE', they do not indicate the number but the categorical characteristics of these things.

(4)

三	岁	的	小女儿	正	对	着	她
sān	*suì*	*de*	*xiǎonǚér*	*zhèng*	*duì*	*zhe*	*tā*
three	year.old	DE	little.daughter	straight	to	ZHE	3SG

唱	着	从	托儿所	中	所	学	来	的
chàng	*zhe*	*cóng*	*tuōérsuǒ*	*zhōng*	*suǒ*	*xué*	*lái*	*de*
sing	ZHE	from	nursery	in	SUO	learn	come	DE

儿歌。（撞墙 81）

érgē

nursery.rhyme

'The three-year-old youngest daughter is singing to her nursery rhymes learned at nursery.' (Zhuàngqiáng 81)

三岁 *sānsuì* 'three years old' in sentence (4) does not indicate the number but the age of the youngest daughter.

8.10 Verb Phrases as Attributes

Generally speaking, single verbs always take 的 *de* 'DE' when they act as attributes of nouns, otherwise we get predicate-object phrases. Let's compare the attribute-head phrases on the left and the predicate-object phrases on the right.

attribute-head phrases			predicate-object phrases	
吃	的	饼干	吃	饼干
chī	*de*	*bǐnggān*	*chī*	*bǐnggān*
eat	DE	biscuit	eat	biscuit
'biscuits for eating'			'eat biscuits'	
写	的	文章	写	文章
xiě	*de*	*wénzhāng*	*xiě*	*wénzhāng*
write	DE	article	write	article
'written articles'			'write articles'	

看	的	电影	看		电影
kàn	de	diànyǐng	kàn		diànyǐng
watch	DE	film	watch		film
'films that have been watched'			'watch a film'		

达到	的	目的	达到		目的
dádào	de	mùdì	dádào		mùdì
reach	DE	goal	achieve		goal
'goals that have been reached'			'achieve goals'		

打扫	的	房间	打扫		房间
dǎsǎo	de	fángjiān	dǎsǎo		fángjiān
clean	DE	room	clean		room
'rooms that have been cleaned'			'clean rooms'		

交纳	的	会费	交纳		会费
jiāonà	de	huìfèi	jiāonà		huìfèi
pay	DE	membership.fee	pay		membership fee
'membership fee that has been paid'			'pay the membership fee'		

However, there are a number of disyllabic verbs that can modify nouns without 的 *de* 'DE'. Here is an example.

(1) 教育　　素质　　（风筝 76）
　　jiàoyù　*sùzhì*
　　educate　quality
　　'educational quality' (*Fēngzhēng* 76)

教育 *jiàoyù* 'educate' in (1) is a disyllabic verb, which can be directly used as the attribute of the noun 素质 *sùzhì* 'quality' without 的 *de* 'DE'. Let's look at more examples.

(2) 教学　　目标（华文教学 135）　　　休息　　时间（一心 7）
　　jiàoxué　*mùbiāo*　　　　　　　　*xiūxi*　*shíjiān*
　　teach　goal　　　　　　　　　　　break　time
　　'teaching goal' (*Huáwénjiàoxué* 135)　'breaktime' (*Yīxīn* 7)

学习　态度（伦理·中三 11）
xuéxí　tàidù
study　attitude
'studying attitude' (*Lúnlǐ* III 11)

统计　数字（华文教材 4A 87）
tǒngjì　shùzì
count　number
'statistics' (*Huáwénjiàocái* 4A 87)

创作　动向（至性 29）
chuàngzuò　dòngxiàng
create　direction
'creation direction' (*Zhìxìng* 29)

发展　理想（平心 131）
fāzhǎn　lǐxiǎng
develop　ideal
'developing ideals' (*Píngxīn* 131)

研究　报告（金狮奖 135）
yánjiū　bàogào
research　report
'research report' (*Jīnshījiǎng* 135)

流浪　生活（回忆 94）
liúlàng　shēnghuó
roam　life
'roaming life' (*Huíyì* 94)

工作　态度（报 1995 年 6 月 7 日 2 版）
gōngzuò　tàidù
work　attitude
'working attitude' (*Bào*, June 7, 1995, Issue no. 2)

拯救　事件（报 1995 年 3 月 10 日 3 版）
zhěngjiù　shìjiàn
save　event
'saving event' (*Bào*, Mar. 10, 1995, Issue no. 3)

比赛　规模（报 1995 年 3 月 9 日 9 版）
bǐsài　guīmó
compete　scale
'the scale of the competition' (*Bào*, Mar. 9, 1995, Issue no. 9)

These disyllabic verbs share certain characteristcs, which will be dicussed in Section 8.12.

Verb phrases are usually followed by 的 *de* 'DE' as well, when they serve as the attributes of nouns, as in (3).

(3)　拟　　兴建　　的　　住宅　　单位（报 1995 年 3 月 15 日 21 版）
　　　nǐ　　xīngjiàn　de　　zhùzhái　dānwèi

plan   found   DE   residential flat

'residential flats to be built' (*Bào*, Mar. 15, 1995, Issue no. 21)

刚刚	点燃	的	香烟（大胡子 118）
gānggāng	*diǎnrán*	*de*	*xiāngyān*
just.now	light	DE	cigarette

'a freshly lit cigarette' (*Dàhúzi* 118)

卷起	的	袖管（今后 18）
juǎnqǐ	*de*	*xiùguǎn*
roll.up	DE	sleeves

'the rolled up sleeves' (*Jīnhòu*, 18)

摘	豆芽、	剥	虾壳	的	女人（风雨 92）
zhāi	*dòuyá*、	*bō*	*xiāké*	*de*	*nǚrén*
pick	bean.sprouts	peel	shrimp.shell	DE	woman

'a woman picking bean sprouts and peeling shrimp' (*Fēngyǔ* 92)

对	足球	赛	了解	不	深	的	人
duì	*zúqiú*	*sài*	*liǎojiě*	*bù*	*shēn*	*de*	*rén*
about	football	game	know	NEG	deep	DE	people

'people who don't know much about football'

现在	造	的	房子（梦 143）
xiànzài	*zào*	*de*	*fángzi*
now	build	DE	house

'houses being built at present' (*Mèng* 143)

来自	新加坡	的	学生 （何 57）
láizì	*xīnjiāpō*	*de*	*Xuéshēng*
from	Singapore	DE	Student

'a student from Singapore' (*Hé* 57)

None of the 的 *de* 'DE' in (3) can be omitted. Nevertheless, a predicate-object phrase composed of a single verb and a single noun can sometimes be used as an attribute without 的 *de* 'DE', as shown in (4).

(4) 做人　　　态度（伦理·中四 111）
　　zuòrén　　tàidù
　　be.a.man　attitude
　　'attitudes towards life' (*Lúnlǐ* IV 111)

　　花钱　　　　方式（报 1995 年 3 月 2 日 6 版）
　　huāqián　　　fāngshì
　　spend.money　way
　　'way of spending money' (*Bào*, Mar. 2, 1995, Issue no. 6)

　　上课　　　时间表（追云 15）
　　shàngkè　　shíjiānbiǎo
　　have.class　timetable
　　'class timetable' (*Zhuīyún* 15)

　　守城　　　人（回忆 21）
　　shǒuchéng　rén
　　defend.city　person
　　'defenders of the city' (*Huíyì* 21)

Of course, these attributes can also take 的 *de* 'DE'. The alternative way of saying 做人态度 *zuòréntàidù* 'life attitude' is 做人的态度 *zuòréndetàidù*, and 花钱方式 *huāqiánfāngshì* 'ways of spending money' is 花钱的方式 *huāqiándefāngshì*, and so on. This type of optional usage of 的 *de* 'DE' is not found for other verbal phrases.

8.11　Subject-Predicate Phrases as Attributes

Subject-predicate phrases used as the attributes take 的 *de* 'DE'. Sentences (1) through (4) are examples of the subject-predicate phrases being the attributes. These sentences would become ungrammatical if 的 *de* 'DE' were removed.

(1)　什么　　　是　　永远　　　呢？　大　　平卖？　　　　众人
　　shénme　　shì　　yǒngyuǎn　ne　　dà　　píngmài　　　zhòngren
　　what　　　be　　eternity　　SFP　big　　clearance.sale　everyone

　　争购　　　的　　牛仔裤？　还是　　画家们　　　摄影师们
　　zhēnggòu　de　　niúzǎikù　　háishì　huàjiāmen　　shèyǐngshīmen
　　snap.up　　DE　jeans　　　　or　　 painters　　　photographers

　　忙　　着　　捕捉　　　　的　　危楼旧垣？（牛车水 15）
　　máng　zhe　bǔzhuō　　　de　　wēilóujiùyuán

	busy	ZHE	catch		DE	rickety.buildings

'What is eternity? A big sale? The jeans that everyone scrambles for? Or the rickety buildings that the painters and photographers are busy catching?' (*Niúchēshuǐ* 15)

(2)
	你	有	看过	她	主演	的
	nǐ	yǒu	kànguò	tā	zhǔyǎn	de
	2SG	YOU	seen	3SG	star	DE

电影	吗？	（大胡子 32）	
diànyǐng	ma		
movie	SFP		

'Have you ever seen a movie that she starred in?' (*Dàhúzi* 32)

(3)
	吃	的	东西	可	好？	（追云 102）
	chī	de	dōngxi	kě	Hǎo	
	eat	DE	things	just	good	

'Do you eat well?' (*Zhuīyún* 102)

(4)
	只有	20	间	交易
	zhǐyǒu	èrshí	jiān	Jiāoyì
	only	twenty	CL	transaction

	最	活跃	的	公司。（报 1995 年 3 月 3 日 13 版）
	zuì	huóyuè	de	Gōngsī
	most	active	DE	Company

'Only 20 companies are the most active in transactions.' (*Bào*, Mar. 3, 1995, Issue no. 13)

8.12 Nominal Verbs

In Section 8.3 and Section 8.10, we mentioned that some disyllabic verbs can directly modify nouns without 的 *de* 'DE'; in Section 6.13, we also mentioned that quasi-predicate-object-taking-verbs (such as 进行 *jìnxíng* 'to conduct') can take disyllabic verbs as their objects (such as 研究 *yánjiū* 'research' in 进行研究 *jìnxíngyánjiū* 'to conduct a study'), and once these disyllabic verbs become the object they will lose their verbal characteristics. These observations are actually connected. It is found that verbs which can take nominal attributes can also be attributes without being followed by 的 *de* 'DE' (such as 研究 *yánjiū* 'research' in 语法研究 *yǔfǎyánjiū* 'grammar research' and 研究课题 *yánjiūkètí* 'research topic') and can also be the objects of quasi predicate-object-taking-verbs. Disyllabic verbs of this kind are called nominal verbs. As revealed in this section, they are distinctive in the following three respects: (1) They can be the objects of quasi predicate-object-taking-verbs. (2) They can modify nouns directly without using 的 *de* 'DE'. (3) They can be modified by nouns directly without 的 *de* 'DE' as well.

Here are more examples of nominal verbs:[1]

研究：	很	有	研究	研究	课题	语法	研究
yánjiū	*hěn*	*yǒu*	*yánjiū*	*yánjiū*	*kètí*	*yǔfǎ*	*Yánjiū*
research	very	have	research	research	topic	grammar	research
	'well researched'			'research topic'		'grammar research'	

教育：	进行	教育	教育	制度	道德	教育
jiàoyù	*jìnxíng*	*jiàoyù*	*jiàoyù*	*zhìdù*	*dàodé*	*Jiàoyù*
educate	conduct	educate	educate	system	moral	educate
	'educate'		'education system'		'moral education'	

调查：	进行	调查	调查	内容	社会	调查
diàochá	*jìnxíng*	*diàochá*	*diàochá*	*nèiróng*	*shèhuì*	*diàochá*
survey	conduct	survey	survey	content	sociaty	survey
	'conduct a survey'		'survey content'		'social survey'	

影响：	很	有	影响	影响	程度	思想	影响
yǐngxiǎng	*hěn*	*yǒu*	*yǐngxiǎng*	*yǐngxiǎng*	*chéngdù*	*sīxiǎng*	*yǐngxiǎng*
influence	very	have	influence	influence	degree	ideology	influence
	'very influential'			'degree of influence'		'ideological influence'	

讨论：	进行	讨论	讨论	时间	课堂	讨论
tǎolùn	*jìnxíng*	*tǎolùn*	*tǎolùn*	*shíjiān*	*kètáng*	*Tǎolùn*
discuss	conduct	discuss	discuss	time	class	discuss
	'have a discussion'		'time for discussion'		'class discussion'	

奖励：	给以	奖励	奖励	方式	物质	奖励
jiǎnglì	*gěiyǐ*	*jiǎnglì*	*jiǎnglì*	*fāngshì*	*wùzhì*	*Jiǎnglì*
reward	give	reward	reward	method	material	reward
	'give rewards'		'way of reward'		'material rewards'	

帮助:	得到	帮助		帮助	方式	经济	帮助
	dédào	bāngzhù		bāngzhù	fāngshì	jīngjì	Bāngzhù
	get	help		help	way	finance	help
	'receive help'			'way of help'		'financial help'	
批评:	接受	批评		批评	方式	文学	批评
	jiēshòu	pīpíng		pīpíng	fāngshì	wénxué	Pīpíng
	accept	criticise		criticise	way	literary	Criticise
	'accept criticism'			'way of criticism'		'literary criticism'	
检讨:	进行	检讨		检讨	内容	书面	检讨
	jìnxíng	jiǎntǎo		jiǎntǎo	nèiróng	shūmiàn	Jiǎntǎo
	conduct	review		review	content	written.form	review
	'conduct a review'			'review content'		'written review'	
斗争:	进行	斗争		斗争	方式	思想	斗争
	jìnxíng	dòuzhēng		dòuzhēng	fāngshì	sīxiǎng	dòuzhēng
	conduct	struggle		struggle	way	ideology	Struggle
	'do battle'			'way of struggle'		'ideological struggle'	
阅读:	进行	阅读		阅读	能力	课外	阅读
	jìnxíng	yuèdú		yuèdú	nénglì	kèwài	yuèdú
	conduct	read		read	ability	extracurricular	read
	'do some reading'			'reading ability'		'extracurricular reading'	

These verbs become nominal when they become the objects of quasi-predicate-object-taking-verbs and lose their verbal characteristics. They can modify nouns without 的 *de* 'DE', and can be modified by nouns without 的 *de* 'DE'. These are all characteristics of nouns. In this way, it seems reasonable to regard these verbs as multi-category words that overlap both verb and noun categories. However, considering that "there should be only be a small number of multi-category words" (Zhu 1982) and these types of disyllabic verb accounts for a rather large proportion of verbs, we do not treat them as multi-category words, but as verbs. Given the fact that they possess the characteristics of nouns in certain contexts, we named them 'nominal verbs', which is a subcategory of verbs.

8.13 Appositive Modifier-Head Phrases

The appositive modifier-head phrase is a special type of the attribute-head endocentric phrases, which is characterised by the fact that the attribute and the head signify the same referent but in different expressions. They are of referential relation or annotative relation. Several examples are illustrated here.

(1) 我们 新加坡 学生
    wǒmén xīnjiāpō xuéshēng
    1PL Singaporean student
    'we Singaporean students'

(2) 你 这 个 人（△大喜 10）
    nǐ zhè gè rén
    2SG this CL person
    'you guy' (*Dàxǐ* 10)

(3) 丁国成 他们（恶梦 62）
    dīngguóchéng tāmén
    Ding Guocheng 3PL
    'those people as Ding Guocheng' (*Èmèng* 62)

(4) 他 老 人家（风雨 4）
    tā lǎo rénjiā
    3SG old person
    'he, that old man' (*Fēngyǔ* 4)

(5) 英 女皇 伊莉莎白二世（风雨 4）
    yīng nǚhuáng yīlìshābáièrshì
    British queen Elizabeth II
    'British Queen Elizabeth II' (*Fēngyǔ* 4)

(6) 父 女 俩（风雨4）
    fù nǚ liǎng
    father daughter two
    'the father and daughter, two of them' (*Fēngyǔ* 4)

(7) 陈成财　　　　大使（报 1995 年 4 月 12 日 1版）
　　 chénchéngcái　*dàshǐ*
　　 Chen Chengcai　ambassador
　　 'Ambassador Chen Chengcai' (*Bào*, Apr. 12, 1995, Issue no. 1)

The seven preceding examples represent seven types of appositive modifier-head phrases, which can be roughly divided into two categories: One is as in (1) through (4), showing a referential relation between the attribute and the head, one of which is a personal pronoun. The other is as in (5) through (7) where the relation between the attribute and the head is annotative.

An appositive modifier-head phrase is different from a typical modifier-head phrase in the sense that the two parts present an appositive relation, referential relation or annotative relation rather than a modifying relation. It seems to deserve its own category, which could be termed appositive phrases. However, it is roughly in line with the typical modifier-head phrase in terms of grammatical function. That is why we do not have a separate category for the appositive modifier-head phrase.

8.14　Words That Can Take Adverbials

8.14.1　Verbs Taking Adverbials

Verbs can take adverbials, as shown in examples (1) through (3).

(1) **冷静**　　思考。（大胡子·序）
　　 lěngjìng　*sīkǎo*
　　 calmly　think
　　 'Think calmly.' (Preface of *Dàhúzi*)

(2) 华语、　　英语　　和　　方言　　**时常**　　混用。（华文教材 4B 31）
　　 huáyǔ　　*yīngyǔ*　*hé*　*fāngyán*　***shícháng***　*Hùnyòng*
　　 Singapore.　English　and　dialects　**often**　mix
　　 Mandarin
　　 'Singapore Mandarin, English and dialects are often mixed.' (*Huáwénjiàocái* 4B 31)

(3) 他们　　**一起**　　出动。（报 1995 年 3 月 10 日 7 版）
　　 tāmen　***yīqǐ***　*Chūdòng*
　　 3PL　　**together**　go.out
　　 'They went out together.' (*Bào*, Mar. 10 1995, Issue no. 7)

The preceding examples are of a single verb taking an adverbial. The following is a set of examples of predicate-object phrases taking adverbials before the verbs.

(4) 多　　留　　点　　吃　　的　　东西。（恶梦 122）
　　 duō　*liú*　*diǎn*　*chī*　*de*　*dōngxī*
　　 more　save　some　eat　DE　things
　　 'Save a little more to eat.' (*Èmèng* 122)

(5) 一共　　　有　　一千一百五十　　　元　　呢！（吾土・小说上 27）
　　 yīgòng　*yǒu*　*yīqiānyībǎiwǔshí*　*yuán*　*Ne*
　　 all.together　have　1,150　　　　　　yuan　SFP
　　 'It's eleven hundred and fifty yuan in all!' (*Wútǔ*(novel) 27)

(6) 刘婶　　　同情地　　　　看看　　　母亲。（醒醒 68）
　　 liúshěn　*tóngqíngde*　*kànkàn*　*Mǔqīn*
　　 aunt.Liu　sympathetically　look-look　mother
　　 'Aunt Liu looked at the mother sympathetically.' (*Xǐngxǐng* 68)

Following are examples of predicate-complement phrases taking adverbials before the verbs.

(7) 轻轻地　　　　飘落　　　下来，...（心情 62）
　　 qīngqīngde　*piāoluò*　*xiàlái*
　　 softly　　　　drift　　　down
　　 'Drift down softly...' (*Xīnqíng* 62)

(8) 方向　　　也　　辨别　　　不　　出，...（晚上 88）
　　 fāngxiàng　*yě*　*biànbié*　*bù*　*chū*
　　 direction　also　tell　　　NEG　out
　　 'I can't tell the direction either...' (*Wǎnshang* 88)

(9) 夜　　已经　　　变得　　　非常　　　　沉寂。（青青 81）
　　 yè　*yǐjīng*　*biànde*　*fēicháng*　*chénjì*
　　 night　already　become　very　　　　quiet
　　 'The night has already become very quiet.' (*Qīngqīng* 81)

8.14.2 Adjectives Taking Adverbials

Adjectives can take adverbials, usually degree adverbs. Here are some adjectives taking adverbials such as 很 *hěn* 'very', 十分 *shífēn* 'very' and 挺 *tǐng* 'quite'.

(10) 写作　　这　　条　　路，很　　漫长，　　很　　寂寞。（青春 110）
　　 xiězuò　zhè　tiáo　lù　hěn　màncháng　hěn　jìmò
　　 writing　this　CL　road　**very　long　very　lonely**

　　 'Writing is a very long and lonely road.' (*Qīngchūn* 110)

(11) 设计　　　十分　　　精巧。（中学 1A 110）
　　 shèjì　　shífēn　　jīngqiǎo
　　 design　**very**　exquisite

　　 'The design is very delicate.' (*Zhōngxué* 1A 110)

(12) 那　　沙发，　躺　　着　　或　　坐　　着，
　　 nà　　shāfā　tǎng　zhe　huò　zuò　zhe
　　 that　soft　lie　ZHE　or　sit　ZHE

　　 挺　　舒服　　的。（报 1995 年 6 月 19 日副刊 7 版）
　　 tǐng　Shūfú　*de*
　　 quite　comfortable　DE

　　 'That sofa is very comfortable whether for lying or sitting.' (*Bào*, June 19, 1995, Issue no. 7, supplementary edition)

8.14.3 Subject-Predicate Phrases Taking Adverbials

Subejct-predicate phrases can take adverbials, as shown in the following example.

　　 忽然　　　电话铃　　　响　　　了。
　　 hūrán　　diànhuàlíng　xiǎng　Le
　　 suddenly　telephone.bell　ring　LE

　　 'Suddenly the telephone rings.'

The adverb 忽然 *hūrán* 'suddenly' is the adverbial of the subject-predicate phrase 电话铃响了 *diànhuàlíngxiǎngle* 'the telephone rings'. The phrase could be analysed as follows.

```
忽然         电话铃        响了
hūrán       diànhuàlíng   xiǎngle

  1              2                    (adverbial-head endocentric phrase)
  ─────────────────────
         3              4             (subject-predicate phrase)
```

Here are more examples.

(13) 忽然   熊猫   啦、 河马   啦、 小   白兔   啦
     hūrán   xióngmāo   lā   hémǎ   lā   xiǎo   báitù   lā
     suddenly panda   TOP   hippo   TOP   little rabbit TOP

小   猴子   啦   一下子   都   围   了   上来。
                                                       （中学 1A 129）
xiǎo   hóuzi   lā   yīxiàzi   dōu   wéi   le   shànglái
little monkey TOP   all.at.once all   gather   LE   come

'All of a sudden, pandas, hippos, rabbits and monkeys all gathered around.'
(*Zhōngxué* 1A 129)

(14) 两   项   控状   **都**   罪名成立。（报 1995 年 6 月 7 日 7 版）
     liǎng   xiàng   kòngzhuàng   **dōu**   zuìmíngchénglì
     two   CL   pleading   **all**   be.convicted

'Be convicted on both charges.' (*Bào*, July 7, 1995, Issue no. 7)

(15) 一般上   "续集"   都   比   "正集"   差劲。（八方 27–28）
     yībānshàng   xùjí   dōu   bǐ   zhèngjí   chàjìn
     generally   sequel   all   than   last.   bad
                                               episode

'Generally, sequels are worse than the originals.' (*Bāfāng* 27–28)

(16) 在   1981   年   4 月，   他   成为   劳工   基金   产业
     zài **yījiǔbāyī** **nián** **sìyuè** tā   chéngwéi   láogōng   jījīn   chǎnyè
     in **1981**   **year** **April** 3SG   become   labor   fund   industry

私人   有限公司   的   董事。（报 1995 年 5 月 1 日 13 版）
sīrén   yǒuxiàngōngsī   de   dǒngshì

private   limited.company   DE   director

'In April 1981, he became a director of the labor fund industries private limited company.' (*Bào*, May 1, 1995, Issue no. 13)

In sentences (13) through (15), the adverbs 忽然 *hūrán* 'suddenly', 都 *dōu* 'all' and 一般上 *yībānshàng* 'generally' all modify the subject-predicate phrase that follows. In sentence (16), the prepositional phrase 在 1981 年 4 月 *zài yījiǔbāyī nián sìyuè* 'in April 1981' modifies the following subject-predicate phrase.

8.14.4 Stative Words Seldom Taking Adverbials

In the written data, we don't find any examples of adverbials modifying the stative words. But there are a few examples with adverbials in spoken language, though rare, such as 也 *yě* 'also' and 都 *dōu* 'all'.

(17) 她   的   脸   也   红红的。
     tā   *de*   *liǎn*   *yě*   *hónghóngde*
     3SG   DE   face   also   red

'Her face is red, too.'

(18) 四周   都   静悄悄的。
     sìzhōu   *dōu*   *jìngqiāoqiāode*
     all.round   all   quiet

'It was quiet all around.'

8.14.5 Nouns Taking Adverbials

Examples (19) through (21) reveal that nouns can take adverbials like the adverbs 也 *yě* 'also', 已经 *yǐjīng* 'already' and 才 *cái* 'just'. This is commonly found in spoken language.

(19) 我,   潮州,   人,   他   也   潮州,   人。
     wǒ   *cháozhōu*   *rén*   *tā*   *yě*   *cháozhōu*   *rén*
     1SG   Chaozhou   person   3SG   also   Chaozhou   person

'I'm from Chaozhou, and he's from Chaozhou, too.'

(20) 他   已经   大学生   了。
     tā   *yǐjīng*   *dàxuéshēng*   *le*
     3SG   already   college.student   LE

'He is a college student.'

(21) 你   才   傻瓜！
    nǐ   cái   shǎguā
    2SG   just   fool
    'You're a fool!'

8.14.6 Numeral-Classifier Phrases Taking Adverbials

Examples (22) through (24) show that the adverbials of numeral-classifier phrases are usually adverbs.

(22) 你   那时   才   三   岁。（跳舞 58）
    nǐ   nàshí   cái   sān   suì
    2SG   that.time just three year.old
    'You were only three years old.' (*Tiàowǔ* 58)

(23) 足足   五   个   多   小时（石头 223）
    zúzú   wǔ   gè   duō   xiǎoshí
    full   five   CL   more   hour
    'more than five hours' (*Shítou* 223)

(24) 我   已经   十七   岁   了（华文教材 2A 205）
    wǒ   yǐjīng   shíqī   suì   le
    1SG   already 17   year.old LE
    'I'm already 17 years old.' (*Huáwénjiàocái* 2A 205)

8.15 Words That Can Function as Adverbials

Due to the influence of English, it is generally believed that only adverbs can be used as adverbials. In fact, in the lingua franca of modern Chinese nationalities, including Singapore Mandarin, adverbials are not restricted to adverbs. Details are given next.

8.15.1 Adverbs Being Typical Adverbials

Adverbs are defined by the function of being adverbials, and naturally all of them can be used as adverbials. Adverb adverbials are most commonly used among all types of adverbials. Here are a few examples.

(1) 旧时   的   情怀   又   涌上心头。（华韵 47）
    jiùshí   de   qínghuái yòu   yǒngshàngxīntóu

```
old.time    DE   complex   **again**   come.flooding.back
```
'The old feelings about the old time came flooding back again.' (*Huáyùn* 47)

(2) 身上　　　　一　　件　　圆领　　　　短袖　　　　的　　白　　线衣，
　　shēnshàng　*yī*　*jiàn*　*yuánlǐng*　*duǎnxiù*　*de*　*bái*　*xiànyī*,
　　body　　　　one　CL　round.neck　short.sleeves　DE　white　sweater

已经　　　发　　　黄　　　了。（华文教材 3A18）
yǐjīng　*fā*　*huáng*　*le*
already　turn　yellow　LE

'The white sweater with a round neck and short sleeves he was wearing has already turned yellow.' (*Huáwénjiàocái* 3A18)

(3) 匆匆地　　　赶到　　　洗手间　　　洗　　个　　脸，　　就　　下楼
　　cōngcōngdi　*gǎndào*　*xǐshǒujiān*　*xǐ*　*gè*　*liǎn*　*jiù*　*xiàlóu*
　　hastily　　　rush.to　rest.room　wash　CL　face　then　go.downstairs

吃　　　早餐。（金狮奖 103）
chī　*zǎocān*
eat　breakfast

'I hurried to the bathroom and washed my face, then went downstairs to have breakfast.' (*Jīnshījiǎng* 103)

Next, we will look at two groups of adverbs whose usages differ from those in Chinese Mandarin.

1　有 *yǒu* 'YOU', 太过 *tàiguò* 'too much', 一般上 *yìbānshàng* 'generally'

There are some adverbs in Singapore Mandarin that are absent in Chinese Mandarin. Three of the most common ones will be introduced in this section.

　　A　有 *yǒu* 'YOU'

It is widely acknowledged that there are two 没有 *méiyǒu* in the lingua franca of modern Chinese nationalities, one is the verb 没有 *méiyǒu* 'not have', which can be followed by a nominal object, such as 没有钱 *méiyǒu qián* 'have no money', 没有房子 *méiyǒu fángzi* 'have no house', 没有词典 *méiyǒu cídiǎn* 'have no dictionary'; the other is an adverb 没有 *méiyǒu* 'NEG', used before verbs and adjectives, such as 没有看电视 *méiyǒu kàn diànshì* 'not watching TV', 没有洗干净 *méiyǒu xǐ gānjìng* 'not cleaned', 没有熟 *méiyǒu shóu* 'not ripe', 没有亮 *méiyǒu liàng* 'not lighted'.

　　In Singapore Mandarin, there are two usages of 有 *yǒu* corresponding to 没有 *méiyǒu*. One is the verb 有 *yǒu* 'have/there be', taking a nominal object, such as 有许多人 *yǒu xǔduō rén* 'there are many people', 有两个苹果 *yǒu liǎng gè* píngguǒ 'have two apples', 有五块钱 yǒu wǔ kuài qián 'have five dollars'. The other is the adverb 有 yǒu 'YOU', mainly used as an adverbial before verbs, such as 你有去过吗? nǐ yǒu qùguò ma 'Have you been there?', 我有去过 wǒ yǒu qùguò 'I have been there.' In Singapore Mandarin, the adverb 有 yǒu 'YOU' is widely used. It orginates from the Min and Cantonese dialects, expressing the grammatical meaning of "affirming the existence or occurrence of events or facts". Here are some examples of 有 yǒu 'YOU' used as adverbials before the verb.

(4) 学生   时代   有   读过   一点   历史。（八方 12）
    xuésheng shídài yǒu   dúguò   yīdiǎn lìshǐ
    student era   YOU   read   a.bit.of history
    'I have read a little history when I was a student.' (Bāfāng 12)

(5) "这   几天   有   下雨   呀！"   我   说。（吾土·小说上 127）
    zhè   jǐtiān yǒu   xiàyǔ   ya   wǒ   shuō
    These few.days YOU rain   SFP   1SG   say
    '"It has rained these few days!" I said.' (Wútǔ(novel) 127)

(6) "他   几时   有   说过？"   子昀   一   脸   迷惑。(金狮奖 155)
    tā   jǐshí   yǒu   shuōguò?   zǐyún   yī   liǎn míhuò
    3SG   when   YOU   said   Zi Yun a   face confusion
    '"When did he say that?" Zi Yun looked confused.' (Jīnshījiǎng 155)

The following are examples of 有 yǒu 'YOU' used as adverbials before the adjective.

(7) 她   哪里   有   生气，   她   也是   在   跟   你   开玩笑
    tā   nǎlǐ   yǒu   shēngqì   tā   yěshì   zài   gēn   nǐ   kāiwánxiào
    3SG   where   YOU   angry   3SG   also   in.   with 2SG   joke.with
                                                  process.of

    呀，   不   信，   我   去   叫   她   来！（追云 111）
    ya   bú   xìn,   wǒ   qù   jiào tā   lái
    SFP   NEG   believe   1SG   go   call 3SG   come
    'She is not angry at all! She is also joking with you. If you don't believe it, I'll call her!' (Zhuīyún 111)

(8) "有   乖   一点   吗？"
    yǒu   guāi   yīdiǎn ma?
    YOU   behaved a.little SFP
    'Is she better behaved?'

    "她   会   乖   一点   就   好   了。"（春风 114）
    tā   huì   guāi   yīdiǎn jiù   hǎo   le
    3SG will behaved a.little just good LE
    'It would be nice if she behaved a little better.' (*Chūnfēng* 114)

In sentences (7) and (8), 有 *yǒu* 'YOU' is used to indicate realis. But it can also be employed for irrealis and assumptive sentences as follows.

(9) 明天   国庆   大   检阅， 我们   有   参加
    míngtiān guóqìng   dà   jiǎnyuè, wǒmen yǒu   cānjiā
    tomorrow the.National.Day grand review 1PL   YOU   participate

    表演   节目。（吾土·戏剧59）
    biǎoyǎn   jiémù
    performance   program

    'We will participate in a performance in the National Day review tomorrow.' (*Wútǔ*(drama) 59)

(10) 今天   晚上   如果   她   有   回来，   我   可得   要
     jīntiān wǎnshàng rúguǒ   tā   yǒu   huílai, wǒ   kěděi   yào
     today   night   if   3SG YOU   come.back, 1SG have.to will

     好好   教训   她   一   顿。（吾土·小说上 120）
     hǎohǎo jiàoxùn tā   yī   dùn
     well   lesson   3SG one   CL

     'If she comes back tonight, I will teach her a lesson.' (*Wútǔ*(novel) 120)

The adverb 有 *yǒu* 'YOU' can also be used on its own, just like the adverb 不 *bù* 'NEG', 没有 *méiyǒu* 'NEG'.

(11) "难道   你   的   公司   没   替你   投保？"
    nándào nǐ   de   gōngsī   méi   tìnǐ   tóubǎo ?
    don't   2SG   DE   company NEG   for.you   insure
    'Didn't your company insure you?'

    "**有**,   不过,   那   是   劳工   险,…"（微型 82）
    yǒu   búguò   nà   shì   láogōng   xiǎn
    YOU   but   that   be   labor   insurance
    'Yes, but that is labour insurance…." (*Wēixíng* 82)

(12) "他   没有   告诉   你   买   刀   的   意图？"
    tā   méiyǒu   gàosù   nǐ   mǎi   dāo   de   yìtú
    3SG   NEG   tell   2SG   buy   knife   DE   intention
    'He didn't tell you the intention to buy a knife?'

    "**有**。"（微型 212）
    yǒu
    YOU
    'Yes.' (*Wēixíng* 212)

In Chinese Mandarin, 有 *yǒu* can only be used as a verb not as an adverb. However, influenced by advertisement language in Cantonese, the expressions of 有售 *yǒushòu* 'for sale', 有出售 *yǒuchūshòu* 'be on sale' have also appeared in advertisements used in Chinese Mandarin, but that's the only case. This usage has not spread widely yet.

　　B　太过 *tàiguò* 'too much'

In Singapore Mandarin, 太过 *tàiguò* 'too much' is frequently used for expressing both a high and excessive degree, as shown in sentences (13) through (15).

(13) 那   也   未免   **太过**   天真   了。（报 1995 年 3 月 14 日
                                                            15版）
    nà   yě   wèimiǎn   **tàiguò**   tiānzhēn   le
    that also   rather   **too.much** naive   LE
    'That would be rather too naive.' (*Bào*, Mar.14, 1995, Issue no. 15)

(14) 做   事情   不   可   **太过**   野蛮。（新马·剧本 23）
    zuò   shìqíng   bú   kě   **tàiguò**   yěmán

| do | things | NEG | can | **too.much** | savage |

'Don't do things too savagely.' (*Xīnmǎ*(drama) 23)

(15)
不要	**太过**	掉以轻心，	文笔	好	的
búyào	**tàiguò**	diàoyqīngxīn	wénbǐ	hǎo	de
don't	**too.much**	let.down.one's.guard	write	good	DE

人	通常	历史	考	得	不	好。（牛车水 119）
rén	tōngcháng	lìshǐ	kǎo	dé	bú	hǎo
person	usually	history	examine	DE	NEG	well

'Don't be too careless. People who write well usually don't do well in history tests.' (*Niúchēshuǐ* 119)

Chinese Mandarin does not have such an adverb. To convey the same meaning, we use either 太 *tài* 'too' or 过于 *guòyú* 'excessively'.

C 一般上 *yībānshàng* 'generally'

一般上 *yībānshàng* 'generally' is an adverb peculiar to Singapore Mandarin Chinese, and it is used with high frequency. Some examples are listed here.

(16)
一	本	微型	小说集，	**一般上**	都	有	好	几十
yī	běn	wēixíng	xiǎoshuōjí	**yībānshàng**	dōu	yǒu	hǎo	jǐshí
one	CL	miniature	novel.collection	**generally**	all	have	well	dozens

篇	作品。（胜利·序）
piān	zuòpǐn
CL	work

'Generally, there are dozens of works in a collection of flash fiction.' (Preface of *Shènglì*)

(17)
自主学校	的	师生	比例	一般上
zìzhǔxuéxiào	de	shīshēng	bǐlì	yībānshàng
independent.school	DE	teachers.and.students	proportion	generally

较	小。（报 1995 年 3 月 5 日 1 版）
jiào	xiǎo
less	small

'The proportion of teachers and students in independent schools is generally small.' (*Bào*, Mar. 5, 1995, Issue no. 1)

(18) 一般上　　在　一　所　监狱　里　　工作　　几　　年　　后，
yībānshàng zài yī suǒ jiānyù lǐ gōngzuò jǐ nián hòu
generally at one CL prison inside work several year later

就　　会　　被　　调到　　另　　一　　所　　监狱。（牛车水 119）
jiù huì bèi diàodào lìng yī suǒ jiānyù
then will BEI transfer another one CL prison

'Generally, after working in one prison for a few years, they will be transferred to another prison.' (*Niúchēshuǐ* 119)

一般上 *yībānshàng* 'generally' here is roughly equivalent to 一般 *yībān* 'generally' and 一般说来 *yībānshuōlái* 'generally speaking' in Chinese Mandarin.

2　才 *cái* 'CAI' and 太 *tài* 'too'

It should further be noted that the grammatical meaning of some adverbs in Singapore Mandarin is different from that in Chinese Mandarin, especially 才 *cái* 'then' and 太 *tài* 'too'.

A　才 *cái* 'then'

In Chinese Mandarin, both 才 *cái* 'then' and 再 *zài* 'again/then' can be used in irrealis sentences.

(19) 他　　明天　　**才**　　走。
tā míngtiān **cái** zǒu
3SG tomorrow **then** go

'He won't leave until tomorrow.'

(20) 你　　唱　　得　　真好，　**再**　　给　　大家　　唱
nǐ chàng de zhēnhǎo **zài** gěi dàjiā chàng
2SG sing DE really.well **again** give everyone sing

一　　个。
yī gè
one CL

'You sing so well. Just sing one more for everyone.'

(21) 今天　　没　　买　　到　　电影票　　　没关系，　　我们
jīntiān méi mǎi dào diànyǐngpiào méiguānxì wǒmen
today NEG buy get movie.ticket no.matter 1PL

明天	**再**	看	好了。
míngtiān	***zài***	*kàn*	*hǎole*
tomorrow	**then**	watch	ok

'It doesn't matter if we cann't get the movie tickets today, we can watch it tomorrow.'

However, the grammatical meanings of the two are different: 才 *cái* 'then' used in an irrealis context implies that certain events have happeneds late, as in (19); 再 *zài* 'again/then' means repetition, including actual repetition and vacant repetition. The former implies that the action to be repeated has been performed previously, as shown in (20), while the later means that the action to be repeated has not actually been performed before but will be carried out as planned, as shown in (21). In Singapore Mandarin, 才 *cái* 'then' and 再 *zài* 'again/then' also have the same usage as in Chinese Mandarin, but there is no difference between them when being used in irrealis context. That is to say, 才 *cái* 'then' in an irrealis sentence also means repetition (especially the grammatical meaning of vacant repetition). This kind of usage is very common, as illustrated in sentences (22) through (24).

(22)
婆婆，	叫	人家	十五	**才**	来	看	花灯	吧！（今后 76）
pópó	*jiào*	*rénjiā*	*shíwǔ*	***cái***	*lái*	*kàn*	*huādēng*	*ba*
grandma	tell	people	fifteen	**then**	come	see	lantern	SFP

'Grandma, tell people come to see the lantern on the 15th.' (*Jīnhòu* 76)

(23)
妈！	让	我	考虑	一天，	明晚	**才**	说。（微型 98）
mā	*ràng*	*wǒ*	*kǎolǜ*	*yītiān*	*míngwǎn*	***cái***	*shuō*
Mum	let	1SG	think	one.day	tomorrow.night	**then**	say

'Mum! Let me think about it for a day. I will tell you tomorrow night.' (*Wēixíng* 98)

(24)
吃	了	饭	**才**	走	吧！（华文教材 1A 65）
chī	*le*	*fàn*	***cái***	*zǒu*	*ba*
eat	LE	food	**then**	leave	SFP

'Leave after having the meal, please.' (*Huáwénjiàocái* 1A 65)

This usage of 才 *cái* 'then' can only be found in Singapore Mandarin. In Chinese Mandarin, 才 *cái* 'then' in the preceding three sentences will have to be replaced by 再 *zài* 'again/then'.

B   太 *tài* 'too'

In Chinese Mandarin, 太 *tài* 'too' has two grammatical meanings. One denotes an extremely high degree, usually being used for admiration. In this case it always co-occurs with 了 *le* 'LE', such as 这太棒了 *zhètàibàngle* 'that's great' and 这节目太精彩了 *zhèjiémùtàijīngcǎi* 'what a wonderful show'.

The other implies excessiveness, such as 他太保守了 *tātàibǎoshǒule* 'he's too conservative' and 这衣服太贵 *zhèyīfútàiguì* 'that dress is too expensive'.

In Singapore Mandarin, 太 *tài* 'too' can also have both such grammatical meanings as exemplified here.

(25) 哇！ 香喷喷 的 炸鸡翅膀， 太 好 了。（小学 6A 32）
wā xiāngpēnpēn de zhàjīchìbǎng **tài** hǎo le
wow appetizing DE fried.chicken. **too** good LE
wings

'Wow! Appetizing fried chicken wings, that's great.' *(Xiǎoxué* 6A 32)

(26) 有些 司机 把 车子 开 得 太 快，
yǒuxiē sījī bǎ chēzi kāi de **tài** kuài
some driver BA cars drive DE **too** fast

是 很 危险 的。（小学 6A 15）
shì hěn wēixiǎn de
be very dangerous DE

'It is dangerous for some drivers to drive too fast.' *(Xiǎoxué* 6A 15)

太 *tài* 'too' in (25) means an extremely high degree, being used to express grateful emotion; 太 *tài* 'too' in (26) means excessiveness.

However, in Singapore Mandarin, 太 *tài* 'too' may have another grammatical meaning similar to 很 *hěn* 'very', simply expressing a high degree without any tone of compliment or excessiveness. It is most commonly used to modify 多 *duō* 'many'. See examples that follow.

(27) 也许， 我 秉承 了 太 多 父亲 的 性格，
yěxǔ wǒ bǐngchéng le **tài** **duō** fùqīn de xìnggé
maybe 1SG inherit LE **too** **much** father DE characters

尤其是 那 一 股 倔强。（青青 116）
yóuqíshì nà yī gǔ juèjiàng
especially that one CL stubborness

'Perhaps I inherited too much of my father's character, especially his stubbornness.' *(Qīngqīng* 116)

(28) 你   有   太   多   知识分子   的   缺点。（吾土·戏剧 31）
    nǐ   yǒu   tài   duō   zhīshifènzǐ   de   quēdiǎn
    2SG   have too   much intellectual DE   flaw
    'You have too many flaws of intellectuals.' (*Wútǔ*(drama) 31)

(29) 有   太   多   的   感觉   不   是   这些   还   没
    yǒu   tài   duō   de   gǎnjué   bú   shì   zhèxiē hái   méi
    have too   much DE   feelings NEG   be   these   yet   NEG

    经历   过   的   人   能够   体会   的。（金狮奖 77）
    jīnglì   guò   de   rén   nénggòu   tǐhuì   de
    experience GUO   DE   people can   sense   DE
    'There are too many feelings that cannot be sensed by those who have not experienced them yet.' (*Jīnshījiǎng* 77)

太多 *tàiduō* 'too much' simply means 很多 *hěnduō* 'a lot' and the adverb 太 *tài* 'too' is sometimes used to modify adjectives, as shown in sentence (30).

(30) 我   知道   太久   没   来   这儿   了，不然   怎么   会
    wǒ   zhīdào tài jiǔ   méi   lái   zhèer   le bùrán   zěnme   huì
    1SG   know   too long NEG   come here   LE otherwise how   will

    相见   不   相识   呢？（微型 59）
    xiāngjiàn bù   xiāngshí   ne
    meet   NEG   know   SFP
    'I know it's been a long time since I've been here. How would we meet and not know each other?' (*Wēixíng* 59)

Here, 太久 *tàijiǔ* 'too long' means 很久 *hěnjiǔ* 'very long'. The adverb 太 *tài* 'too' in Chinese Mandarin does not convey such a meaning.

8.15.2 Some Disyllabic Adjectives Being Adverbials

Disyllabic adjectives are usually used as adverbial modifiers with 地 *de* 'DE'. Here are some examples.

(31) 刘婶   同情   地   看看   母亲。（醒醒 68）
    liúshěn   tóngqíng   de   kànkàn   mǔqīn
    aunt.Liu   sympathetic DE   look-look mother
    'Aunt Liu looked sympathetically at my mother.' (*Xǐngxǐng* 68)

(32) 他   大胆   地   打量   那   金铺，...（金狮奖 186）
    tā   dàdǎn   de   dǎliàng nà   jīnpù
    3SG   bold   DE   look   that   gold.shop
    'He looked boldly at the gold shop . . .' (*Jīnshījiǎng* 186)

(33) 自省   就   是   冷静   地   自己   检讨
    zìxǐng   jiù   shì   lěngjìng de   zìjǐ   jiǎntǎo
    self-examination just   is   calm   DE   self   review

    自己   的   思想   和   行为。（伦理·中三 66）
    zìjǐ   de   sīxiǎng   hé   xíngwéi
    self   DE   thoughts   and   action
    'Self-examination is the calm review of one's thoughts and actions.'
    (*Lúnlǐ* III 66)

(34) 我   诚恳   地   表示   意见。（△含羞草 50）
    wǒ   chéngkěn   de   biǎoshì   yìjiàn
    1SG   honest   DE   put.forward   opinion
    'I put forward my opinion honestly.' (*Hánxiūcǎo* 50)

There are also examples without 地 *de* 'DE'.

(35) 冷静   思考。（大胡子·序）
    lěngjìng   sīkǎo
    calmly   think
    'Think calmly.' (Preface of *Dàhúzi*)

(36) 女歌星   邓丽君   最近   突然   在   泰国   清迈
    nǚgēxīng   dènglìjūn   zuìjìn   tūrán   zài   tàiguó   qīngmài
    female.   Teresa.   recently suddenly in   Thailand   Chiang Mai
    singer   Teng

    逝世...(报 1995 年 5 月 20 日 21 版)
    shìshì
    die
    'Recently, Teresa Teng passed away suddenly in Chiang Mai, Thailand
    . . .' (*Bào*, May 20, 1995, Issue no. 21)

There are also examples like 认真学习 *rènzhēnxuéxí* 'study hard' and 努力工作 *nǔlìgōngzuò* 'work hard' and so on.

Notably, there are a few monosyllabic adjectives that can be used as adverbial modifiers, but these adjectives never take 地 *de* 'DE'. For example, we can say that 慢走 *mànzǒu* 'walk slowly', 大喊大叫 *dàhǎndàjiào* 'scream loudly', 高喊（心情 27）*gāohǎn* 'shout loudly' (*Xīnqíng*, 27), 远看 *yuǎnkàn* 'look from a long distance' and 静坐（短篇 5）*jìngzuò* 'sit quietly' (*Duǎnpiān*, 5), but we can't say *慢地走 *màndezǒu*, *大地喊大地叫 *dàdehǎndàdejiào*, *高地喊 *gāodehǎn*, *远地看 *yuǎndekàn* and *静地坐 *jìngdezuò*.

8.15.3 Stative Words Being Adverbials

All stative words can function as adverbials. Here are some examples.

(37) 留　在　家里　**静静**　地　欣赏　心爱　的　唱片
*liú　zài　jiālǐ　**jìngjìng**　de　xīnshǎng　xīnài　de　chàngpiàn*
stay　at　home　**quiet**　DE　enjoy　favourite　DE　record

歌曲，...（△浮萍 80）
gēqǔ
songs

'Stay at home and quietly enjoy the music of your favorite records . . .' (*Fúpíng* 80)

(38) 非要　先　**好好**　地　洗　它　一　洗，...（孤寂 91）
*fēiyào　xiān　**hǎohǎ**　de　xǐ　tā　yì　xǐ*
must　firstly　**good**　DE　wash　3SG　one　wash

'We must give it a good wash first . . .' (*Gūjì* 91)

(39) 他　**匆匆忙忙**　地　写　了　八　封　信，
*tā　**cōngcōngmángmáng**　de　xiě　le　bā　fēng　xìn*
3SG　**hurried**　DE　write　LE　eight　CL　letters

紧紧张张　地　把　信　寄　出去　后，才
***jǐnjǐnzhāngzhāng*　de　bǎ　xìn　jì　chūqù　hòu，cái*
nervous　DE　BA　letter　mail　out　after　then

松松　地　哼起　小调。（胜利 72）
***sōngsōng*　de　hēngqǐ　xiǎodiào*
relaxed　DE　hum.up　tune

'He scribbled eight letters in a hurry, and then, after nervously mailing them off, he began to relax and hum a little tune.' (*Shènglì* 72)

8.15.4 Prepositional Phrases Being Adverbials

The primary function of a prepositional phrase is being an adverbial. When it is used as an adverbial, it does not take 地 *de* 'DE', as shown here.

(40) 蜡烛   的   亮光   把   我们   的   影子
    làzhú   *de*   *liàngguāng* *bǎ*   *wǒmen*   *de*   *yǐngzi*
    candle   DE   light   BA   1PL   DE   shadow

    拉   得   长长。(风雨 17)
    lā   *de*   *chángcháng*
    pull   DE   long

    'The candlelight lengthened our shadows.' (*Fēngyǔ* 17)

(41) 没关系,   我   **在**   外面   等   一会。(金狮奖 156)
    méiguānxi *wǒ*   **zài**   *wàimiàn*   *děng* *yīhuì*
    no.matter   1SG   **at**   outside   wait   a.while

    'That's all right. I will wait outside for a while.' (*jīnshījiǎng* 156)

(42) 你   有没有   **替**   我   **向**   我   姐姐
    nǐ   *yǒuméiyǒu*   **tì**   *wǒ*   **xiàng** *wǒ*   *jiějiě*
    2SG   YOU-NEG-YOU   **for**   1SG   **to**   1SG   elder.sister

    说?(吾土 · 戏剧 124)
    shuō
    speak

    'Did you speak to my elder sister for me?' (*Wútǔ*(drama) 124)

(43) 多   磨练磨练   **对**   你   总是   好   的。
    duō   *móliànmóliàn*   **duì**   *nǐ*   *zǒngshì*   *hǎo*   *de*
    more   practise-practise **for**   2SG   always   good   DE
    (华文教材 1A137)

    'It's always good for you to practise more.' (*Huáwénjiàocái* 1A 137)

8.15.5 A Few Subject-Predicate Phrases Being Adverbials

There are mainly two types of subject-predicate phrases that function as adverbials. One uses an isomorphic form of subject and object, as in sentences

(44) and (45). The other uses a quadrisyllabic unit, as in (46) through (48). Both types usually take 地 *de* 'DE' when they serve as adverbial.

(44) 和　　　父亲　　　面对面　　　地　　　坐　　　着，...（狮子 5）
　　　hé　　　fùqīn　　　miàn-duì-miàn　　de　　　zuò　　　zhe
　　　with　　father　　face.to.face　　DE　　　sit　　　ZHE
　　　'I sat face to face with my father . . .' (*Shizi* 5)

(45) 一个接一个　　地　　　快步　　　滑　　　下　　　河滩　　　去，
　　　yīgè-jiē-yīgè　　de　　　kuàibù　　huá　　　xià　　　hétān　　　qù
　　　one.follow.one　DE　　　quickly　　glide　　down　　beach　　　go

　　　从不会　　　跌倒。（风雨 2）
　　　cóngbúhuì　　diēdǎo
　　　never　　　　stumble
　　　'They quickly glide down the beach, one after another, and never stumble.' (*Fēngyǔ* 2)

(46) 爸爸...　脸无表情　　　地　　　在　　　沉思　　　着。（短篇 5）
　　　bàba　　liǎn-wú-biǎoqíng　de　　　zài　　　chénsī　　zhe
　　　Dad　　expressionless　　DE　　　in.process.of　think　　ZHE
　　　'Dad . . . He was in deep thought with an expressionless face.' (*Duǎnpiān* 5)

(47) 大家　　情绪饱满　　　地　　　唱　　　着，　　跳　　　着。
　　　dàjiā　　qíngxù-bǎomǎn　　de　　　chàng　　zhe　　　tiào　　　zhe
　　　everyone　full.spirits　　　DE　　　sing　　　ZHE　　　dance　　ZHE
　　　'Everyone was singing and dancing in high spirits.'

(48) 他　　信心百倍　　　地　　　报考　　　了　　　南大　　　电脑
　　　tā　　xìnxīn-bǎibèi　　de　　　bàokǎo　　le　　　nándà　　　diànnǎo
　　　3SG　confident　　　DE　　　apply.for　LE　　　NanJing.University　computer

　　　系。
　　　xì
　　　major
　　　'He was confident enough to register for the computer major exam of Nanjing University.'

8.15.6 Onomatopoeias Being Adverbials

As shown in the following examples, onomatopoeias can serve as adverbials.

(49) 豆大的　　　　雨点，　　随　　着　　风势，
　　　dòudàde　　　yǔdiǎn　　suí　　zhe　　fēngshì
　　　as.big.as.bean　raindrops　follow　ZHE　momentum.of.wind

　　　哗啦啦　　地　　倾盆而下。（吾土・戏剧 146）
　　　huālālā　　de　　qīngpénérxià
　　　clatter　　DE　　pour.down

　　　'Blown by the wind, large raindrops poured down.' (*Wútǔ*(drama) 146)

(50) 唤着，　　唤着，　　眼泪　　哗哗　　地　　流　　了　　下来。(跳舞 44)
　　　huànzhe　huànzhe　yǎnlèi　huāhuā　de　liú　le　xiàlái
　　　calling,　calling,　tear　　gush.out　DE　flow　LE　downward

　　　'As (she/he) called the tears flow down.' (*Tiàowǔ* 44)

(51) 几乎　　一夜　　到　　亮，　　楼板　　老是
　　　jīhū　　yīyè　　dào　　liàng　　lóubǎn　　lǎoshì
　　　almost　overnight　untill　dawn　　floor　　always

　　　叮叮咚咚　　　　响个不停。（吾土・戏剧 126）
　　　dīngdīngdōngdōng　xiǎnggebùtíng
　　　clatter　　　　　rumble.restlessly

　　　'The floor clattered with noise almost the whole night.' (*Wútǔ*(drama) 126)

When serving as an adverbial, onomatopoeias may either take 地 *de* 'DE' or not. Sentences (49) and (50) are still grammatical if 地 *de* 'DE' is removed; in (51), if 叮叮咚咚 *dīngdīngdōngdōng* 'clatter' is added by 地 *de* 'DE', the sentence is still grammatical. However, as shown in (52), if the verb modified by the onomatopoeia is a monosyllabic word, then 地 *de* 'DE' is more likely to occur.

(52) 外面　　的　　雷　　轰轰　　地　　响，
　　　wàimiàn　de　　léi　　hōnghōng　de　　xiǎng
　　　outside　DE　　thunder　rumble　DE　　blast

　　　风　　呼呼　　地　　吹，　　雨　　哗哗　　地　　下，
　　　fēng　hūhū　　de　　chuī　　yǔ　　huāhuā　de　　xià
　　　wind　screech　DE　　blow　　rain　gush　　DE　　drop

Attributes and Adverbials 347

仿佛	要	把	人世	的	脏乱	一扫而光。
fǎngfú	yào	bǎ	rénshì	de	zāngluàn	yìsǎoérguāng
as.if	going.to	BA	society	DE	filth	sweep.away

（吾土·戏剧 147）

'The thunder is rumbing outside, the wind is blowing, and the rain is pouring down, as if to sweep away the filth of society.' (*Wútǔ*(drama) 147)

8.15.7 *Nouns Being Adverbials of Verb Phrases*

In Singapore Mandarin, some nouns can modify verb phrases as adverbials after taking 地 *de* 'DE', as in (53) and (54).

(53) 他 奇迹 地 出现，绅士 地 吻 她 的
    tā *qíjì* *de* *chūxiàn* *shēnshì* *de* *wěn* *tā* *de*
    3SG miracle DE appear gentleman DE kiss 3SG DE

手。（报 1995 年 3 月 5 日副刊 13 版）
shǒu
hand

'He appeared miraculously, and kissed her hand like a gentleman.' (*Bào*, Mar. 5, 1995, Issue no. 13, supplementary edition)

(54) 我 兴趣 地 看着 他。（青青 107）
    wǒ *xìngqù* *de* *kànzhe* *tā*
    1SG interest DE look.at 3SG

'I looked at him with interest.' (*Qīngqīng* 107)

This usage is also found in Chinese Mandarin as well, as in (55).

(55) 我们 要 历史 地 看 问题
    wǒmen *yào* *lìshǐ* *de* *kàn* *wèntí*
    1PL should history DE look.at problem

'We need to look at the problem from a historical perspective.'

Nevertheless, the frequency of such usage is pretty rare in Chinese Mandarin. For instance, the nouns in the preceding sentences, such as 兴趣 *xìngqu* 'interest', 奇迹 *qíjì* 'miracle', 绅士 *shēnshì* 'gentleman', cannot be used as adverbials in Chinese Mandarin.

8.16 Complex Modifier-Head Phrases

The so-called complex modifier-head phrases refer to phrases whose modifier or head itself is a modifier-head phrase. They can be classified into three types.

8.16.1 Modifier-Head Phrases as the Modifier

The modifier itself can be a modifier-head phrase, as in examples (1) and (2).

(1) 我　　妈妈　　的　　头发　　（大胡子 24）
　　 wǒ　　māma　 de　　tóufa
　　 1SG　 mother　DE　　hair
　　 'My mother's hair' (*Dàhúzi* 24)

(2) （大家）　很　　　愉快　　地　　谈论　　着。
　　 dàjiā　　　hěn　　yúkuài　 de　　tánlùn　 zhe
　　 everyone　very　happy　　DE　　talk　　ZHE
　　 '(Everyone is) talking happily.'

Example (1) is an instance where the attribute itself is a modifier-head phrase, and example (2) is an instance where the adverbial itself is a modifier-head phrase. Both 我妈妈的头发 *wǒmāmadetóufa* 'my mother's hair' and 很愉快地谈论着 *hěnyúkuàidetánlùnzhe* 'talking happily' in these two examples can be analysed as follows[2].

```
我      妈妈     的      头发
wǒ     mama    de     tóufà
─────────── ( ) ──────── (attribute-head endocentric phrase)
    1              2
───── ─────                (attribute-head endocentric phrase)
  3     4
```

```
很      愉快     地      谈论着
hěn    yúkuài   de     tánlùnzhe
─────────── ( ) ──────── (adverbial-head endocentric phrase)
    1              2
───── ─────                (adverbial-head endocentric phrase)
  3     4
```

One more example of multilayer embedded attributes is shown in (3).

(3) 马华　　　文艺　　　意识　　　　的　　萌芽（新马·剧本·导论 1）
　　 mǎhuá　　wényì　　yìshí　　　 de　　méngyá
　　 Ma Hua　 literary　consciousness　DE　germination
　　 'The germination of Ma Hua's literary consciousness.' (Introduction of *Xīnmǎ*(drama) 1)

The structure of example (3) can be analysed as follows.

马华	文艺	意识	的	萌芽
mǎhuá	wényì	yìshí	de	méngyá

```
_____              2           (attribute-head endocentric phrase)
       1              ( )
_____                           (attribute-head endocentric phrase)
   3          4                               (attribute-head endocentric phrase)
_____
 5     6
```

- 1 _____ 2 (attribute-head endocentric phrase)
- 3 _____ 4 (attribute-head endocentric phrase)
- 5 __ 6 __ (attribute-head endocentric phrase)

Attribute-head endocentric phrases like that in (1) and (2) are common, however, multilayers of endocentric phrases like that in (3) are relatively less common.

8.16.2 Modifier-Head Phrases as the Head

It is more frequent to see the head of modifier-head phrase being a modifier-head phrase.

(4) 他　　的　　**工作**　　**情况**（微型 50）
    tā　　de　　gōngzuò　　qíngkuàng
    3SG　　DE　　working　　condition

   'his working conditions' (*Wēixíng* 50)

(5) （设计）也　　**十分**　　**精巧**。（中学 1A 110）
    shèjì　　yě　　shífēn　　jīngqiǎo
    design　　also　　very　　ingenious

   'The design is also very ingenious.' (*Zhōngxué* 1A 110)

Sentence (4) is a complex attribute-head endocentric phrase, while sentence (5) is a complex adverbial-head endocentric phrase. Their structures can be analysed in the following way.

他的	工作	情况
tāde	gōngzuò	qíngkuàng

- 1 _____ 2 _____ (attribute-head endocentric phrase)
- 　　　　 3 ____ 4 ____ (attribute-head endocentric phrase)

也	十分	精巧
yě	shífēn	jīngqiǎo

```
___1___ _____2_____              (adverbial-head endocentric phrase)
        ___3___ ___4___          (adverbial-head endocentric phrase)
```

There are also examples that have multiple layers of head phrases.

(6) 中国　　　资深　　乒乓球　　　　教练（报 1995 年 6 月 14 日 22 版）
　　zhōngguó　zīshēn　pīngpāngqiú　jiàoliàn
　　China　　senior　table.tennis　coach

'Chinese senior table tennis coach' (*Bào*, June 14, 1995, Issue no. 22)

(7) （我）　也　　已经　　把　　这些　　情况　　　统统　　　向　　经理
　　wǒ　　yě　　yǐjīng　　bǎ　　zhèxiē　　qíngkuàng　tǒngtǒng　xiàng　jīnglǐ
　　1SG　also　already　BA　these　　conditions　all　　　to　　manager

作　　了　　汇报。
zuò　le　　huìbào
make　LE　report

'(I) have reported all these to the manager.'

The structures of sentences (6) and (7) are analysed respectively.

中国	资深	乒乓球	教练
zhōngguó	zīshēn	pīngpāngqiú	jiàoliàn

```
___1___ _____2_____            (attribute-head endocentric phrase)
        ___3___ _____4_____            (attribute-head endocentric phrase)
                ___5___ ___6___        (attribute-head endocentric phrase)
```

也	已经	把这些情况	统统	向经理	做了汇报
yě	yǐjīng	bǎzhèxiēqíngkuàng	tǒngtǒng	xiàngjīnglǐ	zuòlehuìbào

```
___1___ _____2_____
        ___3___ _____4_____
                _____5_____ _____6_____
                                  ___7___ ___8___
                                          ___9___ ___10___
```

1-2, 3-4, 5-6, 7-8, 9-10 adverbial-head endocentric phrase

8.16.3 Both the Modifier and the Head Being Modifier-Head Phrases

Within this type of complex modifier-head phrases, attribute-head endocentric phrases are more common than adverbial-head endocentric phrases, as shown in examples (8) through (13).

(8) 新加坡　　中产阶级　　　　的　整体　　政治
　　 xīnjiāpō　zhōngchǎnjiējí　de　zhěngtǐ　zhèngzhì
　　 Singapore　middle-class　　DE　overall　political

倾向（报 1995 年 4 月 19 日 4 版）
qīngxiàng
tendency

'the overall political orientation of the middle class in Singapore'
(*Bào*, Apr. 19, 1995, Issue no. 4)

(9) （你　　要）　很好　　　向　　他　　学习。
　　 nǐ　　yào　　hěnhǎo　　xiàng　tā　　xuéxí
　　 2SG　should　very.well　from　3SG　study

'(You should) learn from him well.'

Example (8) is a complex attribute-head endocentric phrase, while example (9) is a complex adverbial-head endocentric phrase. Their structures can be analysed in the following way.

More examples follow.

新加坡　　中产阶级　　　　的　整体　　政治　　倾向
xīnjiāpō　zhōngchǎnjiējí　de　zhěngtǐ　zhèngzhì　qīngxiàng

```
─────    ─────────────  ( )  ──────   ───────────────
   1            2                        2
─────    ─────────────       ─────   ───────
   3            4               5        6
                                     ──────────────────
                                          7        8
```

1-2, 3-4, 5-6, 7-8 attribute-head endocentric phrase

很　好　　向　他　　学习
hěnhǎo　　xiàngtā　　xuéxí

```
──────    ──────    ─────
   1          2          (adverbial-head endocentric phrase)
──  ──    ──  ──
 3   4     5   6         (3-4, 5-6 adverbial-head endocentric phrases)
```

(10) 我国　　　大多数　　人　　的　家庭　　用语（华文教材 4B 31）
　　　wǒguó　　dàduōshù　rén　de　jiātíng　yòngyǔ
　　　our.country　most　people　DE　family　language

'the family language used by most people in our country' (*Huáwénjiàocái* 4B 31)

(11) 大马　　　　移民厅　　　　　　　　的　　工作
    dàmǎ　　*yímíntīng*　　　　　　*de*　*gōngzuò*
    Malaysian　immigration.department　DE　work

态度（报1995年6月7日2版）
tàidù
attitude

'the working attitude of Malaysian Immigration Department' (*Bào*, June 7, 1995, Issue no. 2)

(12) 整个　　社会　　的　　道德　　水平（伦理·中三 38）
    zhěnggè　*shèhuì*　*de*　*dàodé*　*shuǐpíng*
    whole　　society　DE　moral　level

'the moral level of the whole' (*Lúnlǐ* III 38)

Notes

1   Translator's note: Three more examples of nominal verbs are omitted here because of space limitations. They are 准备 *zhǔnbèi* 'prepare', 处罚 *chǔfá* 'punish', 欣赏 *xīnshǎng* 'appreciate'.
2   Translators note: As confirmed by the author, the bracket in the following means that there might be further detailed analysis here, but due to space limit that is omitted.

9 Complex Predicate Phrases

Lu Jianming

9.1 About Complex Predicate Phrases

What is a complex predicate phrase? Let's start with some examples.

(1) （被 关 在 劳动 营地）砍 树 种 菜。（华文教材 2A91）
    bèi guān zài láodòng yíngdì kǎn shù zhòng cài
    BEI lock at labour camp cut tree plant vegetables
    '(I was locked up in a labour camp) cutting down trees and planting vegetables.' (*Huáwénjiāocái* 2A 91)

(2) （我） 想 洗澡（女儿 99）
    wǒ xiǎng xǐzǎo
    1SG want shower
    '(I) want to take a shower.' (*Nǚér* 99)

(3) 听 懂（笑眼 13）
    tīng dǒng
    hear understand
    'I understand.' (*Xiàoyǎn* 13)

(4) 写 字 可以 修身（渐行 50）
    xiě zì kěyǐ xiūshēn
    write word can self-cultivate
    'Writing is good for self-cultivation.' (*Jiànxíng* 50)

(5) 冷静 思考（大胡子·序）
    lěngjìng sīkǎo
    calmly think
    'Think calmly.' (*Dàhúzǐ·xù*)

(6) 派　　你　　上　　阵（狮子 4）
　　 pài   nǐ   shàng zhèn
　　 send 2SG go   battle

'Sending you into battle.' (*Shīzi* 4)

(7) 非　　改　　改　　不　　行（笑眼 5）
　　 fēi   gǎi   gǎi   bù   xíng
　　 NEG change change NEG   ok

'It has to be changed.' (*Xiàoyǎn* 5)

(8) 出　　外　　散心（华文教材 2A92）
　　 chū   wài   sànxīn
　　 go   out   take-a-break

'Go out to take a break.' (*Huáwénjiāocái* 2A 92)

Examples (1) through (8) all contain two predicate words. In example (1), 砍树种菜 *kǎnshù zhòngcài* 'cutting down trees and planting vegetables' is a coordinate phrase consisting of two predicate-object phrases: 砍树 *kǎnshù* 'cut down trees' and 种菜 *zhòngcài* 'plant vegetables'. In example (2), 想洗澡 *xiǎng xǐzǎo* 'want to take a shower' is a predicate-object phrase, with the verb 想 *xiǎng* 'want' as the predicate and 洗澡 *xǐzǎo* 'take a shower' as the object. In example (3), 听懂 *tīngdǒng* 'hear and understand' is a predicate-complement phrase, with the verb 听 *tīng* 'hear' as the predicate and the verb 懂 *tīng* 'understand' as the complement. In example (4), 写字可以修身 *xiězì kěyǐ xiūshēn* 'writing can cultivate one's morality' is a subject-predicate phrase, with the predicate-object phrase 写字 *xiězì* 'write characters' as the subject and the predicate-object phrase and 可以修身 *kěyǐ xiūshēn* 'can cultivate oneself' as the predicate. In example (5), 冷静思考 *lěngjìng sīkǎo* 'think calmly' is an adverbial-head endocentric phrase, with the adjective 冷静 *lěngjìng* 'calm' as the adverbial of the verb 思考 *sīkǎo* 'think'. We have introduced all of these phrases in the preceding chapters. Examples (6) through (8), on the other hand, grammatically speaking, do not belong to any of the predicate phrases that we have discussed so far: coordinate phrases, predicate-object phrases, predicate-complement phrases, subject-predicate phrases or adverbial-head endocentric phrases. They are complex predicate phrases to be discussed in this chapter. Example (6) is a complex predicate phrase composed of the predicate-object phrase 派你 *pàinǐ* 'send you' and the verb 上阵 *shàngzhèn* 'go to battle'. Example (7) consists of two adverbial-head endocentric phrases 非改改 *fēigǎigǎi* 'have to change' and 不行 *bùxíng* 'not ok'. Example (8) comprises of 出外 *chūwài* 'go out' and 散心 *sànxīn* 'take a break'.

A complex predicate phrase is a combination of two predicate phrases which do not form any of the following grammatical relations, such as coordination, predicate-object, predicate-complement, subject-predicate or adverbial-head relation.

The complex predicate phrases, as a special kind of predicate phrase, are unique to the lingua franca of the Han people, including Singapore Mandarin. They have a much more complex internal structure than other predicate phrases and can be divided into at least three categories: pivotal phrase, as in example (6); contracted correlative phrases, as in example (7); and serial predicate phrase, as in example (8).

9.2 Pivotal Phrases

9.2.1 The Major Characteristics of Pivotal Phrases

1. Pivotal phrases are made up of two parts, both of which are verb phrases. For example, in example (6) in Section 9.1, the phrase 派你上阵 *pàinǐshàngzhèn* 'send you into battle' consists of two verbal phrases: 派你 *pàinǐ* 'send you' and 上阵 *shàngzhèn* 'go into battle'.
2. The first part of a pivotal phrase is a predicate-object phrase with a nominal object that has a specific reference. For example, in 派你上阵 *pàinǐshàngzhèn* 'send you into battle', the first part is a predicate-object phrase with the second personal pronoun 你 *nǐ* as the object. This phrase should be grammatically analysed as follows:

```
派      你      上阵
pài     nǐ      shàngzhèn
―――――――  ―――――――――
   1        2            (pivotal phrase)
―――――――
 3    4                  (predicate-object phrase)
```

3. The object in the first predicate-object phrase has a close semantic relation with the second verb phrase, as exemplified in 派你上阵 *pàinǐshàngzhèn* 'send you into battle', in which the object 你 *nǐ* in the predicate-object phrase 派你 *pàinǐ* 'send you' plays the semantic role of the agent of the action denoted by the following verb phrase 上阵 *shàngzhèn* 'go into battle' (meaning it is "you" who is going to battle).

9.2.2 Classification of Pivotal Phrases

Pivotal phrases, according to different semantic relations between the object in the first verb phrase and the verb in the second verb phrase, can be further divided into three types as follows (for convenience, we will mark the first predicate-object phrase as 'V$_1$N' and the verb in the second verb phrase as 'V$_2$').

1. The semantic relation between the N in 'V$_1$N' and V$_2$ is of an 'agent-action' relation. Most often, V$_1$ is a causative verb. For example, in 请先生进来 *qǐngxiānshēngjìnlái* 'invite the gentleman in' (*Jīnhòu*, 46), V$_1$ 请 *qǐng* 'invite' is a causative verb, and 先生 *xiānshēng* 'gentleman', as the object of 请 *qǐng* 'invite', bear an 'agent-action' relation with V$_2$ 进来 *jìnlái* 'come in'. Here are more examples:

(1) 钱　　请　　你　　先　　　　　付，……（华文教材 1B8）
    qián　qǐng　nǐ　　xiān　　　　fù
    money　ask　　2SG　in.advance　pay
    'Would you please pay for it first ...' (*Huáwénjiāocái* 1B 8)

(2) 我们　　以后　　会　　通知　　再　　来　　的。（吾土·小说上 142）
    wǒmen　yǐhòu　huì　tōngzhī　zài　lái　de
    1PL　　later　　will　notice　　again　come　DE
    'We will send you a notice to come again later.' (*Wútǔ·Novel I* 142)

(3) 明天　　　叫　　你　　阿姨　　来　　　学校，……（狮子 42）
    míngtiān　jiào　nǐ　　āyí　　　lái　　xuéxiào
    tomorrow　ask　　2SG　aunt　　come　school
    'Ask your aunt to come to school tomorrow ...' (*Shīzi* 42)

(4) 我　　想　　　要　　　唤　　　　他　　回来，……（牛车水 79）
    wǒ　xiǎng　yào　　huàn　　　tā　　huílái
    1SG　want　　need　summon　　3SG　come.back
    'I want to call him back ...' (*Niúchēshuǐ* 79)

(5) 在　　政治　　　上　　　迫使　　政府　　　　接受　　　他们　　的
    zài　zhèngzhì　shàng　pòshǐ　　zhèngfǔ　　Jiēshòu　　tāmen　de
    at　　political　on　　　force　　government　accept　　　3PL　　DE

建议,……(金狮奖 35)
jiànyì
proposal
'Politically force the government to accept their proposals…'
(*Jīnshījiǎng* 35)

(6) 你　如果　逼　我　回去,　我　就　立刻……(大胡子 47)
　　nǐ　rúguǒ　bī　wǒ　huíqù　wǒ　jiù　likè
　　2SG　if　force　1SG　come.back　1SG　then　immediately
　　'If you force me to go back, I will immediately…' (*Dàhúzi* 47)

(7) 下　一　回　有　演出　时　便　派　你　上阵。(狮子 4)
　　Xià　yī　huí　yǒu　yǎnchū　shí　biàn　pài　nǐ　shàngzhèn
　　next　one　CL　have　show　time　then　send　2SG　go.to.battle
　　'Next time there's a show, you'll be in it.' (*Shīzi* 4)

(8) 一　年　后,　厂　里　劝　他　退　了　休。(太阳 32)
　　yī　nián　hòu　chǎng　lǐ　quàn　tā　tuì　le　xiū
　　one　year　later　factory　insi　persuade　3SG　return　LE　retire
　　'A year later, he was advised to retire from the factory.' (*Tàiyáng* 32)

In the pivotal phrases in examples (1) through (8), the verbs occupying V_1 position are all causative verbs, such as 请 *qǐng* 'request', 通知 *tōngzhī* 'inform', 叫 *jiào* 'ask', 唤 *huàn* 'summon', 迫使 *pòshǐ* 'force', 逼 *bī* 'force', 派 *pài* 'send', 劝 *quàn* 'persuade'. Apart from causative verbs, other verbs may also occur in pivotal phrases with an 'agent-action' semantic relation between N and V_2. Some examples are given here.

(9) 有　人　在　推　门。(大喜 20)
　　yǒu　rén　zài　tuī　mén
　　have　people　at　push　door
　　'Someone is pushing the door.' (*Dàxǐ* 20)

(10) 没有　人　签收,……(狮子 52)
　　 méiyǒu　rén　qiānshōu
　　 not.have　people　sign
　　 'No one signed up…' (*Shīzi* 52)

(11) 我   有   意   推荐   你   到   会计   部
     wǒ   yǒu yì   tuījiàn   nǐ   dào kuàijì   bù
     1SG have intention recommend 2SG to   accountancy department

     去。（大喜 201）
     qù
     go

     'I would like to recommend you for a position in the Accountancy Department.' (*Dàxǐ* 201)

(12) 今晚   你   要   陪   我   玩   个   痛快。（吾土·小说上 187）
     jīnwǎn   nǐ yào péi   wǒ   wán gè   tòngkuài
     tonight 2SG need accompany 1SG play CL   enjoyable

     'Tonight, you're going to have fun with me.' (*Wútǔ·Novel I* 187)

(13) 我   在   英国   时，   便   看到   英国   的   言论，
     wǒ   zài yīngguó   shí   biàn   kàndào   yīngguó   de   yánlùn
     1SG in   Britain   time then   see   Britain   DE   comment

     提醒   英人   不要   忘记   在   第二次大战
     tíxǐng   yīngrén   búyào wàngjì   zài dì-èr-cì-dà-zhàn
     remind   British   NEG   forget   at   the.second.world.war

     所   受   的   痛苦，……（风筝 204）
     suǒ   shòu   de   tòngkǔ
     SUO   suffer   DE   pain

     'When I was in Britain, I read some comments about reminding the British not to forget what they had suffered in the Second World War.' (*Fēngzhēng* 204)

(14) 有没有   给   医生   看   呀？（恶梦 125）
     yǒuméiyǒu   gěi   yīshēng   kàn   ya
     YOU-NEG-YOU   give doctor   see   SFP

     'Did (you) show it to the doctor?' (*Èmèng* 125)

(15) 感谢   你   帮   公司   的   忙。（醒醒 59）
     gǎnxiè   nǐ   bāng   gōngsī   de   máng
     thank   2SG help   company   DE   favour

     'Thank you for helping the company.' (*Xǐngxǐng* 59)

(16) 我   和   弟弟   骂   妹妹   只   懂得   哭。（牛车水 76）
    wǒ   hé   dìdì   mà   mèimèi   zhǐ   dǒngdé   kū
    1SG and   brother scold sister   only know   cry
    'My brother and I scolded our little sister for crying.' (*Niúchēshuǐ* 76)

(17) 孔子．．．．尊称   他   为   "万世师表"。（伦理·中三 11）
    kǒngzǐ   zūnchēng   tā   wéi   wàn-shì-shī-biǎo
    Confucius   respectfully.address   3SG   as   teacher.model
    'Confucius is regarded as the "teacher of all ages."' (*Lúnlǐ·zhōngsān* 11)

In examples (9) through (17), the verbs 有 *yǒu* 'have', 没有 *méiyǒu* 'not have', 推荐 *tuījiàn* 'recommend', 陪 *péi* 'accompany', 提醒 *tíxǐng* 'remind', 给 *gěi* 'give', 感谢 *gǎnxiè* 'thank', 骂 *mà* 'scold' can all take an object and then a verb phrase to form a pivotal phrase.

2 The semantic relation between the N in 'V$_1$N' and V$_2$ is of a 'patient-action' relation, which can be further divided into two subtypes.

   A The second part of the pivotal phrase is a verb phrase with V$_2$ as its core. For example:

(18) 跟   爸爸   讨   江鱼仔   吃。（金狮奖 306）
    gēn   bàbà   tǎo   jiāngyúzǎi   chī
    with   father   ask.for   anchovies   eat
    'Ask my dad for some anchovies to eat.' (*Jīnshījiǎng* 306)

(19) 有   许多   话   要   说。（醒醒 107）
    yǒu   xǔduō   huà   yào   shuō
    have   many   word   need   talk
    '. . . have a lot to talk about' (*Xǐngxǐng* 107)

(20) 今天   客人   没   烘饼   吃   了，......（梦 122）
    jīntiān   kèrén   méi   hōngbǐng chī   le
    today   guest   not.have   biscuit   eat   LE
    'There are no more biscuits for the guests today . . .' (*Mèng* 122)

(21) 我   再   拿   些   吃的   给   你。（狮子 81）
    wǒ   zài   ná   xiē   chīde   gěi   nǐ
    1SG   again   take   some   food   give   2SG
    'I'll bring you more food.' (*Shīzǐ* 81)

(22) 大   金鲤鱼......   抢   面包   吃。（风雨 6）
    dà   jīnlǐyú   qiǎng   miànbāo   chī
    big   golden.fish   seize   bread   eat

'(A) big golden carp. . . . . seized on the bread and ate it.' (*Fēngyǔ* 6)

(23) 他   举起   腕表   一   看，   哇，   快
    tā   jǔqǐ   wànbiǎo   yī   kàn   wa   kuài
    3SG   hold.up   wrist.watch just   look   wow   nearly

一点钟   了。（恶梦 62）
yī-diǎn-zhōng   le
one.o'clock   LE

'He held up his watch and saw that it was almost one o'clock.' (*Èmèng* 62)

In example (18), 江鱼仔 *jiāngyúzǎi* 'fish' is grammatically the object of V₁ 讨 *tǎo* 'ask for' and, semantically, the subject of V₂ 吃 *chī* 'eat'. The other preceding examples follow the same pattern.

    B   The second part of the pivotal phrase is a subject-predicate phrase with V₂ as the predicate. For example:

(24) 商场   上   有   很多   事   我   不   懂。（大喜 201）
    shāngchǎng shàng   yǒu   hěnduō   shì   wǒ   bú   dǒng
    business   on   have   many   thing   1SG   NEG   understand

'There are many things I don't understand about business.' (*Dàxǐ* 201)

(25) 你   等   着，   我   泡   一   杯   龙井茶   你   喝。
    nǐ   děng   zhe   wǒ   pào   yī   Bēi   long-jǐng-chá   nǐ   hē
    2SG   wait   ZHE   1SG   brew   one   CL   long-jing-tea   2SG   drink

'Wait, I will make a cup of Longjing tea for you to drink.'

The pivotal phrases in examples (24) and (25) should be analysed as follows.

有   很多事   我   不懂
yǒu   hěnduōshì   wǒ   bùdǒng
―――――――――――――   ―――――――――――
    1   2
―――――――――――――――――――――――――――
 3   4   5   6

1-2 pivotal phrases; 3-4 predicate-object phrase; 5-6 subject-predicate phrase

泡　　一杯龙井茶　　　你　喝
pào　yìbēilóngjǐngchá　nǐ　hē

```
      _____     _____
          1             2
_   _____   ___  ___
3       4         5    6
```

1-2 pivotal phrases; 3-4 predicate-object phrase; 5-6 subject-predicate phrase

In example (24), 很多事 *hěnduōshì* 'many things' is grammatically the object of V₁ 有 *yǒu* 'have' and semantically the object of V₂ 懂 *dǒng* 'know'. In example (25), 一杯龙井茶 *yìbēilóngjǐngchá* 'a cup of Longjing tea' is grammatically the object of V₁ 泡 *pào* 'make' and semantically the object of V₂ 喝 *hē* 'drink'.

3　The first part of the pivotal phrase is a ditransitive construction with two objects (marked as V₁N₁N₂), one object being the agent of V₂ and the other object being the patient of V₂. For example:

(26) 你　　　能不能　　　给　　我　　一　　杯　　水　　喝？
　　 nǐ　　　néngbùnéng　gěi　wǒ　yī　　bēi　shuǐ　hē
　　 2SG　　can-NEG-can　give　1SG　one　CL　water　drink
　　 'Can you give me a cup of water?'

(27) 我　　借　　你　　一　　本　　武侠　　　　小说　　看　　吧。
　　 wǒ　jiè　nǐ　　yī　　běn　wǔxiá　　　xiǎoshuō　kàn　ba
　　 1SG　lend　2SG　one　CL　martial.arts　novel　　read　SFP
　　 'I'll lend you a martial arts novel to read.'

(28) 过　　　些　　日子　　送　　你们　　一些　　野味　　　　尝尝。
　　 Guò　xiē　rìzi　　song　nǐmen　yīxiē　yěwèi　　　chángcháng
　　 GUO　CL　days　　send　2PL　　some　wile.game　taste
　　 'I'll give you some wild game to taste some other day.'

In example (26), the grammatical structure of 给我一杯水喝 *gěi wǒ yì bēi shuǐ hē* 'give me a cup of water to drink' is shown here:

给　　我　　一杯水　　喝
gěi　wǒ　yìbēishuǐ　hē

```
      _____     ___
         1         2       (pivotal phrase)
_   _____
3       4                  (predicate-object phrase)
_   ___
5   6                      (predicate-object phrase)
```

Semantically, 我 *wǒ* '1SG' and 一杯水 *yìbēishuǐ* 'a glass of water' are the agent and the patient of V₂ 喝 *hē* 'drink' respectively. The other preceding examples can be analysed in the same way.

9.3 Contracted Correlative Phrases

9.3.1 Two Common Types of Contracted Correlative Phrases

A contracted correlative phrase is defined by two predicative components linked by some connectives (mainly adverbs). There are two subtypes.

1   The two connectives are used in pairs. For example:

(1) 不　　　失眠　　　才　　　怪。（八方 120）
    bù　　 *shīmián*　 *cái*　 *guài*
    NEG　　 insomnia　 just　 strange
    'No wonder you suffer from insomnia.' (*Bāfāng* 120)

(2) 那　不　被　大　火　烧　死　才　怪　哪。（微型 15）
    nà　*bú*　*bèi*　*dà*　*huǒ*　*shāo*　*sǐ*　*cái*　*guài*　*nǎ*
    that　NEG　BEI　big　fire　burn　die　just　weird　SFP
    'It's a wonder you didn't get burnt to death by the fire.' (*Wēixíng* 15)

(3) 不　把　饭　吃　完　就　不　准　开　舞会。（牛车水 78）
    bù　*bǎ*　*fàn*　*chī*　*wán*　*jiù*　*bù*　*zhǔn*　*kāi*　*wǔhuì*
    NEG　BA　rice　eat　finish　then　NEG　allow　have　party
    'You can't have a party until you've finished your lunch.' (*Niúchēshuǐ* 78)

(4) （雨伞）不　　带　　又　　不　　行。（壁虎 9）
    yǔsǎn　*bù*　*dài*　*yòu*　*bù*　*xíng*
    umbrella　NEG　take　again　NEG　can
    'You have to take your umbrella.' (*Bìhǔ* 9)

(5) 因为　一　有　怀疑　便　会　想　办法　去　弄
    yīnwéi　*yī*　*yǒu*　*huáiyí*　*biàn*　*huì*　*xiǎng*　*bànfǎ*　*qù*　*nòng*
    because　once　have　doubt　then　will　think　way　go　figure

    个　　　一清二楚。（伦理·中三 51）
    gè　　 *yīqīngèrchǔ*
    CL　　 clearly
    'Because when in doubt, you'll try to figure everything out.' (*Lúnlǐ* III 51)

(6) 火苗　越　扩　越　大，　愈　烧
　　huǒmiáo yuè kuò yuè dà yù shāo
　　flame the.more expand the.more big the.more burn

愈　　　猛。（狮子 28）
yù　　　měng
the.more fierce

'The fire grew bigger, and the more it burned, the fiercer it became.' (*Shīzǐ* 28)

(7) 丽　却　好多　次　因　淋　雨　而
　　lì què hǎoduō cì yīn lín yǔ ér
　　Li but many times because get.wet rain then

病　倒......（壁虎 11）
bìng dǎo
sick down

'Li fell sick many times because of getting caught in the rain.' (*Bìhǔ* 11)

(8) 我　边　说　边　把　志华　的　名字　写　在　纸
　　wǒ biān shuō biān bǎ zhìhuá de míngzì xiě zài zhǐ
　　1SG as talk as BA Zhihua DE name write at paper

上。（牛车水 74）
shàng
on

'I wrote Zhihua's name on the paper as I spoke.' (*Niúchēshuǐ* 74)

(9) 我　一边　唱歌　一边　行走......（南风 75）
　　wǒ yībiān chànggē yībiān hángzǒu
　　1SG as sing as walk

'I sang as I walked...' (*Nánfēng* 75)

In examples (1) through (6), the predicates are linked by adverbs: 不...才... *bù...cái...* 'NEG...just' in examples (1) and (2); 不...不... *bù...bù...* 'NEG...NEG...' in examples (3) and (4); 一...便... *yī...biàn...* 'as soon as... then...' in example (5); 越...越... *yuè...yuè...* 'the more...the more...' and 愈...愈... *yù...yù...* 'the more...the more...' in example (6). In examples (7) through (9), the predicates are linked by conjunctions: 因...而... *yīn...ér...*

'because of... then...' in example (7); 边...边..*biān...biān...* 'as...as...' in example (8); and 一边...一边..*yìbiān...yìbiān...* 'as...as...' in example (9).

In example (1), the contracted correlative phrase 不失眠才怪 *bùshīmiáncáiguài* has the following grammatical structure:

不	失眠		才	怪	
bù	shīmián		cái	guài	
	1			2	(contracted correlative phrase)
3	4		5	6	(3-4, 5-6 adverbial-head endocentric phrases)

More examples of contracted correlative phrases are given here.

A 一...就...*yī...jiù...* 'as soon as...then':

(10) 我 一 没 课 就 回 家......（梦 58）
    wǒ yī méi kè jiù huí jiā
    1SG once not.have lesson then back home
   'I'll go home as soon as I have no lessons...' (*Mèng* 58)

B 非...不...*fēi...bù...* 'NEG...NEG':

(11) 我 非 去 不 可。
    wǒ fēi qù bú kě
    1SG NEG go NEG can
   'I have to go.'

C 再...也...*zài...yě...* 'again...also':

(12) 我 再 怎么 学 也 学 不 会。
    wǒ zài zěnme xué yě xué bú huì
    1SG again how learn also learn NEG can
   'I can't learn anything no matter how hard I try.'

D 不...也...*bù...yě...* 'NEG...also...':

(13) 你 不 去 也 得 去。
    nǐ bú qù yě děi qù
    2SG NEG go also need go
   'You have to go even if you don't want to.'

2 Only one connective is used (at the beginning of the latter predicate). For example:

(14) 要　　　骂　　　就　　　骂　　　好了。（吾土·小说上 155）
　　 yào　　*mà*　　*jiù*　　*mà*　　*hǎole*
　　 want　　scold　　then　　scold　　it.is.fine
　　 'If you want to scold me, go ahead.' (*Wútǔ·xiǎoshuō I* 155)

(15) 说　　　搬家　　　就　　　搬家。（有缘 37）
　　 shuō　　*bānjiā*　　*jiù*　　*bānjiā*
　　 say　　move.house　then　　move.house
　　 '. . . moved to a new place right after talking about it.' (*Yǒuyuán* 37)

(16) 谈　　到　　不　　能　　不　　分手　　的　　时候　　才
　　 tán　*dào*　*bú*　*néng*　*bú*　*fēnshǒu*　*de*　*shíhòu*　*cái*
　　 talk　until　NEG　can　NEG　leave　　DE　　time　　then

离开。（吾土·小说上 159）
líkāi
leave
'We kept talking and didn't leave until we had to.' (*Wútǔ·Novel I* 159)

(17) 卖　　完　　香皂　　才　　上学　　去……（风雨 13）
　　 mài　*wán*　*xiāngzào*　*cái*　*shàngxué*　*qù*
　　 sell　finish　soap　　then　go.to.school　go
　　 'After selling all the soap, he then went to school . . .' (*Fēngyǔ* 13)

(18) 为什么　　要　　拆掉　　又　　重　　织　　呢？（风雨 7）
　　 wéishénme　*yào*　*chāidiào*　*yòu*　*chóng*　*zhī*　*ne*
　　 why　　need　dismantle　then　again　weave　SFP
　　 'Why did they tear it down and re-weave it?' (*Fēngyǔ* 7)

(19) 敢　　怒　　而　　不　　敢　　言。（大喜 200）
　　 gǎn　*nù*　*ér*　*bù*　*gǎn*　*yán*
　　 dare　angry　but　NEG　dare　speak
　　 '. . . dare to be angry but not to speak.' (*Dàxǐ* 200)

In examples (14) through (18), the predicates are linked by adverbs, specifically, 就 *jiù* 'then' in examples (14) and (15), 才 *cái* 'only' in examples (16) and (17), 又 *yòu* 'again' in example (18). In example (19), the predicates are linked by the conjunction 而 *ér* 'but'. Grammatically speaking, the structure of the contracted correlative phrase 要骂就骂 *yàomàjiùmà* 'scold if you want to' in example (14) can be analysed as follows.

```
   要骂      就    骂
   yàomà    jiù   mà
   ─────   ──────
     1       2         (contracted correlative phrase)
           ──  ──
            3   4      (adverbial-head endocentric phrase)
```

The other preceding examples follow the same pattern.

9.3.2 Contracted Correlative Phrases Indicating Dependency Relations

In addition to the two types of contracted correlative phrases described earlier, there is another type which indicates a dependency relation. For example, 谁想去谁就去 *shuíxiǎngqùshuíjiùqù* means 'if you want to go, you go; if he wants to go, he goes'. There must be the same interrogative pronoun in the preceding and following predicate phrases of this type of chain phrase, such as 谁 *shuí* 'who' in this example. More similar examples are illustrated as follows.

(20) 有　　　什么　　就　　吃　　什么　　吧。（有缘 28）
　　 yǒu　 *shénme* *jiù*　*chī*　*shénme*　*ba*
　　 have　 what　　 then　 eat　 what　　 SFP
'Eat what you have.' (*Yǒuyuán* 28)

(21) 她们　去　到　哪　唱　到　哪。（报 1995 年 4 月 5 日 12 版）
　　 tāmen *qù* *dào* *nǎ* *chàng* *dào* *nǎ*
　　 3PL　 go　 arrive where sing arrive where
'They sing wherever they go.' (*Bào*, Apr. 5, 1995, Issue no. 12)

(22) 爱　　往　　哪儿　就　　上　　哪儿。（有缘 78）
　　 ài　*wǎng*　*nǎér*　*jiù*　*shàng*　*nǎér*
　　 like　 go　　 where　 then　 go　　 where
'Go wherever you like.' (*Yǒuyuán* 78)

(23) 你   高兴   什么   时候   来   就   什么   时候   来,
    nǐ   gāoxìng   shénme shíhòu lái   jiù   shénme shíhòu lái
    2SG   happy   what   time   come then what   time   come

    爱   呆   多久   就   呆   多久。（报 1995 年 6 月 19
                                              日副刊 7 版）
    ài   dāi   duōjiǔ   jiù   dāi   duōjiǔ
    like stay   how.long then   stay   how.long

    'Come whenever you like, stay as long as you like.' (*Bào*, June 19, 1995, Issue no. 7, supplementary edition)

9.3.3 Contracted Correlative Phrases and Compound Sentences

There is no phonetic pause in the middle of a contracted correlative phrase, otherwise it will become a compound sentence, as evidenced by the following pairs of examples.

(24) a   我   一   看   就   明白   了。
        wǒ   yí   kàn   jiù   míngbái   le
        1SG   once   look   then   understand LE
        'I knew what happened the moment I looked at it.'

    b   我   一   看,   就   明白   了。
        wǒ   yí   kàn   jiù   míngbái   le
        1SG   once   look   then   understand LE
        'I took a look, and then I understood.'

(25) a   你   做   完   了   功课   才   能   出去   玩。
        nǐ   zuò   wán   le   gōngkè   cái   néng   chūqù   wá
        2SG   do   finish LE   homework then   can   go.out   play
        'You can't go out to play until you've finished your homework.'

    b   你   做   完   了   功课,   才   能   出去   玩。
        nǐ   zuò   wán   le   gōngkè   cái   néng   chūqù   wá
        2SG   do   finish LE   homework then   can   go.out   play
        'Finish your homework, and then you can go out to play.'

(26) a 他   爱   上   哪儿   就   上   哪儿。
        tā   ài   shàng   nǎér   jiù   shàng   nǎér
        3SG   like   go   where   then   go   where
        'He can go wherever he likes.'

    b   他   爱   上   哪儿,   就   上   哪儿。
        tā   ài   shàng   nǎér   jiù   shàng   nǎér
        3SG   like   go   where   then   go   where
        'Where does he like to go? Well, he can go.'

The group of sentences in examples (24a) through (26a) are all simple subject-predicate sentences with a contracted correlative phrase as the predicate. In contrast, the group of sentences in examples (24b) through (26b) are all compound sentences. The only difference between each pair is whether there is a pause between two phrased.

9.4 Serial Predicate Phrases

As has been discussed so far, both the pivotal phrases and the contracted correlative phrases have distinctive features. The first part of the pivotal phrase is always a predicate-object phrase, in which the object is semantically related to the verb that comes after it. A contracted correlative phrase must include a connective to link the two parts of the phrase. Serial predicate phrases, however, have no defining grammatical features. Suffice to say that, excluding pivotal phrases and contracted correlative phrases, the rest of the complex predicate phrases are serial predicate phrases.

Serial predicate phrases in Singapore Mandarin are quite complex, the exact classification of which still needs more investigation. For the time being, some common types are listed here (the former part of a serial predicate phrase is marked as W_1 and the latter W_2 for the sake of convenience).

9.4.1 Purpose Serial Predicate Phrases

There is a purpose relation between W_1 and W_2, with W_2 indicating the purpose of W_1.

For example, in （她决定）进去店铺里看看 (*tā juédìng*) *jìnqù diànpùlǐ kànkàn* '(she decided) to go into the shop and have a look' (*Tiàowǔ* 60), the purpose of 进去店铺里 *jìnqù diànpùlǐ* 'go into the shop' is to 看看 *kànkàn* 'have a look'. This type of serial predicate phrase is most commonly seen in Singapore Mandarin. Here are more examples.

(1) 老头   拿   出   最好的   东西   招待   老太太。（太阳 47）
    lǎotóu   ná   chū   zuìhǎode   dōngxī   zhāodài   lǎotàitài
    old.man   take   out   best   thing   treat   old.lady
    'The old man took out the best things to treat the old lady.' (*Tàiyáng* 47)

(2) 我   留   她   再   坐   一会儿，她   说   还   要
    wǒ   liú   tā   zài   zuò   yīhuìěr tā   shuō hái   yào
    1SG keep 3SG   more   sit   a.while 3SG   say   also need

   赶   回去   预备   晚餐。（风雨 24）
   gǎn   huíqù yùbèi   wǎncān
   hurry back   prepare dinner

   'I asked her to stay for a while, but she said she had to get back in time to prepare dinner.' (Fēngyǔ 24)

(3) 长大   后，   大家   在   外   工作，   除了   经常
    zhǎngdà hòu   dàjiā   zài   wài   gōngzuò chúle   jīngcháng
    grow.up after everybody at   outside   work   apart   often
                                                     from

   互   通   音讯，   总   要   找   机会
   hù   tōng   yīnxùn zǒng   yào   zhǎo   jīhuì
   mutual communicate message always need   find   opportunity

   欢聚欢聚。（伦理·中三 79）
   huānjù-huānjù
   gather-gather

   'When we grew up and worked away from home, we always found opportunities to get together, apart from calling or texting each other.' (Lúnlǐ·zhōngsān 79)

(4) 人家   早   打   电话   向   系里   请假。（金狮奖 81）
    rénjiā zǎo   dǎ   diànhuà xiàng xìlǐ   qǐngjiǎ
    people early call phone   to   departmentin ask.for.leave

   'They called the department to ask for leave a long time ago.' (Jīnshījiǎng 81)

In this type of serial predicate phrase, it is typical that W_1 is a predicate-object phrase with a place object, indicating the movement of the actor; and W_2 indicates the purpose of such a movement. For example:

(5) 你   没有   回去   香港   探望   她   老人家？（风雨 24）
    nǐ   méiyǒu huíqù   xiānggǎng   tànwàng tā   lǎorénjiā
    2SG NEG   come.back   Hongkong   visit   3SG old.person

   'Haven't you gone back to Hong Kong to visit the old laday?' (Fēngyǔ 24)

(6) 进去　　房间　　梳好　　头发……（微型 11）
    Jìnqù　fángjiān　shūhǎo　tóufā
    go.in　room　　brush　　hair
    'Go into the room and brush your hair …' (*Wēixíng* 11)

(7) 我　要　回　　房　　温习　　了。（有缘 51）
    wǒ　yào　huí　fáng　wēnxí　le
    1SG　want　return　room　review　LE
    'I'm going back to my room to do some reviewing.' (*Yǒuyuán* 51)

Sometimes W₁ can be just a directional verb, for example:

(8) 我们　几　个　今天　晚上　　就　　来　　喝　　你　　的
    wǒmen　jǐ　gè　jīntiān　wǎnshàng　jiù　lái　hē　nǐ　de
    2PL　several　CL　today　night　then　come　drink　2SG　DE

    喜酒。（太阳 29）
    xǐjiǔ
    wedding.wine
    'We are coming to drink your wedding wine this evening.' (*Tàiyáng* 29)

(9) 我　要　　去　　环球　　　　旅行。（跳舞 113）
    wǒ　yào　qù　huánqiú　　lǚxíng
    1SG　want　go　around.the.world　travel
    'I'm going on a trip around the world.' (*Tiàowǔ* 113)

9.4.2 Manner Serial Predicate Phrases

W₁ indicates the manner of W₂. For example:

(10) 下　　课　　钟　　一　　响，　敏仪　立即　　　挽　　了　她
     xià　kè　zhōng　yī　xiǎng　mǐnyí　lìjí　wǎn　le　tā
     after　class　clock　once　ring　Minyi　immediately　hold　LE　3SG

     的　　手，　到　食堂　　后面　　的　　草地　去，　坐　　着
     de　shǒu　dào　shítáng　hòumiàn　de　cǎodì　qù　zuò　zhe
     DE　hand　to　canteen　behind　DE　grass　go　sit　ZHE

谈心。（狮子 110）

tánxīn

talk.heart

'As soon as the bell rang, Minyi immediately took her hand and went to the lawn behind the canteen. They sat down to have a heart-to-heart talk.' (*Shīzǐ* 110)

For the phrase 坐着谈心 *zuòzhetánxīn* 'sit and have a talk' in example (10), its semantic head is the latter part 谈心 *tánxīn* 'have a heart-to-heart talk', while the first part 坐着 *zuòzhe* 'sit' indicates the manner of the talking action. Let's look at more examples of this type:

(11) 小妮子　笑　着　把　食盒　推　过去……（金狮奖 217）
xiǎonīzǐ　xiào　zhe　bǎ　shí-hé　tuī　guòqù
Xiaonizi　smile　ZHE　BA　food.box　push　over

'Xiaonizi smiled and pushed the food box over to...' (*Jīnshījiǎng* 217)

(12) 到　了　屋　外　的　庭院，
dào　le　wū　wài　de　tíngyuàn
arrive　LE　house　outside　DE　courtyard

我　才　喘　着　气　说：
wǒ　cái　chuǎn　zhe　qì　shuō
1SG　just　gasp　ZHE　air　say

"你　回去　吧……"（大胡子 47）
nǐ　huíqù　ba
2SG　go.back　SFP

'When we arrived the courtyard outside the house, I gasped and said, "you go back..."' (*Dàhúzǐ* 47)

In this type of manner serial predicate phrase, the verb in W_1 is usually affixed with the auxiliary word 着 *zhe* 'ZHE', as in the preceding examples. However, there are also examples without 着 *zhe* 'ZHE'.

(13) 坐　飞机　回来　好　啦！（风雨 6）
zuò　fēijī　huílái　hǎo　lā
sit　airplane　come.back　good　SFP

'Just come back by plane.' (*Fēngyǔ* 6)

(14) 老师们　　都　　摇头　　　　叹息。（狮子 48）
    lǎoshīmen dōu yáotóu   tànxī
    teachers   all shake.head   sign
'The teachers all shook their heads and sighed.' (*Shīzǐ* 48)

In example (13) 坐飞机 *zuòfēijī* 'take an airplane' describes the way of 回来 *huílái* 'come back', and in example (24), 摇头 *yáotóu* 'shake head' indicates the manner of signing.

9.4.3 Possibility Serial Predicate Phrases

W_1 indicates the possibility of realising the action expressed in W_2. The verb in the predicate-object phrase in W_1 will be 有 *yǒu* 'have', 没有 *méiyǒu* 'not have', 没 *méi* 'not have' or 无 *wú* 'not have'. Some examples follow:

(15) 我　　希望　　天天　　　晚上　　　都　　停　　电，　　　好让
    wǒ   xīwàng tiāntiān wǎnshàng dōu tíng diàn   hǎoràng
    1SG   wish   everyday night   all stop electricity so.that

    我们　　每　　晚　　有　　机会　　点　　蜡烛。（风雨 17）
    wǒmen   měi   wǎn   yǒu   jīhuì   diǎn làzhú
    1PL   every night have chance light candle
'I wish the electricity would go out every night so that we could have a chance to light candles.' (*Fēngyǔ* 17)

(16) 我们　　有　　力量　　帮助　　别人。
    wǒmen   yǒu lìliàng bāngzhù biérén
    1PL   have power   help   others
'We have the power to help others.'

(17) 我　　有　　把握　　　成功。
    wǒ   yǒu   bǎwò   chénggōng
    1SG   have confidence succeed
'I have the confidence to succeed.'

In example (15), 有机会点蜡烛 *yǒujīhuì diǎn làzhú*, which literally says 'have the opportunity to light candles', means "can light candles". In example (16), 有力量帮助别人 *yǒu lìliàng bāngzhù biérén* which literally says 'have the power to help others', means "can help others". In the preceding examples, the verb in

Complex Predicate Phrases 373

W₁ is 有 *yǒu* 'have', while in the following examples the verbs in W₁ are its negative counterpart meaning 'not have', including 没有 *méiyǒu*, 没 *méi*, or 无 *wú*.

(18) 平时   忙   于   功课,   没有   时间   聊天。 (风雨 18)
     píngshí máng yú   gōngkè   méiyǒu   shíjiān   liáotiān
     usually busy at   homework not.have time   chat

'With so much homework, I'm usually too busy to chat.' (*Fēngyǔ* 18)

(19) 爸爸 得   谈   生意,   所以   没有   办法   陪
     bàbà děi tán   shēngyì suǒyǐ méiyǒu   bànfǎ péi
     dad   have discuss business so   not.have way   accompany

小安安......（再见）
xiǎoānān
little.Ann

'Dad had business to attend to, so he was not able to spend time with little Ann . . .' (*Zàijiàn*)

In example (18), 没有时间聊天 *méiyǒu shíjiān liáotiān*, the literal translation of which is 'have no time to chat', means "cannot have a chat" and in example (19), 没有办法陪小安安 *méiyǒu bànfǎ péi xiǎoānān*, the literal translation of which is 'have no way to be with little Ann', means "cannot spend time with little Ann".

9.4.4 Serial Predicate Phrases Describing Something From Two Sides

In this type of serial predicate phrases, W₁ and W₂ state both sides of the same fact. W₁ usually takes an affirmative form and W₂ a negative form. For example, in 怎么愣着不说话 *zěnme lèngzhe bù shuōhuà* 'why are you speechless and saying nothing', 愣着 *lèngzhe* 'speechless' and 不说话 *bù shuōhuà* 'not talking' describe the same fact of saying nothing in both positive and negative terms. Similar examples follow.

(20) 妹妹   在   那   个   部门   硬赖   着   不
     mèimèi zài nà   gè   bùmén   yìnglài   zhe   bù
     sister at   that CL   department stay   ZHE   NEG

肯   走......（牛车水 78）
kěn   Zǒu
want   leave

'My sister refused to leave that department . . .' (*Niúchēshuǐ* 78)

(21) 我   催   了   张芹   好几   遍，
     wǒ   cuī   le   zhāngqín   jǐ   biàn
     1SG urge LE   Zhangqin   several times

    可是   她   还   是   坐   着   不   动。
    kěshì   tā   hái   shì   zuò   zhe   bú   Dòng
    but   3SG   still SHI   sit   ZHE   NEG   move

    'I have urged Zhang Qin several times, but she is still sitting there without moving.'

9.4.5 Causal Serial Predicate Phrases

There is a causal relation between W_1 and W_2, with W1 indicating the cause and W2 the result.

(22) 魏敏   打   篮球   扭   了   腰。
     wèimǐn   dǎ   lánqiú   Niǔ   le   yāo
     Weimin   play basketball twist   LE   back

    'Wei Min twisted his back while playing basketball.'

(23) 阿舅   是   怕   你   遇到   老千   上了当。（追云 57）
     ājiù   shì   pà   nǐ   yùdào   lǎoqiān   shàngledāng
     uncle   SHI   afraid 2SG   meet   crook   fall.into.a.trap

    'Your uncle is afraid that you might meet a crook and be tricked.' (*Zhuīyún* 57)

(24) 那天   她   病   了   没   能   参加   那   次   晚会。
     nà tiān   tā   bìng   Le   méi   néng cānjiā nà   cì   wǎnhuì
     that day   3SG   sick   LE   NEG   can   join   that   CL   party

    'She was sick that day and couldn't attend the party.'

In example (22), 打篮球 *dǎlánqiú* 'play basketball' is the cause of 扭了腰 *niǔleyāo* 'twist the back'. In example (23), 遇到老千 *yùdào lǎoqiān* 'meet a crook' is the cause of 上当 *shàngdàng* 'be tricked'. In example (24), what causes the fact that 'she' couldn't attend the party is that she was sick.

9.4.6 Contrastive Serial Predicate Phrases

There is a contrastive relation between W_1 and W_2. W_1 takes an affirmative form and W_2 a negative form. For example:

(25) 那   件   大衣   买   了   一直   没有   穿。
     nà   jiàn dàyī   mǎi   Le   yīzhí   méiyǒu chuān
     that CL   coat   buy   LE   always NEG   wear

'She bought the coat but has never worn it.'

(26) 有   家   归   不   得,   回想   前事,
     yǒu   jiā   guī   Bú   dé   huíxiǎng qiánshì
     have home back NEG   DE   look.back past

恍如隔世。（风雨 41）
Huǎngrúgéshì
like.a.lifetime.ago

'With a home that I can never return to, when I look back on the past, it's like a lifetime ago.' (*Fēngyǔ* 41)

(27) 那   封   信   当时   我   收   了   没有   拆。
     nà   fēng   xìn   Dāngshí   wǒ   shōu   le   méiyǒu   chāi
     that CL   letter   that.time   1SG   receive LE   NEG   open

'I took the letter but didn't open it at that time.'

In example (25), the coat was bought a long time ago but it has never been worn. In example (26), 'I' have a home that I cannot go back to. In example (27), although the letter has arrived, it was not opened.

9.4.7 Serial Predicate Phrases Describing Perceptions or Senses

In this type of serial predicate phrases, W_2, usually an adjective phrase, describes how people perceive or feel about something, while W_1 specifies the physical senses with a sensory verb in the form of a 'verb + directional complement' or 'verb +着 *zhe* 'ZHE'. For example:

(28) 那   孩子   看上去   很   笨,   其实   他
     nà   háizi   Kànshàngqù   hěn   bèn   qíshí   tā
     that kid   look-go-up   very   stupid   actually   3SG

聪明   绝顶。
cōngmíng   Juédǐng
clever   incredibly

'The boy looks stupid, but in fact he is incredibly clever.'

(29) 我　　　用起来　　　　一点也不　　　自在……（醒醒 93）
　　　wǒ　　yòngqǐlái　　　Yīdiǎnyěbù　　zìzài
　　　1SG　 use-rise-up　　not.at.all　　　comfortable

'I didn't feel comfortable using it ...' (*Xǐngxǐng* 93)

(30) 这　　桔子　　闻　　着　　挺　　香的，　　可是　　味道
　　　zhè　 júzi　　wén　 Zhe　 tǐng　 xiāngde　 kěshì　 wèidào
　　　this　orange　smell　ZHE　 very　 sweet　　but　　 taste

很　　酸。（报 1995 年 6 月 19 日副刊 7 版）
hěn　　Suān
very　 Sour

'This orange smells sweet, but it tastes sour.' (*Bào*, June 19, 1995, Issue no. 7, supplementary edition)

9.4.8 Directional Serial Predicate Phrases

This type of serial predicate phrase is realised by inserting an object or a 了 *le* 'LE' in the middle of a directional predicate-complement phrase.

For example, the phrases 跑回娘家去 *pǎo huí niángjiā qù* 'run back to her mother's home' (*Zhuīyún*, 34) and 流了下来 *liú le xiàlái* 'flowed down' (*Tiàowǔ*, 44) are serial predicate phrases, which are realised by inserting the object 娘家 *niángjiā* 'mother's home' and the auxiliary word 了 *le* 'LE' respectively into the predicate-complement phrases 跑回去 *pǎo huíqù* 'run back' and 流下来 *liú xiàlái* 'flow down'. Their internal grammatical constructions are shown as follows.

```
  跑     回    娘家    去
  pǎo   huí   niángjiā  qù

  ‾‾‾‾‾‾‾‾‾‾‾‾‾‾‾‾‾  ‾‾‾
         1             2       (serial predicate phrase)
  ‾‾‾‾‾‾‾‾‾  ‾‾‾‾‾‾
       3        4               (predicate-object phrase)
  ‾‾‾  ‾‾‾
   5    6                       (predicate-complement phrase)

  流    了    下来
  liú   le   xiàlái

  ‾‾‾‾‾‾‾‾  ‾‾‾‾
      1       2                 (serial predicate phrase)
  ‾‾‾  ‾‾
   3   4                        (auxiliary phrase)
```

Let's see more examples.

(31) 我们　　有　　一　　个　　队员　　就　　差点儿　　掉　　下
     wǒmen yǒu yī gè duìyuán jiù chàdiǎnér diào xià
     1PL   have one CL member   then almost   fall down

   山谷　　去　　了。（华文教材 1B4）
   shāngǔ qù Le
   valley go LE

   'One of our team members almost fell down the valley.' (*Huáwénjiāocái* 1B4)

(32) 过　　了　　几　　分钟，　　乙和尚　　气愤愤地　　跑　　进
     guò le jǐ fēnzhōng yīhéshàng qìfènfende pǎo jìn
     past LE a.few minute   monk.Yi   angrily   rush in

   房　　来……（八方 37）
   fáng Lái
   room come

   'After a few minutes, Monk Yi rushed angrily into the room . . .' (*Bāfāng* 37)

9.4.9 Conditional Serial Predicate Phrases

There is a 'condition-consequence' relation between W$_1$ and W$_2$, with W$_1$ describing the condition and W$_2$ the consequence.

(33) "谢谢　　你，　　有　　缘　　再见。"　　我　　把　　手
     xièxiè nǐ yǒu yuan zàijiàn wǒ bǎ shǒu
     thank   2SG have fate see.again 1SG BA hand

   抽　　出　　时，　　向　　他　　眨　　了　　眨　　眼。
                                              （有缘 3）
   chōu chū shí xiàng Tā zhá le zhá yǎn
   take out time to   3SG wink LE wink eye

   '"Thank you, goodbye." I winked at him as I held my hand out.' (*Yǒuyuán* 3)

(34) 你　　觉得　　肚子　　饿　　可以　　先　　吃　　点　　饼干。
     nǐ   juéde dùzi   è   kěyǐ   xiān chī diǎn bǐnggān
     2SG think belly hungry can first eat some biscuit

   'If you feel hungry, you can have some biscuits first.'

(35) （我） 又 大声地 说： "晚 回来 别 等 我
　　　wǒ　 yòu dàshengde shuō wǎn huílái   bié   děng wǒ
　　　1SG also loudly　　 say   late back NEG   wait 1SG

啊！"（壁虎 10）
ā
SFP

'(I) also said loudly, "Don't wait up for me. I'll be back late."' (Bìhǔ 10)

In example (33), the serial predicate phrase 有缘再见 yǒuyuán zàijiàn means "if fate permits, we'll see each other again". Example (34) means "if you feel hungry, you can have some biscuits first". In example (35), 晚回来别等我 wǎn huílái bié děngwǒ means "If I come back late, don't wait for me".

9.4.10 Consecutive Serial Predicate Phrases

W₁ and W₂ indicate consecutive actions.

(36) 洗　 了　热　 水　 澡　　出来，　窗　　 外
　　　xǐ   le   rè   shuǐ   zǎo   chūlái   chuāng   wài
　　　wash LE hot water shower go.out window   outside

仍然……（壁虎，11）
réngrán
still

'When I came out after the hot shower, outside of the window it was still…' (Bìhǔ 11)

(37) 有　　一　 回，   看　 完　　舞狮　　　 回　 家，
　　　yǒu   yī   huí   kàn   wán   wǔshī   huí   jiā
　　　have one time watch finish dancing.lion back home

父亲　　外出　　　未　　归……（狮子 9）
fùqīn   wàichū   wèi   Guī
father go.outside NEG Back

'One day, when I returned home after watching the lion dance, my father had not returned from his trip…' (Shīzǐ 9)

Different from the first nine types of serial predicate phrases which consist of two parts, this type of consecutive serial predicate phrase can include more than two parts. For examples:

(38) 听到　　喊声，　周小姐　　就　　下　　　床
　　　tīngdào　hǎnsheng　zhōuxiǎojiě　jiù　xià　chuáng
　　　hear　　shout　　Miss.Zhou　then　get.off　bed

穿好　　　衣服　　出去　　开　　门。
chuānhǎo　yīfú　　chūqù　kāi　mén
put.on　　clothes　go.out　open　door

'When she heard the voice, Miss Zhou got off the bed, got dressed and went to open the door.'

In example (38), 下床 *xiàchuáng* 'get off the bed', 穿好衣服 *chuānhǎoyīfú* 'get dressed', 出去 *chūqù* 'go out' and 开门 *kāimén* 'open the door' narrate four consecutive actions. The grammatical structure of this phrase can be analysed into four parts, which are at the same level.

下床	穿好衣服	出去	开门
xiàchuáng	chuānhǎoyīfú	chūqù	kāimén
1	2	3	4	(serial predicate phrase)

The following are more serial predicate phrases with multi-parts:

(39) 你　　把　　冰箱　　　里　　　的　　水果　　　拿　　出来
　　　nǐ　bǎ　bīngxiāng　lǐ　de　shuǐguǒ　ná　chūlái
　　　2SG　BA　fridge　inside　DE　fruit　take　out

削　　皮　　切　　块……（有缘15）
xiāo　pí　qiē　Kuài
peel　skin　cut　Piece

'Take the fruit out of the fridge, peel them and cut them into pieces.' (*Yǒuyuán* 15)

(40) 另外　　　　又　　　有　　一　　批　　好奇的　　观众，
　　　lìngwài　yòu　Yǒu　yī　pī　hǎoqíde　guānzhòng
　　　in.addition　again　have　one　CL　curious　spectator

又　　停　　车　　下来　　　看　　个　　清楚。（风筝187）
yòu　tíng　chē　xiàlái　Kàn　ge　qīngchǔ
again　stop　car　get.down　look　CL　clearly

'Another group of curious spectators pulled the car over to take a closer look.' (*Fēngzhēng* 187)

In example (39), there are three consecutive actions: 拿出来 *náchūlái* 'take out', 削皮 *xiāopí* 'peel' and 切块 *qiēkuài* 'cut into pieces', and in example (40), the three consecutive actions are 停车 *tíngchē* 'pull over the car', 下来 *xiàlái* 'get down' and 看个清楚 *kàngèqīngchǔ* 'take a closer look'.

The preceding ten types of serial predicate phrases are only a general classification in an attempt to reveal the complexity of the internal semantic relations within serial predicate phrases. For some of them, there may be several possible analyses. See the following example.

(41) 她　迅速地　抬起　脸　来　看　她　母亲。（狮子 98）
　　 tā　xùnsùde　táiqǐ　liǎn　lái　kàn　tā　mǔqīn
　　 3SG　quickly　lift.up　face　come　look　3SG　mother
　　 'She quickly lifted her face up to look at her mother.' (*Shīzǐ* 98)

In the phrase 抬起脸来看她母亲 *táiqǐ liǎn lái kàn tā mǔqīn* 'lift her face up to look at her mother', the relation between 抬起脸来 *táiqǐ liǎn lái* 'lift her face' and 看她母亲 *kàn tā mǔqīn* 'look at her mother' can be understood as a relation of purpose, that is, lift her face up to look at her mother, or be interpreted as a consecutive relation.

9.5　有 yǒu 'Have' Complex Predicate Phrases

The majority of complex predicate phrases consist of verbal phrases. Some verbs are quite complex and productive in that they may form a variety of complex predicate phrases, such as 有 *yǒu* 'have' and 给 *gěi* 'give'. This section begins with the 有 *yǒu* 'have' complex predicate phrases.

有 *yǒu* 'have' complex predicate phrases contain predicate-object phrases with 有 *yǒu* 'have' as the verb, followed by another verb phrase. They can be pivotal phrases, contracted correlative phrases or serial predicate phrases (with different subtypes).

9.5.1　有 yǒu *'have' Pivotal Phrases*

1　In this type of phrase, the object of 有 *yǒu* 'have' is also understood as the agent of the following verb. For instance, in 有人扣门 *yǒurén kòumén* 'there is someone knocking the door', 人 *rén* 'people' is the object of 有 *yǒu* 'have', and semantically it is also the agent of the action 扣门 *kòumén* 'knock the door'. Grammatically, this example can be analysed in the following way.

有　人　扣门

yǒu rén　kòumén

　1　　2　　　(pivotal phrase)
　3　4　　　　(predicate-object phrase)

This type of phrase is used with high frequency. Here are more examples:

(1) 她　有　个　朋友　　患有　　严重的　　风湿病......（梦 135）
　　 tā yǒu gè péngyǒu huànyǒu yánzhòngde fēngshībìng
　　 3SG have CL friend   have   severe   rheumatism
　　 'She has a friend with severe rheumatism.' (*Mèng* 135)

(2) 有　位　灵牙利齿的　　　年轻　姑娘　　抢先　　回答。(天长 15)
　　 yǒu wèi língyálìchǐde   niánqīng gūniáng qiǎngxiān huídá
　　 have CL sharp-toungued young   girl   lead.up   answer
　　 'A sharp-tongued young girl was the first to answer.' (*Tiāncháng* 15)

(3) 拨　　电话　　去，　没有　　人　　接；　寄　　挂号信
　　 bō   diànhuà qù   méiyǒu   rén   jiē   jì   guàhàoxìn
　　 dial phone   go   not.have person take send registered letter

　　 去，　没　　人　　签收，　被　　退　　了　回来。（狮子 52）
　　 qù   méi   rén   qiānshōu bèi   tuì   le huílái
　　 go   not.have people receive BEI return LE back
　　 'When I called, no one answered, when I sent a registered letter, no one signed for it and it was returned.' (*Shīzi* 52)

In example (3), the verb 没（有）*méi(yǒu)* 'not have' is the negative form of 有 *yǒu* 'have'. The expressions 没有人接 *méiyǒu rén jiē* 'no one answered' and 没人签收 *méirén qiānshōu* 'no one signed up for it' share the same structure with their positive counterparts 有人接 *yǒurén jiē* 'someone answered it' and 有人签收 *yǒurén qiānshōu* 'someone signed up for it'.

2　The object of 有 *yǒu* 'have' is interpreted as the patient of the following verb. For example, in 有好戏看 *yǒu hǎoxì kàn* 'there's something interesting to watch', 好戏 *hǎoxì* 'something interesting' is the object of 有 *yǒu* 'have', and semantically it is the patient of the following verb 看 *kàn* 'watch'. Its grammatical structure is as follows.

有　　好戏　　看

yǒu　hǎoxì　kàn

1	2	(pivotal phrase)
3	4	(predicate-object phrase)

This type of phrase is also used frequently. More examples follow.

(4) 我　　有　　一　　件　　事情　　想　　告诉　　你……（南风 31）
wǒ　　yǒu　　yí　　jiàn　　shìqíng　　xiǎng　　gàosù　　Nǐ
1SG　have　one　CL　thing　want　tell　2SG
'I have something to tell you . . .' (*Nánfēng* 31)

(5) 商场　　上　　有　　很多　　事　　我　　不　　懂。（大喜 201）
shāngchǎng　shàng　yǒu　hěnduō　shì　wǒ　bù　dǒng
business　in　have　many　thing　1SG　NEG　understand
'There are lots of things in business that I do not understand.' (*Dàxǐ* 201)

(6) 没有　　电视　　看，　　时间　　怎么　　打发？（有缘 74）
méiyǒu　diànshì　kàn　shíjiān　zěnme　dǎfā
not.have　TV　watch　time　how　spend
'Without TV to watch, how am I supposed to kill time?' (*Yǒuyuán* 74)

9.5.2 有 yǒu 'have' Contracted Correlative Phrases

(7) 他　　越　　有　　钱　　越　　贪婪。
tā　yuè　yǒu　qián　yuè　tānlán
3SG　more　have　money　more　greedy
'The richer he is, the greedier he becomes.'

(8) 有　　什么　　就　　吃　　什么　　吧……（有缘 28）
yǒu　shénme　jiù　chī　shénme　ba
have　what　then　eat　what　SFP
'Let's eat whatever there is . . .' (*Yǒuyuán* 28)

Example (7) can be grammatically analysed in the following way.

```
越    有钱      越    贪婪
yuè   yǒuqián   yuè   tānlán
─────────────────────────────
    1             2              (contracted correlative phrase)
─────────────────────────────
  3   4         5    6           (3-4, 5-6 adverbial-head endocentric phrases)
```

'YOU' contracted correlative phrases are relatively rare.

9.5.3 有 yǒu 'have' Serial Predicate Phrases

1. In 有 yǒu 'have' serial predicate phrases, the first part "有 yǒu 'have' + object" expresses the possibility of carrying out the action indicated by the following verb phrase. For example, 有能力养育孩子 yǒunénglì yǎngyù háizi means having the ability or the possibility to raise children. Its grammatical structure is illustrated here.

   This type of serial predicate phrase has a high occurrence as well. For example:

```
有    能力      养育     孩子
yǒu  nénglì    yǎngyù   háizi
_____    _____
    1              2              (serial predicate phrase)
___  ___       _____    _____
 3    4          5        6      (3-4, 5-6 predicate-object phrases)
```

(9) 这些   新秀   肯定   是   有   能力   取代   老将
    zhèxiē xīnxiù kěndìng shì   yǒu   nénglì qǔdài   lǎojiàng
    these rookies must   SHI   have ability replace veteran

   的。（华文教材 2B3）
   de
   DE

   'These rookies are certainly capable of replacing the veterans.' (*Huáwénjiàocái* 2B3)

(10) 让   客人   有   机会   尝到   摩利族   的   古老
     ràng   kèrén   yǒu   jīhuì   chángdào   mólìzú   de   gǔlǎo
     let   guest   have   chance taste   Mori   DE   ancient

   菜肴。（天长 27）
   càiyáo
   dish

   'Give guests a chance to taste the ancient dishes of the Mori people.' (*Tiāncháng* 27)

(11) 你   没有   权力   歧视   别人。（华文教材 4A 49）
     nǐ   méiyǒu   quánlì   qíshì   biérén
     2SG   not.have   power   discriminate   others

   'You don't have any right to discriminate against others.' (*Huáwénjiàocái* 4A 49)

2. The first part "有 *yǒu* 'have' + object" indicates conditions and the following verb phrase expresses the possible outcome. For instance, in 有缘再见 *yǒuyuán zàijiàn* 'have luck to see you soon', 有缘 *yǒuyuán* 'have luck' and 再见 *zàijiàn* 'see you soon' is of such a relationship, meaning that "if luck beholds, we will see each other again". This phrase can be grammatically analysed as follows.

```
有      缘      再      见
yǒu    yuan   zài    jiàn

───────────  ───────────       (serial predicate phrase)
    1             2
───  ───    ───  ───           (3-4 predicate-object phrase; 5-6 adverbial-head phrase)
 3    4      5    6
```

There are more examples of this type. See the following.

(12) 等   以后   有   机会   再   一决雌雄。（华文教材 2A 33）
     děng yǐhòu yǒu   jīhuì   zài   yījuécíxióng
     wait later have chance again fight.it.out
     'We will fight it out when we get the chance.' (*Huáwénjiàocái* 2A 33)

(13) 以后   你   有   什么   事   可以   找   陈   教授。
     yǐhòu   nǐ   yǒu   shénme   shì   kěyǐ   zhǎo   chén   jiàoshòu
     later   2SG   have what   thing can   look.for Chen   professor
     'If you have any problem in the future, you can contact Professor Chen.'

(14) 没有   时间   可以   不   去。
     méiyǒu   shíjiān kěyǐ   bú   qù
     not.have time   can   NEG   go
     'You may not go if you don't have time.'

3. There is a semantic contrastive relation between the preceding "有 *yǒu* 'have' + object" phrase and the following verb phrase. For example, in 有家归不得 *yǒujiā guībùdé*, 有家 *yǒujiā* 'have a home' and 归不得 *guībùdé* 'can't return' are of such a relation, meaning 'he has a home, which he cannot return to'. Its grammatical structure is shown here.

```
有      家       归不得
yǒu    jiā     guībùdé

───────────  ───────────       (serial predicate phrase)
    1             2
───  ───                       (predicate-object phrase)
 3    4
```

Here are more examples.

(15)

世界	上	还	有	什么	比	有	国	不	得
shìjiè	shàng	hái	yǒu	shénme	bǐ	yǒu	guó	bù	dé
world	in	still	have	what	than	have	country	NEG	get

归	还	痛苦的	事。（梦 13）
guī	hái	tòngkǔde	shì
return	more	painful	thing

'What in the world could be more painful than not being able to return to your country?' (*Mèng* 13)

(16)

你们	这些	垃圾，	有	书	不	读，	有	课
nǐmen	zhèxiē	lājī	yǒu	shū	bù	dú	yǒu	kè
2PL	these	trash	have	book	NEG	read	have	class

不	上……（变调 13）
bú	shàng
NEG	attend

'You trash! You have books but you don't read them. You can go to school but you don't attend classes.' (*Biàndiào* 13)

(17)

他	有	钱	不	肯	捐助	点儿，
tā	yǒu	qián	bù	kěn	juānzhù	diǎner
3SG	have	money	NEG	will	donate	some

你	说	他	吝啬	不	吝啬。
nǐ	shuō	tā	lìnsè	bú	Lìnsè
2SG	say	3SG	mean	NEG	mean

'He has money but he doesn't want to donate any. Quite mean, wouldn't you say so?'

The 有 *yǒu* 'have' serial predicate phrases in the preceding examples all express a contrastive relation. Example (15) means "even though you have a country, you cannot return". In example (16), the highlighted phrase means that "they have books, but they don't want to read them; they have classes, but they don't want to take them". Example (17) states "though he has money, he doesn't want to donate any".

4 There is a cause-result relationship between the "有 *yǒu* 'have' + object" phrase and the following verb phrase. For example, in（他今天）有病不能上班了 *(tā jīntiān) yǒubìng bùnéng shàngbān le*, 有病 *yǒubìng* 'have illness' expresses the cause and 不能上班了 *bùnéng shàngbān le* 'can't go to work'

is the result, meaning "he can't go to work today due to illness". The grammatical structure of this phrase is as follows.

有	病	不	能	上班	了
yǒu	bìn	bù	néng	shàngbān	le

```
    1                    2              ( )   (serial predicate phrase)
  3   4         5            6                (3-4, 5-6 predicate-object phrases)
                7   8                         (adverbial-head endocentric phrase)
```

More examples are given next.

(18) 王　　　小姐，　我　　　明天　　　下午　　　有　　　学术　　　报告会
　　　wáng　　xiǎojiě　wǒ　　　míngtiān　xiàwǔ　　yǒu　　xuéshù　　Bàogàohuì
　　　Wang　　lady　　1SG　　　tomorrow　afternoon　have　academic　seminar

　　　不　　　能　　去　　植物园　　　了，　我们　　改天　　　　再
　　　bù　　　néng　qù　　zhíwùyuán　le　　wǒmēn　gǎitiān　　　zài
　　　NEG　　can　　go　　botanical.　LE　　1PL　　another.　　again
　　　　　　　　　　　　garden　　　　　　　　　　day

　　　去　　　吧。
　　　qù　　　ba
　　　go　　　SFP

'Miss Wang, I can't go to the botanical garden tomorrow afternoon because I have to attend an academic seminar. Let's go another day.'

(19) "你　　　妈　　在　　　家　　吗？"
　　　nǐ　　　mā　　zài　　jiā　　ma
　　　2SG　　mum　at　　home　SFP

　　　"我　　　妈　　有　　　事　　出去　　了。"
　　　wǒ　　　mā　　yǒu　　shì　　chùqù　le
　　　1SG　　mum　have　thing　go.out　LE

'"Is your mum home?" "No, my mum is out doing something."'

In example (18), the highlighted part of the sentence means "(I) can't go to the botanical garden because because I have to attend an academic seminar". In example (19), the highlighted phrase means "(my mum) is not home because she has something to do".

9.6 给 gěi 'Give' Complex Predicate Structures

In Singapore Mandarin, 给 *gěi* can either be a verb or a preposition. As a verb, 给 *gěi* means giving, as shown in the following sentence.

(1) 她 的   这   封   信   给   了   我   异常   深刻的   印象。（△断
                                                                    情剪 46）
    tā de zhè fēng xìn   gěi le wǒ yìcháng shēnkède yìnxiàng
    3SG DE this CL   letter give LE 1SG very   deep   impression
    'Her letter left a very deep impression on me.' (*Duànqíngjiǎn* 46)

As a preposition, 给 *gěi* may be interpreted as 'BEI' 'for', 'to' or 'on behalf of'. For example:

(2) 我   那   小   书橱   的   "暗屉"   果然   给
    wǒ   nà   xiǎo   shūchú   de   àntì   guǒrán   gěi
    1SG that small bookcase DE   hidden.drawer unsurprisingly GEI

    他   撬   开   了！（大喜 16）
    tā   qiào   kāi   le
    3SG prise open   LE
    'The "hidden drawer" of my little bookcase had been prised open!' (*Dàxǐ* 16)

(3) 点燃   起   妈妈   给   我   造   的   柚灯笼。（晚上 16）
    diǎnrán qǐ   māmā gěi   wǒ   zào   de   yòudēnglóng
    light   up   mom   GEI   1SG make DE   pomelo.lantern
    'Light up the pomelo lantern my mother made for me.' (*Wǎnshàng* 16)

(4) 你   给   我   看着   这   行李，   我   去   买   点   吃的。
    nǐ gěi   wǒ   kànzhe   zhè xíngli   wǒ qù mǎi diǎn chīde
    2SG GEI 1SG look.after   this baggage 1SG go buy some food
    'You keep an eye on this baggage while I go and get something to eat.'

(5) 我   怎么   给   他   祝贺？   给   他   道喜？（△断情剪 44）
    wǒ zěnme gěi   tā   zhùhè   gěi   tā   dàoxǐ
    1SG how   GEI   3SG congratulate GEI   3SG compliment
    'How do I congratulate him, and offer him a compliment?' (*Duànqíngjiǎn* 44)

In the preceding examples, 给 *gěi* 'GEI' can be understood as meaning 'BEI' 'for', 'on behave of' and 'to' respectively, all of which are prepositions.

In this section, we only discuss complex predicate structures with verb 给 *gěi* 'give', which fall into five types.

9.6.1 Construction 1: V + 给 *gěi* 'give' + NP

In this construction, as well as the following ones, V stands for a verb and NP stands for a nominal phrase. Examples of Construction 1 are given as follows:

(6) 惨　　了　　啦！　这　　次，　一定　　又　　输　　给
    căn　 *le*　 *la*　 *zhè*　*cì*　*yídìng*　*yòu*　*shū*　*gěi*
    miserable LE SFP   this   time surely   again lose   give

　　林小雯　　　　了！（有缘 54）
　　línxiăowén　　*le*
　　Lin.Xiaowen　　 LE

'How awful! This time, I'm definitely going to lose to Lin Xiaowen again!' (*Yǒuyuán* 54)

(7) 他　　把　　纸袋　　　递　　给　　丽明，
    tā　*bă*　*zhǐdài*　*dì*　*gěi*　*lìmíng*
    3SG   BA   paper.bag hand give   Liming

　　说　　着　　就要　　　走　　了。（梦 121）
　　shuō　*zhe*　*jiùyào*　*zǒu*　*le*
　　talk   ZHE   then   walk   LE

'She handed the paper bag to Liming and was about to leave.' (*Mèng* 121)

(8) 随后　　　将　　新　　鱼苗　　　再　　售卖　　　给　　谢先生。（晚上 67）
    suíhòu　*jiāng*　*xīn*　*yúmiáo*　*zài*　*shòumai*　*gěi*　*xièxiānshēng*
    later   BA   new   fry   again sell   give   Mr.Xie

'Later he sold the new fry again to Mr. Xie.' (*Wǎnshang* 67)

Construction 1 is a serial predicate phrase. Taking the highlighted phrase in sentence (6) as example, this construction can be grammatically analysed as follows.

　　输　　给　　林小雯
　　shū　*gěi*　*línxiăowén*

　　—1—　—2—　　　　(serial predicate phrase)
　　　　—3—　—4—　　(predicate-object phrase)

Sometimes there will be two NPs after the verb 给 *gěi* 'give', resulting in a "V + 给 *gěi* 'give' + NP$_1$ + NP$_2$" construction, as exemplified in (9) and (10).

(9) 校长　　分　给　我　一　本　教学　记录簿……
　　　　　　　　　　　　　　　　　　　（吾土·小说上 126）
　　xiàozhǎng fēn gěi wǒ yī běn jiàoxué jìlùbù
　　headmaster give give 1SG one CL teaching record.book
　　'The headmaster gave me a teaching record book.' (*Wútǔ Novel I* 126)

(10) 在　这　种　时代　变迁　中,
　　zài zhè zhǒng shídài biànqiān zhōng
　　at this CL time change amid

　　带　给　我　莫大的　感慨！（晚上 55）
　　dài gěi wǒ mòdàde gǎnkǎi
　　bring give 1SG great feeling
　　'It touches me a lot in such times of change!' (*Wǎnshàng* 17)

The "V + 给 *gěi* 'give' + NP$_1$ + NP$_2$" construction, as a variant of Construction 1, is also a serial predicate phrase. The construction highlighted in example (9) has the following grammatical structure.

分　给　我　一本　教学记录簿

fēn gěi wǒ yīběn jiàoxuéjìlùbù

```
1        2              (serial predicate phrase)
   3        4           (predicate-object phrase)
      5  6              (predicate-object phrase)
```

9.6.2 Construction 2: V + NP$_1$ + 给 *gěi* 'give' + NP$_2$

This construction is a pivotal phrase which can be subdivided into two types.

1　NP$_1$ is the patient of 给 *gěi* 'give'. For example:

(11) 捐　　钱　　给　　孤儿院、老人院……（有缘 56）
　　juān qián gěi gūéryuàn lǎorényuàn
　　donate money give orphanage old.people's.home
　　'Donate money to orphanages and homes for the elderly …' (*Yǒuyuán* 56)

(12) 打   电话   给   你   奶奶……（梦 144）
    dǎ   diànhuà   gěi   nǐ   nǎinai
    call   phone   give   2SG   grandma

    'Call your grandma …' (*Mèng* 144)

(13) 写   个   报告   给   医生   就是了。（断情剪 38）
    xiě   gè   bàogào   gěi   yīshēng   jiùshìle
    write   CL   report   give   doctor   that.is.it

    'Just write a report for the doctor.' (*Duànqíngjiǎn* 38)

2 NP₁ is the agent of 给 *gěi* 'give', but this kind of usage is relatively rare. For example:

(14) 请   你   给   我   现款。（断情剪 15）
    qǐng   nǐ   gěi   wǒ   xiànkuǎn
    please 2SG   give   1SG   cash

    'Please give me cash.' (*Duànqíngjiǎn* 15)

Taking example (11) for instance; its grammatical structure can be analysed as follows.

```
捐       钱       给      孤儿院、    老人院
juān     qián     gěi     gūéryuàn   lǎoréngyuàn
─────────────────  ──────────────────────────   (pivotal phrase)
       1                    2
─────  ─────  ─────   ──────────────────────   (3-4, 5-6 predicate-object phrases)
  3      4      5                6
```

9.6.3 Construction 3: 给 *gěi* 'give' + NP₁ + V + NP₂

In this section and those that follow, NP₁ and NP₂ stand for different nominal phrases. This construction may be either a pivotal phrase or a serial predicate phrase. When it is a pivotal phrase, NP₂ may not appear after the verb, as in example (15).

(14) 这   种   罐子   给   我   煮   面糊。（梦 157）
    zhè   zhǒng   guànzi   gěi   wǒ   zhǔ   miànhú
    this   CL   pot   give   1SG   cook   batter

    'Use this pot to cook batter for me.' (*Mèng* 157)

(15) 那   榴莲   给   奶奶   吃。
    nà   liúlián   gěi   nǎinai   chī
    that durian   give   grandma   eat
    'That durian is for grandma.'

As pivotal phrases, Construction 3 can be analysed in the following way.

给   我   煮   面糊
gěi   wǒ   zhǔ   miànhú

```
___   ___
 1     2              (pivotal phrase)
___  ___  ___  ___
 3    4    5    6     (3-4, 5-6 predicate-object phrases)
```

给   奶奶   吃
gěi   nǎinai   chī

```
___   ___
 1     2              (pivotal phrase)
___  ___
 3    4               (predicate-object phrase)
```

The following examples are slightly different from the preceding examples. Here NP$_2$ appears before the V, immediately following NP$_1$.

(16) 平日   媳妇   只   会   给   他们   脸色   看......（扶轮 57）
    píngrì   xífù   zhǐ   huì   gěi   tāmen   liǎnsè   kàn
    usually   daughter-in-law only   can   give   3PL   long.face   look
    'Usually, the daughter-in-law wears a long face for them.' (*Fúlún* 57)

(17) 给   我   一   点   水   喝！
    gěi   wǒ   yī   diǎn   shuǐ   hē
    give   1SG   one   CL   water   drink
    'Give me some water to drink!'

The preceding examples, as a variant of Construction 3, are still pivotal phrases; their grammatical structures follow:

给　他们　　脸色　　看
gěi　tāmen　liǎnsè　kàn

```
─────────────────   ─────
        1              2      (pivotal phrase)
  ─────────  ─────
      3         4             (predicate-object phrase)
  ───  ───
   5    6                     (predicate-object phrase)
```

给　　我　　一点水　　　喝
gěi　wǒ　yīdiǎnshuǐ　hē

```
───────────────────   ─────
        1                2      (pivotal phrase)
  ─────────  ─────
      3         4               (predicate-object phrase)
  ───  ───
   5    6                       (predicate-object phrase)
```

The following are some examples of serial predicate phrases:

(18) 还　　要　　给　　妈妈　　买　　衣服。（有缘 56）
　　 hái　 yào　 gěi　 māma　 mǎi　 yīfu
　　 still　need　give　mum　　buy　cloth

　　 'I still need to buy my mum some clothes.' (*Yǒuyuán* 56)

(19) 在　医院　　驻守　　的　警员　　给　我　来　了　电话。（△断
　　　　　　　　　　　　　　　　　　　　　　　　　　　　　　情剪 42）
　　 zài　yīyuàn　zhùshǒu　de　jǐngyuán　gěi　wǒ　lái　le　diànhuà
　　 at　hospital　garrison　DE　guard　　give　1SG　come　LE　phone

　　 'The guard that garrisons the hospital called me.' (*Duànqíngjiǎn* 42)

In example (18), 给妈妈买衣服 *gěi māma mǎi yīfu* is ambiguous if understood without context. If we regard 给 *gěi* as a verb, the phrase could mean "buy some clothes and give them to mom"; if we interpret 给 *gěi* as a proposition, it may mean "buy some clothes on behalf of mum". Nevertheless, taking context into consideration, it's more appropriate to understand 给 *gěi* in example (18) as a verb; therefore, the phrase means "buy some clothes and give them to mum".

Construction 3, as a serial predicate phrase, can be grammatically analysed as follows.

给	妈妈	买	衣服
gěi	mama	mǎi	yīfu
1		2		(serial predicate phrase)
3	4	5	6	(3-4, 5-6 predicate-object phrases)

9.6.4 Construction 4: V + 给 gěi 'give' + NP + VP

VP stands for a verb phrase (as in the following section). Let's see some examples first.

(20) a 他   要   吃   我   那   盘   鸡饭,
        tā   yào   chī   wǒ   nà   pán   jīfàn
        3SG   need   eat   1SG   that CL   chicken.rice

        我   就   递   给   他   吃。
        wǒ   jiù   dì   gěi   tā   chī
        1SG   then   pass   give 3SG   eat
        'He wanted to eat my chicken rice, so I passed it to him.'

    b   他   要   吃   鸡饭,
        tā   yào   chī   jīfàn
        3SG   need   eat   chicken.rice

        我   就   煮   给   他   吃。
        wǒ   jiù   zhǔ   gěi   tā   chī
        1SG   then   cook   give 3SG   eat
        'He wanted to eat chicken rice, so I cooked some for him.'

递给他吃 *dìgěi tā chī* 'pass it to him to eat' in sentence (a) and 煮给他吃 *zhǔgěi tā chī* 'cook it for him to eat' in sentence (b) both belong to Construction 4, but there are differences between them. If the verb 吃 *chī* 'eat' is deleted in (a), 递给他 *dìgěi tā* 'pass it to him' is still grammatically correct. However, if we delete 吃 *chī* 'eat' in (b), 煮给他 *zhǔgěi tā* will be ungrammatical. The internal structures and relations of these two are also different.

递　给　他　吃

dì　gěi　tā　chī

```
    ─1──  ─2─          (pivotal phrase)
─3─ ─4─                (serial predicate phrase)
    ─5─ ─6─            (predicate-object phrase)
```

煮　给　他　吃

zhǔ　gěi　tā　chī

```
─1─  ──2──             (serial predicate phrase)
    ─3─ ─4─            (pivotal phrase)
    ─5─ ─6─            (predicate-object phrase)
```

The difference between (a) and (b) lies in the verb preceding 给 *gěi* 'give'. When verbs of giving (including 递 *dì* 'hand over', 送 *sòng* 'send', 卖 *mài* 'sell', 交 *jiāo* 'hand in', 借 *jiè* 'borrow', 租 *zū* 'rent', 留 *liú* 'keep', 扔 *rēng* 'throw away', etc. appear in the V position in Construction 4, we get the (a) structure. When other verbs (such as 煮 *zhǔ* 'cook', 做 *zuò* 'do', 画 *huà* 'print', 炒 *chǎo* 'fry', 打（毛衣）*dǎ(máoyī)*, 'knit (a sweater)', 讲 *jiǎng* 'talk', 沏（茶）*qì(chá)* 'make (tea)', etc.[1]) are in the V position, we get the (b) structure. The following are some (a)-type examples.

(21) （朋友们）将　全盘　生意　交　给　你　掌管……（△断情剪 11）
péngyǒumen jiāng quánpán shēngyì jiāo gěi nǐ zhǎngguǎn
friends BA all business leave give 2SG manage
'Your friends left all the business to you to manage.' (*Duànqíngjiǎn* 11)

(22) （那只　玉佩）留　给　小琪　当　嫁妆。（扶轮 57）
nà zhī yùpèi liú gěi xiǎoqí dāng jiàzhuāng
that CL jade keep give Xiaoqi be.as dowry
'That jade is left for Xiaoqi as her dowry.' (*Fúlún* 57)

If we delete the verb 掌管 *zhǎngguǎn* 'manage' in (21) and 当嫁妆 *dāngjiàzhuang* 'be as dowry' in (22), the remaining sentences will still be grammatical. The following are (b)-type examples.

Complex Predicate Phrases 395

(23) 我   好不好   把   这 个 秘密   讲   给   爹地   听？（微型 25）
     wǒ   hǎo-bù-hǎo bǎ   zhè gè mìmì   jiǎng gěi   diēdi   tīng
     1SG ok-NEG-ok   BA   this CL secret tell give dad   listen
     'Can I tell this secret to dad?' (*Wēixíng* 25)

(24) 他   曾经   用   那   低沉   磁性的   声音   说，
     tā   céngjīng yòng   nà   dīchén   cíxìngde   shēngyīn   shuō
     3SG once   use   that low   magnetic   voice   say

     指   给   他   看。（梦 115）
     zhǐ   gěi   tā   kàn
     point give   3SG   look
     'Once he spoke in his low and magnetic voice, asking me to point it out to him.' (*Mèng* 115)

(25) 徐淑芳   探监   回来   把   黄昆松
     xúshūfāng   tànjiān   huílái   bǎ   huángkūnsōng
     Xu Shufang visit.a.prisoner back   BA   Huang.Kunsong

     的   情况   讲述   给   曾家成   听……（△断情剪 4）
     de   jiǎngshù   jiǎngshù   gěi   zēngjiāchéng   tīng
     DE   situation tell   give Zeng.Jiacheng listen
     'After coming back from prison, Xu Shufang explained Huang Kunsong's current situation to Zeng Jiacheng…' (*Duànqíngjiǎn* 4)

The deletion of the verb 听 *tīng* 'listen' in (23), 看 *kàn* 'look' in (24) and 听 *tīng* 'listen' in (25) will make the remaining sentences unacceptable.

9.6.5 *Construction 5:* V + NP$_1$ + 给 *gěi* 'give' + NP$_2$ + VP

Construction 5 is a complex pivotal phrase containing the verb 给 *gěi* 'give'. Let's see some examples first:

(26) 我   拿   相簿   给   你   看。（狮子 103）
     wǒ   ná   xiàngbù   gěi   nǐ   kàn
     1SG take album   give   2SG   look
     'I'll show you the album.' (*Shīzi* 103)

(27) 煮   点   粥   给   婆婆   吃！（△断情剪 11）
    zhǔ   diǎn   zhōu   gěi   pópó   chī
    cook some porridge give mother-in-law   eat
    'Cook some porridge for your mother-in-law!' (*Duànqíngjiǎn* 11)

In example (26), 相簿 *xiāngbù* 'album' is the object of 拿 *ná* 'take', and semantically it is also the patient of both 给 *gěi* 'give' and 看 *kàn* 'look'; 你 *nǐ* '2SG' is the object of 给 *gěi* 'give', and semantically it is also the agent of the following verb 看 *kàn* 'look'. This is a complex pivotal phrase in which a pivotal phrase is embedded within another. The grammatical structure of example (26) can be analysed as follows.

```
拿      相簿      给      你      看
ná      xiàngbù   gěi     nǐ      kàn
_____       _____
    1                   2                   (pivotal phrase)
___  ___       ___  ___
 3    4         5    6                     (3-4 predicate-object phrase; 5-6 pivotal phrase)
                ___  ___
                 7    8                     (predicate-object phrase)
```

9.7 Complicated Complex Predicate Phrase

The so-called complicated complex predicate phrases contain components that are themselves complex predicate phrases. Construction 5 in Section 9.6 is such a case. In sentence (26), 拿相簿给你看 *ná xiàngbù gěi nǐ kàn* 'show you the album' is a complicated pivotal phrase within which another pivotal phrase is embedded (see Section 9.6).

Various complex predicate phrases may embed into each other, forming varied complicated complex predicate phrases. Let's explain with some examples.

One type is a pivotal phrase containing another pivotal phrase. More examples similar to (26) are given here.

(1) 我   找   几   个   学生   陪   你   回   家。（狮子 58）
    wǒ   zhǎo   jǐ   gè   xuéshēng   péi   nǐ   huí   jiā
    1SG   seek   some   CL   student   company   2SG   back   home
    'I'll ask some students to accompany you home.' (*Shīzi* 58)

In example (1), the highlight part can be grammatically analysed as follows.

```
找      几个学生         陪    你    回家
zhǎo    jǐgèxuéshēng    péi   nǐ    huíjiā
        ─────────────────────
              1                2         (pivotal phrase)
                        ──────────────
                              3     4    (pivotal phrase)
```

Another common type is a serial predicate phrase containing another serial predicate phrase, for example:

(2) 我   曾   两次   请假   回家   侍候   母亲。（独上 15）
    wǒ   céng liǎng cì   qǐngjià   huí jiā   shìhòu   mǔqīn
    1SG once two CL   ask.for.leave   back home tend   mom

'I had asked for leave twice to go home to tend to my mother.' (*Dúshàng* 15)

(3) 校长   会   走   短   路   穿   过   你   的   教室
    xiàozhǎng huì   zǒu   duǎn   lù   chuān   guò   nǐ   de   jiàoshì
    headmaster can   walk   short road cross   pass   2SG   DE   classroom

    回   去   收   衣服……（吾土·小说上 128）
    huí   qù   shōu   yīfu
    back   go   collect cloth

'The headmaster will take a shortcut via your classroom to collect his clothes …' (*Wútǔ xiǎoshuōshàng* 128)

The grammatical structures of the preceding highlighted phrases are as follows.

```
请假       回家      侍候       母亲
qǐngjià    huíjiā    shìhòu    mǔqīn
───────────────────
      1              2                (pivotal phrase)
──────────────
   3       4                          (pivotal phrase)

走短路        穿过你的教室              回去        收衣服
zǒuduǎnlù    chuānguònǐdejiàoshì     huíqù      shōuyīfu
──────────────────────────────────
          1                  2                     (serial predicate phrase)
──────────────────────────────────
   3           4               5         6         (3-4, 5-6 serial predicate phrases)
```

We also have examples in which a serial predicate phrase is embedded into a pivotal phrase.

(4) 老爸 叫 我 回 家 吃 饭。(报 1995 年 3 月 5 日 9 版)
lǎo bà jiào wǒ huí jiā chī fàn
old dad asked 1SG back home eat dinner
'My dad asked me home to have dinner.' (*Bào*, Mar. 5, 1995, Issue no. 9)

(5) 他 母亲 呢, 带 了 妹妹 回返 美国
tā mǔqīn ne dài le mèimèi huífǎn měiguó
3SG mom TOP bring LE sister return America

省亲。(狮子 100)
xǐngqīn
visit.relatives

'His mother brought his sister back to America to visit their relatives.' (*Shīzi* 100)

The preceding highlighted phrases can be grammatically analysed as follows.

叫 我 回家 吃饭
jiào wǒ huíjiā chīfàn

| 1 | 2 | (pivotal phrase) |
| 3 | 4 | (serial predicate phrase) |

带了 妹妹 回返美国 省亲
dàile mèimèi huífǎnměiguó xǐngqīn

| 1 | 2 | (pivotal phrase) |
| 3 | 4 | (serial predicate phrase) |

There are examples where a pivotal phrase is embedded into a serial predicate phrase.

(6) (那 鲤鱼) 冲 过来 抢 面包 吃。(风雨 6)
nà lǐyú chōng guòlái qiǎng miànbāo chī
that carp swim come snatch bread eat
'That carp swam over quickly to snatch some bread.' (*Fēngyǔ* 6)

(7) 我　　去　　叫　　她　　来！（追云 111）
　　 wǒ　 qù　 jiào　 tā　 lái
　　 1SG　go　 call　 3SG　come
　　 'I went and called her over!' (*Zhuīyún* 111)

The grammatical structures of the preceding highlighted phrases are shown here.

冲过来　　　抢　　面包　　吃
chōngguòlái　qiǎng　miànbāo　chī

```
_____
     1              2         (serial predicate phrase)
          _____  ____
            3       4         (pivotal phrase)
```

去　　叫　　她　　来
qù　 jiào tā　 lái

```
___  _____
 1       2                    (serial predicate phrase)
     ___  ___
      3    4                  (pivotal phrase)
```

Finally, let's look some examples in which pivotal phrases and serial predicate phrases are entwined with each other.

(8) 我　　要　　走　　了，赶　　着　　回　　去　　煮　　饭　　给
　　 wǒ　 yào　 zǒu　 le　 gǎn　 zhe　 huí　 qù　 zhǔ　 fàn　 gěi
　　 1SG　need　walk　LE　hurry　ZHE　back　go　cook　rice　GEI

家婆　　吃　　呢！（梦 121）
jiāpó　 chī　 ne
grandma　eat　 SFP

'I've got to go. I have to hurry back to cook for my grandma.' (*Mèng* 121)

(9) 早　　知道　　这样，　我　　宁　　死　　也　　不　　会　　三更半夜
　　 zǎo　 zhīdào　zhèyàng　wǒ　 níng　sǐ　 yě　 bù　 huì　 sāngēngbànyè
　　 early　know　 this　　 1SG　rather　die　also　NEG　will　midnight

叫　　妈妈　　买　　夜宵　　回来　　给　　我　　吃　　了。（南风 33）
jiào　 māmā　 mǎi　 yèxiāo　 huílái　 gěi　 wǒ　 chī　 le

ask   mom   buy   night.snack   back   GEI   1SG   eat   LE

'If I had known this earlier, I would rather die than ask my mother in the middle of the night to buy snacks and bring them back for me to eat.' (*Nánfēng* 33)

The highlighted part in sentence (8) has the following grammatical structure.

赶着　回去　煮　饭　给　家婆　吃
gǎnzhe　huíqù　zhǔ　fàn　gěi　jiāpó　chī

1	2	(serial predicate phrase)
3	4	5	6	(3-4, serial predicate phrase; 5-6 pivotal phrase)
7	8	(pivotal phrase)

And the highlighted part in example (9) can be grammatically analysed as follows.

叫　妈妈　买　夜宵　回来　给　我　吃
jiào　māmā　mǎi　yèxiāoi　huílái　gěi　wǒ　chī

1	2	(serial predicate phrase)
3	4	5	6	(3-4, 5-6 pivotal phrases)
7	8	(7-8 serial predicate phrase)

Note

1. For more discussions on other verbs that may or may not contain the meaning of 'give' one can refer to Yu Dongci Gei Xiangguan De Jufa Wenti 'Syntactic Problems Related to Verb Give' (Zhu Dexi 1979) or *Xiandai Hanyu Yufa Yanjiu* 'Grammatical Studies about Modern Chinese' (Zhu Dexi 1980).

10 Prepositions and Prepositional Phrases

Lu Jianming

10.1 Prepositions and Prepositional Phrases

10.1.1 Frequently Used Prepositions

Prepositions are categorised as functional words. The most frequently used prepositions in Singapore Mandarin are listed as follows:

按 *àn* 'according to'	把 *bǎ* 'BA'	被 *bèi* 'BEI'
比 *bǐ* 'than'	朝 *cháo* 'towards'	从 *cóng* 'from'
当 *dāng* 'when'	到 *dào* 'to'	对 *duì* 'towards'
给 *gěi* 'GEI'	跟 *gēn* 'along with'	和 *hé* 'with'
将 *jiāng* 'BA'	叫 *jiào* 'AM¹'	据 *jù* 'according to'
连 *lián* 'even'	令 *lìng* 'make'	凭 *píng* 'by'
让 *ràng* 'AM'	使 *shǐ* 'make'	随 *suí* 'along with'
替 *tì* 'for'	同 *tóng* 'with'	往 *wǎng* 'towards'
为 *wèi* 'for'	向 *xiàng* 'to'	以 *yǐ* 'by'
用 *yòng* 'with'	由 *yóu* 'by'	于 *yú* 'in'
与 *yǔ* 'with'	在 *zài* 'at/in'	照 *zhào* 'according to'
自 *zì* 'from'		
按照 *ànzhào* 'according to'	除（了）*chú (le)* 'except (for)'	
打从 *dǎcóng* 'from'	对于 *duìyú* 'concerning/with regard to'	
根据 *gēnjù* 'according to'	关于 *guānyú* 'about'	
随着 *suízhe* 'with'	通过 *tōngguò* 'through'	
为了 *wèile* 'in order to'	沿着 *yánzhe* 'along'	
至于 *zhìyú* 'as for'	自从 *zìcóng* 'since'	

Examples for some prepositions are listed here.[2]

(1) 按　　　　　国家　　　图书馆　　　二　　　年　　　来　　　出借　　　华文
　　 àn　　 guójiā　　 túshūguǎn　　 èr　　 nián　　 lái　　 chūjiè　　 huáwén
　　 according.to　 nation　 library　 two　 year　 since　 lent.out　 Chinese

书籍　　的　　　数字　　　看来，……　成人　　　居多。（风筝 18）
shūjí　 de　　 shùzì　　 kànlái　　　　 chéngrén　 jūduō
book　 DE　 number　 seem　　　　 adult　　　 be.in.the.majority

'According to the number of Singapore Mandarin books lent out from the National Library in the past two years, . . . most borrowers are adults.' (*Fēngzhēng* 18)

(2) 在　　 1989　 年，　　按照　　　　妇女　　 宪章　　　 离婚
　　 zài　 1989　 nián　　**ànzhào**　　 fùnǚ　　 xiànzhāng　 líhūn
　　 in　 1989　 year　 **according.to**　 woman　 charter　　 divorce

的　　有　　 4.6%。（风筝 150）
de　　yǒu　　4.6%
DE　 have　 4.6%

'In 1989, 4.6% of women got divorced according to the Women's Charter.' (*Fēngzhēng* 150)

(3) 有些　　 司机　　 把　　 车子　　 开　　　 得　　 太　　 快，　 是　　 很
　　 yǒuxiē　 sījī　　 **bǎ**　 chēzi　　 kāi　　 de　　 tài　　 kuài　 shì　　 hěn
　　 some　 driver　 **BA**　car　　 drive　 DE　　 too　 fast　 SHI　 very

危险的。（小学 6A 15）
wēixiǎn-de
dangerous

'It's dangerous for some drivers to drive too fast.' (*Xiǎoxué* 6A 15)

(4) 她　　 家　　 门前　　　 的　　 几　　 支　　 电线杆　　　 已
　　 tā　　 jiā　　 ménqián　　 de　　 jǐ　　 zhī　　 diànxiàngān　 yǐ
　　 3SG　 house　 gate.front　 DE　 several　 CL　 telegraph.pole　already

被　　　水　　　淹没，……（胜利 31）
bèi　 shuǐ　 yānmò

BEI   water   submerge

'Several telegraph poles in front of her house have been flooded.' (*Shènglì* 31)

(5) 他　　的　　华文　　程度　　在　　当时　　的确　　**比**
　　 tā　　de　　huáwén　chéngdù　zài　dāngshí　díquè　**bǐ**
　　 3SG　 DE　 Chinese　level　　at　　then　　indeed　**than**

　　 我　　好。（牛车水 22）
　　 wǒ　　hǎo
　　 1SG　 good

'At that time, his Singapore Mandarin was indeed better than mine.' (*Niúchēshuǐ* 22)

(6) 那个　　男　　的，　还　　不时　　　　探头探脑地　　　**朝**
　　 nàgè　 nán　 de　　hái　 bùshí　　　　tàntóutànnǎo-de　**cháo**
　　 that　 man　 DE　 even　from.time.　　stealthily　　　**towards**
　　　　　　　　　　　　　　to.time

　　 办公室　　　里　　　　望，　目光　　直射　　墙边　　　的
　　 bàngōngshì　lǐ　　　　wàng　mùguāng　zhíshè　qiángbiān　de
　　 office　　　inside　　look　sight　　 fix　　 wall.side　DE

　　 小　　　房间。（微型 40）
　　 xiǎo　　fángjiān
　　 small　 room

'That man peered into the office from time to time, with his eyes fixed on the small room at the side.' (*Wēixíng* 40)

(7) 在　　中学　　　　　及　　高中，　　　**除了**　　少数　　华文
　　 zài　 zhōngxué　　　 jí　　gāozhōng　　**chúle**　　shǎoshù　huáwén
　　 in　 middle.school　and　high.school　**except.for**　few　Chinese

　　 程度　　　好的　　学生　　　外，　　绝大多数　　　学生　　　只
　　 chéngdù　 hǎode　 xuéshēng　wài　　juédàduōshù　 xuéshēng　zhǐ
　　 level　　 good　　student　　other.than　most　　　student　　only

读	英文	书。（风筝 17）
dú	*yīngwén*	*shū*
read	English	book

'In middle school and high school, except for a few students who are good at Chinese, most students only read English books.' (*Fēngzhēng* 17)

10.1.2 Functions of Prepositions

As explained in Section 3.11, the function of a preposition is to mark the role of an item which relates to an action. For example, the preposition 把 *bǎ* 'BA' usually introduces the patient of an action, as in (8).

(8)
"爸爸，	吃	东西	啦！"	小妮子	笑	着	**把**	食盒
bàba	*chī*	*dōngxī*	*la*	*xiǎonīzi*	*xiào*	*zhe*	***bǎ***	*shíhé*
dad	eat	things	SFP	little.girl	smile	ZHE	**BA**	food.box

推	过去，	顺手	递	过	了	一	双	筷子。（金狮奖 217）
tuī	*guòqù*	*shùnshǒu*	*dì*	*guò*	*le*	*yī*	*shuāng*	*kuàizi*
push	over	by.the.way	pass	over	LE	one	CL	chopstick

'"Dad, let's eat something!" The little girl smiled as she pushed the food box over and handed over a pair of chopsticks.' (*Jīnshījiǎng* 217)

In (8), the preposition 把 *bǎ* 'BA' introduces the noun 食盒 *shíhé* 'food box', which takes the role of "patient" assigned by the verb 推 *tuī* 'push'. Different prepositions in Singapore Mandarin mark different roles of objects. For instance, the prepositions 把 *bǎ* 'BA' and 将 *jiāng* 'BA' can be regarded as the patient markers. 被 *bèi* 'BEI', 给 *gěi* 'GEI' and 让 *ràng* 'AM' can be considered as the agent markers. 用 *yòng* 'with' serves as the marker of the instruments, materials or methods employed in the action. The prepositions 向 *xiàng* 'facing', 替 *tì* 'for' and 为 *wèi* 'for' function as the recipient marker. The prepositions 在 *zài* 'at', 到 *dào* 'to', 自 *zì* 'from', 自从 *zìcóng* 'since' and 于 *yú* 'in' can be regarded as chronological and locative markers. The prepositions 和 *hé* 'and', 跟 *gēn* 'along with', 同 *tóng* 'with' and 与 *yǔ* 'with' can be considered as the companion markers.

A preposition always takes a noun phrase (NP) as its object so as to mark the role of that NP which associates with an action verb. The combination of a preposition and a NP forms a prepositional phrase (PP, with a few exceptions, see Section 10.3). As illustrated in the sentence 他把面包吃光了 *tā bǎ miànbāo chī guāng le* 'He ate up all the bread', the preposition 把 *bǎ* 'BA' is followed by the word 面包 *miànbāo* 'bread', which is the patient of the action verb 吃 *chī* 'eat'. 把 *bǎ* 'BA' and 面包 *miànbāo* 'bread' thus constitute a prepositional phrase 把面包

bǎ miànbāo. Since the component following the preposition is usually regarded as its object, PP is also occasionally called preposition-object construction.

10.1.3 *Differences Between Prepositions and Transitive Verbs*

Prepositions and transitive verbs share similarities in that both of them take objects. However, they are essentially different.

First, prepositions can neither be used independently nor act as predicates, whereas most transitive verbs can be used independently and act as predicates.

Second, transitive verbs can generally be negated by 不 *bù* 'NEG', as in 不吃 *bùchī* 'not eat', 不看 *bùkàn* 'not look', 不买 *bùmǎi* 'not buy', 不学习 *bùxuéxí* 'not study' or 不参观 *bùcānguān* 'not visit'. In contrast, prepositions cannot be modified by 不 *bù* 'NEG'. For instance, expressions such as *不把 *bùbǎ* 'not BA', *不向 *bùxiàng* 'not facing', *不对于 *bùduìyú* 'not concerning' or *不关于 *bù guānyú* 'not as to' are not acceptable in Singapore Mandarin. It is worth noting that in the sentence 不把功课做完，（不能玩。）*bù bǎ gōngkè zuòwán, bù néng wán* '(You can't play) if you don't finish the homework', 不 *bù* 'NEG' negates the whole phrase 把功课做完 *bǎ gōngkè zuòwán* 'finish the homework', but not 把 *bǎ* 'BA'. To illustrate, 不把功课做完 should be structured as in (A) rather than in (B):

A	不	把	功课	做完(√)	B	*不	把	功课	做完(×)
	bù	*bǎ*	*gōngkè*	*zuòwán*		*bù*	*bǎ*	*gōngkè*	*zuòwán*
	NEG	BA	homework	finish		NEG	BA	homework	finish

Third, the object of a transitive verb can be omitted in context, as in (9) and (10).

(9) "喝酒　　　　吗？"
　　hējiǔ　　　　*ma*
　　drink.alcohol　SFP
　　'Have a drink?'

　　"喝。"（金狮奖 244）
　　hē
　　drink
　　'Sure.' (*Jīnshījiǎng* 244)

(10) "勤丽，　平时　　在　　家，　谁　　煮　　晚餐？"
　　 qínlì　　*píngshí*　*zài*　*jiā*　　*shuí*　*zhǔ*　*wǎncān*
　　 Qinli　　usually　　at　　home　who　　cook　dinner
　　'Qinli, who usually cooks dinner at home?'

"我   煮。"（跳舞 84）
wǒ   zhǔ
1SG   cook
'Me.' (*Tiàowǔ* 84)

The transitive verb 喝 *hē* 'drink' is followed by the object 酒 *jiǔ* 'alcohol' in the interrogative sentence in (48), but not in the answer. Similarly, in (49), the transitive verb 煮 *zhǔ* 'cook' is followed by the object 晚餐 *wǎncān* 'dinner' in the interrogative sentence, but not in the answer, either. In contrast, prepositions such as the preposition 把 *bǎ* 'BA' aforementioned have to be followed by objects, which can't be omitted in any cases.

Fourth, predicate-object phrases formed by transitive verbs can be predicates and can be used independently as a sentence in a given context as well. For example, in a conversation, the speaker says: "你吃什么 *nǐ chī shénme* 'What do you eat?'" Then the listener replies: "吃饼干 *chī bǐnggān* '(I) eat biscuits'". Here the predicate-object phrase 吃什么 *chī shénme* 'eat what' serves as the predicate in the interrogative sentence and 吃饼干 *chī bǐnggān* 'eat biscuits' is independently used as a response sentence. More examples are as follows:

(11) "爸，   我   考到,   了   四   优   二   良，
     bà   wǒ   kǎodào   le   sì   yōu   èr   liáng
     dad   1SG   score   LE   four A   two   B

可以   念大学   了。"
kěyǐ   niàndàxué   le
can   go.to.college   LE
'Dad, I got four A's and two B's, which means I can go to college.'

"念 大学？   唉……"   岂知   爸   却   皱   了   皱
niàn dàxué   **ài**   qǐzhī   bà   què   zhòu   le   zhòu
go.to college **alas** who.knows   dad   but   frown LE   frown

眉   慨叹   道。（短篇 4）
méi   kǎitàn   dào
eyebrow sigh   say
'"College? Alas . . ." Unexpectedly, Dad frowned and sighed.' (*Duǎnpiān* 4)

(12) "开   过   枪？"
     kāi   guò   qiāng

	fire	GUO	gun			

"(Have you) fired a gun before?"

" 开	过	一	两	发	子弹。"（浮萍 171）
kāi	guò	yī	liǎng	fā	zǐdàn
fire	GUO	one	two	CL	bullet

'(I've) shot a couple of bullets.' (*Fúpíng* 171)

(13)
啊,	演	叠罗汉！	他	傻兮兮地	对	自己	微笑。（狮子 25）
ā	yǎn	diéluóhàn	tā	shǎxīxī-de	duì	zìjǐ	wēixiào
Ah	play	pyramid	3SG	foolishly	to	oneself	smile

'Ah! (We'll) play the human pyramid! He smiles to himself foolishly.' (*Shīzi* 25)

In these three examples, the predicate-object phrases 念大学 *niàn dàxué* 'go to college', 开过枪 *kāi guò qiāng* 'have opened fire', 开过一两发子弹 *kāi guò yīliǎng fā zǐdàn* 'have fired a couple of bullets' and 演叠罗汉 *yǎn diéluóhàn* 'play the human pyramid' are all used as separate sentences. In contrast to predicate-object phrases, prepositional phrases cannot be used as predicates nor independent sentences even in conversation. Take 把 *bǎ* 'BA' as an example, there are no such sentences like *我把书 *Wǒ bǎ shū* 'I take the book' or *把书 *bǎshū* 'take the book' in Singapore Mandarin. On the contrary, prepositional structures can act as adverbials in sentences (see 10.1.4), whereas predicate-object phrases cannot.

10.1.4 *Grammatical Functions of Prepositional Phrases*

1 The main grammatical function of prepositional phrases in sentences is to act as adverbials, as illustrated in Section 10.1.1. More examples are as follows:

(14)
他	的	华文	程度	在	当时	的确
tā	de	huáwén	chéngdù	zài	dāngshí	díquè
3SG	DE	Chinese	level	at	that.time	indeed

比	我	好。（牛车水 22）
bǐ	wǒ	hǎo
than	1SG	good

'His Singapore Mandarin was indeed better than mine at that time.' (*Niúchēshuǐ* 22)

(15) 中午   猛烈的   阳光，   从   窗口   挤   了   进来，
    zhōngwǔ měngliè-de yángguāng cóng   chuāngkǒu jǐ   le   jìnlái
    noon   fiery   sunlight   from   window   squeeze LE   in

    泼辣地   撒满   一地，   把   个   长方形的
    pōlà-de   sāmǎn   yīdì   bǎ   gè   chángfāngxíng-de
    wantonly   spread.full everywhere BA   CL   rectangular

    厅   转化   成   热不可当的   小   烘炉。(跳舞 21)
    tīng   zhuǎnhuà   chéng   rèbùkědāng-de   xiǎo   hōnglú
    hall   change   become   scorching   small   oven

    'The burning sunlight shone through the window and spread on the ground at noon, making the rectangular hall a little scorching oven.' (*Tiàowǔ* 21)

(16) 那个   第六   届   学生会   理事，
    nàge   dìliù   jiè   xuéshēnghuì   lǐshì
    that   sixth   period   student.union   council.member

    向   我   细数   当年   筹备   庆祝
    xiàng   wǒ   xìshù   dāngnián   chóubèi   qìngzhù
    to   1SG   introduce.in.detail that.year   prepare   celebrate

    中秋   的   事情。（回忆 37）
    zhōngqiū   de   shìqíng
    Mid-Autumn.Day DE   thing

    'The council member for the sixth Student Union introduced to me in detail the preparation work for the Mid-Autumn Day celebration that year.' (*Huíyì* 37)

There are two prepositional phrases in (14): 在当时 *zài dāngshí* 'at that time' serves as the adverbial of 的确比我好 *díquè bǐ wǒ hǎo* 'better than me indeed'; 比我 *bǐwǒ* 'than me' serves as the adverbial of 好 *hǎo* 'better'. Similarly, in (15), 从窗口 *cóng chuāngkǒu* 'from the window' functions as the adverbial of 挤了进来 *jǐlejìnlái* 'squeeze into', and 把个长方形的厅 *bǎ gè chángfāngxíngde tīng* 'make the rectangular hall' functions as the adverbial of 转化成热不可当的小烘炉 *zhuǎnhuà chéng rèbùkědāngde xiǎo hōnglú* 'turn into a scorching oven'. In (16), the prepositional phrase 向我 *xiàngwǒ* 'to me' takes the role of adverbial for 细数当年筹备庆祝中秋的事情 *xì shù dāngnián chóubèi qìngzhù zhōngqiū de shìqíng* 'introduce in detail the preparation work for the Mid-Autumn Day celebration that year'. The hierarchical structure of example (14) is illustrated here.

```
他的华文程度         在    当时      的确      比    我    好
tāde huáwén chéngdù  zài  dāngshí  díquè    bǐ   wǒ   hǎo
─────────────────    ────────────────────────────────────     (subject-predicate phrase)
        1                              2
                     ──────────────    ──────────────────     (adverbial-head phrase)
                             3                  4
                     ───  ───   ───    ─────    ─────         (5-6 prepositional phrase,
                      5    6    7       8                      7-8 adverbial-head phrase)
                                        ─────    ─────        (adverbial-head phrase)
                                          9       10
                                        ───      ───          (prepositional phrase)
                                         11       12
```

2 Prepositional structures formed with a handful of prepositions like 在 *zài* 'at', 到 *dào* 'to', 自 *zì* 'from', 向 *xiàng* 'to' and 于 *yú* 'in' can also act as complements (see Section 7.7), as shown in the following examples:

(17) 我们   总   不   能   一直   站   **在**   **这里**。（想飞 63）
     wǒmen   zǒng   bù   néng   yīzhí   zhàn   zài   zhèlǐ
     1PL   always   NEG   can   always   stand   at   here

   'We cannot always stand here.' (*Xiǎngfēi* 63)

(18) 这时,   有   一   个   瘦子   出现   了,
     zhèshí   yǒu   yī   gè   shòuzi   chūxiàn   le
     at.this.time have   one   CL   a.lean.person   appear   LE

     双手   直直地   伸   **到**   我   面前   来，......（石头 1）
     shuāngshǒu   zhízhí-de   shēn   dào   wǒ   miànqián   lái
     both.hands   straight   stretch to   1SG   front   come

   'At that time, a lean person appeared and stretched out both his hands straight towards me . . .' (*Shítou* 1)

(19) 医院   设备   良好   的   大   讲堂   里,   密密地
     yīyuàn   shèbèi   liánghǎo   de   dà   jiǎngtáng   lǐ   mìmì-de
     hospital equipment   good   DE   big   lecture.hall   in   densely

     坐   满   了   来   **自**   他   国   的   游客。（Δ天长 24）
     zuò   mǎn   le   lái   zì   tā   guó   de   yóukè
     sit   full   LE   come   from   3SG   country   DE   tourist

'The hospital's big well-equipped lecture hall was full of tourists from other countries.' (Δ*Tiānzhǎng* 24)

(20) 这   条   水沟   宽   二十   呎,...... 也   不   知   流
    zhè tiáo shuǐgōu kuān èrshí   chǐ   yě   bù   zhī   liú
    this CL   gutter   wide twenty inch   also NEG know flow

向   何方。（壁虎 61）
xiàng héfāng
to   where

'We don't know where this twenty-inch-wide gutter flows to.' (*Bìhǔ* 61)

(21) 流冰   一九一四   年   出生   于   新加坡,......（Δ新华
                                                              文学 61）
    liúbīng yījiǔyīsì   nián   chūshēng   yú   xīnjiāpō
    Liubing 1914   year   be.born   in   Singapore

'Liubing was born in 1914 in Singapore.' (Δ*Xīnhuáwénxué* 61)

3   Some prepositional phrases with prepositions such as 对 *duì* 'concerning' and 关于 *guānyú* 'about' can act as modifiers after being followed by 的 *de* 'DE', for example:

(22) 对   事物   的   看法（风筝 34）
    duì   shìwù   de   kànfǎ
    concerning   thing   DE   opinion

'opinions about things' (*Fēngzhēng* 34)

(23) 关于   华文   教学   的   几   个   问题（风筝 54）
    guānyú   huáwén   jiàoxué   de   jǐ   gè   wèntí
    concerning   Chinese   teaching   DE   several CL   question

'several questions about teaching' (*Fēngzhēng* 54)

10.1.5 Origins of Prepositions

Most prepositions in modern Singapore Mandarin are grammaticalised from verbs. Some of them are completely grammaticalised and have lost their meanings and usage as verbs. For example, the word 被 *bèi* 'BEI' has evolved from a verb meaning "to cover or to suffer" in ancient Chinese to a preposition in modern Singapore Mandarin. In some cases, although the verbal usages still exist, their meanings as a verb are quite different from that as a preposition and there is no connection between them. A typical example in modern Singapore Mandarin is 把 *bǎ*. Its verbal usage means "to control or to guard", as in 船长把舵 *chuánzhǎng bǎduò* 'The captain controls the rudder' and 他把着大门 *tā bǎ zhe dàmén* 'He guarded the gate'. But when 把 *bǎ* it is used as a preposition only the functional meaning remains, marking the object(s) of the action verb following it. There are also a few prepositions (such as 比 *bǐ* 'than', 朝 *cháo* 'towards', 到 *dào* 'to', 替 *tì* 'for', 用 *yòng* 'with', 在 *zài* 'at', etc.) still being used as both verbs and prepositions, without much differences in meaning. Consider the following example pairs.

(24) a 你们 两 个 不妨 比 一 比 （verb）
      nǐmen *liǎng* *gè* *bùfáng* **bǐ** *yī* **bǐ**
      2PL two CL might.as.well **compare** one **compare**
      'You two may compare.'

    b 他 画 得 比 我 好 (preposition)
      tā *huà* *de* **bǐ** *wǒ* *hǎo*
      3SG draw DE **than** 1SG good
      'He draws better than I do.'

(25) a 这 间 屋子 朝 南 （verb）
      zhè *jiān* *wūzi* **cháo** *nán*
      this CL house **face** south
      'This room faces south.'

    b 他 朝 门 外 望 了 望(preposition)
      tā **cháo** *mén* *wài* *wàng* *le* *wàng*
      3SG **towards** door outside look LE look
      'He looked out of the door.'

(26) a 火车 到 北京 了 （verb）
      huǒchē **dào** *běijīng* *le*
      train **arrive** Beijing LE
      'The train arrived in Beijing.'

    b 我 明天 到 北京 开 会 去(preposition)
      wǒ *míngtiān* **dào** *běijīng* *kāi* *huì* *qù*
      1SG tomorrow **to** Beijing attend meeting go

'I will go to Beijing to attend the meeting.'

(27) a | 下午 | 我 | 来 | 替 | 你（verb）
     | xiàwǔ | wǒ | lái | **tì** | nǐ
     | afternoon | 1SG | come | **replace** | 2SG

'I will cover for you in the afternoon.'

b | 你 | 替 | 我 | 看 | 看 | 孩子(preposition)
  | nǐ | **tì** | wǒ | kān | kan | háizi
  | 2SG | **for** | 1SG | look | look | child

'Take care of the child for me.'

Then a question that arises is how to tell whether the word is a verb or a preposition. The answer is based on the following two criteria:

Criterion I. It is a verb if it is not followed by an object. For example:

(28) | 我们 | 比 | 一 | 比
     | wǒmen | **bǐ** | yī | **bǐ**
     | 1PL | **compare** | one | **compare**

'Let's compare.'

(29) | 我 | 是 | 昨天 | 到 | 的
     | wǒ | shì | zuótiān | **dào** | de
     | 1SG | SHI | yesterday | **arrive** | DE

'I arrived yesterday.'

(30) | 电脑 | 我 | 还 | 不 | 会 | 用
     | diànnǎo | wǒ | hái | bú | huì | **yòng**
     | computer | 1SG | still | NEG | can | **use**

'I don't know how to use a computer yet.'

(31) | 老师 | 不 | 在 | 的 | 时候 | 他们 | 就 | 讲话
     | lǎoshī | bú | **zài** | de | shíhou | tāmen | jiù | jiǎnghuà
     | teacher | NEG | **be** | DE | time | 3PL | then | talk

'They talk when the teacher is not there.'

Prepositions and Prepositional Phrases 413

In the preceding examples, 比 *bǐ* 'compare', 到 *dào* 'arrive', 用 *yòng* 'use' and 在 *zài* 'be' are all used without objects, so they are all verbs.

Criterion II. If it takes an object, whether it is a verb or prepostion depends on its position in the sentence. It is a preposition if it occurs at the adverbial or complement position. Otherwise, it is a verb. Taking 在 *zài* 'at/be' as an example, it is used as a preposition in (32) and (33), while as a verb in (34) to (37).

(32) 我　　在　　书店　　买　　了　　本　　字典（做状语）
　　　wǒ　　zài　　shūdiàn　mǎi　le　　běn　　zìdiǎn
　　　1SG　 at　　bookstore buy　LE　 CL　　 dictionary
　　　'I bought a dictionary at the bookstore.' (*zài* PP as a adverbial)

(33) 别　　睡　　在　　地上（做补语）
　　　bié　　shuì　zài　　dìshàng
　　　NEG　sleep　at　　 floor
　　　'Don't sleep on the floor.' (*zài* PP as complement)

(34) 妈妈　　在　　外婆　　家（做谓语）
　　　māma　zài　　wàipó　　jiā
　　　mum　 be　　Grandma　home
　　　'Mum is at Grandma's.' (*zài* VP as a predicate)

(35) 在　　学校　　的　　老师　　都　　看　　她　　来　　了（带上"的"做定语）
　　　zài　 xuéxiào　de　　lǎoshī　dōu　 kàn　　tā　　lái　　le
　　　be　 school　　DE　 teacher　all　　visit　3SG　 come　LE
　　　'The teachers at school all come to visit her.' (*zài* VP with 的 *de* 'DE' as attribute)

(36) 在　　家　　靠　　父母（做主语）
　　　zài　　jiā　　kào　　fùmǔ
　　　be　　home　rely.on parents
　　　'When being at home, we rely on our parents.' (*zài* VP as a subject)

(37) 你　　的　　笔　　不　　在　　抽屉　　里（带上"不"做谓语）
　　　nǐ　　de　　bǐ　　bú　　zài　　chōutì　　lǐ
　　　2SG　DE　 pen　 NEG　be　　drawer　　in

'Your pen is not in the drawer.' (*zài* VP VP as a predicate being negated by the adverbial 不 *bù* 'NEG')

Consider the following special example.

(38) 我们 都 知道 用 条播 来 种植 小麦
wǒmen dōu zhīdào yòng tiáobō lái zhòngzhí xiǎomài
1PL all know with strip.sow come plant wheat

很 理想, 可是, 条播 需要 用 新式的 条播机,
hěn lǐxiǎng kěshì tiáobō xūyào yòng xīnshì-de tiáobōjī
very ideal but strip.sow need use new-style strip.planter

我们 国家 穷, 哪里 买 得 起 这些
wǒmen guójiā qióng nǎlǐ mǎi dé qǐ zhèxiē
1PL country poor where buy DE up these

新式的 机械 呢！（跳舞 15）
xīnshì-de jīxiè ne
new-style machine SFP

'We all know that strip sowing is ideal for growing wheat, but it requires a new-style strip sowing machine. Our country is poor, so how can we afford such new-style machines?' (*Tiàowǔ* 15)

In (38), 用 *yòng* appears twice, both being followed by an object. The phrase 用条播 *yòng tiáo bō* 'sowing with strips' functions as an adverbial in the sentence, while 用新式的条播机 *yòng xīnshìde tiáobōjī* 'use the new-style strip planter' serves as the object of 需要 *xūyào* 'need'. Based on the criteria previously mentioned, the former 用 *yòng* is a preposition and the latter is a verb.

Some commonly used or representative prepositions will be discussed in the following sections.

10.2 把 bǎ 'BA' and 将 jiāng 'BA'

10.2.1 把 *bǎ* 'BA' and BA Construction

把 *bǎ* 'BA' is a commonly used preposition. 把 *bǎ* 'BA' prepositional phrase can only be used as an adverbial. The most common construction is shown here.

(subject) + (adverbial) + 把 *bǎ* 'BA' + object + verb phrase

Prepositions and Prepositional Phrases 415

This construction can sometimes be simplified into "(X) + 把 *bǎ* 'BA' + Y + action", in which X stands for the subject, and the bracket indicates that the subject can appear overtly or covertly. Such constructions are usually called BA constructions. In addition, the adverbial is also optional, marked in brackets, too. Consider the following examples.

(1) 他　　今天　　晚上　　就　　**把**　　她　　带　　过　　来
　　 tā　 *jīntiān*　*wǎnshàng*　*jiù*　　***bǎ***　*tā*　*dài*　*guò*　*lái*
　　 3SG　today　　evening　　then　　**BA**　3SG　take　GUO　come

我们　　家　　了。（大胡子 25）
wǒmen　*jiā*　*le*
1PL　　home　LE

'He's bringing her over to our home this evening.' (*Dàhúzi* 25)

(2) 他　　**把**　　目光　　调　　　向　　　别　　处。（跳舞 19）
　　 tā　 ***bǎ***　*mùguāng*　*tiáo*　*xiàng*　*bié*　*chù*
　　 3SG　**BA**　sight　　　turn　　towards　other　place

'He turned his gaze elsewhere.' (*Tiàowǔ* 19)

(3) 别　　**把**　　钥匙　　给　　丢　　了！（再见 28）
　　 bié　***bǎ***　*yàoshi*　*gěi*　*diū*　*le*
　　 NEG　**BA**　key　　　GEI　lose　LE

'Don't lose your keys!' (*Zàijiàn* 28)

(4) **把**　　心　　中　　　的　　哀痛　　都　　宣泄　　出来　　吧！（回忆 18）
　　 bǎ　*xīn*　*zhōng*　*de*　*āitòng*　*dōu*　*xuānxiè*　*chūlái*　*ba*
　　 BA　heart　inside　　DE　grief　　all　　abreact　out.come　SFP

'Let out all the grief in your heart!' (*Huíyì* 18)

In (1), both a subject and an adverbial precedes 把 *bǎ* 'BA'; in (2), only a subject precedes 把 *bǎ* 'BA'. In (3), only an adverbial appears ahead of 把 *bǎ* 'BA'; in (4), neither a subject nor an adverbial precedes 把 *bǎ* 'BA'.

Semantically, BA construction is used to express the "disposition" of people or things. In (1), 带过来我们家 *dài guòlái women jiā* 'bring over to our home' is about how he treated 她 *tā* '3SG'. In (2), 调向别处 *tiáo xiàng biéchù* 'turn to other place' describes what he did to his 目光 *mùguāng* 'sight'. In (3), 给丢了 *diū* 'lost' can be seen as the disposition of 钥匙 *yàoshi* 'the key'. In (4), 宣泄出

来 *xuānxiè chūlái* 'let out' expresses how the listener may deal with 心中的哀痛 *xīnzhōng de āitòng* 'the grief in (your) heart'. The "disposition" can be understood as causing certain changes to someone or something or making them in a certain state by active acts or some influences.

BA construction has a number of distinctive grammatical features in the grammar of Singapore Mandarin. The following section starts with discussion about the verb phrases in BA construction first.

10.2.2 Verb Phrase in BA Construction

The following three points need to be noted concerning the verb phrases in BA construction.

1. The verb phrase in BA construction cannot be a single verb. A complex verb phrase is required instead. For instance,

*	（你	/我	/他）	把	鞋	扔
	nǐ	*wǒ*	*tā*	*bǎ*	*xié*	*rēng*
	2SG	1SG	3SG	BA	shoe	throw

'(You/I/he) throw(s) the shoes away.'

The preceding sentence is ungrammatical in any context because the 'verb phrase' 扔 *rēng* 'throw' is a single verb. However, it will become grammatical if more elements are attached to the single verb 扔 *rēng* 'throw', as shown in the following examples.

他	把	鞋	扔	了
tā	*bǎ*	*xié*	*rēng*	*le*
3SG	BA	shoe	throw	LE

'He threw the shoes away.'

你	把	鞋	扔	垃圾桶	里
nǐ	*bǎ*	*xié*	*rēng*	*lājītǒng*	*lǐ*
2SG	BA	shoe	throw	trash.bin	inside

'You throw the shoes into the trash bin.'

我	把	鞋	扔	掉	了
wǒ	*bǎ*	*xié*	*rēng*	*diào*	*le*
1SG	BA	shoe	throw	drop	LE

'I threw the shoes away.'

你	把	鞋	**扔**	**过来**
nǐ	bǎ	xié	**rēng**	**guòlái**
2SG	BA	shoe	throw	pass-come

'You throw the shoes over.'

The verb phrases in BA construction may come in the following forms.

A The verb is followed by a complement, which is the most commonly used. For example:

(5) 衣服 干 了，我 必须 一件件 把 它 **折 好**。（回忆 5）

yīfu	gān	le	wǒ	bìxū	yījiànjiàn	bǎ	tā	**zhé**	**hǎo**
clothes	dry	LE	1SG	must	one.by.one	BA	3SG	fold	well

'When the clothes are dry, I must fold them one by one.' (*Huíyì* 5)

(6) 好 一会 才 把 窗帘布 **拆 下**。（金狮奖 277）

hǎo	yīhuì	cái	bǎ	chuāngliánbù	**chāi**	**xià**
quite	a.while	then	BA	curtain	get	down

'It took me quite a while to remove the curtain.' (*Jīnshījiǎng* 277)

(7) 有些 司机 把 车子 **开 得 太 快**，是 很

yǒuxiē	sījī	bǎ	chēzi	**kāi**	**de**	**tài**	**kuài**	shì	hěn
some	driver	BA	car	drive	DE	too	fast	SHI	very

危险的。（小学 6A 15）

wēixiǎn-de

dangerous

'It is dangerous for some drivers to drive their cars too fast.' (*Xiǎoxué* 6A 15)

(8) 今年 我 和 家人 一起 大 扫除，

jīnnián	wǒ	hé	jiārén	yīqǐ	dà	sǎochú
this.year	1SG	and	family	together	big	clean

把 家里 **收拾 得 整整齐齐、干干净净**。（课本 1 A 18）

bǎ	jiālǐ	**shōushí**	**de**	**zhěngzhěngqíqí**	**gāngānjìngjìng**
BA	home	arrange	DE	neat	clean

'This year, my family and I did a thorough clean, making the house neat and clean.' (*Kèběn* 1A 18)

(9) 听说   他   曾经   把   "大伯公"   的   香炉
    tīngshuō tā   céngjīng   bǎ   dàbógōng   de   xiānglú
    hear   3SG   once   BA   great.grandpa DE incense.burner

    倒个干净,   拿   来   养   一   只   蝌蚪。（胜利36）
    dào-gè-gānjìng   ná   lái   yǎng   yī   zhī   kēdǒu
    empty.completely   take come   raise one CL   tadpole

'I heard that he once emptied his "great grandpa's" incense burner and raised a tadpole in it.' (*Shènglì* 36)

(10) 我   把   文件夹   放   在   桌案   上。（回忆26）
     wǒ   bǎ   wénjiànjiá fàng   zài   zhuōàn   shàng
     1SG BA   folder   put   at   desk   on

'I put the folder on the desk.' (*Huíyì* 26)

In the preceding examples, the verb is followed by a resultative complement in (5), by a directional complement in (6), a state complement in (7) to (9) and a temporal and locative complement in (10).

B   The verb is followed by an object. For example:

(11) 记   不   记得   你   以前   曾经   把
     jì   bú   jìdé   nǐ   yǐqián   céngjīng bǎ
     remember NEG   remember   2SG in.the.past once   BA

     婚姻   比作   "框子"?   （大胡子116）
     hūnyīn   bǐzuò   kuāngzi
     marriage compare.to   frame

'Do you remember that you used to compare marriage to a "frame"?' (*Dàhúzi* 116)

(12) 进   门   后,   阿妈   帮   我   把   行李   搬
     jìn   mén   hòu   āmā   bāng   wǒ   bǎ   xínglǐ   bān
     enter door after mum   help   1SG BA   luggage   move

进   房子。 （微型 13）
jìn   *fángzi*
enter house

'After I entered, mum helped me carry my luggage into the house.' (*Wēixíng* 13)

(13) 太阳   吐   出   一   粒   大   火球，   把   整   条   街
tàiyáng *tǔ*   *chū* *yī* *lì* *dà* *huǒqiú* *bǎ* *zhěng* *tiáo* *jiē*
sun   spit   out   one   CL   big   fire.ball BA   whole   CL   street

烘   成   一   条   面包。 （八方 22）
hōng *chéng*   *yī* *tiáo* *miànbāo*
bake   become   one   CL   bread

'The sun spat out a big ball of fire and baked the whole street into a loaf of bread.' (*Bāfāng* 22)

C   The verb is followed by the auxiliary 了 *le* 'LE' or 着 *zhe* 'ZHE' as shown here:

(14) 我   把   钢琴   卖   了。
wǒ   *bǎ*   *gāngqín* *mài*   *le*
1SG   BA   piano   sell   LE

'I sold the piano.'

(15) 她   把   鞋子   脱   了。 （跳舞 20）
tā   *bǎ*   *xiézi*   *tuō*   *le*
3SG   BA   shoe   take.off LE

'She took her shoes off.' (*Tiàowǔ* 20)

(16) 他们   家   成天   把   大门   开   着。
tāmen   *jiā*   *chéngtiān*   *bǎ*   *dàmén*   *kāi*   *zhe*
3PL   house all.day.long BA   gate   open   ZHE

'They leave the front door of their house open all day long.'

D   The verb phrase is a complex predicate phrase as illustrated here:

(17) 我   好   不   好   把   这个   秘密   讲   给   爹地
wǒ   *hǎo*   *bù* *hǎo*   *bǎ*   *zhègè* *mìmì* *jiǎng* *gěi*   *diēdì*
1SG   good   NEG good   BA   this   secret   tell   give   daddy

听？（微型 25）
tīng
listen

'Shall I tell this secret to Daddy?' (*Wēixíng* 25)

(18) 他们...... 把 孩子 送 到 国外 深造。（回忆 71）
tāmen bǎ háizi sòng dào guówài shēnzào
3PL BA child send to overseas further study

'They ... sent their children abroad for further education.' (*Huíyì* 71)

(19) 关上 门 以后， 杨仲钦 捻亮 了 灯，
guānshàng mén yǐhòu yángzhòngqīn niǎnliàng le dēng
close door after Yang.Zhongqin turn.on LE lamp

把 裤子 **摊开** 来 看。（跳舞 4）
bǎ kùzi **tānkāi** lái kàn
BA pants **spread.out** come look

'After closing the door, Yang Zhongqin turned the light on and spread out his trousers for a look.' (*Tiàowǔ* 4)

E The verb phrase contains verb reduplications. This is frequently seen in imperative sentences and often in colloquial expressions. For example:

(20) 有 时间 的话， 你 把 玻璃 窗 **擦擦**。
yǒu shíjiān dehuà nǐ bǎ bōli chuāng **cā-cā**
have time if 2SG BA glass window **wipe-wipe**

'If you have time, please give the glass windows a wipe.'

(21) 这 屋子 够 乱的，
zhè wūzi gòu luàn-de
this house enough messy

我们 是 不 是 先 把 屋子 **收拾 收拾**
wǒmen shì bú shì xiān bǎ wūzi **shōushi-shōushi**
1PL be NEG be firstly BA house **tidy.up-tidy.up**

'This house is really messy. Shall we tidy it up first?'

It is important to note that although grammatically speaking, there must be some elements following the verb in BA construction as has been discussed earlier; it doesn't matter much whether there is an adverbial preceding the verb or not, as shown by the following examples.

(22) 那个   男人   昨天   把   我   课余   工作   赚来
     nàge   nánrén   zuótiān   bǎ   wǒ   kèyú   gōngzuò   zuànlái
     that   man   yesterday BA   1SG   after.school work   earn

    的   钱   全都   硬硬地   拿   走   了。（跳舞 103）
    de   qián   quándōu   yìngyìng-de   ná   zǒu   le
    DE   money   all   forcibly   take   go   LE

    'Yesterday, that man forcibly took away all the money I earned from my after-school job.' (Tiàowǔ 103)

(23) 别   把   钥匙   给   丢   了。（再见 28）
     bié   bǎ   yàoshí   gěi   diū   le
     NEG   BA   key   GEI   lose   LE

    'Don't lose your keys.' (Zàijiàn 28)

(24) 他   把   濡湿的   唇   重重的、   紧紧的   压
     tā   bǎ   rúshī-de   chún   zhòngzhòng-de   jǐnjǐn-de   yā
     3SG   BA   moist   lip   heavily   tightly   press

    在   她   纤巧的   嘴   上。（跳舞 26）
    zài   tā   xiānqiǎo-de   zuǐ   shàng
    at   3SG   delicate   mouth   on

    'He pressed his moist lips heavily and firmly against her delicate mouth.' (Tiàowǔ 26)

In (22), the sentence remains grammatical if the adverbials 全都 quándōu 'all' and 硬硬地 yìngyìngde 'forcibly' preceding the verb 拿 ná 'take' are omitted. In contrast, the sentence is ungrammatical if the elements 走了 zǒu le 'away' following the verb is omitted. Similarly, (23) is grammatical with the word 给 gěi 'GEI' omitted, but ungrammatical with the omission of 了 le 'LE'. The same goes for sentence (24), in which the adverbials 重重的、紧紧的 zhòngzhòngde jǐnjǐnde 'heavily and tightly' is omittable while the complement 在她纤巧的嘴上 zàitā xiānqiǎode zuǐshàng 'on her delicate mouth' following the verb 压 yā 'press' can never be omitted.

In Chinese Mandarin, the verb phrase in BA constructions can be in the form of "一 *yī* 'one' + Verb"³ as shown in the following sentences:

(25) 他　　把　　大腿　　一　　**拍**，　　就　　站起身　　走　　了。
　　　tā　　*bǎ*　　*dàtuǐ*　　*yī*　　***pāi***，　　*jiù*　　*zhànqǐshēn*　　*zǒu*　　*le*
　　　3SG　　BA　　lap　　one　　slap　　then　　stand.up　　leave　　LE
　　　'He slapped at his thighs and stood up to leave.'

(26) 他　　把　　油门　　一　　**踩**，　　车子　　就　　飞
　　　tā　　*bǎ*　　*yóumén*　　*yī*　　***cǎi***，　　*chēzi*　　*jiù*　　*fēi*
　　　3SG　　BA　　accelerator　　one　　step　　car　　then　　fly

　　　也似的　　奔驰　　而　　去。
　　　yě-shì-de　　*bēnchí*　　*ér*　　*qù*
　　　seemingly　　run　　LIG　　go
　　　'As soon as he stepped on the accelerator, the car raced away.'

Such cases are not found in the written corpus of Singapore Mandarin we collected, but there are a few cases in the spoken genre. For example:

(27) 当时，　　他　　把　　大腿　　一　　**拍**，　　站起身　　就　　走　　了。
　　　dāngshí　　*tā*　　*bǎ*　　*dàtuǐ*　　*yī*　　***pāi***，　　*zhànqǐshēn*　　*jiù*　　*zǒu*　　*le*
　　　then　　3SG　　BA　　lap　　one　　slap　　stand.up　　then　　leave　　LE
　　　'At that time, he slapped his thighs and stood up to leave.'

(28) 他　　把　　油门　　一　　**踩**，
　　　tā　　*bǎ*　　*yóumén*　　*yī*　　***cǎi***，
　　　3SG　　BA　　accelerator　　one　　step

　　　车子　　就　　飞快地　　向　　前　　冲　　去
　　　chēzi　　*jiù*　　*fēikuài-de*　　*xiàng*　　*qián*　　*chōng*　　*qù*
　　　car　　then　　fastly　　toward　　front　　rush　　go
　　　'As soon as he stepped on the accelerator, the car immediately raced forward.'

2　Only a limited number of verbs can appear adjacent to the word 把 *bǎ* 'BA' in BA constructions. Generally speaking, they are mostly transitive verbs indicating actions, like the ones listed here:

吃 *chī* 'eat'　　打 *dǎ* 'beat'　　洗 *xǐ* 'wash'　　看 *kàn* 'look'
说 *shuō* 'say'　　卖 *mài* 'sell'　　写 *xiě* 'write'　　收拾 *shōushi* 'tidy up'
修理 *xiūlǐ* 'repair'　　解释 *jiěshì* 'explain'　　安排 *ānpái* 'arrange'

On the contrary, intransitive verbs as listed next cannot be used in a BA construction.

游泳 *yóuyǒng* 'swim'　　合作 *hézuò* 'cooperate'　　让步 *ràngbù* 'give in'
出发 *chūfā* 'depart'　　会考 *huìkǎo* 'take general exam'
锈 *xiù* 'rust'（那刀锈了 *nà dāo xiù le* 'That knife rusted.'）
谢 *xiè* 'wither'（花谢了 *huā xiè le* 'The flower withered.'）

Other transitive verbs, as listed next, cannot be used in BA constructions either, because they do not denote concrete actions.
Existential verb or copula verbs:

有 *yǒu* 'have'　　在 *zài* 'be'　　存在 *cúnzài* 'exist'
是 *shì* 'be'　　成为 *chéngwéi* 'become'　　好像 *hǎoxiàng* 'seem'

Psychological verbs:

感觉 *gǎnjué* 'feel'　　同意 *tóngyì* 'agree'　　反对 *fǎnduì* 'object'
相信 *xiāngxìn* 'believe'　　知道 *zhīdào* 'know'　　以为 *yǐwéi* 'think'
谢谢 *xièxiè* 'thank'　　看见 *kànjiàn* 'see'　　听见 *tīngjiàn* 'hear'

Directional verbs:

来 *lái* 'come'　　去 *qù* 'go'
进来 *jìnlái* 'come in'　　出去 *chūqù* 'go out'.

Consider two verbs 看 *kàn* 'look' and 看见 *kànjiàn* 'see'. The verb 看 *kàn* 'look' can be used in BA constructions as in (29):

(29) 我　　把　　那些　　材料　　都　　**看**　　了。
　　 wǒ　 *bǎ*　 *nàxiē*　 *cáiliào*　 *dōu*　 **kàn**　 *le*
　　 1SG　 BA　　those　　material　 all　　**look**　 LE
　　 'I read all those materials.'

In contrast, the verb 看见 *kànjiàn* 'see' cannot be used in a BA construction. The following sentence is ungrammatical.

(30) *我   把   那些   材料   都   看见   了。
     wǒ   bǎ   nàxiē   cáiliào   dōu   **kànjiàn** le
     1SG   BA   those   material   all   **see**   LE
     Intended meaning: 'I read all those materials.'

This is because the verb 看 *kàn* 'look' is an activity verb, while 看见 *kànjiàn* 'see' is a psychological verb.

3   When modal verbs (such as 能够 *nénggòu* 'be able to', 可以 *kěyǐ* 'can', 应该 *yīnggāi* 'should', 会 *huì* 'will', 要 *yào* 'want', etc.) or negation adverbs (such as 不 *bù* 'NEG', 没有 *méiyǒu* 'NEG' and 别 *bié* 'NEG') appear in BA constructions, they can only precede but not follow the word 把 *bǎ* 'BA'. In other words, in BA constructions, the 'verb phrase' does not contain any modal verbs or negation adverbs. Examples are as follows:

(31) **不**   把   饭   吃   完，   就   不   准   开   舞会。（牛车水78）
     bù   bǎ   fàn   chī   wán   jiù   bù   zhǔn   kāi   wǔhuì
     NEG BA   meal   eat   finish   then   NEG   allow   have   ball
     'You are not allowed to go to the ball unless the meal is finished.' (*Niúchēshuǐ* 78)

(32) **别**   把   钥匙   给   丢   了。（再见28）
     bié   bǎ   yàoshí   gěi   diū   le
     NEG BA   key   GEI   lose   LE
     'Don't lose your keys.' (*Zàijiàn* 28)

(33) 我   **没**   把   米   洗   干净。（再见15）
     wǒ   **méi**   bǎ   mǐ   xǐ   gānjìng
     1SG   **NEG** BA   rice   wash   clean
     'I didn't wash the rice clean.' (*Zàijiàn* 15)

It will be grammatically wrong to rewrite sentences (31) through (33) as follows:

(31)' *把   饭   **不**   吃   完，   就   不   准   开   舞会。（牛车水78）
      bǎ   fàn   **bù**   chī   wán   jiù   bù   zhǔn   kāi   wǔhuì
      BA   meal   **NEG**   eat   finish   then   NEG   allow   have   ball
      Intended meaning: 'You are not allowed to go to the ball unless the meal is finished.' (*Niúchēshuǐ* 78)

(32)' * 把   钥匙   别   给   丢   了。（再见28）
        bǎ   yàoshí bié   gěi   diū   le
        BA   key   NEG   GEI   lose   LE

Intended meaning: 'Don't lose your keys.' (*Zàijiàn* 28)

(33)' * 我   把   米   没   洗   干净。（再见15）
       wǒ   bǎ   mǐ   méi   xǐ   gānjìng
       1SG BA   rice NEG   wash   clean

Intended meaning: 'I didn't wash the rice clean.' (*Zàijiàn* 15)

10.2.3 The Object of the Preposition 把 bǎ 'BA'

1   Two points should be made regarding the object of the preposition 把 *bǎ* 'BA'.

Firstly, the object of 把 *bǎ* 'BA' is usually definite, which means that the person or the thing that the object refers to is known to the speaker or the listener. For example:

(34) 他   把   《时代新汉语词典》   拿   走   了。
      tā   bǎ   shídài xīn hànyǔ cídiǎn   ná   zǒu   le
      3SG BA   TIMES.New.Chinese.   take   go   LE
                Dictionary

'He took *The TIMES New Chinese Dictionary* away.'

(35) 他   把   那   本   书   拿   走   了。
      tā   bǎ   nà   běn   shū   ná   zǒu   le
      3SG BA   that CL   book   take   go   LE

'He took that book away.'

(36) 他   把   你   的   书   拿   走   了。
      tā   bǎ   nǐ   de   shū   ná   zǒu   le
      3SG BA   2SG   DE   book   take   go   LE

'He took your book away.'

(37) 他   把   昨天   刚   买   的   书   拿   走   了。
      tā   bǎ   zuótiān   gāng   mǎi   de   shū   ná   zǒu   le
      3SG BA   yesterday just   buy   DE   book   take   go   LE

'He took away the book he had just bought yesterday.'

(38) 他   把   书   拿   走   了。
    tā   bǎ   shū   ná   zǒu   le
    3SG   BA   book   take go   LE
    'He took the book away.'

In (34), the object of 把 *bǎ* 'BA' is a proper noun 时代新汉语词典 *shídài xīn hànyǔ cídiǎn* '*TIMES New Chinese Dictionary*', the reference of which is definite. In examples (35) to (37), the objects, all being modified by an 'attribute-head' endocentric phrase whose function is to specify the range of reference, are thereby definite in reference too. The same is true for the object in (38). Although the object 书 *shū* 'book' is a bare noun, it also refers to a confirmed subject – the book that both the speaker and the listener know.

Given the fact that the object of 把 *bǎ* 'BA' is usually definite, it cannot be a 'numeral + classifier + noun' phrase, because the person or thing designated by such phrase is indefinite. The following two examples are unacceptable:

(39) *他   把   一   本   书   拿   走   了。
    tā   bǎ   yī   běn   shū   ná   zǒu   le
    3SG   BA   one   CL   book   take go   LE
    *Intended meaning: 'He took away a book.'

(40) *你   把   三   个   苹果   吃   了⁴。
    nǐ   bǎ   sān   gè   píngguǒ chī   le
    2SG   BA   three CL   apple   eat   LE
    *Intended meaning: 'You ate three apples.'

Second, from the perspective of semantic relations, the object of 把 *bǎ* 'BA' takes the patient role of the activity verb that follows. For example:

(41) 罗涵珊   伸   手   把   额   上   的   汗
    luóhánshān   shēn   shǒu   bǎ   é   shàng   de   hàn
    Luo.Hanshan stretch   hand   BA   forehead   on   DE   sweat

    拭   干   把   火   转   小。(跳舞 2)
    shì   gān   bǎ   huǒ   zhuǎn   xiǎo
    wipe   dry   BA   fire   turn   small

    'Luo Hanshan reached out to wipe off the sweat on her forehead and turned the fire down.' (*Tiàowǔ* 2)

(42)

衣服	干	了	我	必须	一	件	件	把	它
yīfú	gān	le	wǒ	bìxū	yī	jiàn	jiàn	bǎ	tā
clothes	dry	LE	1SG	must	one	CL	CL	BA	3SG

折	好。（回忆 5）
zhé	hǎo
fold	done

'The clothes are dry. I have to fold them one by one.' (*Huíyì* 5)

In (41), the objects of 把 *bǎ* 'BA', that is, 额上的汗 *é shàng de hàn* 'sweat on the forehead' and 火 *huǒ* 'fire', take the patient role of the verbs 拭 *shì* 'wipe' and 转 *zhuǎn* 'turn' respectively. In (42), the word 它 *tā* '3SG' (referring to the clothes mentioned earlier in the sentence), the object of 把 *bǎ* 'BA', is the patient of the verb 折 *zhé* 'fold'.

2   There is a particular type of BA construction in Chinese Mandarin: the object of 把 *bǎ* 'BA' is the agent, rather than the patient, of the action indicated by the verb that follows. For example:

(43)

别	把	犯人	跑	了。
bié	bǎ	fànrén	pǎo	le
NEG	BA	prisoner	run	LE

'Don't let the prisoner run away.'

(44)

偏偏	把	老李	病	了。
piānpiān	bǎ	lǎolǐ	bìng	le
coincidentally	BA	Lao.Li	ill	LE

'It happened that Lao Li was ill.'

Such type of BA construction is not found in our corpus of written Singapore Mandarin.

10.2.4 *The Subject of the BA Construction*

In Singapore Mandarin, the subject of the 把 *bǎ* 'BA' construction is semantically the agent of the action specified by the verb that follows. For example:

(45)

我	好不好	把	这个	秘密	讲	给	爹地
wǒ	hǎo-bù-hǎo	bǎ	zhège	mìmì	jiǎng	gěi	diēdì
1SG	ok-NEG-ok	BA	this	secret	tell	give	daddy

听？（微型25）

tīng

listen

'Is it ok for me to tell this secret to Daddy?' (*Wēixíng* 25)

(46) 有些 司机 把 车子 开 得 太 快，......（小学 6A 15）

yǒuxiē sījī bǎ chēzi kāi de tài kuài

some driver BA car drive DE too fast

'Some drivers drive too fast. . . .' (*Xiǎoxué* 6A 15)

(47) 我们 兄弟姐妹们 都 把 孩子 带 回 家

wǒmen xiōngdìjiěmèimen dōu bǎ háizi dài huí jiā

1Pl brother.and.sister all BA child take back home

来。（回忆 66）

lái

come

'We brothers and sisters all took our children home.' (*Huíyì* 66)

The subject 我 *wǒ* '1SG' in (45) is the agent of the verb 讲 *jiǎng* 'say'. The subject 有些司机 *yǒuxiē sījī* 'some drivers' in (46) is the agent of the verb 开 *kāi* 'drive'. And in (47), the subject 我们兄弟姐妹们 *wǒmenxiōngdìjiěmèimen* 'we brothers and sisters' serves as the agent of the verb 带 *dài* 'take'.

10.2.5 将 jiāng 'BA'

The meaning and usage of the preposition 将 *jiāng* 'BA' is basically the same as that of the preposition 把 *bǎ* 'BA', both of which indicate the disposal of a person or a thing. The only difference between them is that the preposition 把 *bǎ* 'BA' is used in both spoken and written language, while the preposition 将 *jiāng* 'BA' is only used in written langue. In terms of frequency of use, 将 *jiāng* 'BA' is far less used than 把 *bǎ* 'BA'. Here are some examples:

(48) 她 将 落地的 玻璃窗门 都 拉 拢

tā jiāng luòdìde bōlíchuāngmén dōu lā lǒng

3SG BA landing glass.window all pull close

来， 然后 回去 厨房。（吾土·戏剧 146）

lái ránhòu huíqù chúfáng

| | come | then | go.back | kitchen | | | |

'She closed the glass French windows and went back to the kitchen.'
(*Wútǔ*(drama) 146)

(49) 随后　　将　　新　　鱼苗　　再　　售卖　　给　　谢先生（晚上 67）

	suíhòu	jiāng	xīn	yúmiáo	zài	shòumài	gěi	xièxiānshēng
	afterwards	BA	new	fry	again	sell		give	Mr. Xie

'Afterwards, the new fry were sold to Mr. Xie.' (*Wǎnshàng* 67)

(50) 将　　全盘　　生意　　交　　给　　你　　去　　管理。（Δ断情剪 11）

jiāng	quánpán	shēngyì	jiāo	gěi	nǐ	qù	guǎnlǐ
BA	whole	business	hand.over	give	2SG	go	manage

'Leave the whole business to you.' (Δ*Duànqíngjiǎn* 11)

10.3 被 bèi 'BEI'

10.3.1 Differences Between BEI Constructions and BA Constructions

From the perspective of semantic relations, the preposition 被 *bèi* 'BEI' seems to be the counterpart of the prepostion 把 *bǎ* 'BA' with 把 *bǎ* 'BA' introducing the patient of the action and 被 *bèi* 'BEI' introducing the agent. As mentioned in the previous section, the format of the BA construction is as follows:

X + 把 *bǎ* 'BA' + Y + action

While 被 *bèi* 'BEI' construction is of the following format:

Y + 被 *bèi* 'BEI' + X + action

It is obvious that X and Y have switched their positions in the two constructions. Compare the two sentences in (1).

(1) a 妈妈　　把　　所有的　　水梅　　盆栽　　都　　丢

	māma	bǎ	suǒyǒude	shuǐméi	pénzāi	dōu	diū
	mum	BA	all	water.jasmine	bonsai	all	throw

　　　　进　　垃圾桶　　里。（跳舞 5）

	jìn	lājītǒng	lǐ
	into	rubbish.bin	in

'Mum threw all the water plum pots into the rubbish bin.' (*Tiàowǔ* 5)

b. 所有的　　水梅　　　　盆栽　　都　　**被**　　妈妈　　丢
   *suǒyǒude shuǐméi   pénzāi dōu **bèi** māma diū*
   all   water.jasmine bonsai all **BEI** mum   throw

   进   垃圾桶   里。
   jìn lājītǒng   lǐ
   into rubbish.bin in

   'Mum threw all the water jasmine pots into the rubbish bin.'

In (1a) and (1b), 妈妈 *māma* 'mum' is the agent of the verb 丢 *diū* 'throw' and 所有的水梅盆栽 *suǒyǒu de shuǐméi pénzāi* 'all water jasmine bonsai' is the patient. In the BA construction of (1a), the subject is the agent and the object of 把 *bǎ* 'BA' is the patient. In contrast, in the BEI construction of (1b), the order reverses in that the subject is the patient and the object of 被 *bèi* 'BEI' is the agent. The meanings expressed are slightly different: sentence (1a) emphasises the subjectivity by using a BA construction to describe how the subject will dispose of 'all water plum bonsai'; while sentence (1b) indicates passivity by using a BEI construction to imply what has been done to the things denoted by the subject.

Apart from the differences in surface order and semantic meaning, there are two more major differences between BEI construction and BA construction.

First, as we have seen before, the predicate in a BA construction needs to be a complex verb phrase rather than a single verb. But the BEI construction does not have such a restriction, as shown in the following examples:

(2) 她   家   附近的   几   支   电线杆   已   被
    tā   jiā   fùjìnde   jǐ   zhī   diànxiàngǎn   yǐ   bèi
    3SG home nearby   several CL   telegraph.pole already BEI

    水   **淹没**，   可见   水   有   多   深。（胜利 31）
    *shuǐ **yānmò**   kějiàn   shuǐ   yǒu   duō   shēn*
    water **flood**   can.be.seen water   have how.much   deep

    'Several telegraph poles near her house had been flooded, showing how deep the water was.' (*Shènglì* 31)

(3) 直至   尸体   发出   了   恶臭，   才   被   人   **发觉**。
（回忆 61）
    *zhízhì shītǐ   fāchū   le   èchòu   cái   bèi rén **fājué***
    until   corpse give.off LE stench   then BEI people **notice**
'The corpse was not noticed until it gave off a stench.' (*Huíyì* 61)

(4) 他   被   乱鞭   **扫打**，   却   不   知   缘由！
（狮子 10）
    *tā   bèi   luànbiān **sǎodǎ**   què   bù   zhī   yuányóu*
    3SG BEI violent.whip **beat**   but   NEG know reason
'He was violently beaten with a whip without knowing the reason!' (*Shīzi* 10)

However, only disyllabic verbs can be used this way but monosyllabic verbs cannot. The following sentences seem to be ungrammatical in Singapore Mandarin:

(5) *那   苹果   **被**   我   吃。
    *nà   píngguǒ **bèi**   wǒ   chī*
    that apple   **BEI** 1SG   eat
'Intended meaning: That apple was eaten by me.'

(6) *电线杆   已经   **被**   水   淹。
    *diànxiàngǎn yǐjīng **bèi** shuǐ yān*
    telegraph.pole already **BEI** water flood
'Intended meaning: The telegraph poles have been flooded.'

(7) *他   的   小提琴   昨天   **被**   他   卖。
    *tā   de   xiǎotíqín zuótiān **bèi** tā   mài*
    3SG DE violin   yesterday **BEI** 3SG sell
Intended meaning: 'His violin was sold by him yesterday.'

Second, the object of 把 *bǎ* 'BA' can never be omitted since it is definite, whereas the object of 被 *bèi* 'BEI' can be omitted, which is acutally more often seen, because it does not necessarily have definite meaning. This is illustrated as follows:

(8) 凶手　　　胡立国　　去年　　**被**　　判　　　死刑。（报1995
年5月20日13
版）

xiōngshǒu　húlìguó　qùnián　**bèi**　pàn　sǐxíng
murderer　Hu.Liguo　last.year　**BEI**　sentence　death.penalty

'Last year, the murderer, Hu Liguo, was sentenced to death.' (*Bào*, May 20, 1995, Issue no. 13)

(9) 突然　　　一　　股　　巨　　浪　　猛　　　扑　　　过来，
tūrán　　　yī　　gǔ　　jù　　làng　měng　　pū　　guòlái
suddenly　one　CL　huge　wave　violently　slam　come

我　　　**被**　　抛　　　了　　　起来。（建屋16）
wǒ　　**bèi**　　pāo　　le　　qǐlái
1SG　　**BEI**　　throw　LE　up

'Suddenly, a huge wave slammed into me and I was thrown up into the sky.' (*Jiànwū* 16)

(10) 蓦地，　　他　　的　　思潮　　**被**　　打断　　了。（回忆28）
mòde　　tā　　de　　sīcháo　**bèi**　dǎduàn　le
suddenly　3SG　DE　thought　**BEI**　interrupt　LE

'Suddenly, his thought was interrupted.' (*Huíyì* 28)

10.3.2 *Passive Markers and Markers of 'Adverseness'*

Although the BEI construction indicates passivity, it is not reasonable to assume that the preposition 被 *bèi* 'BEI' in Singapore Mandarin is a marker of passiveness. People who have been influenced by English grammar tend to treat 被 *bèi* 'BEI' as a passive marker. Passive constructions in English have obvious markers, that is, the predicate of passive sentences must be in the form of 'to be + past participle of transitive verbs'. In contrast, the predicate verb in passive constructions in Singapore Mandarin are not necessarily overtly marked (see Section 5.12). In fact, unmarked passive sentences are even more pervasive. Consider the following examples of English and Singapore Mandarin.

(11) a *The TIMES New Chinese Dictionary* has already been published.

　　b 《时代新汉语词典》　　　　　　已经　　出版　　了。
　　　　shídài xīn hànyǔ cídiǎn　　　　yǐjīng　chūbǎn　le
　　　　The.TIMES.New.Chinese.Dictionary　already　publish　LE

'*The TIMES New Chinese Dictionary* has already been published.'

Sentences (11a) and (11b) are both passive sentences with the same meaning. (11a) is an English sentence with an obvious passive marker (as shown in 'been published') and (11b) is a Singapore Mandarin sentence, in which there is no passive marker and 被 *bèi* 'BEI' cannot be added. We have already mentioned in Section 5.12 that in Singapore Mandarin, patient-subject sentences are indeed passive sentences. In fact, in terms of the functions the marker shows, the preposition 被 *bèi* 'BEI' is better treated as a marker of 'adverseness' rather than passiveness.

It is acknowledged that the preposition 被 *bèi* 'BEI' in modern Singapore Mandarin has been grammaticalised from the verb 被 *bèi*, which initially meant 'to cover' and then meant 'to suffer' in ancient Chinese. In the modern Chinese lingua franca including Singapore Mandarin, although 被 *bèi* 'BEI' has been fully grammaticalised into a preposition and the verb usage of 被 *bèi* 'BEI' no longer exists, the original meaning of 'to suffer' is still retained in the prepositional usage. Our study shows that about 80% of sentences with the preposition 被 *bèi* 'BEI' contain the meaning of 'suffering adversity' as shown in the examples cited earlier. More examples follow:

(12) 布质　　粗厚的　衣衫，　**被**　　汗水　　　浸透　　　了。（狮子 140）
　　　 bùzhì　*cūhòude*　*yīshān*　***bèi***　*hànshuǐ*　*jìntòu*　　*le*
　　　 cloth　　thick　　　clothes　**BEI**　sweat　　　soak　　　LE
　　　 'The thick-cloth of the clothes was soaked in sweat.' (*Shīzi* 140)

(13) 日子　　是　　一　　　张　　　一　　　张　　　的　　　饭票，
　　　 rìzi　　*shì*　*yī*　　*zhāng*　*yī*　　*zhāng*　*de*　　*fànpiào*
　　　 day　　　be　　one　　CL　　　one　　CL　　　DE　　meal.ticket

　　　 而　　饭票　　　**被**　　我们　　撕　　了。（牛车水 134）
　　　 ér　　*fànpiào*　***bèi***　*wǒmen*　*sī*　　*le*
　　　 and　 meal.ticket　**BEI**　1PL　　　tear　LE
　　　 'The days are pieces of meal tickets, which have been torn by us.'[5] (*Niúchēshuǐ* 134)

(14) 她　　家　　附近的　　几　　　支　　电线杆　　　　　已
　　　 tā　　*jiā*　*fùjìnde*　　*jǐ*　　　*zhī*　*diànxiàngǎn*　　*yǐ*
　　　 3SG　home　nearby　　several　CL　　telegraph.pole　already

　　　 被　水　　　淹没，　可　　见　　水　　有　　多　　深。（胜利，31）
　　　 bèi　*shuǐ*　*yānmò*　*kě*　*jiàn*　*shuǐ*　*yǒu*　*duō*　*shēn*
　　　 BEI　water　flood　　able　see　　water　have　how.much　deep
　　　 'Several telegraph poles near her house had been flooded, showing how deep the water was.' (*Shènglì* 31)

10.3.3 The Usage of BEI Constructions

Since its meaning is related to adverseness, the preposition 被 *bèi* 'BEI' is used much less frequently than the preposition 把 *bǎ* 'BA'. We have conducted two sample surveys using two works. One is 《不凋萎的回忆》 *Memories That Do Not Wither* by Feng Huanhao, published by Singapore Translation and Publishers in 1989. In this book, the preposition 把 *bǎ* 'BA' appears 38 times and the preposition 被 *bèi* 'BEI' appears 10 times among the approximate 60,000 characters and the proportion of 把 *bǎ* 'BA' and 被 *bèi* 'BEI' is roughly four to one. The other book is the 30,000-character short novel 《跳舞的向日葵》 *The Dancing Sunflower* by You Jin, published by the Educational Publishing Pte Ltd in 1992, in which 把 *bǎ* 'BA' appears 56 times and 被 *bèi* 'BEI' appears eight times, and the ratio between them is seven to one. Therefore, it can be concluded that BEI constructions and BA constructions are not exact counterparts of passive and positive constructions and are not freely interchangeable.

However, since Singapore Mandarin is deeply influenced by English, BEI sentences are used much more widely than those in Chinese Mandarin. For instance, the BEI sentences in the following are all grammatical in Singapore Mandarin. But if these are sentences in Chinese Mandarin, the 被 *bèi* 'BEI' in each sentence is supposed to be deleted:

(16) 信　　　已　　　**被**　　投　　入　　了　　邮筒。（都市1）
　　　xìn　　　yǐ　　　**bèi**　　tóu　　rù　　le　　yóutǒng
　　　letter　 already　**BEI**　put　 into　LE　mailbox
'The letter had already been put into the mailbox.' (*Dūshì* 1)

(17) 君子　　　抛弃　　　了　　　仁德，　　怎么　　还　　能
　　　jūnzǐ　　　pāoqì　　　le　　　réndé　　　zěnme　 hái　　néng
　　　gentleman　abandon　　LE　　virtue　　　how　　still　can

　　　被　　称　　　为　　　君子　　　呢？（伦理 · 中四5）
　　　bèi　chēng　　wéi　　jūnzǐ　　　ne
　　　BEI　call　　　as　　　gentleman　SFP
'How can a gentleman still be regarded as a gentleman when he has abandoned his virtues?' (*Lúnlǐ* IV 5)

(18) 这　　件　　事，　　立刻　　　　流传开　　　　去，　　成　　　了
　　　zhè　jiàn　shì　　lìkè　　　　　liúchuánkāi　　qù　　　chéng　le
　　　this　CL　thing　immediately　spread.out　　go　　　become　LE

美谈,	一直	到	今天,	还	**被**	传颂
měitán	yīzhí	dào	jīntiān	hái	**bèi**	chuánsòng
good.story	all.the.time	to	today	still	**BEI**	appreciate

着。（伦理·中四37）

zhe

ZHE

'Immediately the story spread and became a beautiful story which even today is still being appreciated.' (*Lúnlǐ* IV 37)

10.4 在 zài 'Be/At/In Process'

10.4.1 Three 在 *zài 'be/at/in process' in Singapore Mandarin*

The first 在 *zài* in Singapore English is a verb meaning 'be', which usually takes a place object and together acts as a predicate. For example:

(1)
我	的	启蒙	学校	叫做	通志	学校,
wǒ	de	qǐméng	xuéxiào	jiàozuò	tōngzhì	xuéxiào
1SG	DE	enlightenment	school	call	Tong.Chi	school

在	牛车水	沙莪街	一	间	屋子	的	二	楼,
zài	niúchēshuǐ	shāéjiē	yī	jiān	wūzi	de	èr	lóu
be	Chinatown	Shah.Cur.Street	one	CL	house	DE	two	floor

我	的	家	也	**在**	同	一	条	街	上,
wǒ	de	jiā	yě	**zài**	tóng	yī	tiáo	jiē	shàng
1SG	DE	home	also	**be**	same	one	CL	street	on

约	有	十	间	店铺	之	距。（回忆2）
yuē	yǒu	shí	jiān	diànpù	zhī	jù
about	have	ten	CL	store	LIG	distance

'My elementary school was called Tong Chi School, which was located on the second floor of a house on Shah Cur Street in Chinatown and my home was also located on the same street, about ten stores away.' (*Huíyì* 2)

In (1), both 在 *zài* 'be' are verbs. The first 在 *zài* 'be' serves as a predicate and the subject 我的启蒙学校 *wǒ de qǐméng xuéxiào* 'my elementary school' is omitted since it already appears in the previous clause. The second 在 *zài* 'be' is also a predicate precedeed by an adverbial 也 *yě* 'also' with 我的家 *wǒdejiā* 'my home' being the subject. There are cases without objects as shown in the following example:

(2) 张先生　　　　不　　**在,**　运载　　黄梨　　去　　各处
　　zhāngxiānshēng bú ***zài*** *yùnzǎi huánglí qù gèchù*
　　Mr. Zhang　　NEG　**be**　carry　pineapple go　everywhere

配售。（一心 201）
pèishòu
distribute

'Mr. Zhang is not here and he is carrying pineapples to various places for distribution.' (*Yixin* 201)

The second 在 *zài* is as an adverb meaning 'in process'. It usually functions as an adverbial preceding verbal phrases, for instance:

(3) 火炎树　　　开　　得　　很　　绚烂,　　鲜红的　　　树叶,
　　huǒyánshù kāi de hěn xuànlàn xiānhóngde shùyè
　　fireflame.tree blossom DE very glorious bright.red leaf

像　　一　　个　　个　　火球,　　在　　　迎风　　　招展,
xiàng yī gè gè huǒqiú ***zài*** *yíngfēng zhāozhǎn*
like one CL CL fire.ball **in.process** in.the.wind wave

在　　　随风　　　摇曳。（回忆 58）
zài *suífēng yáoyè*
in.process in.the.wind sway

The fireflame trees were in glorious bloom, and their bright red leaves, like fire balls, were waving and swaying in the wind. (*Huíyì* 58)

(4) 鼓声　　　响起　　时,　一家之主　　　　江兆邦
　　gǔshēng xiǎngqǐ shí yījiāzhīzhǔ jiāngzhàobāng
　　drum.sound ring.p time the.head.of.a.family Jiang.Zhaobang

在　　　读报......（跳舞7）
zài *dúbào*

in.process read.newspaper

'The head of the family, Jiang Zhaobang, was reading a newspaper when the drums started to beat . . .' (*Tiàowǔ* 7)

在 *zài* 'in process' in examples (3) and (4) are all adverbs acting as the adverbials ofﬂ 风招展 *yíngfēngzhāozhǎn* 'wave with the wind', 随风摇曳 *suífēngyáoyè* 'sway with the wind' and 读报 *dúbào* 'read newspapers'.

The third 在 *zài*, also one of the most frequently used in Singapore Mandarin, is the preposition meaning 'at'. The prepositional phrase '在 *zài* "at" + X' can be used as both an adverbial and a complement, which is different from the prepositions 把 *bǎ* 'BA' and 被 *bèi* 'BEI' mentioned earlier. For example:

(5) 在   潺潺   溪水   中   涉足   嬉戏； 在   丛林   灌木
    zài *chánchán* *xīshuǐ* *zhōng* *shèzú* *xīxì*   *zài* *cónglín* *guànmù*
    at   babble   stream   inside   wade   play   at   jungle   bush

间   捉迷藏；   在   澄蓝的   大海边   拾   彩色
jiān   *zhuōmícáng*   *zài* *chénglánde* *dàhǎi-biān* *shí*   *cǎisè*
between hide-and.seek   at   azure   seaside   pick.up colourful

贝壳；   或   在   星空   下   摇   着   葵扇   听
bèiké *huò*   *zài* *xīngkōng* *xià*   *yáo*   *zhe*   *kuíshàn*   *tīng*
shell   or   at   starry.sky below   fan   ZHE   palm-leaf.fan listen

牛郎织女、   嫦娥奔月   的
niúlángzhīnǚ   *chángébènyuè*   *de*
the.Cowboy.and.the.   the.Goddess.Chang'e.fly.to.the.moon   DE
Weaving.Girl

故事。（回忆 1）
gùshì
story

'Wade and play in a babbling brook; play hide-and-seek in the bushes; pick up colourful shells by the azure sea; or shake a palm-leaf fan under the starry sky, listening to the story of the Cowboy and the Weaving Girl and Chang 'e Flying to the Moon."' (*Huíyì* 1)

(6) 走   在   路上，   穿插   在   人群   中，
    zǒu   zài   lùshàng   chuānchā zài   rénqún zhōng
    walk on   road   shuttle in   crowd   inside

    我   仿佛   来   到   香港。（回忆 74）
    wǒ   fǎngfú   lái   dào   xiānggǎng
    1SG   seem   come   to   Hong.Kong

    'Walking on the road among the crowds, I felt as if I had come to Hong Kong.' (*Huíyì* 74)

The prepositional phrases 在潺潺溪水中 *zài chánchán xīshuǐ zhōng* 'in the babbling brook', 在丛林灌木间 *zài cónglín guànmù jiān* 'among the bushes', 在澄蓝的大海边 *zài chénglán de dàhǎi biān* 'by the azure sea' and 在星空下 *zài xīngkōng xià* 'under the starry sky' are all adverbials in (5); 在路上 *zài lù shàng* 'on the road' and 在人群中 *zài rénqún zhōng* 'among the crowds' are both complements in (6). A further explanation of the prepositional phrase '在 *zài* "at" + X' as an adverbial and a complement are given respectively in the following sections.

10.4.2 *The Prepositional Phrase '在 zài "at" + X' as an Adverbial*

The prepositional phrase '在 *zài* "at" + X' is often used as an adverbial following a subject, for example:

(7) 她   在   屋   里   栽种   了   许多   盆景。（跳舞 5）
    tā   zài   wū   lǐ   zāizhòng   le   xǔduō   pénjǐng
    3SG   at   house   inside   plant   LE   many   bonsai

    'She planted many bonsai in her house.' （*Tiàowǔ* 5）

(8) 几   只   小   麻雀，   在   树   下   蹦跳   追逐。（回忆 59）
    jǐ   zhī   xiǎo   máquè   zài   shù   xià   bèngtiào   zhuīzhú
    several CL   small   sparrow at   tree   under   hop   chase

    'A few little sparrows were hopping and chasing around under the tree.' (*Huíyì* 59)

(9) 我   在   上   个   月   被   调升   到
    wǒ   zài   shàng   gè   yuè   bèi   diàoshēng   dào
    1SG   at   last   CL   month BEI   promote   to

教育部　　　　　　　　去。
jiāoyùbù　　　　　　　qù
Ministry.of.Education　go

'I was promoted to the Ministry of Education last month.'

(10) 没关系，　我　在　外面　等　一会。（金狮奖 156）
méiguānxì　wǒ　zài　wàimiàn　děng　yīhuì
it.doesn't.matter　1SG　at　outside　wait　a.while

'That's all right. I'll wait outside for a while.' (*Jīnshījiǎng* 156)

However, it can also precede the subject as an adverbial, and in this case there is often a pause after the prepositional phrase '在 *zài* "at" + X'. For example:

(11) 在　夜色　　　　迷茫　中，　我　重　临
zài　yèsè　　　　mímáng　zhōng　wǒ　chóng　lín
at　the.shades.of.night　haze　inside　1SG　again　come

黄城，　　启开　城门。（回忆 21）
huángchéng　qǐkāi　chéngmén
Huangcheng　open　gate

'In the hazy night, I returned to Huangcheng and opened its gate.' (*Huíyì* 21)

(12) 在　回家　的　路程　上，　他　觉得　自己
zài　huíjiā　de　lùchéng　shàng　tā　juéde　zìjǐ
at　go.home　DE　road　on　3SG　think　oneself

变成　了　一　只　鸟。（狮子 14–15）
biànchéng　le　yī　zhī　niǎo
change　LE　one　CL　bird

'On the way home, he felt himself change into a bird.' (*Shīzi* 14–15)

(13) 在　儿女　的　恳求　下，
zài　érnǚ　de　kěnqiú　xià
at　child　DE　implore　under

双方　才　答应　把　儿女　带大。（短篇 64）
shuāngfāng　cái　dāyìng　bǎ　érnǚ　dàidà
two.side　then　agree　BA　child　bring.up

'After the pleas of the children, both sides finally agreed to bring them up.' (*Duǎnpiān* 64)

When serving as an adverbial, the prepositional phrase '在 *zài* "at" + X' mainly expresses the following grammatical meanings:

1. Denoting time. In such cases, the position of X as the object of 在 *zài* 'at' is mainly filled by the following two types of words:

    A   Nominal phrases that denote time, for example:

(14) 它   在   今天， 在   五月   八日   早上，
     tā   *zài* *jīntiān* *zài* *wǔyuè* *bārì*   *zǎoshàng*
     3SG   at   today   at   May   8th.day morning

   已   被   宣判   为   危楼。（回忆 18）
   yǐ   *bèi* *xuānpàn* *wéi* *wēilóu*
   already BEI   declare   be   a.dangerous.building

'Today, on the morning of May 8th it was declared a dangerous building.' (*Huíyì* 18)

(15) 上   一   次   的   演习   是   在
     shàng *yī*   *cì* *de* *yǎnxí*   *shì* *zài*
     last   one   CL   DE   exercise be   at

   前年   举行   的。（报 1995 年 3 月 3 日 8 版）
   qiánnián   *jǔháng*   *de*
   the.year.before.last.year   hold   DE

'The last exercise was held the year before last.' (*Bào*, Mar. 3, 1995, Issue no. 8)

(16) 请问   在   服役   期间   你   担任   的   是   什么
     qǐngwèn   *zài* *fúyì*   *qījiān* *nǐ* *dānrèn* *de* *shì* *shénme*
     excuse.me   at   enlist   period   2SG   serve   DE   be   what

   职位？（吾土·小说上171）
   zhíwèi
   post

'What position did you hold during your service?' (*Wútǔ*, Novel I 171)

B Verb phrase + 前 qián 'before'/后 hòu 'after'/时 shí 'when', for instance:

(17) 在   新   学年   开始   前,
     zài   xīn   xuénián   kāishǐ   qián
     at   new   term   begin   before

   我   总   要   回   学校   一   趟,．．．．．．．
                                                        （回忆 25）
   wǒ   zǒng   yào   huí   xuéxiào   yī   tàng
   1SG   always need   return   school   one   CL

   'Before a new term starts, I always have to go back to school one time...'
   (*Huíyì* 25)

(18) 在   会考   来临   前,   我   开   了
     zài   huìkǎo   láilín   qián   wǒ   kāi   le
     at   a.general.exam   come   before 1SG   have LE

   不少   夜车。（回忆27）
   bùshǎo   yèchē
   many   revise.late.to.the night

   'Before the examination I spent many late nights revising.' (*Huíyì* 27)

(19) 尼克逊   准备   在   伤势   痊愈   后   回去   印尼
     níkèxùn   zhǔnbèi   zài   shāngshì   quányù   hòu   huíqù   yìnní
     Nixon   prepare   at   wound   recover   after   return   Indonesia

   工作。（报1995年3月7日11版）
   gōngzuò
   work

   'When he recovers from his injuries, Nixon plans to return to Indonesia to work.' (*Bào*, Mar. 7, 1995, Issue no. 11)

2 Denoting place. In such cases, the position X is mainly filled by the following two types of phrases:

   A Nominal phrases that denote places, for example:

(20) 女   歌星   邓丽君   最近   突然   在
     nǚ   gēxīng   dènglìjūn   zuìjìn   tūrán   zài
     female singer   Teresa.Teng   recently   suddenly   at

泰国　　　清迈　　　　逝世。（报 1995 年 5 月 20 日 21 版）
tàiguó　　*qīngmài*　　*shìshì*
Thailand　Chiangmai　pass.away

'The singer, Teresa Teng suddenly died in Chiang Mai, Thailand.' (*Bào*, May 20, 1995, Issue no. 21)

(21) 我　　在　　小　　公园　　里　　找到　　作画　　的
　　 wǒ　*zài*　*xiǎo*　*gōngyuán*　*lǐ*　*zhǎodào*　*zuòhuà*　*de*
　　 1SG　at　small　park　inside　find　draw　DE

　　 灵感，......（梦 87）
　　 línggǎn
　　 inspiration

'I found my inspiration for painting in a small park.' (*Mèng* 87)

(22) 杨仲钦　　**在**　我们　学校　读　了　四　年。（跳舞 36）
　　 yángzhòngqīn　*zài*　*wǒmen*　*xuéxiào*　*dú*　*le*　*sì*　*nián*
　　 Yang.Zhongqin　at　1PL　school　study　LE　four　year

'Yang Zhongqin has studied in our school for four years.' (*Tiàowǔ* 36)

B　Pronouns that denote places, for example:

(23) 如果　　不　　是　　**在**　这里　　碰见　　你，
　　 rúguǒ　*bú*　*shì*　*zài*　*zhèlǐ*　*pèngjiàn*　*nǐ*
　　 if　NEG　be　at　here　meet　2SG

　　 我　　真　　不敢　　认　　你。（金狮奖 131）
　　 wǒ　*zhēn*　*bùgǎn*　*rèn*　*nǐ*
　　 1SG　really　dare.not　recognise　2SG

'If I hadn't met you here, I would not have dared to say hello to you.' (*Jīnshījiǎng* 156)

(24) 让　　你　　**在**　那里　　日叫夜叫，
　　 ràng　*nǐ*　*zài*　*nàlǐ*　*rìjiàoyèjiào*
　　 let　2SG　at　there　cry.all.day.and.all.night

叫	得	你	痛痛快快！（跳舞 21）
jiào	de	nǐ	tòngtòngkuàikuài
shout	DE	2SG	heartily

'Cry as much as you want. Then you will be happy!' (*Tiàowǔ* 21)

(25)
当时	的	华工们，	都	有	着
dāngshí	de	huágōngmen	dōu	yǒu	zhe
at.that.time	DE	Chinese.workers	all	posses	ZHE

浓厚的	乡土观念，	纯粹	为	采金	而来，
nónghòude	xiāngtǔguānniàn	chúncuì	wèi	cǎijīn	érlái
profound	parochialism	purely	for	gold.mining	come

无意	**在**	**此**	久居。（回忆 51）
wúyì	**zài**	**cǐ**	jiǔjū
have.no.intention	**at**	**here**	inhabit

'At that time, those Chinese workers all were extremely parochial, coming only for gold and not intending to settle down here.' (*Huíyì* 51)

3 Denoting scope. In this case, as the object of 在 *zài* 'at', X may be broadly filled by the following two types of collocations:

A Abstract noun + 上 *shàng* 'on', for example:

(26)
他	不但	要	**在**	**功课**	**上**	帮忙	小薇，
tā	búdàn	yào	**zài**	**gōngkè**	**shàng**	bāngmáng	xiǎowēi
3SG	not.only	need	**at**	**homework**	**on**	help	Xiaowei

更	要	帮助	她	改掉	以前的	坏脾气。（短篇 69）
gèng	yào	bāngzhù	tā	gǎidiào	yǐqiánde	huàipíqi
more	need	help	3SG	correct	previous	bad.temperament

'Not only does he want to help Xiaowei with her homework, but he also wants to help her change her previously bad temper.' (*Duǎnpiān* 69)

(27)
校方	**在**	**路**	**税**	**上**	每	年	可
xiàofāng	**zài**	**lù**	**shuì**	**shàng**	měi	nián	kě
school.authority	**at**	**road**	**tax**	**on**	every	year	can

	节省	整	千	元。（报1995年3月15日18版）
	jiēshěng	*zhěng*	*qiān*	*yuán*
	save	whole	thousand	dollar

'The school can save a whole thousand dollars a year on road tax.' (*Bào*, Mar. 15, 1995, Issue no. 18)

(28) 明明 是 血脉 相连的 两 个 人，
míngmíng shì xuèmài xiāngliánde liǎng gè rén
obviously be blood.lineage connected two CL person

可是， **在** **感觉** **上** 竟 是 那么 的
kěshì **zài gǎnjiào shàng** *jìng shì nàme de*
but **at feeling on** unexpectedly be so DE

陌生。（跳舞51）
mòshēng
strange

'Two people are clearly linked by blood, but they unexpectedly feel so alien to each other.' (*Tiàowǔ* 51)

(29) 学生 吟咏 诗词 时， **在** **个人的** **情操** **上，**
xuéshēng yínyǒng shīcí shí **zài gèrénde qíngcāo shàng**
student chant poetry time **at personal sentiment on**

也 受到 培养。（华文24）
yě shòu dào péiyǎng
also receive nurture

'When students chant poems, they also nurture their personal sentiments.' (*Huáwén* 24)

In the preceding examples, 在…上 *zài…shàng* 'at…' is roughly equivalent to 在…方面 *zài…fāngmiàn* 'in terms of…'. In (26), 在功课上 *zàigōngkèshàng* 'homework' means in terms of homework. The rest is analogous.

B   Concrete noun + 中/里（头）*zhōng/ lǐ (tou)* 'inside'. For example:

(30) **在** 所有 出生 的 儿童 **中，**
    zài *suǒyǒu chūshēng de értóng* **zhōng**
    at all born DE child **inside**

有	1/4	是	私	生	的；	
yǒu	sìfēnzhīyī	shì	sī	shēng	de	
have	quarter	be	secret	born	DE	

有	1/8	的	儿童	是	由	单身
yǒu	bāfēnzhīyī	de	értóng	shì	yóu	dānshēn
have	one.eighth	DE	child	be	by	single

母亲	养育	的。（风筝148）
mǔqīn	yǎngyù	de
mother	raise	DE

'One quarter of all children born are born out of wedlock; one in eight children are raised by a single mother.' (*Fēngzhēng* 148)

(31)
类似	这样	的	情感	直觉	造型
lèisì	zhèyàng	de	qínggǎn	zhíjiào	zàoxíng
similar	this	DE	emotion	intuition	moulding

在	话剧	《茶馆》	中	也	有	一	篇。（科学27）
zài	huàjù	cháguǎn	zhōng	yě	yǒu	yī	piān
at	stage.play	Teahouse	inside	also	have	one	CL

'There is also a kind of moulding of emotional intuition in the stage play *Teahouse*.' (*Kēxué* 27)

(32)
像	这种	口号	一样的	诗，	在
xiàng	zhèzhǒng	kǒuhào	yīyàngde	shī	**zài**
seem	this	slogon	same	poetry	**at**

《马华新文学大系》	里，	占	了	大	部分。（新华文学99）
mǎhuáxīnwénxuédàxì	lǐ	zhàn	le	dà	bùfen
Chinese.Literature.in.Malaysia	inside	occupy	LE	big	part

'Slogan-like poems like this one make up the bulk of the *Chinese Literature in Malaysia*.' (*Xīnhuáwénxué* 99)

(33)
启蒙	班	最初	在	67	所	华文
qǐméng	bān	zuìchū	**zài**	liùshíqī	suǒ	huáwén
enlightenment	class	initial	**at**	sixty-seven	CL	Chinese

小学	里	办,	到	了	1989年,
xiǎoxué	lǐ	bàn	dào	le	yījiǔbājiǔnián
primary.school	inside	hold	reach	LE	1989

也	就	是	10	年	后,	在	全国
yě	jiù	shì	shí	nián	hòu	zài	quánguó
also	just	be	ten	year	after	at	whole.country

的	210	所	小学	里头,
de	èrbǎiyīshí	suǒ	xiǎoxué	lǐtou
DE	210	CL	primary.school	inside

只	有	39	所	继续	开办	启蒙	班。

(华文 65)

zhǐ	yǒu	sānshíjiǔ	suǒ	jìxù	kāibàn	qǐméng	bān
only	have	thirty-nine	CL	continue	hold	enlightenment	class

'Initially there were beginner's class in 67 Chinese primary schools. By 1989, 10 years later, only 39 out of the 210 primary schools in the country continued to run such classes.' (*Huáwén* 65)

(34)
在	日常	运用	的	华文	字	里头,
zài	rìcháng	yùnyòng	de	huáwén	zì	lǐtou
at	daily	apply	DE	Chinese	word	inside

有	三	个	虚字,	最	容易	使	人	困惑。
yǒu	sān	gè	xūzì	zuì	róngyì	shǐ	rén	kùnhuò
have	three	CL	functional.word	most	easy	make	person	confused

这	三	个	字	是	"地"	"底"	"的"。(△华语 16)
zhè	sān	gè	zì	shì	de	dǐ	de
this	three	CL	word	be	DE	DI	DE

'In the everyday use of Chinese words, there are three functional words that are most confusing. These three words are 地 *de* "DE" 底 *dǐ* "DI" and 的 *de* "DE."' (△*Huáyǔ* 16)

4 Denoting a condition, a circumstance or a situation. In this case, as the object of 在 *zài* 'at', X may come in the following two forms:

A Abstract noun/nominal verb ＋下 *xià* 'under'. For example:

(35) 年轻　　　一　　　代　　　的　　　新加坡人，
　　 niánqīng　 yī　　 dài　　　de　　 xīnjiāpōrén
　　 young　　　one　　CL　　　DE　　 Singaporean

　　 在　　比较　　　安逸的　　环境　　　下　　成长　　　起来......
　　 zài bǐjiào　 　ānyìde　 huánjìng xià chéngzhǎng qǐlái
　　 at   relative comfor-   environ- under grow   up
　　 table   ment

　　 不　　能　　　了解　　贫困　　是　　什么　　一　　回　　事。（文艺 4）
　　 bù   néng   liǎojiě pínkùn shì shénme yī   huí   shì
　　 NEG   can   know   poor   be   what   one CL   thing

'The younger generation of Singaporeans, who grew up in a more comfortable environment ... cannot understand what poverty is all about.' (*Wényì* 4)

(36) 县长　　　　　　　在　　不得已的　　　情况　　　　下，
　　 xiànzhǎng　　　　zài　 búdéyǐde　　 qíngkuàng　 xià
　　 the.head.of.a.county at   have.no.choice situation   under

　　 只好　　　宣布　　　紧急　　　状态。（报 1995 年 6 月 3 日副刊 21 版）
　　 zhǐ hǎo　 xuānbù　　jǐnjí　　 zhuàngtài
　　 but.to   announce urgent   state

'Under such uncontrollable circumstances the governor had no choice but to declare a state of emergency.' (*Bào*, June 3, 1995, Issue no. 21, supplementary edition)

(37) 在　　我们　　的　　双语　　　　教育　　　　政策　　　实施
　　 zài　 wǒmen　 de　 shuāngyǔ　 jiāoyù　　 zhèngcè　 shíshī
　　 at   1PL   DE   bilingual   education   policy   implement

	下,	我们	不	会	逐渐	变成	单语
	xià	*wǒmen*	*bú*	*huì*	*zhújiàn*	*biànchéng*	*dānyǔ*
	under	1PL	NEG	can	gradually	become	monolingual

社会。（风筝 4）
shèhuì
society

'With the implementation of our bilingual education policy, we will not gradually become a monolingual society.' (*Fēngzhēng* 4)

(38) 美专同人　　　　　　　在　　文工团　　　　　的
měizhuāntóngrén　　　　*zài*　*wéngōngtuán*　　*de*
colleague.specializing.in.fine.arts　at　song.and.dance.ensemble　DE

领引　　下,　　负责　　　　　　宣传　　　画......（香沱11）
lǐngyǐn　*xià*　*fùzé*　　　　*xuānchuán*　*huà*
guide　under　be.responsible.for　propaganda　painting

'Colleagues specializing in fine arts led by the 'song-and-dance ensemble' are in charge of the posters.' (*Xiāngtuó* 11)

B　Abstract noun/nominal verb ＋中 *zhōng* 'middle/inside'. For example,

(39) 在　　一　　阵　　汽　　笛　　声　　中,
zài　*yī*　*zhèn*　*qì*　*dí*　*shēng*　*zhōng*
at　one　CL　steam　whistle　sound　middle

告别　了　这　文化　古　城——日惹。（晚上 83）
gàobié　*le*　*zhè*　*wénhuà*　*gǔ*　*chéng*　　　*rìrě*
leave　LE　this　culture　ancient　city　　Yogyakarta

'With the sound of a siren, we bid farewell to this ancient cultural city – Yogyakarta.' (*Wǎnshàng* 83)

(40) 她们　　与　　四　　勇士　　合　　跳　　一　　舞,
tāmen　*yǔ*　*sì*　*yǒngshì*　*hé*　*tiào*　*yī*　*wǔ*
3PL　with　four　warrior　together　leap　one　dance

便	在	掌声	中	下	台。（晚上 93）
biàn	*zài*	*zhǎngshēng*	*zhōng*	*xià*	*tái*
then	at	applause	middle	leave	stage

'They danced with the four warriors and left the stage to applause.' (*Wǎnshàn* 93)

(41)
一	个	隆重的	仪式，	就	在	愉快的
yī	*gè*	*lóngzhòngde*	*yíshì*	*jiù*	*zài*	*yúkuàide*
one	CL	solemn	ceremony	thus	at	pleasing

气氛	中	结束，	大家	尽兴	离	座，
qìfēn	*zhōng*	*jiéshù*	*dàjiā*	*jìnxìng*	*lí*	*zuò*
atmosphere	middle	end	everyone	content	leave	seat

步	出	礼堂。（一心 122）
bù	*chū*	*lǐtáng*
walk	out	auditorium

'A solemn ceremony ended on a happy note, with everyone leaving the auditorium in good spirits.' (*Yīxīn* 122)

(42)
美专	同人......	虽	在	大	轰炸
měizhuān tóngrén		*suī*	*zài*	*dà*	*hōngzhà*
colleague.specializing.in.fine.arts		although	at	big	bombardment

中	仍然	不	避	危难，	继续	工作。（Δ香沱 11）
zhōng	*réngrán*	*bú*	*bì*	*wēinàn*	*jìxù*	*gōngzuò*
middle	still	NEG	shun	danger	continue	work

'Colleagues specializing in fine arts ... continued to work despite the devastating bombardment.' (Δ*Xiāngtuó* 11)

在…过程中 *zài…guòchéngzhōng* 'in the process of…' can also be included in this subcategory. For example:

(43)
即使	在	学习	过程	中，	忽略	了	一
jíshǐ	*zài*	*xuéxí*	*guòchéng*	*zhōng*	*hūluè*	*le*	*yī*
even.if	at	study	process	middle	overlook	LE	one

些	原则	与	方法,	以致	"南腔北调",	那	也
xiē	yuánzé	yǔ	fāngfǎ	yǐzhì	nánqiāngběidiào	nà	yě
some	principle	and	method	so.that	with.mixed.accents	that	also

绝对	不	会	影响	语意	的	表达。	(△华语55)
juéduì	bú	huì	yǐngxiǎng	yǔyì	de	biǎodá	
definitely	NEG	can	influence	meaning	DE	express	

'In the process of learning, even if some principles and methods are overlooked, resulting in mixed accents, this will in no way affect the expression of the meaning.' (△*Huáyǔ* 55)

(44)
在	迈	向	21	世纪	的	过程	中,
zài	mài	xiàng	èrshíyī	shìjì	de	guòchéng	zhōng
at	walk	towards	twenty-first	century	DE	process	middle

我	国	所	面临	的	社会	问题、	文化	问题,
wǒ	guó	suǒ	miànlín	de	shèhuì	wèntí	wénhuà	wèntí
1SG	country	SUO	face	DE	society	problem	culture	problem

是	既	复杂	且	繁多的。	(文艺 105)
shì	jì	fùzá	qiě	fánduōde	
be	not.only	complex	but.also	complicated.and.numerous	

'As we enter the 21st century, the social and cultural issues facing our country are both numerous and complex.' (*Wényì* 105)

Finally, there is the construction of 在 X 看来 *zài X kànlái* 'in X's opinion', a fixed format meaning roughly the same as 按 X 的看法 *àn X de kànfǎ* 'according to the opinion of X'. X as the object of 在 *zài* 'at' can only be filled by a personal pronoun or a noun referring to a person. For example:

(45)
上述		问题	在	他们	看来,	根本	就
shàngshù		wèntí	zài	tāmen	kànlái	gēnběn	jiù
above-mentioned		problem	at	3PL	view	at.all	just

不	像	是	问题。	(报 1995 年 3 月 12 日副刊 9 版)
bú	xiàng	shì	wèntí	
NEG	like	be	problem	

'The above-mentioned problems are not problems at all in their opinion.' (*Bào*, Mar. 12, 1995, Issue no. 9, supplementary edition)

(46) 在   我   看来， 目前的   青少年，   进行   高等
    zài   wǒ   kànlái mùqiánde   qīngshàonián jìnxíng   gāoděng
    at   1SG view   current   teenager   enter   higher

    教育   机关   前   选课   是   非常   现实的。
                                                                （风筝 93）
    jiàoyù   jīguān   qián   xuǎnkè   shì   fēicháng   xiànshíde
    education institution before select.lesson be   very   realistic

    'Currently, it seems to me that it is very realistic for young people to make pre-institutional course selections before starting their higher education.' (*Fēngzhēng* 93)

(47) 在   当代人   看来，
    zài   dāngdàirén   kànlái
    at   the.present.generation   view

    演员   都   不   年轻   了......（科学 64）
    yǎnyuán dōu   bù   niánqīng   le
    actor   all   NEG   young   LE

    'In the opinion of the present generation, actors are no longer young.' (*Kēxué* 64)

10.4.3 The Prepositional Phrase '在 zài "at" + X' as a Complement

The prepositional phrase '在 *zài* "at" + X' mainly indicates a location when serving as a complement. There are four subcategories for this usage:

1 Denoting the place where a person or thing exists. For example:

(48) 我们   总   不   能   一直   站   在   这里。
                                                              （想飞 63）
    wǒmen   zǒng   bù   néng yīzhí   zhàn   zài   zhèlǐ
    1PL   always NEG can   always   stand at   here

    'We can't stand here forever.' (*Xiǎngfēi* 63)

(49) 那   孩子   整   天   就   一   个   人   呆
    nà   háizi   zhěng   tiān   jiù   yī   gè   rén   dāi
    that kid   whole   day   just one CL   person stay

在	家	里，	怪	可怜的。（跳舞 8）
zài	*jiā*	*lǐ*	*guài*	*kěliánde*
at	home	inside	quite	pitiful

'It is pitiful that the poor boy stays at home alone all day.' (*Tiàowǔ* 8)

(50)
没有	他，	你	的	金牙	早	就	葬	在
méiyǒu	*tā*	*nǐ*	*de*	*jīnyá*	*zǎo*	*jiù*	*zàng*	*zài*
without	3SG	2SG	DE	golden.tooth	already	thus	bury	at

阴沟	里	了。（金狮奖 193）
yīngōu	*lǐ*	*le*
drain	inside	LE

'Without him, your golden tooth would have long been buried in the ditch.' (*Jīnshījiǎng* 193)

(51)
我们	的	办公室	座落	在	亚历山大	军营
wǒmen	*de*	*bàngōngshì*	*zuòluò*	*zài*	*yàlìshāndà*	*jūnyíng*
1PL	DE	office	locate	at	Alexander	barrack

的	小	山	坡。（△青春 8）
de	*xiǎo*	*shān*	*pō*
DE	small	hill	slope

'Our office is situated on the hill near the Alexander barracks.' (△*Qīngchūn* 8)

2 Denoting the endpoint of the movement of a person or thing. For example:

(52)
他	搓	了	搓	手，	端端正正 地	坐
tā	*cuō*	*le*	*cuō*	*shǒu*	*duānduānzhèngzhèng-de*	*zuò*
3SG	rub	LE	rub	hand	upright	sit

在	椅子	上。（胜利 92）
zài	*yǐzi*	*shàng*
at	chair	on

'He rubbed his hands and sat upright in his chair.' (*Shènglì* 92)

(53) 哭 累 了, 两 个 人 一起 倒 在
    kū lèi le liǎng gè rén yīqǐ dǎo **zài**
    cry tired LE two CL person together fall **at**

铺 了 地毯 的 地板 上。（跳舞 42）
pū le dìtǎn de dìbǎn shàng
spread LE carpet DE floor on

'Tired from crying, the two collapsed together on the carpeted floor.' (*Tiàowǔ* 42)

(54) 我 把 全部 旧 篇 都 翻 阅 过 一 遍,
    wǒ bǎ quánbù jiù piān dōu fān yuè guò yī biàn
    1SG BA all old article all flip read GUO one CL

然后 分别 装 在 两 个 大 塑胶袋 中。（回忆 28）
ránhòu fēnbié zhuāng **zài** liǎng gè dà sùjiāodài zhōng
then respectively put **at** two CL big plastic.bag inside

'I browsed through all the old articles and separated them into two large plastic bags.' (*Huíyì* 28)

(55) 紫杆 把 石 弹 拣 起来, 丢 在 池塘 里。（胜利 9）
    Zǐgǎn bǎ shí dàn jiǎn qǐlái diū **zài** chítáng lǐ
    Zigan BA stone bullet pick up throw **at** pond inside

'Zigan picked up the stone bullets and dropped them in the pond.' (*Shènglì* 9)

(56) 杯子 落 在 她 的 脚 边, "咯啷"
    bēizi luò **zài** tā de jiǎo biān gēlāng
    cup fall **at** 3SG DE foot side smash

一 声, 碎 了。（跳舞 50）
yī shēng suì le
one CL broke LE

'The cup fell down at her feet and shattered with a clatter.' (*Tiàowǔ* 50)

Examples (52) and (53) indicate the endpoint of the movement by the agent of the predicate verb, and examples (54) through (56) indicate the endpoint of the movement by the patient of the predicate verb.

3 Denoting the place or area where the action or activity takes place. For example:

(57) 纽约　　　自　　　　有　她　万般　　迷人的　　风情……
　　 niǔyuē　 zì　　　 yǒu　tā　wànbān　mírénde　fēngqíng
　　 New.York obviously have 3SG a.lot charming flavour

　　 单是　　走　　**在**　街　　上,　叫　　人　　　如　　置身
　　 dānshì　zǒu　**zài**　jiē　shàng　jiào　rén　　rú　　zhìshēn
　　 just　 walk　**at**　 street　on　　let　person　seem　stay

　　 山阴道　　　　　上,　　　目不暇接。（怀旧 69）
　　 shānyīndào　　shàng　　mùbùxiájiē
　　 mountain.path　on　　　have.no.time.to.take.in.the.scene.as.a.whole

　　 'New York has its own charm.... Walking on its streets one feels like walking down a mountain path, with too much to take in.' (*Huáijiù* 69)

(58) 也　　有　　不少　　**在**　　海外　　获得　　一等　　荣誉　　学位,
　　 yě　 yǒu　 bùshǎo　**zài**　hǎiwài　huòdé　yīděng　róngyù　xuéwèi
　　 also　have　many　　**at**　abroad　obtain　first.class　honour　degree

　　 驰骋　　**在**　　学术　　疆场　　　上。（回忆 26）
　　 chíchěng　**zài**　xuéshù　jiāngchǎng　shàng
　　 gallop　　**at**　academic　battlefield　on

　　 'Many have also obtained overseas first-class honour degrees and are galloping on the frontiers of academia.' (*Huíyì* 26)

(59) 我　　的　　血液　要　　奔流　　**在**　祖国　　的　　土地
　　 wǒ　de　xuèyè　yào　bēnliú　**zài**　zǔguó　de　tǔdì
　　 1SG　DE　blood　want　run.flow　**at**　homeland　DE　land

　　 上。（回忆59）
　　 shàng
　　 on

　　 'My blood shall run in the land of my country.' (*Huíyì* 59)

4 Denoting the exact contact point of a striking instrument. For example:

(60) 哨　　　棒　　　刚好　　　打　在　树枝　　　上，　断　了。
　　　shào　　bàng　　gānghǎo　dǎ　zài　shùzhī　　shàng　duàn　le
　　　whistle　stick　just　　　hit　at　tree.branch　on　　　break　LE
（跳舞 9）

'The club happened to hit the branch and broke.' (*Tiàowǔ* 9)

(61) 涵珊　　　把　　杂志　　　卷　　　起来，
　　　hánshān　bǎ　zázhì　　　juǎn　　qǐlái
　　　Hanshan　BA　magazine　roll　　up

　　　猛力　　打　在　江兆邦　　　　的　肩膀　　　上。
　　　měnglì　dǎ　zài　jiāngzhàobāng　de　jiānbǎng　shàng
　　　violently　hit　at　Jiang.Zhaobang　DE　shoulder　on
（跳舞 8）

'Hanshan rolled up the magazine and slammed it hard on Jiang Zhaobang's shoulder.' (*Tiàowǔ* 8)

The prepositional phrase '在 *zài* "at" + X' may, in rare cases, be used as a complement indicating time. For example:

(62) 今天，　我们　　是　　生活　　　在　　九十　　年代，
　　　jīntiān　wǒmen　shì　shēnghuó　zài　jiǔshí　niándài
　　　today　1PL　　SHI　live　　　　at　　ninety　age

　　　我们　　的　　思想　　　不　　能　　停留　　在　过去，
　　　wǒmen　de　　sīxiǎng　　bù　　néng　tíngliú　zài　guòqù
　　　1PL　　DE　　mind　　　NEG　can　　stay　　at　past

　　　要　　跟上　　　时代　　的　　步伐。（报 1995 年 4 月 18 日 11 版）
　　　yào　gēnshàng　shídài　de　　bùfá
　　　need　follow　　age　　DE　pace

'Today, living in the nineties, our minds cannot stick in the past, but rather, we have to keep up with the times.' (*Bào*, Apr. 18, 1995, Issue no. 11)

Occasionally it is used as the complement of the verb 停留 *tíngliú* 'to stay' to indicate certain state or level. For example:

(63) 他们   种   小麦，
    tāmen zhòng   xiǎomài
    3PL   plant   wheat

还   停留   在   点播   和   撒播   的   阶段。（跳舞 14）
hái   tíngliú   zài   diǎnbō   hé   sǎbō   de   jiēduàn
still stay   at   dibbling and broadcasting DE   stage

'They are still growing wheat using dibbling and broadcasting methods.' (*Tiàowǔ* 14)

10.5 比 bǐ 'Than'

In Singapore Mandarin, 比 *bǐ* mainly functions as a preposition marking comparison. But sometimes it can be used as a verb meaning 'to compare'. For example:

(1) 我   的   球艺   还是   比   不   上   他。（胜利 52）
    wǒ   de   qiúyì   háishì   **bǐ**   bú   shàng tā
    1SG DE   ball.game.skills still   **compare** NEG up   3SG

'As for ball game skills, I still can't compare with him.' (*Shènglì* 52)

In (1), 比 *bǐ* 'compare' is a verb which takes a potential complement. The predicate-complement phrase 比不上 *bǐ búshàng* 'not as good as' takes an object 他 *tā* '3SG'. The verbal usage of 比 *bǐ* 'compare' is not commonly found.

When functioning as a preposition, the frequently used construction of 比 *bǐ* 'than' is shown as follows, where X and Y are entities to be compared.

X   比   Y   怎么样
X   ***bǐ***   Y   zěnmeyàng
X   than   Y   How(properties of comparison)

'X is . . . than Y.'

The preceding sentence pattern is usually called BI construction. For example:

(2) 他   比   你   乖！   （今后 8）
    tā   bǐ   nǐ   guāi
    3SG than   2SG   well-behaved

'He's better behaved than you.' (*Jīnhòu* 8)

(3) 康:　　　爸爸　　比　　妈妈　　重要。
　　　kāng:　*bàba*　*bǐ*　*māma*　*zhòngyào*
　　　Kang　dad　than　mum　important

　　仁:　我　说，妈妈　比　爸爸　重要。（吾土·戏剧 119）
　　rén　*wǒ*　*shuō*　*māma*　*bǐ*　*bàba*　*zhòngyào*
　　Ren　1SG　say　mum　than　dad　important

　　'Kang: Dad is more important than mum.
　　Ren: I think mum is more important than dad.' (*Wútǔ* (drama) 119)

(4) 没　　受　　过　　多少　　教育　　的　　小贩　　也
　　méi　*shòu*　*guò*　*duōshǎo*　*jiāoyù*　*de*　*xiǎofàn*　*yě*
　　NEG　receive　GUO　much　education　DE　pedlar　also

　　比　　护士们　　有礼。（风筝 168）
　　bǐ　*hùshìmen*　*yǒulǐ*
　　than　nurses　polite

　　'Peddlers with little education are more polite than nurses.' (*Fēngzhēng* 168)

The structural analysis of (2) is shown as follows:

```
他      比      你      乖
tā      bǐ      nǐ      guāi
────
 1       2                      (subject-predicate relation)
        ─────────
         3       4              (adverbial-head modifying relation)
        ─────
         5       6              (prepositional phrase)
```

BI construction implies the difference in degree between the property of X and Y and the phrases modified by the prepositional phrase '比 *bǐ* "than"+ Y' are usually adjectives. For instance, in examples (2) and (3), 乖 *guāi* 'well-behaved' and 重要 *zhòngyào* 'important' are both adjectives. Here are some more examples:

(5) 这　　两　　个　　都市　　的　　市民　　比　　我们　　忙。（风筝 165）
　　zhè　*liǎng*　*gè*　*dūshì*　*de*　*shìmín*　*bǐ*　*wǒmen*　**máng**
　　this　two　CL　city　DE　citizen　than　1Pl　busy

　　'The citizens of these two cities are busier than we are.' (*Fēngzhēng* 165)

(6) 你   难道   比   我   勤劳？（恶梦 79）
    nǐ   nándào   bǐ   wǒ   qínláo
    2SG   aren't   than 1SG   diligent

    'Aren't you more diligent than I am?' (È mèng 165)

(7) 他   的   华文   程度   在   当时   的确
    tā   de   huáwén   chéngdù   zài   dāngshí   díquè
    3SG   DE   Chinese level   at   then   indeed

    比   我   好。（牛车水 22）
    bǐ   wǒ   hǎo
    than 1SG   good

    'His Chinese was indeed better than mine at that time.' (Niúchēshuǐ 22)

(8) 我们   比   他   幸运。（报 1995年3月5日9版）
    wǒmen bǐ   tā   xìngyùn
    1Pl   than 3SG   lucky

    'We are luckier than he is.' (Bào, Mar. 5, 1995, Issue no. 9)

(9) 活   着   时，   也许   有人   会   以为   自己   比
    huó   zhe   shí   yěxǔ   yǒurén   huì   yǐwéi   zìjǐ   bǐ
    living ZHE   time   perhaps someone will think   oneself than

    别人   伟大。（八方 142）
    biérén wěidà
    other   great

    'While alive, some people may think that they are greater than others.' (Bāfāng 142)

(10) 在   你   心目   中，   我   比   你   儿子   重要？（吾土
     zài   nǐ   xīnmù   zhōng   wǒ   bǐ   nǐ   érzi   zhòngyào 戏剧 25）
     in   2SG   mind   middle   1SG   than 2SG   son   important

     'In your mind, am I more important than your son?' (Wútǔ (drama) 25)

(11) 海伦   比   她   漂亮、   活泼、   讨人欢心。（恶梦 103）
     hǎilún   bǐ   tā   piàoliàng huópō   tǎorénhuānxīn

| Helen | **than** | 3SG | beautiful | lively | pleasing |

'Helen is more beautiful, lively and pleasing than she is.' (*Èmèng* 103)

(12) 我们　　呀，　只是　　**比**　　他　　机警　　一点。（金狮奖 198）
　　 wǒmen　ya　　zhǐshì　**bǐ**　　tā　　jījǐng　yīdiǎn
　　 1Pl　　TOP　just　　**than**　3SG　alert　a.little

'We are just a little more alert than he is.' (*Jīnshījiǎng* 198)

(13) 梁文福　　　的　　心灵　　**比**　　一般人　　　　敏锐　　太
　　 liángwénfú　de　　xīnlíng　**bǐ**　　yībānrén　　　mǐnruì　tài
　　 Liang.Wenfu　DE　mind　　**than**　common.people　sharp　too

多，......（牛车水・序 11）
duō
much

'Liang Wenfu has a much sharper mind than others ...' (*Niúchēshuǐ* (preface) 11)

(14) 克仁　　的　　工资　　　**比**　　你　　高　　出　　许多。（恶梦 2）
　　 kèrén　de　　gōngzī　**bǐ**　　nǐ　　gāo　chū　xǔduō
　　 Keren　DE　salary　**than**　2SG　high　out　a.lot

'Keren's salary is much higher than yours.' (*Èmèng* 2)

(15) 他　　的　　容貌　　　**比**　　舞台　　上　　　芒速沙苏丹
　　 tā　　de　　róngmào　**bǐ**　　wǔtái　　shàng　mángsùshāsūdān
　　 3SG　DE　appearance　**than**　stage　　on　　Mansur.Shah.Sultan

年轻、　　清秀　　　得　　多。　（报 1995 年 3 月 8 日 10 版）
niánqīng　qīngxiù　de　　duō
young　　handsome　DE　much

'His appearance is much younger and more handsome than that of Mansur Shah Sultan on stage.' (*Bào*, Mar. 8, 1995, Issue no. 10)

In examples (5) through (10), the prepositional phrase '比 *bǐ* "than"+ Y' modifies a single adjective; in examples (11) to (15) it modifies an adjective phrase. Sometimes, the modified components can be verb phrases. For example:

(16) 他们　　却　　**比**　　我　　更　　**有**　　礼貌，　　更
　　　tāmen　què　**bǐ**　wǒ　gèng　**yǒu**　lǐmào　gèng
　　　3Pl　　yet　**than**　1SG　more　**have**　polite　more

　　　乐于助人。（风筝 165）
　　　lèyúzhùrén
　　　helpful

　　　'They are more polite and helpful than I am.' (*Fēngzhēng* 165)

(17) 这些　　界限，　　似乎　　**比**　　任何　　有形的　　界限　　更
　　　zhèxiē　jièxiàn　sìhū　**bǐ**　rènhé　yǒuxíngde　jièxiàn　gèng
　　　these　boundary　seem　**than**　any　tangible　boundary　more

　　　划　　得　　仔细　　分明　　更　　是　　难以抹去。（牛车水 63）
　　　huá　de　zǐxì　fēnmíng　gèng　shì　nányǐmǒqù
　　　divide　DE　careful　clear　more　SHI　difficult.to.erase

　　　'It seems that these boundaries are more carefully and sharply drawn, thus more difficult to erase than any tangible one.' (*Niúchēshuǐ* 63)

Since BI construction indicates comparison, the adjective modified by the 比 *bǐ* 'than' prepositional structure can be modified by the degree adverb 更 *gèng* 'more' or 还（要）*hái(yào)* 'even' which contains comparative meaning, but not by the degree adverb 很 *hěn* 'very' and 挺 *tǐng* 'quite' which contain a comparative meaning, nor by the degree adverb indicating superlative degree 最 *zuì* 'most'. For example:

(18) 中四　　　　　　　　是　　会考　　班，　　功课　　比
　　　zhōngsì　　　　　shì　huìkǎo　bān　gōngkè　bǐ
　　　secondary.school.grade.four　be　exam　class　homework　than

　　　中三　　**更**　　多、　　**更**　　繁、　　**更**　　重。（风筝 76）
　　　zhōngsān　**gèng**　duō　**gèng**　fán　**gèng**　zhòng
　　　grade.three　**more**　much　**more**　difficult　**more**　heavy

　　　'The fourth year of secondary school is the preparation class for the examination, and the homework is more difficult and heavier than the third year.' (*Fēngzhēng* 76)

(19) 外面　　是　　个　　众雨纷扰的　　黯湿　　世界，
　　　wàimiàn　shì　gè　zhòngyǔfēnrǎo-de　ànshī　shìjiè
　　　outside　be　CL　very.rainy　dim.and.wet　world

在	学校	的	办公室		里,	我	的	心	却
zài	xuéxiào	de	bàngōngshì		lǐ	wǒ	de	xīn	què
at	school	DE	office		inside	1SG	DE	heart	yet

比	外面	更	暗淡	**更**	冷湿。（回忆 63）
bǐ	wàimiàn	gèng	àndàn	**gèng**	lěngshī
than	outside	more	dim	**more**	wet

'Outside is a dim and wet world, but my heart is dimmer and wetter inside the school office than outside.' (*Huíyì* 63)

(20)
我	的	前途	也许	比	你	**更**	光明
wǒ	de	qiántú	yěxǔ	bǐ	nǐ	**gèng**	guāngmíng
1SG	DE	future	maybe	than	2SG	**more**	bright

哩！（新马·剧本 22）
li
SFP

'My future may be brighter than yours!' (*Xīnmǎ* (script) 22)

(21)
赐福	的	叛逆	性	比	我	**还**	强。（胜利 36）
cìfú	de	pànnì	xìng	bǐ	wǒ	**hái**	qiáng
Cifu	DE	rebellious	nature	than	1SG	**even**	strong

'Cifu's rebelliousness is even stronger than mine.' (*Shènglì* 36)

(22)
我	妈妈	的	头发	比	我	的	**还要**	滑
wǒ	māmā	de	tóufā	bǐ	wǒ	de	**háiyào**	huá
1SG	mother	DE	hair	than	1SG	DE	**even**	smooth

还要	亮	哩。（大胡子 24）
háiyào	liàng	li
even	shiny	SFP

'My mother's hair is even smoother and shinier than mine.' (*Dàhúzǐ* 24)

In examples (18) to (22), the words 更 *gèng* 'more', 还 *hái* 'even', 还 (要) *hái(yào)* 'even' can neither be replaced by 很 *hěn* 'very', 挺 *tǐng* 'quite', nor by 最 *zuì* 'most'.

It should be noted that the meaning of the sentence varies slightly depending on whether 更 *gèng* 'more'/还（要）*hái(yào)* 'even' is used or not. Compare the following two sentences.

(23) a 他　　比　　我　　高。
　　　tā　*bǐ*　*wǒ*　*gāo*
　　　3SG　than　1SG　tall
　　　'He is taller than I am.'

　　 b 他　　比　　我　　**更/还**　　　　高。
　　　tā　*bǐ*　*wǒ*　***gèng/hái***　*gāo*
　　　3SG　than　1SG　**more/even**　tall
　　　He is taller/still taller than me.'

Sentence (23a) without degree adverb 更 *gèng* 'more' or 还 *hái* 'more' only shows that 'he' is tall, but does not affirm whether 'I' am tall or not. In contrast, the use of 更 *gèng* 'more' or 还 *hái* 'even' in (23b) not only indicates that 'he' is tall but also implies that 'I' am also tall.

Similarly, in (18) the use of 更 *gèng* 'more' indicates that the homework in the fourth year of secondary school is more difficult and heavier than that in the third year, even though homework in both years is difficult and onerous. Without 更 *gèng* 'more', it only tells of the difficulty in the fourth year, indicating nothing about the third year. Thus, the use of degree adverbs 更 *gèng* 'more'/还 *hái* 'even' in BI construction implies comparison over the same basis.

Two more points should be clarified about the BI construction in Singapore Mandarin:

First, in BI construction, 来得 *láide* 'LAIDE' is often inserted in between the prepositional phrase '比 *bǐ* "than"+ Y' and the adjective following behind, for example:

(24) 自己　　　承认　　　　总　　　比　　人家　　　审问　　　　　**来得**
　　　zìjǐ　　*chéngrèn*　*zǒng*　*bǐ*　*rénjiā*　*shěnwèn*　　***láide***
　　　self　　admit　　　always　than　others　interrogate　**LAIDE**

干净利落。（吾土・戏剧 38）
gànjìnglìluò
neat.and.tidy

'Confessing onself is better than being interrogated by others.' (*Wútǔ*(drama) 38)

(25) 他　　比　　谁　　　都　　**来得**　　沉默、　　安静。（金狮奖 69）
　　　tā　*bǐ*　*shuí*　*dōu*　***láide***　*chénmò*　*ānjìng*

Prepositions and Prepositional Phrases 463

| 3SG | **than** | who | all | **LAIDE** | silent | quiet |

'He is quieter than anyone else.' (*Jīnshíjiǎng* 69)

(26) 不论 ② 句 或 ③ 句, 都 比
  búlùn *èr* *jù* *huò* *sān* *jù* *dōu* ***bǐ***
  no.matter second sentence or third sentence all **than**

  ① 句 **来得** 生动。(华文教材 2A 150)
  yī *jù* ***láidé*** *shēngdòng*
  first sentence **LAIDE** vivid

'No matter whether the second sentence or the third one, both of them are more vivid than the first one.' (*Huáwénjiàocái* 2A 150)

There are no such usages in Chinese Mandarin.

Second, BI construction is one of the four comparative constructions showing differences between two entities in Singapore Mandarin. They are:

A 'X 比 *bǐ* "than" Y . . .'. This is the aforementioned construction (with examples omitted).

B 'XAY + numeral-classifier compound' (X and Y represent entities to be compared, and A represents adjectives). For example:

(28) 男 的 大 女 的 三 岁。(胜利 64)
  nán *de* *dà* *nǚ* *de* *sān* *suì*
  man DE old woman DE three year

'The man is three years older than the woman.' (*Shènglì* 64)

(29) 我 父亲 虽然 只 小 他 四 岁, 但. . . . . .
                                                        (新马 255)
  wǒ *fùqīn* *suīrán* *zhǐ* *xiǎo* *tā* *sì* *suì* *dàn*
  1SG father although only young 3SG four year but

'My father was only four years younger than him, but . . .'(*Xīnmǎ* 255)

C 'XA 过 *guò* "pass" Y' (X and Y represent entities to be compared and A represents adjectives). For example:

(30) 和 邻居 和睦相处, 总 好 过
  hé *línjū* *hémùxiāngchǔ* *zǒng* *hǎo* ***guò***
  with neighbour live.harmoniously always good **pass**

正面冲突。（吾土・戏剧 149）
zhèngmiànchōngtū
head-on.confrontation

'Getting along well with neighbours is always better than head-on confrontations.' (*Wútǔ*(drama) 149)

(31) 小时候， 他 跟 别的 孩子 打架， 伤 了
xiǎoshíhòu tā gēn biéde háizi dǎjià shāng le
childhood 3SG with other child fight injure LE

些儿， 我 心里 痛 **过** 他 百倍。（金狮奖 287）
xiēr wǒ xīnlǐ tòng **guò** *tā bǎibèi*
a.bit 1SG heart painful **pass** 3SG hundred.times

'When he was a child, he got hurt while fighting with other kids, and I felt much more pain than he did.' (*Jīnshīijiǎng* 287)

(32) 他们 自己 所 订 的 公务员 起薪
tāmen zìjǐ suǒ dìng de gōngwùyuán qǐxīn
3Pl self SUO stipulate DE civil.servant starting.salary

却 低 **过** 最低 生活费。（报 1995 年 3 月 9 日 26 版）
què dī **guò** *zuìdī shēnghuófèi*
yet low **pass** the.lowest living.cost

'The starting salary of civil servants that they stipulated themselves is lower than the minimus cost of living.' (*Bào*, Mar. 9, 1995, Issue no. 26)

(33) 曾经 在病中 被 逼 看 土产 电视剧，
céngjīng zàibìngzhōng bèi bī kàn tǔchǎn diànshìjù
once in.illness.period BEI force watch local TV.series

其 难受 程度 "惨 **过** 吃药"。（报 1995 年 3 月 22 日副刊 5 版）
qí nánshòu chéngdù cǎn **guò** *chīyào*
its pain degree bad **pass** take.medicine

'I was once forced to watch a local TV series when I was ill, which was "worse than taking medicine."' (*Bào*, Mar. 22, 1995, Issue no. 5, supplementary edition)

D 'XA 于 *yú* 'than' Y" (X and Y represent entities to be compared and A represents adjectives). For example:

(34)
新加坡	中产	阶级	的	政治	倾向	是
xīnjiāpō	*zhōngchǎn*	*jiējí*	*de*	*zhèngzhì*	*qīngxiàng*	*shì*
Singapore	middle	class	DE	political	tendency	be

冷漠	多	于	热诚,	对		现有的	体制
lěngmò	*duō*	*yú*	*rèchéng*	*duì*		*xiànyǒu-de*	*tǐzhì*
indifference	more	than	zeal	concerning		existing	system

是	拥护	多	于	反对,	甚至	是	"保守"
shì	*yōnghù*	*duō*	*yú*	*fǎnduì*	*shènzhì*	*shì*	*bǎoshǒu*
SHI	advocacy	more	than	objection	even	SHI	conservation

多	于	"自由化"。(报 1995 年 4 月 19 日 4 版)
duō	*yú*	*zìyóuhuà*
more	than	liberalisation

'The political tendency of the middle classes in Singapore is more indifference than enthusiasm, more support than opposition to the existing system, even "conservativism" over "liberalization."' (*Bào*, Apr. 19, 1995, Issue no. 4)

(35)
新加坡	的	年工资	增长率	高	于
xīnjiāpō	*de*	*niángōngzī*	*zēngzhǎnglǜ*	*gāo*	*yú*
Singapore	DE	yearly.salary	increasing.rate	high	than

通货膨胀率。
tōnghuòpéngzhànglǜ
inflation.rate

'The rate of increase of annual salaries in Singapore is higher than the inflation rate.'

Generally speaking, the adjectives in the latter two kinds of comparative constructions are monosyllabic adjectives.

Among the four types of comparative constructions mentioned earlier, A, B and D are also seen in Chinese Mandarin, while type C is only used in Singapore Mandarin.

In addition to the BI sentences, the preposition 比 *bǐ* 'than' can also constitute a special construction as illustrated here:

一 *yī* 'one' + classifier + 比 *bǐ* 'than' + 一 *yī* 'one' + classifier + adjective phrase

Such 比 *bǐ* 'than' format usually functions as a predicate, indicating the property increases by degree, which is similar to "越来越 *yuèláiyuè* 'more and more'. The two classifiers in this construction are identical. Based on the classifiers used, this construction can be further categorised into two subtypes. The first subtype employs general classifiers, indicating a succession of things in which the latter one is much better than the previous one in certain properties. For example:

(36) 自　　　三　　年　　前　　她　　以　　一　　篇　　同性恋
zì　　*sān*　*nián*　*qián*　*tā*　*yǐ*　*yī*　*piān*　*tóngxìngliàn*
since　three　year　before　3SG　with　one　CL　homosexual

小说　　　在　　文艺界　　　　引起　　轩然大波　　　之后，
xiǎoshuō　*zài*　*wényìjiè*　　*yǐnqǐ*　*xuānrándàbō*　*zhīhòu*
novel　in　literature.circle　cause　uproar　after

她　　的　　小说　　　便　　一　　**篇**　　**比**　　一　　**篇**
tā　*de*　*xiǎoshuō*　*biàn*　*yī*　***piān***　***bǐ***　*yī*　***piān***
3SG　DE　novel　then　one　CL　than　one　CL

精彩。（想飞 47–48）
jīngcǎi
exciting

'Ever since her homosexual novel caused an uproar in literary circles three years ago, her works have been more and more exciting.' (*Xiǎngfēi* 47–48)

(37) 我　　看看　　坐　　在　　车后　　　　的　　三　　个
wǒ　*kànkàn*　*zuò*　*zài*　*chēhòu*　　*de*　*sān*　*gè*
1SG　look　sit　at　the.back.of.the.car　DE　three　CL

孩子：　九岁、　　　　四岁、　　　　三岁，　　　　一　　个
háizi　*jiǔsuì*　　　　*sìsuì*　　　　*sānsuì*　　　　*yī*　*gè*
kid　nine.year.old　Four.year.old　three.years.old　one　CL

比　　一　　个　　可爱。（天长 65）
bǐ　*yī*　*gè*　*kěài*
than　one　CL　cute

'I looked at the three children sitting in the back of the car, aged nine, four and three, each one more adorable than the previous one.' (*Tiāncháng* 65)

The second subtype uses temporal classifiers such as 天 *tiān* 'day' and 年 *nián* 'year', indicating that certain nature of the object is increasingly reinforced as time goes by, which is shown in the following examples:

(38) 春天　　来　　了，　天气　　一　　天　　比　　一　　天
　　　chūntiān　*lái*　*le*　*tiānqì*　*yī*　*tiān*　*bǐ*　*yī*　*tiān*
　　　spring　　come　LE　weather　one　day　than　one　day

暖和。（中学 1A 93）
nuǎnhuo
warm

'With the arrival of spring, the weather is getting warmer every day.' (*Zhōngxué* 1A 93)

(39) 人　　却　　一　　天　　比　　一　　天　　枯老，
　　　rén　*què*　*yī*　*tiān*　*bǐ*　*yī*　*tiān*　*kūlǎo*
　　　person　yet　one　day　than　one　day　emaciated

一　　日　　比　　一　　日　　憔悴。（金狮奖（四）40）
yī　*rì*　*bǐ*　*yī*　*rì*　*qiáocuì*
one　day　than　one　day　haggard

'But one grows more emaciated and more haggard day by day.' (*Jīnshījiǎng* (IV) 40)

(40) 会考　　成绩　　一　　年　　比　　一　　年　　辉煌。（薪传 63）
　　　huìkǎo　*chéngjì*　*yī*　*nián*　*bǐ*　*yī*　*nián*　*huīhuáng*
　　　exam　result　one　year　than　one　year　glorious

'The results of the examination become more promising every year.' (*Xīnchuán* 63)

In terms of structural analysis, 她的小说一篇比一篇精彩 *tā de xiǎoshuō yī piān bǐ yī piān jīngcǎi* 'her works have been more and more exciting' in (36) and 天气一天比一天暖和 *tiānqì yī tiān bǐ yī tiān nuǎnhuo* 'the weather is getting warmer every day' in (38) can be analysed in the following way:

```
她的小说    一篇    比    一篇    精彩
tādexiǎoshuō  yīpiān  bǐ    yīpiān  jīngcǎi
```

```
  1        2                              (subject-predicate relation)
           3              4                (subject-predicate relation)
                    5           6          (adverbial-head endocentric phrase)
                    7    8                 (prepositional phrase)
```

```
天气      一天    比    一天    暖和
tiānqì   yītiān  bǐ    yītiān  nuǎnhuo
```

```
  1        2                              (subject-predicate relation)
           3              4                (subject-predicate relation)
                    5           6          (adverbial-head endocentric phrase)
                    7    8                 (prepositional phrase)
```

10.6 对 duì 'To/Towards/With regard to' and 对于 duìyú 'Towards/With regard to'

10.6.1 Four 对 duì in Singapore Mandarin

In Singapore Mandarin, 对于 *duìyú* 'towards/with regard to' can only be a preposition, while 对 *duì* has three more usages with different meanings in addition to being a preposition. First, 对 *duì* is used as a verb meaning 'to face'. For example:

(1) 有   一   张   毛茸茸的   脸   正   **对**   着
    yǒu   yī   zhāng máoróngróng-de liǎn   zhèng   **duì**   zhe
    have   one   CL   hairy   face   right   **face** ZHE

我。（大胡子 2）
wǒ
1SG

'There is a hairy face facing me directly.' (*Dàhúzi* 2)

Second, 对 *duì* can be used as an adjective meaning 'right'. For example:

(2) **对**！   你   说   得   很   **对**！   人类   原本
    duì   nǐ   shuō   de   hěn   **duì**   rénlèi   yuánběn
    right 2SG   say   DE   very   **right** human.being   originally

Prepositions and Prepositional Phrases 469

就	是	团结一致、	齐心协力		去	战胜
jiù	shì	tuánjiéyīzhì	qíxīnxiélì		qù	zhànshèng
just	SHI	unite.as.one	make.concert.effort		go	defeat

自然灾害		的。（Δ 断情剪 89）
zìránzāihài		de
natural.disaster		DE

'Yes! You're right! Human beings should be united to make joint efforts to overcome natural disasters.' (Δ *Duànqíngjiǎn* 89)

Third, 对 *duì* can be used as a classifier denoting duality. For example:

(3)
半年	前,	有	一	对	来自	日本	的	情侣,
bànnián	qián	yǒu	yī	duì	láizì	rìběn	de	qínglǚ
half.year	ago	have	one	CL	from	Japan	DE	couple

也	是	以	同样	方式	来	结束	生命...
							（跳舞 56）
yě	shì	yǐ	tóngyàng	fāngshì	lái	jiéshù	shēngmìng
also	be	by	same	way	come	end	life

'Half a year ago, a couple from Japan ended their lives in the same way...' (*Tiàowǔ* 56)

The examples just mentioned indicate that in Singapore Mandarin, there are four usages of 对 *duì*, namely, being a preposition, a verb, an adjective and a classifier. In this chapter, the discussion merely covers the preposition 对 *duì* 'towards/with regard to/to' and 对于 *duìyú* 'Towards/with regard to'.

10.6.2 Grammatical Meanings of 对 duì *'Towards With regard to/To'* and 对于 duìyú *'towards/with regard to'*

The grammatical function of preposition 对于 *duìyú* 'towards/with regard to' simply denotes the relating relation between people and things, whereas the grammatical functions of 对 *duì* towards/with regard to/to are diversified. In addition to indicating the aboutness relation as 对于 *duìyú* 'towards/with regard to' does, 对 *duì* can also express the meaning of "to". For example:

(4)
她	对	光业	说:	"阿业,	你	赌马
tā	duì	guāngyè	shuō	āyè	nǐ	dǔmǎ
3SG	to	Guangye	say	A.Ye	2SG	bet.on.the.horse

我	不	说	你,	但	你	不	做生意,
wǒ	bù	shuō	nǐ	dàn	nǐ	bú	zuòshēngyì
1SG	NEG	say	2SG	but	2SG	NEG	do.business

叫	我们	以后	吃	什么	呢?..."（追云 61）
jiào	wǒmen	yǐhòu	chī	shénme	ne
let	1PL	later	eat	what	SFP

'She said to Guangye, "A Ye, I won't complain if you bet on horses, but if you don't do business, how can we make a living in the future?"...' (*Zhuīyún* 61)

(5)
小萱	已经	**对**	大家	讲	过,
xiǎoxuān	yǐjīng	**duì**	dàjiā	jiǎng	guò
Xiaoxuan	already	**to**	everyone	say	GUO

说	姐姐	不	允许	一切	新潮	玩意。（梦 76）
shuō	jiějie	bù	yǔnxǔ	yīqiè	xīncháo	wányì
say	sister	NEG	allow	all	new-fashioned	thing

'Xiaoxuan has already told everyone that her sister doesn't allow any new things.' (*Mèng* 76)

(6)
"又	是	一	个	忘	了	照	镜子	的	人。"
yòu	shì	yī	gè	wàng	le	zhào	jìngzi	de	rén
again	be	one	CL	forget	LE	look	mirror	DE	person

子昀	心里	叹	道,	却	只是	**对**	方愫
zǐyún	xīnlǐ	tàn	dào	què	zhǐshì	**duì**	fāngsù
Ziyun	in.heart	sigh	say	but	only	**at**	Fang.Su

笑笑。（金狮奖 140）
xiàoxiào
smile

'"There is another one who forgot to look at herself in the mirror." Sighing in her heart, Ziyun just smiled at Fang Su.' (*Jīnshījiǎng* 140)

In examples (4) and (5), 对 *duì* 'towards' can be substituted by the preposition 向 *xiàng* 'to'; in (6), it can be substituted by the preposition 朝 *cháo* 'towards'. However, in none of the three examples can 对 *duì* 'to' be replaced by 对于 *duìyú* 'towards/ with regard to'. The following section only focuses on 对 *duì* 'towards with regard to' and 对于 *duìyú* 'towards/with regard to' when they denote relating relation.

10.6.3 The Usage of "对（于）..." duì(yú) 'Towards/With Regard To...'

The "对（于）..." *duì(yú)* 'towards/with regard to' prepositional phrase has two main usages.

1 Being used as an adverbial. The prepositional phrase can function as an adverbial, following the subject with or without a pause. For example:

(7) 一向　　　最　　　多话的　　　老刘　　　对　　　我们　　　之间
　　yīxiàng　*zuì*　*duōhuà-de*　*lǎoliú*　*duì*　*wǒmen*　*zhījiān*
　　always　　most　　talkative　　Lao.Liu　towards　1Pl　　between

　　共有的　　　顾虑　　避而不谈。（华韵 27）
　　gòngyǒu-de　*gùlǜ*　*bìérbùtán*
　　shared　　　concern　be.evasive.about

　　'Lao Liu, who has always been the most talkative, was evasive about our shared concerns.' (*Huáyùn* 27)

(8) 作者　　　对　　　这些　　　下层　　　　人物　　　的　　挣扎
　　zuòzhě　*duì*　*zhèxiē*　*xiàcéng*　　*rénwù*　*de*　*zhēngzhá*
　　author　　towards　these　　lower.class　people　DE　　struggling

　　生活，　　　的确　　处处　　　　露出　　爱怜的
　　shēnghuó　*díquè*　*chùchù*　　*lùchū*　*àilián-de*
　　life　　　　indeed　in.all.aspect　show　　affectionate

　　精神。（新马·剧本·导论 4）
　　jīngshén
　　spirit

　　'The author shows tender affection for the struggling life of these lower class characters in all aspects.' (*Xīnmǎ* (drama) (introduction) 4)

(9) 温朵朵　　　　对于　　　屋　　里　　邋里邋遢的　　情况，
　　wēnduǒduǒ　*duìyú*　*wū*　*lǐ*　*lālǐlātā-de*　*qíngkuàng*
　　Wen.Duoduo　towards　　room　inside　messy　　　condition

早　　　已　　　习以为常　　　　了。（跳舞 20）
zǎo　　　yǐ　　　xíyǐwéicháng　　le
early　　already　be.used.to　　　LE

'Wen Duoduo has long been used to the mess in the room.' (*Tiàowǔ* 20)

The prepositional phrase can also precede the subject with a pause. For example:

(10) 对　　　　母亲，　她　　是　　彻底地　　　麻木　　　了。（跳舞 50）
　　　duì　　　mǔqīn　tā　　shì　chèdǐ-de　　mámù　　　le
　　　towards　mother　3SG　be　completely　indifferent　LE

'She has become completely indifferent to her mother.' (*Tiàowǔ* 50)

(11) 对　　　　欧洲大陆　　　其他　　语系　　　　　地区，
　　　duì　　　ōuzhōudàlù　　qítā　　yǔxì　　　　　dìqū
　　　towards　Europe　　　　other　language.family　region

我们　　做　　过　　多少　　　努力？（△小小鸟 23）
wǒmen　zuò　guò　duōshǎo　nǔlì
1Pl　　do　　GUO　how.many　effort

'How much effort have we made for regions in Europe where other language families are spoken?' (△*Xiǎoxiǎoniǎo* 23)

(12) 对于　　　　　　这样的　　　事实，　跟　　　他们　　呼吸　　同
　　　duìyú　　　　zhèyàngde　shìshí　gēn　　tāmen　hūxī　　tóng
　　　with.regard.to　such　　　　fact　　with　3Pl　　breathe　same

一　　种　　空气　的　　我们　　会　　有　　什么　　　感想
yī　　zhǒng　kōngqì　de　　wǒmen　huì　　yǒu　shénme　gǎnxiǎng
one　CL　　air　　　DE　　1Pl　　will　have　what　　thought

呢？（华文教材2B 165）
ne
SFP

'For us, who breathe the same air as them, what feelings may be generated with regard to this kind of fact?' (*Huáwénjiāocái* 2B 165)

The structure of examples (9) and (10) can be respectively analysed as follows:

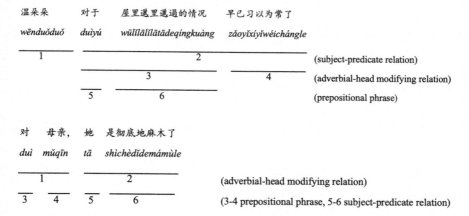

Preposition 对（于） *duì(yú)* 'towards/with regard to' denotes aboutness relation and its role is to introduce the relating object as shown in the preceding examples. It should be noted that the relating object, that is, the object of 对（于） *duì(yú)* 'towards/with regard to', sometimes serves as the patient of its following verb. For instance, in (7) the object of 对 *duì* 'towards' 我们之间共有的顾虑 *wǒmén zhījiān gòngyǒu de gùlǜ* 'the concerns we share' is the patient of the following verb 谈 *tán* 'talk'. Here is another example:

(13) 在　　某　　个　意义上，　人　　已　　向　机器　　臣服，
     zài　*mǒu*　*gè*　*yìyì shàng*　*rén*　*yǐ*　*xiàng*　*jīqì*　*chénfú*
     at　certain　CL　sense on　people　already　to　machine　surrender

     对　　　它　　　绝对　　　　信任。（△ 小小鸟 56）
     duì　　*tā*　　*juéduì*　　　*xìnrèn*
     towards　3SG　absolutely　trust

'In a sense, people have surrendered to machines and absolutely trusted them.' (△ *Xiǎoxiǎoniǎo* 56)

In (13), 它 *tā* '3SG' (referring to the machine), the object of 对 *duì* 'towards', is the patient of the verb 信任 *xìnrèn* 'trust'. Sometimes, the objects of 对 *duì* 'towards' and the following verbs are not of direct 'action-patient' relations, as shown in examples (8) to (12), but they are still semantically related. For instance, in (8) the object of 对 *duì* 'towards', namely 这些下层人物的挣扎生活 *zhèxiē xiàcéngrénwù de zhēngzhá shēnghuó* 'the struggling life of the lower class' is not the patient of the verb 露出 *lùchū* 'show'. Nevertheless, it's apparent that 'the author' 露出爱怜的精神 *lùchū àilián de jīngshén* 'show empathetic feelings' because of 这些下层人物的挣扎生活 *zhèxiē xiàcéng rénwù de zhēngzhá shēnghuó* 'the struggling life of the lower class'. Thus they are still semantically related. "对（于）...来说" *duì(yú)...láishuō* or "对（于）...而言" *duì(yú)...éryán*', has become a fixed form, meaning 'as far as ... is concerned...'. For example:

(14)

嫦娥奔月			的	表演，	**对**	一	个	在	这里
chángébēnyuè			*de*	*biǎoyǎn*	***duì***	*yī*	*gè*	*zài*	*zhèlǐ*
Chang'e.flies.to.the.moon			DE	show	**for**	one	CL	in	here
moon									

度过	十余	个	中秋		的	人	**来说，**		
dùguò	*shíyú*	*gè*	*zhōngqiū*		*de*	*rén*	***láishuō***		
spend	about.ten	CL	Mid-Autumn.Day		DE	person	**be.concerned**		

似乎	更	没什么		趣味	可言		了。（回忆 36）		
sìhū	*gèng*	*méishénme*		*qùwèi*	*kěyán*		*le*		
seem	more	have.no		interest	to.mention		LE		

'For a person who has spent over ten Mid-Autumn Festivals here, there seems to be nothing interesting in the show of Chang'e flying to the moon.' (*Huíyì* 36)

(15)

对于	我们	这些	"城市佬"	**来说，**	坐	牛车	回去
duìyú	*wǒmen*	*zhèxiē*	*chéngshìlǎo*	***láishuō***	*zuò*	*niúchē*	*huíqù*
for	1Pl	these	city.slicker	**be.concerned**	sit	oxcart	back

大象营	可说	是	一	种	全新的		
dàxiàngyíng	*kěshuō*	*shì*	*yī*	*zhǒng*	*quánxīnde*		
elephant.camp	can	be	one	CL	brand.new		

经验。（南北 16）

jīngyàn

experience

'For us "city slickers", it's a brand new experience to take an oxcart back to the elephant camp.' (*Nánběi* 16)

(16)

对	我	**而言，**	除非	不	爱，	不然	的话，
duì	*wǒ*	***éryán***	*chúfēi*	*bú*	*ài*	*bùrán*	*dehuà*
for	1SG	**be.concerned**	unless	NEG	love	otherwise	if

轰轰烈烈的	爱情	肯定	是	我	人生中	一
hōnghōnglièliè-de	àiqíng	kěndìng	shì	wǒ	rénshēngzhōng	yī
passionate	romance	surely	be	1SG	life.in	one

种	必须	履行	的	信约。（无月98）
zhǒng	bìxū	lǚxíng	de	xìnyuē
CL	must	honour	DE	promise

'As far as I am concerned, passionate romance is a promise that must be honoured in my life unless I have no one to love.' (*Wúyuè* 98)

对一个在这里度过十余个中秋的人来说 *duì yīge zài zhèlǐ dùguò shí yú ge zhōngqiū de rén láishuō* in (14) means 'as far as a person who has spent over ten Mid-Autumn Days here is concerned'. Other examples are in the same token.

2 Being an attribute after taking 的 *de* 'DE'. This usage is only found for 对 *duì* 'to/towards' but not for 对于 *duìyú* 'towards/with regard to'. When 的 *de* 'DE' is attached to the prepositional structure 对...*duì* 'to/towards...' to act as attribute, the head word can be nouns, for example:

(17)
乡下人	对	土地	的	观念	总是	充满	情感的。（科学30）
xiāngxiàrén	**duì**	tǔdì	de	guānniàn	zǒngshì	chōngmǎn	qínggǎnde
rustic	to	land	DE	view	always	fill	affectionate

'A rustic's attitude towards the land is always filled with affection.' (*Kēxué* 30)

(18)
目前的	华文	试题	主要	考查	学生	的	语文
mùqián-de	huáwén	shìtí	zhǔyào	kǎochá	xuéshēng	de	yǔwén
present	Chinese	test	mainly	examine	student	DE	Chinese

程度，	不	是	对	教材	的	熟悉	程度。（华文233）
chéngdù	bú	shì	**duì**	jiàocái	de	shúxī	chéngdù
level	NEG	be	to	textbook	DE	familiar	level

'The present tests of Chinese mainly examine students' language level instead of how familiar they are with the textbooks.' (*Huáwén* 233)

(19)
对	人性	的	看法（伦理·中三25）
duì	rénxìng	de	kànfǎ
to	humanity	DE	view

'the view of humanity' (*Lúnlǐ* III 25)

Sentence (17) is analysed as follows:

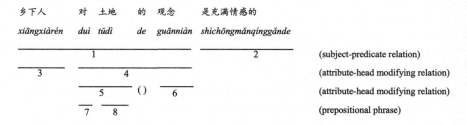

The prepositional phrase 对土地 *duì tǔdì* 'to the land', together with 的 *de* 'DE', acts as the attribute of the noun 观念 *guānniàn* 'view'.

However, it is more common for the head to be a nominal verb (see Section 8.12). In this case, the object of the preposition 对 *duì* 'to towards' is also understood as the patient of the following nominal verb, the head. For example:

(20) 学生　　读　了　这些　资料，　对　　问题　的
　　　 xuéshēng dú le zhèxiē zīliào　**duì**　*wèntí de*
　　　 student　read LE these material **towards** issue DE

　　 了解　　　　会　 更　　 彻底　 和　　 全面。（华文 193）
　　 liǎojiě　　huì　gèng　chèdǐ　hé　　quánmiàn
　　 understanding will more thorough and comprehensive

'Students will have a more thorough and comprehensive understanding of the issues after reading these materials.' (*Huáwén* 193)

(21) 我　 来到　　 李家　　 只不过　 两　 天　 光景，　 始终
　　 wǒ　*láidào*　*lǐjiā*　*zhǐbúguò*　*liǎng*　*tiān*　*guāngjǐng*　*shǐzhōng*
　　 1SG come Li'house only two day time always

　　 未　 曾　　 断　　 过　 对　　 蝴蝶　　 的　 注意。（短篇 29）
　　 wèi　*céng*　*duàn*　*guò*　**duì**　*húdié*　*de*　*zhùyì*
　　 NEG ever stop GUO **towards** butterfly DE attention

'Since I came to Li's house only two days ago, I have never stopped paying attention to the butterflies.' (*Duǎnpiān* 29)

(22) 五十　　年　　后，　她　　对　　　世界　　的　　影响，
　　　wǔshí　nián　hòu　tā　　duì　　shìjiè　de　yǐngxiǎng
　　　fifty　year　later　3SG　towards　world　DE　influence

　　　将　　　是　　巨大的。（薪传 180）
　　　jiāng　shì　jùdà-de
　　　will　be　immense

'In fifty years, her influence on the world will be immense.' (*Xīnchuán* 180)

(23) 《父亲　冷冷的　　目光》　还　　引起　　我　　对
　　　fùqīn　lěnglěng-de　mùguāng　hái　yǐnqi　wǒ　duì
　　　father　cold　　gaze　　even　elicit　1SG　towards

　　　一些　艺术　创作　　欣赏　　　规律　的　思考。（科学 9）
　　　yìxiē　yìshù　chuàngzuò　xīnshǎng　guīlǜ　de　sīkǎo
　　　some　art　creation　appreciation　rule　DE　thinking

'*The Cold Gaze of Father* even caused me to contemplate the appreciation rules of art creation.' (*Kēxué* 9)

(24) 那个　问题　　所　　测量　　的　是　学生　　的　背景
　　　nàge　wèntí　suǒ　cèliáng　de　shì　xuéshēng　de　bèijǐng
　　　that　problem　SUO　measure　DE　be　student　DE　background

　　　知识，　而　　不　　是　对　　选文　　的　理解。（华文 249）
　　　zhīshí　ér　bú　shì　duì　xuǎnwén　de　lǐjiě
　　　knowledge　but　NEG　be　towards　excerpt　DE　understanding

'That question was testing the students' background knowledge, not their understanding of the excerpt.' (*Huáwén* 249)

The heads in examples (20) through (24), that is, 了解 *liǎojiě* 'understanding', 注意 *zhùyì* 'attention', 影响 *yǐngxiǎng* 'influence', 思考 *sīkǎo* 'thinking' and 理解 *lǐjiě* 'understanding' (which are modified by the prepositional construction 对 *duì* 'to . . .') are all nominal verbs.

10.7　关于 *guānyú* 'About'

关于 *guānyú* 'about' is a preposition used in written Singapore Mandarin, not with high frequency. Nevertheless, it has some unique features which need to be mentioned.

The meaning expressed by 关于 *guānyú* is 'about' or 'regarding', whose function is to denote the scope or content of activities or things. For example:

(1) 关于   战后   马华   文学   之   演变,   王赓武
    guānyú zhànhòu mǎhuá   wénxué   zhī   yǎnbiàn   wánggēngwǔ
    about   post.war Malaysian literature LIG evolution Wang.Gungwu

   在   《马华文学简论》   中   有   很好的
   zài mǎhuáwénxuéjiǎnlùn   *zhōng yǒu   hěnhǎo*de
   in   A.Brief.Essay.on.Malaysian.Chinese.Literature middle have   great

   分析。(科学 14)
   fēnxī
   analysis

   'On the evolution of post-war Malaysian Chinese literature, Wang Gungwu has a good analysis in his *A Brief Essay on Malaysian Chinese Literature*.' (*Kēxué* 14)

In (1), the object of 关于 *guānyú* 'about' clarifies the scope or content analysed by Wang Gungwu in *A Brief Essay on Malaysian Chinese Literature*.

Prepositional phrases with 关于 *guānyú* 'about' act as adverbial in the same way as the prepositional phrase "对（于）..." *duì(yú)* 'with regard to...' does as in (1). Here are some more examples:

(2) 关于   鄞碧乐   自杀   的   原因   说法   颇   为   纷纭。
                                                              (变调 16)
    guānyú yínbìlè zìshā   de   yuányīn   shuōfǎ   pō   wéi   fēnyún
    about   Yin.Bile suicide   DE   reason   theory   very be   diverse

   'People have conflicting speculations on the reasons for Yin Bile's suicide.' (*Biàndiào* 16)

(3) 关于   小一   至   小四   的   奠基   阶段,
    guānyú xiǎoyī   zhì   xiǎosì   de   diànjī   jiēduàn
    about   first.grade to   fourth.grade DE   foundation   Stage

   在   语文   课程   方面   还   须   仔细   研究
   zài yǔwén   kèchéng   fāngmiàn   hái   xū   zǐxì   Yánjiū
   in   language course   aspect   still   need   careful   examine

一下。（风筝 85）

yīxià

a.bit

'With regard to the foundation stage from the first to the fourth grade in primary school, the language curriculum still needs to be closely examined.' (*Fēngzhēng* 85)

Or they may, with 的 *de* 'DE' attached, act as attribute, as shown here:

(4) 翻　　到　　徐勤丽　　的　　那　　一　　页，　**关于**　　父母　　的
　　 fān　*dào*　*xúqínlì*　*de*　*nà*　*yī*　*yè*　***guānyú***　*fùmǔ*　*de*
　　 turn　 to　　Xu.Qinli　 DE　that　one　page　**about**　parent　DE

　　那个　　栏目，　　清清楚楚地　　　　写　　着：. . .（跳舞71）
　　nàgè　*lánmù*　*qīngqīngchǔchǔ-de*　*xiě*　*Zhe*
　　that　 column　 clearly　　　　　　　write　ZHE

'Turning to the page about Xu Qinli, you'll clearly see in the column about parents that . . .' (*Tiàowǔ* 71)

(5) 我　　跟　　颜　　同学. . .　望　　着　　碧海　　蓝天
　　 wǒ　*gēn*　*yán*　*tóngxué*　*wàng*　*zhe*　*bìhǎi*　*lántiān*
　　 1SG　with　Yan　classmate　 look　　ZHE　green.sea　blue.sky

　　谈　　些　　**关于**　　学校　　的　　事情。（晚上 152）
　　tán　*xiē*　***guānyú***　*xuéxiào*　*de*　*Shìqing*
　　talk　some　**about**　 school　　DE　thing

'Yan and I . . . looking at the turquoise sea and the azure sky, talked about our school.' (*Wǎnshàng* 152)

The structure of 关于父母的那个栏目 *guānyú fùmǔ de nàgè lánmù* 'the column about parents' in (4) and 关于学校的事情 *guānyú xuéxiào de shìqing* 'things about the school' in (5) can be analysed as shown here:

关于　　　父母　　　的　　　那个栏目
guānyú　*fùmǔ*　*de*　*nàgèlánmù*

———1———　( )　———2———　　(attribute-head modifying relation)
—3—　—4—　　　　　　　　　　(prepositional phrase)

关于	学校	的		事情
guānyú	xuéxiào	de		shìqíng
___1___		( )		___2___	(attribute-head modifying relation)
___3___	___4___				(prepositional phrase)

The features for the usage of the prepositional phrase "关于..." *guānyú* 'about...' are summarised next.

First, as an adverbial, the prepositional phrase "关于..." *guānyú* 'about...' can only precede, but not follow, the subject, as evidenced by the following examples.

关于	这个	问题,	我们	正在	研究。
guānyú	**zhègè**	**wèntí**	wǒmen	zhèngzài	yánjiū
about	this	issue	1PL	in.process	research

'About this issue, we are still working on it.'

The subject 我们 *women* '1PL' cannot precede "关于..." *guānyú* 'about...' as shown here.

*我们	关于	这个	问题,	正在	研究。
wǒmen	guānyú	zhègè	wèntí	zhèngzài	yánjiū
1PL	about	this	issue	in.process	research

Intended meaning: 'About this issue, we are still working on it.'

Back to (1) and (2), 关于战后马华文学之演变 *guānyú zhànhòu mǎhuá wénxué zhī yǎnbiàn* 'about the evolution of post-war Malaysian Chinese literature' and 关于鄞碧乐自杀的原因 *guānyú yínbìlè zìshā de yuányīn* 'about the reasons for Yin Bile's suicide' are both placed before the subject. They can never follow the subjects of 王赓武 *wānggēngwǔ* 'Wang Gungwu' and 说法 *shuōfǎ* 'sayings' respectively. More examples follow:

(6)
关于	这	一	点,	笔者	颇	具	同感。	（薪传163）
guānyú	**zhè**	**yī**	**diǎn**	bǐzhě	pō	jù	tónggǎn	
about	this	one	point	author	very	have	same.feeling	

'About this view, the author agrees.' (*Xīnchuán* 163)

(7)
关于	口语词	及	惯用语,	工具书	渐多。（△语言文字51）
guānyú	**kǒuyǔcí**	**jí**	**guànyòngyǔ**	gōngjùshū	jiànduō

about	colloquial and idiom			reference.book	gradually.more	

'There is a growing number of reference books on colloquial words and idioms.' (△*Yǔyánwénzì* 51)

In (6), 关于这一点 *guānyú zhè yīdiǎn* 'about this view' cannot be placed after the subject 笔者 *bǐzhě* 'author'; likewise, in (7), 关于口语词及惯用语 *guānyú kǒuyǔcí jí guànyòngyǔ* 'about colloquial words and idioms' cannot follow the subject 工具书 *gōngjùshū* 'reference book'.

In cases where the subjects do not appear, the prepositional phrase "关于..." *guānyú* 'about...' seems to directly act as an adverbial of the verb phrase, as in (3) and the following example:

(8) 关于 "是"字句 的 让步 用法, 素无
guānyú *shìzìjù* *de* *ràngbù* *yòngfǎ* *sùwú*
about SHI.construction DE concession usage NEG

争议。(△ 语言文字72)
zhēngyì
dispute

'The concessive usage of the 是 *shì* 'be' construction is never in dispute.' (△ *Yǔyánwénzì* 72)

However, in (3), if the subject 我们 *wǒmen* 'we' is to be added, then it can only appear either before 在语文课程方面 *zài yǔwén kèchéng fāngmiàn* 'in the aspect of language curriculum' or before 还须仔细研究一下 *hái xū zǐxì yánjiū yīxià* 'still need to be closely examined', as follows:

(9) 关于 小一 至 小四 的 奠基 阶段,
guānyú *xiǎoyī* *zhì* *xiǎosì* *de* *diànjī* *jiēduàn*
about first.grade to fourth.grade DE foundation stage

我们 在 语文 课程 方面 还 须 仔细
wǒmen *zài* *yǔwén* *kèchéng* *fāngmiàn* *hái* *Xū* *zǐxì*
1PL in language course aspect still Need careful

研究 一下。(风筝 85)
yánjiū *yīxià*
examine a.bit

'With regard to the foundation stage from the first to the fourth grade in primary school, the language course needs to be closely examined.' (*Fēngzhēng* 85)

(10) 关于 小一 至 小四 的 奠基 阶段，
    guānyú xiǎoyī zhì xiǎosì de diànjī jiēduàn
    about first.grade to fourth.grade DE foundation Stage

    在 语文 课程 方面 **我们** 还 须 仔细
    zài yǔwén kèchéng fāngmiàn **wǒmen** hái xū zǐxì
    in language course aspect **1PL** still need careful

    研究 一下。（风筝 85）
    yánjiū yīxià
    examine a.bit

    'With regard to the foundation stage from the first to the fourth grade in primary school, the language course needs to be closely examined.' (*Fēngzhēng* 85)

The subject 我们 *wǒmen* 'we' can never be added ahead of the prepositional phrase "关于..." *guānyú* 'about...'. The following example is ungrammatical.

(11) ***我们** 关于 小一 至 小四 的 奠基 阶段，
    wǒmen guānyú xiǎoyī zhì xiǎosì de diànjī jiēduàn
    1PL about first.grade to fourth.grade DE foundation stage

    在 语文 课程 方面 还 须 仔细
    zài yǔwén kèchéng fāngmiàn hái xū zǐxì
    in language course aspect still need careful

    研究 一下。（风筝85）
    yánjiū yīxià
    examine a.bit

    Intended meaning: 'With regard to the foundation stage from the first to the fourth grade in primary school, the language curriculum needs to be closely examined.' (*Fēngzhēng* 85)

Similarly, in (8), the subject 学术界 *xuéshùjiè* 'academic circles' can only be added before the verb phrase 素无争议 *sùwúzhēngyì* 'never in dispute' but not the "关于..." *guānyú* 'about' prepositional phrase.

Second, the prepositional phrase "关于..." *guānyú* 'about..' can be used in headlines or titles of articles, a function that is shared by no other prepositional phrase. For example, on Dec. 17, 1947, Mr. Li Liewen published an article entitled 《关于郁达夫》 *guānyú yùdáfū* '*About Yu Dafu*'[6] in the eighth section of Singapore's *Nan Chiau Daily*. The other example is Dr. Lin Wanjing's article 《略论汉语教学中一些棘手问题》 '*luèlùn hànyǔ jiàoxué zhōng yīxiē jíshǒu wèntí* '*A Brief Discussion on Some Difficult Issues in Teaching Chinese*',[7] where the subheadings are almost all in the format of "关于..." *guānyú* 'about', as listed here.

一、引言 *yǐnyán* 'introduction'
二、关于字形与笔顺 *guānyú zìxíng yǔ bǐshùn* 'about the shape and stroke order of characters'
三、关于语音 *guānyú yǔyīn* 'about phonetics'
四、关于词汇 *guānyú cíhuì* 'about vocabulary'
五、关于语法 *guānyú yǔfǎ* 'about grammar'
六、关于语意 *guānyú yǔyì* 'about semantics'
七、结语 *jiéyǔ* 'conclusion'

Notes

1. Translator's note: The semantic meaning of 叫 *jiàoe* is similar to 'let', 'make', or 'ask', marking the agent of the verb followed. In this book, this word is classified as a preposition.
2. Translator's note: There are 46 examples illustrating the use of each preposition listed here in the original text. Due to the space limit, many of the examples are omitted.
3. See Section 13.7.1, Zhu (1982).
4. If the adverb 都 *dōu* 'all' is inserted ahead of the verb 吃 *chī* 'eat' in this sentence, that is, 你把三个苹果都吃了 *nǐ bǎ sāngè píngguǒ dōu chī le* 'You ate all the three apples', the sentence is acceptable. This is because the adverb 都 *dōu* 'all' expresses the entirety, which means that there is no exception for the people or things it covers. Therefore, 'numeral + classifier + noun' phrase becomes definite via 都 *dōu* 'all' assertion.
5. Translator's note: In old days of planned enconomy people used to use meal tickets, which was one part of the salary, rather than cash to buy meals from the canteen of the working institution. Once the meal ticket is used, it would be torn into pieces.
6. Quoted from the bibliography of Lin Wanjing's 《中国作家在新加坡极其影响》 '*Chinese Writers in Singapore: A Critical Impact*' (Miles Books, 1994, Singapore).
7. The article was published in *Euphoria*, No. 3, May 1993; see also Lim Wan Ching, 《语言文字论集》 '*Essays on Language and Script*', Centre for Chinese Studies, National University of Singapore, 1996.

Appendix 1
English-Chinese Term List

Terms in English	Terms in Chinese
abstract noun	抽象名词
accusative object	受事宾语
act as complement	充任补语
action	行为动作
action-patient	动作-受事
activity verb	动作动词
actor	动作者
actual discourse	实际话语
adjectival predicate sentence	形容词谓语句
adjective phrase	形容词性词语
adverbial	状语
adverbial-head	状语-中心语
adverbial-head endocentric phrase	状中偏正词组
adversative complex sentence	转折复句
adversative conjunction	转折连词
adversative relation	转折关系
affected object	对象宾语
affiliated relation	隶属关系
affiliation	隶属
agent	施事
agent of the predicate verb	述语动词施事
agentive object	施事宾语
agent-subject sentence	施事主语句
alternative question	选择问句
ancient Chinese	古代汉语
annotative conjunctive sentence	注解复句
annotative relation	注释关系
answer	答话
appositive modifier-head construction	同位性偏正结构
appositive relation	同位关系
approximate number	约数
approximation	概数
aspect auxiliary	状态助词
assertion	陈述性说明
assumptive complex sentence	假设复句
assumptive concession	假设让步
assumptive concessive sentence	假设让步转折复句
assumptive mood	假设语气

assumptive relation	假设关系
attribute	定语
attribute-head phrase	定中偏正词组
auxiliary structure	助词结构
auxiliary	助词
BA construction/sentence	把字句
BEI construction/sentence	被字句
binary	一分为二
cardinal	基数词
categorical nominal classifier	种类名量词
categorical relation	类别关系
causative object	致使宾语
causative verb	使令意义的动词
cause-result complex sentence	因果复句
cause-result relation	因果关系
character	字
Chinese mandarin	普通话
classifier	量词（个、只）
clause	分句
collective nominal classifier	集合名量词
companion	伴随者
comparative construction	比较句式
comparative relation	比况关系
comparative sentence	比较句
complement	补语
complement of time and place	时地补语
complex predicate phrase	复谓词组
complex sentence/compound sentence	复句
compound and complex sentence/composite sentence	复句
compound cardinal	系位结构
compound directional verb	复合趋向动词
compound nominal classifier	复合名量词
concession	让步
concessive transitional complex sentence	让步转折复句
concrete noun	具体名词
conditional complex sentence	条件复句
conjunction	连词
connective word	关联词语
consecutive actions	前后连贯的行为动作
consecutive conjunctive sentence	连贯复句
construction	格式
content word	实词
continuation of dynamic situation	动态状况持续义
contracted correlative phrase	连锁词组
contrastive	对举
contrastive conjunctive sentence	对立复句
coordinate conjunctive sentence	并列复句，联合复句
coordinate phrase	联合词组
coordinate relation	并列关系
copula verb	判断动词
correlative complex sentence	倚变复句
dative object	与事宾语
DE construction	"的"字结构

decimal	小数
declarative mood	陈述语气
declarative sentence	陈述句
definite	有定
degree adverb	程度副词
degree complement	程度补语
demonstrative pronoun	指示代词
demonstrative classifier compound	指量词
dependency relations	倚变关系
direct object	直接宾语
directional complement	趋向补语
directional verb	趋向动词
discourse linguistics	话语语言学
disjunctive	或此或彼
disjunctive sentence	选择复句
displacement	位移
disposal	处置
distinguishing word	区别词
distributive subject sentence	周遍性主语句
disyllabic verb	双音节动词
disyllable	双音节
ditransitive construction	带双宾语的述宾词组
dominating grammatical relation	支配关系
double object construction	双宾结构
dynamic auxiliary	动态助词
entity to be compared with	比较项
erhua, rhotacisation	儿化
Europeanised sentences	欧化句式
exclamative mood	感叹语气
exclamative sentence	感叹句
exclusive conditional complex sentence	排除条件的条件复句
exhaustive conditional complex sentence	无条件复句
existential meaning	存在义
existential verb	存在动词
extensional meaning	引申意义
fixed phrase	固定词组
forming relationship	组成关系
fraction	分数
functional word	虚词
general classifier	一般量词
grammar study	语法学
grammatical construction	语法结构
grammatical function	语法功能
grammatical unit	语法单位
grammaticalised from verbs	从动词虚化而来
head	中心语
Hierarchical Analysis	层次分析法
high level tone	阴平调
homomorphic pattern/construction	同形句式
idiom	成语
Immediate Constituent Analysis (IC analysis)	直接成分分析法
imperative sentence	祈使句
indefinite nominal classifier	不定名量词

indefinite temporal classifier	不定时量词
indirect object	间接宾语
individual nominal classifier	个体名量词
instrument	工具
instrument object	工具宾语
integer	整数
interrogative mood	疑问语气
interrogative pronoun	疑问代词
interrogative sentence	问话
intonation	句调
intransitive verb	不及物动词
irrealis	未然
kinship relation	亲属关系
kinship term	亲属称谓的名词
lingua franca of the Han people	现代汉民族共同语
linked object	表称宾语，系事宾语
localiser	方位词
magnitude number	位数词
major subject	大主语
maker of adverseness	"不如意"的标志
manner object	方式宾语
material relation	质料关系
matrix clause	主句
meaning of appearance	出现义
measure word	度量名量词
minor subject	小主语
modal verb	能愿动词
modern Singapore Mandarin	现代华语
modern standard lingua franca	华族共同语
modifier	修饰语
modifier-head	定语-中心语
modifier-head phrase	偏正词组
monosyllabic adjective	单音节形容词
monosyllabic verb	单音节动词
monosyllable	单音节
mood	语气
morpheme	语素
morphological marker	形态标记
morphological transformation	形态变化
multi-category	兼类
multi-category word	兼类词
multilayer embedded attribute	定语多层套叠
multilayered complex sentence	多重复句
multiple	倍数
multi-syllable	多音节
mutually exclusive	非此即彼
natural stress	自然重音
necessary conditional complex sentence	唯一条件的条件复句
negative adverb	否定副词
neutral tone	轻音
nominal classifier	名量词
nominal object	体词性宾语
nominal phrase	名词性词语

nominal predicate	体词性谓语
nominal predicate sentence	名词谓语句
nominal pronoun	体词性代词
nominal subject	体词性主语
nominal verb	名动词
nominal word	体词
non-subject-predicate sentence	非主谓句
non-word	非词
numeral	数词
numeral-classifier compound	数量词
numeral-classifier phrase/compound	数量词词组（如，三个）
numeral-classifier-noun object	"数 量 名"宾语
object	宾语
numeral-classifier phrase as objects	数量宾语
numeral-nominal classifier phrase as object	名量宾语
numeral-temporal classifier phrase as object	时量宾语
verb classifier as object	动量宾语
one-word sentence	独词句
onomatopoeia	拟声词
ordinal	序数词
parataxis	意合法
passive marker	被动标志
passive voice	被动式
passivity	被动性
patient	受事
patient of the predicate verb	述语动词受事
patient-subject sentence	受事主语句
personal pronoun	人称代词
phonological principle	语音规则
phrase	词组
pivotal phrase	递系词组
place object	处所宾语
place words	处所词
polyfunctionality	多重性
possession relationship	领有关系
potential complement	可能补语
pragmatic principle	语用规则
predicate	述语, 谓语
predicate word	谓词
predicate-complement	述语–补语
predicate-complement construction	述补结构
predicate-complement phrase	述补词组
predicate-object construction	述宾结构
predicate-object phrase	述宾词组
predicative object	谓词性宾语
predicative-object-taking verbs	真谓宾动词
prefix	前缀
preposition	介词
preposition-object structure	介宾结构
primary-subordinate	主次
progressive conjunctive sentence	递进复句
progressive relation	递进关系
pronoun	代词

English	Chinese
proper noun	专有名词
psychological verb	心理感受动词
purpose relation	目的关系
purposive complex sentence	目的复句
purposive relation	目的关系
quadrisyllabic unit	四字格
quantifier	量词（例如，每, 些）
quasi directional complement	准趋向补语
quasi-predicate-object-taking verb	准谓宾动词
quasi-object	准宾语
realis	已然
realising relationship	实现关系
recipient	与事
reduplication of adjective	形容词重叠式
reduplication	重叠式
reduplication of verb	动词重叠式
referent	所指
referential relation	称代关系
result object	结果宾语
resultative complement	结果补语
rhotacisation of syllable final	儿化韵
rising tone	上声声调
sample survey	抽样调查
semantic orientation	语义指向
semantic principle	语义规则
semantic relation	语义关系
sentence-final particle	语气词
sentence-final pause	句末停顿
sentence-making unit	造句单位
serial predicate phrase	连谓词组
shape of characters	字形
simple adjective	单个形容词
simple sentence	单句
Singapore Mandarin	新加坡华语
single cardinal	系数词
slight adversative complex sentence	轻转的转折复句
slight-pause mark	顿号
sound combination	合音
specialised temporal classifier	专用时量词
specialised verb classifier	专用动量词
specific-general conjunctive sentence	分合复句
speculative complex sentence	推论复句
standard Chinese	标准华语
state complement	状态补语
stative adjective	状态形容词
stative word	状态词
stative word-predicate sentence	状态词谓语句
stroke order of characters	笔顺
strong adversative complex sentence	重转的转折复句
structural auxiliary	结构助词
subject-predicate construction	主谓关系
subject-predicate phrase	主谓词组
subject-predicate predicate sentence	主谓谓语句

subjunctive sentence	假设句
subsidiary word formation	附带说构词
sufficient conditional complex sentence	充足条件的条件复句
suffix	后缀
supplement	追加
supplementary relation	追加补充关系
systematicity	系统性
temporal classifiers	时量词
temporal complex sentence	时间复句
temporary nominal classifier	借用名量词
time word	时间词
topic	话题
transitive verb	及物动词
transliterated word	音译词
regular object	真宾语
unit(s) of sound and meaning	音义结合体
universality	普遍性
verb classifier	动量词
verb phrase	动词性词语
verbal predicate sentence	动词谓语句
verb-object construction	动宾结构
verbs taking nominal object	体宾动词
verbs taking predicative object	谓宾动词
vernacular	白话
vocative sentence	呼应句
VP-Neg question	反复问
word class	词类
word class shift	词性转移
word order	词序
word of overlapping classes	一词多类

Appendix 2
Translation of Examples and Glossary

There are abundant Singapore Mandarin examples in this book and they are translated into two ways, depending on their length and location in the text. For examples in the main text or short – phrase examples on separate lines, the translation version includes the Chinese characters, Chinese Pinyin with tones and English translations. For sentences or long – phrase examples on separate lines, the translation has four lines, showing, respectively, Chinese characters, Chinese Pinyin, word glossaries and translations.

In the original book the author has cited numerous authentic examples from various sources to demonstrate that the language phenomena discussed are quite common in the Singapore Mandarin language. In the translated version, all the original examples discussed in the main text are kept and translated, and, if it is a long sentence, the example is put in a separate line with a number. Owing to space limitations, long sentence examples, appearing on separate lines with numbers, are not all translated, omitted with the author's consent under the condition that the omission will not affect the main discussion. Therefore, the number of examples in the translation version is different from that in the original version.

The glossary words that indicate distincti grammatical functions in the examples are listed here in alphabetical order:

Glossary	Grammatical Meaning	Singapore Mandarin
1PL	First person plural	我们
1SG	First person singular	我
2PL	Second person plural	你们
2SG	Second person singular	你
3PL	Third person plural	他们、她们、它们
3SG	Third person singular	他、她、它
AM	Agent marker	叫, 让
BA	Disposal marker	把、将
BEI	Adverseness marker	被
DAO	Post verbal auxiliary word taking state complement	到
DE	Postverbal auxiliary word	的, 得, 地
GE	Post verbal auxiliary word taking state complement	个 （例 "看个清楚"）

(*Continued*)

(Continued)

Glossary	Grammatical Meaning	Singapore Mandarin
GEI	Grammaticalised form of verb give	给
GUO	Postverbal auxiliary word indicating the experienced aspect	过
LAIDE	Auxiliary word in BI comparative construction	来得
LE	Postverbal auxiliary word indicating the perfective aspect; Auxiliary word at Sentence final position.	了
LIG	Ligature	而，之
NEG	Negative adverb	不、没、没有、不是
SFP	Sentence final particle	吗、吧、呢
SHI	Focus marker	是
SUO	Preverbal auxiliary word	所
TOP	Topic marker	呀、啦、呢
YOU	Adverb before verbs and adjective	有
ZHE	Postverbal auxiliary word indicating durative and progressive aspect	着

Appendix 3
The Sources of Examples

The examples in this book are adapted from the following works, which are listed alphabetically under the authors' name. Due to space limit, only the abbreviations of the name of the work are referred at the end of each example in the book, which are shown in square brackets as indicated here.

Ai, Hua. (1993). *Kēxué yǔ shī de huìhé* [The incorporation of science and poetry]. Sino-foreign Translation Book Press [Lēxué].
Bai, He. (1981). *Dúshàng gāolóu Xīnjiāpō huáwén zhōngxué jiàoshīhuì* [Alone on tall buildings, Singapore Chinese Secondary School Teachers Association]. [Dúshàng].
Bai, He. (1989). *Fēngyǔ gùrén lái* [Old friends come]. Shengyou Bookstore [Fēngyǔ].
Chen, Huashu. (1988). *Zhuī yúnyuè* [Chasing the cloud and the moon]. Shengyou Bookstore, Singapore Writers Association [Zhuīyún].
Chen, Huashu. (1994). *Bīngdēng huīyìng de wǎnshàng* [The night of the ice lantern]. Singapore Chaozhou Bayi Hall [Bīngdēng].
Chen, Miaohua. (1995). *Héshàng fēngyún* [Storms on the River]. Favorite Publishing Service Press [Héshàng].
Dìèrjiè shīchéng fúlún wénxuéjiǎng déjiǎng zuòpǐnjí [The 2nd Lion City Rotary Literature Award Winning Works Collection]. (1990). Rotary Club of Lion City. Chinese Society of Huachu Alumni Association [Fúlún].
Ding, Zhiping. (1977). *Èyútán biān de èmèng* [The nightmare by the Crocodile Pond]. Education Press [Èmèng].
Duǎnpiān xiǎoshuō chuàngzuò bǐsài·jiāzuò tèjí [Short story writing competition·Excellent Works Special]. (1997). Education Press [Duǎnpiān].
Editorial Board of xinsha New Chinese Literature Department. (1971). *Xīnmǎ huáwén wénxué dàxì: jùběn* [Chinese Literature in Singapore and Malaysia: the scripts]. Education Press [Xīnmǎ·jùběn].
Fei, Xin. (1990). *Jiànxíngjiànyuǎn* [Drifting away]. Huazhong Junior College [Jiànxíng].
Feng, Bingzhang. (1992). *Xīnlíng zhī yǎn* [The eye of the mind]. Dot Line Press [Xīnlíng].
Feng, Huanhao. (1989). *Bù diāowěi de huíyì* [Memories unfaded]. Sino-foreign Translation Book Press [Huíyì].
Feng, Shayan. (1993). *Wényì xùyǔ jí* [Collections of Literary Talks]. Sino-foreign Translation Book Press [Wényì].
Guang, Hui. (1991). *Méiyǒu diàndēng de wǎnshàng* [Nights without lights]. Shengyou Bookstore [Wǎnshàng].
Guang, Hui. (1994). *Yīxīnxiǎngxiě* [Writing heart and soul]. Shengyou Bookstore [Yīxīn].

Guo, Baokun. (1969). *Wèi xǐngxǐng* [Hey! Wake up]. Performing Arts Publishing Press [Xǐngxǐng].

Guo, Yi. (1983). *Chūnfēnghuàyǔ* [Breeze and rain in spring: the beneficial influence of education]. Education Press Pte Ltd. [Chūnfēng].

Guo, Yongxiu. (1989). *Bìhǔ zhī liàn* [Gecko love]. Publishing Group, Cultural and Educational Committee of Bayi Guild Hall [Bìhǔ].

Han, Laoda. (1986). *Láodá jùzuò* [Lauda's plays]. Publishing Group, Cultural and Educational Committee of Bayi Guild Hall [Láodájùzuò].

He, Naiqiang. (1987). *Értóng bìngfáng* [Children's Ward]. Sino-foreign Translation Book Press [értóng].

Hong, Youhe. (1995). *Huàjù biǎoyǎn xùnliàn bǎilì* [One hundred cases of drama performance training]. Cultural Publishing Press [Huàjù].

Hu, Yuebao. (1993). *Zhuàngqiáng* [Hitting the wall]. Huazhong Junior College [Zhuàngqiáng].

Hu, Yuebao. (1994). *Yǒuyuán zàijiàn* [Goodbye by fate]. Singapore Authors Association, Dadi Cultural Enterprise Co., Ltd. [Zàijiàn].

Hua, Zhifeng. (1988). *Wǔtái èrjuàn* [Stage of two volums]. Publishing Group, Cultural and Educational Committee of Bayi Guild Hall, Singapore [Wǔtái].

Huai, Ying. Zhang, Hui. Hong, Di. Tian, Liu. (1989). *Lántiān zài xuánzhuǎn* [The spinning blue sky]. New Cultural Institution, Shin Min Daily [Lántiān].

Huang, Mengwen. (1982). *Xiězuòrén xiǎoshuōxuǎn* [Selected stories of writers]. World Bookstore [Xiězuòrén].

Huáyùn·dìshíbāqī [Huayun·Eighteenth issue]. (1993). Huazhong Junior College [Huáyùn].

Jīnshījiǎng huòjiǎng zuòpǐnjí dìyījiè 1981–1982 [The First Golden Lion award winning works 1981–1982). (1982). Nanyang Commercial Daily, Sin Chew Daily [Jīnshījiǎng].

Jīnshījiǎng huòjiǎng zuòpǐnjí·dìsìjiè1990 [The forth Golden Lion award winning works 1990]. (1990). Lianhe Zaobao, Education Publishing Private Limited [Jīnshījiǎngsì].

Ke, Siren. (1988). *Xúnmiào* [Finding the temple]. Singapore Junior College [Xúnmiào].

Li, Guo. (1984). *Fénchéngjì* [The story of burning the city]. Education Press [Fénchéngjì].

Li, Jian. (1990). *Shānchéng gùshì* [Tales of the mountain city]. Shengyou Bookstore [Shānchéng].

Li, Jian. (1991). *Fàngxià nǐ de biānzǐ* [Put down your whip]. Mountain View Publishing House [Biānzǐ].

Li, Yixiang. Xu, Fuji. Zeng, Jifeng. (1991). *Xīnqíng dié zài qīngqīng de rìjìlǐ* [Moods folded in Qingqing's diary]. Mood Studio [Xīnqíng].

Li, Yueqing. (1993). *Nánběi yóuzōng* [North-South Journey]. Pisces Advertising Design Pte Ltd, U.S. China Printing Pte Ltd [Nánběi].

Liang, Wenfu. (1988). *Zuìhòu de Niú chēshuǐ* [The last Chinatown]. Guanhe Production Publishing House [Niúchēshuǐ].

Liánhézǎobào.1995.2.-1995.8. [Lianhe zaobao1995.2–1995.8). [Bào].

Lin, Chen. (1961). *Jiànwū gōngdìshàng* [On the building site of the house]. Nanyang Literature and Art Publishing House [Jiànwū].

Lin, Jin. (1990). *Wǒ búyào shènglì* [I don't want victory]. New Asia Publishing House [Shènglì].

Lin, Kang. (1986). *Chǎnggēdàngkū* [The song of cry]. Publishing Group, Cultural and Educational Committee of Bayi Guild Hall, Singapore [Chǎnggēdàngkū].

Lin, Kang. (1988). *Xièhòu yītiáo hēigǒu* [Encountering with a black dog]. Cactus Press [Xièhòu].

Lin, Qiuxia. (1993). *Xiǎngfēi* [Wanna fly]. Dot Line Press [Xiǎngfēi].

Ling, Xi. (1989). *Huāyǔzhōng de mèng* [Dreams in the rain of flowers]. Wanli Bookstore [Huāyǔ].
Liu, Huixia. (1992). *Bié zuò duànlexiàn de fēngzhēng* [Don't be a kite with a broken string]. Mountain View Publishing House [fēngzhēng].
Liu, Jun. (1987). *Zhuóliú* [Turbid flow]. Publishing Group, Cultural and Educational Committee of Bayi Guild Hall, Singapore [Zhuóliú].
Liu, Shun. (1987). *MD shì zhèyàng xuǎnchūlái de* [This is how MD is selected]. Cactus Press [MD].
Liu, Su. (1991). *Rénshēng shì huā* [Life is a flower]. Life is a Flower [Rénshēng].
Liu, Wenzhu. (1989). *Huànbìng de tàiyáng* [The sick sun]. Singapore Writers Association [Huànbìng].
Lu, Tao. (1989). *Hénjì* [Trace]. Mountain View Publishing House [Hénjì].
Meng, Zi. (1988). *Jīnhòu wǒ shì zhēnde* [I'm sure from now on]. Shengyou Bookstore, Singapore Writers Association [Jīnhòu].
Mu, Zi. (1990). *Mùzǐ xiǎoshuō* [Muzi's Novels]. Xinhua Cultural Enterprise [New]. Co., Ltd. [Mùzǐ].
Mu, Zi. (1990). *Wǒ yǒu huà yào shuō* [I have something to say]. Shengyou Bookstore [Wǒyǒu].
Mu, Zi. (1993). *Wǒ hái yǒu huà yào shuō* [I still have something to say]. Shengyou Bookstore [Wǒháiyǒu].
Nan, Zi. (1985). *Bāfāng fēngyǔ* [Floating all the directions]. Literature Bookstore [Bāfāng].
Nan, Zi. (1987). *Niánsuì de chīhén* [The marks of years]. Publishing Group, Cultural and Educational Committee of Bayi Guild Hall, Singapore [Niánsuì].
Nanyang University Academic Staff Association. (1986). *Xīngmǎ xiǎoshuō jiāzuò xuǎnjí* [Selected Works of Xingma Novels]. Education Press [Xīngmǎ].
Peng, Zhifeng. (1989). *Xīnjiāpō wēixíng xiǎoshuōxuǎn* [A selection of Singapore mini stories]. Aljunied Literary Creation and Translation Society Publishing Press [Wēixíng].
Qu, Rubai. (1993). *Lúnxiàn suìyuè* [Colonised years]. Shengyou Bookstore [Lúnxiàn].
Singapore Class Development Board. (1984). *Zhōngxué huáwén jiāocái* [Middle School Chinese Textbook 1A]. Education Publishing Private Limited [Huáwénjiāocái1A].
Singapore Class Development Board. (1985). *Zhōngxué huáwén jiāocái* [Middle School Chinese Textbook 2A]. Education Publishing Private Limited [Huáwénjiāocái2A].
Singapore Class Development Board. (1986). *Zhōngxué huáwén jiāocái* [Middle School Chinese Textbook 3A]. Education Publishing Private Limited [Huáwénjiāocái3A].
Singapore Class Development Board. (1987). *Zhōngxué huáwén jiāocái* [Middle School Chinese Textbook 4A]. Education Publishing Private Limited [Huáwénjiāocái4A].
Singapore Class Development Board. (1988). *Rújiālǐlùn·zhōngsìkèběn* [Confucian theory: Textbook of the fourth year of middle school]. Education Publishing Private Limited [Lúlǐ·zhōngsì].
Singapore Class Development Board. (1988). *Rújiālǐlùn·zhōngsānkèběn* [Confucian theory: Textbook of the third year of middle school]. Education Publishing Private Limited [Lúlǐ·zhōngsān].
Singapore Class Development Board. (1989). *Zhōngxué huáwén jiāocái* [Middle School Chinese Textbook 1B]. Education Publishing Private Limited [Huáwénjiāocái1B].
Singapore Class Development Board. (1989). *Zhōngxué huáwén jiāocái* [Middle School Chinese Textbook 2B]. Education Publishing Private Limited [Huáwénjiāocái2B].
Singapore Class Development Board. (1990). *Zhōngxué huáwén jiāocái* [Middle School Chinese Textbook 3B]. Education Publishing Private Limited [Huáwénjiāocái3B].

Singapore Class Development Board. (1992). *Xiǎoxué huáwén jiāocái* [Primary School Chinese Textbook 6A]. Education Publishing Private Limited [Xiǎoxué6A].
Singapore Class Development Board. (1992). *Zhōngxué huáwén jiāocái* [Middle School Chinese Textbook 4B]. Education Publishing Private Limited [Huáwénjiāocái4B].
Singapore Class Development Board. (1993). *Shíyòng huáwén kèběn* [Practical Chinese Textbook 1A]. Education Publishing Private Limited [Kèběn1A].
Singapore Class Development Board. (1993). *Xiǎoxué huáwén jiāocái* [Primary School Chinese Textbook 6B]. Education Publishing Private Limited [Xiǎoxué6B].
Singapore Class Development Board. (1994). *Shíyòng huáwén kèběn* [Practical Chinese Textbook 1B]. Education Publishing Private Limited [Kèběn1B].
Singapore Class Development Board. (1994). *Shíyòng huáwén kèběn* [Practical Chinese Textbook 2A]. Education Publishing Private Limited [Kèběn2A].
Singapore Class Development Board. (1994). *Zhōngxué huáwén kèběn* [Middle School Chinese Textbook 1A]. Education Publishing Private Limited [Zhōngxué1A].
Sun, Ailing. (1988). *Bìluó shílǐ xiāng* [The aroma of green tea]. Singapore Art Research Association [Bìluó].
Sun, Ailing. (1993). *Shuǐjīng jí* [The crystal collection]. Shengyou Bookstore [Shuǐjīngjí].
Tian, Liu. (1980). *Xīnmǎ xiǎoshuō xuǎnjí* [Selected Malaysian and Singaporean stories]. Dadi Cultural Enterprise Co., Ltd. [Xīnmǎ].
Tian, Liu. (1989). *Xiàoyǎn kàn rénshēng* [A glimpse of life with a smile]. Shengyou Bookstore [Xiàoyǎn].
Wu, Cisu. (1986). *Mèng* [Dream]. Wanli Bookstore [Mèng].
Wu, Mu. (1989). *Wúxiányuè* [Moon without a quarter]. Seven Oceans Publishing House [Wúxiányuè].
Wu, Mu. (1993). *Zhìxìng de yìqíng* [The empathy of the supreme nature]. Publishing Group, Cultural and Educational Committee of Bayi Guild Hall, Singapore [Zhìxìng].
Wu, Weicai. (1989). *Wú Wěicái guàitán* [Wu Weicai's odd tales]. Pan Pacific Press Pte Ltd [Wú Wěicái].
Wu, Yuanhua. (1991). *Píngxīnérlùn* [A fair discussion]. Victory Publishing Pte Ltd [Píngxīn].
Wútǔ wúmín chuàngzuòxuǎn·xiǎoshuōshàng [Selected Literature of Wutuwumin·novel]. (1982). Nanyang Commercial Daily [Wútǔ·xiǎoshuōshàng].
Wútǔ wúmín chuàngzuòxuǎn xìjù [Selected Literature of Wutuwumin·play]. (1982). Nanyang Commercial Daily [Wútǔ·xìjù].
Xi, Nier. (1992). *Shēngmìnglǐ nányǐchéngshòu de zhòng* [The unbearable weight of life]. Publishing Group, Cultural and Educational Committee of Bayi Guild Hall, Singapore [Shēngmìng].
Xiao, Xin. (1991). *Nǚér huílái le* [The return of the daughter]. South Asia Press [Nǚér].
Xie, Qing. (1988). *Shuǐyánzhūyǔ* [The words of water drops]. Publishing Group, Cultural and Educational Committee of Bayi Guild Hall, Singapore [Shuǐyánzhūyǔ].
Xie, Zewen. (1994). *Xīnjiāpō huáwén jiàoxué lùnwénjí* [Collected essays of Singapore Chinese teaching]. Beijing Language Institute Press [Huáwén].
Xin, Zhu. (1992). *Dìyīgèmèng* [First dream]. Shengyou Bookstore [Dìyī].
Xīnchuán guānghuá xuéxiào sìshí zhōunián jìniàn tèkān [Xinchuan-Guanghua School's 40th Anniversary Special Issue]. (1990). Victory Publishing Pte Ltd. [Xīnchuán].
Xīnjiāpō diànshìjīgòu dìbābōdào.1995.3.-1995.8. Some Chinese programs on the 8th Channel of Singapore Television from March 1995 to August 1995). [Xīnshìdìbābōdào].
Xu, Fuji. Li, Yixiang. Zeng, Jifeng. (1987). *Qīngchūn zhī lǚ* [The journey of youth]. People's Bookstore [Qīngchūn].

Yao, Zi. (1988). *Jiǔyuè de yuányě* [September's Wilderness]. Chen Longyue [Jiǔyuè].
Yi, Fan. (1990). *Dàshùxià liǎnggè lǎorén* [Two old people under the big tree]. Pan Pacific Press Pte Ltd [Dàshùxià].
Ying, Peian. (1988). *Gūjì de liǎn* [The face of solitude]. Grassroots Press [Gūjì].
You, Jin. (1988). *Tàiyáng bù kěn huíjiāqù* [The sun won't go home]. Dongsheng Publishing House [Tàiyáng].
You, Jin. (1989). *Dàhúzi de chūn yǔ dōng* [The spring and winter of the bearded man]. New Asia Publishing Press [Dàhúzi].
You, Jin. (1989). *Rénjiān lètǔ* [Paradise on earth]. New Asia Publishing Press [Rénjiān].
You, Jin. (1990). *Chénshì fúdiāo* [Earthly relief]. Success Press [Chénshì].
You, Jin. (1990). *Ránshāo de shīzi* [The burning lion]. Education Publishing House Private Limited [Shīzi].
You, Jin. (1991). *Ránshāo de shīzi* [The burning lion]. Education Publishing House Private Limited [Ránshāo].
You, Jin. (1992). *Shítouchéng* [The city of stone]. New Asia Publishing Press [Shítou].
You, Jin. (1992). *Tiàowǔ de xiàngrìkuí* [The dancing sunflower]. Education Publishing House Private Limited [Tiàowǔ].
Yun, Kai. (1984). *Wù suǒ nányáng* [Fog covered Nanyang]. Singapore Broadcasting Bureau [Wùsuǒ].
Zhang, Hui. (1990). *45·45Huìyì jīmì* [45·45 Meeting confidential]. Singapore Authors Association [jīmì].
Zhang, Hui. (1992). *Shí mèng lù* [Records of ten dreams]. Singapore Authors Association [Shímènglù].
Zhang, Xina. (1990). *Biàndiào* [Tone change]. Grassroots Library [iàndiào].
Zhou, Can. (1980). *Liúlián shùxià* [Under the durian tree]. Pan Pacific Book Pte Ltd [Liúlián].
Zhou, Can. (1983). *Fāngkuài wénzhāng* [A cubic Article]. Book Publishing Department, Singapore Press and Publishing Co., Ltd. [Fāngkuài].
Zhou, Can. (1988). *Dūshì de liǎn* [The urban Face]. Shengyou Bookstore [Dūshì].
Zhou, Can. (1988). *Èmó zhī yè* [A devil night]. Dongsheng Publishing Press, Tropical Press [èmó].
Zhou, Can. (1990). *Mílù de tóngnián* [The lost childhood]. Success Press [Mílù].
Zhou, Can. (1991). *Cíhuàrén* [The magnetized man]. Shengyou Bookstore [Cíhuàrén].
Zhou, Can. (1994). *Wànhuātǒng* [Kaleidoscope]. Singapore Writers Association, Dadi Cultural Enterprise Co., Ltd. [Wànhuātǒng].
Zhuang, Xin. (1993). *Yě shì huáijiù* [Also nostalgic]. Intellectual Publishing House [Huáijiù].

Bibliography

Chen, Chuimin. (1994). Minnanhua he Putonghua "You" Zi Yongfa de Bijiao [A comparison of '有 you' in Southern Min and Putonghua]. In *Shuangyu Shuang Fangyan III* [Bilingual and dual dialects III]. Shenzhen: Hanxue Press.

Chen, Chung-yu. (1993). Xinjiapo Huayu Yufa yu Cihui Tezheng [The grammatical and lexical features of Singapore Mandarin]. In *Huayu Yanjiu Lunwenji* [Essays on Chinese studies]. National University of Singapore Mandarin Language Research Centre. (Note: This paper was first published as a separate paper by the Centre for Chinese Studies, National University of Singapore in 1981. Parts of its contents were published under the title of Features of Singaporean Chinese Grammar on the first issue of *Yuyan Yanjiu* [Language studies], 1986.)

Chen, Enquan. (1990). Shi Lun Yueyu Zai Zhongguo Yuyan Shenghuo Zhong de Diwei [On the status of Cantonese in Chinese language life]. In *Di Er Jie Yuefangyan Yantaohui Lunwenji* [Proceedings of the second conference on Cantonese dialects]. Guangzhou: Jinan University Press.

Chen, Jianmin. (1984). *Hanyu Kouyu* [Spoken Chinese]. Beijing: Beijing Press.

Cheng, Robert Liang. (1990). Cong Taiwan Dangdai Xiaoshuo Kan Hanyu Yufa Yanbian [Chinese grammatical change from the perspective of Taiwan contemporary novels]. In *Xinjiapo Shijie Huawen Jiaoxue Yantaohui Lunwenji* [Selected papers of international symposium of Chinese teaching, Singapore]. Singapore: Singapore Society of Culture Studies.

Chew Chenghai. (1994). Yufa Yanjiu yu Yufa Jiaoxue [Grammar studies and grammar teaching]. In *Xinjiapo Huawen Jiaoxue Lunwenji* [Essays of Singapore Mandarin teaching]. Beijing: Beijing Language and Culture Press.

Ding, Shengshu, et al. (1961). *Xiandai Hanyu Yufa Jianghua* [Speeches on modern Chinese Grammar]. Beijing: Commercial Press.

Gao, Huanian. (1980). *Guangzhou Fangyan Yanjiu* [The study of Guangzhou dialect]. Hong Kong: Commercial Press.

Goh, Nguen Wah. (1978). *Xinjiapo de Shehui Yuyan* [The social languages of Singapore]. Singapore: Educational Publishing.

Goh, Yeng Seng. (1986). *Xinjiapo Huayu Yufa Yanjiu* [Studies on Singapore Mandarin grammar]. Singapore: Singapore Society of Culture Studies.

Goh, Yeng Seng. (1990). Cong Xinjiapo Huayu Jufa Shikuang Diaocha Taolun Huayu Jufa Guifanhua Wenti [The standardization of Chinese from the fact-finding investigation of Singapore Mandarin syntax].in *Shijie Huawen Jiaoxue Yantaohui Lunwenji* [Proceedings of Chinese language teaching in the world]. Singapore: Singapore Society of Culture Studies.

Hsieh, Yun-Fei. (1976). Huayu de Biaozhun Wenti [On the standardization of Singapore Mandarin]. *Huayu Yanjiu Zhongxin Xueshu Jiangyan Huilu* [Proceedings of academic speeches of Chinese Research Center]. Singapore: Chinese Research Center of Nanyang University.

Huang, Guoying. (1988). *Taiwan Dangdai Xiaoshuo de Cihui Yufa Tedian* [Lexical and syntactical features of contemporary Taiwan Novels]. Zhongguo Yuwen [Chinese linguistics], (3), 194–201.

Kuo, Chen-Yu. (1976). Cong Shehuixue de Guandian Lun Xinjiapo de Yuyan [On the languages of Singapore from the perspective of sociology]. *Huayu Yanjiu Zhongxin Xueshu Jiangyan Huilu* [Proceedings of academic speeches of Chinese Research Centre]. Singapore: Chinese Research Centre of Nanyang University.

Kuo, Chen-Yu. (1985). *Xinjiapo de Yuyan yu Shehui* [The languages and society of Singapore]. Taibei: Cheng Chung Book.

Lee, Seng Giap. (Ed.). (1989). *Tuiguang Huayu Yundong Kaimu Yanjiang Zhuanji 1979–1989* [Lectures on the opening of promoting mandarin movements 1979–1989]. Promote Mandarin Council Secretariat of Ministry of of Communications and Information.

Li, Rulong. (1986). Minnanhua de "u4" and "mo2" ['有 u4' and '无 mo2' in Southern Min]. *Journal of Fujian Normal University*, (6), 76–83.

Li, Ying-Che. (1988). Huayu Yufa Biaozhun Wenti de Tantao [Discussions on Chinese standardization]. *Di Er Jie Shijie Huayuwen Jiaoxue Yantaohui Lunwenji: Jiaoxue yu Yingyong Pian (Shang Ce)* [Proceedings of the 2nd international symposium of Chinese language teaching: teaching and application I]. Taibei: Global Chinese Press.

Lu, Shaochang. (1984). *Huayu Lunji* [Selected papers on Chinese]. Singapore: Jin Chang Press.

Lü, Shuxiang. (1979). *Hanyu Yufa Fenxi Wenti* [Problems on Chinese grammar analysis]. Beijing: Commercial Press.

Lü, Shuxiang. (Ed). (1980). *Xiandai Hanyu Babai Ci* [800 Words in Modern Chinese]. Beijing: Commercial Press.

Ma, Zhen. (1991). Nanchonghua Li de Fanfu Wenju yu "Meide" He "Meiyou" [VP-Neg interrogatives and 'Meide' and 'Meiyou' in Nanchong dialect]. *Yuyanxue Luncong* [Essays on linguistics], (16), 99–111. Beijing: Commercial Press.

Section of Modern Chinese, Department of Chinese, Peking University. (1993). *Xiandai Hanyu* [Modern Chinese]. Beijing: Commercial Press.

Soh, BengMui. (1995). *Xinjiapo Huayu Zhong Yantan Biaozhi Yanjiu* [A study of speech markers in Singapore Mandarin]. BA(Hons) Thesis. Singapore: Chinese Language Department, National University of Singapore.

The Grammar Section of Singapore Standard Chinese Committee. (1985). *Huayu Yufa Yanjiu Baogao Cifa he Jufa* [Reports on Chinese grammar studies: lexicology and syntax]. Singapore: Singapore Standard Chinese Committee.

Tian, Huigang. (1994). Haiwai Huayu yu Xiandai Hanyu de Yitong [Similarities and differences between overseas chinese and modern Chinese]. *Journal of Hubei University (Philosophy and Social Science Edition)*, (4), 73–79.

Wang, Huidi. (1995). ×× Zu [××Family]. In *Shicheng Yuwen Xiantan* [Language talk of Singapore Mandarin]. Singapore: Federal Publications.

Wu, Yongde. (1989). Xianggang Hanyu yu Dalu Hanyu de Cihui Yufa Chayi [The lexical and grammatical differences of Chinese between Hong Kong and Mainland China]. In E. Chen (Ed.), *Shuangyu Shuang Fangyan* [Bilingual and dual dialects]. Guangzhou: Sun Yat-sen University Press.

Bibliography

Xing, Fuyi. (1989). "Youmeiyou VP" Yiwen Jushi [Interrogative construction of 'Youmeiyou VP']. In E. Chen (Ed.), *Shuangyu Shuang Fangyan* [Bilingual and dual dialects]. Guangzhou: Sun Yat-sen University Press.

Yuan, Jiaye. (1960). *Hanyu Fangyan Gaiyao* [Outline of Chinese dialects]. Beijing: Wenzi Gaige Press.

Zhang, Xianliang. (1994). Shilun Chongdieshi Dongci de Yufa Gongneng [On the grammatical functions of reduplicated forms of verbs]. *Yuyan Yanjiu* [Language studies], (1), 21–29.

Zhou, Xiaobing. (1989). Xinjiapo Huayu Xiaoshuo de Yufa Tedian [Grammatical features of Singapore Chinese novels]. In E. Chen (Ed.), *Shuangyu Shuang Fangyan* [Bilingual and dual dialects]. Guangzhou: Sun Yat-sen University Press.

Zhu, Dexi. (1961). Shuo "de" [On *de*]. *Zhongguo Yuwen* [Chinese linguistics], 12.

Zhu Dexi. (1979). Yu Dongci Gei Xiangguan De Jufa Wenti [Syntactic problems related to verb give]. *Fangyan* [Dialects], (2).

Zhu Dexi. (1980). *Xiandai Hanyu Yufa Yanjiu* [Grammatical studies about modern Chinese]. Beijing: Commercial Press.

Zhu, Dexi. (1982). *Yufa Jiangyi* [Lectures on grammar]. Beijing: Commercial Press.

Zhu, Dexi. (1985). *Yufa Dawen* [Questions and answers on grammar]. Beijing: Commercial Press.

Index

abstract noun 308, 443, 447–448
accusative object 158–159, 186–187, 191–194
action: agent of 114; duration of 62; quantity of 177; verb 228–229, 237, 242, 404, 411
action-patient 152, 473
activity verb 424, 426
actor 60, 137, 229, 369
actual discourse 246
adjectival predicate sentences 79–80
adjective phrase 110, 168, 300, 375, 459, 465
adverbial-head 20, 32, 284, 288, 349
adverbial-head endocentric phrase 102, 349, 351, 354
agent: -action relation 356–357; agentive object 159, 180–183, 200; of the predicate verb 454; -subject sentence 137–139
ancient Chinese 410, 433
annotative relation 326–327
appositive relation 327
attribute-head phrase 19–20, 103, 107, 135, 288, 318

categorical relation 309
causative object 162
causative verb 356–357
clause predicate 128–129
companion 404
comparative: construction 463, 465; sentence 260, 281
complex predicate phrase i, v, 245, 353–355, 383, 395–397, 419
compound directional verb 187–188, 190, 244
concession 148
concrete noun 444

conjunction 27, 37, 39, 61–62, 157, 363, 366
connective words 91
consecutive actions 378–380
content word 39–40, 94–95, 102
contracted correlative phrase 355, 362, 364, 366–368, 380, 382–383
contrastive 117–118, 123, 184, 226, 374, 384–385
coordinative phrases 16, 26–27, 102, 354
copula verb 98, 423

dative object 159, 191–193, 196
declarative: mood 77; sentence 85, 199
DE construction 63, 104, 134–135, 146, 293
degree: adverb 47, 53–54, 329, 460, 462; complement 232, 253, 257, 262, 282
demonstrative pronoun 57–58, 102, 292–296, 314–315
dependency relations 366
directional complement 183, 235–240, 242–246, 375, 418
directional verb 183, 187–188, 190, 244, 370, 423
direct object ix, 9, 191, 193, 196
discourse linguistics 76
disposal 428
distinguishing word 35, 56–57, 72, 102, 109, 316
distributive subject sentences 143
disyllabic verb 54, 289, 319–320, 323–325, 431
disyllable 202
ditransitive construction 361
dominating grammatical relation 32
double object construction ix, 9
dynamic auxiliary 62, 115, 182, 215

exclamative: mood 65; sentence 85, 87
existential verb 423

forming relationship 17
functional words i, 8–9, 59–61, 401, 446

grammatical: construction 29, 77, 376; function 40–44, 47–49, 204, 284, 327, 407; units 10, 12, 17, 76

Hierarchical Analysis 29

idiom 269, 278
imperative sentence 85–86, 199, 420
instrument 114; object 160
interrogative: mood 65, 77; pronoun 58, 102, 144–145, 170, 366; sentence 85, 87, 106, 406
intonation 12, 15, 17, 76–77, 90, 93
intransitive verb 53, 138, 153, 173–174, 178, 197, 202–206, 423
irrealis 335, 338–339

kinship relation 304–305

lingua franca of the Han people 227, 355
linked objects 162–163

manner object 160–161
material relation 304
modal verb 215–220, 222, 224–225, 247, 282, 424
modern Singapore Mandarin 64, 236, 410–411, 433
modifier-head phrase 17, 283, 326, 347–349, 351
monosyllable 12; adjective 55; noun 307; verb 54, 212
mood 50, 65, 76–77, 85
morpheme 2, 10–13, 17, 92, 150
morphological: marker 6; transformation 6, 17
multi-category 71–75, 325
multi-syllable 12

negation adverb 424
neutral tone 5, 54–55, 62–63
nominal: object 156, 158, 163, 206; phrase 156; predicate 79, 82, 130, 135; pronouns 107, 157; subject 102, 130; verb 323–325, 352, 447–448; word 102, 130

non-subject-predicate sentence 78–79, 83–84
non-word 125
numeral-classifier phrase 109, 130, 175, 316, 332

one-word sentence 93
onomatopoeia 40, 346

passive: marker 142–143, 282, 432–433; voice 143
passivity 430, 432
patient-action relation 359
patient-subject sentence 141–142, 433
personal pronoun 58, 290, 311
place object 161–162, 183, 185–188
possession relationship 305
potential complement 231, 245–250, 252, 265, 456
pragmatic principle 2
predicate-complement: construction 64, 187–188, 190; phrase 23–25, 227–228, 230–233, 243–246
predicate-object: construction 31; phrase 16, 21–23
predicate word 102, 354
proper noun 155, 426
psychological verb 423–424

quasi-object 170–175, 178, 195–197

realis 335
recipient 158–159, 191, 404
reduplication 54–55, 179–180, 420
referent 143–145, 326
resultative complement 232–235, 245–246, 262, 418
result object 159
rising tone 12

sample survey 434
sentence-making unit 77, 90
serial predicate phrase 355, 368–380, 383, 385, 388–390, 392–393
simple sentence 90
slight-pause mark 27
standard Chinese 5, 9, 64
state complement x, 232, 261–263, 265–268, 271, 418
stative adjectives 293, 302
stative word 55–57, 124–127, 292, 302–304, 331, 343

stative word-predicate sentences 79, 81
structural auxiliary 38, 62–63
subject-predicate: construction 8, 31; phrase 25, 112–113, 322, 329–331, 344, 354; predicate sentences 79, 82
supplement 142
systematicity xi

true object 195

universality xi, 10

verb-object construction 8
verbs taking nominal object 206, 216
verbs taking predicative object 206–209, 213, 215–216
vernacular 249
vocative sentence 85, 88–89
VP-Neg question 5

word order i, ix, 8–9, 248–249